Wheelock's Latin

The WHEELOCK'S LATIN Series

WHEELOCK'S LATIN
Frederic M. Wheelock, revised by Richard A. LaFleur

WORKBOOK FOR WHEELOCK'S LATIN
Paul Comeau, revised by Richard A. LaFleur

WHEELOCK'S LATIN READER:
SELECTIONS FROM LATIN LITERATURE
Frederic M. Wheelock, revised by Richard A. LaFleur

Wheelock's Latin

Frederic M. Wheelock

Revised by
Richard A. LaFleur

6th Edition, Revised

HarperResource
An Imprint of HarperCollins *Publishers*

ACKNOWLEDGMENTS

Maps

pages xlvi–xlviii: All maps copyright by Richard A. LaFleur and Thomas R. Elliott with materials courtesy of the Ancient World Mapping Center (http://www.unc.edu/awmc)

Photographs

cover (detail) and page 289: Virgil between two Muses, mosaic, early 3rd century A.D., Musée National du Bardo, Tunis, Tunisia—Giraudon/Art Resource, NY; **page xxxiv:** Giraudon/Art Resource, NY; **pages xl, 7, 8, 23, 30, 73, 88, 102, 108, 120, 127, 139, 154, 176, 177, 201, 208, 209, 216, 227, 282:** Scala/Art Resource, NY; **pages 42, 47, 87, 153, 160, 217, 241:** Erich Lessing/Art Resource, NY; **pages 53, 169, 170:** Nimatallah/Art Resource, NY; **pages 60, 244:** SEF/Art Resource, NY; **p. 80:** The Pierpont Morgan Library/Art Resource, NY; **page 96:** Fine Art Photographic Library, London/Art Resource, NY; **page 114:** Philadelphia Museum of Art: The George W. Elkins Collection; **pages 133, 199:** Alinari/Art Resource, NY; **page 192:** Tate Gallery, London/Art Resource, NY; **page 265:** James C. Anderson, jr.

Editorial consultant: Prof. Ward Briggs, University of South Carolina

ISBN 0-06-078371-0 (pbk.)   05   06   07   08   09   GC/RRD   10 9 8 7 6 5 4 3
ISBN 0-06-078423-7   05   06   07   08   09   GC/RRD   10 9 8 7 6 5 4 3

Contents

Foreword

The genesis of, and inspiration for, *Wheelock's Latin* was the 1946 G.I. Education bill which granted World War II Veterans a college education upon their return from service. "Why would a vet, schooled on the battle-fields of Europe and Asia, want to study Latin?" asked our father, then a Professor of Classics at Brooklyn College. What could this language say to those who had already seen so much reality? How could a teacher make a *dead* language become alive, pertinent, and viable? How could one teach Latin, not as an extinct vehicle, but as the reflection of a lively culture and philosophy? This was the challenge our father undertook.

Frederic Wheelock set about to create a Latin text that would give students something to think about, a humanistic diet to nurture them both linguistically and philosophically. The book began with lessons he designed especially for his Brooklyn College students. As children we smelled regularly the pungent hectograph ink which allowed him to painstakingly reproduce the chapters of a book he was designing, page by page on a gelatin pad, for one student at a time. In 1950, on Frederic's six-month sabbatical leave, the Wheelock family travelled to the remote village of San Miguel De Allende in Mexico, where Frederic conscientiously wrote his text, and our diligent mother, Dorothy, meticulously typed the manuscript on an old portable typewriter. We young children scampered irreverently underfoot or played with native children and burros.

Twelve years of refinement, revision, and actual usage in our father's classrooms resulted in the book's first edition. When students needed to learn grammar, they read lessons and literature from the great ancient writers who used the grammar in a meaningful context. Our father sought to graft the vital flesh and blood of Roman experience and thinking onto the basic bones of forms, syntax, and vocabulary; he wanted students to transcend mere gerund grinding by giving them literary and philosophical substance on which to sharpen their teeth.

As early as we can remember classical heritage filled our house. The etymology of a word would trigger lengthy discussion, often tedious for us as adolescents but abiding as we became adults. Knowing Latin teaches us English, we were constantly reminded; 60% of English words are derived from Latin. Students who take Latin are more proficient and earn higher scores on the verbal SAT exam. The business world has long recognized the importance of a rich vocabulary and rates it high as evidence of executive potential and success. Understanding the etymological history of a word gives the user vividness, color, punch, and precision. It also seems that the clearer and more numerous our verbal images, the greater our intellectual power. *Wheelock's Latin* is profuse with the etymological study of English and vocabulary enrichment. Our own experiences have shown that students will not only remember vocabulary words longer and better when they understand their etymologies, but also will use them with a sharper sense of meaning and nuance.

Why, then, exercise ourselves in the actual translation of Latin? "Inexorably accurate translation from Latin provides a training in observation, analysis, judgment, evaluation, and a sense of linguistic form, clarity, and beauty which is excellent training in the shaping of one's own English expression," asserted Frederic Wheelock. There is a discipline and an accuracy learned in the translation process which is transferable to any thinking and reasoning process, such as that employed by mathematicians. In fact, our father's beloved editor at Barnes & Noble, Dr. Gladys Walterhouse, was the Math Editor there and yet an ardent appreciator of Latin and its precision.

Our father loved the humanistic tradition of the classical writers and thinkers. And he shared this love not only with his students through the *Sententiae Antīquae* sections of his Latin text, but also with his family and friends in his daily life. As young girls, we were peppered with phrases of philosophical power from the ancients, and our father would show how these truths and lessons were alive and valid today. Some of the philosophical jewels which students of Latin will find in this book are: *carpe diem,* "seize the day"; *aurea mediocritās,* "the golden mean"; *summum bonum,* "the Highest Good"; and the derivation of "morality" from *mōrēs* ("good habits create good character," as our father used to tell us).

If learning the Latin language and the translation process are important, then getting to know the messages and art of Horace, Ovid, Virgil, and other Roman writers is equally important. Wheelock presents these Classical authors' writings on such illuminating topics as living for the future, attaining excellence, aging, and friendship. The *summum bonum* of Latin studies,

Frederic Wheelock wrote, "is the reading, analysis and appreciation of genuine ancient literary humanistic Latin in which our civilization is so deeply rooted and which has much to say to us in our 20th century."

For the 45 years that Frederic Wheelock was a Professor of Latin, he instilled in his students the love of Latin as both language and literature, and he did so with humor and humility. He dearly loved teaching, because he was so enthusiastic about what he taught. He had a deep and abiding respect for his students and demanded discipline and high standards. He wished for Latin to be loved and learned as he lived it, as a torch passed down through the ages, to help light our way today.

In 1987, as Frederic Wheelock was dying at the end of 85 richly lived years, he recited Homer, Horace, and Emily Dickinson. He, like the ancients, leaves a legacy of the love of learning and a belief that we stand on the shoulders of the ancients. He would be delighted to know that there are still active and eager students participating in the excitement and enjoyment of his beloved Latin.

Martha Wheelock and Deborah Wheelock Taylor
Fīliae amantissimae

Preface

Why a new beginners' Latin book when so many are already available? The question may rightly be asked, and a justification is in order.

It is notorious that every year increasing numbers of students enter college without Latin; and consequently they have to begin the language in college, usually as an elective, if they are to have any Latin at all. Though some college beginners do manage to continue their study of Latin for two or three years, a surprising number have to be satisfied with only one year of the subject. Among these, three groups predominate: Romance language majors, English majors, and students who have been convinced of the cultural and the practical value of even a little Latin.[1] Into the hands of such mature students (and many of them are actually Juniors and Seniors!) it is a pity and a lost opportunity to put textbooks which in pace and in thought are graded to high-school beginners. On the other hand, in the classical spirit of moderation, we should avoid the opposite extreme of a beginners' book so advanced and so severe that it is likely to break the spirit of even mature students in its attempt to cover practically everything in Latin.

Accordingly, the writer has striven to produce a beginners' book which is mature, humanistic, challenging, and instructive, and which, at the same time, is reasonable in its demands. Certainly it is not claimed that Latin can be made easy and effortless. However, the writer's experience with these

---

[1] I have even had inquiries about my lessons from graduate students who suddenly discovered that they needed some Latin and wanted to study it by themselves—much as I taught myself Spanish from E. V. Greenfield's *Spanish Grammar* (College Outline Series of Barnes & Noble) when I decided to make a trip to Mexico. Such instances really constitute a fourth group, adults who wish to learn some Latin independently of a formal academic course.

chapters in mimeographed form over a number of years shows that Latin can be made interesting despite its difficulty; it can give pleasure and profit even to the first-year student and to the student who takes only one year; it can be so presented as to afford a sense of progress and literary accomplishment more nearly commensurate with that achieved, for instance, by the student of Romance languages. The goal, then, has been a book which provides both the roots and at least some literary fruits of a sound Latin experience for those who will have only one year of Latin in their entire educational career, and a book which at the same time provides adequate introduction and encouragement for those who plan to continue their studies in the field. The distinctive methods and devices employed in this book in order to attain this goal are here listed with commentary.

1. SENTENTIAE ANTĪQUAE AND LOCĪ ANTĪQUĪ

It can hardly be disputed that the most profitable and the most inspiring approach to ancient Latin is through original Latin sentences and passages derived from the ancient authors themselves. With this conviction the writer perused a number of likely ancient works,[2] excerpting sentences and passages which could constitute material for the envisioned beginners' book. A prime desideratum was that the material be interesting per se and not chosen merely because it illustrated forms and syntax. These extensive excerpts provided a good cross section of Latin literature on which to base the choice of the forms, the syntax, and the vocabulary to be presented in the book. All the sentences which constitute the regular reading exercise in each chapter under the heading of *Sententiae Antīquae* are derived from this body of original Latin, as is demonstrated by the citing of the ancient author's name after each sentence. The same holds for the connected passages which appear both in the chapters and in the section entitled *Locī Antīquī*. Experience has shown that the work of the formal chapters can be covered in about three-quarters of an academic year, and that the remaining quarter can be had free and clear for the crowning experience of the year—the experience of reading additional real Latin passages from ancient authors,[3] passages which cover a wide range of interesting topics such as love, biography, philosophy, religion, morality, friendship, philanthropy, games, laws of war, anecdotes, wit, satirical comment. These basic exercises, then, are derived from

---

[2] Caesar's works were studiously avoided because of the view that Caesar's traditional place in the curriculum of the first two years is infelicitous, and that more desirable reading matter can be found.

[3] A half-dozen passages from late Latin and medieval authors are included to illustrate, among other things, the continuance of Latin through the Middle Ages.

Latin literature[4]; they are not "made" or "synthetic" Latin. In fact, by the nature of their content they constitute something of an introduction to Roman experience and thought; they are not mere inane collections of words put together simply to illustrate vocabulary, forms, and rules—though they are intended to do this too.

2. VOCABULARIES AND VOCABULARY DEVICES

Every chapter has a regular vocabulary list of new Latin words to be thoroughly learned. Each entry includes: the Latin word with one or more forms (e.g., with all principal parts, in the case of verbs); essential grammatical information (e.g., the gender of nouns, case governed by prepositions); English meanings (usually with the basic meaning first); and, in parentheses, representative English derivatives. The full vocabulary entry must be memorized for each item; in progressing from chapter to chapter, students will find it helpful to keep a running vocabulary list in their notebooks or a computer file, or to use vocabulary cards (with the Latin on one side, and the rest of the entry on the other). With an eye to the proverb *repetītiō māter memoriae,* words in the chapter vocabularies are generally repeated in the sentences and reading passages of the immediately following chapters, as well as elsewhere in the book.

In order to avoid overloading the regular chapter vocabularies, words that are less common in Latin generally or which occur infrequently (sometimes only once) in this book are glossed in parentheses following the *Sententiae Antīquae* and the reading passages. These glosses are generally less complete than the regular vocabulary entries and are even more abbreviated in the later chapters than in the earlier ones, but they should provide sufficient information for translating the text at hand; for words whose meanings can be easily deduced from English derivatives, the English is usually not provided. The instructor's requirements regarding these vocabulary items may vary, but in general students should be expected to have at least a "passive" mastery of the words, i.e., they should be able to recognize the words if encountered in a similar context, in a later chapter, for example, or on a test; full entries for most of these "recognition" items will also be found in the end Vocabulary.

---

[4] To be sure, at times the Latin has had to be somewhat edited in order to bring an otherwise too difficult word or form or piece of syntax within the limits of the student's experience. Such editing most commonly involves unimportant omissions, a slight simplification of the word order, or the substitution of an easier word, form, or syntactical usage. However, the thought and the fundamental expression still remain those of the ancient author.

3. SYNTAX

Although the above-mentioned corpus of excerpts constituted the logical guide to the syntactical categories which should be introduced into the book, common sense dictated the mean between too little and too much, as stated above. The categories which have been introduced should prove adequate for the reading of the mature passages of *Locī Antīquī* and also provide a firm foundation for those who wish to continue their study of Latin beyond the first year. In fact, with the skill acquired in handling this mature Latin and with a knowledge of the supplementary syntax provided in the Appendix, a student can skip the traditional second-year course in Caesar and proceed directly to the third-year course in Cicero and other authors. The syntax has been explained in as simple and unpedantic a manner as possible, and each category has been made concrete by a large number of examples, which provide both the desirable element of repetition and also self-tutorial passages for students. Finally, in light of the sad experience that even English majors in college may have an inadequate knowledge of grammar, explanations of most grammatical terms have been added, usually with benefit of etymology; and these explanations have not been relegated to some general summarizing section (the kind that students usually avoid!) but have been worked in naturally as the terms first appear in the text.

4. FORMS AND THEIR PRESENTATION

The varieties of inflected and uninflected forms presented here are normal for a beginners' book. However, the general practice in this text has been to alternate lessons containing noun or adjective forms with lessons containing verb forms. This should help reduce the ennui which results from too much of one thing at a time. The same consideration prompted the postponement of the locative case, adverbs, and most irregular verbs to the latter part of the book, where they could provide temporary respite from subjunctives and other heavy syntax.

Considerable effort has been made to place paradigms of more or less similar forms side by side for easy ocular cross reference in the same lesson[5] and also, as a rule, to have new forms follow familiar related ones in natural sequence (as when adjectives of the third declension follow the **i**-stem nouns).

The rate at which the syntax and the forms can be absorbed will obviously depend on the nature and the caliber of the class; the instructor will have to adjust the assignments to the situation. Though each chapter forms a logical unit, it has been found that at least two assignments have to be allotted to many of the longer chapters: the first covers the English text,

---

[5] The same device has been carefully employed in the Appendix.

the paradigms, the vocabularies, the *Practice and Review,* and some of the *Sententiae Antīquae;* the second one requires review, the completion of the *Sententiae,* the reading passage, and the section on etymology. Both these assignments are in themselves natural units, and this double approach contains the obvious gain of repetition.

5. PRACTICE AND REVIEW

The *Practice and Review* sentences were introduced as additional insurance of repetition of forms, syntax, and vocabulary, which is so essential in learning a language. If the author of a textbook can start with a predetermined sequence of vocabulary and syntax, for example, and is free to compose sentences based thereon, then it should be a fairly simple matter to make the sentences of succeeding lessons repeat the items of the previous few lessons, especially if the intellectual content of the sentences is not a prime concern. On the other hand, such repetition is obviously much more difficult to achieve when one works under the exacting restrictions outlined above in Section 1. Actually, most of the items introduced in a given chapter do re-appear in the *Sententiae Antīquae* of the immediately following chapters as well as passim thereafter, but the author frankly concocted the *Practice and Review* sentences[6] to fill in the lacunae, to guarantee further repetition than could otherwise have been secured, and to provide exercises of continuous review. The English-into-Latin sentences, though few in number on the grounds that the prime emphasis rests on learning to read Latin, should, however, be done regularly, but the others need not be assigned as part of the ordinary outside preparation. They are easy enough to be done at sight in class as time permits; or they can be used as a basis for review after every fourth or fifth chapter in lieu of formal review lessons.

6. ETYMOLOGIES

Unusually full lists of English derivatives are provided in parentheses after the words in the vocabularies to help impress the Latin words on the student, to demonstrate the direct or indirect indebtedness of English to Latin, and to enlarge the student's own vocabulary. Occasionally, English cognates have been added. At the end of each chapter a section entitled *Etymology* covers some of the recognition vocabulary items introduced in the sentences and reading passages, as well as other interesting points which could not be easily indicated in the vocabulary. From the beginning, the student should be urged to consult the lists of prefixes and suffixes given in the Appendix under the heading of *Some Etymological Aids.* To interest

---

[6] Ancient Latin sentences suggested some of them.

students of Romance languages and to suggest the importance of Latin to the subject, Romance derivatives have been listed from time to time.

7. THE INTRODUCTION

In addition to discussing the Roman alphabet and pronunciation, the book's general introduction sketches the linguistic, literary, and palaeographical background of Latin. This background and the actual Latin of the *Sententiae Antīquae* and the *Locī Antīquī* give the student considerable insight into Roman literature, thought, expression, and experience, and evince the continuity of the Roman tradition down to our own times. It is hoped that the Introduction and especially the nature of the lessons themselves will establish this book as not just another Latin grammar but rather as a humanistic introduction to the reading of genuine Latin.

The book had its inception in a group of mimeographed lessons put together rather hurriedly and tried out in class as a result of the dissatisfaction expressed above at the beginning of this Preface. The lessons worked well, despite immediately obvious imperfections traceable to their hasty composition. To Professor Lillian B. Lawler of Hunter College I am grateful for her perusal of the mimeographed material and for her suggestions. I also wish to acknowledge the patience of my students and colleagues at Brooklyn College who worked with the mimeographed material, and their helpfulness and encouragement in stating their reactions to the text. Subsequently these trial lessons were completely revised and rewritten in the light of experience. I am indebted to Professor Joseph Pearl of Brooklyn College for his kindness in scrutinizing the 40 chapters of the manuscript in their revised form and for many helpful suggestions. To the Reverend Joseph M.-F. Marique, S.J., of Boston College I herewith convey my appreciation for his encouraging and helpful review of the revised manuscript. Thomas S. Lester of Northeastern University, a man of parts and my *alter īdem amīcissimus* since classical undergraduate years, has my heartfelt thanks for so often and so patiently lending to my problems a sympathetic ear, a sound mind, and a sanguine spirit. To my dear wife, Dorothy, who so faithfully devoted herself to the typing of a very difficult manuscript, who was often asked for a judgment, and who, in the process, uttered many a salutary plea for clarity and for compassion toward the students, I dedicate my affectionate and abiding gratitude. My final thanks go to Dr. Gladys Walterhouse and her colleagues in the editorial department of Barnes & Noble for their friendly, efficient, and often crucial help in many matters. It need hardly be added that no one but the author is responsible for any infelicities which may remain.

The Second and Third Editions

Because of the requests of those who found that they needed more reading material than that provided by the *Locī Antīquī,* the author prepared a second edition which enriched the book by a new section entitled *Locī Immūtātī.* In these passages the original ancient Latin texts have been left unchanged except for omissions at certain points. The footnotes are of the general character of those in the *Locī Antīquī.* It is hoped that these readings will prove sufficiently extensive to keep an introductory class well supplied for the entire course, will give an interesting additional challenge to the person who is self-tutored, and will provide a very direct approach to the use of the regular annotated texts of classical authors.

Because of the indisputable value of repetition for establishing linguistic reflexes, the third edition includes a new section of Self-Tutorial Exercises. These consist of questions on grammar and syntax, and sentences for translation. A key provides answers to all the questions and translations of all the sentences.

The second and third editions would be incomplete without a word of deep gratitude to the many who in one way or another have given kind encouragement, who have made suggestions, who have indicated emendanda. I find myself particularly indebted to Professors Josephine Bree of Albertus Magnus College, Ben L. Charney of Oakland City College, Louis H. Feldman of Yeshiva College, Robert J. Leslie of Indiana University, Mr. Thomas S. Lester of Northeastern University, the Reverend James R. Murdock of Glenmary Home Missioners, Professors Paul Pascal of the University of Washington, Robert Renehan of Harvard University, John E. Rexine of Colgate University, George Tyler of Moravian College, Ralph L. Ward of Hunter College, Dr. Gladys Walterhouse of the Editorial Staff of Barnes & Noble, and most especially, once again, to my wife.

Frederic M. Wheelock

The Revised Edition

When Professor Frederic Wheelock's *Latin* first appeared in 1956, the reviews extolled its thoroughness, organization, and concision; at least one reviewer predicted that the book "might well become the standard text" for introducing college students and other adult learners to elementary Latin. Now, half a century later, that prediction has certainly been proven accurate. A second edition was published in 1960, retitled *Latin: An Introductory Course Based on Ancient Authors* and including a rich array of additional reading passages drawn directly from Latin literature (the *Locī Immūtātī*); the third edition, published in 1963, added Self-Tutorial Exercises, with an answer key, for each of the 40 chapters and greatly enhanced the book's usefulness both for classroom students and for those wishing to study the language independently. In 1984, three years before the author's death, a list of passage citations for the *Sententiae Antīquae* was added, so that teachers and students could more easily locate and explore the context of selections they found especially interesting; and in 1992 a fourth edition appeared under the aegis of the book's new publisher, HarperCollins, in which the entire text was set in a larger, more legible font.

The fifth edition, published in 1995 and aptly retitled *Wheelock's Latin,* constituted the first truly substantive revision of the text in more than 30 years. The revisions which I introduced were intended, not to alter the basic concept of the text, but to enhance it; indeed, a number of the most significant changes were based on Professor Wheelock's own suggestions, contained in notes made available for the project by his family, and others reflected the experiences of colleagues around the country, many of whom (myself included) had used and admired the book for two decades or more and had in the process arrived at some consensus about certain basic ways in which it might be improved for a new generation of students.

The most obvious change in the fifth edition reflected Wheelock's own principal desideratum, shared by myself and doubtless by most who had used the book over the years, and that was the addition of passages of continuous Latin, based on ancient authors, to each of the 40 chapters. These are in the early chapters quite brief and highly adapted, but later on are more extensive and often excerpted verbatim from a variety of prose and verse authors; some had appeared in previous editions among the *Locī Antīquī* and the *Locī Immūtātī,* while many were included for the first time in the fifth edition. Some of the Practice and Review sentences were revised or replaced, as were a few of the *Sententiae Antīquae* (which in some instances were expanded into longer readings), again as suggested in part by Professor Wheelock himself.

The chapter vocabularies, generally regarded as too sparse, were expanded in most instances to about 20–25 words, a quite manageable list including new items as well as many found previously as parenthetical glosses to the *Sententiae Antīquae.* Full principal parts were provided for all verbs from the beginning, as colleagues around the country had agreed should be done, so students would not be confronted with the somewhat daunting list previously presented in Chapter 12.

There was only minimal shifting of grammar, but in particular the imperfect tense was introduced along with the future in Chapters 5, 8, and 10, so that a past tense would be available for use in the readings at a much earlier stage. Numerals and the associated material originally in Chapter 40 were introduced in Chapter 15; and a half dozen or so important grammatical constructions previously presented in the Supplementary Syntax were instead introduced in Chapter 40 and a few of the earlier chapters. Many of the grammatical explanations were rewritten; essential information from the footnotes was incorporated into the text, while some less important notes were deleted.

Finally, I included at the end of each chapter in the fifth edition a section titled *Latīna Est Gaudium—et Ūtilis,* which presents, in a deliberately informal style, a miscellany of Latin mottoes and well-known quotations, familiar abbreviations, interesting etymologies, classroom conversation items, occasional tidbits of humor, and even a few ghastly puns, all intended to demonstrate, on the lighter side, that Latin can indeed be pleasurable as well as edifying.

The Sixth Edition and Sixth Edition, Revised

The very considerable success of the fifth edition encouraged all of us involved—Professor Wheelock's daughters, Martha Wheelock and Deborah Wheelock Taylor, our editor Greg Chaput and his associates at HarperCollins, and myself—to proceed with the further revisions I had proposed for this new sixth edition. We all hope that teachers and students alike will benefit from the numerous improvements, the most immediately apparent of which are: the handsome new cover art, a Roman mosaic from Tunisia depicting Virgil with a copy of the *Aeneid* in his lap and flanked by two Muses representing his work's inspiration; the three maps of ancient Italy, Greece and the Aegean area, and the Mediterranean, which have been specially designed to include, inter alia, all the placenames mentioned in the book's readings and notes (except a few situated on the remotest fringes of the empire); and the numerous photographs selected primarily from classical and later European art to illustrate literary and historical figures and aspects of classical culture and mythology presented in the chapter readings. Among the less obvious but, we hope, equally helpful changes are: revision of chapter readings, especially the Practice and Review sentences, for greater clarity and increased reinforcement of new and recently introduced chapter vocabulary items; expansion of derivatives lists in the chapter vocabularies and of cross-references to related words in other chapters; and enlargement of the English-Latin end vocabulary.

The "sixth edition, revised," first published in 2005, contains a variety of additional enhancements, including slight revisions to the Introduction and to some of the sentences, reading passages, and accompanying notes, as well as further expansion of the English-Latin vocabulary designed to render even more useful the popular companion text, *Workbook for Wheelock's Latin* (in its revised third edition by Paul Comeau and myself, published concurrently with the sixth edition of *Wheelock's Latin*). The sixth edition, revised, is also the first in many years to appear in a hardbound version, along with the traditional paperback; audio is now available online for all the chapter vocabularies and other pronunciation help; and, for the first time ever, a teacher's guide has been written and is available online, password-protected, to instructors who provide verification of their faculty status.

A final note for professors, teachers, and those engaged in independent study: This revised edition of *Wheelock's Latin* very likely contains more material for translation than can actually be covered in the two or three days typically allotted to a chapter in a semester course or the week or so allotted in high school. Instructors may thus pick and choose and be selective in the material they assign: my suggestion for the first day or two is to assign for written homework only limited selections from the Practice and Review sentences and the *Sententiae Antīquae,* while reserving the others (or some of the others, carefully selected in advance) for in-class sight translation; assignments for the second or third day should nearly always include the reading passages following the *Sententiae Antīquae,* which will give students the experience they need with continuous narrative. Students should regularly be encouraged to practice new material at home with the Self-Tutorial Exercises located at the back of the book, checking their accuracy with the answer key that follows, and sentences from these exercises, again pre-selected for the purpose, can be used to drill mastery of new concepts via sight translation in class.

Most instructors will also want their students to use the *Workbook for Wheelock's Latin,* which contains a wide range of additional exercises, including for each chapter a detailed set of objectives, a series of questions designed to focus directly on the newly introduced grammar, a variety of transformation drills, word, phrase, and sentence translations, questions on etymologies, synonyms, antonyms, and analogies for new vocabulary items, and reading comprehension questions to test the student's understanding of the chapter's reading passages.

Those who may not have time to complete all of the many *Workbook* items provided for each chapter are advised at least to review each of the *Intellegenda* (chapter objectives), answer all the *Grammatica* (grammar review) questions and then complete at least one or two items from each section of the *Exercitātiōnēs* (i.e., one or two from the section A exercises, one or two from section B, etc.), all the *Vīs Verbōrum* (etymology and English word power) items, one or two of the Latin-to-English translations in section A of the *Lēctiōnēs* (readings), and all the items in *Lēctiōnēs* B (questions on the chapter's continuous reading passages).

There are numerous other materials designed to complement *Wheelock's Latin* and the *Workbook for Wheelock's Latin,* including supplemental readers, computer software, and a wealth of internet resources, many of which, along with further suggestions on teaching and learning Latin via Wheelock, are listed at the official Wheelock's Latin Series Website, www.wheelockslatin.com, and described in my book *Latin for the 21st Century: From Concept to Classroom* (available from Prentice Hall Publishers).

There are many whom I am eager to thank for their support of the fifth and sixth editions of *Wheelock's Latin:* my children, Jean-Paul, Laura Caroline, and Kimberley Ellen, for their constant affection; my colleague Jared Klein, a distinguished Indo-European linguist, for reading and offering his judicious advice on my revisions to both the Introduction and the individual chapters; graduate assistants Cleve Fisher, Marshall Lloyd, Sean Mathis, Matthew Payne, and Jim Yavenditti, for their energetic and capable help with a variety of tasks; Mary Wells Ricks, long-time friend and former Senior Associate Editor for the *Classical Outlook,* for her expert counsel on a variety of editorial matters; our department secretaries, JoAnn Pulliam and Connie Russell, for their generous clerical assistance; my editors at HarperCollins, Erica Spaberg, Patricia Leasure, and especially Greg Chaput, each of whom enthusiastically supported my proposals for the revised editions; Tim McCarthy of Art Resource in New York, as well as colleagues Jim Anderson, Bob Curtis, Timothy Gantz†, and Frances Van Keuren, for their assistance with the graphics; Tom Elliott, with the Ancient World

Mapping Center, for the lion's share of the work involved in designing the sixth edition's maps; students and associates at the University of Georgia who field-tested the new material or provided other helpful assistance, among them Bob Harris and Richard Shedenhelm; colleagues around the country who offered suggestions for specific revisions to one or both of these editions, especially Ward Briggs at the University of South Carolina (whose biographies of Professor Wheelock appear in his book, *A Biographical Dictionary of American Classicists,* Westport CT: Greenwood Press, 1994, and in the Winter, 2003, *Classical Outlook*), Rob Latousek, John Lautermilch, John McChesney-Young, Braden Mechley, Betty Rose Nagle, John Ramsey, Joseph Riegsecker, Cliff Roti, Les Sheridan, David Sider, Alden Smith, Cliff Weber, and Stephen Wheeler; Dean Wyatt Anderson, for his encouragement of my own work and all our Classics Department's endeavors; Martha Wheelock and Deborah Wheelock Taylor, my "sisters-in-Latin," for their steadfast advocacy of my work on the revised editions and their generous sharing of their father's notes; and finally, Professor Frederic M. Wheelock himself, for producing a textbook that has truly become a classic in its own right and one whose revision, therefore, became for me a *labor amōris.*

Richard A. LaFleur
University of Georgia
Autumn, 2004

I love the language, that soft bastard Latin,
Which melts like kisses from a female mouth.

> George Noel Gordon, Lord Byron
> *Beppo*

I would make them all learn English: and then I would
let the clever ones learn Latin as an honor, and Greek
as a treat.

> Sir Winston Churchill
> *Roving Commission: My Early Life*

He studied Latin like the violin, because he liked it.

> Robert Frost
> *The Death of the Hired Man*

Introduction

Wer fremde Sprachen nicht kennt, weiss nichts von seiner eigenen. (Goethe)
Apprendre une langue, c'est vivre de nouveau. (French proverb)

Interest in learning Latin can be considerably increased by even a limited knowledge of some background details such as are sketched in this introduction. The paragraphs on the position of the Latin language in linguistic history provide one with some linguistic perspective not only for Latin but also for English. The brief survey of Latin literature introduces the authors from whose works have come the *Sententiae Antīquae* and the *Locī Antīquī* of this book; and even this abbreviated survey provides some literary perspective which the student may never otherwise experience. The same holds for the account of the alphabet; and, of course, no introduction would be complete without a statement about the sounds which the letters represent.

THE POSITION OF THE LATIN LANGUAGE IN LINGUISTIC HISTORY

Say the words "I," "me," "is," "mother," "brother," "ten," and you are speaking words which, in one form or another, men and women of Europe and Asia have used for thousands of years. In fact, we cannot tell how old these words actually are. If their spelling and pronunciation have changed somewhat from period to period and from place to place, little wonder; what does pique the imagination is the fact that the basic elements of these symbols of human thought have had the vitality to traverse such spans of time and space down to this very moment on this new continent. The point is demonstrated in the considerably abbreviated and simplified table that follows.[1]

English	*I*	*me*	*is*	*mother*	*brother*	*ten*
Sanskrit[2]	aham	mā	asti	mātar-	bhrātar-	daśam
Greek	egō	me	esti	mētēr	phrātēr[3]	deka
Latin	ego	mē	est	māter	frāter	decem
Anglo-Saxon[4]	ic	mē	is	mōdor	brōthor	tīen
Old Irish[5]		mé	is	máthir	bráthir	deich
Lithuanian[6]	aš	manè	esti	motè	broterèlis	dešimtis
Russian[7]	ja	menja	jest'	mat'	brat	desjat'

You can see from these columns of words that the listed languages are related.[8] And yet, with the exception of the ultimate derivation of English from Anglo-Saxon,[9] none of these languages stems directly from another in the list. Rather, they all go back through intermediate stages to a common ancestor, which is now lost but which can be predicated on the evidence of the languages which do survive. Such languages the philologist calls "cognate" (Latin for "related" or, more literally, "born together," i.e., from the same ancestry). The name most commonly given to the now lost ancestor of all these "relatives," or cognate languages, is *Indo-European,* because its descendants are found both in or near India (Sanskrit, Iranian) and also in Europe (Greek and Latin and the Germanic, Celtic, Slavic, and Baltic languages).[10] The oldest of these languages on the basis of documents writ-

---

[1] Some elements have been omitted from this table as not immediately necessary. The words in the table are only a few of the many which could be cited.

[2] The language of the sacred writings of ancient India, parent of the modern Indo-European languages of India.

[3] Though cognate with the other words in this column, classical Greek **phrātēr** meant *member of a clan.*

[4] As an example of the Germanic languages; others are Gothic, German, Dutch, Danish, Norwegian, Swedish, Icelandic, English.

[5] As an example of the Celtic languages; others are Gaulish, Breton, Scots (Gaelic). Old Irish **mé** in the chart is actually nominative case, equivalent to "I" in meaning and usage but to "me" in form.

[6] As an example of the Baltic group; others are Latvian and Old Prussian.

[7] As an example of the Slavic group; others are Polish, Bulgarian, Czech.

[8] This large family of languages shows relationship in the matter of inflections also, but no attempt is made here to demonstrate the point. An inflected language is one in which the nouns, pronouns, adjectives, and verbs have variable endings by which the relationship of the words to each other in a sentence can be indicated. In particular, note that Anglo-Saxon, like Latin, was an inflected language but that its descendant English has lost most of its inflections.

[9] The later connection between English and Latin will be pointed out below.

[10] Note that many languages (e.g., the Semitic languages, Egyptian, Basque, Chinese, the native languages of Africa and the Americas) lie outside the Indo-European family.

ten in them are Sanskrit, Iranian, Greek, and Latin, and these documents go back centuries before the time of Christ.

The difference between *derived* (from roots meaning "to flow downstream from" a source) and *cognate* languages can be demonstrated even more clearly by the relationship of the Romance languages to Latin and to each other. For here we are in the realm of recorded history and can see that with the Roman political conquest of such districts as Gaul (France), Spain, and Dacia (Roumania) there occurred also a Roman linguistic conquest. Out of this victorious ancient Latin as spoken by the common people (**vulgus,** hence "vulgar" Latin) grew the Romance languages, such as French, Spanish, Portuguese, Roumanian, and, of course, Italian. Consequently, we can say of Italian, French, and Spanish, for instance, that they are *derived* from Latin and that they are *cognate* with each other.

Parent	Cognate Romance Derivatives			
Latin	**Italian**	**Spanish**	**French**	**English Meaning**
amīcus	amico	amigo	ami	friend
liber	libro	libro	livre	book
tempus	tempo	tiempo	temps	time
manus	mano	mano	main	hand
bucca	bocca	boca	bouche	mouth (cheek *in classical Lat.*)[11]
caballus[12]	cavallo	caballo	cheval	horse
fīlius	figlio	hijo	fils	son
ille	il	el	(le)[13]	the (that *in classical Lat.*)
illa	la	la	la	the (that *in classical Lat.*)
quattuor	quattro	cuatro	quatre	four
bonus	buono	bueno	bon	good
bene	bene	bien	bien	well (*adv.*)
facere	fare	hacer	faire	make, do
dīcere	dire	decir	dire	say
legere	leggere	leer	lire	read

Although it was noted above that English ultimately stems from Anglo-Saxon, which is cognate with Latin, there is much more than that to the story of our own language. Anglo-Saxon itself had early borrowed a few words from Latin; and then in the 7th century more Latin words[14] came in as a result of the work of St. Augustine (the Lesser), who was sent by Pope Gregory to Christianize the Angles. After the victory of William the Con-

---

[11] The classical Latin word for *mouth* was **ōs, ōris.**

[12] The classical Latin word for *horse* was **equus.**

[13] Derived from **ille** but not actually cognate with *il* and *el.*

[14] Many of these were of Greek and Hebrew origin but had been Latinized. The Latin *Vulgate* played an important role.

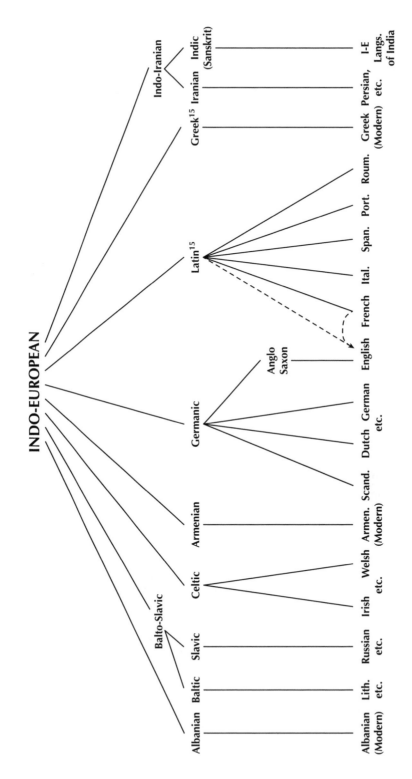

INDO-EUROPEAN

Indo-Iranian

Indic (Sanskrit) — I-E Langs. of India

Iranian — Persian, etc.

Greek[15] — Greek (Modern)

Latin[15] — French, Ital., Span., Port., Roum.

Germanic

Anglo Saxon — English

Scand., Dutch, German etc.

Armenian — Armen. (Modern)

Celtic — Irish, Welsh etc.

Slavic — Russian etc.

Baltic — Lith. etc.

Balto-Slavic

Albanian — Albanian (Modern)

[15] Actually, Latin was only one of a number of Italic dialects (among which were Oscan and Umbrian), and some time passed before Latin won out over the other dialects in Italy. Similarly, among the Greeks there were a number of dialects (Aeolic, Attic, Ionic, Doric).

queror in 1066, Norman French became the polite language and Anglo-Saxon was held in low esteem as the tongue of vanquished men and serfs. Thus Anglo-Saxon, no longer the language of literature, became simply the speech of humble daily life. Some two centuries later, however, as the descendants of the Normans finally amalgamated with the English natives, the Anglo-Saxon language reasserted itself; but in its poverty it had to borrow hundreds of French words (literary, intellectual, cultural) before it could become the language of literature. Borrow it did abundantly, and in the 13th and 14th centuries this development produced what is called Middle English, known especially from Chaucer, who died in 1400. Along with the adoption of these Latin-rooted French words there was also some borrowing directly from Latin itself, and the renewed interest in the classics which characterized the Renaissance naturally intensified this procedure during the 16th and the 17th centuries.[16] From that time to the present Latin has continued to be a source of new words, particularly for the scientist.[17]

Consequently, since English through Anglo-Saxon is cognate with Latin and since English directly or indirectly has borrowed so many words from Latin, we can easily demonstrate both cognation and derivation by our own vocabulary. For instance, our word "brother" is *cognate* with Latin **frāter** but "fraternal" clearly is *derived* from **frāter.** Other instances are:

English	**Latin Cognate**[18]	**English Derivative**
mother	māter	maternal
two	duo	dual, duet
tooth	dēns, *stem* dent-	dental
foot	pēs, *stem* ped-	pedal
heart	cor, *stem* cord-	cordial
bear	ferō	fertile

[16] Thomas Wilson (16th century) says: "The unlearned or foolish fantastical, that smells but of learning (such fellows as have been learned men in their days), will so Latin their tongues, that the simple cannot but wonder at their talk, and think surely they speak by some revelation." Sir Thomas Browne (17th century) says: "If elegancy still proceedeth, and English pens maintain that stream we have of late observed to flow from many, we shall within a few years be fain to learn Latin to understand English, and a work will prove of equal facility in either." These statements are quoted by permission from the "Brief History of the English Language" by Hadley and Kittredge in Webster's *New International Dictionary,* Second Edition, copyright, 1934, 1939, 1945, 1950, 1953, 1954, by G. & C. Merriam Co.

[17] And apparently even our 20th-century composers of advertisements would be reduced to near beggary if they could not draw on the Latin vocabulary and the classics in general.

[18] Grimm's law catalogues the Germanic shift in certain consonants (the stops). This shows how such apparently different words as English *heart* and Latin **cor, cord-,** are in origin the same word.

In fact, here you see one of the reasons for the richness of our vocabulary, and the longer you study Latin the more keenly you will realize what a limited language ours would be without the Latin element.

Despite the brevity of this survey you can comprehend the general position of Latin in European linguistic history and something of its continuing importance to us of the 20th century. It is the cognate[19] of many languages and the parent of many; it can even be called the adoptive parent of our own. In summary is offered the much abbreviated diagram on page xxx above.[20]

A BRIEF SURVEY OF LATIN LITERATURE

Since throughout this entire book you will be reading sentences and longer passages excerpted from Latin literature, a brief outline is here sketched to show both the nature and the extent of this great literature. You will find the following main divisions reasonable and easy to keep in mind, though the common warning against dogmatism in regard to the names and the dates of periods should certainly be sounded.

    I. Early Period (down to ca. 80 B.C.)
   II. Golden Age (80 B.C.–14 A.D.)
      A. Ciceronian Period (80–43 B.C.)
      B. Augustan Period (43 B.C.–14 A.D.)
  III. Silver Age (14–ca. 138 A.D.)
  IV. Patristic Period (late 2nd–5th cens. of our era)
   V. Medieval Period (6th–14th cens. of our era)
  VI. Period from the Renaissance (ca. 15th cen.) to the Present

THE EARLY PERIOD (DOWN TO CA. 80 B.C.)

The apogee of Greek civilization, including the highest development of its magnificent literature and art, was reached during the 5th and the 4th centuries before Christ. In comparison, Rome during those centuries had little to offer. Our fragmentary evidence shows only a rough, accentual na-

---

[19] Take particular care to note that Latin is simply cognate with Greek, not derived from it.

[20] In the interests of simplicity and clarity a number of languages and intermediate steps have been omitted. In particular it should be noted that no attempt has been made to indicate the indebtedness of English to Greek. Two branches of the Indo-European language family, Anatolian and Tocharian, are now extinct and are not shown on the chart.

tive meter called Saturnian, some native comic skits, and a rough, practical prose for records and speeches.

In the 3d century B.C., however, the expansion of Roman power brought the Romans into contact with Greek civilization. Somehow the hard-headed, politically and legally minded Romans were fascinated by what they found, and the writers among them went to school to learn Greek literature. From this time on, Greek literary forms, meters, rhetorical devices, subjects, and ideas had a tremendous and continuing influence on Roman literature, even as it developed its own character and originality in a great many ways.

In fact, the Romans themselves did not hesitate to admit as much. Although the Romans now composed epics, tragedies, satires, and speeches, the greatest extant accomplishments of this period of apprenticeship to Greek models are the comedies of Plautus (ca. 254–184 B.C.) and Terence (185–159 B.C.). These were based on Greek plays of the type known as New Comedy, the comedy of manners, and they make excellent reading today. Indeed, a number of these plays have influenced modern playwrights; Plautus' *Menaechmi,* for instance, inspired Shakespeare's *Comedy of Errors.*

THE GOLDEN AGE (80 B.C.–14 A.D.)

During the first century before Christ the Roman writers perfected their literary media and made Latin literature one of the world's greatest. It is particularly famous for its beautiful, disciplined form, which we know as classic, and for its real substance as well. If Lucretius complained about the poverty of the Latin vocabulary, Cicero so molded the vocabulary and the general usage that Latin remained a supple and a subtle linguistic tool for thirteen centuries and more.[21]

THE CICERONIAN PERIOD (80–43 B.C.). The literary work of the Ciceronian Period was produced during the last years of the Roman Republic. This was a period of civil wars and dictators, of military might against constitutional right, of selfish interest, of brilliant pomp and power, of moral and religious laxity. Outstanding authors important for the book which you have in hand are:

Lucretius (Titus Lūcrētius Cārus, ca. 98–55 B.C.): author of *Dē Rērum Nātūrā,* a powerful didactic poem on happiness achieved through the Epicurean philosophy. This philosophy was based on pleasure[22] and was buttressed by an atomic theory which made the universe a realm of natural, not divine, law and thus eliminated the fear of the gods and the tyranny of religion, which Lucretius believed had shattered men's happiness.

Catullus (Gāius Valerius Catullus, ca. 84–54 B.C.): lyric poet, the Robert

---

[21] See below under Medieval and Renaissance Latin.

[22] However, that it meant simply "eat, drink, and be merry" is a vulgar misinterpretation.

Burns of Roman literature, an intense and impressionable young provincial from northern Italy who fell totally under the spell of an urban sophisticate, Lesbia (a literary pseudonym for her real name, Clodia), but finally escaped bitterly disillusioned; over 100 of his poems have survived.

Cicero (Mārcus Tullius Cicerō, 106–43 B.C.): the greatest Roman orator, whose eloquence thwarted the conspiracy of the bankrupt aristocrat Catiline[23] in 63 B.C. and 20 years later cost Cicero his own life in his patriotic opposition to Anthony's high-handed policies; admired also as an authority on Roman rhetoric, as an interpreter of Greek philosophy to his countrymen, as an essayist on friendship (*Dē Amīcitiā*) and on old age (*Dē Senectūte*), and, in a less formal style, as a writer of self-revealing letters. Cicero's vast contributions to the Latin language itself have already been mentioned.

Caesar (Gāius Iūlius Caesar, 102 or 100–44 B.C.): orator, politician, general, statesman, dictator, author; best known for his military memoirs, *Bellum Gallicum* and *Bellum Cīvīle.*

[23] See the introductory notes to "Cicero Denounces Catiline" in Ch. 11 and "Evidence and Confession" in Ch. 30.

Julius Caesar
1st century B.C.
Museo Archeologico Nazionale
Naples, Italy

Nepos (Cornēlius Nepōs, 99–24 B.C.): friend of Catullus and Caesar and a writer of biographies noted rather for their relatively easy and popular style than for greatness as historical documents.

Publilius Syrus (fl. 43 B.C.): a slave who was taken to Rome and who there became famous for his mimes, which today are represented only by a collection of epigrammatic sayings.

THE AUGUSTAN PERIOD (43 B.C.–14 A.D.). The first Roman Emperor gave his name to this period. Augustus wished to correct the evils of the times, to establish civil peace by stable government, and to win the Romans' support for his new regime. With this in mind he and Maecenas, his unofficial prime minister, sought to enlist literature in the service of the state. Under their patronage Virgil and Horace became what we should call poets laureate. Some modern critics feel that this fact vitiates the noble sentiments of these poets; others see in Horace a spirit of independence and of genuine moral concern, and maintain that Virgil, through the character of his epic hero Aeneas, is not simply glorifying Augustus but is actually suggesting to the emperor what is expected of him as head of the state.[24]

Virgil (Pūblius Vergilius Marō, 70–19 B.C.): from humble origins in northern Italy; lover of nature; profoundly sympathetic student of humankind; Epicurean and mystic; severe and exacting self-critic, master craftsman, linguistic and literary architect, "lord of language"; famous as a writer of pastoral verse (the *Eclogues*) and of a beautiful didactic poem on farm life (the *Georgics*); best known as the author of one of the world's great epics,[25] the *Aeneid,* a national epic with ulterior purposes, to be sure, but one also with ample universal and human appeal to make it powerful 20th-century reading.

Horace (Quīntus Horātius Flaccus, 65–8 B.C.): freedman's son who, thanks to his father's vision and his own qualities, rose to the height of poet laureate; writer of genial and self-revealing satires; author of superb lyrics both light and serious; meticulous composer famed for the happy effects of his linguistic craftsmanship (**cūriōsa fēlīcitās,** *painstaking felicity*); synthesist of Epicurean **carpe diem** (*enjoy today*) and Stoic **virtūs** (*virtue*); preacher and practitioner of **aurea mediocritās** (*the golden mean*).

Livy (Titus Līvius, 59 B.C.–17 A.D.): friend of Augustus but an admirer of the Republic and of olden virtues; author of a monumental, epic-spirited history of Rome, and portrayer of Roman character at its best as he judged it.

---

[24] See, for instance, E. K. Rand, *The Builders of Eternal Rome* (Harvard Univ. Press, 1943).

[25] The *Aeneid* is always associated with Homer's *Iliad* and *Odyssey,* to which it owes a great deal, and with Dante's *Divine Comedy* and Milton's *Paradise Lost,* which owe a great deal to it.

Propertius (Sextus Propertius, ca. 50 B.C.–ca. 2 A.D.): author of four books of romantic elegiac poems, much admired by Ovid.

Ovid (Pūblius Ovidius Nāsō, 43 B.C.–17 A.D.): author of much love poetry which was hardly consonant with Augustus' plans; most famous today as the writer of the long and clever hexameter work on mythology entitled *Metamorphōsēs,* which has proved a thesaurus for subsequent poets. Ovid, like Pope, "lisped in numbers, for the numbers came."

THE SILVER AGE (14–CA. 138 A.D.)

In the Silver Age there is excellent writing; but often there are also artificialities and conceits, a striving for effects and a passion for epigrams, characteristics which often indicate a less sure literary sense and power—hence the traditional, though frequently overstated, distinction between "Golden" and "Silver." The temperaments of not a few emperors also had a limiting or blighting effect on the literature of this period.

Seneca (Lūcius Annaeus Seneca, 4 B.C.–65 A.D.): Stoic philosopher from Spain; tutor of Nero; author of noble moral essays of the Stoic spirit, of tragedies (which, though marred by too much rhetoric and too many conceits, had considerable influence on the early modern drama of Europe), and of the *Apocolocyntōsis* ("Pumpkinification"), a brilliantly witty, though sometimes cruel, prosimetric satire on the death and deification of the emperor Claudius.

Petronius (exact identity and dates uncertain, but probably Titus Petrōnius Arbiter, d. 65 A.D.): Neronian consular and courtier; author of the *Satyricon,* a satiric, prosimetric novel of sorts, famous for its depiction of the nouveau-riche freedman Trimalchio and his extravagant dinner-parties.

Quintilian (Mārcus Fabius Quīntiliānus, ca. 35–95 A.D.): teacher and author of the *Īnstitūtiō Ōrātōria,* a famous pedagogical work which discusses the entire education of a person who is to become an orator; a great admirer of Cicero's style and a critic of the rhetorical excesses of his own age.

Martial (Mārcus Valerius Mārtiālis, 45–104 A.D.): famed for his more than 1,500 witty epigrams and for the satirical twist which he so often gave to them. As he himself says, his work may not be great literature but people do enjoy it.

Pliny (Gāius Plīnius Caecilius Secundus, ca. 62–113 A.D.): a conscientious public figure, who is now best known for his *Epistulae,* letters which reveal both the bright and the seamy sides of Roman life during this imperial period.

Tacitus (Pūblius Cornēlius Tacitus, 55–117 A.D.): most famous as a satirical, pro-senatorial historian of the period from the death of Augustus to the death of Domitian.

Juvenal (Decimus Iūnius Iuvenālis, ca. 55-post 127 A.D.): a relentless, intensely rhetorical satirist of the evils of his times, who concludes that the only thing for which one can pray is a **mēns sāna in corpore sānō** (*a sound mind in a sound body*). His satires inspired Dr. Samuel Johnson's *London* and *The Vanity of Human Wishes* and the whole conception of caustic, "Juvenalian" satire.

THE ARCHAISING PERIOD. The mid- to late 2nd century may be distinguished as an archaizing period, in which a taste developed for the vocabulary and style of early Latin and for the incorporation of diction from vulgar Latin; characteristic authors of the period were the orator Fronto and the antiquarian Aulus Gellius, known for his miscellaneous essays *Noctēs Atticae* ("Nights in Attica").

THE PATRISTIC PERIOD (Late 2nd Cen.–5th Cen.)

The name of the Patristic Period comes from the fact that most of the vital literature was the work of the Christian leaders, or fathers (**patrēs**), among whom were Tertullian, Cyprian, Lactantius, Jerome, Ambrose, and Augustine. These men had been well educated; they were familiar with, and frequently fond of, the best classical authors; many of them had even been teachers or lawyers before going into service of the Church. At times the classical style was deliberately employed to impress the pagans, but more and more the concern was to reach the common people (**vulgus**) with the Christian message. Consequently, it is not surprising to see vulgar Latin re-emerging[26] as an important influence in the literature of the period. St. Jerome in his letters is essentially Ciceronian, but in his Latin edition of the Bible, the *Vulgate* (383–405 A.D.), he uses the language of the people. Similarly St. Augustine, though formerly a teacher and a great lover of the Roman classics, was willing to use any idiom that would reach the people (**ad ūsum vulgī**) and said that it did not matter if the barbarians conquered Rome provided they were Christian.

THE MEDIEVAL PERIOD (6th–14th Cens.)

During the first three centuries of the Medieval Period, vulgar Latin underwent rapid changes[27] and, reaching the point when it could no longer be called Latin, it became this or that Romance language according to the locality.

---

[26] Vulgar Latin has already been mentioned as the language of the common people. Its roots are in the early period. In fact, the language of Plautus has much in common with this later vulgar Latin, and we know that throughout the Golden and the Silver Ages vulgar Latin lived on as the colloquial idiom of the people but was kept distinct from the literary idiom of the texts and the polished conversation of those periods.

[27] E.g., the loss of most declensional endings and the increased use of prepositions; extensive employment of auxiliary verbs; anarchy in the uses of the subjunctive and the indicative.

On the other hand, Latin, the literary idiom more or less modified by the *Vulgate* and other influences, continued throughout the Middle Ages as the living language of the Church and of the intellectual world. Though varying considerably in character and quality, it was an international language, and Medieval Latin literature is sometimes called "European" in contrast to the earlier "national Roman." In this Medieval Latin was written a varied and living literature (religious works, histories, anecdotes, romances, dramas, sacred and secular poetry), examples of which are included below, in the excerpt from the 7th century writer Isidore of Seville (in Ch. 29) and selections from other authors in the *Locī Antīquī*. The long life of Latin is attested in the early 14th century by the facts that Dante composed in Latin the political treatise *Dē Monarchiā,* that he wrote in Latin his *Dē Vulgārī Ēloquentiā* to justify his use of the vernacular Italian for literature, and that in Latin pastoral verses he rejected the exhortation to give up the vernacular, in which he was writing the *Divine Comedy,* and compose something in Latin.[28]

THE PERIOD FROM THE RENAISSANCE (ca. 15th Cen.) TO THE PRESENT

Because of Petrarch's new-found admiration of Cicero, Renaissance scholars scorned Medieval Latin and turned to Cicero in particular as the canon of perfection. Although this return to the elegant Ciceronian idiom was prompted by great affection and produced brilliant effects, it was an artificial movement which made Latin somewhat imitative and static compared with the spontaneous, living language which it had been during the Middle Ages. However, Latin continued to be effectively employed well into the modern period,[29] and the ecclesiastical strain is still very much alive (despite its de-emphasis in the early 1960s) as the language of the Roman Catholic Church and seminaries. Furthermore, the rediscovery of the true, humanistic spirit of the ancient Latin and Greek literatures and the fresh attention to literary discipline and form as found in the classics proved very beneficial to the native literature of the new era.

The purpose of this abbreviated outline has been to provide some sense of the unbroken sweep of Latin literature from the 3rd century B.C. down to our own times. Besides enjoying its own long and venerable history, Latin literature has also inspired, schooled, and enriched our own English and other occidental literatures to a degree beyond easy assessment. Add to this

---

[28] At the same time, by token of Dante's success and that of others in the use of the vernacular languages, it must be admitted that Latin had begun to wage a losing battle.

[29] For instance, note its use by Erasmus and Sir Thomas More in the 16th century, by Milton, Bacon, and Newton in the 17th century, and by botanists, classical scholars, and poets of the later centuries.

the wide influence of the Latin language itself as outlined above and you can hardly escape the conclusion that Latin is dead only in a technical sense of the word, and that even a limited knowledge of Latin is a great asset to anyone who works with or is interested in English and the Romance languages and literatures.

THE ALPHABET AND PRONUNCIATION

The forms of the letters which you see on this printed page are centuries old. They go back through the earliest Italian printed books of the 15th century[30] and through the finest manuscripts of the 12th and 11th centuries to the firm, clear Carolingian bookhand of the 9th century as perfected under the inspiration of the Carolingian Renaissance by the monks of St. Martin's at Tours in France. These monks developed the small letters from beautiful clear semi-uncials, which in turn lead us back to the uncials[31] and square capitals of the Roman Empire. Today we are in the habit of distinguishing the Roman alphabet from the Greek, but the fact is that the Romans learned to write from the Etruscans, who in turn had learned to write from Greek colonists who had settled in the vicinity of Naples during the 8th century B.C. Actually, therefore, the Roman alphabet is simply one form of the Greek alphabet. But the Greeks were themselves debtors in this matter, for, at an early but still undetermined date, they had received their alphabet from a Semitic source, the Phoenicians.[32] And finally the early Semites appear to have been inspired by Egyptian hieroglyphs. This brief history of the forms of the letters which you see in our books today provides one more illustration of our indebtedness to antiquity.

The Roman alphabet was like ours except that it lacked the letters **j** and **w.** Furthermore, the letter **v** originally stood for both the sound of the vowel

---

[30] Called "incunabula" because they were made in the "cradle days" of printing. The type is called "Roman" to distinguish it from the "black-letter" type which was used in northern Europe (cp. the German type). The Italian printers based their Roman type on that of the finest manuscripts of the period, those written for the wealthy, artistic, exacting Renaissance patrons. The scribes of those manuscripts, seeking the most attractive kind of script with which to please such patrons, found it in manuscripts written in the best Carolingian book-hand.

[31] The uncial letters are similar to the square capitals except that the sharp corners of the angular letters have been rounded so that they can be written with greater rapidity. An illustration can be found in Webster's *Collegiate Dictionary,* entry *uncial.*

[32] The 22 letters of the Phoenician alphabet represented only consonant sounds. The Greeks showed their originality in using some of these letters to designate vowel sounds.

Portrait of a young woman with stilus and tabella, fresco from Pompeii
Museo Archeologico Nazionale, Naples, Italy

u and the sound of the consonant **w.**[33] Not till the second century of our era did the rounded **u**-form appear, but for convenience both **v** and **u** are employed in the Latin texts of most modern editions. The letter **k** was rarely

[33] Note that our letter **w** is simply double **u** of the **v**-shaped variety.

used, and then only before **a,** in a very few words. The letters **y**[34] and **z** were introduced toward the end of the Republic to be used in spelling words of Greek origin.

The following tables indicate approximately the sounds of Latin and how the letters were used by Romans of the classical period to represent those sounds (there are several differences of pronunciation in medieval and ecclesiastical Latin).

Vowels

Vowels in Latin had only two possible pronunciations, long and short. Long vowels were generally held about twice as long as short vowels (cf. half notes to quarter notes in music) and are marked in this book, as in most beginning texts (though not in the actual classical texts), with a "macron" or "long mark" (e.g., **ā**); vowels without a macron are short. Students should regard macrons as part of the spelling of a word, since the differences of pronunciation they indicate are often crucial to meaning (e.g., **liber** is a noun meaning *book,* while **līber** is an adjective meaning *free*). The pronunciations are approximately as follows:

Long	Short
ā as in *father:* **dās, cārā**	**a** as in *Dinah:* **dat, casa**
ē as in *they:* **mē, sēdēs**	**e** as in *pet:* **et, sed**
ī as in *machine:* **hīc, sīca**	**i** as in *pin:* **hic, sicca**
ō as in *clover:* **ōs, mōrēs**	**o** as in *orb, off:* **os, mora**
ū as in *rude:* **tū, sūmō**	**u** as in *put:* **tum, sum**

y, either short or long, as in French **tu** or German **über**

Diphthongs

Latin has the following six diphthongs, combinations of two vowel sounds that were collapsed together into a single syllable:

ae as *ai* in *aisle:* **cārae, saepe**
au as *ou* in *house:* **aut, laudō**
ei as in *reign:* **deinde**
eu as Latin **e** + **u**, pronounced rapidly as a single syllable: **seu.**
    The sound is not found in English and is rare in Latin.
oe as *oi* in *oil:* **coepit, proelium**
ui as in Latin **u** + **i**, spoken as a single syllable like Spanish **muy** (or like Eng. *gooey,* pronounced quickly as a single syllable). This diphthong occurs only in **huius, cuius, huic, cui, hui.** Elsewhere the two letters are spoken separately as in **fu-it, frūctu-ī.**

---

[34] This was really Greek **u,** upsilon (Y), a vowel with a sound intermediate between **u** and **i,** as in French **u.**

Consonants

Latin consonants had essentially the same sounds as the English consonants with the following exceptions:

bs and **bt** were pronounced *ps* and *pt* (e.g., **urbs, obtineō**); otherwise Latin
b had the same sound as our letter (e.g., **bibēbant**).

c was always hard as in *can,* never soft as in *city:* **cum, cīvis, facilis.**

g was always hard as in *get,* never soft as in *gem:* **glōria, gerō.** When it
appeared before **n,** the letter **g** represented a nasalized *ng* sound as in
hangnail: **magnus.**

h was a breathing sound, as in English, only less harshly pronounced:
hic, haec

i (which also represented a vowel) usually functioned as a consonant
with the sound of *y* as in *yes* when used before a vowel at the beginning of a word (**iūstus** = yustus); between two vowels within a word
it served in double capacity: as the vowel *i* forming a diphthong with
the preceding vowel, and as the consonant *y* (**reiectus** = rei-yectus,
maior = mai-yor, **cuius** = cui-yus); otherwise it was usually a vowel.
This so-called "consonantal" **i** regularly appears in English derivatives as a *j* (a letter added to the alphabet in the Middle Ages); hence
maior = *major,* **Iūlius** = *Julius.*

m had the sound it has in English, pronounced with the lips closed:
monet. There is some evidence, however, that in at least certain instances final **-m** (i.e., **-m** at the end of a word), following a vowel,
was pronounced with the lips open, producing a nasalization of the
preceding vowel: **tum, etiam.**

q, as in English, is always followed by consonantal **u,** the combination
having the sound *kw:* **quid, quoque.**

r was trilled; the Romans called it the **littera canīna,** because its sound
suggested the snarling of a dog: **Rōma, cūrāre.**

s was always voiceless as in *see,* never voiced as in our word *ease:* **sed,
posuissēs, mīsistis.**

t always had the sound of *t* as in *tired,* never of *sh* as in *nation* or *ch* as
in *mention:* **taciturnitās, nātiōnem, mentiōnem.**

v had the sound of our *w:* **vīvō** = wīwō, **vīnum** = wīnum.

x had the sound of *ks* as in *axle,* not of *gz* as in *exert:* **mixtum, exerceō.**

ch represented Greek *chi* and had the sound of *ckh* in *block head,* not of
ch in *church:* **chorus, Archilochus.**

ph represented Greek *phi* and had the sound of *ph* in *uphill,* not the *f*
sound in our pronunciation of *philosophy:* **philosophia.**

th represented Greek *theta* and had the sound of *th* in *hot house,* not of
th in *thin* or *the:* **theātrum.**

The Romans quite appropriately pronounced double consonants as two
separate consonants; we in our haste usually render them as a single conso-

nant. For instance, the **rr** in the Latin word **currant** sounded something like the two *r*'s in *the cur ran* (except that in Latin each **r** was trilled); and the **tt** in **admittent** sounded like the two *t*'s in *admit ten.*

Syllables

In Latin as in English, a word has as many syllables as it has vowels and diphthongs.

Syllabification: In dividing a word into syllables:

1. Two contiguous vowels or a vowel and a diphthong are separated: **dea, de-a; deae, de-ae.**

2. A single consonant between two vowels goes with the second vowel: **amīcus, a-mī-cus.**

3. When two or more consonants stand between two vowels, generally only the last consonant goes with the second vowel: **mittō, mit-tō; servāre, ser-vā-re; cōnsūmptus, cōn-sūmp-tus.** However, a stop **(p, b, t, d, c, g)** + a liquid **(l, r)** generally count as a single consonant and go with the following vowel:[35] **patrem, pa-trem; castra, cas-tra.** Also counted as single consonants are **qu** and the aspirates **ch, ph, th,** which should never be separated in syllabification: **architectus, ar-chi-tec-tus; loquācem, lo-quā-cem.**

Syllable quantity: A syllable is long *by nature* if it contains a long vowel or a diphthong; a syllable is long *by position* if it contains a short vowel followed by two or more consonants[36] or by **x,** which is a double consonant (= *ks*). Otherwise a syllable is short; again, the difference is rather like that between a musical half-note and a quarter-note.

Syllables long by nature (here underlined): **lau-dō, Rō-ma, a-mī-cus.**
Syllables long by position (underlined): **ser-vat, sa-pi-en-ti-a, ax-is** (= *ak-sis*).
Examples with all long syllables, whether by nature or by position, underlined: **lau-dā-te, mo-ne-ō, sae-pe, cōn-ser-vā-tis, pu-el-lā-rum.**

Even in English, syllables have this sort of temporal quantity, i.e., some syllables take longer to pronounce than others (consider the word "enough," with its very short, clipped first syllable, and the longer second syllable), but it is not a phenomenon we think much about. The matter is important in Latin, however, for at least two reasons: first, syllable quantity was a major determinant of the rhythm of Latin poetry, as you will learn later in your

---

[35] But in poetry the consonants may be separated according to the rule for two consonants.

[36] But remember that a stop + a liquid as well as **qu** and the aspirates **ch, ph,** and **th** regularly count as a single consonant: e.g., **pa-trem, quo-que.**

study of the language; and, of more immediate importance, syllable quantity determined the position of a word's stress accent, as explained below.

Accent

Words in Latin, like those in English, were pronounced with extra emphasis on one syllable (or more than one, in the case of very long words); the placement of this "stress accent" in Latin (unlike English) followed these strict and simple rules:

1. In a word of two syllables the accent always falls on the first syllable: **sér-vo, saé-pe, ní-hil.**

2. In a word of three or more syllables (a) the accent falls on the next to last syllable (sometimes called the "penult"), if that syllable is long (**ser-vá-re, cōn-sér-vat, for-tú-na**); (b) otherwise, the accent falls on the syllable before that (the "antepenult": **mó-ne-ō, pá-tri-a, pe-cú-ni-a, vó-lu-cris**).

Because these rules for accentuation are so regular, accent marks (as opposed to macrons) are not ordinarily included when writing Latin; in this text, however, accents are provided in both the "paradigms" (sample declensions and conjugations) and the chapter vocabularies, as an aid to correct pronunciation.

Although oral-aural communication and conversational skills are sometimes—and unfortunately—given little stress in the Latin classroom, nevertheless a "correct" or at least a consistent pronunciation is essential to the mastery of any language. An ability to pronounce Latin words and sentences aloud according to the rules provided in this introduction will also enable you to "pronounce" correctly in your mind and, as you think of a word, to spell it correctly.

As you begin your study of Latin, remember that it did not merely consist of written texts to be silently read (in fact, the Romans themselves nearly always read aloud!), but it was for centuries a spoken language—a language learned and spoken by Roman boys and girls, in fact, just as your own native language was acquired and spoken by you in your childhood, and not only by famous orators, poets, and politicians. You should apply all four language learning skills in your study every day, listening and speaking as well as reading and writing; always pronounce paradigms and vocabulary items aloud, and most especially *read aloud every Latin sentence or passage you encounter,* and always read *for comprehension,* before attempting a translation into English.

MAPS

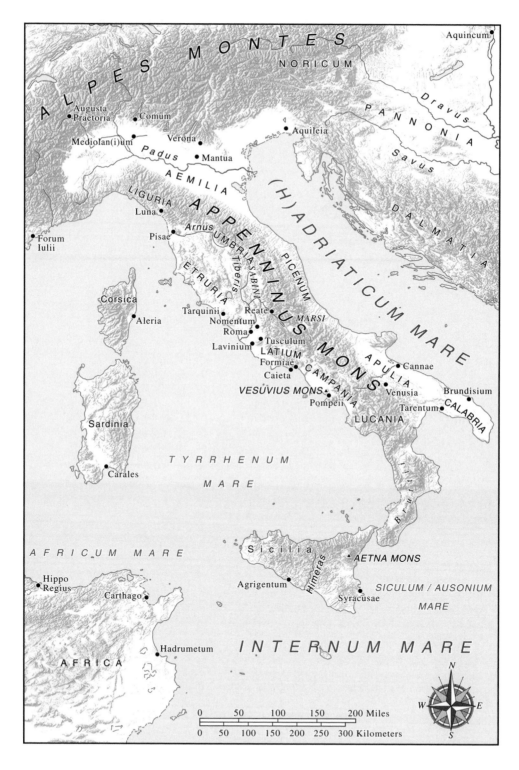

Map 1: ANCIENT ITALY

Map by Richard A. LaFleur and Thomas R. Elliott, using materials provided by the Ancient World Mapping Center (http://www.unc.edu/awmc)

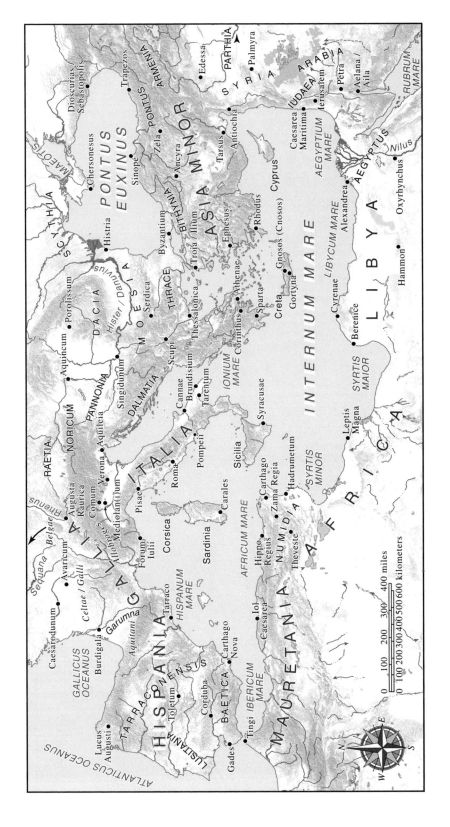

Map 2: THE ROMAN EMPIRE

Map by Richard A. LaFleur and Thomas R. Elliott, using materials provided by the Ancient World Mapping Center (http://www.unc.edu/awmc)

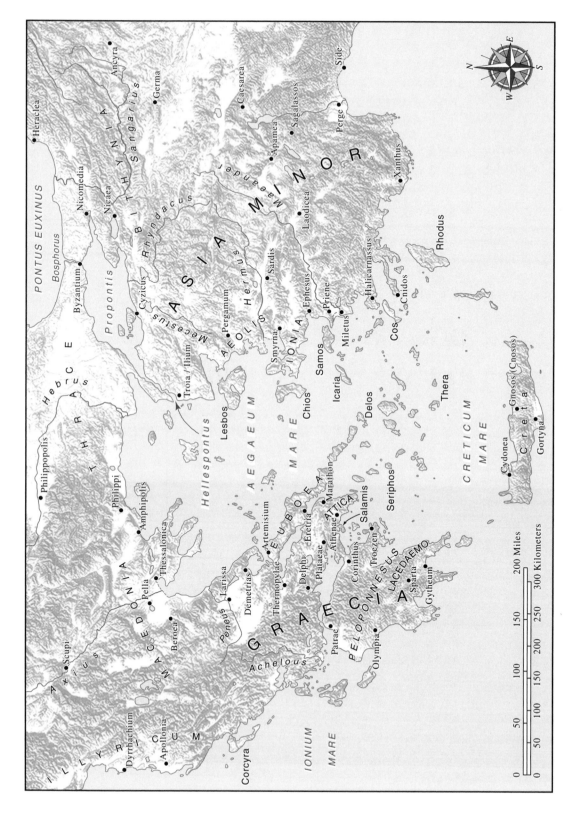

Map 3: *ANCIENT GREECE AND THE AEGEAN*

Map by Richard A. LaFleur and Thomas R. Elliott, using materials provided by the Ancient World Mapping Center (http://www.unc.edu/awmc)

1

Verbs; First and Second Conjugations: Present Infinitive, Indicative, and Imperative Active; Translating

VERBS

One might properly consider the verb (from Lat. **verbum,** *word*), which describes the subject's activity or state of being, to be the most important word in a sentence, and so we may best begin our study of Latin with a look at that part of speech (the other parts of speech in Latin are the same as those in English: nouns, pronouns, adjectives, adverbs, prepositions, conjunctions, interjections).

In Latin as in English, verbs exhibit the following five characteristics:

PERSON (Lat. **persōna**): who is the subject, i.e., who performs (or, in the passive, receives) the action, from the speaker's point of view; 1st person = the speaker(s), *I, we;* 2nd = the person(s) spoken to, *you;* 3rd = the person(s) spoken about, *he, she, it, they.*

NUMBER (**numerus**): how many subjects, singular or plural.

TENSE (**tempus,** *time*): the time of the action; Latin has six tenses, present, future, imperfect, perfect (or present perfect), future perfect, and pluperfect (or past perfect).

MOOD (**modus,** *manner*): the manner of indicating the action or state of being of the verb; like English, Latin has the indicative (which "indicates" facts) and the imperative (which orders actions), introduced in this chapter, and the subjunctive (which describes, in particular, hypothetical or potential actions), introduced in Ch. 28.

VOICE (**vōx**): an indication, with transitive verbs (those that can take direct objects), of whether the subject performs the action (the active voice) or receives it (passive).

CONJUGATION

To conjugate (Lat. **coniugāre,** *join together*) a verb is to list together all its forms, according to these five variations of person, number, tense, mood, and voice. If asked to conjugate the English verb *to praise* in the present tense and the active voice of the indicative mood, you would say:

	Singular	**Plural**
1st person	I praise	we praise
2nd person	you praise	you praise
3rd person	he (she, it) praises	they praise

The person and the number of five of these six forms cannot be determined in English without the aid of pronouns *I, you, we, they.* Only in the third person singular can you omit the pronoun *he (she, it)* and still make clear by the special ending of the verb that *praises* is third person and singular.

PERSONAL ENDINGS

What English can accomplish in only one of the six forms, Latin can do in all six by means of "personal endings," which indicate distinctly the person, the number, and the voice of the verb. Since these personal endings will be encountered at every turn, the time taken to memorize them at this point will prove an excellent investment. For the active voice they are:

Singular

1st person	**-ō** or **-m,** which corresponds to *I.*
2nd person	**-s,** which corresponds to *you.*
3rd person	**-t,** which corresponds to *he, she, it.*

Plural

1st person	**-mus,** which corresponds to *we.*
2nd person	**-tis,** which corresponds to *you.*
3rd person	**-nt,** which corresponds to *they.*

The next step is to find a verbal "stem" to which these endings can be added.

PRESENT INFINITIVE[1] ACTIVE AND PRESENT STEM

The present active infinitives of the model verbs used in this book for the first and second conjugations are respectively:

laudāre, *to praise*   monēre, *to advise*

You see that **-āre** characterizes the first conjugation and **-ēre** characterizes the second.

Now from the infinitives drop the **-re,** which is the actual infinitive ending, and you have the "present stems":

laudā-   monē-

To this present stem add the personal endings (with the few modifications noted below), and you are ready to read or to say something in Latin about the present: e.g., **laudā-s,** *you praise;* **monē-mus,** *we advise.*

This leads to the first of many paradigms. "Paradigm" (pronounced pár-adime) derives from Greek **paradeigma,** which means *pattern, example;* and paradigms are used at numerous points throughout the chapters and in the Appendix to provide summaries of forms according to convenient patterns. Of course, the ancient Romans learned the many inflected forms from their parents and from daily contacts with other people by the direct method, as we ourselves learn English today. However, since we lack this natural Latin environment and since we usually begin the study of Latin at a relatively late age under the exigencies of time, the analytical approach through paradigms, though somewhat artificial and uninspiring, is generally found to be the most efficacious method.

In the process of memorizing all paradigms, be sure always to say them *aloud,* for this gives you the help of two senses, both sight and sound; speak-

---

[1] The *infinitive* (**īnfīnītus, īnfīnītīvus,** *not limited*) simply gives the basic idea of the verb; its form is "not limited" by person and number, though it does indicate tense and voice.

ing and listening to the language, to its basic sounds and rhythms, will be an enormous aid to acquiring mastery.

PRESENT INDICATIVE ACTIVE OF Laudō & Moneō

Singular

1. laúdō, *I praise, am praising, do praise*   móneō, *I advise,* etc.
2. laúdās, *you praise, are praising, do praise*   mónēs, *you advise,* etc.
3. laúdat, *he (she, it) praises, is praising,*   mónet, *he (she, it) advises,*
    does praise   etc.

Plural

1. laudámus, *we praise, are praising, do praise*   monémus, *we advise,* etc.
2. laudátis, *you praise, are praising, do praise*   monétis, *you advise,* etc.
3. laúdant, *they praise, are praising, do praise*   mónent, *they advise,* etc.

Note that Latin has only these present active indicative forms, and so simple or progressive or emphatic translations are possible, depending on context; e.g., **mē laudant,** *they praise me* or *they are praising me* or *they do praise me.*

Remember that the accent marks are provided in the paradigm only for convenience; they follow the strict rules for accentuation explained in the Introduction, and need not be included in your own conjugation of Latin verbs (unless you are asked to do so by your instructor).

The macrons, however, must be included, and the vowel sounds they indicate must be taken into account in memorizing the paradigm and in conjugating other first and second conjugation verbs. Notice that the stem vowel has no macron in certain forms (e.g., **moneō, laudant**); you should learn the following rule, which will make it easier to account for macrons that seem to disappear and reappear arbitrarily:

> Vowels that are normally long are usually shortened when they occur immediately before another vowel (hence **moneō** instead of ***monēō**[2]), before **-m, -r,** or **-t** at the end of a word (hence **laudat,** not ***laudāt**), or before **nt** or **nd** in any position (hence **laudant**).

In the case of first conjugation, or **-ā-,** verbs (by contrast with the second conjugation, **-ē-** verbs), the stem vowel is not merely shortened but disappears entirely in the first person singular, through contraction with the final **-ō** (hence **laudō,** not ***laudāō**).

---

[2] The asterisk here and elsewhere in this book indicates a form not actually occurring in classical Latin.

PRESENT ACTIVE IMPERATIVE

The imperative mood is used for giving commands; the singular imperative form is identical to the present stem and the plural imperative (employed when addressing two or more persons) is formed simply by adding **-te** to the stem:

2nd person singular	laúdā, *praise!*	mónē, *advise!*
2nd person plural	laudā́te, *praise!*	monḗte, *advise!*

E.g., **Monē mē!** *Advise me!* **Servāte mē!** *Save me!*

READING AND TRANSLATING LATIN

The following simple rules will assist you with translating the sentences and the reading passage in this chapter; further assistance will be provided in subsequent chapters. First, always read each sentence from beginning to end aloud; read for comprehension, thinking about the meanings of the individual words and the likely sense of the whole sentence. The verb often comes last in a Latin sentence: remember that if its ending is either first or second person, you already know the subject ("I," "we," or "you"); if the verb is third person, look for a noun that might be the subject (frequently the first word in the sentence). Subject-object-verb (SOV) is a common pattern. Now, once you have memorized the paradigms above and the vocabulary in the following list, and practiced conjugating some of the verbs in the list, try your hand at reading and translating the sentences and short passage that conclude the chapter. **BONAM FORTŪNAM!** (*Good luck!*)

VOCABULARY

Remember, in memorizing the vocabularies always be sure to say all the Latin words *aloud* as you learn the meanings. N.B.: Like an English verb, a Latin verb has "principal parts" (usually four, vs. three in English) which must be memorized in order to conjugate the verb in all its forms. As you will see from the following list, the first principal part is the first person singular present active indicative, and the second principal part is the present active infinitive; the function of the remaining principal parts will be explained in subsequent chapters.

mē, pronoun, *me, myself*
quid, pronoun, *what* (quid pro quo)
níhil, noun, *nothing* (nihilism, annihilate)

nōn, adverb, *not*

saépe, adverb, *often*

sī, conjunction, *if*

ámō, amā́re, amā́vī, amā́tum, *to love, like;* **amā́bō tē,** idiom, *please* (lit., *I will love you*) (amatory, Amanda)

cốgitō, cōgitā́re, cōgitā́vī, cōgitā́tum, *to think, ponder, consider, plan* (cogitate)

dḗbeō, dēbḗre, dḗbuī, dḗbitum, *to owe; ought, must* (debt, debit, due, duty)

dō, dáre, dédī, dátum, *to give, offer* (date, data)

érrō, errā́re, errā́vī, errā́tum, *to wander; err, go astray, make a mistake, be mistaken* (erratic, errant, erroneous, error, aberration)

laúdō, laudā́re, laudā́vī, laudā́tum, *to praise* (laud, laudable, laudatory)

móneō, monḗre, mónuī, mónitum, *to remind, advise, warn* (admonish, admonition, monitor, monument, monster, premonition)

sálveō, salvḗre, *to be well, be in good health;* **sálvē, salvḗte,** *hello, greetings* (salvation, salver, salvage)

sérvō, servā́re, servā́vī, servā́tum, *to preserve, save, keep, guard* (observe, preserve, reserve, reservoir)

cōnsérvō, cōnservā́re, cōnservā́vī, cōnservā́tum (con-servō), a stronger form of **servō,** *to preserve, conserve, maintain* (conservative, conservation)

térreō, terrḗre, térruī, térritum, *to frighten, terrify* (terrible, terrific, terrify, terror, terrorist, deter)

váleō, valḗre, váluī, valitū́rum, *to be strong, have power; be well;* **válē (valḗte),** *good-bye, farewell* (valid, invalidate, prevail, prevalent, valedictory)

vídeō, vidḗre, vī́dī, vī́sum, *to see; observe, understand* (provide, evident, view, review, revise, revision, television)

vócō, vocā́re, vocā́vī, vocā́tum, *to call, summon* (vocation, advocate, vocabulary, convoke, evoke, invoke, provoke, revoke)

SENTENTIAE (SENTENCES)[3]

1. Labor mē vocat. (**labor,** a noun, and one of hundreds of Latin words that come into English with their spelling unchanged; such words are often not defined in the chapters but may be found in the end Vocab., p. 470–90 below.)
2. Monē mē, amābō tē, sī errō.
3. Festīnā lentē. (a saying of Augustus.—**festīnō, festīnāre,** *to hasten, make haste.*—**lentē,** adv., *slowly.*)
4. Laudās mē; culpant mē. (**culpō, culpāre,** *to blame, censure.*)
5. Saepe peccāmus. (**peccō, peccāre,** *to sin.*)

---

[3] All these sentences are based on ancient Roman originals but most of them had to be considerably adapted to meet the exigencies of this first chapter.

6. Quid dēbēmus cōgitāre?

7. Cōnservāte mē!

8. Rūmor volat. (**volō, volāre,** *to fly.*)

9. Mē nōn amat.

10. Nihil mē terret.

11. Apollō mē saepe servat.

12. Salvēte!—quid vidētis? Nihil vidēmus.

13. Saepe nihil cōgitās.

14. Bis dās, sī cito dās. (**bis,** adv., *twice.*—**cito,** adv., *quickly.*—What do you suppose this ancient proverb actually means?)

15. Sī valēs, valeō. (A friendly sentiment with which Romans often commenced a letter.)

16. What does he see?

17. They are giving nothing.

18. You ought not to praise me.

19. If I err, he often warns me.

20. If you love me, save me, please!

THE POET HORACE CONTEMPLATES AN INVITATION

Maecēnās et Vergilius mē hodiē vocant. Quid cōgitāre dēbeō? Quid dēbeō respondēre? Sī errō, mē saepe monent et culpant; sī nōn errō, mē laudant. Quid hodiē cōgitāre dēbeō?

(For Horace, and the other authors cited in these chapter reading passages, review the Introd.; the patron Maecenas and the poet Virgil were both friends of Horace, and this brief passage is very freely adapted from autobiographical references in his poetry.—**et,** conj., *and.*—**hodiē,** adv., *today.*—**respondeō, respondēre,** *to reply, respond.*)

Roman portrait medal of Horace
Museo Nazionale Romano delle Terme
Rome, Italy

LATĪNA EST GAUDIUM—ET ŪTILIS!

Salvēte! Here and at the close of each subsequent chapter, you will find a variety of Latin "tidbits," for your pleasure and edification! (**Gaudium,** by the way, is the Lat. noun for *joy* or just plain *fun,* and **ūtilis** is an adj. meaning *useful.*) To start with, here is some "first day" conversational Latin:

Salvē, discipula or **discipule!** *Hello, student!* (The **-a/-e** variants distinguish between female and male students respectively.)

Salvēte, discipulae et discipulī! *Hello, students!* (Feminine and masculine plural.)

Salvē, magister or **magistra!** *Greetings, teacher!* (Again, masculine or feminine.)

Valēte, discipulī et discipulae! Valē, magister (magistra)! *Good-bye, students . . . ,* etc.

Quid est nōmen tibi? *What's your name?*

Nōmen mihi est "Mark." *My name is Mark.* (Or, better yet, how about a Latin name: **nōmen mihi est "Mārcus."**)

Remember that **labor** in sentence 1 above is just one of a great many Latin words that come directly into English without any alteration in spelling? Well, **rūmor** in sentence 8 is another, and so is **videō** in the Vocabulary. **Amō,** however, does not mean "bullets," nor is **amat** "a small rug," so beware of . . . **iocī terribilēs** (*terrible jokes*): **valēte!**

Model of Rome in the 4th century A.D.
Museo della Civilta Romana, Rome, Italy

2

Nouns and Cases; First Declension; Agreement of Adjectives; Syntax

NOUNS AND CASES

As a Latin verb has various inflections or terminations which signal its particular role in a given sentence, so a Latin noun (from **nōmen,** *name*) has various terminations to show whether it is used as the subject or the object of a verb, whether it indicates the idea of possession, and so on. The various inflected forms of a noun are called "cases," the more common uses and meanings of which are catalogued below; you will encounter several other case uses in subsequent chapters, all of which you must be able to identify and name, so it is advisable to begin now keeping a list for each case, with definitions and examples, in your notebook or computer file. For illustrative purposes it will be convenient to refer to the following English sentences,[1] which later in the chapter will be translated into Latin for further analysis.

A. The poet is giving the girl large roses (*or* is giving large roses to the girl).
B. The girls are giving the poet's roses to the sailors.
C. Without money the girls' country (*or* the country of the girls) is not strong.

---

[1] These sentences have been limited to the material available in Chs. 1 and 2 so that they may readily be understood when turned into Latin.

Nominative Case   The Romans used the nominative case most commonly to indicate the *subject* of a finite verb; e.g., *poet* in sentence A and *girls* in sentence B.

Genitive Case   When one noun was used to modify[2] another, the Romans put the modifying, or limiting, noun in the genitive case, as we do in such instances as *poet's* in sentence B and *girls'* in sentence C. One idea very commonly conveyed by the genitive is *possession* and, although other categories besides the genitive of possession are distinguished, the meaning of the genitive can generally be ascertained by translating it with the preposition *of.* A Latin noun in the genitive case usually follows the noun it modifies.

Dative Case   The Romans used the dative to mark the person or thing indirectly affected by the action of the verb, as *girl* (*to the girl*) in sentence A and *to the sailors* in B; both of these nouns are *indirect objects,* the most common use of the dative. In most instances the sense of the dative can be determined by using *to* or *for* with the noun.

Accusative Case   The Romans used the accusative case to indicate the *direct object* of the action of the verb, the person or thing directly affected by the action of the verb. It can also be used for the object of certain prepositions: e.g., **ad,** *to;* **in,** *into;* **post,** *after, behind.*[3] In sentences A and B, *roses* is the direct object of *is* (*are*) *giving.*

Ablative Case   The ablative case we sometimes call the adverbial[4] case because it was the case used by the Romans when they wished to modify, or limit, the verb by such ideas as *means* ("by what"), *agent* ("by whom"), *accompaniment* ("with whom"), *manner* ("how"), *place* ("where; from which"), *time* ("when or within which"). The Romans used the ablative sometimes with a preposition and sometimes without one. There is no simple rule of thumb for translating this complex case. However, you will find little difficulty when a Latin preposition is used (**ab,** *by, from;* **cum,** *with;* **dē** and **ex,** *from;* **in,** *in, on*); and in general you can associate with the ablative such English preposi-

---

[2] Modify derives its meaning from Latin **modus** in the sense of "limit"; it means to limit one word by means of another. For example, in sentence B *roses* by itself gives a general idea but the addition of *poet's* modifies, or limits, *roses* so that only a specific group is in mind. The addition of *red* would have modified, or limited, *roses* still further by excluding white and yellow ones.

[3] A preposition is a word placed before (**prae-positus**) a noun or pronoun, the "object of the preposition," to indicate its relationship to another word in a sentence; prepositional phrases can function adjectivally ("a man *of wisdom*") or adverbially ("he came *from Rome*").

[4] Latin **ad verbum** means *to* or *near the verb;* an adverb modifies a verb, an adjective, or another adverb.

tions as *by, with, from, in, on, at.*[5] The more complex uses will be taken up at convenient points in the following chapters.

Vocative Case

The Romans used the vocative case, sometimes with the interjection[6] **Ō,** to address (**vocāre,** *to call*) a person or thing directly; e.g., (**Ō**) **Caesar,** (*O*) *Caesar;* **Ō fortūna,** *O fortune.* In modern punctuation the vocative (or noun of *direct address*) is separated from the rest of the sentence by commas. With one major exception to be studied in Ch. 3, the vocative has the same form as that of the nominative, and so it is ordinarily not listed in the paradigms.

FIRST DECLENSION[7] — NOUN AND ADJECTIVE

The listing of all the cases of a noun—or an adjective—is called a "declension." Just as we conjugate verbs by adding endings to a stem, so we "decline" nouns and adjectives by adding endings to a "base." The nominative and genitive singular forms of a noun are provided in the vocabulary entry, which must be completely memorized, and the base is then found by dropping the genitive ending; the procedure for an adjective is similar and will be clarified in Chs. 3–4. The following paradigm, which should be memorized (and remember to practice *aloud!*), illustrates the declension of a noun/adjective phrase, **porta magna,** *the large gate:*

porta, *gate* **Base: port-**	**magna,** *large* **Base: magn-**		**Endings**
Singular			
Nom. pórta	mágna	*the (a)*[8] *large gate*	**-a**
Gen. pórtae	mágnae	*of the large gate*	**-ae**
Dat. pórtae	mágnae	*to/for the large gate*	**-ae**
Acc. pórtam	mágnam	*the large gate*	**-am**
Abl. pórtā	mágnā	*by/with/from,* etc., *the large gate*	**-ā**
Voc. pórta	mágna	*O large gate*	**-a**

[5] For instance: **pecūniā,** *by* or *with money;* **ab puellā,** *by* or *from the girl;* **cum puellā,** *with the girl;* **cum īrā,** *with anger, angrily;* **ab (dē, ex) patriā,** *from the fatherland;* **in patriā,** *in the fatherland;* **in mēnsā,** *on the table;* **ūnā hōrā,** *in one hour.*

[6] Lat. **interiectiō** means, lit., *throwing something in,* i.e., without syntactical connection to the rest of the sentence.

[7] The term *declension* is connected with the verb **dē-clīnāre,** *to lean away from.* The idea of the ancient grammarians was that the other cases "lean away from" the nominative; they deviate from the nominative.

[8] Since classical Latin had no words corresponding exactly to our definite article *the* or our indefinite article *a,* **porta** can be translated as *gate* or *the gate* or *a gate.*

Plural

Nom.	pórtae	mágnae	*the large gates* or *large gates*	**-ae**
Gen.	portárum	magnárum	*of the large gates*	**-árum**
Dat.	pórtīs	mágnīs	*to/for the large gates*	**-īs**
Acc.	pórtās	mágnās	*the large gates*	**-ās**
Abl.	pórtīs	mágnīs	*by/with/from,* etc., *the large gates*	**-īs**
Voc.	pórtae	mágnae	*O large gates*	**-ae**

GENDER OF FIRST DECLENSION = FEMININE

Like English, Latin distinguishes three genders: masculine, feminine, and neuter. While Latin nouns indicating male beings are naturally masculine and those indicating female beings are feminine, the gender of most other nouns was a grammatical concept, not a natural one, and so a noun's gender must simply be memorized as part of the vocabulary entry.

Nouns of the first declension are normally feminine; e.g., **puella,** *girl;* **rosa,** *rose;* **pecūnia,** *money;* **patria,** *country.* A few nouns denoting individuals engaged in what were among the Romans traditionally male occupations are masculine; e.g., **poēta,** *poet;* **nauta,** *sailor;* **agricola,** *farmer* (others not employed in this book are **aurīga,** *charioteer;* **incola,** *inhabitant;* **pīrāta,** *pirate*).

In this book, as a practical procedure the gender of a noun will not be specifically labeled *m., f.,* or *n.* in the notes, if it follows the general rules.

AGREEMENT OF ADJECTIVES

The normal role of adjectives is to accompany nouns and to modify, or limit, them in size, color, texture, character, and so on; and, like nouns, adjectives are declined. Naturally, therefore, an adjective agrees with its noun in gender, number, and case (an adjective that modifies more than one noun usually agrees in gender with the nearest one, though sometimes the masculine predominates). An adjective (**adiectum,** *set next to, added*) is a word *added* to a noun. As its Latin root meaning also suggests, an adjective was usually positioned next to its noun (except in poetry, where word order is much freer). Most often the adjective followed the noun, a logical arrangement since the person or thing named is generally more important than the attribute; exceptions were adjectives denoting size or number, as well as demonstratives (**hic,** *this;* **ille,** *that*), which normally precede, as do any adjectives which the speaker or writer wishes to emphasize.

SYNTAX

The Greek verb **syntattein** means *to arrange* or, in particular, to draw up an army in orderly array. Similarly, in grammatical terminology "syntax" is the orderly marshaling of words according to the service which they are to perform in a sentence. To explain the syntax of a given noun or adjective, you should state its form, the word on which it most closely depends, and the reason for the form (i.e., its grammatical use or function in the sentence). The sample sentences given above, here translated into Latin, provide some examples. Notice in the subject and verb endings the rule that *a verb must agree with its subject in person and number;* notice too that where a noun ending such as **-ae** can represent more than one case, word order and context provide necessary clues to a sentence's meaning (hence **puellae** is the indirect object in A, subject in B).

A. Poēta puellae magnās rosās dat.
B. Puellae nautīs rosās poētae dant.
C. Patria puellārum sine pecūniā nōn valet.

The syntax of some of these words can be conveniently stated thus:

Word	Form	Dependence	Reason
Sentence A			
poēta	nom. sg.	dat	subject
puellae	dat. sg.	dat	indirect object
magnās	acc. pl.	rosās	modifies and agrees with noun
Sentence B			
puellae	nom. pl.	dant	subject
nautīs	dat. pl.	dant	indirect object
rosās	acc. pl.	dant	direct object
poētae	gen. sg.	rosās	possession
Sentence C			
pecūniā	abl. sg.	sine	object of preposition

Be ready to explain the syntax of all nouns and adjectives in the sentences and reading passage below.

VOCABULARY

fắma, fắmae, f., *rumor, report; fame, reputation* (famous, defame, infamy)

fốrma, fốrmae, f., *form, shape; beauty* (formal, format, formula, formless, deform, inform, etc.; but not formic, formidable)

fortū́na, fortū́nae, f., *fortune, luck* (fortunate, unfortunate)

ī́ra, ī́rae, f., *ire, anger* (irate, irascible; but not irritate)

naú́ta, naú́tae, m., *sailor* (nautical)

pátria, pátriae, f., *fatherland, native land, (one's) country* (expatriate, re-patriate)

pecúnia, -ae,[9] f., *money* (pecuniary, impecunious; cp. peculation)

philosóphia, -ae, f. (Greek **philosophia,** *love of wisdom*), *philosophy*

poéna, -ae, f., *penalty, punishment;* **poénās dáre,** idiom, *to pay the penalty* (penal, penalize, penalty, pain, subpoena)

poéta, -ae, m., *poet* (poetry)

pórta, -ae, f., *gate, entrance* (portal, portico, porch, porthole)

puélla, -ae, f., *girl*

rósa, -ae, f., *rose* (rosary, roseate, rosette)

senténtia, -ae, f., *feeling, thought, opinion, vote, sentence* (sententious, sentencing)

vīta, -ae, f., *life; mode of life* (vital, vitals, vitality, vitamin, vitalize, devitalize, revitalize)

antīqua, -ae, adjective,[10] *ancient, old-time* (antique, antiquities, antiquated, antiquarian)

mágna, -ae, adj., *large, great; important* (magnify, magnificent, magnate, magnitude, magnanimous)

méa, -ae, adj., *my*

múlta, -ae, adj., *much, many* (multitude, multiply, multiple; multi-, a prefix as in multimillionaire)

túa, -ae, adj., *your,* used when speaking to only one person

et, conjunction, *and; even;* **et . . . et,** *both . . . and*

sed, conj., *but*

Ō, interjection, *O!, Oh!,* commonly used with the vocative

síne, preposition + abl., *without* (sinecure, sans)

est, *is*

SENTENTIAE ANTĪQUAE[11]

1. Salvē, Ō patria! (Plautus.)
2. Fāma et sententia volant. (Virgil.—**volāre,** *to fly, move quickly.*)

---

[9] **pecúnia, -ae** = **pecúnia, pecúniae;** this abbreviated format will be employed in all subsequent entries for regular first decl. nouns.

[10] Given here are the adjectives' nom. and gen. forms, the latter abbreviated as with first decl. nouns; after the masculine and neuter forms are learned in the next two chapters, adj. entries will provide the nom. endings only for all three genders (see, e.g., **bónus, -a, -um** in the Ch. 4 Vocab.).

[11] Sentences of ancient Roman origin. Henceforth, the author of every ancient Latin sentence will be named. An asterisk before an author's name means that the sentence is quoted verbatim. The lack of an asterisk means that the original sentence had to be somewhat altered to bring it into line with the student's limited knowledge of Latin, but the student may be assured that the thought and the expression are those of the ancient author indicated. The specific passage from which each sentence is adapted is identified below, p. 508–10, for students who are interested in the context and wish to do further reading.

3. Dā veniam puellae, amābō tē. (Terence.—**venia, -ae,** *favor, pardon.*)
4. Clēmentia tua multās vītās servat. (Cicero.—**clēmentia, -ae,** *clemency.*)
5. Multam pecūniam dēportat. (Cicero.—**dēportāre,** *to carry away.*)
6. Fortūnam et vītam antīquae patriae saepe laudās sed recūsās. (Horace.—**recūsāre,** *to refuse, reject.*)
7. Mē vītāre turbam iubēs. (*Seneca.—**vītāre,** *to avoid;* do not confuse this verb with the noun **vīta.**—**turba, -ae,** *crowd, multitude.*—**iubēre,** *to order.*)
8. Mē philosophiae dō. (Seneca.)
9. Philosophia est ars vītae. (*Cicero.—**ars,** nom. sg., *art.*)
10. Sānam fōrmam vītae cōnservāte. (Seneca.—**sāna, -ae,** adj., *sound, sane.*)
11. Immodica īra creat īnsāniam. (Seneca.—**immodica, -ae,** adj., *immoderate, excessive.*—**creāre,** *to create.*—**īnsānia, -ae,** *unsoundness, insanity.*)
12. Quid cōgitās?—dēbēmus īram vītāre. (Seneca.)
13. Nūlla avāritia sine poenā est. (*Seneca.—**nūlla, -ae,** adj., *no.*—**avāritia, -ae,** *avarice.*)
14. Mē saevīs catēnīs onerat. (Horace.—**saeva, -ae,** adj., *cruel.*—**catēna, -ae,** *chain.*—**onerāre,** *to load, oppress.*)
15. Rotam fortūnae nōn timent. (Cicero—**rota, -ae,** *wheel.*—**timēre,** *to fear.*)
16. The girls save the poet's life.
17. Without philosophy we often go astray and pay the penalty.
18. If your land is strong, nothing terrifies the sailors and you ought to praise your great fortune.
19. We often see the penalty of anger.
20. The ancient gate is large.

CATULLUS BIDS HIS GIRLFRIEND FAREWELL

Puella mea mē nōn amat. Valē, puella! Catullus obdūrat: poēta puellam nōn amat, fōrmam puellae nōn laudat, puellae rosās nōn dat, et puellam nōn bāsiat! Īra mea est magna! Obdūrō, mea puella—sed sine tē nōn valeō.

(Catullus 8; prose adaptation. For this 1st cen. B.C. poet, see the Introd., and for unadapted excerpts from the original poem, see Ch. 19.—Note the poet's shift from first person, to third, and back to first; what is the intended emotional effect?—**obdūrāre,** *to be firm, tough.*—**bāsiāre,** *to kiss.*—**tē,** *you.*)

ETYMOLOGY

Note that "etymology" comes from the Greek **etymos,** *true, real,* and **logos,** *word, meaning.* Consequently, the etymology of a word traces the derivation of the word and shows its original meaning. Under this heading will be introduced various items not covered by the derivatives listed in the vocabularies. Each chapter so abounds in such material, however, that complete coverage cannot be attempted.

Pecūnia is connected with **pecus,** *cattle,* just as English *fee* is related to German **Vieh,** *cattle.*

Fortūna derives from **fors,** *chance, accident.*

Explain the meanings of the following English words on the basis of the appropriate Latin words found in the sentences indicated. Further aid, if needed, can be obtained from a good dictionary; *Webster's New World Dictionary* and the *American Heritage Dictionary* are especially helpful with etymologies.

volatile (2)	tenet (10)	onerous (14)
venial (3)	creature (11)	rotary, rotate (15)
turbulent (7)	nullify (13)	obdurate ("Catullus")
insane (10)	concatenation (14)	

LATĪNA EST GAUDIUM—ET ŪTILIS!

Salvēte, discipulī et discipulae! From the Vocab.: To do something **sub rosā** is to do it secretly or in confidence (the rose was in antiquity a symbol of secrecy); **aqua vītae,** lit., *the water of life,* is an old Latin phrase for "whiskey"; and a "sinecure" (from **sine** + **cūra,** *care*) is an office or position that is largely *without responsibility.*

And here's some more conversational Latin:

Quid agis hodiē? *How are you today?*
   Optimē! *Great!*
   Pessimē! *Terrible!*
   Bene! *Good!*
   Satis bene. *So-so* or *Okay.*
   Nōn bene. *Not well.*
   Et tū? *And you?*

Discipulae et discipulī, valēte!

3

Second Declension: Masculine Nouns and Adjectives; Apposition; Word Order

THE SECOND DECLENSION

The second declension follows the rule already given for the first declension: base + endings. However, the endings differ from those of the first declension, except in the dative and the ablative plural. The nouns of this declension are regularly either masculine or neuter; the masculines are introduced below, the neuters in Ch. 4. Most second declension masculine nouns have a nominative singular ending in **-us,** while a few end in **-er** (the neuters, as we shall see in the next chapter, end with **-um**).

MASCULINES IN -us

Base:	**amīcus,** *friend* **amīc-**	**magnus,** *great* **magn-**		**Endings**
Singular				
Nom.	amīcus	mágnus	*a/the great friend*	**-us**
Gen.	amī́cī	mágnī	*of a great friend*	**-ī**
Dat.	amī́cō	mágnō	*to/for a great friend*	**-ō**
Acc.	amī́cum	mágnum	*a great friend*	**-um**
Abl.	amī́cō	mágnō	*by/with/from a great friend*	**-ō**
Voc.	amī́ce	mágne	*O great friend*	**-e**

Plural

Nom.	amícī	mágnī	*great friends*	**-ī**
Gen.	amīcṓrum	magnṓrum	*of great friends*	**-ōrum**
Dat.	amícīs	mágnīs	*to/for great friends*	**-īs**
Acc.	amícōs	mágnōs	*great friends*	**-ōs**
Abl.	amícīs	mágnīs	*by/with/from[1] great friends*	**-īs**
Voc.	amícī	mágnī	*O great friends*	**-ī**

MASCULINES IN -er

Of the second declension **-er** masculines, some like **puer** retain the **-e-** in the base, while most, like **ager,** drop the **-e-,** hence the special importance of learning the genitive as part of the full vocabulary entry (though a knowledge of such English derivatives as "puerile" and "agriculture" will also help you remember the base). Similar is the unique **-ir** masculine, **vir, virī,** *man.*

Base:	**puer,** *boy* **puer-**	**ager,** *field* **agr-**		**Endings**
Singular				
Nom.	púer[2]	áger[2]	mágnus[3]	(none)
Gen.	púerī	ágrī	mágnī	**-ī**
Dat.	púerō	ágrō	mágnō	**-ō**
Acc.	púerum	ágrum	mágnum	**-um**
Abl.	púerō	ágrō	mágnō	**-ō**
Voc.	púer	áger	mágne	(none)
Plural				
Nom.	púerī	ágrī	mágnī	**-ī**
Gen.	puerṓrum	agrṓrum	magnṓrum	**-ōrum**
Dat.	púerīs	ágrīs	mágnīs	**-īs**
Acc.	púerōs	ágrōs	mágnōs	**-ōs**
Abl.	púerīs	ágrīs	mágnīs	**-īs**
Voc.	púerī	ágrī	mágnī	**-ī**

[1] Remember that this is only an imperfect, makeshift way of representing the ablative, and remember that prepositions are commonly used with the ablative, especially when the noun indicates a person; in English translation a preposition is virtually always used.

[2] The underlined forms are the ones which call for special attention.

[3] Added for the sake of comparison and contrast. Note the combination of **puer magnus,** *a big boy,* and **Ō puer magne,** O *big boy.*

COMMENTS ON CASE ENDINGS

It should be helpful to note that some second declension endings are identical to those in the first (the dat. and abl. pl. in **-īs**) and others are similar (e.g., **-am/-um** in the acc. sg., **-ārum/-ōrum** gen. pl., and **-ās/-ōs** acc. pl.). As in the first declension, some second declension endings are used for different cases (e.g., what different cases may the forms **amīcī, amīcō,** and **amīcīs** represent?); again, word order and context will be in such instances essential aids to reading comprehension and translation.

It is especially important to note that only in the singular of **-us** nouns and adjectives of the second declension does the vocative ever differ in spelling from the nominative: singular **amīcus, amīce;** but plural **amīcī, amīcī.** Nouns in **-ius** (e.g., **fīlius,** *son,* **Vergilius,** *Virgil*) and the adjective **meus,** *my,* have a single **-ī** in the vocative singular: **mī fīlī,** *my son;* **Ō Vergilī,** *O Virgil.*

APPOSITION

Gāium, fīlium meum, in agrō videō.
I see Gaius, my son, in the field.

In this sentence **fīlium** is in apposition with **Gāium.** An appositive is a noun which is "put beside"[4] another noun as the explanatory equivalent of the other noun; nouns in apposition always agree in case, usually in number, and often in gender as well. An appositive is commonly separated from the preceding noun by commas.

WORD ORDER

A typical order of words in a simplified Latin sentence or subordinate clause is this: (1) the subject and its modifiers, (2) the indirect object, (3) the direct object, (4) adverbial words or phrases, (5) the verb. In formal composition, the tendency to place the verb at the end of its clause is probably connected with the Romans' fondness for the periodic style, which seeks to keep the reader or listener in suspense until the last word of a sen-

---

[4] **ad** (*to, near*) + **pōnō, positus** (*put*).

tence has been reached. Remember, too, that adjectives and genitive nouns commonly follow the words they modify. However, although the patterns described above should be kept in mind, the Romans themselves made many exceptions to these rules for the purposes of variety and emphasis. In fact, in highly inflected languages like Latin, the order of the words can be relatively unimportant to the sense, thanks to the inflectional endings, which tell so much about the interrelationship of the words in a sentence. On the other hand, in English, where the inflections are relatively few, the sense commonly depends on stricter conventions of word order.

For example, study the following idea as expressed in the one English sentence and the four Latin versions, which all mean essentially the same despite the differences of word order.

(1) *The boy is giving the pretty girl a rose.*
(2) Puer puellae bellae rosam dat.
(3) Bellae puellae puer rosam dat.
(4) Bellae puellae rosam dat puer.
(5) Rosam puer puellae bellae dat.

Whatever the order of the words in the Latin sentence, the sense remains the same (though the emphasis does vary). Note also that according to its ending, **bellae** must modify **puellae** no matter where these words stand. But if you change the order of the words in the English sentence, you change the sense:

(1) *The boy is giving the pretty girl a rose.*
(2) *The pretty girl is giving the boy a rose.*
(3) *The girl is giving the boy a pretty rose.*
(4) *The girl is giving the pretty boy a rose.*
(5) *The rose is giving the boy a pretty girl.*

In all these sentences the same words are used with the same spellings, but the sense of each sentence is different in accordance with the conventions of English word order. Furthermore, where the fifth English sentence is senseless, the fifth Latin sentence, though in much the same order, makes perfectly good sense.

VOCABULARY

áger, ágrī, m., *field, farm* (agrarian, agriculture, agronomy; cp. **agricola**)
agrícola, -ae, m., *farmer*
amíca, -ae, f., and **amícus, amícī,** m., *friend* (amicable, amiable, amity; cp. **amō**)
fémina, -ae, f., *woman* (female, feminine, femininity)
fília, -ae, f., dat. and abl. pl. **fīliábus,** *daughter* (filiation, affiliation, affiliate, filial, hidalgo)
fílius, fíliī, m., *son* (see **fília**)

númerus, -ī,[5] m., *number* (numeral, innumerable, enumerate)

pópulus, -ī, m., *the people, a people, a nation* (populace, population, popularity, popularize, populous)

púer, púerī, m., *boy;* pl. *boys, children* (puerile, puerility)

sapiéntia, -ae, f., *wisdom* (sapience, sapient, sage, savant)

vir, vírī, m., *man, hero* (virtue, virile, triumvirate; *not* virulent)

avắrus (m.), **avắra** (f.), adj., *greedy, avaricious* (avarice)

paúcī (m.), **paúcae** (f.), adj., usually pl., *few, a few* (paucity)

Rōmắnus (m.), **Rōmắna** (f.), adj., *Roman* (Romance, romance, romantic, romanticism, Romanesque, Roumania)

dē, prep. + abl., *down from, from; concerning, about;* also as a prefix **dē-** with such meanings as *down, away, aside, out, off* (demote, from **dēmoveō**; decline, descend)

in, prep. + abl., *in, on*

hódiē, adv., *today*

sémper, adv., *always* (sempiternal)

hábeō, habére, hábuī, hábitum, *to have, hold, possess; consider, regard* (inhabit, "hold in"; ex-hibit, "hold forth"; habit, habitat)

sátiō (1),[6] *to satisfy, sate* (satiate, insatiable, satiety, satisfaction; cp. **satis,** Ch. 5)

PRACTICE AND REVIEW

1. Fīlium nautae Rōmānī in agrīs vidēmus.
2. Puerī puellās hodiē vocant.
3. Sapientiam amīcārum, Ō fīlia mea, semper laudat.
4. Multī virī et fēminae philosophiam antīquam cōnservant.
5. Sī īra valet, Ō mī fīlī, saepe errāmus et poenās damus.
6. Fortūna virōs magnōs amat.
7. Agricola fīliābus pecūniam dat.
8. Without a few friends life is not strong.
9. Today you have much fame in your country.
10. We see great fortune in your daughters' lives, my friend.
11. He always gives my daughters and sons roses.

SENTENTIAE ANTĪQUAE

1. Dēbētis, amīcī, dē populō Rōmānō cōgitāre. (Cicero.)
2. Maecēnās, amīcus Augustī, mē in numerō amīcōrum habet. (Hor-

---

[5] Regular second declension **-us** nouns will be abbreviated this way in subsequent Vocab. entries (i.e., **númerus, -ī** = **númerus, númerī**).

[6] Regular first conjugation verbs with principal parts following the pattern **-ō/-āre/ -āvī/-ātum** will be indicated with this (1) in subsequent Vocab. entries.

ace.—**Maecēnās,** a name in nom. sg.; see Ch. 1 reading passage.—**Augustus, -ī.**)

3. Libellus meus et sententiae meae vītās virōrum monent. (Phaedrus.—**libellus, -ī,** *little book.*)
4. Paucī virī sapientiae student. (Cicero.—**studēre** + dat., *to be eager for.*)
5. Fortūna adversa virum magnae sapientiae nōn terret. (Horace.—**adversus, adversa,** adj. = English.)
6. Cimōn, vir magnae fāmae, magnam benevolentiam habet. (Nepos.—**Cimōn,** proper name nom. sg.—**benevolentia, -ae** = Eng.)
7. Semper avārus eget. (*Horace.—**avārus** = **avārus vir.**—**egēre,** *to be in need.*)
8. Nūlla cōpia pecūniae avārum virum satiat. (Seneca.—**nūllus, nūlla,** adj., *no.*—**cōpia, -ae,** *abundance.*)
9. Pecūnia avārum irrītat, nōn satiat. (Publilius Syrus.—**irrītāre,** *to excite, exasperate.*)
10. Sēcrētē amīcōs admonē; laudā palam. (*Publilius Syrus.—**sēcrētē,** adv., *in secret.*—**admonē** = **monē.**—**palam,** adv., *openly.*)
11. Modum tenēre dēbēmus. (*Seneca.—**modus, -ī,** *moderation.*—**tenēre,** *to have, observe.*)

THE GRASS IS ALWAYS GREENER

Agricola et vītam et fortūnam nautae saepe laudat; nauta magnam fortūnam et vītam poētae saepe laudat; et poēta vītam et agrōs agricolae laudat. Sine philosophiā avārī virī dē pecūniā semper cōgitant: multam pecūniam habent, sed pecūnia multa virum avārum nōn satiat.

(Horace, *Sermōnēs* 1.1; free prose adaptation.)

ETYMOLOGY

The following are some of the Romance words which you can recognize on the basis of the vocabulary of this chapter.

Latin	Italian	Spanish	French
amīcus	amico	amigo	ami
fīlius	figlio	hijo	fils
numerus	numero	número	numéro
populus	popolo	pueblo	peuple
paucī	poco	poco	peu
semper	sempre	siempre	
habēre	avere	haber	avoir
dē	di	de	de

LATĪNA EST GAUDIUM—ET ŪTILIS!

Salvēte, amīcae et amīcī! Quid agitis hodiē? Well, if you are in the Coast Guard, you are **semper parātus,** *always prepared,* or if you're a U.S. Marine, it's **semper fidēlis,** *always faithful* (from the same Latin root as "Fido," your trusty hound). These are just two (suggested by this chapter's Vocab.) of countless Latin mottoes representing a wide range of modern institutions and organizations. **Valēte et habēte fortūnam bonam!**

Augustus of Prima Porta
Late 1st century B.C.
Vatican Museums
Vatican State

4

Second Declension Neuters; Adjectives; Present Indicative of Sum; Predicate Nouns and Adjectives; Substantive Adjectives

SECOND DECLENSION—NEUTERS

In the first declension there are no nouns of neuter gender but in the second declension there are many. They are declined as follows, again by adding endings to a base:

Base:	**dōnum,** *gift* **dōn-**	**cōnsilium,** *plan* **cōnsili-**	**magnum,** *great* **magn-**	**Endings**
Singular				
Nom.	dṓnum	cōnsílium	mágnum	**-um**
Gen.	dṓnī	cōnsíliī[1]	mágnī	**-ī**
Dat.	dṓnō	cōnsíliō	mágnō	**-ō**
Acc.	dṓnum	cōnsílium	mágnum	**-um**
Abl.	dṓnō	cōnsíliō	mágnō	**-ō**

[1] The gen. sg. of second declension nouns ending in **-ius** or **-ium** was spelled with a single **-ī** (**fīlius**, gen. **fīlī**; **cōnsilium**, gen. **cōnsilī**) through the Ciceronian Period. However,

Plural

Nom.	dṓna	cōnsília	mágna	**-a**
Gen.	dōnṓrum	cōnsiliṓrum	magnṓrum	**-ōrum**
Dat.	dṓnīs	cōnsíliīs	mágnīs	**-īs**
Acc.	dṓna	cōnsília	mágna	**-a**
Abl.	dṓnīs	cōnsíliīs	mágnīs	**-īs**

Notice that the second declension neuter endings are the same as the masculine endings, except that the nominative, accusative, and vocative are identical to one another (this is true of all neuters of all declensions): **-um** in the singular, **-a** in the plural. Word order and context will often enable you to distinguish between a neuter noun used as a subject and one used as an object (vocatives are even more easily distinguished, of course, as they are regularly set off from the rest of the sentence by commas). The plural **-a** ending might be mistaken for a first declension nominative singular, so you can see again how important it is to memorize all vocabulary entries completely, including the gender of nouns. Regular second declension neuters will be presented in the vocabularies in the following abbreviated form: **dṓnum, -ī** (= **dṓnum, dṓnī**), n.

DECLENSION AND AGREEMENT OF ADJECTIVES

The paradigms of **magnus** presented in Chs. 2–4 have illustrated the point that, while the base remains constant, the adjective has masculine, feminine, or neuter endings according to the gender of the noun with which it is used, and it likewise agrees with its noun in number and case. The full declension of **magnus** below provides a good review of the first two declensions.

	Masc.	**Fem.**	**Neut.**
Singular			
Nom.	mágnus	mágna	mágnum
Gen.	mágnī	mágnae	mágnī
Dat.	mágnō	mágnae	mágnō
Acc.	mágnum	mágnam	mágnum
Abl.	mágnō	mágnā	mágnō
Voc.	mágne	mágna	mágnum

---

since the genitive form **-ī** (**fīliī, cōnsiliī**) became established during the Augustan Period and since **-ī** was always the rule in adjectives (**eximius,** gen. **eximiī**), this is the form which will be employed in this text.

Plural

Nom.	mágnī	mágnae	mágna
Gen.	magnṓrum	magnā́rum	magnṓrum
Dat.	mágnīs	mágnīs	mágnīs
Acc.	mágnōs	mágnās	mágna
Abl.	mágnīs	mágnīs	mágnīs
Voc.	mágnī	mágnae	mágna

Henceforth, such first and second declension adjectives will appear thus in the vocabularies:

méus, -a, -um   múltus, -a, -um   paúcī, -ae, -a (pl. only)

Sum: PRESENT INFINITIVE AND PRESENT INDICATIVE

As the English verb *to be* is irregular, so is the Latin **sum.** Although the personal endings can be distinguished, the stem varies so much that the best procedure is to memorize these very common forms as they are given. Notice that, because **sum** is an intransitive linking verb, we do not refer to its voice as either active or passive.

PRESENT INFINITIVE OF Sum: esse, to be

PRESENT INDICATIVE OF Sum

Singular
1. sum, *I am*
2. es, *you are*
3. est, *he (she, it) is, there is*

Plural
súmus, *we are*
éstis, *you are*
sunt, *they are, there are*

PREDICATE NOUNS AND ADJECTIVES

As an intransitive verb, **sum** cannot take a direct object. Instead, like a coupling which connects two cars in a train, **sum** (and other linking verbs to be learned later) serves to connect the subject of a clause with a noun or adjective in the predicate[2]. Such predicate nouns and adjectives—or "predicate nominatives," as they are often called—are connected or even equated

---

[2] The two main divisions of a sentence are the subject and the predicate. The predicate is composed of the verb and all its dependent words and phrases.

with the subject by the linking verb, and so they naturally agree with the subject in number and case (usually the nominative, of course) and, wherever possible, in gender as well. In the case of compound subjects of different gender, a predicate adjective usually agrees in gender with the nearest, though the masculine often predominates. Study the following examples, and be prepared to identify the predicate nouns and adjectives in the chapter's sentences and reading passage.

> Vergilius est amīcus Augustī, *Virgil is the friend of Augustus.*
> Vergilius est poēta, *Virgil is a poet.*
> Vergilius est magnus, *Virgil is great.*
> Fāma Vergiliī est magna, *the fame of Virgil is great.*
> Amīcae sunt bonae, *the girlfriends are good.*
> Puerī dēbent esse bonī, *the boys ought to be good.*
> Puer et puella sunt bonī, *the boy and girl are good.*
> Dōnum est magnum, *the gift is large.*
> Dōna sunt magna, *the gifts are large.*
> Sumus Rōmānī, *we are Romans (Roman men).*
> Sumus Rōmānae, *we are Roman women.*

SUBSTANTIVE ADJECTIVES

The Romans often used an adjective as a "substantive," i.e., in place of a noun, just as we do in English ("The meek shall inherit the earth"—i.e., "the meek *people*"). Such a substantive adjective should generally be translated as a noun, often by supplying *man* or *men, woman* or *women, thing* or *things,* in accordance with its number and gender, as illustrated in the following examples:

> Bonās saepe laudant, *they often praise the good women.*
> Multī sunt stultī, *many (men) are foolish.*
> Puerī mala nōn amant, *the boys do not love bad things.*
> Paucī dē perīculō cōgitant, *few (men) are thinking about the danger.*

VOCABULARY

bāsium, -iī (= **bāsiī**), n., *kiss*

béllum, -ī, n., *war* (bellicose, belligerent, rebel, rebellion, revel)

cōnsílium, -iī, n., *plan, purpose, counsel, advice, judgment, wisdom* (counsel, counselor)

cūra, -ae, f., *care, attention, caution, anxiety* (cure, curator, curious, curiosity, curio, curettage, sinecure; cp. **cūrō,** Ch. 36))

dōnum, -ī, n., *gift, present* (donate, donation, condone; cp. **dō**)

exítium, -iī, n., *destruction, ruin* (exit; cp. **exeō,** Ch. 37)

magíster, magístrī, m., and **magístra, -ae,** f., *schoolmaster* or *school-mistress, teacher, master* or *mistress* (magistrate, magistracy, magiste-rial, maestro, mastery, mister, miss; cp. **magnus**)

móra, -ae, f., *delay* (moratorium, demur)

níhil, indeclinable, n., *nothing* (see Ch. 1)

óculus, -ī, m., *eye* (ocular, oculist, binoculars, monocle)

offícium, -iī, n., *duty, service* (office, officer, official, officious; cp. **faciō,** Ch. 10)

ótium, -iī, n., *leisure, peace* (otiose, negotiate)

perículum, -ī, n., *danger, risk* (peril, perilous, imperil, parlous)

remédium, -iī, n., *cure, remedy* (remedial, irremediable, remediation)

béllus, -a, -um, *pretty, handsome, charming* (belle, beau, beauty, embel-lish, belladonna, belles-lettres). Do not confuse with **bellum,** *war.*

bónus, -a, -um, *good, kind* (bonus, bonanza, bonny, bounty, bona fide)

hūmā́nus, -a, -um, *pertaining to man* (**homō,** Ch. 7), *human; humane, kind; refined, cultivated* (humanity, humanitarian, humanism, the humani-ties, humanist, inhuman, superhuman)

málus, -a, -um, *bad, wicked, evil* (malice, malicious, malign, malignant, malaria, malady, malefactor, malfeasance, malevolent; mal-, a prefix as in maladjustment, malnutrition, maltreat, malapropos)

párvus, -a, -um, *small, little* (parvovirus, parvule, parvicellular)

stúltus, -a, -um, *foolish;* **stúltus, -ī,** m., *a fool* (stultify, stultification)

vḗrus, -a, -um, *true, real, proper* (verify, verisimilitude, very, veracity)

iúvō (or **ádiuvō**), **iuvā́re, iū́vī, iū́tum,** *to help, aid, assist; please* (adjutant, coadjutant, aid, aide-de-camp)

sum, ésse, fúī, futū́rum, *to be, exist* (essence, essential, future, futurity)

PRACTICE AND REVIEW

1. Ōtium est bonum, sed ōtium multōrum est parvum.
2. Bella (from **bellum, -ī,** n.) sunt mala et multa perīcula habent.
3. Officium nautam dē ōtiō hodiē vocat.
4. Paucī virī avārī multās fōrmās perīculī in pecūniā vident.
5. Sī multam pecūniam habētis, saepe nōn estis sine cūrīs.
6. Puellae magistram dē cōnsiliō malō sine morā monent.
7. Ō magne poēta, sumus vērī amīcī; mē iuvā, amābō tē!
8. Fēmina agricolae portam videt.
9. You (sg.) are in great danger.
10. My son's opinions are often foolish.
11. The daughters and sons of great men and women are not always great.
12. Without wisdom the sailors' good fortune is nothing and they are paying the penalty.

SENTENTIAE ANTĪQUAE

1. Fortūna est caeca. (*Cicero.—**caecus, -a, -um,** *blind.*)
2. Sī perīcula sunt vēra, īnfortūnātus es. (Terence.—**īnfortūnātus, -a, -um,** *unfortunate.*)
3. Salvē, Ō amīce; vir bonus es. (Terence.)
4. Nōn bella est fāma fīliī tuī. (Horace.)
5. Errāre est hūmānum. (Seneca.—As an indeclinable neuter verbal noun, an infinitive can be the subject of a verb.)
6. Nihil est omnīnō beātum. (Horace—**omnīnō,** adv., *wholly.*—**beātus, -a, -um,** *happy, fortunate.*)
7. Remedium īrae est mora. (Seneca.)
8. Bonus Daphnis, amīcus meus, ōtium et vītam agricolae amat. (Virgil.—Daphnis is a pastoral character.)
9. Magistrī parvīs puerīs crūstula et dōna saepe dant. (Horace.—**crūstulum, -ī,** *cookie.*)
10. Amīcam meam magis quam oculōs meōs amō. (Terence.—**magis quam,** *more than.*)
11. Salvē, mea bella puella—dā mihi multa bāsia, amābō tē! (Catullus.—**mihi,** dat., *to me.*)
12. Īnfīnītus est numerus stultōrum. (Ecclesiastes.—**īnfīnītus, -a, -um** = Eng.)
13. Officium mē vocat. (Persius.)
14. Malī sunt in nostrō numerō et dē exitiō bonōrum virōrum cōgitant. Bonōs adiuvāte; cōnservāte populum Rōmānum. (Cicero.—**nostrō,** *our.*)

THE RARITY OF FRIENDSHIP

Paucī virī vērōs amīcōs habent, et paucī sunt dignī. Amīcitia vēra est praeclāra, et omnia praeclāra sunt rāra. Multī virī stultī dē pecūniā semper cōgitant, paucī dē amīcīs; sed errant: possumus valēre sine multā pecūniā, sed sine amīcitiā nōn valēmus et vīta est nihil.

(Cicero, *Dē Amīcitiā* 21.79–80.—**dignus, -a, -um,** *worthy, deserving.* **amīcitia, -ae,** *friendship.*—**omnia,** *all* [*things*].—**praeclārus, -a, -um,** *splendid, remarkable.*—**rārus, -a, -um** =Eng.—**possumus,** *we are able.*)

ETYMOLOGY

Some Romance derivatives:

Latin	Italian	Spanish	French
oculus	occhio	ojo	œil
ōtium	ozio	ocio	oisiveté
perīculum	pericolo	peligro	péril

officium	officio	oficio	office
bonus	buono	bueno	bon
vērus	vero	verdadero	vrai
magister	maestro	maestro	maître
bellus	bello	bello	belle
hūmānus	umano	humano	humain
beātus	beato	beato	béat
bāsium	bacio	beso	baiser
rārus	raro	raro	rare

LATĪNA EST GAUDIUM—ET ŪTILIS!

Salvē, amīce! There are countless Latin expressions in current English usage (remember **sub rosā**?); one of them, related to an adjective encountered in this chapter, is **rāra avis,** lit. *a rare bird,* but used for an exceptional or unusual individual or a rarity. The student of Latin in the United States was becoming a **rāra avis** in the 1960s and early 70s, but there has been a remarkable resurgence of interest since then. **Ergō,** *therefore,* is another Latin word that has come straight into English; ergo, you now know what Descartes meant in his *Discourse on Method* when he said **cōgitō ergō sum. Semper cōgitā, amīce, et valē!**

Cicero
Uffizi
Florence, Italy

5

First and Second Conjugations: Future and Imperfect; Adjectives in -er

THE FUTURE AND IMPERFECT TENSES

The Romans indicated future time in the first two conjugations by inserting the future tense sign (**-bi-** in most forms) between the present stem and the personal endings. The tense sign **-bā-** was similarly employed (in all four conjugations) for the imperfect tense, a past tense generally equivalent to the English past progressive. The forms of these future and imperfect endings are seen in the following paradigms:

FUTURE AND IMPERFECT INDICATIVE ACTIVE OF Laudō AND Moneō

Future	Imperfect
Singular	
1. laudā́-bō, *I shall praise*	laudā́-ba-m, *I was praising, kept praising, used to praise, praised*
2. laudā́-bi-s, *you will praise*	laudā́-bā-s, *you were praising,* etc.
3. laudā́-bi-t, *he, she, it will praise*	laudā́-ba-t, *he was praising,* etc.
Plural	
1. laudā́bimus, *we shall praise*	laudābā́mus, *we were praising,* etc.
2. laudā́bitis, *you will praise*	laudābā́tis, *you were praising,* etc.
3. laudā́bunt, *they will praise*	laudā́bant, *they were praising,* etc.

Singular

1. monḗ-bō, *I shall advise*   monḗ-ba-m, *I was advising, kept advising, used to advise, advised*

2. monḗ-bi-s, *you will advise*   monḗ-bā-s, *you were advising,* etc.

3. monḗ-bi-t, *he, she, it will advise*   monḗ-ba-t, *he was advising,* etc.

Plural

1. monḗbimus, *we shall advise*   monēbā́mus, *we were advising,* etc.

2. monḗbitis, *you will advise*   monēbā́tis, *you were advising,* etc.

3. monḗbunt, *they will advise*   monḗbant, *they were advising,* etc.

Notice the vowel change in the first person singular and third plural future endings (remember **bō/bi/bi/bi/bi/bu**—sounds like baby talk!), and the shortened -**a**- in the first and third singular and third plural of the imperfect (remember that vowels which are normally long are regularly shortened before -**m, -r,** and -**t** at the end of a word, and before **nt** or another vowel in any position).

The "infixes" -**bi**- and -**bā**- (with the distinctive -**i**- and -**ā**-) can be easily remembered as signs of the future and imperfect tenses, respectively, if they are associated with the English auxiliary verbs "will" and "was" (also spelled with -*i*- and -*a*-), which are generally used to translate those two tenses. Note that, where English requires three separate words for the ideas *he will praise* or *he was praising,* Latin requires only a single word with the three components of stem + tense sign + personal ending (**laudā** + **bi** + **t** = *praise-will-he* or **laudā-ba-t** = *praising-was-he*).

TRANSLATION

Translation of the future tense, usually with *shall* in the first person and *will* in the second and third, should present no difficulty: **dē amīcō cōgitābō,** *I shall think about my friend;* **multam sapientiam habēbunt,** *they will have much wisdom.*

The imperfect tense commonly indicates an action that was continuing or progressive in the past, as suggested by the term "imperfect" (from **imperfectum,** *not completed*), including actions that were *going on, repeated, habitual, attempted,* or *just beginning.* All the following translations are possible, *depending upon the context in which the sentence appears:*

Nautam monēbam, *I was warning (kept warning, used to warn, tried to warn, was beginning to warn) the sailor.*

Poētae vītam agricolae laudābant, *poets used to praise the farmer's life.*

Magister puerōs vocābat, *the teacher kept calling (was calling) the boys.*

Occasionally the imperfect may be translated as a simple past tense, especially with an adverb that in itself indicates continuing action: **nautam saepe monēbam,** *I often warned the sailor.*

ADJECTIVES OF THE FIRST AND SECOND DECLENSION IN -er

The problem with **e** before **r** appears in adjectives as well as in nouns like **puer** and **ager** (Ch. 3). This problem is no great one if you memorize the forms of the adjectives as given in the vocabularies (nominative masculine, feminine, neuter), since the base, whether with or without the **-e-,** appears in the feminine and the neuter forms, as seen in the following examples; likewise, just as with the **-er** nouns, your familiarity with English derivatives can be an aid to remembering the base ("liberal" from **līber,** "pulchritude" from **pulcher,** "miserable" from **miser,** etc.).

līber	līber-a	līber-um	*free*
pulcher	pulchr-a	pulchr-um	*beautiful*

The rest of the paradigm continues with the base and the regular endings:

	Masc.	**Fem.**	**Neut.**	**Masc.**	**Fem.**	**Neut.**
Nom.	líber	líbera	líberum	púlcher	púlchra	púlchrum
Gen.	líberī	líberae	líberī	púlchrī	púlchrae	púlchrī
Dat.	líberō	líberae	líberō	púlchrō	púlchrae	púlchrō
		(etc.)			(etc.)	

For the singular of these samples fully declined, see the Summary of Forms, p. 447, and remember to refer to this Summary on a regular basis, when reviewing declensions and conjugations.

VOCABULARY

adulēscéntia, -ae, f., *youth, young manhood; youthfulness* (adolescence, adolescent)

ánimus, -ī, m., *soul, spirit, mind;* **ánimī, -órum,** *high spirits, pride, courage* (animus, animosity, magnanimous, unanimous, pusillanimous)

caélum, -ī, n., *sky, heaven* (ceiling, celestial, Celeste, cerulean)

cúlpa, -ae, f., *fault, blame* (cp. **culpō** below; culpable, culprit, exculpate, inculpate)

glória, -ae, f., *glory, fame* (glorify, glorification, glorious, inglorious)

vérbum, -ī, n., *word* (verb, adverb, verbal, verbiage, verbose, proverb)

tē, abl. and acc. sg., *you; yourself;* cp. **mē**

līber, lībera, līberum, *free* (liberal, liberality, libertine; cp. **lībertās,** Ch. 8, **līberō,** Ch. 19)

nóster, nóstra, nóstrum, *our, ours* (nostrum, paternoster)

púlcher, púlchra, púlchrum, *beautiful, handsome; fine* (pulchritude)

sắnus, -a, -um, *sound, healthy, sane* (sanity, sanitary, sanitation, sanitarium, insane)

ígitur, conj., postpositive,[1] *therefore, consequently*

-ne, enclitic or suffix added to the emphatic word placed at the beginning of a sentence to indicate a question the answer to which is uncertain. (For other types of direct questions, see **nōnne** and **num** in Ch. 40.)

própter, prep. + acc., *on account of, because of*

crās, adv., *tomorrow* (procrastinate, procrastination)

herī, adv., *yesterday*

quándō, interrogative and relative adv. and conj., *when;* **sī quándō,** *if ever*

sátis, indecl. noun, adj., and adv., *enough, sufficient* (-*ly*) (cp. **satiō;** satisfy, satisfactory, satiate, insatiable, sate; assets, from **ad,** *up to* + **satis**)

tum, adv., *then, at that time; thereupon, in the next place*

cḗnō (1), *to dine* (cenacle; cp. **cēna,** Ch. 26)

cúlpō (1), *to blame, censure* (cp. **culpa** above)

remáneō, remanḗre, remắnsī, remánsum, or **máneō, manḗre, mắnsī, mắnsum,** *to remain, stay, stay behind, abide, continue* (permanent, remnant, mansion, manor, immanent—do not confuse with imminent)

súperō (1), *to be above* (cp. **super,** adv. and prep. + abl. or acc., *above*), *have the upper hand, surpass; overcome, conquer* (superable, insuperable)

PRACTICE AND REVIEW

1. Officium līberōs virōs semper vocābat.
2. Habēbimusne multōs virōs et fēminās magnōrum animōrum?
3. Perīcula bellī nōn sunt parva, sed patria tua tē vocābit et agricolae adiuvābunt.
4. Propter culpās malōrum patria nostra nōn valēbit.
5. Mora animōs nostrōs superābat et remedium nōn habēbāmus.
6. Multī in agrīs herī manēbant et Rōmānōs iuvābant.
7. Paucī virī dē cūrā animī cōgitābant.
8. Propter īram in culpā estis et crās poenās dabitis.
9. Vērum ōtium nōn habēs, vir stulte!
10. Nihil est sine culpā; sumus bonī, sī paucās habēmus.
11. Poēta amīcae multās rosās, dōna pulchra, et bāsia dabat.

---

[1] A postpositive word is one which does not appear as the first word of a sentence; it is put after (**post-pōnō**) the first word or phrase.

12. Will war and destruction always remain in our land?
13. Does money satisfy the greedy man?
14. Therefore, you (sg.) will save the reputation of our foolish boys.
15. Money and glory were conquering the soul of a good man.

SENTENTIAE ANTĪQUAE

1. Invidiam populī Rōmānī crās nōn sustinēbis. (Cicero.—**invidia, -ae,** *dislike.*—**sustinēre,** *to endure, sustain.*)
2. Perīculumne igitur herī remanēbat? (Cicero.)
3. Angustus animus pecūniam amat. (Cicero.—**angustus, -a, -um,** *narrow.*)
4. Superā animōs et īram tuam. (Ovid.)
5. Culpa est mea, Ō amīcī. (Cicero.)
6. Dā veniam fīliō et fīliābus nostrīs. (Terence.—**venia, -ae,** *favor, pardon.*)
7. Propter adulēscentiam, fīliī meī, mala vītae nōn vidēbātis. (Terence.)
8. Amābō tē, cūrā fīliam meam. (Cicero.—**cūrāre,** *to take care of.*)
9. Vīta hūmāna est supplicium. (Seneca.—**supplicium, -iī,** *punishment.*)
10. Satisne sānus es? (Terence.)
11. Sī quandō satis pecūniae habēbō, tum mē cōnsiliō et philosophiae dabō. (Seneca.—**pecūniae,** gen. case.)
12. Semper glōria et fāma tua manēbunt. (Virgil.)
13. Vir bonus et perītus aspera verba poētārum culpābit. (Horace.—**perītus, -a, -um,** *skillful.*—**asper, aspera, asperum,** *rough, harsh.*)

HIS ONLY GUEST WAS A REAL BOAR!

Nōn cēnat sine aprō noster, Tite, Caeciliānus:
    bellum convīvam Caeciliānus habet!

(*Martial 7.59. This is the first of several selections included in this book from the *Epigrams* of Martial, a popular poet of the late 1st cen. A.D., briefly discussed in the Introd.; these poems are generally quite short, like this two-verse elegiac couplet, satirical, and targeted at a specific, but usually fictitious, character, here the glutton Caecilianus.—**Titus,** the poem's addressee, but not its victim.—**aper, aprī,** *boar, pig.*—**convīva, -ae,** one of a few masc. first decl. nouns, *dinner-guest.*)

THERMOPYLAE: A SOLDIER'S HUMOR

"Exercitus noster est magnus," Persicus inquit, "et propter numerum sagittārum nostrārum caelum nōn vidēbitis!" Tum Lacedaemonius respondet: "In umbrā, igitur, pugnābimus!" Et Leōnidās, rēx Lacedaemoniōrum, exclāmat: "Pugnāte cum animīs, Lacedaemoniī; hodiē apud īnferōs fortasse cēnābimus!"

(Cicero, *Tusculānae Disputātiōnēs* 1.42.101; an anecdote from the battle of Thermopylae, 480 B.C., in which the Persians under king Xerxes defeated the Spartans under Leonidas.—**exercitus**, *army.*—**Persicus, -ī,** *a Persian.*—**inquit,** *says.*—**sagitta, -ae,** *arrow.*—**Lacedaemonius, -ī,** *a Spartan.*—**respondēre** = Eng.—**umbra, -ae,** *shade, shadow; ghost.*—**pugnāre,** *to fight.*—**rēx,** *king.*—**exclāmāre,** *to shout.*—**cum** + abl., *with.*—**apud** + acc., *among.*—**īnferī, -ōrum,** *those below, the dead.*—**fortasse,** adv., *perhaps.*)

ETYMOLOGY

Related to **animus** is **anima, -ae,** *the breath of life;* hence: animal, animated, inanimate.

"Envy" came to us from **invidia** (sent. 1) indirectly through French; "invidious" we borrowed directly from Latin.

"Expert" and "experience" are both related to **perītus** (13). The **ex** here is intensive (= *thoroughly*) and the stem **perī-** means *try, make trial of.* What, then, is an "experiment"? Apparently there is no experiment without some risk (**perī-culum**).

In sent. 13: asperity, exasperate (**ex** again intensive). In "Thermopylae": sagittate; umbrella (through Italian, with diminutive ending), umbrage, adumbrate; pugnacious, pugilist.

LATĪNA EST GAUDIUM—ET ŪTILIS!

Salvēte, et amīcī et amīcae meae! Quid agitis hodiē? In fact, I hope you are **sānī et sānae,** both physically and spiritually; if so, you have attained what the 1st cen. A.D. Roman satirist Juvenal suggested was the highest good in life, **mēns sāna in corpore sānō,** *a healthy mind in a healthy body* (you'll encounter the two third decl. nouns **mēns** and **corpus** later on, but in the meantime you can keep this famous quotation **in mente**). It's rumored, by the way, that the athletic gear brand-name ASICS is an acronym for **animus sānus in corpore sānō;** with a glance back at the Vocab. you can figure that one out too. NIKE, an ASICS competitor, takes its name from the Greek word for "victory," which in Latin is **victōria,** a winning name for a queen or any powerful lady (whose male counterpart might well be dubbed "Victor," from Lat. **victor**).

You may have encountered the expressions **verbum sap** and **mea culpa** before; if not, you will. The former is an abbreviation of **verbum satis sapientī est: sapientī** is dat. of the third decl. adj. **sapiēns,** *wise,* used here as a noun (remember substantive adjs. from Ch. 4?), so you should already have deduced that the phrase means *a word to the wise is sufficient.* If you couldn't figure that out, just shout **"mea culpa!"** and (here's a **verbum sap**) go back and review the vocabulary in Chs. 1–5. **Valēte!**

6

Sum: Future and Imperfect Indicative; Possum: Present, Future, and Imperfect Indicative; Complementary Infinitive

FUTURE AND IMPERFECT INDICATIVE OF Sum

As we return to the irregular verb **sum, esse,** the best procedure for learning the future and imperfect tenses is again simply to memorize the paradigms below; these forms are more regular than those for the present tense, however, each formed on the stem **er-** and with the familiar present system personal endings (**-ō/-m, -s, -t, -mus, -tis, -nt**).

	Future Indicative	Imperfect Indicative
Sg.	1. érō, *I shall be*	éram, *I was*
	2. éris, *you will be*	érās, *you were*
	3. érit, *he (she, it, there) will be*	érat, *he (she, it, there) was*
Pl.	1. érimus, *we shall be*	erámus, *we were*
	2. éritis, *you will be*	erátis, *you were*
	3. érunt, *they (there) will be*	érant, *they (there) were*

IRREGULAR *Possum, Posse, Potuī:* To Be Able, Can, Could

The very common verb **possum, posse, potuī,** is simply a compound of **pot-,** from the irregular adjective **potis** (*able, capable;* cp. "potent," "potential") + **sum.** Before forms of **sum** beginning with **s-,** the **-t-** was altered or "assimilated" to **-s-** (hence **possum** from *potsum); otherwise the **-t-** remained unchanged. The irregular present infinitive **posse** developed from an earlier form which followed this rule (**potesse**).

		Present Indicative	Future Indicative	Imperfect Indicative
		I am able, can	*I shall be able*	*I was able, could*
	1.	pós-sum	pót-erō	pót-eram
Sg.	2.	pót-es	pót-eris	pót-erās
	3.	pót-est	pót-erit	pót-erat
	1.	pós-sumus	pot-érimus	pot-erā́mus
Pl.	2.	pot-éstis	pot-éritis	pot-erā́tis
	3.	pós-sunt	pót-erunt	pót-erant

For both **sum** and **possum** it may be helpful to note the similarity of the future and imperfect endings, **-ō/-is/-it,** etc., and **-am/-ās/-at,** etc., to the first and second conjugation future and imperfect endings, **-bō/-bis/-bit,** etc., and **-bam/-bās/-bat,** etc., which were introduced in the previous chapter.

COMPLEMENTARY INFINITIVE

Possum, exactly like the English *to be able* or *can,* regularly requires an infinitive to complete its meaning. Hence we have the term "complementary" infinitive, which simply means "completing" infinitive, a point that is emphasized by the spelling: comp*le*mentary in contrast to comp*li*mentary. You have already seen the complementary infinitive used with **dēbeō,** and you will find it employed with other verbs.

Our friends were able to overcome (*could overcome*) *many dangers.*
Amīcī nostrī poterant superāre multa perīcula.

My friend is not able to remain (*cannot remain*).
Amīcus meus nōn potest remanēre.

You ought to save your money.
Dēbēs cōnservāre pecūniam tuam.

Note that a complementary infinitive has no separate subject of its own; its subject is the same as that of the verb on which it depends.

VOCABULARY

déa, -ae, f., dat. and abl. pl. **deābus,** *goddess,* and **déus, -ī,** m., voc. sg. **deus,** nom. pl. **dī,** dat. and abl. pl. **dīs** (the plurals **deī** and **deīs** became common during the Augustan Period), *god* (adieu, deify, deity)

discípula, -ae, f., and **discípulus, -ī,** m., *learner, pupil, student* (disciple, discipline, disciplinary; cp. **discō,** Ch. 8)

īnsídiae, -árum, f. pl., *ambush, plot, treachery* (insidious)

líber, líbrī, m., *book* (library, libretto); not to be confused with **līber,** *free*

tyránnus, -ī, m., *absolute ruler, tyrant* (tyrannous, tyrannicide)

vítium, -iī, n., *fault, crime, vice* (vitiate, vicious; but not vice in vice versa)

Graécus, -a, -um, *Greek;* **Graécus, -ī,** m., *a Greek*

perpétuus, -a, -um, *perpetual, lasting, uninterrupted, continuous* (perpetuate, perpetuity)

plénus, -a, -um, *full, abundant, generous* (plenary, plenteous, plentiful, plenitude, plenty, replenish, plenipotentiary)

sálvus, -a, -um, *safe, sound* (cp. **salveō**)

secúndus, -a, -um, *second; favorable* (secondary)

véster, véstra, véstrum, *your* (pl., i.e., used in addressing more than one person, vs. **tuus, -a, -um**), *yours*

-que, enclitic conj., *and.* It is appended to the second of two words to be joined: **fāma glōriaque,** *fame and glory.*

úbi: (1) rel. adv. and conj., *where, when;* (2) interrog. adv. and conj., *where?* (ubiquitous)

íbi, adv., *there* (ib. or ibid.)

nunc, adv., *now, at present* (quidnunc)

quárē, adv., lit. *because of which thing* (**quā rē**), *therefore, wherefore, why*

póssum, pósse, pótuī, *to be able, can, could, have power* (posse, possible, potent, potentate, potential, puissant, omnipotent)

tólerō (1), *to bear, endure* (tolerate, toleration, tolerable, intolerable, intolerance; cp. **tollō,** Ch. 22, **ferō,** Ch. 31)

PRACTICE AND REVIEW

1. Oculī nostrī nōn valēbant; quārē agrōs bellōs vidēre nōn poterāmus.
2. Sine multā pecūniā et multīs dōnīs tyrannus satiāre populum Rōmānum nōn poterit.
3. Nōn poterant, igitur, tē dē poenā amīcōrum tuōrum herī monēre.
4. Parvus numerus Graecōrum crās ibi remanēre poterit.
5. Magister puerōs malōs sine morā vocābit.

6. Fīliae vestrae dē librīs magnī poētae saepe cōgitābant.
7. Quandō satis sapientiae habēbimus?
8. Multī librī antīquī propter sapientiam cōnsiliumque erant magnī.
9. Glōria bonōrum librōrum semper manēbit.
10. Possuntne pecūnia ōtiumque cūrās vītae hūmānae superāre?
11. Therefore, we cannot always see the real vices of a tyrant.
12. Few free men will be able to tolerate an absolute ruler.
13. Many Romans used to praise the great books of the ancient Greeks.
14. Where can glory and (use **-que**) fame be perpetual?

SENTENTIAE ANTĪQUAE

1. Dionȳsius tum erat tyrannus Syrācūsānōrum. (Cicero.—**Dionȳsius, -iī,** a Greek name.—**Syrācūsānus, -ī,** *a Syracusan.*)
2. Optāsne meam vītam fortūnamque gustāre? (Cicero.—**optāre,** *to wish.*—**gustāre,** *to taste.*)
3. Possumusne, Ō dī, in malīs īnsidiīs et magnō exitiō esse salvī? (Cicero.—Can you explain why the nom. pl. **salvī** is used here?)
4. Propter cūram meam in perpetuō perīculō nōn eritis. (Cicero.)
5. Propter vitia tua multī tē culpant et nihil tē in patriā tuā dēlectāre nunc potest. (Cicero.—**dēlectāre,** *to delight.*)
6. Fortūna Pūnicī bellī secundī varia erat. (Livy.—**Pūnicus, -a, -um,** *Punic, Carthaginian.*—**varius, -a, -um,** *varied.*)
7. Patria Rōmānōrum erat plēna Graecōrum librōrum statuārumque pulchrārum. (Cicero.—**statua, -ae,** Eng.)
8. Sine dīs et deābus in caelō animus nōn potest sānus esse. (Seneca.)
9. Sī animus īnfīrmus est, nōn poterit bonam fortūnam tolerāre. (Publilius Syrus.—**īnfīrmus, -a, -um,** *not strong, weak.*)
10. Ubi lēgēs valent, ibi populus līber potest valēre. (Publilius Syrus.—**lēgēs,** nom. pl., *laws.*)

"I DO NOT LOVE THEE, DOCTOR FELL"

Nōn amo tē, Sabidī, nec possum dīcere quārē.
   Hoc tantum possum dīcere: nōn amo tē.

(*Martial 1.32; meter: elegiac couplet. **amo:** final -ō was often shortened in Latin poetry.—**Sabidius, -iī.—nec = et nōn.—dīcere,** *to say.*—**hoc,** *this,* acc. case.—**tantum,** adv., *only.*)

THE HISTORIAN LIVY LAMENTS THE DECLINE OF ROMAN MORALS

Populus Rōmānus magnōs animōs et paucās culpās habēbat. Dē officiīs nostrīs cōgitābāmus et glōriam bellī semper laudābāmus. Sed nunc multum ōtium habēmus, et multī sunt avārī. Nec vitia nostra nec remedia tolerāre possumus.

(Livy, from the preface to his history of Rome, *Ab Urbe Conditā;* see Introd.—
nec . . . nec, conj., *neither . . . nor.*)

ETYMOLOGY

Eng. "library" is clearly connected with **liber.** Many European languages, however, derive their equivalent from **bibliothēca,** a Latin word of Greek origin meaning in essence the same thing as our word. What, then, do you suppose **biblos** meant in Greek? Cp. the *Bible.*

In the readings[1]

2. option, adopt.—gusto, disgust. 5. delectable, delight. 10. legal, legislative, legitimate, loyal.

French **y** in such a phrase as **il y a** (*there is*) may prove more understandable when you know that **y** derives from **ibi.**

The following French words are derived from Latin as indicated: **êtes** =
estis; nôtre = **noster; vôtre** = **vester; goûter** = **gustāre.** What, then, is one thing which the French circumflex accent indicates?

LATĪNA EST GAUDIUM—ET ŪTILIS!

Salvēte, discipulī et discipulae! Quid hodiē agitis, amīcī? Cōgitātisne dē linguā Latīnā? Well, I assume by now that your etymological sense will tell you that **lingua Latīna** means . . . *the Latin language* or just "Latin," your favorite subject. Now that you've developed a taste for the language, I know that you study with great "gusto"! (If you missed that bit of etymologizing, see S.A. 2 above.) The new Vocab. item **deus** turns up in the expression **deus ex machinā,** *god from a machine,* which refers (in drama and other contexts) to any person or mechanism that performs an amazing rescue from some seemingly hopeless dilemma.

Do you know that **sub** is a preposition meaning *under,* as in "subterranean," under the **terra,** *earth;* if so, you can laugh at this old favorite: **semper ubi sub ubi!** (Good hygiene and prevents rash!) And speaking of **ubi,** it asks the question that **ibi** answers; a compound form of the latter constructed with the intensifying suffix **-dem,** *the same* (see Ch. 11 for a similar use of **-dem**), **ibidem,** gives us **ibid.,** *in the same place cited,* just one of many Latin-based abbreviations commonly employed in English. Here are some others:

cf. = **cōnfer,** *compare*
cp. = **comparā,** *compare*
e.g. = **exemplī grātiā,** *for the sake of example*
et al. = **et aliī/aliae,** *and others* (of persons)

[1] For the sake of brevity this phrase will henceforth be used to direct attention to words etymologically associated with words in the sentences indicated.

etc. = **et cētera,** *and others* (of things)

i.e. = **id est,** *that is*

n.b. = **nōtā bene,** *note carefully* (i.e., pay close attention)

v.i. and v.s. = **vidē īnfrā** and **vidē suprā,** *see below* and *see above*

Semper ubi sub ubi AND the scholarly **ibid.** both in the same lesson? Well, that's what the title means: **Latīna EST gaudium—et ūtilis! Valēte!**

Paquius Proculus (?) and wife
Wallpainting from Pompeii, house at region VII.ii.6, 1st century A.D.
Museo Archeologico Nazionale, Naples, Italy

7

Third Declension Nouns

The third of Latin's five declensions contains nouns of all three genders with a great variety of nominative singular endings, but all characterized by the genitive singular in **-is;** because of this variety of gender and nominative form, it is especially important to memorize the full vocabulary entry (which in the chapter vocabularies will include the complete, unabbreviated genitive form—abbreviations will be used only in the notes). The declension itself is a simple matter, following the same principles already learned for first and second declension nouns: find the base (by dropping the genitive singular **-is**[1]) and add the endings. Because the vocative is always identical to the nominative (with the sole exception of second declension **-us/-ius** words), it will not appear in any subsequent paradigms.

NOUNS OF THE THIRD DECLENSION

| | **rēx,** m.
king | **virtūs,** f.
merit | **homō,** m.
man | **corpus,** n.
body | **Case**
Endings | |
Base	**rēg-**	**virtūt-**	**homin-**	**corpor-**	**M./F.**	**N.**
Nom.	rēx (rēg-s)	vírtūs	hómō	córpus	—	—
Gen.	rḗg-is	virtū́tis	hóminis	córporis	**-is**	**-is**
Dat.	rḗg-ī	virtū́tī	hóminī	córporī	**-ī**	**-ī**
Acc.	rḗg-em	virtū́tem	hóminem	córpus	**-em**	—
Abl.	rḗg-e	virtū́te	hómine	córpore	**-e**	**-e**

[1] As has been pointed out before, English derivatives can also be helpful in remembering the base; e.g., **iter, itineris,** *journey:* itinerary; **cor, cordis,** *heart:* cordial; **custōs, custōdis,** *guard:* custodian.

Nom.	rḗg-ēs	virtū́tēs	hómines	córpora	**-ēs**	**-a**
Gen.	rḗg-um	virtū́tum	hóminum	córporum	**-um**	**-um**
Dat.	rḗg-ibus	virtū́tibus	homínibus	corpóribus	**-ibus**	**-ibus**
Acc.	rḗg-ēs	virtū́tēs	hómines	córpora	**-ēs**	**-a**
Abl.	rḗg-ibus	virtū́tibus	homínibus	corpóribus	**-ibus**	**-ibus**

GENDER

Rules have been devised to assist you in remembering the gender of the many third declension nouns, but, aside from the fact that those denoting human beings are masculine or feminine according to sense, the exceptions to most of the other rules are numerous.[2] The safest procedure is to learn the gender of each noun as you first encounter it.[3]

TRANSLATION

In translating (as well as declining), take very careful note of the fact that a third declension noun may be modified by a first or second declension adjective; e.g., *great king* in Latin is **magnus rēx, magnī rēgis,** etc., *true peace* is **vēra pāx, vērae pācis,** etc. While an adjective and noun must agree in number, gender, and case, the spelling of their endings will not necessarily be identical.

Because some of the endings of third declension nouns are identical to the endings of different cases of nouns in other declensions (e.g., the dative singular **-ī** is the same as the genitive singular and the masculine nominative plural in the second declension), it is absolutely essential when reading and translating not only to pay attention to word order and context but also to recognize a particular noun's declension. Again, meticulous study of the vocabulary is the key to success.

---

[2] However, the following rules have few or no exceptions:

Masculine
-or, -ōris (amor, -ōris; labor, -ōris; arbor, *tree,* is a principal exception)
-tor, -tōris (victor, -tōris; scrīptor, -tōris, *writer*)
Feminine (including a large group of abstract nouns)
-tās, -tātis (vēritās, -tātis, *truth;* lībertās, -tātis)
-tūs, -tūtis (virtūs, -tūtis; senectūs, -tūtis, *old age*)
-tūdō, -tūdinis (multitūdō, -tūdinis; pulchritūdō, -tūdinis)
-tiō, -tiōnis (nātiō, -tiōnis; ōrātiō, -tiōnis)
Neuter
-us (corpus, corporis; tempus, temporis; genus, generis)
-e, -al, -ar (mare, maris, *sea;* animal, animālis)
-men (carmen, carminis; nōmen, nōminis)

The gender of nouns following these rules will not be given in the notes.
[3] A helpful device is to learn the proper form of some adjective like **magnus, -a, -um,** with each noun. This practice provides an easily remembered clue to the gender and is comparable to learning the definite article with nouns in Romance languages. For example: **magna virtūs, magnum corpus, magnus labor.**

VOCABULARY

ámor, amóris, m., *love* (amorous, enamored; cp. **amō, amícus**)

cármen, cárminis, n., *song, poem* (charm)

cívitās, cīvitátis, f., *state, citizenship* (city; cp. **cívis,** Ch. 14)

córpus, córporis, n., *body* (corps, corpse, corpuscle, corpulent, corporal, corporeal, corporate, corporation, incorporate, corsage, corset)

hómō, hóminis, m., *human being, man* (homicide, homage; homo sapiens, but not the prefix homo-; cp. **hūmānus** and **vir**)

lábor, labóris, m., *labor, work, toil; a work, production* (laboratory, belabor, laborious, collaborate, elaborate; cp. **labōrō,** Ch. 21)

líttera, -ae, f., *a letter of the alphabet;* **lítterae, -árum,** pl., *a letter (epistle), literature* (literal, letters, belles-lettres, illiterate, alliteration)

mōs, móris, m., *habit, custom, manner;* **mórēs, mórum,** pl., *habits, morals, character* (mores, moral, immoral, immorality, morale, morose)

nómen, nóminis, n., *name* (nomenclature, nominate, nominative, nominal, noun, pronoun, renown, denomination, ignominy, misnomer)

pāx, pácis, f., *peace* (pacify, pacific, pacifist, appease, pay)

rēgína, -ae, f., *queen* (Regina, regina, reginal; cp. **regō,** Ch. 16)

rēx, régis, m., *king* (regal, regalia, regicide, royal; cp. rajah)

témpus, témporis, n., *time; occasion, opportunity* (tempo, temporary, contemporary, temporal, temporize, extempore, tense [of a verb])

térra, -ae, f., *earth, ground, land, country* (terrestrial, terrace, terrier, territory, inter [verb], parterre, subterranean, terra cotta)

úxor, uxóris, f., *wife* (uxorial, uxorious, uxoricide)

vírgō, vírginis, f., *maiden, virgin* (virgin, virginal, virginity, Virginia)

vírtūs, virtútis, f., *manliness, courage; excellence, character, worth, virtue* (virtuoso, virtuosity, virtual; cp. **vir**)

nóvus, -a, -um, *new; strange* (novel, novelty, novice, innovate)

post, prep. + acc., *after, behind* (posterity, posterior, posthumous, post mortem, P.M. = post meridiem, preposterous, post- as a prefix, postgraduate, postlude, postwar, etc.; cp. **postrēmum,** Ch. 40)

sub, prep. + abl. with verbs of rest, + acc. with verbs of motion, *under, up under, close to* (sub- or by assimilation suc-, suf-, sug-, sup-, sus-, in countless compounds: subterranean, suburb, succeed, suffix, suggest, support, sustain)

aúdeō, audére, aúsus sum (the unusual third principal part of this "semi-deponent" verb is explained in Ch. 34), *to dare* (audacious, audacity)

nécō (1), *to murder, kill* (internecine; related to **noceō,** Ch. 35, and **necro-** from Gk. **nekros**).

PRACTICE AND REVIEW

1. Secundās litterās discipulae herī vidēbās et dē verbīs tum cōgitābās.
2. Fēminae sine morā cīvitātem dē īnsidiīs et exitiō malō monēbunt.

3. Rēx et rēgīna igitur crās nōn audēbunt ibi remanēre.
4. Mōrēs Graecōrum nōn erant sine culpīs vitiīsque.
5. Quandō hominēs satis virtūtis habēbunt?
6. Corpora vestra sunt sāna et animī sunt plēnī sapientiae.
7. Propter mōrēs hūmānōs pācem vēram nōn habēbimus.
8. Poteritne cīvitās perīcula temporum nostrōrum superāre?
9. Post bellum multōs librōs dē pāce et remediīs bellī vidēbant.
10. Officia sapientiamque oculīs animī possumus vidēre.
11. Without sound character we cannot have peace.
12. Many students used to have small time for Greek literature.
13. After bad times true virtue and much labor will help the state.
14. The daughters of your friends were dining there yesterday.

SENTENTIAE ANTĪQUAE

1. Homō sum. (*Terence.)
2. Nihil sub sōle novum (*Ecclesiastes.—**sōl, sōlis,** m., *sun.*—**novum:** sc. **est.**)
3. Carmina nova dē adulēscentiā virginibus puerīsque nunc cantō. (Horace.—**cantāre,** *to sing.*)
4. Laudās fortūnam et mōrēs antīquae plēbis. (*Horace.—**plēbs, plēbis,** f., *the common people.*)
5. Bonī propter amōrem virtūtis peccāre ōdērunt. (Horace.—**peccāre,** *to sin.*—**ōdērunt,** defective vb., 3d per. pl., *to hate.*)
6. Sub prīncipe dūrō temporibusque malīs audēs esse bonus. (Martial.—**prīnceps, -cipis,** m., *chief, prince;* **dūrus, -a, -um,** *hard, harsh.*)
7. Populus stultus virīs indignīs honōrēs saepe dat. (Horace.—**honor, -nōris,** *honor, office.*—**indignus, -a, -um,** *unworthy.*)
8. Nōmina stultōrum in parietibus et portīs semper vidēmus. (Cicero.—The desire to scribble names and sentiments in public places is as old as antiquity!—**pariēs, -etis,** m., *wall of a building.*)
9. Ōtium sine litterīs mors est. (*Seneca.—**mors, mortis,** f., *death.*)
10. Multae nātiōnēs servitūtem tolerāre possunt; nostra cīvitās nōn potest. Praeclāra est recuperātiō lībertātis. (Cicero.—**nātiō, -ōnis** = Eng.—**servitūs, -tūtis,** *servitude.*—**praeclārus, -a, -um,** *noble, remarkable.*—**recuperātiō, -ōnis,** *recovery.*—**lībertās, -tātis** = Eng.)
11. Nihil sine magnō labōre vīta mortālibus dat. (Horace.—**mortālis, -tālis,** *a mortal.*)
12. Quōmodo in perpetuā pāce salvī et līberī esse poterimus? (Cicero.—**quōmodo,** *how.*)
13. Glōria in altissimīs Deō et in terrā pāx hominibus bonae voluntātis. (*Luke.—**altissimīs,** abl. pl., *the highest.*—**voluntās, -tātis,** *will.*)

THE RAPE OF LUCRETIA

Tarquinius Superbus erat rēx Rōmānōrum, et Sextus Tarquinius erat fīlius malus tyrannī. Sextus Lucrētiam, uxōrem Collātīnī, rapuit, et fēmina bona, propter magnum amōrem virtūtis, sē necāvit. Rōmānī antīquī virtūtem animōsque Lucrētiae semper laudābant et Tarquiniōs culpābant.

(Livy 1.58; Tarquinius Superbus was Rome's last king, Collatinus a Roman nobleman; according to legend, the rape of Lucretia led to the overthrow of the Tarquin dynasty, the end of monarchy, and the establishment of the Roman Republic in 509 B.C.—**rapuit,** *raped.*—**sē,** *herself.*—**necāvit,** a past tense form.)

Tarquin and Lucretia
Titian, 1570–75
Akademie der Bildenden Kuenste, Vienna, Austria

CATULLUS DEDICATES HIS POETRY BOOK

Cornēliō, virō magnae sapientiae, dabō pulchrum librum novum. Cornēlī, mī amīce, librōs meōs semper laudābās, et es magister doctus litterārum! Quārē habē novum labōrem meum: fāma librī (et tua fāma) erit perpetua.

(Catullus 1, prose adaptation; see L.I. 1. Catullus dedicated his first book of poems to the historian and biographer Cornelius Nepos.—**doctus, -a, -um,** *learned, scholarly.*)

ETYMOLOGY

From what Latin word do you suppose It. **uomo,** Sp. **hombre,** and Fr. **homme** and **on** are derived?

"Tense" meaning the "time" of a verb comes from **tempus** through old

Fr. **tens;** but "tense" meaning "stretched tight" goes back to **tendō, tendere, tetendī, tēnsum,** *to stretch.*

In late Latin **cīvitās** came to mean *city* rather than *state,* and thus it became the parent of the Romance words for city: It. **città,** Sp. **ciudad,** Fr. **cité.**

In the readings

2. solar, solstice.—novel, novelty, novice, novitiate, innovate, renovate. 3. chant, enchant, incantation, cant, recant, canto, cantabile, precentor. 4. plebeian, plebe, plebiscite. 5. peccant, peccadillo. 6. dour, duration, endure, obdurate. 13. volunteer, involuntary.

It may prove helpful to list the Romance and English equivalents of three of the suffixes given in n. 2.

Latin	Italian	Spanish	French	English
-tās, -tātis	-tà	-dad	-té	-ty
vēritās	verità	verdad	vérité	verity (truth)
antīquitās	antichità	antigüedad	antiquité	antiquity
-tiō, -tiōnis	-zione	-ción	-tion	-tion
nātiō	nazione	nación	nation	nation
ratiō	razione	ración	ration	ration
-tor, -tōris	-tore	-tor	-teur	-tor
inventor	inventore	inventor	inventeur	inventor
actor	attore	actor	acteur	actor

LATĪNA EST GAUDIUM—ET ŪTILIS!

Salvēte, et discipulī et discipulae! Quid nunc agitis? You are beginning to see by now that Latin is living everywhere in our language; in fact, it's a **rāra avis** these days who considers Latin a dead language. To anyone who does, you might quip, **quot hominēs, tot sententiae**—an old proverb from the 2nd cen. B.C. comic playwright Terence meaning, freely, *there are as many opinions as there are men.*

Notice **terra** in the Vocab.: we met "subterranean" in the last chapter, now do you think of ET? In the 1980s the little guy was everybody's favorite *ExtraTerrestrial* (from **extrā,** prep. + acc., *beyond,* + **terra**). Until he became familiar with the terrain, he was in a **terra incognita;** but once he'd learned the territory he felt he was on **terra firma** (look all four of those up in your Funk and Wagnall's—if you need to!). And, speaking of movies, Stephen Spielberg's top-grossing *Jurassic Park* reminded us all that Tyrannosaurus rex was truly both a "tyrant" and a "king" (though Spielberg's "velociraptors" were certainly terrifying "swift-snatchers," from the Lat. adj. **vēlōx,** *fast,* as in "velocity," + **raptor,** a third decl. noun based on the verb **rapere,** *to seize, snatch, grab*). **Latīnam semper amābitis—valēte!**

8

Third Conjugation: Present Infinitive, Present, Future, and Imperfect Indicative, Imperative

The third conjugation, particularly in its present system tenses (present, future, and imperfect), is the most problematic of the four Latin conjugations. Because the stem vowel was short (**-e-**) and generally unaccented, unlike the stem vowels of the other three conjugations (**-ā-** in the first, **-ē-** in the second, and **-ī-** in the fourth, introduced in Ch. 10—cf. **laudā́re, monḗre,** and **audī́re** with **ágere**), it had undergone a number of sound and spelling changes by the classical period. The surest procedure, as always, is to memorize the following paradigms; a little extra effort invested in mastering these forms now will pay rich dividends in every subsequent chapter.

PRESENT INDICATIVE ACTIVE			**FUTURE INDICATIVE ACTIVE**		
	1. ág-ō	(*I lead*)		1. ág-am	(*I shall lead*)
Sg.	2. ág-is	(*you lead*)		2. ág-ēs	(*you will lead*)
	3. ág-it	(*he, she, it leads*)		3. ág-et	(*he, she, it will lead*)
	1. ágimus	(*we lead*)		1. agḗmus	(*we shall lead*)
Pl.	2. ágitis	(*you lead*)		2. agḗtis	(*you will lead*)
	3. águnt	(*they lead*)		3. ágent	(*they will lead*)

IMPERFECT INDICATIVE ACTIVE

	1. ag-ḗbam	(*I was leading, used to lead,* etc.)
Sg.	2. ag-ḗbās	(*you were leading,* etc.)
	3. ag-ḗbat	(*he, she, it was leading,* etc.)
	1. agēbā́mus	(*we were leading,* etc.)
Pl.	2. agēbā́tis	(*you were leading,* etc.)
	3. agḗbant	(*they were leading,* etc.)

PRESENT IMPERATIVE ACTIVE

2. **Sg.** ā́ge (*lead*)   2. **Pl.** ā́gite (*lead*)

PRESENT INFINITIVE

As **-āre** and **-ēre** by this time immediately indicate to you the first and the second conjugations respectively, so **-ere** will indicate the third. Once again you can see the importance of meticulous vocabulary study, including attention to macrons: you must be especially careful to distinguish between second conjugation verbs in **-ēre** and third conjugation verbs in **-ere.**

PRESENT STEM AND PRESENT INDICATIVE

According to the rule for finding the present stem, you drop the infinitive ending **-re** and have **age-** as the present stem. To this you would naturally expect to add the personal endings to form the present indicative. But in fact the short, unaccented stem vowel disappears altogether in the first person singular, and it was altered to **-i-** in the second and third persons singular and the first and second persons plural, and appears as **-u-** in the third plural. Consequently, the practical procedure is to memorize the endings.[1]

FUTURE INDICATIVE

The striking difference of the future tense in the third conjugation (and the fourth, as we shall see in Ch. 10) is the lack of the tense sign **-bi-.** Here **-ē-** is the sign of the future in all the forms except the first singular, and by contraction the stem vowel itself has disappeared.

IMPERFECT INDICATIVE

The imperfect tense is formed precisely according to the rules learned for the first two conjugations (present stem + **-bam, -bās,** etc.), except that

---

[1] This mnemonic device may help: (a) for the present use an IOU (**i** in 4 forms, **o** in the first, **u** in the last); (b) for the future you have the remaining vowels, **a** and **e.** It may also be helpful to note that the vowel alternation is exactly the same as that seen in the future endings of first and second conjugation verbs (**-bō, -bis, -bit, -bimus, -bitis, -bunt**).

the stem vowel has been lengthened to **-ē-,** yielding forms analogous to those in the first and second conjugations.

PRESENT IMPERATIVE

Also in accordance with the rule already learned, the second person singular of the present imperative is simply the present stem; e.g., **mitte** (from **mittere,** *to send*), **pōne** (**pōnere,** *to put*). In the plural imperative, however, we see again the shift of the short, unaccented **-e-** to **-i-:** hence, **mittite** and **pōnite** (not **mittete* or **pōnete*).

The singular imperative of **dūcere** was originally **dūce,** a form seen in the early writer Plautus. Later, however, the **-e** was dropped from **dūce,** as it was from the imperatives of three other common third conjugation verbs: **dīc** (**dīcere,** *say*), **fac** (**facere,** *do*), and **fer** (**ferre,** *bear*). The other verbs of this conjugation follow the rule as illustrated by **age, mitte,** and **pōne;** the four irregulars, **dīc, dūc, fac,** and **fer,** should simply be memorized.

VOCABULARY

Cícerō, Cicerónis, m., (*Marcus Tullius*) *Cicero* (Ciceronian, cicerone)

cópia, -ae, f., *abundance, supply;* **cópiae, -árum,** pl., *supplies, troops, forces* (copious, copy, cornucopia)

fráter, frátris, m., *brother* (fraternal, fraternity, fraternize, fratricide)

laus, laúdis, f., *praise, glory, fame* (laud, laudable, laudation, laudatory, magna cum laude; cp. **laudō**)

lībértās, lībertátis, f., *liberty* (cp. **līber, lībero,** Ch. 19, **līberālis,** Ch. 39)

rátiō, ratiónis, f., *reckoning, account; reason, judgment, consideration; system; manner, method* (ratio, ration, rational, irrational, ratiocination)

scríptor, scrīptóris, m., *writer, author* (scriptorium; cp. **scrībō** below)

sóror, soróris, f., *sister* (sororal, sororate, sororicide, sorority)

victória, -ae, f., *victory* (victorious; see **Latīna Est Gaudium,** Ch. 5, and cp. **vincō** below)

dum, conj., *while, as long as, at the same time that;* + subjunctive, *until*

ad, prep. + acc., *to, up to, near to,* in the sense of "place to which" with verbs of motion; contrast the dat. of indirect object (administer, ad hoc, ad hominem). In compounds the **d** is sometimes assimilated to the following consonant so that **ad** may appear, for instance, as **ac-** (**accipiō: ad-capiō**), **ap-** (**appellō: ad-pellō**), **a-** (**aspiciō: ad-spiciō**).

ex or **ē,** prep. + abl., *out of, from, from within; by reason of, on account of;* following cardinal numbers, *of* (exact, except, exhibit, evict). The Romans used **ex** before consonants or vowels; **ē** before consonants only. Like **ad** and many other prepositions, **ex/ē** was often used as a prefix in compounds, sometimes with the **x** assimilated to the following consonant; e.g., **excipiō, ēdūcō, ēventus, efficiō** from **ex** + **faciō,** etc.

númquam, adv., *never* (cp. **umquam,** Ch. 23)

támen, adv., *nevertheless, still*

ágō, ágere, ḗgī, ā́ctum, *to drive, lead, do, act; pass, spend* (life or time); **grātiās agere** + dat., *to thank someone,* lit., *to give thanks to* (agent, agenda, agile, agitate, active, actor, action, actual, actuate)

dēmṓnstrō (1), *to point out, show, demonstrate* (demonstrable, demonstration, demonstrative; see the demonstrative pronouns in Ch. 9)

díscō, díscere, dídicī, *to learn* (cp. **discipulus, discipula**)

dóceō, docḗre, dócuī, dóctum, *to teach* (docent, docile, document, doctor, doctrine, indoctrinate)

dū́cō, dū́cere, dū́xī, dū́ctum, *to lead; consider, regard; prolong* (ductile, abduct, adduce, deduce, educe, induce, produce, reduce, seduce)

gérō, gérere, géssī, géstum, *to carry; carry on, manage, conduct, wage, accomplish, perform* (gerund, gesture, gesticulate, jest, belligerent, congest, digest, suggest, exaggerate, register, registry)

scrī́bō, scrī́bere, scrī́psī, scrī́ptum, *to write, compose* (ascribe, circumscribe, conscript, describe, inscribe, proscribe, postscript, rescript, scripture, subscribe, transcribe, scribble, scrivener, shrive)

tráhō, tráhere, trā́xī, trā́ctum, *to draw, drag; derive, acquire* (attract, contract, retract, subtract, tractor, etc.; see Etymology section below)

víncō, víncere, vī́cī, víctum, *to conquer, overcome* (convince, convict, evince, evict, invincible, Vincent, victor, Victoria, vanquish)

PRACTICE AND REVIEW

1. Tempora nostra nunc sunt mala; vitia nostra, magna.
2. Quārē soror mea uxōrī tuae litterās scrībit (scrībet, scrībēbat)?
3. Tyrannus populum stultum ē terrā vestrā dūcet (dūcit, dūcēbat).
4. Ubi satis ratiōnis animōrumque in hominibus erit?
5. Cōpia vērae virtūtis multās culpās superāre poterat.
6. In līberā cīvitāte adulēscentiam agēbāmus.
7. Rēgem malum tolerāre numquam dēbēmus.
8. Post parvam moram multa verba dē īnsidiīs scrīptōrum stultōrum scrībēmus.
9. The body will remain there under the ground.
10. Write (sg. and pl.) many things about the glory of our state.
11. Does reason always lead your (pl.) queen to virtue?
12. We shall always see many Greek names there.

SENTENTIAE ANTĪQUAE

1. Frāter meus vītam in ōtiō semper aget. (Terence.)
2. Age, age! Iuvā mē! Dūc mē ad secundum fīlium meum. (Terence.— **age, age** = *come, come!*)

3. Ō amīcī, lībertātem perdimus. (Laberius.—**perdere,** *to destroy.*)
4. Nova perīcula populō Rōmānō expōnam sine morā. (Cicero.—**expōnere,** *to set forth.*)
5. Numquam perīculum sine perīculō vincēmus. (Publilius Syrus.)
6. Ex meīs errōribus hominibus rēctum iter dēmōnstrāre possum. (Seneca.—**error, -rōris.**[2]—**rēctus, -a, -um,** *right.*—**iter, itineris,** *n., road, way.*)
7. Catullus Mārcō Tulliō Cicerōnī magnās grātiās agit. (Catullus.—See "Thanks a Lot, Tully!" Ch. 27.)
8. Eximia fōrma virginis oculōs hominum convertit. (Livy.—**eximius, -a, -um,** *extraordinary.*—**convertere,** *to turn around, attract.*)
9. Agamemnon magnās cōpiās ē terrā Graecā ad Trōiam dūcet, ubi multōs virōs necābit. (Cicero.—**Agamemnon, -nonis.**)

Gold funerary mask of "Agamemnon"
Mycenae, 16th century B.C.
National Archaeological Museum, Athens, Greece

10. Amor laudis hominēs trahit. (Cicero.)
11. Auctōrēs pācis Caesar cōnservābit. (Cicero.—**auctor, -tōris,** *author.*—**Caesar, -saris.**)
12. Inter multās cūrās labōrēsque carmina scrībere nōn possum. (Horace.—**inter,** prep. + acc., *among.*)
13. Dum in magnā urbe dēclāmās, mī amīce, scrīptōrem Trōiānī bellī in ōtiō relegō. (Horace.—**urbs, urbis,** f., *city.*—**dēclāmāre,** *to declaim.*—**Trōiānus, -a, -um.**—**relegere,** *to re-read.*)
14. Nōn vītae, sed scholae, discimus. (*Seneca.—**vītae** and **scholae,** datives expressing purpose; see S.S., p. 443—**schola, -ae,** *school.*)
15. Hominēs, dum docent, discunt. (*Seneca.)
16. Ratiō mē dūcet, nōn fortūna. (Livy.)

---

[2] Hereafter in the notes, when a Latin word easily suggests an English derivative, the English meaning will be omitted.

CICERO ON THE ETHICS OF WAGING WAR

Cīvitās bellum sine causā bonā aut propter īram gerere nōn dēbet. Sī fortūnās et agrōs vītāsque populī nostrī sine bellō dēfendere poterimus, tum pācem cōnservāre dēbēbimus; sī, autem, nōn poterimus esse salvī et servāre pātriam lībertātemque nostram sine bellō, bellum erit necessārium. Semper dēbēmus dēmōnstrāre, tamen, magnum officium in bellō, et magnam clēmentiam post victōriam.

(Cicero, *Dē Officiīs* 1.11.34–36 and *Dē Rē Pūblicā* 3.23.34–35, and see L.A. 7 for a fuller adaptation.—**causa, -ae.**—**dēfendere.**—**autem,** conj., *however.*—**necessārius, -a, -um.**—**clēmentia, -ae.**)

ETYMOLOGY

Also connected with **trahō** are: abstract, detract, detraction, distract, distraction, distraught, extract, protract, portray, portrait, retreat, trace, tract, tractable, intractable, traction, contraction, retraction, trait, treat, treaty, train, training.

In the readings   6. rectitude; cp. Eng. cognate "right."—itinerary, itinerant. 11. kaiser, czar. 14. "School" comes through Lat. **schola** from Greek **scholē,** *leisure.* "Waging War": causation; defense, defensive; necessary; clement, clemency.

LATĪNA EST GAUDIUM—ET ŪTILIS!

Salvēte! With this chapter's copious new vocabulary, you can see again what a veritable linguistic cornucopia (a "horn of plenty," from **cōpia** + **cornū,** *horn,* which is cognate with "cornet"!) you have in Latin. **Scrīptor** is one of a large group of masc. third decl. nouns formed by replacing the **-um** of a verb's fourth principal part with **-or,** a suffix meaning essentially *one who performs the action of the verb.* So, a **monitor, -tōris,** is *one who advises,* i.e., *an advisor;* an **amātor** is *a lover;* etc. What would be the similarly formed nouns from **docēre** and **agō?** Look at the other verbs introduced in this chapter and at the vocabularies in the previous chapters; what other such **-or** nouns can you form and recognize?

The point is that if you know one Latin root word, then you will often discover and be able to deduce the meanings of whole families of words: the verb **discere,** e.g., is related to **discipulus** and **discipula,** of course, and also to the noun **disciplīna.** I like to point out that "discipline" is *not* "punishment" but "learning." If you saw the popular 1993 film *Man Without a Face,* you heard lots of Latin, including a favorite old injunction and the motto of England's Winchester College, **aut disce aut discēde,** *either learn or leave* (I have this posted on my office door). You'll be learning, not leaving, I have no doubt, but for now, **valēte, discipulī et discipulae!**

9

Demonstratives Hic, Ille, Iste; Special -īus Adjectives

DEMONSTRATIVES

The Latin demonstratives (from **dēmōnstrāre,** *to point out*) function either as pronouns or adjectives equivalent to English *this/these* and *that/those;* the declension generally follows that of **magnus, -a, -um** (see Ch. 4), with the exception of the forms underlined in the following paradigms (which, as always, should be memorized by repeating the forms aloud, from left to right, **hic, haec, hoc; huius, huius, huius;** etc.).

| | **ille,** *that, those* | | | **hic,** *this, these* | | |
	M.	**F.**	**N.**	**M.**	**F.**	**N.**
Singular						
Nom.	ílle	ílla	íllud	hic	haec	hoc
Gen.	illíus	illíus	illíus	húius	húius	húius
Dat.	íllī	íllī	íllī	huic	huic	huic
Acc.	íllum	íllam	íllud	hunc	hanc	hoc
Abl.	íllō	íllā	íllō	hōc	hāc	hōc
Plural						
Nom.	íllī	íllae	ílla	hī	hae	haec
Gen.	illṓrum	illā́rum	illṓrum	hṓrum	hā́rum	hṓrum
Dat.	íllīs	íllīs	íllīs	hīs	hīs	hīs
Acc.	íllōs	íllās	ílla	hōs	hās	haec
Abl.	íllīs	íllīs	íllīs	hīs	hīs	hīs

DECLENSION

Iste, ista, istud, *that* (*near you*), *that of yours, such,* follows the declension of **ille:** *nom.* íste, ísta, ístud; *gen.* istíus, istíus, istíus; *dat.* ístī, ístī, ístī; etc. Be ready to give all the forms orally.

Again, all three demonstratives follow the pattern of **magnus, -a, -um** quite closely, entirely in the plural with the exception of the neuter **haec.** The most striking differences are in the distinctive genitive and dative singular forms (shared by the nine other special adjectives discussed below) and the **-c** in several forms of **hic,** a shortened form of the demonstrative enclitic **-ce.** Note that **huius** and **huic** are among the few words in which **ui** functions as a diphthong; for the special pronunciation of **huius** (= **huí-yus**) see the Introduction (p. xli).

USAGE AND TRANSLATION

In general the demonstratives point out persons or things either near the speaker (**hic liber,** *this book* = *this book of mine, this book here*) or near the addressee (**iste liber,** *that book, that book of yours, that book next to you*), or distant from both (**ille liber,** *that book* = *that book over there, that book of his or hers*). **Ille** and **hic** are sometimes equivalent to *the former* and *the latter,* respectively, and occasionally they have little more force than our personal pronouns, *he, she, it, they;* **ille** can also mean *the famous . . . ;* **iste** is sometimes best translated *such,* and occasionally has a disparaging sense, as in **ista īra,** *that awful anger of yours.*

When demonstratives modify nouns, they function as adjectives; since they are by nature emphatic, they regularly precede the nouns they modify. The following examples will provide practice with some of the more troublesome forms.

hic liber, *this book*	hanc cīvitātem, *this state*
ille liber, *that book*	huic cīvitātī, *to this state*
illīus librī, *of that book*	illī cīvitātī, *to that state*
illī librī, *those books*	illae cīvitātēs, *those states*
illī librō, *to that book*	haec cīvitās, *this state*
illō librō, *by that book*	haec cōnsilia, *these plans*
istīus amīcī, *of that friend* (*of yours*)	hoc cōnsilium, *this plan*
istī amīcī, *those friends* (*of yours*)	hōc cōnsiliō, *by this plan*
istī amīcō, *to that friend* (*of yours*)	huic cōnsiliō, *to this plan*

When used alone, demonstratives function as pronouns (from Lat. **prō,** *for, in place of,* + **nōmen,** *name, noun*) and can commonly be translated as *this man, that woman, these things,* and the like, according to their gender, number, and context.

hic, *this man*	ille, *that man*
hanc, *this woman*	illa, *that woman*
hunc, *this man*	illa, *those things*
haec, *this woman*	huius, *of this man or woman*[1]
haec, *these things*	illī, *to that man or woman*[1]
istum, *that man*	illī, *those men*
istārum, *of those women*	

SPECIAL -*īus* ADJECTIVES

The singular of nine adjectives of the first and the second declensions is irregular in that the genitive ends in **-īus** and the dative in **-ī**, following the pattern of **illīus** and **illī** above. Elsewhere in the singular and throughout the plural these are regular adjectives of the first and the second declensions, following the pattern of **magnus, -a, -um.**[2]

	sōlus, -a, -um, *alone, only*			**alius, alia, aliud,** *another, other*		
Singular						
Nom.	sṓlus	sṓla	sṓlum	álius	ália	áliud
Gen.	sōlī́us	sōlī́us	sōlī́us	alterī́us[3]	alterī́us	alterī́us
Dat.	sṓlī	sṓlī	sṓlī	áliī	áliī	áliī
Acc.	sṓlum	sṓlam	sṓlum	álium	áliam	áliud
Abl.	sṓlō	sṓlā	sṓlō	áliō	áliā	áliō
Plural						
Nom.	sṓlī	sṓlae	sṓla	áliī	áliae	ália
		etc.			etc.	

The nine adjectives in this group can be easily remembered via the acronym UNUS NAUTA, each letter of which represents the first letter of one of the adjectives (and which at the same time includes one of the nine words, **ūnus,** and even reminds you that **nauta,** though a first declension noun, is masculine, hence the masculine form **ūnus**). Note, too, that each of the nine words indicates some aspect of number:

---

[1] As a rule, the neuter was used as a pronoun only in the nominative and the accusative. In the genitive, the dative, and the ablative cases the Romans preferred to use the demonstrative as an adjective in agreement with the noun for "thing"; e.g., **huius reī,** *of this thing.*

[2] Except for the neuter singular form **aliud** (cp. **illud**).

[3] This form, borrowed from **alter,** is more common than the regular one, **alīus.**

UNUS:

ūnus, -a, -um (ūnīus, etc.), *one*
nūllus, -a, -um (nūllīus, etc.), *no, none*
ūllus, -a, -um, *any*
sōlus, -a, -um, *alone, only*

NAUTA:

neuter, neutra, neutrum, *neither*
alius, -a, -ud, *another, other*
uter, utra, utrum, *either, which (of two)*
tōtus, -a, -um, *whole, entire*
alter, altera, alterum, *the other (of two)*

VOCABULARY

lócus, -ī, m., *place; passage in literature;* pl., **lóca, -órum,** n., *places, region;* **lócī, -órum,** m., *passages in literature* (allocate, dislocate, locality, locomotion)

mórbus, -ī, m., *disease, sickness* (morbid, morbidity)

stúdium, -iī, n. *eagerness, zeal, pursuit, study* (studio, studious; cp. **studeō,** Ch. 35)

hic, haec, hoc, *this; the latter;* at times weakened to *he, she, it, they* (ad hoc)

ílle, ílla, íllud, *that; the former; the famous; he, she, it, they*

íste, ísta, ístud, *that of yours, that; such;* sometimes with contemptuous force

álius, -a, -ud, *other, another;* **áliī . . . áliī,** *some . . . others* (alias, alibi, alien)

álter, áltera, álterum, *the other (of two), second* (alter, alteration, alternate, alternative, altercation, altruism, adulterate, adultery)

neúter, neútra, neútrum, *not either, neither* (neutrality, neutron)

nū́llus, -a, -um, *not any, no, none* (null, nullify, nullification, annul)

sólus, -a, -um, *alone, only, the only;* **nōn sólum . . . sed étiam,** *not only . . . but also* (sole, solitary, soliloquy, solo, desolate, sullen)

tótus, -a, -um, *whole, entire* (total, totality, factotum, in toto)

úllus, -a, -um, *any*

únus, -a, -um, *one, single, alone* (unit, unite, union, onion, unanimous, unicorn, uniform, unique, unison, universal, university)

úter, útra, útrum, *either, which (of two)*

énim, postpositive conj., *for, in fact, truly*

in, prep. + acc., *into, toward; against* (also **in** + abl., *in, on,* see Ch. 3). In compounds **in-** may also appear as **il-, ir-, im-;** and it may have its literal meanings or have simply an intensive force. (Contrast the inseparable negative prefix **in-,** *not, un-, in-.*)

nímis or **nímium,** adv., *too, too much, excessively*

PRACTICE AND REVIEW

1. Hic tōtus liber litterās Rōmānās semper laudat.
2. Hī igitur illīs deābus herī grātiās agēbant.
3. Illud dē vitiīs istīus rēgīnae nunc scrībam, et ista poenās dabit.
4. Neuter alterī plēnam cōpiam pecūniae tum dabit.
5. Potestne laus ūllīus terrae esse perpetua?
6. Labor ūnīus numquam poterit hās cōpiās vincere.
7. Mōrēs istīus scrīptōris erant nimis malī.
8. Nūllī magistrī, tamen, sub istō vēra docēre audēbant.
9. Valēbitne pāx in patriā nostrā post hanc victōriam?
10. Dum illī ibi remanent, aliī nihil agunt, aliī discunt.
11. Cicero was writing about the glory of the other man and his wife.
12. The whole state was thanking this man's brother alone.
13. On account of that courage of yours those (men) will lead no troops into these places tomorrow.
14. Will either book be able to overcome the faults of these times?

SENTENTIAE ANTĪQUAE

1. Ubi illās nunc vidēre possum? (Terence.)
2. Hic illam virginem in mātrimōnium dūcet. (Terence.—**mātrimō-nium, -iī.**)
3. Huic cōnsiliō palmam dō. (Terence.—**palma, -ae,** *palm branch* of victory.)
4. Virtūtem enim illīus virī amāmus. (Cicero.)
5. Sōlus hunc iuvāre potes. (Terence.)
6. Poena istīus ūnīus hunc morbum cīvitātis relevābit sed perīculum semper remanēbit. (Cicero.—**relevāre,** *to relieve, diminish.*)
7. Hī enim dē exitiō huius cīvitātis et tōtīus orbis terrārum cōgitant. (Cicero.—**orbis, orbis,** m., *circle, orb;* **orbis terrārum,** idiom, *the world.*)
8. Est nūllus locus utrī hominī in hāc terrā. (Martial.)
9. Nōn sōlum ēventus hoc docet—iste est magister stultōrum!—sed etiam ratiō. (Livy.—**ēventus,** *outcome.*)

WHEN I HAVE . . . ENOUGH!

Habet Āfricānus mīliēns, tamen captat.
Fortūna multīs dat nimis, satis nūllī.

(*Martial 12.10; meter: choliambic.—**Āfricānus, -ī,** a personal name.—**mīliēns,** call it *millions.*—**captāre,** *to hunt for legacies.*)

Sī vīs studēre philosophiae animōque, hoc studium nōn potest valēre sine frūgālitāte. Haec frūgālitās est paupertās voluntāria. Tolle, igitur, istās excūsātiōnēs: "Nōndum satis pecūniae habeō. Sī quandō illud 'satis' habēbō, tum mē tōtum philosophiae dabō." Incipe nunc philosophiae, nōn pecūniae, studēre.

(Seneca, *Epistulae* 17.5.—**vīs,** irreg. form, *you wish.*—**studēre** + dat., *to be eager for, devote oneself to.*—**frūgālitās -tātis.**—**paupertās, -tātis,** *small means, poverty.*—**voluntārius, -a, -um.**—**tollere,** *to take away.*—**excūsātiō, -ōnis.**—**nōndum,** adv., *not yet.*—**incipe,** imper., *begin.*)

Seneca (the Younger)
Museo Archeologico Nazionale
Naples, Italy

ETYMOLOGY

A few examples of **in-** as a prefix connected with the preposition: invoke, induce, induct, inscribe, inhibit, indebted.

Some examples of **in-** as an inseparable negative prefix: invalid, innumerable, insane, insuperable, intolerant, inanimate, infamous, inglorious, impecunious, illiberal, irrational.

Latin **ille** provided Italian, Spanish, and French with the definite article and with pronouns of the third person; and Latin **ūnus** provided these languages with the indefinite article. Some of these forms and a few other derivatives are shown in the following table:

Latin	Italian	Spanish	French
ille, illa	il, la	el, la	le, la
ille, illa	egli, ella	él, ella	il, elle
ūnus, ūna	un(o), una	un(o), una	un, une
tōtus	tutto	todo	tout
sōlus	solo	solo	seul
alter	altro	otro	autre

Fr. **là** (*there*) comes from **illāc** (**viā**), an adverbial form meaning *there* (*that way*); similarly, It. **là** and Sp. **allá**.

LATĪNA EST GAUDIUM—ET ŪTILIS!

Salvēte! Here is a mysterious old inscription, found on a hitching post out west in Dodge City:

TOTI

EMUL

ESTO

Aha!—looks like the newly learned dat. of **tōtus** + **emul**, like **simul,** *simultaneously?* + some form of **sum, es, est,** the exotic future imperative, perhaps? (NOT!—that old post was just "to tie mules to"!)

Here are some more vocab. items useful for Latin conversation and other classroom activities: **surgere,** *to rise, stand up* (surge, resurgence, insurgence); **sedēre,** *to sit* (sedentary); **ambulāre,** *to walk* (ambulatory, amble, ambulance); **aperīre** (fourth conj.), *to open* (aperture); **claudere,** *to close* (clause, closet); **dēclīnāre; coniugāre; crēta, -ae,** *chalk* (cretaceous); **ērāsūra, -ae,** *eraser;* **stilus, -ī,** *pen* or *pencil* (actually a stylus); **tabula, -ae,** *chalkboard* (tabular, tabulate); **tabella, -ae,** the diminutive form of **tabula,** *notebook, writing pad* (tablet); **iānua, -ae,** *door* (janitor, Janus, January); **fenestra, -ae,** *window;* **cella, -ae,** *room* (cell); **sella, -ae,** *chair;* **mēnsa, -ae,** *table;* **podium, -ī.** Now you'll know just what to do when your instructor says to you, **Salvē, discipula** (or **discipule)! Quid agis hodiē? Surge ex sellā tuā, ambulā ad tabulam, et dēclīnā "hic, haec, hoc."** Next thing you know, you'll be speaking Latin—not so difficult (even Roman toddlers did!): **semper valēte, amīcae amīcīque!**

10

Fourth Conjugation and -iō Verbs of the Third

This chapter introduces the last of the regular conjugations, in the active voice, the fourth conjugation (illustrated here by **audiō, audīre, audīvī, audītum,** *to hear*) and **-iō** verbs of the third (illustrated by **capiō, capere, cēpī, captum,** *to take, seize*). Like the first two conjugations, the fourth is characterized by a long stem vowel; as seen in the paradigm below, the **-ī-** is retained through all the present system tenses (present, future, imperfect), although it is shortened before vowels as well as before final **-t.** Certain third conjugation verbs are formed in the same way in the present system, except that the **-i-** is everywhere short and **e** appears as the stem vowel in the singular imperative (**cape**) and the present active infinitive (**capere**). **Agō** is presented alongside these new paradigms for comparison and review (see Ch. 8).

PRESENT INDICATIVE ACTIVE

	1. ágō	aúdi-ō	cápi-ō	(*I hear, take*)
Sg.	2. ágis	aúdī-s	cápi-s	(*you hear, take*)
	3. ágit	aúdi-t	cápi-t	(*he, she, it hears, takes*)
	1. ágimus	audímus	cápimus	(*we hear, take*)
Pl.	2. ágitis	audítis	cápitis	(*you hear, take*)
	3. águnt	aúdiunt	cápiunt	(*they hear, take*)

FUTURE INDICATIVE ACTIVE

Sg.	1. ágam	aúdi-am	cápi-am	(*I shall hear, take*)
	2. ágēs	aúdi-ēs	cápi-ēs	(*you will hear, take*)
	3. áget	aúdi-et	cápi-et	(*he, she, it will hear, take*)
	1. agḗmus	audiḗmus	capiḗmus	(*we shall hear, take*)
Pl.	2. agḗtis	audiḗtis	capiḗtis	(*you will hear, take*)
	3. ágent	aúdient	cápient	(*they will hear, take*)

IMPERFECT INDICATIVE ACTIVE

Sg.	1. agḗbam	audi-ḗbam	capi-ḗbam	(*I was hearing, taking*)
	2. agḗbās	audi-ḗbās	capi-ḗbās	(*you were hearing, taking*)
	3. agḗbat	audi-ḗbat	capi-ḗbat	(*he, she, it was hearing, taking*)
	1. agēbámus	audiēbámus	capiēbámus	(*we were hearing, taking*)
Pl.	2. agēbátis	audiēbátis	capiēbátis	(*you were hearing, taking*)
	3. agḗbant	audiḗbant	capiḗbant	(*they were hearing, taking*)

PRESENT IMPERATIVE ACTIVE

Sg.	2. áge	aúdī	cápe	(*hear, take*)
Pl.	2. ágite	audí-te	cápi-te	(*hear, take*)

CONJUGATION OF Audiō

The **-īre** distinguishes the infinitive of the fourth conjugation from the infinitives of the other conjugations (**laud-áre, mon-ére, ág-ere, aud-íre, cá-pere**).

As in the case of the first two conjugations, the rule for the formation of the present indicative is to add the personal endings to the present stem (**audī-**). In the third person plural this rule would give us *audi-nt but the actual form is **audi-unt,** an ending reminiscent of **águnt.**

For the future of **audiō** a good rule of thumb is this: shorten the **ī** of the present stem, **audi-,** and add the future endings of **agō: -am, -ēs, -et, -ēmus, -ētis, -ent.** Once again, as in the third conjugation, **-ē-** is the characteristic vowel of the future.

The imperfect is formed with **-iē-**, instead of simply the stem vowel **-ī-**, before the **-bā-** tense sign, so that the forms are **audiēbam, audiēbās,** etc. (rather than *audībam, etc., as might be expected).

The imperatives, however, follow exactly the pattern of the first and second conjugations, i.e., the singular is the same as the present stem (**audī**) and the plural merely adds **-te** (**audīte**).

CONJUGATION OF *Capiō*

The infinitive **capere** is clearly an infinitive of the third conjugation, not of the fourth. The imperative forms also show that this is a verb of the third conjugation.

The present, future, and imperfect indicative of **capiō** follow the pattern of **audiō,** except that **capiō,** like **agō,** has a short **-i-** in **cápis, cápimus, cápitis.**

Note again very carefully the rule that the **-i-** appears in all present system active indicative forms for both fourth and third **-iō** verbs, and remember that two vowels, **-iē-,** appear before the **-bā-** in the imperfect.

VOCABULARY

amīcítia, -ae, f., *friendship* (cp. **amō, amīca, amīcus**)

cupíditās, cupiditātis, f., *desire, longing, passion; cupidity, avarice* (cp. **cupiō,** Ch. 17)

hóra, -ae, f., *hour, time*

nātúra, -ae, f., *nature* (natural, preternatural, supernatural; cp. **nāscor,** Ch. 34)

senéctūs, senectūtis, f., *old age* (cp. **senex,** Ch. 16)

tímor, timóris, m., *fear* (timorous; cp. **timeō,** Ch. 15)

vēritās, vēritātis, f., *truth* (verify, veritable, verity; cp. **vērus, vērō,** Ch. 29)

vía, -ae, f., *way, road, street* (via, viaduct, deviate, devious, obvious, pervious, impervious, previous, trivial, voyage, envoy)

volúptās, voluptátis, f., *pleasure* (voluptuary, voluptuous)

beátus, -a, -um, *happy, fortunate, blessed* (beatific, beatify, beatitude, Beatrice)

quóniam, conj., *since, inasmuch as*

cum, prep. + abl., *with.* As a prefix **cum** may appear as **com-, con-, cor-, col-, co-,** and means *with, together, completely,* or simply has an intensive force (complete, connect, corroborate, collaborate)

aúdiō, audīre, audīvī, audītum, *to hear, listen to* (audible, audience, audit, audition, auditory; cp. **audītor,** Ch. 16)

cápiō, cápere, cépī, cáptum, *to take, capture, seize, get.* In compounds the **-a-** becomes **-i-, -cipiō: ac-cipiō, ex-cipiō, in-cipiō, re-cipiō,** etc. (capable, capacious, capsule, captious, captive, captor)

dícō, dícere, díxī, díctum, *to say, tell, speak; name, call* (dictate, dictum, diction, dictionary, dight, ditto, contradict, indict, edict, verdict)

fáciō, fácere, fécī, fáctum, *to make, do, accomplish.* In compounds the **-a-** becomes **-i-, -ficiō: cōn-ficiō, per-ficiō,** etc. (facile, fact, faction, factotum, facsimile, faculty, fashion, feasible, feat)

fúgiō, fúgere, fúgī, fúgitūrum, *to flee, hurry away; escape; go into exile; avoid, shun* (fugitive, fugue, centrifugal, refuge, subterfuge)

vénió, veníre, vénī, véntum, *to come* (advent, adventure, avenue, convene, contravene, covenant, event, inconvenient, intervene, parvenu, prevent, provenience)

invénió, inveníre, -vénī, -véntum, *to come upon, find* (invent, inventory)

vívō, vívere, víxī, víctum, *to live* (convivial, revive, survive, vivacity, vivid, vivify, viviparous, vivisection, victual, vittle; cp. **vīta**)

PRACTICE AND REVIEW

1. Quid discipulae hodiē discere dēbent?
2. Frātrēs nihil cum ratiōne herī gerēbant.
3. Ille magnam virtūtem labōris et studiī docēre saepe audet.
4. Hic dē senectūte scrībēbat; ille, dē amōre; et alius, dē lībertāte.
5. Ex librīs ūnīus virī nātūram hārum īnsidiārum dēmōnstrābimus.
6. Istī sōlī victōriam nimis amant; neuter dē pāce cōgitat.
7. Ubi cīvitās ūllōs virōs magnae sapientiae audiet?
8. Ex illīs terrīs in hunc locum cum amīcīs vestrīs venīte.
9. Post paucās hōrās sorōrem illīus invenīre poterāmus.
10. Cōpiae vestrae utrum virum ibi numquam capient.
11. Alter Graecus remedium huius morbī inveniet.
12. Carmina illīus scrīptōris sunt plēna nōn sōlum vēritātis sed etiam virtūtis.
13. We shall then come to your land without any friends.
14. While he was living, nevertheless, we were able to have no peace.
15. The whole state now shuns and will always shun these vices.
16. He will, therefore, thank the queen and the whole people.

SENTENTIAE ANTĪQUAE

1. Cupiditātem pecūniae glōriaeque fugite. (Cicero.)
2. Officium meum faciam. (*Terence.)
3. Fāma tua et vīta fīliae tuae in perīculum crās venient. (Terence.)
4. Vīta nōn est vīvere sed valēre. (Martial.)
5. Semper magnō cum timōre incipiō dīcere. (Cicero.— **incipiō, -ere,** *to begin.*)
6. Sī mē dūcēs, Mūsa, corōnam magnā cum laude capiam. (Lucretius.—**Mūsa, -ae,** *Muse.*—**corōna, -ae,** *crown.*)
7. Vīve memor mortis; fugit hōra. (Persius.—**memor,** adj. nom. sg. m. or f., *mindful.*—**mors, mortis,** f., *death.*)
8. Rapite, amīcī, occāsiōnem dē hōrā. (Horace.— **rapiō, -ere,** *to snatch, seize.*—**occāsiō, -ōnis,** f., *opportunity.*)
9. Paucī veniunt ad senectūtem. (*Cicero.)
10. Sed fugit, intereā, fugit tempus. (Virgil.—**intereā,** adv., *meanwhile.*— The verb is repeated for emphasis.)
11. Fāta viam invenient. (*Virgil.—**fātum, -ī,** *fate.*)

12. Bonum virum nātūra, nōn ōrdō, facit. (*Publilius Syrus.—**ōrdō, -dinis,** m., *rank.*)

13. Obsequium parit amīcōs; vēritās parit odium. (Cicero.—**obsequium, -iī,** *compliance.*—**pariō, -ere,** *to produce.*—**odium, -iī,** *hate.*)

THE INCOMPARABLE VALUE OF FRIENDSHIP

Nihil cum amīcitiā possum comparāre; dī hominibus nihil melius dant. Pecūniam aliī mālunt; aliī, corpora sāna; aliī, fāmam glōriamque; aliī, voluptātēs—sed hī virī nimium errant, quoniam illa sunt incerta et ex fortūnā veniunt, nōn ex sapientiā. Amīcitia enim ex sapientiā et amōre et mōribus bonīs et virtūte venit; sine virtūte amīcitia nōn potest esse. Sī nūllōs amīcōs habēs, habēs vītam tyrannī; sī inveniēs amīcum vērum, vīta tua erit beāta.

(Cicero, *Dē Amīcitiā,* excerpts; see L.A. 6.—**comparāre.—melius,** *better.*—**mālunt,** *prefer.*—**incertus, -a, -um,** *uncertain.*)

ETYMOLOGY

Audiō is the ultimate ancestor of these surprising descendants: "obey" through Fr. **obéir** from Lat. **obēdīre (ob + audīre)**; "obedient" (**ob + audiēns**); "oyez, oyez" from Fr. **ouir,** Lat. **audīre.**

In the readings   5. incipient, inception. 6. museum, music.—corona, coronation, coronary, coroner, corolla, corollary. 7. memory, memoir, commemorate. 8. rapid, rapture, rapacious. 13. obsequious.—odium, odious. "Friendship": comparable.—certainty.

LATĪNA EST GAUDIUM—ET ŪTILIS!

Salvēte! Do you remember being introduced to masc. **-or** nouns formed from the fourth principal parts of verbs? (That was back in Ch. 8.) Well, there are lots of others related to the new verbs in this chapter: **audītor,** Eng. *auditor, listener,* is one; can you find others? Look at the section on Etymological Aids in the App., p. 435–42 below, and you'll learn a great deal more about word families, including another group of third decl. nouns, mostly fem., formed by adding the suffix **-iō (-iōnis, -iōnī,** etc.) to the same fourth principal part. Such nouns generally indicate the performance or result of an action, e.g., **audītiō, audītiōnis,** f., *listening, hearing,* and many have Eng. derivatives in *-ion* (like "audition"). Another example from this chapter's Vocab. is **dictiō,** (*the act of*) *speaking, public speaking,* which gives us such Eng. derivatives as "diction" (the manner or style of one's speaking or writing), "dictionary," "benediction," "contradiction," etc. How many other Latin nouns and Eng. derivatives can you identify from the new verbs in this chapter? Happy hunting, but in the meantime **tempus fugit,** so I'll have to say **valēte!**

11

Personal Pronouns Ego, Tū, and Is; Demonstratives Is and Īdem

PERSONAL PRONOUNS

A personal pronoun is a word used in place of a noun (remember **prō + nōmen**) to designate a particular person, from the speaker's point of view: the first person pronoun indicates the speaker himself or herself (Lat. **ego/ nōs,** *I/me, we/us*), the second person pronoun indicates the person(s) addressed by the speaker (**tū/vōs,** *you*), and the third person indicates the person(s) or thing(s) the speaker is talking about (**is, ea, id,** and their plurals, *he/him, she/her, it, they/them*).

THE FIRST AND SECOND PERSON PRONOUNS Ego/Nōs, Tū/Vōs

While the first and second person pronouns are irregular in form, their declensions are quite similar to one another and are easily memorized; note that there are two different forms for the genitive plural.

1st Person—Ego, *I*			2nd Person—Tū, *You*	
Singular				
Nom.	égo	(*I*)	tū	(*you*)
Gen.	méī	(*of me*)	túī	(*of you*)
Dat.	míhi	(*to/for me*)	tíbi	(*to/for you*)
Acc.	mē	(*me*)	tē	(*you*)
Abl.	mē	(*by/with/from me*)	tē	(*by/with/from you*)

Plural

Nom.	nōs	(*we*)	vōs	(*you*)
Gen.	nóstrum	(*of us*)	véstrum	(*of you*)
	nóstrī	(*of us*)	véstrī	(*of you*)
Dat.	nṓbīs	(*to/for us*)	vṓbīs	(*to/for you*)
Acc.	nōs	(*us*)	vōs	(*you*)
Abl.	nṓbīs	(*by/with/from us*[1])	vṓbīs	(*by/with/from you*)

THE THIRD PERSON/DEMONSTRATIVE PRONOUN Is, Ea, Id

The declension of the pronoun **is, ea, id** is comparable to those of **hic** and **ille** (Ch. 9), i.e., the pattern is that of **magnus, -a, -um** (Ch. 4), with the exception of the forms underlined below; note that the base is **e-** in all but four forms (including the alternate nominative plural **iī**).

	Masculine		**Feminine**		**Neuter**	
Singular						
N.	is	(*he*[2])	éa	(*she*[2])	id	(*it*[2])
G.	éius[3]	(*of him, his*)	éius	(*of her, her*)	éius	(*of it, its*)
D.	éī	(*to/for him*)	éī	(*to/for her*)	éī	(*to/for it*)
A.	éum	(*him*)	éam	(*her*)	id	(*it*)
A.	éō	(*by/w./fr. him*)	éā	(*by/w./fr. her*)	éō	(*by/w./fr. it*)
Plural						
N.	éī, íī	(*they,* masc.)	éae	(*they,* fem.)	éa	(*they,* neut.)
G.	eṓrum	(*of them, their*)	eā́rum	(*of them, their*)	eṓrum	(*of them, their*)
D.	éīs	(*to/for them*)	éīs	(*to/for them*)	éīs	(*to/for them*)
A.	éōs	(*them*)	éās	(*them*)	éa	(*them*)
A.	éīs	(*by/w./fr. them*)	éīs	(*by/w./fr. them*)	éīs	(*by/w./fr. them*)

USAGE

Since these pronouns are employed as substitutes for nouns, they are in general used as their corresponding nouns would be used: as subjects, direct objects, indirect objects, objects of prepositions, and the like.

Ego tibi (vōbīs) librōs dabō, *I shall give the books to you.*
Ego eī (eīs) librōs dabō, *I shall give the books to him* or *her* (*to them*).
Tū mē (nōs) nōn capiēs, *you will not capture me* (*us*).

---

[1] You will find that a preposition is used in Latin with most ablatives when the noun or pronoun in the ablative indicates a person.

[2] Also *this/that man, woman, thing.*

[3] Pronounced **eí-yus** (cp. **huius**, Ch. 9).

Eī id ad nōs mittent, *they* (masc.) *will send it to us.*
Vōs eōs (eās, ea) nōn capiētis, *you will not capture them* (*them*).
Eae ea ad tē mittent, *they* (fem.) *will send them* (*those things*) *to you.*

Notice, however, that the Romans used the nominatives of the pronouns (**ego, tū,** etc.) *only* when they wished to stress the subject. Commonly, therefore, the pronominal subject of a Latin verb is not indicated except by the ending.

Eīs pecūniam dabō, *I shall give them money.*
Ego eīs pecūniam dabō; quid tū dabis? *I shall give them money; what will you give?*

Another point of usage: when **cum** was employed with the ablative of the personal pronouns (as well as the relative and reflexive pronouns, to be studied later), it was generally suffixed to the pronoun, rather than preceding it as a separate preposition: **eōs nōbīscum ibi inveniēs,** *you will find them there with us.*

Notice also that the genitives of **ego** and **tū** (namely **meī, nostrum, nostrī; tuī, vestrum, vestrī**) were *not* used to indicate possession.[4] To convey this idea, the Romans preferred the possessive pronominal adjectives, which you have already learned:

meus, -a, -um, *my*   tuus, -a, -um, *your*
noster, -tra, -trum, *our*   vester, -tra, -trum, *your*

English usage is comparable: just as Latin says **liber meus,** not **liber meī,** so English says *my book,* not *the book of me.*

The genitives of **is, ea, id,** on the other hand, *were* quite commonly used to indicate possession. Hence, while **eius** can sometimes be translated *of him/ of her/of it,* it is very often best translated *his/her/its;* likewise **eōrum/eārum/ eōrum** can be rendered *of them,* but its common possessive usage should be translated *their.* Study the possessives in the following examples, in which **mittam** governs all the nouns.

Mittam (*I shall send*)

pecūniam meam (*my money*).   amīcōs meōs (*my friends*).
pecūniam nostram (*our money*).   amīcōs nostrōs (*our friends*).
pecūniam tuam (*your money*).   amīcōs tuōs (*your friends*).

---

[4] **Meī** and **tuī** were used as objective genitives (e.g., **timor tuī,** *fear of you*—see S.S., p. 442–43 below) and partitive genitives (or "genitives of the whole," e.g., **pars meī,** *part of me*—see Ch. 15), **nostrī** and **vestrī** only as objective gens., and **nostrum** and **vestrum** only as partitive gens.

pecūniam vestram (*your money*).   amīcōs vestrōs (*your friends*).
pecūniam eius (*his, her money*).   amīcōs eius (*his, her friends*).
pecūniam eōrum (*their money*).   amīcōs eōrum (*their friends*).
pecūniam eārum (*their money*).   amīcōs eārum (*their friends*).

The possessive pronominal adjectives of the first and the second persons naturally agree with their noun in *gender, number,* and *case,* as all adjectives agree with their nouns. The possessive genitives **eius, eōrum,** and **eārum,** being genitive pronouns, remain unchanged regardless of the gender, number, and case of the noun on which they depend.

A last important point regarding possessives is the fact that Latin frequently omits them, except for emphasis or to avoid ambiguity. English, on the other hand, employs possessives regularly, and so you will often need to supply them in translating from Latin (just as you do the articles "a," "an," and "the"), in order to produce an idiomatic translation; e.g., **patriam amāmus,** *we love our country.*

Is, Ea, Id AS DEMONSTRATIVE

While commonly serving as Latin's third person pronoun, **is** was also used as a demonstrative, somewhat weaker in force than **hic** or **ille** and translatable as either *this/these* or *that/those.* In general you should translate the word in this way when you find it immediately preceding and modifying a noun (in the same number, gender, and case); contrast the following:

Is est bonus, *he is good.*
Is amīcus est vir bonus, *this friend is a good man.*

Vidēsne eam, *do you see her?*
Vidēsne eam puellam, *do you see that girl?*

DEMONSTRATIVE Īdem, Eadem, Idem, *the Same*

The very common demonstrative **īdem, eadem, idem,** *the same* (*man, woman, thing*), is formed simply by adding **-dem** directly to the forms of **is, ea, id,** e.g., gen. **eiusdem,** dat. **eīdem,** etc.; besides the singular nominatives **īdem** (masc., for **isdem*) and **idem** (neut., rather than **iddem*), the only forms not following this pattern exactly are those shown below, where final **-m** changes to **-n-** before the **-dem** suffix (for the full declension of **īdem,** see the Summary of Forms, p. 449 below).

	Masculine	Feminine	Neuter
Singular			
Acc.	eúndem[5]	eándem	ídem
Plural			
Gen.	eōrúndem[5]	eārúndem	eōrúndem

Like other demonstratives, **īdem** may function as an adjective or a pronoun: **eōsdem mittō,** *I am sending the same men;* **dē eādem ratiōne cōgitābāmus,** *we were thinking about the same plan.*

VOCABULARY

> **cáput, cápitis,** n., *head; leader; beginning; life; heading; chapter* (cape = headland, capital, capitol, capitulate, captain, chief, chieftain, chef, cattle, chattels, cadet, cad, achieve, decapitate, recapitulate, precipice, occiput, sinciput, kerchief)
>
> **cónsul, cónsulis,** m., *consul* (consular, consulate, consulship; cp. **cōnsilium**)
>
> **némō, nūllíus,**[6] **némini, néminem, núllō**[6] or **núllā,** m. or f., *no one, nobody*
>
> **égo, méī,** *I* (ego, egoism, egotism, egotistical)
>
> **tū, túī,** *you*
>
> **is, éa, id,** *this, that; he, she, it* (i.e. = **id est,** *that is*)
>
> **ídem, éadem, ídem,** *the same* (id., identical, identity, identify)
>
> **amícus, -a, -um,** *friendly* (amicable, amiable, amiably—cp. **amō** and the nouns **amícus, amíca,** and **amícitia**).
>
> **cárus, -a, -um,** *dear* (caress, charity, charitable, cherish)
>
> **quod,** conj., *because*
>
> **néque, nec,** conj. *and not, nor;* **néque . . . néque** or **nec . . . nec,** *neither . . . nor*
>
> **aútem,** postpositive conj., *however; moreover*
>
> **béne,** adv. of **bonus,** *well, satisfactorily, quite* (benediction, benefit, benefactor, beneficent, benevolent)
>
> **étiam,** adv., *even, also*
>
> **intéllegō, intellégere, intelléxī, intelléctum,** *to understand* (intelligent, intellegentsia, intelligible, intellect, intellectual; cp. **legō,** Ch. 18)
>
> **míttō, míttere, mísī, míssum,** *to send, let go* (admit, commit, emit, omit, permit, promise, remit, submit, transmit, compromise, demise)
>
> **séntiō, sentíre, sénsī, sénsum,** *to feel, perceive, think, experience* (assent, consent, dissent, presentiment, resent, sentimental, scent)

---

[5] Try pronouncing *****eumdem** or *****eōrumdem** rapidly and you will probably end up changing the **-m-** to **-n-** before **-d-,** just as the Romans did.

[6] The genitive and ablative forms of **nūllus** are usually found in place of **nēminis** and **nēmine.**

PRACTICE AND REVIEW

1. Eum ad eam cum aliō agricolā herī mittēbant.
2. Tū autem fīliam beātam eius nunc amās.
3. Propter amīcitiam, ego hoc faciō. Quid tū faciēs, mī amīce?
4. Vōsne eāsdem litterās ad eum mittere crās audēbitis?
5. Dūc mē ad eius discipulam (ad eam discipulam), amābō tē.
6. Post labōrem eius grātiās magnās eī agēmus.
7. Tūne vēritātem in eō librō dēmōnstrās?
8. Audē, igitur, esse semper īdem.
9. Venitne nātūra mōrum nostrōrum ex nōbīs sōlīs?
10. Dum ratiō nōs dūcet, valēbimus et multa bene gerēmus.
11. Illum timōrem in hōc virō ūnō invenīmus.
12. Sine labōre autem nūlla pāx in cīvitātem eōrum veniet.
13. Studium nōn sōlum pecūniae sed etiam voluptātis hominēs nimium trahit; aliī eās cupiditātēs vincere possunt, aliī nōn possunt.
14. His life was always dear to the whole people.
15. You will often find them and their friends with me in this place.
16. We, however, shall now capture their forces on this road.
17. Since I was saying the same things to him about you and his other sisters, your brother was not listening.

SENTENTIAE ANTĪQUAE

1. Virtūs tua mē amīcum tibi facit. (Horace.)
2. Id sōlum est cārum mihi. (Terence.—**cārus** and other adjectives indicating relationship or attitude often take the dat., translated *to* or *for;* see Ch. 35).
3. Sī valēs, bene est; ego valeō. (Pliny.—**bene est,** idiom, *it is well.*)
4. Bene est mihi quod tibi bene est. (Pliny.)
5. "Valē." "Et tū bene valē." (Terence.)
6. Quid hī dē tē nunc sentiunt? (Cicero.)
7. Omnēs idem sentiunt. (*Cicero.—**omnēs,** *all men,* nom. pl.)
8. Videō nēminem ex eīs hodiē esse amīcum tibi. (Cicero.—The subject of an infinitive is regularly in the acc., hence **nēminem;** add this to your list of acc. case uses, and see Ch. 25.)
9. Hominēs vidēre caput Cicerōnis in Rōstrīs poterant. (Livy.—Antony proscribed Cicero and had the great orator's head cut off and displayed on the Rostra!—**Rōstra, -ōrum;** see Etymology below.)
10. Nōn omnēs eadem amant aut eāsdem cupiditātēs studiaque habent. (Horace.)
11. Nec tēcum possum vīvere nec sine tē (*Martial.)
12. Vērus amīcus est alter īdem. (Cicero.—Explain how **alter īdem** can mean "a second self.")

CICERO DENOUNCES CATILINE IN THE SENATE

Quid facis, Catilīna? Quid cōgitās? Sentīmus magna vitia īnsidiāsque tuās. Ō tempora! Ō mōrēs! Senātus haec intellegit, cōnsul videt. Hic tamen vīvit. Vīvit? Etiam in senātum venit; etiam nunc cōnsilia agere audet; oculīs dēsignat ad mortem nōs! Et nōs, bonī virī, nihil facimus! Ad mortem tē, Catilīna, cōnsul et senātus dūcere dēbent. Cōnsilium habēmus et agere dēbēmus; sī nunc nōn agimus, nōs, nōs—apertē dīcō—errāmus! Fuge nunc, Catilīna, et dūc tēcum amīcōs tuōs. Nōbīscum remanēre nōn potes; nōn tē, nōn istōs, nōn cōnsilia vestra tolerābō!

(Cicero, *In Catilīnam* 1.1.ff. Lucius Sergius Catilina, "Catiline," masterminded a conspiracy against the Roman government during Cicero's consulship; this excerpt is adapted from the first oration Cicero delivered against him, before the senate, in 63 B.C. See L.I. 5–6 and the reading passage in Ch. 14 below.—**senātus,** *senate.*—**dēsignāre.**—**mors, mortis,** f., *death.*—**apertē,** adv., *openly.*)

Cicero Denouncing Catiline in the Roman Senate
Cesare Maccari, 19th century
Palazzo Madama, Rome, Italy

ETYMOLOGY

Cārus was sometimes used in the sense of *expensive* just as Eng. "dear" and Fr. **cher** can be used.

In the sentences   9. **Rōstra,** the ramming beaks of captured ships affixed to the speakers' platform in the Roman Forum to attest a victory won in 338 B.C. at Antium (Anzio). These beaks gave their name to the platform. Though the pl. *rostra* is still the regular Eng. form, we sometimes use the sg. *rostrum.* "Cicero Denounces Catiline": senator, senatorial; senile.—designate, designation.—mortal, mortality.—aperture; cp. **aperīre,** *to open.*

Some Romance derivatives from the Lat. personal pronouns follow.

Latin	Italian	Spanish	French
ego, tū	io, tu	yo, tu	je, tu
mihi, tibi	mi, ti		
mē, tē	me, te	me, te	me, moi, te, toi[7]
nōs, vōs (nom.)	noi, voi	nosotros, vosotros[8]	nous, vous
nōs, vōs (acc.)		nos, os	nous, vous

LATĪNA EST GAUDIUM—ET ŪTILIS!

Salvēte, discipulī et discipulae cārae! Notice the ending on that adj. **cārae?**—remember that when adjs. modify two nouns of different gender, the tendency is to have it agree with the one closer to it in the sentence. By the way, now you know the source of Freud's **ego** and **id,** and the meaning of the salutation **pāx vōbīscum/pāx tēcum.** And, you Caesar fans, can you believe that all three of the following have the same translation (well . . . sort of!): **Caesar, Caesar! Caesar eam videt. Caesar, cape eam!** According to tradition, Caesar's last words to the assassin Brutus were **et tū, Brūte?** (To which Brutus hungrily replied, according to the late great Brother Dave Gardner, "Nah, I ain't even et one yet!")

Did you notice in the Vocab. the origin of the abbreviations **i.e.** and **id.?** There are dozens of Latin abbreviations in current usage; for some others, besides those at the end of Ch. 6, see the list below, p. 492–93.

And remember those **-or/-iō** nouns? From the verbs in this Vocab. come **missor, missōris,** m., *a shooter* (of "missiles"—lit., *a sender*) and **missiō, missiōnis,** f., lit. *a sending forth* and used in classical Lat. for *release from captivity, liberation* (itself from **līberāre,** *to free*), *discharge* (from military service), *dismissal,* and, of course, *mission;* from compounds of **mittō** come a host of Latin nouns with further English derivatives such as "admission," "commission," "emission," "permission," etc. Can you think of others, both the Lat. nouns and the Eng. derivatives, from **mittō?** And how about **sentiō?**

Well, **tempus fugit,** so **pāx vōbīscum et valēte!**

---

[7] Fr. **moi, toi** came from accented Lat. **mē, tē,** and Fr. **me, te** came from unaccented Lat. **mē, tē.**

[8] **-otros** from **alterōs.**

12

Perfect Active System of All Verbs

You are already familiar with the formation and translation of the present, future, and imperfect tenses, the three tenses that constitute the present system, so-called because they are all formed on the present stem and all look at time from the absolute perspective of the present. In Latin, as in English, there are three other tenses, the perfect (sometimes called the "present perfect"), the future perfect, and the pluperfect (or "past perfect"), which constitute the "perfect system," so-called because they are formed on a perfect (active or passive) stem and look at time from a somewhat different perspective.

Learning the forms for these three tenses in the active voice (the perfect passive system is taken up in Ch. 19) is a relatively easy matter, since verbs of all conjugations follow the same simple rule: perfect active stem + endings.

PRINCIPAL PARTS

To ascertain the perfect active stem of a Latin verb you must know the principal parts of the verb, just as you must similarly know the principal parts of an English verb if you want to use English correctly.[1] As you have

---

[1] In fact the principal parts of an English verb to some extent parallel those of a Latin verb:

    (1) Present Tense:

praise	lead	take	see	sing	be/am

    (2) Past Tense:

praised	led	took	saw	sang	was

    (3) Past Participle:

praised	led	taken	seen	sung	been

Note that, since the pres. indic. and the pres. inf. are normally identical in English, only one form need be given. Note also that the past participle is really a past passive participle like the Latin **laudātum.**

seen from your vocabulary study, most regular Latin verbs have four principal parts, as illustrated by **laudō** in the following paradigm:

1. Present Active Indicative: laúdō, *I praise*
2. Present Active Infinitive: laudā́re, *to praise*
3. Perfect Active Indicative: laudā́vī, *I praised, have praised*
4. Perfect Passive Participle: laudā́tum, *praised, having been praised*

The principal parts of the verbs which have appeared in the paradigms
are as follows:

Pres. Ind.	Pres. Inf.	Perf. Ind.	Perf. Pass. Partic.
laúdō	laudā́re	laudā́vī, *I praised*	laudā́tum, *having been praised*
móneō	monḗre	mónuī, *I advised*	mónitum, *having been advised*
ágō	ágere	ḗgī, *I led*	áctum, *having been led*
cápiō	cápere	cḗpī, *I took*	cáptum, *having been taken*
aúdiō	audī́re	audī́vī, *I heard*	audī́tum, *having been heard*
sum	ésse	fúī, *I was*	futū́rum, *about to be*
póssum	pósse	pótuī, *I was able*	———

The first two principal parts, necessary for conjugating a verb in the present
system, have been dealt with extensively already. As the first person singular
of the perfect active indicative, which always ends in **-ī,** a verb's third principal part is analogous to its first (which is, of course, the first person singular
of the present active indicative and regularly ends in **-ō**). The fourth principal part, while given in its neuter form in this book, is for regular transitive
verbs the perfect passive participle, a fully declinable verbal adjective of the
-us/-a/-um variety (**laudātus, -a, -um,** etc.—some uses of participles will be
explained in Chs. 19 and 23–24). Verbs lacking a perfect passive participle
substitute the accusative supine (see Ch. 38), and some verbs like **sum** and
other intransitives substitute a future active participle (e.g., **futūrum** = **futūrus, -a, -um**), while others like **possum** have no fourth principal part at all.

THE PERFECT ACTIVE STEM

While the first and second principal parts for regular verbs follow a very
consistent pattern, there are no simple rules to cover the many variations in
the third and fourth principal parts (though, as we have seen, most first
conjugation verbs, marked by a [1] in the vocabularies, do follow the **-ō/
-āre/-āvī/-ātum** pattern of **laudō,** and many second and fourth conjugation
verbs follow the patterns of **moneō** and **audiō**); hence, as pointed out earlier,
it is crucial to memorize all the principal parts in the vocabulary entry for
each verb by both *saying them aloud* and *writing them out.* Your knowledge
of English will help you in this memorization, since there are many derivatives from both the present stem and the perfect participial stem, as you have
already discovered (e.g., "docile" and "doctor," "agent" and "action," etc.).

Once you know a verb's principal parts, finding the perfect active stem is easy: simply drop the final **-ī** which characterizes the third principal part of every verb. The stems for the sample verbs in the preceding list are: **laudāv-, monu-, ēg-, cēp-, audīv-, fu-,** and **potu-.** The following paradigms show you the endings for the three perfect system tenses.

Perfect Active Indicative

		I praised, have praised	*I led, have led*	*I was, have been*	**Endings**
Sg.	1.	laudáv-ī	ēg-ī	fú-ī	-ī
	2.	laudāv-ístī	ēg-ístī	fu-ístī	-istī
	3.	laudáv-it	ēg-it	fú-it	-it
Pl.	1.	laudávimus	ēgimus	fúimus	-imus
	2.	laudāvístis	ēgístis	fuístis	-istis
	3.	laudāvḗrunt	ēgḗrunt	fuḗrunt	-ērunt, -ēre[2]

Pluperfect Active Indicative

Future Perfect Active Indicative

		I had praised	*I had been*	*I shall have praised*	*I shall have been*
Sg.	1.	laudáv-eram	fú-eram	laudáv-erō	fú-erō
	2.	laudáv-erās	fú-erās	laudáv-eris	fú-eris
	3.	laudáv-erat	fú-erat	laudáv-erit	fú-erit
Pl.	1.	laudāvérāmus	fuerámus	laudāvérimus	fuérimus
	2.	laudāverátis	fuerátis	laudāvéritis	fuéritis
	3.	laudáverant	fúerant	laudáverint	fúerint

The perfect endings (**-ī, -istī, -it,** etc.) are quite new and must be memorized. The pluperfect is in effect the perfect stem **+ eram,** the imperfect of **sum.** The future perfect is in effect the perfect stem **+ erō,** the future of **sum,** except that the third person plural is **-erint,** not **-erunt.**

USAGE, TRANSLATION, AND DISTINCTION FROM THE IMPERFECT

The perfect tense, like the imperfect, is sometimes translated as a simple past tense, hence both **puer amīcum monuit** and **puer amīcum monēbat** may in certain contexts be translated *the boy warned his friend.* But whereas the imperfect tense is like a video of the past, the perfect tense (from **perficiō, perficere, perfēcī, perfectum,** *to finish, complete*) is rather like a snapshot: with the imperfect the action is viewed as going on, repeated, or habitual, so a more exact translation of **puer amīcum monēbat,** depending upon the

---

[2] The alternate ending **-ēre (laudāvēre, ēgēre, fuēre),** while fairly common, especially in Lat. poetry, appears only once or twice in this book.

context, might be *the boy was warning/kept warning/used to warn his friend.* Conversely, the more static perfect tense looks back at an action as a single, completed event (*he warned his friend once*), or as an event that, although completed, has consequences for the present; in this latter case, you should regularly translate using the auxiliary "has/have" (*he has warned his friend, and so his friend is now prepared*).

The pluperfect (from **plūs quam perfectum,** *more than complete,* i.e., time "prior to the perfect") and the future perfect are employed generally as they are in English and, like the perfect tense, generally look at the consequences of completed actions. Consider these English sentences, illustrating the pluperfect, perfect, and future perfect, respectively, and note the use of the English auxiliary verbs "had," "has," and "will have" (the past, present, and future tenses of the verb "to have"): "he had studied the material and so he knew it well"; "he has studied the material and so he knows it well"; "he will have studied the material and so he will know it well." You can see from these examples how the three perfect system tenses parallel the three tenses of the present system; in the latter we simply look at events of the past, present, or future, while in the former we look at events of the past, present, or future and consider the impact of previously completed actions on those events.

VOCABULARY

aduléscēns, adulēscéntis, m. and f., *young man* or *woman* (adolescent, adolescence, adult; cp. **adulēscentia**)

ánnus, -ī, m., *year* (annals, anniversary, annuity, annual, biennial, perennial, centennial, millennium, superannuated)

Ásia, -ae, f., *Asia,* commonly referring to Asia Minor

Caésar, Caésaris, m., *Caesar* (Caesarian, Caesarism, kaiser, czar, tsar)

máter, mátris, f., *mother* (maternal, maternity, matriarchy, matrimony, matricide, matriculate, matrilineal, matrix, matron)

médicus, -ī, m., and **médica, -ae,** f., *doctor, physician* (medic, medical, medicate, medicine, medicinal)

páter, pátris, m., *father* (paternal, paternity, patrician, patrimony, patron, patronage, patronize, patter, padre, père; cp. **patria**)

patiéntia, -ae, f., *suffering; patience, endurance* (patient, impatient; cp. **patior,** Ch. 34)

prīncípium, -íī, n., *beginning* (principal, principle; cp. **prīnceps,** Ch. 28)

acérbus, -a, -um, *harsh, bitter, grievous* (acerbity, exacerbate)

prō, prep. + abl., *in front of, before, on behalf of, for the sake of, in return for, instead of, for, as;* also as prefix (pros and cons, pro- as a prefix)

díū, adv., *long, for a long time*

nűper, adv., *recently*

āmíttō, -míttere, -mísī, -míssum, *to lose, let go*

cádō, cádere, cécidī, cāsū́rum, *to fall* (cadence, case, casual, cascade, chance, accident, incident, decadence, decay, deciduous)

créō (1), *to create* (creation, creativity, creature, procreate)

PRACTICE AND REVIEW

1. Vōs nōbīs dē voluptātibus adūlēscentiae tum scrīpsistis.
2. Ratiōnēs alterīus fīliae herī nōn fuērunt eaedem.
3. Nēmō in hanc viam ex utrā portā fūgerat.
4. Illī autem ad nōs cum medicā eius nūper vēnērunt.
5. Illī adulēscentēs ad nōs propter amīcitiam saepe veniēbant.
6. Eundem timōrem in istō cōnsule sēnsimus.
7. Post paucās hōrās Caesar Asiam cēpit.
8. Illa fēmina beāta sōla magnam cupiditātem pācis sēnsit.
9. Potuistisne bonam vītam sine ūllā lībertāte agere?
10. Vēritās igitur fuit tōtī populō cāra.
11. Neuter medicus nōmen patris audīverat.
12. That friendly queen did not remain there a long time.
13. Our mothers had not understood the nature of that place.
14. However, we had found no fault in the head of our country.
15. They kept sending her to him with me.

SENTENTIAE ANTĪQUAE

1. In prīncipiō Deus creāvit caelum et terram; et Deus creāvit hominem. (Genesis.)
2. In triumphō Caesar praetulit hunc titulum: "Vēnī, vīdī, vīcī." (Suetonius.—**triumphus, -ī,** *triumphal procession,* here celebrating his quick victory at Zela in Asia Minor in 47 B.C.—**praeferō, -ferre, -tulī, -lātum,** *to display.*—**titulus, -ī,** *placard.*)
3. Vīxit, dum vīxit, bene. (*Terence.)
4. Adulēscēns vult diū vīvere; senex diū vīxit. (Cicero.—**vult,** irreg., *wishes.*—**senex, senis,** m., *old man.*)
5. Nōn ille diū vīxit, sed diū fuit. (*Seneca.)
6. Hui, dīxistī pulchrē! (*Terence.—**hui,** interj., comparable to Eng. "whee!"—**pulchrē,** adv. from **pulcher**; advs. were commonly formed from adjs. in this way. See Chs. 26–27, and cp., e.g., **vērē** from **vērus, lībere** from **līber,** and the irregular **bene** from **bonus.**)
7. Sophoclēs ad summam senectūtem tragoediās fēcit. (*Cicero.—**Sophoclēs, -clis,** the famous Athenian playwright.—**summus, -a, -um,** *extreme.*—**tragoedia, -ae,** *tragedy.*)
8. Illī nōn sōlum pecūniam sed etiam vītam prō patriā prōfūdērunt. (Cicero.—**prōfundō, -ere, -fūdī, -fūsum,** *to pour forth.*)
9. Rēgēs Rōmam ā prīncipiō habuērunt; lībertātem Lūcius Brūtus Rōmānīs dedit. (Tacitus.—**ā** + abl., *from.*)

10. Sub Caesare autem lībertātem perdidimus. (Laberius.—**perdō, -ere, -didī, -ditum,** *to destroy, lose.*)

11. Quandō lībertās ceciderit, nēmō līberē dīcere audēbit. (Publilius Syrus.)

PLINY WRITES TO MARCELLINUS ABOUT THE DEATH OF FUNDANUS' DAUGHTER

Salvē, Marcellīne! Haec tibi scrībō dē Fundānō, amīcō nostrō; is fīliam cāram et bellam āmīsit. Illa puella nōn XIII annōs vīxerat, sed nātūra eī multam sapientiam dederat. Mātrem patremque, frātrem sorōremque, nōs et aliōs amīcōs, magistrōs magistrāsque semper amābat, et nōs eam amābāmus laudābāmusque. Medicī eam adiuvāre nōn poterant. Quoniam illa autem magnōs animōs habuit, morbum nimis malum cum patientiā tolerāvit. Nunc, mī amīce, mitte Fundānō nostrō litterās dē fortūnā acerbā fīliae eius. Valē.

(Pliny, *Epistulae* 5.16; see L.I. 40.—**XIII annōs,** *for 13 years,* acc. of duration of time, Ch. 37. Minicius Fundanus was a consul in A.D. 107; his daughter's funerary urn and the following epitaph were found in the family's tomb outside of

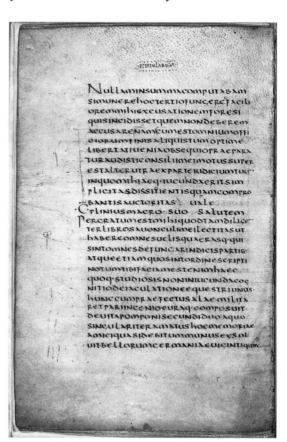

Page from manuscript of Pliny's Epistulae
(Epist. III.4.8–9 and III.5.1–3)
6th century A.D., Italy
The Pierpont Morgan Library, New York

Rome: **D[īs] M[ānibus] Miniciae Marcellae Fundānī f[īliae]; v[īxit] a[nnōs] XII m[ēnsēs] XI d[iēs] VII.**—The bracketed text was abbreviated in the original inscription.—The **dī mānēs** were the *spirits of the dead,* who protected the deceased.—**mēnsēs,** *months.*—**diēs,** *days.*)

DIAULUS STILL BURIES HIS CLIENTS

Nūper erat medicus, nunc est vespillo Diaulus.
Quod vespillo facit, fēcerat et medicus.

(*Martial 1.47; meter: elegiac couplet.—**vespillō, -lōnis,** m., *undertaker.*—Diaulus' name is delayed for suspense.—**quod,** *what.*—**et = etiam.**)

ETYMOLOGY

Further examples of the help of English words in learning principal parts of Latin verbs are:

Latin Verb	Pres. Stem in Eng. Word	Perf. Partic. Stem in Eng. Word
videō	provide (vidēre)	provision (vīsum)
maneō	permanent (manēre)	mansion (mānsum)
vīvō	revive (vīvere)	victuals (vīctum)
sentiō	sentiment (sentīre)	sense (sēnsum)
veniō	intervene (venīre)	intervention (ventum)
faciō	facile (facere)	fact (factum)

The connection between Latin **pater** and **patria** (*father-land*) is obvious. However, although English "patriarch," "patriot," and "patronymic" have in them a stem, **patr-,** which is meaningful to one who knows the Latin words, nevertheless these English words are actually derived from Greek, in which the stem **patr-** is cognate with the same stem in Latin; cp. Greek **patér,** *father,* **pátrā** or **patrís,** *fatherland,* **patriá,** *lineage.*

In the readings   2. prefer, prelate.—title, titular. 8. confound, confuse, effuse, effusive, fuse, fusion, refund, refuse, transfusion. 10. perdition.

LATĪNA EST GAUDIUM—ET ŪTILIS!

Salvēte, discipulae discipulīque cārī! As we saw in S. A. 2 above, Caesar is said to have proclaimed **vēnī, vīdī, vīcī** in propagandizing his victory at Zela—a good example of the perfect tense, a "snapshot" of the action whose rapid conclusion the general wanted to emphasize. There are now some 20th-cen. variants on this boast: from the mall-masters, **VENI, VIDI, VISA,** "I came, I saw, I bought everything in sight!" and from the vegetarians, **VENI, VIDI, VEGI,** "I came, I saw, I had a salad." Are you groaning?!!—but remember, **patientia est virtūs,** and there may yet be worse to come: meantime, **rīdēte** (from **rīdēre,** *to smile*) **et valēte!**

13

Reflexive Pronouns and Possessives; Intensive Pronoun

REFLEXIVE PRONOUNS

Reflexive pronouns differ from other pronouns in that they are used ordinarily only in the predicate and refer back to the subject. "Reflexive," which derives from **re-flexus, -a, -um (reflectō, -ere, -flexī, -flexum,** *to bend back*) means "bent back," and so reflexive pronouns "bend back" to the subject, or, to put it another way, they "reflect" or refer to the subject. English examples are:

Reflexive Pronouns	Personal Pronouns
I praised *myself.*	You praised *me.*
Cicero praised *himself.*	Cicero praised *him* (Caesar).

DECLENSION OF REFLEXIVE PRONOUNS

Since reflexive pronouns refer to the subject, they cannot serve as subjects of finite[1] verbs and they have no nominative case. Otherwise, the declension of the reflexives of the first and the second persons is the same as that of the corresponding personal pronouns.

---

[1] "Finite" verb forms are those which are limited (**fīnītus, -a, -um,** *having been limited, bounded*) by person and number; reflexives can serve as the subject of an infinitive, however, as you will see in Ch. 25.

The reflexive pronoun of the third person, however, has its own peculiar forms; these are easily recognizable because, as seen from the following chart, they are identical to the singular of **tū**, except that the nominative is lacking and the forms begin with **s-** rather than **t-**. Note also that the singular and plural are identical, or, to put it another way, singular and plural were not distinguished and did not need to be, since reflexives in fact "reflect" the number (as well as the gender) of the subject; e.g., **sē** is easily understood to mean *herself* in the sentence **fēmina dē sē cōgitābat** (*the woman was thinking about herself*) and *themselves* in the sentence **virī dē sē cōgitābant** (*the men were thinking about themselves*).

	1st Pers.	2nd Pers.	3rd Pers.
Singular			
Nom.	—	—	—
Gen.	méī (*of myself*)	túī	súī (*of himself, herself, itself*)
Dat.	míhi (*to/for myself*)	tíbi	síbi (*to/for himself*, etc.)
Acc.	mē (*myself*)	tē	sē (*himself, herself, itself*)
Abl.	mē (*by/w./fr. myself*[2])	tē	sē (*by/w./fr. himself*, etc.)
Plural			
Nom.	—	—	—
Gen.	nóstrī (*of ourselves*)	véstrī	súī (*of themselves*)
Dat.	nṓbīs (*to/for ourselves*)	vṓbīs	síbi (*to/for themselves*)
Acc.	nōs (*ourselves*)	vōs	sē (*themselves*)
Abl.	nṓbīs (*by/w./fr. ourselves*)	vṓbīs	sē (*by/w./fr. themselves*)

PARALLEL EXAMPLES OF REFLEXIVE AND PERSONAL PRONOUNS OF 1ST AND 2ND PERSONS.[3]

1. Tū laudāvistī **tē,** *you praised* **yourself.**

2. Cicerō laudāvit **tē,** *Cicero praised* **you.**

3. Nōs laudāvimus **nōs,** *we praised* **ourselves.**

4. Cicerō laudāvit **nōs,** *Cicero praised* **us.**

5. Ego scrīpsī litterās **mihi,** *I wrote a letter to* **myself.**

6. Cicerō scrīpsit litterās **mihi,** *Cicero wrote a letter to* **me.**

PARALLEL EXAMPLES OF REFLEXIVE AND PERSONAL PRONOUNS OF 3RD PERSON

1. Cicerō laudāvit **sē,** *Cicero praised* **himself.**

2. Cicerō laudāvit **eum,** *Cicero praised* **him** (e.g., Caesar).

---

[2] See Ch. 11, n. 1.
[3] The word order in these examples is modified for the sake of clarity.

3. Rōmānī laudāvērunt **sē,** *the Romans praised* **themselves.**
4. Rōmānī laudāvērunt **eōs,** *the Romans praised* **them** (e.g., the Greeks).

5. Puella servāvit **sē,** *the girl saved* **herself.**
6. Puella servāvit **eam,** *the girl saved* **her** (i.e., another girl).

REFLEXIVE POSSESSIVES

The reflexive possessives of the first and the second persons are identical with the regular possessives already familiar to you: **meus, tuus, noster, vester** (i.e., *my, my own; your, your own;* etc.). They will never cause you any difficulty.

The reflexive possessive of the third person, however, is the adjective **suus, sua, suum,** *his (own), her (own), its (own), their (own).* While the forms themselves are easily declined (on the same pattern as **tuus, -a, -um,** a regular first/second declension adjective), a few important points must be kept in mind regarding the word's usage and translation. First, like any adjective, **suus, -a, -um,** must agree with the noun it modifies in number, gender, and case. Its English translation, however, like that of the reflexive pronoun, must naturally reflect the gender and number of the subject to which it refers (e.g., **vir fīlium suum laudat,** *the man praises his [own] son,* vs. **fēmina fīlium suum laudat,** *the woman praises her [own] son,* and **virī patriam suam laudant,** *the men praise their [own] country*). Finally, the reflexive possessive adjective **suus, -a, -um** must be carefully distinguished from the nonreflexive possessive genitives **eius, eōrum, eārum** (*his/her, their:* see Ch. 11), which do not refer to the subject.

1. Cicerō laudāvit amīcum **suum,** *Cicero praised his (own) friend.*
2. Cicerō laudāvit amīcum **eius,** *Cicero praised his* (Caesar's) *friend.*

3. Rōmānī laudāvērunt amīcum **suum,** *the Romans praised their (own) friend.*
4. Rōmānī laudāvērunt amīcum **eōrum,** *the Romans praised their* (the Greeks') *friend.*

5. Fēmina scrīpsit litterās amīcīs **suīs,** *the woman wrote a letter to her (own) friends.*
6. Fēmina scrīpsit litterās amīcīs **eius,** *the woman wrote a letter to his* (or *her,* i.e., someone else's) *friends.*
7. Fēmina scrīpsit litterās amīcīs **eōrum,** *the woman wrote a letter to their* (some other persons') *friends.*

THE INTENSIVE PRONOUN Ipse, Ipsa, Ipsum

The intensive **ipse, ipsa, ipsum** follows the peculiar declensional pattern of the demonstratives in the genitive and the dative singular (i.e., gen. **ipsīus, ipsīus, ipsīus,** dat. **ipsī, ipsī, ipsī**); otherwise, it is like **magnus, -a, -um.**[4] The Romans used the intensive pronoun to emphasize a noun or pronoun of any person in either the subject or the predicate of a sentence; consequently its possible translations include *myself/ourselves* (1st pers.), *yourself/yourselves* (2nd pers.), and *himself/herself/itself/themselves* (3rd pers.), as well as *the very* and *the actual,* as illustrated in the following examples:

Cicerō **ipse** laudāvit mē, *Cicero himself praised me.*

Cicerō laudāvit mē **ipsum,** *Cicero praised me myself* (i.e., *actually praised me*)

Ipse laudāvī eius amīcum, *I myself praised his friend.*

Fīlia scrīpsit litterās vōbīs **ipsīs,** *your daughter wrote a letter to you yourselves.*

Cicerō vīdit Caesaris litterās **ipsās,** *Cicero saw Caesar's letter itself* (i.e., *Caesar's actual letter*).

VOCABULARY

dīvítiae, -árum, f. pl., *riches, wealth* (cp. **dīves,** Ch. 32)

fáctum, -ī, n., *deed, act, achievement* (fact, faction, feat; cp. **faciō**)

sígnum, -ī, n., *sign, signal, indication; seal* (assign, consign, countersign, design, ensign, insignia, resign, seal, signet)

ípse, ípsa, ípsum, intensive pron., *myself, yourself, himself, herself, itself,* etc., *the very, the actual* (ipso facto, solipsistic)

quísque, quídque (gen. **cuiúsque;** dat. **cuíque**—cp. **quis,** Ch. 19), indefinite pron., *each one, each person, each thing*

súī, reflexive pron. of 3rd pers., *himself, herself, itself, themselves* (suicide, sui generis, per se)

dóctus, -a, -um, *taught, learned, skilled* (doctor, doctorate, doctrine, indoctrinate; cp. **doceō**)

fortūnátus, -a, -um, *lucky, fortunate, happy* (unfortunate; cp. **fortūna**)

súus, -a, -um, reflexive possessive adj. of 3rd pers., *his own, her own, its own, their own*

nam, conj., *for*

ánte, prep. + acc., *before* (in place or time), *in front of;* adv., *before, previously;* not to be confused with Greek **anti,** *against* (antebellum, antedate, ante-room, anterior, antediluvian, A.M. = **ante merīdiem,** advance, advantage)

---

[4] See the Summary of Forms, p. 448, for the full declension.

per, prep. + acc., *through;* with reflexive pron., *by;* **per-** (assimilated to **pel-** before forms beginning with **l-**), as a prefix, *through, through and through = thoroughly, completely, very* (perchance, perforce, perhaps, perceive, perfect, perspire, percolate, percussion, perchloride, pellucid)

ṓlim, adv., *at that time, once, formerly; in the future*

álō, álere, áluī, áltum, *to nourish, support, sustain, increase; cherish* (alible, aliment, alimentary, alimony, coalesce, adolescence)

dīligō, dīlígere, dīlḗxī, dīlḗctum, *to esteem, love* (diligent, diligence; cp. **legō,** Ch. 18)

iúngō, iúngere, iū́nxī, iū́nctum, *to join* (join, joint, junction, juncture, adjunct, conjunction, enjoin, injunction, subjunctive)

stō, stā́re, stétī, státum, *to stand, stand still* or *firm* (stable, state, station, statue, stature, statute, establish, instant, instate, reinstate, stay; cp. **praestō,** Ch. 28)

PRACTICE AND REVIEW

1. Cōnsulēs sē nec tēcum nec cum illīs aliīs iungēbant.
2. Tōtus populus Rōmānus lībertātem āmīsit.
3. Rēx malus enim mē ipsum capere numquam potuit.
4. Ad patrem mātremque eōrum per illum locum tum fūgistis.
5. Dī animōs creant et eōs in corpora hominum ē caelō mittunt.
6. Ipsī per sē eum in Asiā nūper vīcērunt.
7. In hāc viā Cicerō medicum eius vīdit, nōn suum.
8. Nēmō fīliam acerbam cōnsulis ipsīus diū dīligere potuit.
9. Hī Cicerōnem ipsum sēcum iūnxērunt, nam eum semper dīlēxerant.
10. Fēmina ante illam hōram litterās suās mīserat.
11. Ille bonam senectūtem habuit, nam bene vīxerat.
12. Māter fīlium bene intellēxit, et adulēscēns eī prō patientiā grātiās ēgit.
13. However, those young men came to Caesar himself yesterday.
14. Cicero, therefore, will never join his (Caesar's) name with his own.
15. Cicero always esteemed himself and even you esteem yourself.
16. Cicero used to praise his own books and I now praise my own books.
17. The consul Cicero himself had never seen his (Caesar's) book.

SENTENTIAE ANTĪQUAE

1. Ipse ad eōs contendēbat equitēsque ante sē mīsit. (Caesar.—**contendō, -ere,** *to hasten.*—**eques, equitis,** m., *horseman.*)
2. Ipsī nihil per sē sine eō facere potuērunt. (Cicero.)
3. Ipse signum suum et litterās suās ā prīncipiō recognōvit. (Cicero.—**recognōscō, -ere, -cognōvī, -cognitum,** *to recognize.*)
4. Quisque ipse sē dīligit, quod quisque per sē sibi cārus est. (Cicero.)

5. Ex vitiō alterīus sapiēns ēmendat suum. (*Publilius Syrus.—**sapiēns, -entis,** m., *wise man, philosopher.*—**ēmendāre,** *to correct.*)
6. Recēde in tē ipsum. (*Seneca.—**recēdō, -ere,** *to withdraw.*)
7. Animus sē ipse alit. (*Seneca.)
8. Homō doctus in sē semper dīvitiās habet. (Phaedrus.)

ALEXANDER THE GREAT AND THE POWER OF LITERATURE

Magnus ille Alexander multōs scrīptōrēs factōrum suōrum sēcum semper habēbat. Is enim ante tumulum Achillis ōlim stetit et dīxit haec verba: "Fuistī fortūnātus, ō adulēscēns, quod Homērum laudātōrem virtūtis tuae invēnistī." Et vērē! Nam, sine *Īliade* illā, īdem tumulus et corpus eius et nōmen obruere potuit. Nihil corpus hūmānum cōnservāre potest; sed litterae magnae nōmen virī magnī saepe cōnservāre possunt.

(Cicero, *Prō Archiā* 24. —**ille,** usually when placed after the word it modifies, can mean *that famous.*—**tumulus, -ī,** *tomb, grave.*—**Achillēs, -lis,** m.—**Homērus, -ī.**—**laudātor, -tōris,** *one who praises* [see Ch. 8, **Latīna Est Gaudium**], here *chronicler.*—**vērē,** adv. of **vērus.**—**Īlias, -adis,** f.—**obruō, -ere,** *to overwhelm, bury.*)

Alexander the Great
Pergamon, 3rd century B.C.
Archaeological Museum, Istanbul, Turkey

THE AUTHORITY OF A TEACHER'S OPINION

Magistrī bonī discipulīs sententiās suās nōn semper dīcere dēbent. Discipulī Pȳthagorae in disputātiōnibus saepe dīcēbant: "Ipse dīxit!" Pȳthagorās, eōrum magister philosophiae, erat "ipse": sententiae eius etiam sine ratiōne valuērunt. In philosophiā autem ratiō sōla, nōn sententia, valēre dēbet.

(Cicero, *Dē Nātūrā Deōrum* 1.5.10.—**Pȳthagorās, -ae,** m.—**disputātiō, -ōnis,** *argument, debate.*—sc. **id** as direct obj. of **ipse dīxit.**)

ETYMOLOGY

The adj. **altus, -a, -um,** *high,* literally means *having been nourished,* and so, *grown large;* hence altitude, alto, contralto, exalt, hautboy, oboe.

In the readings   1. contend, contention, contentious.—equestrian; cp. **equus,** *horse.* 5. emend, emendation, mend. 6. recede, recession. "Alexander": tumulus, tumular, tumulose.—laudatory. "Authority": disputable, dispute, disputant, disputation, disputatious.

LATĪNA EST GAUDIUM—ET ŪTILIS!

Salvēte! If you've spent much time in court, or even watching *Perry Mason* reruns, you've doubtless encountered some legal Latin. **Ipse** turns up more than once in the lawyer's lexicon: there's **ipsō factō,** *by that very fact;* **ipsō jūre** (classical **iūre**), *by the law itself;* and **rēs ipsa loquitur,** *the matter speaks for itself.* And from the third pers. reflexive there's **suī jūris (iūris),** lit. *of his own right,* i.e., legally competent to manage one's own affairs. Not a legal term, but from the reflexive and common in Eng. is **suī generis,** lit. *of his/her/its own kind* (see **genus,** Ch. 18), used of a person or thing that is unique. Another common Eng. phrase, seen in the above reading on Pythagoras, is **ipse dīxit,** used of any dogmatic or arbitrary statement; likewise from the intensive pronoun are the phrase **ipsissima verba,** *the very words* (of a person being quoted), the medical term "ipsilateral," meaning "on or affecting the same side of the body" (from Lat. **latus, lateris,** n., *side*), and the word "solipsism," for the philosophical theory that the self alone is the only reality or that it conditions our perception of reality.

By now you've had all the vocabulary needed to translate the famous quotation from Constantine, **in hōc signō vincēs** (*under this standard*—i.e., the cross—*you shall prevail*), seen in more recent decades on a well-known brand of cigarettes; freely it means, *You'll win with this brand* (but would the U.S. Surgeon General agree?). Well, **tempus iterum fūgit: valēte!**

School of Athens, detail of Pythagoras and a boy
Raphael, 1508
Stanza della Segnatura
Vatican Palace, Vatican State

14

I-Stem Nouns of the Third Declension; Ablatives of Means, Accompaniment, and Manner

Some nouns of the third declension differ from those introduced in Ch. 7 in that they have a characteristic **i** in certain case endings. Because of this **i** these nouns are called **i**-stem nouns, and the rest are known as consonant-stems. As you will see from the following paradigms, the only new ending shared by all **i**-stems is the genitive plural in **-ium** (rather than simply **-um**); neuters have, in addition, **-ī** instead of **-e** in the ablative singular and **-ia** instead of **-a** in the nominative, accusative, and vocative plural; **vīs** is a common irregular **i**-stem and should be memorized (its gen. and dat. sg., given in parentheses, are rarely used).

	Cons.-stem Reviewed	Parisyllabics		Base in 2 Consonants	Neut. in -e, -al, -ar	Irregular
	rēx, rēgis, m., *king*	**cīvis, -is,** m., *citizen*	**nūbēs, -is,** f., *cloud*	**urbs, -is,** f., *city*	**mare, -is,** n., *sea*	**vīs, vīs,** f., *force;* pl. *strength*
N.	rḗx	cī́vis	nū́bēs	úrbs	mā́re	vīs
G.	rḗgis	cī́vis	nū́bis	úrbis	mā́ris	(vīs)
D.	rḗgī	cī́vī	nū́bī	úrbī	mā́rī	(vī)
A.	rḗgem	cī́vem	nū́bem	úrbem	mā́re	**vim**
A.	rḗge	cī́ve	nū́be	úrbe	mā́rī	vī

N.	rḗgēs	cī́vēs	nū́bēs	ū́rbēs	mária	vī́rēs
G.	rḗgum	cī́vium	nū́bium	ū́rbium	márium	vī́rium
D.	rḗgibus	cī́vibus	nū́bibus	ū́rbibus	máribus	vī́ribus
A.	rḗgēs	cī́vēs	nū́bēs	ū́rbēs	mária	vī́rēs
A.	rḗgibus	cī́vibus	nū́bibus	ū́rbibus	máribus	vī́ribus

An important alternate masculine and feminine accusative plural ending in **-īs** (e.g., **cīvīs** for **cīvēs**), though rarely appearing in this book, was frequently employed throughout Republican literature and into the Augustan Period and should be remembered.

Besides learning these few new endings, it is also important to be able to recognize that a noun is an **i**-stem when you encounter it in a vocabulary list or a reading. The following three rules will enable you to do so and should be memorized.

MASCULINE AND FEMININE i-STEMS

1.   Masculine and feminine nouns with a nominative singular in **-is** or **-ēs** and having the same number of syllables in both the nominative and genitive (often called "parisyllabic," from **pār**, *equal,* + **syllaba**).[1]

> hostis, hostis, m.; hostium; *enemy*
> nāvis, nāvis, f.; nāvium; *ship*
> mōlēs, mōlis, f.; mōlium; *mass, structure*

2.   Masculine and (chiefly) feminine nouns with a nominative singular in **-s** or **-x** which have a base ending in two consonants; most, like the following examples, have monosyllabic nominatives.

> ars, art-is, f.; artium; *art, skill*
> dēns, dent-is, m.; dentium; *tooth*
> nox, noct-is, f.; noctium; *night*
> arx, arc-is, f.; arcium; *citadel*

Again, the only ending ordinarily distinguishing these masculine and feminine nouns from consonant stems is the genitive plural in **-ium**.

NEUTER i-STEMS

3.   Neuter nouns with a nominative singular in **-al, -ar,** or **-e.** Again, these have the characteristic **i** not only in the genitive plural **-ium** but also in the ablative singular **-ī** and the nominative/accusative/vocative plural **-ia.**

---

[1] **Canis, canis,** *dog,* and **iuvenis, -is,** *youth,* are exceptions, having **-um** in the gen. pl. There are a few nouns with **-er** nominatives in this category, e.g., **imber, imbris,** m., *shower, rain* (gen. pl. **imbrium**).

animal, animālis, n., *animal*
exemplar, exemplāris, n., *model, pattern, original*
mare, maris, n., *sea*

IRREGULAR Vīs

The common and irregular **vīs** must be thoroughly memorized and must be carefully distinguished from **vir.** Note that the characteristic ī appears in most forms. Practice with the following forms: **virī, vīrēs, virīs, vīrium, vīribus, virōs, virum.**

ABLATIVE CASE USES

So far the ablative has generally appeared along with prepositions and for that reason has occasioned little difficulty. However, the Romans frequently used a simple ablative without a preposition to express ideas which in English are introduced by a preposition. The proper interpretation of such ablatives requires two things: (1) a knowledge of the prepositionless categories and (2) an analysis of the context to see which category is the most logical.

Following are three common uses (or "constructions") of the ablative case, which should be added to the one you have already learned (i.e., object of certain prepositions); several additional uses for this case will be introduced in later chapters, so it is important to maintain a list in your notebook or computer file, complete with the name, a definition, and examples for each (you should be maintaining similar lists, of course, for all of the other cases as well).

ABLATIVE OF MEANS OR INSTRUMENT

The ablative of means or instrument is one of the most important of the prepositionless categories. It answers the questions *by means of what (instrument)?, by what?, with what?* and its English equivalent is a phrase introduced by the prepositions *by, by means of, with.*

Litterās stilō scrīpsit, *he wrote the letter with a pencil* (stilus, -ī).
Cīvēs pecūniā vīcit, *he conquered the citizens with/by money.*
Id meīs oculīs vīdī, *I saw it with my own eyes.*
Suīs labōribus urbem cōnservāvit, *by his own labors he saved the city.*

You have already encountered this construction a few times in the reading and translation exercises.

ABLATIVES OF ACCOMPANIMENT AND MANNER

You have also already encountered the use of **cum** + ablative to indicate (1) accompaniment, which answers the question *with whom?* and (2) manner, which answers the question *how?*

Cum amīcīs vēnērunt, *they came with friends* (= with whom?)
Cum celeritāte vēnērunt, *they came with speed* (= how?; *speedily.* —celeritās, -tātis).
Id cum eīs fēcit, *he did it with them* (= with whom?).
Id cum virtūte fēcit, *he did it with courage* (= how?; *courageously*).

You will notice that each of these three constructions may be translated using the English preposition "with" (among other possibilities), but the three constructions are conceptually different and must be very carefully distinguished. Remember that ablative constructions generally function adverbially, telling you something about the action of the verb; in these three instances they tell you, respectively, by what means or with what instrument the action was performed, with whom the action was performed, and in what manner the action was performed.

Your only real difficulty will come in translating from English to Latin. If *with* tells *with whom* or *in what manner,* use **cum** + ablative; if *with* tells *by means of what,* use the ablative without a preposition.

VOCABULARY

ánimal, animális, n., *a living creature, animal* (related to **anima,** Ch. 34, *breath, air, spirit, soul,* and **animus;** animate, animation)

áqua, -ae, f., *water* (aquatic, aquarium, Aquarius, aqueduct, subaqueous, ewer, sewer, sewage, sewerage)

ars, ártis, f., *art, skill* (artifact, artifice, artificial, artless, artist, artisan, inert, inertia)

aúris, aúris, f., *ear* (aural, auricle, auricular, auriform; not to be confused with "auric," "auriferous," from **aurum,** *gold*)

cívis, cívis, m. and f., *citizen* (civil, civilian, civility, incivility, civilize, civic; cp. **cívitās, cívilis,** *related to one's fellow citizens*)

iūs, iúris, n., *right, justice, law* (jurisdiction, jurisprudence, juridical, jurist, juror, jury, just, justice, injury; cp. **iniūria,** Ch. 39, **iūstus,** Ch. 40)

máre, máris, n., *sea* (marine, mariner, marinate, maritime, submarine, cormorant, rosemary, mere = Eng. cognate, archaic for "small lake.")

mors, mórtis, f., *death* (mortal, immortal, mortify, mortgage; murder = Eng. cognate; cp. **mortālis,** Ch. 18, **immortālis,** Ch. 19)

nŭbēs, nŭbis, f., *cloud* (nubilous)

ōs, ōris, n., *mouth, face* (oral, orifice)

pars, pártis, f., *part, share; direction* (party, partial, partake, participate, participle, particle, particular, partisan, partition, apart, apartment, depart, impart, repartee)

Rŏma, -ae, f., *Rome* (romance, romantic, romanticism; cp. **Rōmānus**)

túrba, -ae, f., *uproar, disturbance; mob, crowd, multitude* (cp. **turbāre,** *to disturb, throw into confusion;* turbid, turbulent, turbine, turbo, disturb, perturb, imperturbable, trouble)

urbs, úrbis, f., *city* (urban, urbane, urbanity, suburb, suburban)

vīs, vīs, f., *force, power, violence;* **vīrēs, vīrium,** pl., *strength* (vim, violate, violent; do not confuse with **vir**)

ā (before consonants), **ab** (before vowels or consonants), prep. + abl., *away from, from; by* (personal agent); frequent in compounds (aberration, abject, abrasive, absolve, abstract, abundant, abuse)

trāns, prep. + acc., *across;* also a prefix (transport, transmit)

appéllō (1), *to speak to, address (as), call, name* (appellation, appellative, appeal, appellant, appellate)

cúrrō, cúrrere, cucúrrī, cúrsum, *to run, rush, move quickly* (current, cursive, cursory, course, coarse, discursive, incur, occur, recur)

mŭtō (1), *to change, alter; exchange* (mutable, immutable, mutual, commute, permutation, transmutation, molt)

téneō, tenḗre, ténuī, téntum, *to hold, keep, possess; restrain;* **-tineō, -ēre, -tinuī, -tentum** in compounds, e.g., **contineō** (tenable, tenacious, tenant, tenet, tenure, tentacle, tenor, continue, content, continent, pertinent, pertinacity, lieutenant, appertain, detain, retain, sustain)

vītō (1), *to avoid, shun;* not to be confused with **vīvō** (inevitable)

PRACTICE AND REVIEW

1. Magnam partem illārum urbium post multōs annōs vī et cōnsiliō capiēbat.
2. Ante Caesaris ipsīus oculōs trāns viam cucurrimus et cum amīcīs fūgimus.
3. Nēmō vitia sua videt, sed quisque illa alterīus.
4. Monuitne nūper eōs dē vīribus illārum urbium in Asiā?
5. Ipsī autem lībertātem cīvium suōrum magnā cum cūrā aluerant.
6. Nōmina multārum urbium nostrārum ab nōminibus urbium antīquārum trāximus.
7. Pars cīvium dīvitiās cēpit et per urbem ad mare cucurrit.

8. Hodiē multae nūbēs in caelō sunt signum īrae acerbae deōrum.
9. Illud animal herī ibi cecidit et sē trāns terram ab agrō trahēbat.
10. That wicked tyrant did not long preserve the rights of these citizens.
11. Great is the force of the arts.
12. His wife was standing there with her own friends and doing that with patience.
13. Cicero felt and said the same thing concerning his own life and the nature of death.

SENTENTIAE ANTĪQUAE

1. Et Deus aquās maria in prīncipiō appellāvit. (Genesis; **aquās** is direct object; **maria** is predicate acc. or objective complement.[2])
2. Terra ipsa hominēs et animālia ōlim creāvit. (Lucretius.)
3. Pān servat ovēs et magistrōs fortūnātōs ovium. (Virgil.—Pan, the god of pastures and shepherds.—**ovis, ovis,** f., *sheep.*)
4. Parva formīca onera magna ōre trahit. (Horace.—**formīca, -ae,** *ant.*—**onus, oneris,** n., *load.*)
5. Auribus teneō lupum. (*Terence.—a picturesque, proverbial statement of a dilemma, like Eng. "to have a tiger by the tail."—**lupus, -ī,** *wolf.*)
6. Ille magnam turbam clientium sēcum habet. (Horace.—**cliēns, -entis,** m., *client, dependent.*)
7. Hunc nēmō vī neque pecūniā superāre potuit. (Ennius.)
8. Animus eius erat ignārus artium malārum. (Sallust.—**ignārus, -a, -um,** *ignorant.*)
9. Magna pars meī mortem vītābit. (Horace.—**meī,** partitive gen., Ch. 15.)
10. Vōs, amīcī doctī, exemplāria Graeca semper cum cūrā versāte. (Horace.—**exemplar, -plāris,** *model, original.*—**versāre,** *to turn; study.*)
11. Nōn vīribus et celeritāte corporum magna gerimus, sed sapientiā et sententiā et arte. (Cicero.—**celeritās, -tātis,** *swiftness.*)
12. Istī caelum, nōn animum suum, mūtant, sī trāns mare currunt. (Horace.)

STORE TEETH

Thāis habet nigrōs, niveōs Laecānia dentēs.
    Quae ratiō est? Ēmptōs haec habet, illa suōs.

(*Martial 5.43; meter: elegiac couplet.—**Thāis** and **Laecānia** are names of women; take **habet . . . dentēs** with both these subjects.—**niger, -gra, -grum,**

---

[2] Such verbs as *to call* (**appellō, vocō**), *consider* (**dūcō, habeō**), *choose* (**legō**), *make* (**faciō, creō**) may be followed by two accusatives: one is the direct object; the other is a type of predicate noun or adjective sometimes called an "objective complement."

black.—**niveus, -a, -um,** *snowy.*—**dēns, dentis,** m., *tooth.*—**quae** (interrogative adj. modifying **ratiō**), *what.*—**ēmptōs [dentēs],** perf. pass. partic., *bought, purchased.*)

CICERO IMAGINES THE STATE OF ROME ITSELF URGING HIM TO PUNISH THE CATILINARIAN CONSPIRATORS

M. Tullī Cicerō, quid agis? Istī prō multīs factīs malīs poenās dare nunc dēbent; eōs enim ad mortem dūcere dēbēs, quod Rōmam in multa perīcula traxērunt. Saepe Rōmānī in hāc cīvitāte etiam cīvēs morte multāvērunt. Sed nōn dēbēs cōgitāre hōs malōs esse cīvēs, nam numquam in hāc urbe prōditōrēs patriae iūra cīvium tenuērunt; hī iūra sua āmīsērunt. Populus Rōmānus tibi magnās grātiās aget, M. Tullī, sī istōs cum virtūte nunc multābis.

(Cicero, *In Catilīnam* 1.11.27–28; see the readings in Ch. 11 above and Ch. 20 below.—**M. = Mārcus.**—**multāre,** *to punish.*—**prōditor, -tōris,** *betrayer.*)

ETYMOLOGY

In the readings   4. formic, formaldehyde.—onus, onerous. 11. celerity, accelerate, accelerator. "Store Teeth": Negro (Spanish from **niger**), Negroid; dental, dentist, dentifrice, dentil, indent, dandelion (Fr. **dent de lion**), tooth = Eng. cognate.

Pan (sent. 3), the Greek god of woods and countryside, was accredited with the power of engendering sudden fear in people. Hence from Greek comes our word "panic." (However, "pan-," as in "Pan-American," comes from another Greek word meaning *all.*)

Study the following Romance derivatives:

Latin	Italian	Spanish	French
ars, artis; artem	arte	arte	art
mors, mortis; mortem	morte	muerte	mort
pars, partis; partem	parte	parte	parti
pēs, pedis; pedem	piede	pie	pied
dēns, dentis; dentem	dente	diente	dent
nāvis, nāvis; nāvem	nave	nave	navire nef (*nave*)
nox, noctis; noctem	notte	noche	nuit

Clearly these Romance derivatives do not come from the nominative of the Latin words. The rule is that Romance nouns and adjectives of Latin origin generally derive from the accusative form, often with the loss of some sound or feature of the final syllable.[3]

---

[3] One exception thus far in this book has been Fr. **fils,** *son,* from Lat. **fīlius.** (Old Fr. **fiz,** whence Eng. "Fitz-," *natural son,* e.g., Fitzgerald.)

LATĪNA EST GAUDIUM—ET ŪTILIS!

Quid agitis, amīcī et amīcae! Here's hoping yours is a **mēns sāna in corpore sānō,** in all of its **partēs.** You've now learned the Latin names for several: **oculus, auris, ōs,** and **dēns** (remember Thais and Laecania?). Here are some others, from the **caput** up only, that can be easily remembered from their Eng. derivatives: **collum, -ī,** *neck* ("collar"); **nāsus, -ī,** *nose* ("nasal"); **supercilium, -ī,** *eyebrow* (let's hope you've never raised an eyebrow superciliously at a friend); **coma, -ae,** *hair* (astronomy buffs know the constellation **Coma Berenīcēs,** *Berenice's lock*—sorry, no connection with "comb," but "comet" is related); **lingua, -ae,** *tongue* as well as *language* ("multilingual," "lingo," and even "linguine," which is long and flat like a tongue!). For more **partēs corporis,** see Ch. 20.

Languages, by the way, should be learned with "oral-aural" techniques, and not just through reading and writing, so I hope you're remembering to practice your declensions and conjugations aloud, and to say **salvē** or **tē amō** to someone everyday.

Oops—looking back at the Vocab. and the new **i**-stems, I am reminded of **ars grātiā artis,** *art for the sake of art,* the motto of M.G.M. film studios, and **B.A.** and **M.A.** for **Baccalaureus Artium** and **Magister Artium,** academic degrees you may have or aspire to. Then there's the familiar Latin phrase, **mare nostrum,** which is either what the Romans used to call the Mediterranean (*our sea*) or, perhaps somewhat less likely, Caesar's critical comment on his unmusical equine ("my horse doesn't play the guitar"—groan!!!). **Valēte!**

The Forum, Rome, Giovanni Paolo Pannini, 18th century
Private Collection

15

Numerals; Genitive of the Whole; Genitive and Ablative with Cardinal Numerals; Ablative of Time

NUMERALS

The commonest numerals in Latin, as in English, are the "cardinals" (from **cardō, cardinis,** m., *hinge,* the "pivotal" numbers in counting, "one, two, three . . . ," etc.) and the "ordinals" (from **ōrdō, ōrdinis,** m., *rank, order,* the numerals indicating "order" of occurrence, "first, second . . . ," etc.).

CARDINAL NUMERALS

In Latin most cardinal numerals through 100 are indeclinable adjectives; the one form is used for all cases and genders. The following, however, are declined as indicated.

únus, úna, únum, *one* (see Ch. 9.)

| | **duo,** *two* | | | **trēs,** *three* | | **mīlle,** *thousand* **mīlia,** *thousands* | |
	M.	F.	N.	M. & F.	N.	M.F.N.	N.
N.	dúo	dúae	dúo	trēs	tría	mílle	mília
G.	duốrum	duấrum	duốrum	tríum	tríum	mílle	mílium
D.	duốbus	duấbus	duốbus	tríbus	tríbus	mílle	mílibus
A.	dúōs	dúās	dúo	trēs	tría	mílle	mília
A.	duốbus	duấbus	duốbus	tríbus	tríbus	mílle	mílibus

The cardinals indicating the hundreds from 200 through 900 are declined like plural adjectives of the first and second declensions; e.g., **ducentī, -ae, -a,** *two hundred.*

Mīlle, 1,000, is an indeclinable *adjective* in the singular, but in the plural it functions as a neuter **i**-stem *noun* of the third declension (e.g., **mīlle virī,** *a thousand men;* **mīlia virōrum,** *thousands of men*).

The cardinals from **ūnus** through **vīgintī quīnque** should be memorized (see the list in the Appendix, p. 451) and with them **centum** (100) and **mīlle.** The following sentences illustrate these various forms and uses of cardinal numerals:

> Trēs puerī rosās dedērunt duābus puellīs, *three boys gave roses to two girls.*
> Octō puerī librōs dedērunt decem puellīs, *eight boys gave books to ten girls.*
> Ūnus vir vēnit cum quattuor amīcīs, *one man came with four friends.*
> Cōnsul vēnit cum centum virīs, *the consul came with 100 men.*
> Cōnsul vēnit cum ducentīs virīs, *the consul came with 200 men.*
> Cōnsul vēnit cum mīlle virīs, *the consul came with 1,000 men.*
> Cōnsul vēnit cum sex mīlibus virōrum, *the consul came with six thousand(s) (of) men.*

ORDINAL NUMERALS

The ordinal numerals, which indicate the order of sequence, are regular adjectives of the first and the second declensions (**prīmus, -a, -um; secundus, -a, -um;** etc.—see Appendix, p. 451). The ordinals from **prīmus** through **duodecimus** should be learned.

GENITIVE OF THE WHOLE

The genitive of a word indicating the whole of some thing or group is used after a word designating a part of that whole.

> pars urbis, *part of the city* (city = the whole)
> nēmō amīcōrum meōrum, *no one of my friends*

This genitive of the whole (sometimes called the "partitive genitive") can also be used after the neuter nominative and accusative of certain pronouns and adjectives such as **aliquid, quid, multum, plūs, minus, satis, nihil, tantum, quantum.**

nihil temporis, *no time (nothing of time)*
quid cōnsiliī, *what plan?*
satis ēloquentiae, *sufficient eloquence*

The genitive of the whole may itself be the neuter singular of a *second* declension adjective.

multum bonī, *much good* (lit. *of good*)
quid novī, *what (is) new?*
nihil certī, *nothing certain*

GENITIVE AND ABLATIVE WITH CARDINAL NUMERALS

With **mīlia** the genitive of the whole is used.

decem mīlia virōrum, *10,000 men (but* mīlle virī, *1,000 men)*

With other cardinal numerals and with **quīdam** (*a certain one*, introduced in Ch. 26) the idea of the whole is regularly expressed by **ex** or **dē** and the ablative. This construction is sometimes found after other words.

trēs ex amīcīs meīs, *three of my friends (but* trēs amīcī = *three friends)*
quīnque ex eīs, *five of them*
centum ex virīs, *100 of the men*
quīdam ex eīs, *a certain one of them*

ABLATIVE OF TIME WHEN OR WITHIN WHICH

The Romans expressed the idea of "time when" or "within which" using the ablative without a preposition. The English equivalent is usually a prepositional phrase introduced by *at, on, in,* or *within,* depending on the English idiom (*for,* which indicates "duration of time," is *not* an option: see Ch. 37).

Eō tempore nōn poteram id facere, *at that time I could not do it.*
Agricolae bonīs annīs valēbant, *in good years the farmers flourished.*
Eōdem diē vēnērunt, *they came on the same day* (**diē,** abl. of **diēs,** *day*).
Aestāte lūdēbant, *in the summer they used to play.* (**aestāte,** abl. of **aestās,** *summer*)
Paucīs hōrīs id faciet, *in (within) a few hours he will do it.*

Since this construction always involves some noun indicating a unit of time, without a preposition, you should easily distinguish it from the other ablative case uses you have now learned (object of certain prepositions, means, manner, and accompaniment, abl. with cardinal numerals); you must be able to recognize, name, and translate each of the six types of ablative usages.

VOCABULARY

Itália, -ae, f., *Italy* (italics, italicize)

memória, -ae, f., *memory, recollection* (memoir, memorial, memorize, memorandum, commemorate)

tempéstās, tempestátis, f., *period of time, season; weather, storm* (tempest, tempestuous; cp. **tempus**)

Cardinal numerals from **únus** to **vīgíntī quínque** (App., p. 451)

Ordinal numerals from **prímus** to **duodécimus** (App., p. 451)

céntum, indecl. adj., *a hundred* (cent, centenary, centennial, centi-, centigrade, centimeter, centipede, centurion, century, bicentenary, bicentennial, sesquicentennial, tercentenary)

mílle, indecl. adj. in sg., *thousand;* **mília, mílium,** n. pl., *thousands* (millennium, millennial, mile, milli-, milligram, millimeter, millipede, million, mill (= 1/10 cent), bimillennium, millefiori)

míser, mísera, míserum, *wretched, miserable, unfortunate* (misery, Miserere, commiserate)

ínter, prep. + acc., *between, among* (intern, internal; common as Eng. prefix, e.g., interact, intercept, interdict)

ítaque, adv., *and so, therefore*

committō, -míttere, -mísī, -míssum, *to entrust, commit* (committee, commission, commissary, commitment, noncommissioned, noncom)

exspéctō (1), *to look for, expect, await* (expectancy, expectation)

iáciō, iácere, iḗcī, iáctum, *to throw, hurl.* This verb appears in compounds as **-iciō, -icere, -iḗcī, -iectum:** e.g., **ēiciō, ēicere, ēiḗcī, ēiectum,** *to throw out, drive out* (abject, adjective, conjecture, dejected, eject, inject, interject, object, project, subject, reject, trajectory)

tímeō, timḗre, tímuī, *to fear, be afraid of, be afraid* (timid, timorous, intimidate; cp. **timor**)

PRACTICE AND REVIEW

1. Illae quīnque fēminae inter ea animālia mortem nōn timēbant.
2. Duo ex fīliīs ā portā per agrōs cum patre suō herī currēbant et in aquam cecidērunt.
3. Prīmus rēx dīvitiās in mare iēcit, nam magnam īram et vim turbae timuit.
4. Nēmō eandem partem Asiae ūnō annō vincet.

5. Rōmānī quattuor ex eīs urbibus prīmā viā iūnxērunt.
6. Itaque mīlia librōrum eius ab urbe trāns Italiam mīsistis.
7. Lībertātem et iūra hārum urbium artibus bellī cōnservāvimus.
8. Dī Graecī sē inter hominēs cum virtūte saepe nōn gerēbant.
9. Cicerō mīlia Rōmānōrum vī sententiārum suārum dūcēbat.
10. Sententiae medicī eum cārum mihi numquam fēcērunt.
11. The tyrant used to entrust his life to those three friends.
12. The greedy man never has enough wealth.
13. At that time we saved their mother with those six letters.
14. Through their friends they conquered the citizens of the ten cities.

SENTENTIAE ANTĪQUAE

1. Diū in istā nāve fuī et propter tempestātem nūbēsque semper mortem exspectābam. (Terence.—**nāvis, nāvis,** *f., ship.*)
2. Septem hōrīs ad eam urbem vēnimus. (Cicero.)
3. Italia illīs temporibus erat plēna Graecārum artium, et multī Rōmānī ipsī hās artēs colēbant. (Cicero.—**artēs,** in the sense of studies, literature, philosophy.—**colō, -ere,** *to cultivate, pursue.*)
4. Inter bellum et pācem dubitābant. (Tacitus.—**dubitāre,** *to hesitate, waver.*)
5. Eō tempore istum ex urbe ēiciēbam. (Cicero.)
6. Dīcēbat quisque miser: "Cīvis Rōmānus sum." (Cicero.)
7. Mea puella passerem suum amābat, et passer ad eam sōlam semper pīpiābat nec sē ex gremiō movēbat. (Catullus.—**passer, -seris,** m., *sparrow,* a pet bird.—**pīpiāre,** *to chirp.*—**gremium, -iī,** lap.—**movēre.**)
8. Fīliī meī frātrem meum dīligēbant, mē vītābant; mē patrem acerbum appellābant et meam mortem exspectābant. Nunc autem mōrēs meōs mūtāvī et duōs fīliōs ad mē crās traham. (Terence.)
9. Dionȳsius tyrannus, quoniam tōnsōrī caput committere timēbat, fīliās suās barbam et capillum tondēre docuit; itaque virginēs tondēbant barbam et capillum patris. (Cicero.—**tōnsor, -sōris,** *barber.*—**barba, -ae,** *beard.*—**capillus, -ī,** *hair.*—**tondēre,** *to shave, cut.*)

CYRUS' DYING WORDS ON IMMORTALITY

Ō meī fīliī trēs, nōn dēbētis esse miserī. Ad mortem enim nunc veniō, sed pars meī, animus meus, semper remanēbit. Dum eram vōbīscum, animum nōn vidēbātis, sed ex factīs meīs intellegēbātis eum esse in hōc corpore. Crēdite igitur animum esse eundem post mortem, etiam sī eum nōn vidēbitis, et semper cōnservāte mē in memoriā vestrā.

(Cicero, *Dē Senectūte* 22.79–81.—Cyrus the Great, whom Cicero quotes here, was a Persian king of the 6th cen. B.C.—**crēdō, -ere,** *to believe.*)

FABIAN TACTICS

Etiam in senectūte Quīntus Fabius Maximus erat vir vērae virtūtis et bella cum animīs adulēscentis gerēbat. Dē eō amīcus noster Ennius, doctus ille poēta, haec verba ōlim scrīpsit: "Ūnus homō cīvitātem fortūnātam nōbīs cūnctātiōne cōnservāvit. Rūmōrēs et fāmam nōn pōnēbat ante salūtem Rōmae. Glōria eius, igitur, nunc bene valet et semper valēbit."

(Ibid. 4.10.—Quintus Fabius Maximus enjoyed considerable success against Hannibal in the Second Punic War [218–201 B.C.] through his delaying tactics, thus earning the epithet **Cūnctātor,** *the Delayer.*—**Ennius,** an early Roman poet.—**cūnctātiō, -ōnis,** *delaying.*—**rūmor, -mōris,** *rumor, gossip.*—**pōnō, -ere,** *to put, place.*—**salūs, salūtis,** f., *safety.*)

Hamilcar Asks Hannibal to Swear His Hatred Against the Romans
Giovanni Battista Pittoni, 18th century
Pinacoteca di Brera, Milan, Italy

ETYMOLOGY

The following are some of the Eng. derivatives from the Lat. cardinals and ordinals 2–12: (2) dual, duel, duet, double (cp. doubt, dubious), duplicity; second; (3) trio, triple, trivial; (4) quart, quarter, quartet, quatrain; (5) quinquennium, quintet, quintuplets, quincunx; (6) sextet, sextant; (7) September; (8) October, octave, octavo; (9) November, noon; (10) December, decimal, decimate, dime, dean; (12) duodecimal, dozen.

The following table lists some Romance cardinal numbers derived from Latin.

Latin	Italian	Spanish	French
ūnus	un(o)	un(o)	un
duo	due	dos	deux
trēs	tre	tres	trois
quattuor	quattro	cuatro	quatre
quīnque	cinque	cinco	cinq
sex	sei	seis	six
septem	sette	siete	sept
octō	otto	ocho	huit
novem	nove	nueve	neuf
decem	dieci	diez	dix
ūndecim	undici	once	onze
duodecim	dodici	doce	douze
centum	cento	ciento	cent
mīlle	mille	mil	mille

In the readings

3. cult, culture, agriculture, horticulture (**hortus,** *garden*), colony. 7. passerine.—"pipe," both verb and noun, an onomatopoetic (imitative) word widely used; e.g., Gk. **pipos,** *a young bird,* and **pipizein** or **peppizein,** *to peep, chirp,* Ger. **piepen** and **pfeifen,** Eng. "peep," Fr. **piper.** 9. tonsorial, tonsure.—barber, barb, barbed, barbate.—capillary, capillaceous. "Cyrus": credo, creed, credible, credulous (see Vocab., Ch. 25). "Fabian": cunctation.—component, etc. (Ch. 27).—salutation, salutary; cf. **salvēre.**

LATĪNA EST GAUDIUM—ET ŪTILIS!

Salvēte! Quid novī, meī amīcī amīcaeque? Latin has other types of numerals, besides the cardinals and ordinals, which you will encounter later in your study of the language and many of which are already familiar. "Roman numerals" developed from counting on the fingers: I = one finger, II = two, etc., V = five (the hand held outstretched with the thumb and index finger making a "V"), VI = a "handful of fingers" plus one, etc., X = two V's, one inverted on the other, and so on. There were also "distributive" numerals, **singulī, -ae, -a** (*one each*); **bīnī, -ae, -a** (*two each*), **ternī, -ae, -a,** etc., and "multiplicatives," **simplex, simplicis** (*single*), **duplex** (*double*), **triplex,** etc.; likewise numeral adverbs, **semel** (*once*), **bis** (*twice*), **ter** (*three times*), etc. All these words have numerous (pardon the pun) Eng. derivatives!

"Me, I believe in grammar, but I did not really know about it until I learnt a little Latin—and that is a gift, an absolute gift."—Margaret Thatcher. **Id est bonum cōnsilium,** whatever your politics. **Valēte!**

16

Third Declension Adjectives

Latin has two major categories of adjectives. You are already quite familiar with those having first and second declension forms like **magnus, -a, -um** (Ch. 4) and the small sub-category of first/second declension adjectives that have **-īus** in the genitive singular and **-ī** in the dative singular (Ch. 9).

Adjectives of the second major group generally have third declension **i**-stem forms and are declined exactly like **i**-stem nouns of the third declension, except that the ablative singular of all genders (not just the neuter) ends with **-ī.**

Adjectives of this group fall into three categories that differ from each other in simply one respect. Some, called "adjectives of three endings," have distinct forms of the *nominative singular* that differentiate each of the three genders, just as **magnus, magna,** and **magnum** do (e.g., **ācer** M., **ācris** F., and **ācre** N.); those of "two endings" (the largest category of third declension adjectives) have a single nominative form for both masculine and feminine, and another for the neuter (e.g., **fortis** M. and F., **forte** N.); and those of "one ending" do not differentiate the genders at all in the nominative singular (e.g., **potēns** is the M., F., and N. nom. sg. form). In all other respects the adjectives of all three categories are the same, with the masculine and feminine endings differing from the neuters only in the accusative singular and the nominative (= vocative) and accusative plural.

Paradigms are given below, with the distinctive **i**-stem endings in bold; the nouns **cīvis** and **mare** are provided for comparison (review Ch. 14, if necessary) and to show that there is very little new to be learned in order to master third declension adjectives.

	I-Stem Nouns Reviewed		**Adj. of 2 Endings**	
			fortis, forte, *strong, brave*	
	M. or F.	**N.**	**M. & F.**	**N.**
Nom.	cívis	máre	fórtis	fórte
Gen.	cívis	máris	fórtis	fórtis
Dat.	cívī	márī	fórtī	fórtī
Acc.	cívem	máre	fórtem	fórte
Abl.	cíve	márī	fórtī	fórtī
Nom.	cívēs	már**ia**	fórt**ēs**	fórt**ia**
Gen.	cív**ium**	már**ium**	fórt**ium**	fórt**ium**
Dat.	cívibus	máribus	fórtibus	fórtibus
Acc.	cívēs[1]	már**ia**	fórtēs[1]	fórt**ia**
Abl.	cívibus	máribus	fórtibus	fórtibus

	Adj. of 3 Endings		**Adj. of 1 Ending**	
	ācer, ācris, ācre,		**potēns,** gen. **potentis,**	
	keen, severe, fierce		*powerful*	
	M. & F.	**N.**	**M. & F.**	**N.**
Nom.	ácer, ácris	ácre	pótēns	pótēns
Gen.	ácris	ácris	poténtis	poténtis
Dat.	ácrī	ácrī	poténtī	poténtī
Acc.	ácrem	ácre	poténtem	pótēns
Abl.	ácrī	ácrī	poténtī	poténtī
Nom.	ácrēs	ácr**ia**	poténtēs	potént**ia**
Gen.	ácr**ium**	ácr**ium**	potént**ium**	potént**ium**
Dat.	ácribus	ácribus	poténtibus	poténtibus
Acc.	ácrēs[1]	ácr**ia**	poténtēs[1]	potént**ia**
Abl.	ácribus	ácribus	poténtibus	poténtibus

OBSERVATIONS

Note carefully the places in which the characteristic **i** appears,[2] as indicated in the paradigms:

(1) **-ī** in the ablative singular of all genders.
(2) **-ium** in the genitive plural of all genders.
(3) **-ia** in the nominative and accusative plural of the neuter.

[1] Remember that **i**-stem nouns and adjectives have an alternate **-īs** ending in the acc. pl. (the regular ending until the Augustan Period), but it will rarely be used in this book.

[2] A few third-declension adjectives of one ending are declined without this characteristic **i** in one or more of the three places; e.g., **vetus, veteris,** *old:* **vetere** (abl. sg.), **veterum** (gen. pl.), **vetera** (neut. nom. and acc. pl.). The forms of comparatives and present participles will be taken up later.

Note also that an adjective of the third declension can be used with a noun of any declension just as an adjective of the first and the second declensions can. In the following illustrations **omnis, -e,** *every, all,* is used as the example of an adjective of two endings.

omnis amīcus *or* homō	ācer amīcus/homō	potēns amīcus/homō
omnis rēgīna *or* māter	ācris rēgīna/māter	potēns rēgīna/māter
omne bellum *or* animal	ācre bellum/animal	potēns bellum/animal

For the sake of practice, study and analyze the forms in the following phrases:

omnī fōrmae	in omnī fōrmā	omnium fōrmārum
omnī animō	in omnī animō	omnium animōrum
omnī hominī	in omnī homine	omnium hominum
omnī urbī	in omnī urbe	omnium urbium
omnī marī	in omnī marī	omnium marium

The vocabulary entries for adjectives of three endings (**-er** words like **ācer,** some of which retain the **-e-** in the base, some of which drop it) and two endings (of the **-is/-e** variety) list the different nominative endings; the base can be determined from the feminine or neuter form. For adjectives of one ending (many of these end in **-ns** or **-x**) the genitive is provided so that you can determine the base (by dropping the **-is** ending, e.g., **potēns, potent-is**).

USAGE

Third declension adjectives function in the same ways as other adjectives: they modify nouns (**omnēs agricolae,** *all the farmers,* sometimes called the "attributive" use); they can serve as "predicate nominatives" (**virī erant ācrēs,** *the men were fierce*) or "objective complements" (**virtūs fēcit virōs fortēs,** *virtue made the men brave*); they can take the place of nouns (**fortūna fortēs adiuvat,** *fortune helps the brave,* sometimes called the "substantive" use). Remember, too, that attributive adjectives usually follow the nouns they modify, except those that denote size or quantity, demonstratives, and any that are meant to be emphasized.

VOCABULARY

aétās, aetātis, f., *period of life, life, age, an age, time* (eternal, eternity)

audítor, audītóris, m., *hearer, listener, member of an audience* (auditor, auditory, auditorium; cp. **audiō**)

clēméntia, -ae, f., *mildness, gentleness, mercy* (clement, clemency, inclement, Clement, Clementine)

mēns, méntis, f., *mind, thought, intention* (mental, mentality, mention, demented; Minerva [?]; cp. mind)

sátura, -ae, f., *satire* (satirist, satirical, satirize)

ácer, ácris, ácre, *sharp, keen, eager, severe, fierce* (acrid, acrimony, acrimonious, eager, vinegar)

brévis, bréve, *short, small, brief* (brevity, breviary, abbreviate, abridge)

céler, céleris, célere, *swift, quick, rapid* (celerity, accelerate)

difficilis, difficile, *hard, difficult, troublesome* (difficulty)

dúlcis, dúlce, *sweet; pleasant, agreeable* (dulcify, dulcet, dulcimer)

fácilis, fácile, *easy, agreeable* (facile, facility, facilitate; cp. **faciō**)

fórtis, fórte, *strong, brave* (fort, forte, fortify, fortitude, force, comfort)

íngēns, gen. **ingéntis,** *huge*

iūcúndus, -a, -um, *pleasant, delightful, agreeable, pleasing* (jocund)

lóngus, -a, -um, *long* (longitude, longevity, elongate, oblong, prolong; Eng. "long" is cognate.)

ómnis, ómne, *every, all* (omnibus, bus, omnipresent, omnipotent, omniscient, omnivorous; cp. **omnīnō,** Ch. 40)

pótēns, gen. **poténtis,** pres. part. of **possum** as an adj., *able, powerful, mighty, strong* (potent, impotent, omnipotent, potentate, potential)

sénex, gen. **sénis,** adj. and noun, *old, aged; old man* (senate, senator, senescent, senile, senior, seniority, sir, sire)

quam, adv., *how*

régō, régere, réxī, réctum, *to rule, guide, direct* (regent, regime, regiment, regular, regulate, correct, direction, rectitude; cp. **rēx, rēgīna**)

PRACTICE AND REVIEW

1. Fortēs virī et fēminae ante aetātem nostram vīvēbant.
2. Eōs centum senēs miserōs ab Italiā trāns maria difficilia herī mittēbat.
3. Illī duo virī omnēs cupiditātēs ex sē ēiēcērunt, nam nātūram corporis timuērunt.
4. Potēns rēgīna, quoniam sē dīlēxit, istōs trēs vītāvit et sē cum eīs numquam iūnxit.
5. Itaque inter eōs ibi stābam et signum cum animō fortī diū exspectābam.
6. Celer rūmor per ōra aurēsque omnium sine morā currēbat.
7. Vīs bellī acerbī autem vītam eius paucīs hōrīs mūtāvit.
8. Quīnque ex nautīs sē ex aquā trāxērunt sēque Caesarī potentī commīsērunt.
9. Caesar nōn poterat suās cōpiās cum celeribus cōpiīs rēgis iungere.
10. Themistoclēs omnēs cīvēs ōlim appellābat et nōmina eōrum ācrī memoriā tenēbat.
11. In caelō sunt multae nūbēs et animālia agricolae tempestāte malā nōn valent.
12. The father and mother often used to come to the city with their two sweet daughters.

13. The souls of brave men and women will never fear difficult times.
14. Does he now understand all the rights of these four men?
15. The doctor could not help the brave girl, for death was swift.

SENTENTIAE ANTĪQUAE

1. Quam dulcis est lībertās! (Phaedrus.)
2. Labor omnia vīcit. (*Virgil.)
3. Fortūna fortēs adiuvat. (Terence.)
4. Quam celeris et ācris est mēns! (Cicero.)
5. Polyphēmus erat mōnstrum horrendum, īnfōrme, ingēns. (Virgil.—**mōnstrum, -ī.**—**horrendus, -a, -um.**—**īnfōrmis, -e,** *formless, hideous.*)

The blinding of Polyphemus
Hydria from Cerveteri, 525 B.C.
Museo Nazionale di Villa Giulia, Rome, Italy

6. Varium et mūtābile semper fēmina. (*Virgil.—Order: **fēmina semper [est] varium et mūtābile.**—**varius, -a, -um,** *varying, fickle.*—**mūtābilis, -e,** *changeable;* the neuters **varium** and **mūtābile** are used to mean "a fickle and changeable *thing.*")
7. Facile est epigrammata belle scrībere, sed librum scrībere difficile est. (*Martial.—**epigramma, -matis,** n., *short poem, epigram.*—**belle,** adv. from **bellus, -a, -um.**)
8. Īra furor brevis est; animum rege. (*Horace.—**furor, -rōris,** *madness.*)
9. Ars poētica est nōn omnia dīcere. (*Servius.—**poēticus, -a, -um.**)
10. Nihil est ab omnī parte beātum. (*Horace.)
11. Liber meus hominēs prūdentī cōnsiliō alit. (Phaedrus.—**prūdēns,** gen. **prūdentis.**)
12. Māter omnium bonārum artium sapientia est. (*Cicero.)
13. Clēmentia rēgem salvum facit; nam amor omnium cīvium est inexpugnābile mūnīmentum rēgis. (Seneca.—**inexpugnābilis, -e,** *impregnable.*—**mūnīmentum, -ī,** *fortification, defense.*)
14. Vīta est brevis; ars, longa. (Hippocrates, quoted by Seneca.)
15. Breve tempus aetātis autem satis longum est ad bene vīvendum. (Cicero.—**vīvendum,** *living,* verbal noun obj. of **ad,** *for.*)
16. Vīvit et vīvet per omnium saeculōrum memoriam. (*Velleius Paterculus.—**saeculum, -ī,** *century, age.*)

JUVENAL EXPLAINS HIS IMPULSE TO SATIRE

Semper ego audītor erō? Est turba poētārum in hāc urbe—ego igitur erō poēta! Sunt mīlia vitiōrum in urbe—dē istīs vitiīs scrībam! Difficile est saturam nōn scrībere. Sī nātūra mē adiuvāre nōn potest, facit indignātiō versum. In librō meō erunt omnia facta hominum—timor, īra, voluptās, culpa, cupiditās, īnsidiae. Nunc est plēna cōpia vitiōrum in hāc miserā urbe Rōmae!

(Juvenal, *Saturae* 1.1ff; prose adaptation from the opening of Juvenal's programmatic first satire.—**indignātiō, -ōnis.**—**versus,** *verse, poetry.*)

ON A TEMPERAMENTAL FRIEND

Difficilis facilis, iūcundus acerbus—es īdem:
    nec tēcum possum vīvere nec sine tē.

(*Martial, 12.46; meter: elegiac couplet.)

ETYMOLOGY

In the readings

5. monstrous.—horrendous.—informal, inform (adj. with neg. prefix **in-**) 6. variety, variegated, vary, unvaried, invariable. 8. furor. 11. **prūdēns,** syncopated form of **prōvidēns** as seen in "providence," "providential." "Juvenal": indignation, indignant.—verse, versify, versification.

LATĪNA EST GAUDIUM—ET ŪTILIS!

Salvēte! Quid agitis? Quid hodiē est tempestās? Here are some possible answers, many of which you can again recognize from Eng. derivatives: **frīgida (tempestās** is fem., as you recall from Ch. 15, hence the fem. adj., from **frīgidus, -a, -um**); **calida** (Eng. "scald" is a derivative); **nimbōsa** (from **nimbus,** which means the same as **nūbēs,** + the common suffix **-ōsus, -a, -um,** *full of,* hence "cloudy"—cp. Eng. "cumulonimbus clouds"); **ventōsa** (an identical formation from **ventus,** *wind*); **sōl lūcet,** *the sun is shining* (cp. "solar," "translucent"); **pluit,** *it's raining* ("pluvial," "pluviometer"); **ningit,** *it's snowing* (Eng. "niveous" from Lat. **niveus, -a, -um** is related).

Well, enough of the weather. Here's an omnibus of **omni-** words and phrases to delight you all: If you were "omnific" (from **facere**) and "omnipresent" (-*sent* from **sum**) and your appetite "omnivorous" (**vorāre,** *to eat,* cp. "carnivorous," "herbivorous") and your sight were "omnidirectional" (see **regō** in the Vocab. above), then you might potentially be "omnipotent" and even "omniscient" (**scīre,** *to know*). But as a proverbial saying from Virgil reminds us, **nōn omnēs possumus omnia.** (By the way **regō,** mentioned above, does NOT mean *to go again* nor should **regit** be translated *leave, and this time I mean it!*)

Valēte, omnēs amīcī et amīcae meae, et semper amāte Latīnam!

17

The Relative Pronoun

The relative pronoun **quī, quae, quod,** as common in Latin as its English equivalent *who/which/that,* ordinarily introduces a subordinate clause and refers back to some noun or pronoun known as its "antecedent"; the relative clause itself has an adjectival function, providing descriptive information about the antecedent (e.g., "the man who was from Italy" . . . = "the Italian man").

The forms of the relative pronoun are so diverse that the only practical procedure is to memorize them. However, it is easy to see that the endings of the genitive **cuius** and dative **cui** are related to those of **illīus** and **illī;** and it is easy to identify the case, the number, and often the gender of most of the remaining forms.

QUĪ, QUAE, QUOD, *who, which, that*

Singular			Plural		
M.	**F.**	**N.**	**M.**	**F.**	**N.**
quī	quae	quod	quī	quae	quae
cuíus[1]	cuíus	cuíus	quốrum	quárum	quốrum
cui[1]	cui	cui	quíbus	quíbus	quíbus
quem	quam	quod	quōs	quās	quae
quō	quā	quō	quíbus	quíbus	quíbus

USAGE AND AGREEMENT

Since the relative pronoun (from Lat. **referō, referre, rettulī, relātum,** Ch. 31) refers to and is essentially equivalent to its antecedent (from **antecēdere,**

---

[1] For the pronunciation of the **ui** in **cuius** (as if spelled *cui-yus*) and in **cui,** cp. **huius** and **huic** (Ch. 9) and see the Introd., p. xli.

to go before, since the antecedent usually appears in a preceding clause), the two words naturally agree in number and gender; the case of the relative, however, like that of any noun or pronoun, is determined by its use within its own clause. The logic of this can be demonstrated by analyzing and translating the following sentence:

The woman whom you are praising is talented.

1. The main clause of the sentence reads:

    The woman . . . is talented. Fēmina . . . est docta.

2. *Whom* introduces a subordinate, relative clause modifying *woman.*

3. *Woman* (**fēmina**) stands before the relative *whom* and is its antecedent.

4. *Whom* has a double loyalty: (1) to its antecedent, **fēmina,** and (2) to the subordinate clause in which it stands.

    a. Since the antecedent, **fēmina,** is feminine and singular, *whom* in Latin will have to be feminine and singular.
    b. Since in the subordinate clause *whom* is the direct object of (*you*) *are praising* (**laudās**), it must be in the accusative case in Latin.
    c. Therefore, the Latin form must be *feminine* and *singular* and *accusative:* **quam.**

The complete sentence in Latin appears thus:

Fēmina quam laudās est docta.

Again, succinctly, the rule is this: the *gender* and the *number* of a relative are determined by its antecedent; the *case* of a relative is determined by its use in its own clause.

Analyze the gender, the number, and the case of each of the relatives in the following sentences:

1. Dīligō puellam **quae** ex Italiā vēnit, *I admire the girl who came from Italy.*

2. Homō dē **quō** dīcēbās est amīcus cārus, *the man about whom you were speaking is a dear friend.*

3. Puella **cui** librum dat est fortūnāta, *the girl to whom he is giving the book is fortunate.*

4. Puer **cuius** patrem iuvābāmus est fortis, *the boy whose father we used to help is brave.*

5. Vītam meam committam eīs virīs **quōrum** virtūtēs laudābās, *I shall entrust my life to those men whose virtues you were praising.*

6. Timeō idem perīculum **quod** timētis, *I fear the same danger which you fear.*

In translating, be sure not to introduce words from the relative clause into the main clause or vice versa; e.g., in the third sentence above, **puella** should not be mistaken as the subject of **dat.** Note that a relative clause is a self-contained unit, beginning with the relative pronoun and often ending with the very first verb you encounter (**cui . . . dat** in the third sample sentence); in complex sentences, like S.A. 3 below, you may find it helpful first to identify and actually even bracket the relative clause(s):

Multī cīvēs aut ea perīcula [quae imminent] nōn vident aut ea [quae vident] neglegunt.

Begin next to read the rest of the sentence and then, as soon as you have translated the relative pronoun's antecedent (which very often precedes the relative pronoun immediately), translate the relative clause.

VOCABULARY

libéllus, -ī, m., *little book* (libel, libelous; diminutive of **liber**)

quī, quae, quod, rel. pron., *who, which, what, that* (quorum)

caécus, -a, -um, *blind* (caecum, caecal, caecilian)

lévis, léve, *light; easy; slight, trivial* (levity, lever, levy, levee, Levant, leaven, legerdemain, alleviate, elevate, relevant, irrelevant, relieve)

aut, conj., *or;* **aut . . . aut,** *either . . . or*

cíto, adv., *quickly* (excite, incite, recite; cp. **recitō,** below)

quóque, adv., *also, too*

admíttō, -míttere, -mīsī, -míssum, *to admit, receive, let in* (admission, admissible, inadmissible, admittedly)

coépī, coepísse, coéptum, *began,* defective verb used in the perfect system only; the present system is supplied by **incipiō** (below).

cúpiō, cúpere, cupī́vī, cupī́tum, *to desire, wish, long for* (Cupid, cupidity, concupiscence, covet, covetous, Kewpie doll; cp. **cupidītās, cupī́dō,** Ch. 36, **cupidus,** Ch. 39)

déleō, dēlére, dēlévī, dēlétum, *to destroy, wipe out, erase* (delete, indelible)

dēsī́derō (1), *to desire, long for, miss* (desiderate, desideratum, desiderative, desire, desirous)

incípiō, -cípere, -cépī, -céptum, *to begin* (incipient, inception; cp. **capiō**)

návigō (1), *to sail, navigate* (navigation, navigable; cp. **nauta**)

néglegō, neglégere, negléxī, negléctum, *to neglect, disregard* (negligent, negligee, negligible; cp. **legō,** Ch. 18)

récitō (1), *to read aloud, recite* (recital, recitation, recitative)

PRACTICE AND REVIEW

1. Potēns quoque est vīs artium, quae nōs semper alunt.
2. Miserōs hominēs, autem, sēcum iungere coeperant.
3. Nam illā aetāte pars populī in Italiā iūra cīvium numquam tenuit.
4. Incipimus vēritātem intellegere, quae mentēs nostrās semper regere dēbet et sine quā valēre nōn possumus.
5. Quam difficile est bona aut dulcia ex bellō trahere!
6. Centum ex virīs mortem diū timēbant et nihil clēmentiae exspectābant.
7. Puer mātrem timēbat, quae eum saepe neglegēbat.
8. Inter omnia perīcula illa fēmina sē cum sapientiā gessit.
9. Itaque celer rūmor ācris mortis per ingentēs urbēs cucurrit.
10. Quoniam memoria factōrum nostrōrum dulcis est, beātī nunc sumus et senectūtem facilem agēmus.
11. Multī audītōrēs saturās ācrēs timēbant quās poēta recitābat.
12. They feared the powerful men whose city they were ruling by force.
13. We began to help those three pleasant women to whom we had given our friendship.
14. We fear that book with which he is beginning to destroy our liberty.

SENTENTIAE ANTĪQUAE

1. Salvē, bone amīce, cui fīlium meum herī commīsī. (Terence.)
2. Dionȳsius, dē quō ante dīxī, ā Graeciā ad Siciliam per tempestātem nāvigābat. (Cicero.—**Sicilia, -ae,** *Sicily.*)
3. Multī cīvēs aut ea perīcula quae imminent nōn vident aut ea quae vident neglegunt. (Cicero.—**imminēre,** *to impend, threaten.*)
4. Bis dat quī cito dat. (Publilius Syrus.—**bis,** adv., *twice.*)
5. Quī coepit, dīmidium factī habet. Incipe! (Horace.—**dīmidium, -iī,** *half.*)
6. Levis est fortūna: id cito repōscit quod dedit. (Publilius Syrus.—**repōscō, -ere,** *to demand back.*)
7. Fortūna eum stultum facit quem nimium amat. (Publilius Syrus.)
8. Nōn sōlum fortūna ipsa est caeca sed etiam eōs caecōs facit quōs semper adiuvat. (Cicero.)
9. Bis vincit quī sē vincit in victōriā. (*Publilius Syrus.)
10. Simulātiō dēlet vēritātem, sine quā nōmen amīcitiae valēre nōn potest. (Cicero.—**simulātiō, -ōnis,** *pretense, insincerity.*)
11. Virtūtem enim illīus virī amāvī, quae cum corpore nōn periit. (Cicero.—**pereō, -īre, -iī, -itum,** *to perish.*)
12. Turbam vītā. Cum hīs vīve quī tē meliōrem facere possunt; illōs admitte quōs tū potes facere meliōrēs. (Seneca.—**melior,** *better.*)

ON THE PLEASURES OF LOVE IN OLD AGE

Estne amor in senectūte? Voluptās enim minor est, sed minor quoque est cupiditās. Nihil autem est cūra nōbīs, sī nōn cupimus, et nōn caret is quī nōn dēsīderat. Adulēscentēs nimis dēsīderant; senēs satis amōris saepe habent et multum sapientiae. Cōgitō, igitur, hoc tempus vītae esse iūcundum.

(Cicero, *Dē Senectūte* 14.47–48.—**minor,** *less.*—**carēre,** *to lack, want.*)

IT'S ALL IN THE DELIVERY

Quem recitās meus est, ō Fīdentīne, libellus;
    sed male cum recitās, incipit esse tuus!

(*Martial, 1.38; meter: elegiac couplet.—**Fīdentīnus,** a fellow who had publicly recited some of Martial's poems.—**libellus,** diminutive of **liber,** is the delayed antecedent of **quem;** in prose the order would be **libellus quem recitās est meus.**—**male,** adv. of **malus.**—**cum,** conj., *when.*)

A Reading from Homer, Sir Lawrence Alma-Tadema, 1885
Philadelphia Museum of Art: The George W. Elkins Collection

ETYMOLOGY

The Lat. rel. pron. was the parent of the following Romance forms: It. **chi, che;** Sp. **que;** Fr. **qui, que.**

If the suffix **-scō** shows a Latin verb to be an "inceptive" verb, what force or meaning does this ending impart to the verb?—**tremō,** *tremble;* **tremēscō** = ?

In medieval manuscripts many texts begin with an "incipit"; e.g., **liber prīmus Epistulārum Plīniī incipit.**

To Latin **aut** can be traced It. **o,** Sp. **o,** Fr. **ou.**

In the readings

3. imminent. 10. simulation, simulator, dissimulation. 11. **perīre:** Fr. **périr, périssant:** Eng. "perish." 12. ameliorate. "Old Age": minority.—caret.

LATĪNA EST GAUDIUM—ET ŪTILIS!

Iterum salvēte! There are a couple of Eng. abbreviations from **quī, quae, quod** which you may have seen: **q.v.** = **quod vidē,** *which see* (i.e., "see this item"), and **Q.E.D.** = **quod erat dēmōnstrandum,** *that which was to be proved* (used, e.g., in mathematical proofs—for the verbal form, a "passive periphrastic," see Ch. 24). Less common are **q.e.** = **quod est,** *which is,* and **Q.E.F.** = **quod erat faciendum,** *which was to be done.* You are beginning to see that for a truly literate person Latin is **sine quā nōn** (*indispensable,* lit. something *without which* one can *not* manage), and that's a point we needn't "quibble" over (a diminutive derived from the frequent use of **quibus** in legal documents).

The root meaning of **recitāre,** by the way, is *to arouse again* (cp. "excite," "incite"); when we "recite" a text, we are quite literally "reviving" or bringing it back to life, which is why we—just like the Romans—should always read literature, especially poetry, aloud!

Here's some good advice on doing your translations: **semper scrībe sententiās in tabellā tuā** (*your notebook*). An ancient proverb tells you why: **quī scrībit, bis discit!** And here's an old proverb with the new Vocab. item **cito: cito matūrum, cito putridum,** *quickly ripe, quickly rotten.* So let's not go too fast: **valēte!**

18

First and Second Conjugations: Passive Voice of the Present System; Ablative of Agent

FIRST AND SECOND CONJUGATION: PRESENT SYSTEM PASSIVE VOICE

In Latin as in English there are passive verb forms and passive sentence types, in which the subject is *recipient* of the action (rather than *performing* the action, as in the active voice). The rule for forming the passive of first and second conjugation present system passives (i.e., passives of the present, future, and imperfect tenses) is an easy one: simply substitute the new passive endings (**-r, -ris, -tur; -mur, -minī, -ntur**) for the active ones learned in Ch. 1 (**-ō/-m, -s, -t; -mus, -tis, -nt**). The few exceptions to this rule are highlighted in bold in the following paradigms.

PRESENT INDICATIVE PASSIVE OF Laudō and Moneō

PASSIVE
ENDINGS

1. -r	laúd**or**	móne**or**	*I am (am being) praised, warned*
2. -ris	laudắ-ris	monḗris	*you are (are being) praised, warned*
3. -tur	laudắ-tur	monḗtur	*he is (is being) praised, warned*

1. -mur	laudá-mur	monḗmur	*we are (are being) praised, warned*
2. -minī	laudá-minī	monḗminī	*you are (are being) praised, warned*
3. -ntur	laudá-ntur	monéntur	*they are (are being) praised, warned*

IMPERFECT INDICATIVE PASSIVE

I was (being) praised,	*I was (being) warned,*
used to be praised, etc.	*used to be warned,* etc.
1. laudá-ba-r	monḗbar
2. laudā-bá-ris	monēbáris
3. laudā-bá-tur	monēbátur
1. laudā-bá-mur	monēbámur
2. laudā-bá-minī	monēbáminī
3. laudā-bá-ntur	monēbántur

FUTURE INDICATIVE PASSIVE

I shall be praised	*I shall be warned*
1. laudá-**b-or**	monḗ**bor**
2. laudá-**be**-ris	monḗ**be**ris
3. laudá-bi-tur	monḗbitur
1. laudá-bi-mur	monḗbimur
2. laudā-bí-minī	monēbíminī
3. laudā-bú-ntur	monēbúntur

The exceptional forms, highlighted in bold above, are few: in the first person singular, present and future, the **-r** is added *directly* to the full active form (with the **-o-** shortened before final **-r**); **-bi-** is changed to **-be-** in the future second person singular. Notice, too, that the stem vowel remains short in **laudantur/monentur** but is long in **laudātur/monētur** (review the rule in Ch. 1: vowels are generally shortened before **nt** in any position but only before a *final* **-m, -r,** or **-t,** hence **laudat** but **laudātur**). You should note the existence of an alternate second person singular passive ending in **-re** (e.g., **laudābere** for **laudāberis**); this ending is not employed in this book, but you will certainly encounter it in your later readings.

THE PRESENT PASSIVE INFINITIVE

The present passive infinitive of the first and the second conjugations is formed simply by changing the final **-e** of the active to **-ī.**

laudár-ī, *to be praised*   monḗr-ī, *to be warned*

THE PASSIVE VOICE

When the verb is in the active voice (from **agō, agere, ēgī, āctum,** *to act*), the subject performs the action of the verb. When the verb is in the passive voice (from **patior, patī, passus sum,** *to undergo, experience*) the subject is acted upon: it suffers or passively permits the action of the verb. As a rule, only transitive verbs can be used in the passive; and what had been the object of the transitive verb (receiving the action of the verb) now becomes the subject of the passive verb (still receiving the action of the verb).

Caesarem admonet, *he is warning Caesar.*
Caesar admonētur, *Caesar is being warned.*

Urbem dēlēbant, *they were destroying the city.*
Urbs dēlēbātur, *the city was being destroyed.*

Patriam cōnservābit, *he will save the country.*
Patria cōnservābitur, *the country will be saved.*

ABLATIVE OF PERSONAL AGENT

The personal *agent by whom* the action of a passive verb is performed is indicated by **ab** and the "ablative of agent"; the *means by which* the action is accomplished is indicated by the "ablative of means" without a preposition, as you have already learned in Ch. 14.

Dī Caesarem admonent, *the gods are warning Caesar.*
Caesar ā dīs admonētur, *Caesar is warned by the gods.* (Agent)
Caesar hīs prōdigiīs admonētur, *Caesar is warned by these omens.* (Means); prōdigium, -iī, *omen.*
Malī virī urbem dēlēbant, *evil men were destroying the city.*
Urbs ab malīs virīs dēlēbātur, *the city was being destroyed by evil men.* (Agent)
Urbs flammīs dēlēbātur, *the city was being destroyed by flames.* (Means); flamma, -ae.
Hī cīvēs patriam cōnservābunt, *these citizens will save the country.*
Patria ab hīs cīvibus cōnservābitur, *the country will be saved by these citizens.* (Agent)
Patria armīs et vēritāte cōnservābitur, *the country will be saved by arms and truth.* (Means)

In summary, and as seen in the preceding examples, an active sentence construction can generally be transformed to a passive construction as follows: what was the direct object becomes the subject, the recipient of the action; what was the subject becomes an ablative of agent (remember to add this to your list of ablative uses), if a person, or an ablative of means, if a thing; and the appropriate passive verb form is substituted for the active.

VOCABULARY

flū́men, flū́minis, n., *river* (flume; cp. **fluō,** below)

génus, géneris, n., *origin; kind, type, sort, class* (genus, generic, genitive, gender, general, generous, genuine, degenerate, genre, congenial; cp. **gēns,** Ch. 21, **ingenium,** Ch. 29)

hóstis, hóstis, m., *an enemy* (of the state); **hóstēs, -ium,** *the enemy* (hostile, hostility, host)

lū́dus, -ī, m., *game, sport; school* (ludicrous, delude, elude, elusive, allude, allusion, illusion, collusion, interlude, prelude, postlude)

próbitās, probitā́tis, f., *uprightness, honesty* (probity; cp. **probāre,** Ch. 27)

sciéntia, -ae, f., *knowledge* (science, scientific; cp. **sciō,** Ch. 21)

clā́rus, -a, -um, *clear, bright; renowned, famous, illustrious* (clarify, clarity, claret, clarinet, clarion, declare, Clara, Clarissa, Claribel)

mortā́lis, mortā́le, *mortal* (mortality, immortality; cp. **mors**)

cūr, adv., *why*

deínde, adv., *thereupon, next, then*

flúō, flúere, flū́xī, flū́xum, *to flow* (fluid, fluent, flux, influx, affluence, effluence, influence, confluence, influenza, flu, mellifluous, super-fluous)

légō, légere, lḗgī, lḗctum, *to pick out, choose; read* (elect, elegant, eligible, lecture, legend, legible, intellect; cp. **intellegō, neglegō**)

mísceō, miscére, míscuī, míxtum, *to mix, stir up, disturb* (miscellanea, miscellaneous, miscellany, miscible, meddle, meddlesome, medley, melee, admixture, intermixture, promiscuous)

móveō, movḗre, mṓvī, mṓtum, *to move; arouse, affect* (mobile, motion, motive, motor, commotion, emotion, remote, locomotive, mutiny)

vídeor, vidḗrī, vī́sus sum, pass. of **videō,** *to be seen, seem, appear*

PRACTICE AND REVIEW

1. Multī morte etiam facilī nimis terrentur.
2. Beāta memoria amīcitiārum dulcium numquam dēlēbitur.
3. Illa fēmina caeca omnia genera artium quoque intellēxit et ab amīcīs iūcundīs semper laudābātur.
4. Pater senex vester, ā quō saepe iuvābāmur, multa dē celeribus perī-culīs ingentis maris herī dīcere coepit.
5. Mentēs nostrae memoriā potentī illōrum duōrum factōrum cito moventur.
6. Cōnsilia rēgīnae illō tertiō bellō longō et difficilī dēlēbantur.

7. Itaque māter mortem quartī fīliī exspectābat, quī nōn valēbat et cuius aetās erat brevis.
8. Bella difficilia sine cōnsiliō et clēmentiā numquam gerēbāmus.
9. Tē cum novem ex aliīs miserīs ad Caesarem crās trahent.
10. Rēgem ācrem, quī officia neglēxerat, ex urbe suā ēiēcērunt.
11. Ille poēta in tertiō libellō saturārum scrīpsit dē hominibus avārīs quī ad centum terrās aliās nāvigāre cupiunt quod pecūniam nimis dēsīderant.
12. Mercy will be given by them even to the citizens of other cities.
13. Many are moved too often by money but not by truth.
14. The state will be destroyed by the powerful king, whom they are beginning to fear.
15. Those ten women were not frightened by plans of that trivial sort.

SENTENTIAE ANTĪQUAE

1. Possunt quia posse videntur. (*Virgil.—**quia,** conj., *because.*)
2. Etiam fortēs virī subitīs perīculīs saepe terrentur. (Tacitus.—**subitus, -a, -um,** *sudden.*)
3. Tua cōnsilia sunt clāra nōbīs; tenēris scientiā hōrum cīvium omnium. (Cicero.)
4. Malum est cōnsilium quod mūtārī nōn potest. (*Publilius Syrus.)
5. Fās est ab hoste docērī. (Ovid.—**fās est,** *it is right.*)
6. Eō tempore erant circēnsēs lūdī, quō genere levī spectāculī numquam teneor. (Pliny.—**circēnsēs lūdī,** *contests in the Circus.*—As here with **genere,** the antecedent is often attracted into the rel. clause.—**spectāculum, -ī.**)

Relief with scene of Circus Maximus Museo Archeologico Foligno, Italy

7. Haec est nunc vīta mea: admittō et salūtō bonōs virōs quī ad mē veniunt; deinde aut scrībō aut legō; post haec omne tempus corporī datur. (Cicero.—**salutāre,** *to greet* at the early morning reception.)
8. Nihil igitur mors est, quoniam nātūra animī habētur mortālis. (Lucretius.)

9. Amor miscērī cum timōre nōn potest. (*Publilius Syrus.)

10. Numquam enim temeritās cum sapientiā commiscētur. (*Cicero.— **temeritās, -tātis,** *rashness.*)

11. Dīligēmus eum quī pecūniā nōn movētur. (Cicero.)

12. Laudātur ab hīs; culpātur ab illīs. (*Horace.)

13. Probitās laudātur—et alget. (*Juvenal.—**algēre,** *to be cold, be neglected.*)

ON DEATH AND METAMORPHOSIS

Ō genus hūmānum, quod mortem nimium timet! Cūr perīcula mortis timētis? Omnia mūtantur, omnia fluunt, nihil ad vēram mortem venit. Animus errat et in alia corpora miscētur; nec manet, nec eāsdem fōrmās servat, sed in fōrmās novās mūtātur. Vīta est flūmen; tempora nostra fugiunt et nova sunt semper. Nostra corpora semper mūtantur; id quod fuimus aut sumus, nōn crās erimus.

(Ovid, *Metamorphōsēs* 15.153–216; prose adaptation.—The ancients had some imaginative views on the transmigration of souls.)

ETYMOLOGY

Hostis meant originally *stranger* and then *enemy,* since any stranger in early times was a possible enemy. From **hostis,** *enemy,* stems our "host" in the sense of "army." **Hospes, hospitis,** which is an ancient compound of **hostis,** *stranger,* and **potis,** *having power over, lord of* (cf. Russ. **gospodin,** *lord, gentleman*), means *host* (one who receives strangers or guests) and also *guest;* cp. "hospital," "hospitality," "hostel," "hotel" (Fr. **hôtel**), and Eng. cognate "guest."

In the readings   6. circus.—spectator, spectacle, specter, spectacular. 10. temerity (contrast "timidity").

LATĪNA EST GAUDIUM—ET ŪTILIS!

Salvēte! Wondering how the same verb, **legere,** can mean both *to pick out* and *to read?* Because the process of reading was likened to gathering and collecting the words of a text. What a splendid metaphor: we are all of us (especially Latin students) "word collectors"! "Gather ye rosebuds while ye may" . . . and also the delights of language.

Remember the special pass. meaning of **videor** introduced in this Vocab.; here it is in the pres. pass. inf. form, also newly introduced in this chapter: **esse quam vidērī,** *to be rather than to seem,* the state motto of North Carolina. **Scientia** also turns up in several mottoes: **scientia est potentia,** *knowledge is power,* is one favorite, and another is **scientia sōl mentis est,** *knowledge is the sun of the mind* (motto of the University of Delaware). **Valēte, discipulae discipulīque!**

19

Perfect Passive System of All Verbs; Interrogative Pronouns and Adjectives

THE PERFECT PASSIVE SYSTEM

The construction of the forms of the perfect passive system is quite simple: a verb's perfect passive participle (the fourth principal part) is combined with **sum, erō,** and **eram** to form the perfect, future perfect, and pluperfect passive, respectively. The same pattern is employed for verbs of all conjugations; thus, in the following paradigms, **monitus, āctus, audītus, captus,** or any other perfect passive participle could be substituted for **laudātus.**

PERFECT INDICATIVE PASSIVE

1. laudā́tus, -a, -um sum	*I was praised, have been praised*
2. laudā́tus, -a, -um es	*you were praised, have been praised*
3. laudā́tus, -a, -um est	*he, she, it was praised, has been praised*
1. laudā́tī, -ae, -a súmus	*we were praised, have been praised*
2. laudā́tī, -ae, -a éstis	*you were praised, have been praised*
3. laudā́tī, -ae, -a sunt	*they were praised, have been praised*

FUTURE PERFECT PASSIVE

I shall have been praised, etc.
1. laudā́tus, -a, -um érō
2. laudā́tus, -a, -um éris
3. laudā́tus, -a, -um érit

PLUPERFECT INDICATIVE PASSIVE

I had been praised, etc.
1. laudā́tus, -a, -um éram
2. laudā́tus, -a, -um érās
3. laudā́tus, -a, -um érat

1. laudātī, -ae, -a érimus
2. laudātī, -ae, -a éritis
3. laudātī, -ae, -a érunt

1. laudātī, -ae, -a erāmus
2. laudātī, -ae, -a erātis
3. laudātī, -ae, -a érant

USAGE AND TRANSLATION

Although **sum** + the participle function together in Latin as a verbal unit, the participle in essence is a type of predicate adjective; i.e., **puella laudāta est** = **puella est laudāta,** cp. **puella est bona.** Consequently, and logically, the participle agrees with the subject in gender, number, and case.

Just as Latin uses the present, future, and imperfect of **sum, esse** to form these perfect system passive verbs, so English uses the present, future, and past tenses of the verb *to have* as perfect system (active and passive) auxiliaries: **laudātus est,** *he has been praised* (or, simple past, *was praised*); **laudātus erit,** *he will have been praised;* **laudātus erat,** *he had been praised.*[1] Be careful to avoid such common mistranslations as *is praised* for **laudātus est** and *was praised* for **laudātus erat** (caused by looking at the forms of **esse** and the participle separately, rather than seeing them as a unit).

The following examples illustrate these rules of form, usage, and translation:

Puella laudāta est, *the girl has been* (or *was*) *praised.*
Puellae laudātae erant, *the girls had been praised.*
Puellae laudātae erunt, *the girls will have been praised.*
Puerī monitī sunt, *the boys have been* (*were*) *warned.*
Perīculum nōn vīsum erat, *the danger had not been seen.*
Perīcula nōn vīsa sunt, *the dangers were not seen.*
Litterae scrīptae erunt, *the letter will have been written.*

THE INTERROGATIVE PRONOUN

As with the English interrogative pronoun (who, whose, whom? what, which?), the Latin interrogative pronoun **quis, quid** asks for the identity of a person or thing: e.g., **quid legis?** *what are you reading?* and **quis illum librum legit?** *who is reading that book?* In the plural the forms of the Latin interrogative pronoun are identical to those of the relative pronoun; in the singular, also, it follows the pattern of the relative with two exceptions: (1) the mascu-

---

[1] The perfect system tenses are sometimes (and with greater clarity, in fact) called the present perfect, future perfect, and past perfect; from the use of present, future, and past tense auxiliaries discussed in this chapter, you can see the appropriateness of this terminology.

line and the feminine have the same forms, (2) the nominative forms have their distinctive spellings **quis, quid** (and **quid** is also, of course, the neut. acc. form).

	Singular		Plural		
	M. & F.	**N.**	**M.**	**F.**	**N.**
Nom.	quis	quid	quī	quae	quae
Gen.	cuíus	cuíus	quốrum	quárum	quốrum
Dat.	cui	cui	quíbus	quíbus	quíbus
Acc.	quem	quid	quōs	quās	quae
Abl.	quō	quō	quíbus	quíbus	quíbus

THE INTERROGATIVE ADJECTIVE

As with the English interrogative adjective (which, what, what kind of), the Latin interrogative adjective **quī, quae, quod** asks for more specific identification of a person or thing: e.g., **quem librum legis?** *which (or what) book are you reading?* and **quae fēmina illum librum legit?** *which woman is reading that book?* The forms of the interrogative adjective are identical to those of the relative pronoun, in both the singular and the plural.

THE INTERROGATIVES AND RELATIVE DISTINGUISHED

The forms **quis** and **quid** are easily recognized as interrogative pronouns, but otherwise the interrogative pronoun, the interrogative adjective, and the relative pronoun can only be distinguished by their function and context, not by their forms. The following points will make the distinction simple:

the *relative pronoun* usually introduces a subordinate clause, has an antecedent, and does not ask a question (in fact, relative clauses *answer* questions, in the sense that they are adjectival and provide further information about their antecedents: e.g., **liber quem legis est meus,** *the book which you are reading is mine*);

the *interrogative pronoun* asks a question about the identity of a person or thing, has no antecedent, and often introduces a sentence with a question mark at the end (an exception is the "indirect question," introduced in Ch. 30); and

the *interrogative adjective* asks for more specific identification of a person or thing and both precedes and agrees in gender, number, and case with the noun it is asking about.

Consider these additional examples, and determine whether a relative pronoun, an interrogative pronoun, or an interrogative adjective is used in each one:

Quis librum tibi dedit? *Who gave the book to you?*

Vir **quī** librum tibi dedit tē laudāvit, *the man who gave the book to you praised you.*

Quem librum tibi dedit? *Which book did he give you?*

Cuius librum Cicerō tibi dedit? *Whose book did Cicero give to you?*

Cuius librī fuit Cicerō auctor? *Of which book was Cicero the author?*

Vir **cuius** librum Cicerō tibi dedit tē laudāvit, *the man whose book Cicero gave to you praised you.*

Cui amīcō librum dedistī? *To which friend did you give the book?*

Cui librum Cicerō dedit? *To whom did Cicero give the book?*

Vir **cui** Cicerō librum dedit tē laudāvit, *the man to whom Cicero gave the book praised you.*

Quid dedit? *What did he give?*

Quod praemium dedit? *What reward did he give?* (**praemium, -iī**.)

Praemium **quod** dedit erat magnum, *the reward which he gave was large.*

Ā quō praemium datum est? *By whom was the reward given?*

Vir ā **quō** praemium datum est tē laudāvit, *the man by whom the reward was given praised you.*

Quō praemiō ille mōtus est? *By which reward was that man motivated?*

VOCABULARY

argūméntum, -ī, n., *proof, evidence, argument* (argumentation, argumentative)

aúctor, auctóris, m., *increaser; author, originator* (authority, authorize)

benefícium, -iī, n., *benefit, kindness; favor* (benefice, beneficence, beneficial, beneficiary; cp. **faciō**)

família, -ae, f., *household, family* (familial, familiar, familiarity, familiarize)

Graécia, -ae, f., *Greece*

iúdex, iúdicis, m., *judge, juror* (judge, judgment; cp. **iūdicium**, below, **iūs, iniūria,** Ch. 39, **iūstus,** Ch. 40)

iūdícium, -iī, n., *judgment, decision, opinion; trial* (adjudge, adjudicate, judicial, judicious, injudicious, misjudge, prejudge, prejudice)

scélus, scéleris, n., *evil deed, crime, sin, wickedness*

quis? quid?, interrog. pron., *who? whose? whom? what? which?* (quiddity, quidnunc, quip)

quī? quae? quod? interrog. adj., *what? which? what kind of?* (quo jure)

cértus, -a, -um, *definite, sure, certain, reliable* (ascertain, certify, certificate)

grávis, gráve, *heavy, weighty; serious, important; severe, grievous* (aggravate, grief, grievance, grieve, grave, gravity)

immortális, immortále, *not subject to death, immortal* (cp. **mors**)

at, conj. *but; but, mind you; but, you say;* a more emotional adversative than **sed**

nísi, conj., *if . . . not, unless; except* (nisi prius)

cóntrā, prep. + acc., *against* (contra- in compounds such as contradict, contrast, contravene, contrapuntal; contrary, counter, encounter, country, pro and con)

iam, adv., *now, already, soon*

dēléctō (1), *to delight, charm, please* (delectable, delectation; cp. **dēlectātiō,** Ch. 27)

líberō (1), *to free, liberate* (liberate, liberation, liberal, deliver; cp. **līber, lībertās**)

párō (1), *to prepare, provide; get, obtain* (apparatus, compare, parachute, parapet, parasol, pare, parry, repair, reparation, separate, several)

PRACTICE AND REVIEW

1. Quis lībertātem eōrum eō tempore dēlēre coepit?
2. Cuius lībertās ab istō auctōre deinde dēlēta est?
3. Quōs librōs bonōs poēta caecus herī recitāvit?
4. Fēminae librōs difficilēs crās legent quōs mīsistī.
5. Omnia flūmina in mare fluunt et cum eō miscentur.
6. Itaque id genus lūdōrum levium, quod ā multīs familiīs laudābātur, nōs ipsī numquam cupimus.
7. Puerī et puellae propter facta bona ā mātribus patribusque laudātae sunt.
8. Cūr istī vēritātem timēbant, quā multī adiūtī erant?
9. Hostis trāns ingēns flūmen in Graeciā deinde nāvigāvit.
10. Quī vir fortis clārusque, dē quō lēgistī, aetātem brevem mortemque celerem exspectābat?
11. Quae studia gravia tē semper dēlectant, aut quae nunc dēsīderās?
12. Who saw the six men who had prepared this?
13. What was neglected by the second student yesterday?
14. We were helped by the knowledge which had been neglected by him.
15. Whose plans did the old men of all cities fear? Which plans did they esteem?

SENTENTIAE ANTĪQUAE

1. Quae est nātūra animī? Est mortālis. (Lucretius.)
2. Illa argūmenta vīsa sunt et gravia et certa. (Cicero.)

3. Quid nōs facere contrā istōs et scelera eōrum dēbēmus? (Cicero.)

4. Quid ego ēgī? In quod perīculum iactus sum? (Terence.)

5. Ō dī immortālēs! In quā urbe vīvimus? Quam cīvitātem habēmus? Quae scelera vidēmus? (Cicero.)

6. Quī sunt bonī cīvēs nisi eī quī beneficia patriae memoriā tenent? (Cicero.)

7. Alia, quae pecūniā parantur, ab eō stultō parāta sunt; at mōrēs eius vērōs amīcōs parāre nōn potuērunt. (Cicero.)

THE AGED PLAYWRIGHT SOPHOCLES HOLDS HIS OWN

Quam multa senēs in mentibus tenent! Sī studium grave et labor et probitās in senectūte remanent, saepe manent etiam memoria, scientia, sapientiaque.

Sophoclēs, scrīptor ille Graecus, ad summam senectūtem tragoediās fēcit; sed propter hoc studium familiam neglegere vidēbātur et ā fīliīs in iūdicium vocātus est. Tum auctor eam tragoediam quam sēcum habuit et quam proximē scrīpserat, "Oedipum Colōnēum," iūdicibus recitāvit. Ubi haec tragoedia recitāta est, senex sententiīs iūdicum est līberātus.

(Cicero, *Dē Senectūte,* 7.22.—**summam,** *extreme.*—**tragoedia, -ae;** the diphthong **oe** has become **e** in the English word.—**proximē,** adv., *shortly before.*—"Oedipus at Colonus.")

Sophocles
Roman copy, 4th century B.C.
Museo Gregoriano Profano
Vatican Museums, Vatican State

CATULLUS BIDS A BITTER FAREWELL TO LESBIA

Valē, puella—iam Catullus obdūrat.

. . .

15   Scelesta, vae tē! Quae tibī manet vīta?
Quis nunc tē adībit? Cui vidēberis bella?
Quem nunc amābis? Cuius esse dīcēris?
Quem bāsiābis? Cui labella mordēbis?
At tū, Catulle, dēstinātus obdūrā.

(*Catullus 8.12, 15–19; meter: choliambic. See L.A. 1, below (and cp. the adaptation of this passage in Ch. 2). **obdūrāre,** *to be hard.*—**scelestus, -a, -um,** *wicked, accursed.*—**vae tē,** *woe to you.*—**Quae,** with **vīta.**—**adībit,** *will visit.*—**dīcēris,** *will you be said.*—**bāsiāre,** *to kiss.*—**cui,** here = **cuius.**—**labellum, -ī,** *lip.*—**mordēre,** *to bite.*—**dēstinātus, -a, -um,** *resolved, firm.*)

MESSAGE FROM A BOOKCASE

Sēlectōs nisi dās mihī libellōs,
admittam tineās trucēsque blattās!

(*Martial 14.37; meter: hendecasyllabic.—**sēlectus, -a, -um,** *select, carefully chosen.*—**tinea, -ae,** *maggot, bookworm.*—**trux,** gen. **trucis,** *fierce, savage.*—**blatta, -ae,** *cockroach.*)

ETYMOLOGY

In the readings

"Catullus": obdurate, mordant, mordent.—destine, destination, destiny. "Sophocles": sum, summary, consummate—proximate, approximate. "Message": truculent.

LATĪNA EST GAUDIUM—ET ŪTILIS!

Salvēte!—**quid agitis?** We've been seeing **quid** in that idiom (*how are you doing?* not *what are you doing?*) ever since Ch. 2, and do you recall **quid novī,** *what's new?,* from the discussion of the gen. of the whole in Ch. 15? Even before beginning your study of Latin you'd likely encountered the common phrase **quid prō quō,** *one thing in return for another* (= "tit for tat"—**quid** was often equivalent to the indefinite *something*) and you may even have run into **quidnunc,** a "busybody" (lit., *what-now?!*). The interrogative adj. has also come into Eng.: **quō jūre** (= classical **iūre**), *by what* (*legal*) *right,* **quō animō,** *with what intention,* and **quō modō,** *in what manner.*

You learned **iaciō, iacere, iēcī, iactum** in Ch. 15: you can now recognize the perfect passive form in Julius Caesar's famous dictum, **alea iacta est,** *the die has been cast,* a remark he made when crossing the Rubicon river in northern Italy in 49 B.C. and embarking upon civil war with Pompey the Great. **Discipulī discipulaeque, valēte!**

20

Fourth Declension; Ablatives of Place from Which and Separation

FOURTH DECLENSION

The fourth declension presents fewer problems than the third and contains fewer nouns; most are masculine, with the nominative singular in **-us,** but there are some feminines, also in **-us** (**manus,** *hand,* and **domus,** *house,* appear in this book), and a very few neuters, with the nominative singular in **-ū.**

As with all nouns, in order to decline, simply add the new endings presented below to the base; note that the characteristic vowel **u** appears in all the endings except the dative and ablative plural (and even there a few nouns have **-ubus** for **-ibus**) and that, of all the **-us** endings, only the masculine and feminine nominative singular has a short **-u-.**

	frūctus, -ūs, m. *fruit*	**cornū, -ūs,** n. *horn*	**Endings** **M. & F.**	**N.**
Nom.	frŭctus	córnū	-us	-ū
Gen.	frŭctūs	córnūs	-ūs	-ūs
Dat.	frŭctuī	córnū	-uī	-ū
Acc.	frŭctum	córnū	-um	-ū
Abl.	frŭctū	córnū	-ū	-ū

Nom.	frúctūs	córnua	-ūs	-ua
Gen.	frúctuum	córnuum	-uum	-uum
Dat.	frúctibus	córnibus	-ibus	-ibus
Acc.	frúctūs	córnua	-ūs	-ua
Abl.	frúctibus	córnibus	-ibus	-ibus

Remember that there are also **-us** nouns in the second and third declensions, e.g., **amīcus** and **corpus;** it is a noun's genitive ending, not the nominative, that determines its declension, so it is imperative that you memorize the full vocabulary entry for every new noun you encounter. Remember, too, that a noun and modifying adjective, though they must agree in number, gender, and case, will not necessarily have the same endings, hence **frūctus dulcis, frūctūs dulcis,** etc., *sweet fruit;* **manus mea, manūs meae,** etc., *my hand;* **cornū longum, cornūs longī,** etc., *a long horn;* etc.

ABLATIVES OF PLACE FROM WHICH AND SEPARATION

The ablatives of place from which and separation are two very common and closely related constructions (which should be added now to your list of ablative case uses). The principal difference is that the former, which you have in fact already encountered in your readings, virtually always involves a *verb of active motion* from one place to another; nearly always, too, the ablative is governed by one of the prepositions **ab, dē,** or **ex** (*away from, down from, out of*):

Graecī ā patriā suā ad Italiam navigāvērunt, *the Greeks sailed from their own country to Italy.*

Flūmen dē montibus in mare flūxit, *the river flowed down from the mountains into the sea.*

Multī ex agrīs in urbem venient, *many will come from the country into the city.*

Cicerō hostēs ab urbe mīsit, *Cicero sent the enemy away from the city.*

The ablative of separation, as the terminology suggests, implies only that some person or thing is separated from another; there is no active movement from one place to another; and sometimes there is no preposition, particularly with certain verbs meaning "to free," "to lack," and "to deprive," which commonly take an ablative of separation:

Cicerō hostēs ab urbe prohibuit, *Cicero kept the enemy away from the city* (cp. the similar example above).

Eōs timōre līberāvit, *he freed them from fear.*

Agricolae pecūniā saepe carēbant, *the farmers often lacked money.*

VOCABULARY

coniūrátī, -órum, m. pl., *conspirators* (conjure, conjurer; cp. **coniūrātiō,** *conspiracy,* conjuration)

córnū, córnūs, n., *horn* (corn—not the grain, but a thick growth of skin; cornea, corner, cornet, cornucopia, unicorn)

frúctus, frúctūs, m., *fruit; profit, benefit, enjoyment* (fructify, fructose, frugal)

génū, génūs, n., *knee* (genuflect, genuflection; *knee* and **genū** are cognates)

mánus, mánūs, f., *hand; handwriting; band* (manual, manufacture, manumit, manuscript, emancipate, manacle, manage, manicle, maneuver)

métus, -ūs (= **métūs;** subsequent 4th decl. nouns will be abbreviated in this way), m., *fear, dread, anxiety* (meticulous; cp. **metuō,** Ch. 38)

mōns, móntis, m., *mountain* (mount, mountainous, Montana, amount, catamount, paramount, surmount, tantamount)

senátus, -ūs, m., *senate* (senatorial; cp. **senex**)

sénsus, -ūs, m., *feeling, sense* (sensation, sensory, sensual, sensuous, senseless, insensate, sensible, sensitive; cp. **sentiō**)

sérvitūs, servitútis, f., *servitude, slavery* (cp. **servō**)

spíritus, -ūs, m., *breath, breathing; spirit, soul* (spiritual, spiritous, conspire, inspire, expire, respiratory, transpire; cp. **spīrāre,** *to breathe*)

vérsus, -ūs, m., *line of verse* (versify, versification; cp. **vertō,** Ch. 23)

commúnis, commúne, *common, general, of/for the community* (communal, commune, communicate, communicable, communion, communism, community, excommunicate)

déxter, déxtra, déxtrum, *right, right-hand* (dexterity, dextrous, ambidextrous)

siníster, sinístra, sinístrum, *left, left-hand; harmful, ill-omened* (sinister, sinistral, sinistrodextral, sinistrorse)

cáreō, carḗre, cáruī, caritúrum + abl. of separation, *to be without, be deprived of, want, lack; be free from* (caret)

dēféndō, -féndere, -féndī, -fénsum, *to ward off; defend, protect* (defendant, defense, defensible, defensive, fence, fencing, fend, fender, offend)

discḗdō, -cḗdere, -céssī, -céssum, *to go away, depart* (cp. **cēdō,** Ch. 28)

ódī, ōdísse, ōsúrum (a so-called "defective" verb, having only perf. system forms and a fut. act. participle), *to hate* (odious; cp. **odium,** Ch. 38)

prohíbeō, -hibḗre, -híbuī, -híbitum, *to keep (back), prevent, hinder, restrain, prohibit* (prohibitive, prohibition, prohibitory; cp. **habeō**)

prōnū́ntiō (1), *to proclaim, announce; declaim; pronounce* (pronounce-ment, pronunciation; cp. **nūntius,** *messenger, message*)

PRACTICE AND REVIEW

1. Etiam senēs frūctibus sapientiae et cōnsiliīs argūmentīsque certīs saepe carent.
2. Aut ingentēs montēs aut flūmina celeria quae dē montibus fluēbant hostēs ab urbe prohibēbant.
3. Quoniam nimis fortia facta faciēbat, aetās eius erat brevis.
4. Illa medica facere poterat multa manū dextrā sed sinistrā manū pauca.
5. Vēritās nōs metū gravī iam līberābit quō diū territī sumus.
6. Quibus generibus scelerum sinistrōrum illae duae cīvitātēs dēlētae sunt?
7. Quī mortālis sine amīcitiā et probitāte et beneficiō in aliōs potest esse beātus?
8. Pater pecūniam ex Graeciā in suam patriam movēre coeperat, nam familia discēdere cupīvit.
9. Ā quibus studium difficilium artium eō tempore neglēctum est?
10. Ubi versūs illīus auctōris clārī lēctī sunt, audītōrēs delectātī sunt.
11. Sē citō iēcērunt ad genua iūdicum, quī autem nūllam clēmentiam dēmōnstrāvērunt.
12. We cannot have the fruits of peace, unless we ourselves free our families from heavy dread.
13. Those bands of unfortunate men and women will come to us from other countries in which they are deprived of the benefits of citizenship.
14. The old men lacked neither games nor serious pursuits.
15. Who began to perceive our common fears of serious crime?

SENTENTIAE ANTĪQUAE

1. Cornua cervum ā perīculīs dēfendunt. (Martial.—**cervus, -ī,** *stag.*)
2. Oedipūs duōbus oculīs sē prīvāvit. (Cicero.—**prīvāre,** *to deprive.*)
3. Themistoclēs bellō Persicō Graeciam servitūte līberāvit. (Cicero.—**Persicus, -a, -um,** *Persian.*)
4. Dēmosthenēs multōs versūs ūnō spīritū prōnūntiābat. (Cicero.)
5. Persicōs apparātūs ōdī. (Horace.—**apparātus, -ūs,** *equipment, display.*)
6. Iste commūnī sēnsū caret. (Horace.)
7. Senectūs nōs prīvat omnibus voluptātibus neque longē abest ā morte. (Cicero.—**longē,** adv. of **longus.**—**absum,** *to be away.*)
8. Nūllus accūsātor caret culpā; omnēs peccāvimus. (Seneca.—**accūsātor, -tōris.**—**peccāre,** *to sin.*)

9. Nūlla pars vītae vacāre officiō potest. (Cicero.—**vacāre,** *to be free from.*)

10. Prīma virtūs est vitiō carēre. (Quintilian.)

11. Vir scelere vacuus nōn eget iaculīs neque arcū. (Horace.—**vacuus, -a, -um,** *free from.*—**egēre,** *to need.*—**iaculum, -ī,** *javelin.*—**arcus, -ūs,** *bow.*)

12. Magnī tumultūs urbem eō tempore miscēbant. (Cicero.—**tumultus, -ūs.**)

13. Litterae senātuī populōque Allobrogum manibus coniūrātōrum ipsōrum erant scrīptae. (Cicero.—**Allobrogēs, -gum,** m. pl., a Gallic tribe whom the Catilinarian conspirators tried to arouse against Rome.)

CICERO URGES CATILINE'S DEPARTURE FROM ROME

Habēmus senātūs cōnsultum contrā tē, Catilīna, vehemēns et grave; ācre iūdicium habēmus, et vīrēs et cōnsilium cīvitās nostra habet. Quid est, Catilīna? Cūr remanēs? Ō dī immortālēs! Discēde nunc ex hāc urbe cum malā manū scelerātōrum; magnō metū mē līberābis, sī omnēs istōs coniūrātōs tēcum ēdūcēs. Nisi nunc discēdēs, tē cito ēiciēmus. Nihil in cīvitāte nostrā tē dēlectāre potest. Age, age! Deinde curre ad Manlium, istum amīcum malum; tē diū dēsīderāvit. Incipe nunc; gere bellum in cīvitātem! Brevī tempore tē omnēsque tuōs, hostēs patriae, vincēmus, et omnēs vōs poenās gravēs semper dabitis.

(Cicero, *In Catilīnam* 1.1.3ff; see the readings in Chs. 11 and 14 above, and "Evidence and Confession," Ch. 30.—**cōnsultum, -ī,** *decree.*—**vehemēns,** gen. **vehementis.**—**scelerātus, -a, -um,** adj. from **scelus.**—Manlius was one of Catiline's principal fellow conspirators.)

Cicero
Museo Capitolino, Rome, Italy

ETYMOLOGY

The Roman *senate* was in origin a council of elders, hence the connection with **senex.**

If one knows the derivation of "caret," one is not likely to confuse this word with "carat."

In the readings   5. peach (Persian apple). 7. absent. 9. vacant, vacuous, vacate, vacation, vacuity, evacuate. 11. arc, arcade. 12. tumult, tumultuous. "Cicero": consult, consultation.—vehement, vehemence.)

LATĪNA EST GAUDIUM—ET ŪTILIS!

Salvēte! This chapter's Vocab. provides some "handy" items: can you explain the etymologies of "manumit," "manuscript," and "manufacture"? A "manual" is the Latinate equivalent of the Germanic "handbook." Then there's the old Roman proverb **manus manum lavat (lavāre,** *to bathe,* gives us "lavatory"), *one hand washes the other.* You can see the right-handed bias in the etymologies of "dexterity" and "sinister" (from the ancient superstition that bad signs and omens appeared to one's left) and even "ambidextrous" (from **ambo,** *both, two:* is having "two right hands" better than having two left hands?).

And speaking of hands, how about fingers? The Latin word is **digitus, -ī,** which gives us "digit," "digital," "prestidigitation" (for a magician's quick fingers), and even "digitalis," a heart medication from a plant whose flowers are finger-shaped. These appendages are also handy for counting (**numerāre**): **prīmus digitus, secundus digitus, tertius . . .** etc. (**Potestisne numerāre omnēs digitōs vestrōs, discipulī et discipulae?** If not, look back at Ch. 15 and review your **numerī!**) The Romans had special names for each of the fingers, beginning with the thumb, **pollex,** then **index** (from **indicāre,** *to point*), **medius** (*middle*) or **īnfāmis** (*infamous, evil*—not all our body language is new!), **quartus** or **ānulārius** (where they often wore **ānulī,** *rings:* see "Ringo," Ch. 31), and **minimus** (*the smallest*) or **auriculārius** (the **parvus digitus,** and so handy for scratching or cleaning one's **aurēs!**). **Valēte!**

21

Third and Fourth Conjugations: Passive Voice of the Present System

The pattern of substituting passive endings for active endings, which you learned in Ch. 18 for the present system passives of first and second conjugation verbs, generally applies to third and fourth conjugation verbs as well; the only exceptions are in the second person singular present tense (set in bold in the following paradigms) and the present infinitive of third conjugation verbs.

PRESENT INDICATIVE PASSIVE

1. ágor	aúdior	cápior
2. ág**eris**	audī́ris	cáp**eris**
3. ágitur	audī́tur	cápitur

1. ágimur	audī́mur	cápimur
2. agíminī	audī́minī	capíminī
3. agúntur	audiúntur	capiúntur

FUTURE INDICATIVE PASSIVE

1. ágar	aúdiar	cápiar
2. agḗris	audiḗris	capiḗris
3. agḗtur	audiḗtur	capiḗtur

1. agḗmur	audiḗmur	capiḗmur
2. agḗminī	audiḗminī	capiḗminī
3. agéntur	audiéntur	capiéntur

IMPERFECT INDICATIVE PASSIVE

1. agḗbar	audiḗbar	capiḗbar
2. agēbā́ris	audiēbā́ris	capiēbā́ris
3. agēbā́tur	audiēbā́tur	capiēbā́tur
1. agēbā́mur	audiēbā́mur	capiēbā́mur
2. agēbā́minī	audiēbā́minī	capiēbā́minī
3. agēbántur	audiēbántur	capiēbántur

Be careful not to confuse the second person singular present and future third conjugation forms, which are distinguished only by the vowel quantity (**ageris** vs. **agēris**). Note that **capiō** and **audiō** are identical throughout the present system active and passive, except for variations in -i- vs. -ī- (in the present tense only) and the second singular passive **caperis** vs. **audīris.** Remember that the perfect passive system for third and fourth conjugation verbs follows the universal pattern introduced in Ch. 19.

PRESENT INFINITIVE PASSIVE

The present infinitive passive of the fourth conjugation is formed by changing the final -e to -ī, as in the first two conjugations; but in the third conjugation, including -iō verbs, the whole -ere is changed to -ī.

audī́re, *to hear*	audī́rī, *to be heard* (cp. laudā́rī, monḗrī)
ágere, *to lead*	ágī, *to be led*
cápere, *to take*	cápī, *to be taken*

SYNOPSIS

To test your ability to conjugate a Latin verb completely, you may be asked to provide a labelled "synopsis" of the verb in a specified person and number, in lieu of writing out all of the verb's many forms. Following is a sample third person singular synopsis of **agō** in the indicative mood:

	Pres.	Fut.	Impf.	Perf.	Fut. Perf.	Plupf.
Act.	ágit	áget	agḗbat	ḗgit	ḗgerit	ḗgerat
Pass.	ágitur	agḗtur	agēbā́tur	áctus est	áctus érit	áctus érat

VOCABULARY

cása, -ae, f., *house, cottage, hut* (casino)

caúsa, -ae, f., *cause, reason; case, situation;* **caúsā,** abl. with a preceding gen., *for the sake of, on account of* (accuse, because, excuse)

fenéstra, -ae, f., *window* (fenestra, fenestrated, fenestration, fenestella, defenestration)

fínis, fínis, m., *end, limit, boundary; purpose;* **fínēs, -ium,** *boundaries, territory* (affinity, confine, define, final, finale, finance, fine, finesse, finial, finicky, finish, finite, infinite, paraffin, refine)

gēns, géntis, f., *clan, race, nation, people* (gentile, gentle, genteel, gentry; cp. **genus, ingenium,** Ch. 29)

múndus, -ī, m., *world, universe* (mundane, demimonde)

nӑvis, nӑvis, f., *ship, boat* (naval, navy, navigable, navigate, nave; cp. **nāvigāre, nauta**)

sálūs, salútis, f., *health, safety; greeting* (salubrious, salutary, salutation, salute, salutatorian, salutatory; cp. **salveō, salvus**)

Tróia, -ae, f., *Troy*

vīcínus, -ī, m., and **vīcína, -ae,** f., *neighbor* (vicinity)

vúlgus, -ī, n. (sometimes m.), *the common people, mob, rabble* (vulgar, vulgarity, vulgarize, vulgate, divulge)

ásper, áspera, ásperum, *rough, harsh* (asperity, exasperate, exasperation)

átque or **ac** (only before consonants), conj., *and, and also, and even*

íterum, adv., *again, a second time* (iterate, iterative, reiterate, reiteration)

contíneō, -tinére, -tínuī, -téntum, *to hold together, contain, keep, enclose, restrain* (content, discontent, malcontent, continual, continuous, incontinent, countenance; cp. **teneō**)

iúbeō, iubére, iússī, iússum, *to bid, order, command* (jussive)

labӧrō (1), *to labor; be in distress* (laboratory, laborer, belabor; cp. **labor**)

rápiō, rápere, rápuī, ráptum, *to seize, snatch, carry away* (rapacious, rapid, rapine, rapture, ravage, ravine, ravish; cp. **ēripiō,** Ch. 22)

relínquō, -línquere, -lίquī, -líctum, *to leave behind, leave, abandon, desert* (relinquish, reliquary, relict, relic, delinquent, dereliction)

scíō, scíre, scívī, scítum, *to know* (science, scientific, conscience, conscious, prescience, scilicet; cp. **scientia, nesciō,** Ch. 25)

tángō, tángere, tétigī, tӑctum, *to touch* (tangent, tangible, tact, tactile, contact, contagious, contiguous, contingent, integer, taste, tax)

PRACTICE AND REVIEW

1. Laus autem nimis saepe est neque certa neque magna.
2. Senēs in gente nostrā ab fīliīs numquam neglegēbantur.
3. Quis tum iussus erat Graeciam metū līberāre, familiās dēfendere, atque hostēs ā patriā prohibēre?

4. Salūtis commūnis causā eōs coniūrātōs ex urbe discēdere ac trāns flūmen ad montēs dūcī iussit.

5. Aliī auctōrēs coepērunt spīritūs nostrōs contrā iūdicium atque argūmenta senātūs iterum movēre, quod omnēs metū novō territī erant.

6. Omnia genera servitūtis nōbīs videntur aspera.

7. Rapiēturne igitur Cicerō ex manibus istōrum?

8. Quī fīnis metūs atque servitūtis in eā cīvitāte nunc potest vidērī?

9. At senectūtis bonae causā iam bene vīvere dēbēmus.

10. In familiā eōrum erant duae fīliae atque quattuor fīliī.

11. Casa vīcīnī nostrī habuit paucās fenestrās per quās vidēre potuit.

12. Quandō cornū audīvit, senex in genua cecidit et deīs immortālibus grātiās prōnūntiābat.

13. Propter beneficia et sēnsum commūnem tyrannī, paucī eum odērunt.

14. The truth will not be found without great labor.

15. Many nations which lack true peace are being destroyed by wars.

16. Their fears can now be conquered because our deeds are understood by all.

17. Unless serious pursuits delight us, they are often neglected for the sake of money or praise.

SENTENTIAE ANTĪQUAE

1. Numquam perīculum sine perīculō vincitur. (Publilius Syrus.)

2. Novius est vīcīnus meus et manū dextrā tangī dē fenestrīs meīs potest. (Martial.—**Novius,** a personal name.)

3. Nōnne iūdicēs iubēbunt hunc in vincula dūcī et ad mortem rapī? (Cicero.—**nōnne** introduces a question which anticipates the answer "yes"; see Ch. 40.—**vinculum, -ī,** *chain.*)

4. Altera aetās bellīs cīvīlibus teritur et Rōma ipsa suīs vīribus dēlētur. (Horace.—**cīvīlis, -e.—terō, -ere, trīvī, trītum,** *to wear out.*)

5. At amīcitia nūllō locō exclūditur; numquam est intempestīva aut sinistra; multa beneficia continet. (Cicero.—**exclūdō, -ere,** *to shut out.*—**intempestīvus, -a, -um,** *untimely.*)

6. Futūra scīrī nōn possunt. (Cicero.—**futūrus, -a, -um.**)

7. Prīncipiō ipse mundus deōrum hominumque causā factus est, et quae in eō sunt, ea parāta sunt ad frūctum hominum. (Cicero.)

8. Quam cōpiōsē ā Xenophonte agrīcultūra laudātur in eō librō quī "Oeconomicus" īnscrībitur. (Cicero.—**cōpiōsē,** adv., cp. **cōpia.**—**Xenophōn, -phontis.—agrīcultūra, -ae.—īnscrībō, -ere,** *to entitle.*)

9. Vulgus vult dēcipī. (*Phaedrus.—**vult,** *want* (irreg. form).—**dēcipiō, -ere,** *to deceive.*)

10. Ubi scientia ac sapientia inveniuntur? (Job.)

11. Vēritās nimis saepe labōrat; exstinguitur numquam. (Livy.—**exstinguō, -ere.**)

VIRGIL'S MESSIANIC ECLOGUE

Venit iam magna aetās nova; dē caelō mittitur puer, quī vītam deōrum habēbit deōsque vidēbit et ipse vidēbitur ab illīs. Hic puer reget mundum cui virtūtēs patris pācem dedērunt. Pauca mala, autem, remanēbunt, quae hominēs iubēbunt labōrāre atque bellum asperum gerere. Erunt etiam altera bella atque iterum ad Trōiam magnus mittētur Achillēs. Tum, puer, ubi iam longa aetās tē virum fēcerit, erunt nūllī labōrēs, nūlla bella; nautae ex navibus discēdent, agricolae quoque iam agrōs relinquent, terra ipsa omnibus hominibus omnia parābit. Currite, aetātēs; incipe, parve puer, scīre mātrem, et erit satis spīritūs mihi tua dīcere facta.

(Virgil, *Eclogae* 4; written ca. 40 B.C., the poem from which this reading is adapted was taken by many early Christians as a prophecy of the birth of Christ.—**altera bella,** *the same wars over again.*—**scīre mātrem,** i.e., to be born.)

Relief of warship, temple of Fortuna Primigenia, Praeneste
1st century A.D., Museo Pio Clementino, Vatican Museums, Vatican State

ETYMOLOGY

Exemplī causā was Cicero's equivalent of the somewhat later **exemplī grātiā,** whence our abbreviation **e.g.**

Romance derivatives from some of the words in the vocabulary:

Latin	Italian	Spanish	French
causa	cosa	cosa	chose
fīnis	fine	fin	fin
gēns	gente	gente	gent; gens (pl.)
continēre	continere	contener	contenir
mundus	mondo	mundo	monde

In the readings   3. vinculum (in mathematics). 4. civil; cp. **cīvis, cīvitās.**—trite, contrite, contrition, attrition, detriment. 5. **ex + claudō** (-ere, clausī, clausum, *to shut, close*): conclude, include, preclude, seclude, recluse, clause, close, closet, cloister.

LATĪNA EST GAUDIUM—ET ŪTILIS!

Salvēte, discipulae atque discipulī! Quid novī? Well, how about some more well-known Latin phrases and mottoes related to the **verba nova** in this chapter's Vocab.? First, for you *Godfather* fans, there's It. **cosa nostra,** from **causa nostra** (shh!). **Vestra causa tōta nostra est** is the motto of the American Classical League, one of our national professional organizations for teachers of Latin, Greek, and classical humanities. The University of Georgia's motto is **et docēre et rērum exquīrere causās,** *both to teach and to seek out the causes of things* (i.e., to conduct research—for **rērum,** see the next chapter). Here are some others: **fīnis corōnat opus,** *the end crowns the work;* **gēns togāta,** *the toga-clad nation* (a phrase Virgil applies to Rome, where the toga was a man's formal attire); **tangere ulcus,** *to touch a sore spot* (lit., *ulcer*); **sīc trānsit glōria mundī,** *so passes the glory of the world* (Thomas à Kempis, on the transitory nature of worldly things—some comedian who shall forever remain nameless has offered an alternate translation, to wit, "Gloria always gets sick on the subway at the beginning of the week"!!!); and the abbreviation **sc.,** meaning *supply* (something omitted from a text but readily understood), comes from **scīlicet,** short for **scīre licet,** lit. *it is permitted for you to understand.* **Hic est fīnis: valēte!**

22

Fifth Declension; Ablative of Place Where; Summary of Ablative Uses

THE FIFTH DECLENSION

This chapter introduces the fifth and last of the Latin noun declensions. The characteristic vowel is **-ē-,** and **-ēī** or **-eī** is the genitive and dative ending (the gen./dat. **-e-** is long when preceded by a vowel, short when preceded by a consonant; cp. **diēī** and **reī** below); to avoid confusion, the genitive form will be spelled out in full for fifth declension nouns (as they are with third declension nouns) in the chapter vocabularies. Nouns of this declension are all feminine, except **diēs** (*day*) and its compound **merīdiēs** (*midday*), which are masculine.

To decline, follow the usual pattern, i.e., drop the genitive ending to find the base, then add the new endings.

	rēs, reī, f. *thing*	**diēs, diēī,** m. *day*	**Case Endings**
Nom.	rēs	díēs	-ēs
Gen.	réī	diéī	-eī, -ēī
Dat.	réī	diéī	-eī, -ēī
Acc.	rem	díem	-em
Abl.	rē	díē	-ē
Nom.	rēs	díēs	-ēs
Gen.	rérum	diérum	-ērum
Dat.	rébus	diébus	-ēbus
Acc.	rēs	díēs	-ēs
Abl.	rébus	diébus	-ēbus

OBSERVATIONS

Notice that the genitive and dative singular are identical (true of the first declension also), as are the nominative singular and the nominative and accusative plural (the vocatives, too, of course), and the dative and ablative plural (true of all declensions); word order, context, and other cues such as subject-verb agreement will help you distinguish them in a sentence.

ABLATIVE OF PLACE WHERE AND SUMMARY OF ABLATIVE USES

You have thus far been introduced to these specific ablative case uses: ablative of means, manner, accompaniment (Ch. 14), ablative with cardinal numerals and ablative of time (Ch. 15), ablative of agent (Ch. 18), place from which and separation (Ch. 20).

You have in fact also encountered frequently the construction known as ablative of "place where," which consists most commonly of the preposition **in,** *in/on,* or **sub,** *under,* plus a noun in the ablative to describe where someone or something is located or some action is being done:

In magnā casā vīvunt, *they live in a large house.*

Nāvis sub aquā fuit, *the ship was under water.*

Some of these case uses require a preposition in Latin, others do not, and in some instances the practice was variable. A case in point, and something to be carefully noted, is that in the ablative of manner construction, when the noun is modified by an adjective, **cum** is frequently omitted; if **cum** is used, it is usually preceded by the adjective (e.g., **id magnā cūrā fēcit** and **id magnā cum cūrā fēcit,** both meaning *he did it with great care*).

The following summary reviews each of the ablative uses studied thus far:

I. THE ABLATIVE WITH A PREPOSITION

The ablative is used with:

1. **cum** to indicate *accompaniment*
   Cum amīcō id scrīpsit, *he wrote it with his friend.*
2. **cum** to indicate *manner*; cp. II.2 below
   Cum cūrā id scrīpsit, *he wrote it with care.*
   Magnā cum cūrā id scrīpsit, *he wrote it with great care.*
3. **in** and **sub** to indicate *place where*
   In urbe id scrīpsit, *he wrote it in the city.*

4. **ab, dē, ex** to indicate *place from which*
   Ex urbe id mīsit, *he sent it from the city.*
5. **ab, dē, ex** to indicate *separation;* cp. II. 4 below
   Ab urbe eōs prohibuit, *he kept them from the city.*
6. **ab** to indicate *personal agent*
   Ab amīcō id scrīptum est, *it was written by his friend.*
7. **ex** or **dē** following certain *cardinal numerals* to indicate a group of which some part is specified
   Trēs ex nāvibus discessērunt, *three of the ships departed.*

II. THE ABLATIVE WITHOUT A PREPOSITION

The ablative is used without a preposition to indicate:

1. *means*
   Suā manū id scrīpsit, *he wrote it with his own hand.*
2. *manner,* when an adjective is used
   Magnā cūrā id scrīpsit, *he wrote it with great care.*
3. *time when or within which*
   Eō tempore *or* ūnā hōrā id scrīpsit, *he wrote it at that time* or *in one hour.*
4. *separation,* especially with ideas of freeing, lacking, depriving
   Metū eōs līberāvit, *he freed them from fear.*

VOCABULARY

díēs, diéī, m., *day* (diary, dial, dismal, diurnal, journal, adjourn, journey, meridian, sojourn)

férrum, -ī, n., *iron; sword* (ferric, ferrite, ferro-, farrier)

fídēs, fideī, f., *faith, trust, trustworthiness, fidelity; promise, guarantee, protection* (confide, diffident, infidel, perfidy, fealty)

ígnis, ígnis, m., *fire* (igneous, ignite, ignition)

módus, -ī, m., *measure, bound, limit; manner, method, mode, way* (model, moderate, modern, modest, modicum, modify, mood)

rēs, réī, f., *thing, matter, business, affair* (real, realistic, realize, reality, real estate)

rēs pública, réī públicae, f., *state, commonwealth, republic* (Republican)

spēs, spéī, f., *hope* (despair, desperate; cf. **spērō,** Ch. 25)

aéquus, -a, -um, *level, even; calm; equal, just; favorable* (equable, equanimity, equation, equator, equilateral, equilibrium, equinox, equity, equivalent, equivocal, inequity, iniquity, adequate, coequal)

fēlíx, gen. **fēlícis,** *lucky, fortunate, happy* (felicitate, felicitation, felicitous, infelicitous, felicity, infelicity, Felix)

incértus, -a, -um (in-certus), *uncertain, unsure, doubtful* (incertitude)

Latínus, -a, -um, *Latin* (Latinate, Latinist, Latinity, Latinize, Latino)

médius, -a, -um, *middle;* used partitively, *the middle of:* **media urbs,** *the middle of the city* (mediterranean, medium, median, mediate, mean, medieval, meridian, demimonde, immediate, intermediary; cp. **mediocris,** Ch. 31)

quóndam, adv., *formerly, once* (quondam)

últrā, adv. and prep. + acc., *on the other side of, beyond* (ultra, ultrasonic, ultrasound, ultraviolet, outrage, outrageous)

prótinus, adv., *immediately*

cérnō, cérnere, crḗvī, crḗtum, *to distinguish, discern, perceive* (discern, discernible, discreet, discrete, discretion; cp. **dēcernō,** Ch. 36)

ērípiō, -rípere, -rípuī, -réptum (ē-rapiō), *to snatch away, take away; rescue*

ínquit, defective verb, *he says* or *said,* placed after one or more words of a direct quotation but usually translated first

tóllō, tóllere, sústulī, sublắtum, *to raise, lift up; take away, remove, destroy* (extol; cp. **tolerō, ferō,** Ch. 31)

PRACTICE AND REVIEW

1. Vīcīnī nostrī sē in genua prōtinus iēcērunt et omnēs deōs in mundō laudāvērunt.
2. Gentēs Graeciae ingentibus montibus et parvīs fīnibus continēbantur.
3. Quis iussit illam rem pūblicam servitūte asperā līberārī?
4. "Iste," inquit, "sceleribus suīs brevī tempore tollētur."
5. Contrā aliās manūs malōrum cīvium eaedem rēs iterum parābuntur; rem pūblicam dēfendēmus et istī cito discēdent.
6. Senectūs senēs ā mediīs rēbus saepe prohibet.
7. At rēs gravēs neque vī neque spē geruntur sed cōnsiliō.
8. Sī versūs hōrum duōrum poētārum neglegētis, magnā parte Rōmānārum litterārum carēbitis.
9. Eōdem tempore nostrae spēs salūtis commūnis vestrā fidē altae sunt, spīritūs sublātī sunt, et timōrēs relictī sunt.
10. Nova genera scelerum in hāc urbe inveniuntur quod multī etiam nunc bonīs mōribus et sēnsū commūnī carent ac nātūram sinistram habent.
11. Vulgus multa ex fenestrīs casārum ēiciēbat.
12. Great fidelity can now be found in this commonwealth.
13. His new hopes had been destroyed by the common fear of uncertain things.
14. On that day the courage and the faith of the brave Roman men and women were seen by all.
15. With great hope the tyrant ordered those ships to be destroyed.
16. He could not defend himself with his left hand or his right.

SENTENTIAE ANTĪQUAE

1. Dum vīta est, spēs est. (Cicero.)
2. Aequum animum in rēbus difficilibus servā. (Horace.)
3. Ubi tyrannus est, ibi plānē est nūlla rēs pūblica. (*Cicero.—**plānē**, adv., *clearly.*)
4. Fuērunt quondam in hāc rē pūblicā virī magnae virtūtis et antīquae fideī. (Cicero.)
5. Hanc rem pūblicam salvam esse volumus. (*Cicero.—**volumus**, *we wish.*)
6. Spēs coniūrātōrum mollibus sententiīs multōrum cīvium alitur. (Cicero.—**mollis, -e,** *soft, mild.*)
7. Rēs pūblica cōnsiliīs meīs eō diē ex igne atque ferrō ērepta est. (Cicero.)
8. Quod bellum ōdērunt, prō pāce cum fidē labōrābant. (Livy.)
9. Dīc mihi bonā fidē: tū eam pecūniam ex eius manū dextrā nōn ēripuistī? (Plautus.)
10. Amīcus certus in rē incertā cernitur. (Ennius.)
11. Homērus audītōrem in mediās rēs rapit. (Horace.)
12. Fēlīx est quī potest causās rērum intellegere; et fortūnātus ille quī deōs antīquōs dīligit. (Virgil.)
13. Stōicus noster, "Vitium," inquit, "nōn est in rēbus sed in animō ipsō." (Seneca.—**Stōicus, -ī,** *a Stoic.*)
14. Et mihi rēs subiungam, nōn mē rēbus. (Horace.—**subiungō, -ere,** *to subject.*)
15. Est modus in rēbus; sunt certī fīnēs ultrā quōs virtūs invenīrī nōn potest. (Horace.)
16. Hoc, Fortūna, tibi vidētur aequum? (*Martial.)

A VISIT FROM THE YOUNG INTERNS

Languēbam: sed tū comitātus prōtinus ad mē
    vēnistī centum, Symmache, discipulīs.
Centum mē tetigēre manūs aquilōne gelātae:
    nōn habuī febrem, Symmache, nunc habeō!

(*Martial 5.9; meter: elegiac couplet.—**languēre,** *to be weak, sick.*—**comitātus, -a, -um,** *accompanied (by).*—**Symmachus,** a Greek name, used here for a medical school professor.—**centum . . . discipulīs,** abl. of agent with **comitātus;** the preposition was often omitted in poetry.—**tetigēre = tetigērunt;** for this alternate ending, see Ch. 12.—**aquilō, -lōnis,** m., *the north wind.*—**gelātus, -a, -um,** *chilled,* here modifying **centum . . . manūs;** cp. Eng. gel, gelatin.—**febris, febris,** f., *fever.*)

ON AMBITION AND LITERATURE, BOTH LATIN AND GREEK

Poētae per litterās hominibus magnam perpetuamque fāmam dare possunt; multī virī, igitur, litterās dē suīs rēbus scrībī cupiunt. Trahimur omnēs studiō laudis et multī glōriā dūcuntur, quae aut in litterīs Graecīs aut Latīnīs invenīrī potest. Quī, autem, videt multum frūctum glōriae in versibus Latīnīs sed nōn in Graecīs, nimium errat, quod litterae Graecae leguntur in omnibus ferē gentibus, sed Latīnae in fīnibus suīs continentur.

(Cicero, *Prō Archiā* 11.26, 10.23.—**ferē,** adv., *almost.*)

ETYMOLOGY

Connected with **diēs** is the adj. **diurnus,** *daily,* whence come the words for "day" in Italian and French: It. **giorno,** Fr. **jour, journée;** cp. Sp. **día.** In late Latin there was a form **diurnālis,** from which derive It. **giornale,** Fr. **journal,** Eng. "journal"; cp. Sp. **diario.** English "dismal" stems ultimately from **diēs malus.**

The stem of **fidēs** can be found in the following words even though it may not be immediately obvious: affidavit, defy, affiance, fiancé. Eng. "faith" is from early Old Fr. **feit, feid,** from Latin **fidem.**

Other words connected with **modus** are: modulate, accommodate, commodious, discommode, incommode, à la mode, modus operandi.

In the readings   6. mollify, emollient, mollusk. 13. The Stoic philosophy was so called because Zeno, its founder, used to teach in a certain stoa (portico) at Athens. 14. subjunctive.

LATĪNA EST GAUDIUM—ET ŪTILIS!

Salvēte! Now that you've encountered **merīdiēs,** you understand **a.m.** and **p.m.,** from **ante** and **post merīdiem.** Your physician might prescribe a medication **diēbus alternīs,** *every other day,* or **diēbus tertiīs,** *every third day,* or even **b.i.d.** or **t.i.d., bis in diē** or **ter in diē** (if you've thought about those last two twice or thrice and still can't figure them out, look back at Ch. 15!). Other items you might encounter one of these days: **diem ex diē,** *day by day;* **diēs fēlīx,** *a lucky day;* the legal terms **diēs jūridicus** and **nōn jūridicus,** days when court is and is not in session; and the **Diēs Īrae,** a medieval hymn about the Day of Judgment, part of the requiem mass. And surely you follow Horace's advice every day and **carpe diem** (an agricultural metaphor, since **carpō, carpere** really means *to pluck* or *harvest* from the vine or stalk—so your day, once seized, should be a bountiful cornucopia).

Now you know, too, what is meant by the common phrase, **amīcus certus in rē incertā;** a **bonā fidē** agreement is made *with good faith* (recognize the abl. usage?); and if your "friend indeed" is your trusty dog, you should consider dubbing him "Fido." **Carpite omnēs diēs, discipulī discipulaeque, et valēte!**

23

Participles

Like English, Latin has a set of verbal adjectives, i.e., adjectives formed from a verb stem, called "participles." Regular transitive verbs in Latin have four participles, two of them in the active voice (the present and future), and two in the passive (future and perfect); they are formed as follows:

	Active	**Passive**
Pres.	present stem + **-ns** (gen. **-ntis**)	————
Perf.	————	partic. stem + **-us, -a, -um**
Fut.	participial stem + **-ūrus,** **-ūra, -ūrum**[1]	pres. stem + **-ndus, -nda, -ndum**

It is important to know the proper stem for each participle as well as the proper ending. Note that the present active and the future passive are formed on the present stem, while the perfect passive and future active are formed on the so-called "participial stem" (found by dropping the endings from the perfect passive participle, which is itself most often a verb's fourth principal part: i.e., **laudāt-** from **laudātus, -a, -um**). This pattern can perhaps best be recalled by memorizing the participles of **agō,** in which the difference between the present stem and the participial stem is sufficient to eliminate any confusion. It is also helpful to note that the base of the present participle is marked by **-nt-,** the future active by **-ūr-**[1], and the future passive, often called the "gerundive," by **-nd-.**

---

[1] The ending of the future active participle is very easy to remember if you keep in mind the fact that our word *future* comes from **futūrus, -a, -um,** the future (and, incidentally, the only) participle of sum.

agō, agere, ēgi, āctum, *to lead*

	Active	**Passive**
Pres.	ágēns, agéntis, *leading*	————
Perf.	————	áctus, -a, -um, *led, having been led*
Fut.	āctū́rus, -a, -um, *about to lead, going to lead*	agéndus, -a, -um, *(about)* to be led, deserving or *fit to be led*

English derivatives are illustrative of the sense of three of these participles: "agent" (from **agēns**), *a person doing something;* "act" (**āctus, -a, -um**), *something done;* "agenda" (**agendus, -a, -um**), *something to be done.* The participles of three of the model verbs follow.

	Act.	**Pass.**	**Act.**	**Pass.**	**Act.**	**Pass.**
Pres.	ágēns	————	aúdiēns	————	cápiēns	————
Perf.	————	áctus	————	audítus	————	cáptus
Fut.	āctū́rus	agéndus	audītū́rus	audiéndus	captū́rus	capiéndus

Note carefully that fourth conjugation and third conjugation **-iō** verbs have **-ie-** in both the present active participle (**-iēns, -ientis**) and the future passive (**-iendus, -a, -um**). Notice too that while Latin has present active, perfect passive, and future active and passive participles, the equivalents of *praising, having been praised, about to praise,* and (*about*) *to be praised,* it lacks both a present passive participle (*being praised*) and a perfect active participle (*having praised*).

DECLENSION OF PARTICIPLES

Three of the four participles are declined on the pattern of **magnus, -a, -um.** Only the present participle has third declension forms, following essentially the model of **potēns** (Ch. 16), except that the ablative singular sometimes ends in **-e,** sometimes **-ī**[2]; the vowel before **-ns** in the nominative singular is always long, but before **-nt-** (according to the rule learned earlier) it is always short.

	M. & F.	**N.**
Nom.	ágēns	ágēns
Gen.	agéntis	agéntis
Dat.	agéntī	agéntī
Acc.	agéntem	ágēns
Abl.	agéntī, agénte	agéntī, agénte

[2] The present participle has **-ī** in the ablative singular when used strictly as an attributive adjective (**ā patre amantī**, *by the loving father*) but **-e** when it functions verbally (e.g., with an object, **patre fīlium amante**, *with the father loving his son*) or as a substantive (**ab amante**, *by a lover*).

Nom.	agéntēs	agéntia
Gen.	agéntium	agéntium
Dat.	agéntibus	agéntibus
Acc.	agéntēs	agéntia
Abl.	agéntibus	agéntibus

PARTICIPLES AS VERBAL ADJECTIVES

The etymology of the term participle, from **participere,** *to share in* (**pars + capere**), reflects the fact that participles share in the characteristics of both adjectives and verbs. As *adjectives,* participles naturally agree in gender, number, and case with the words which they modify. Sometimes also, like adjectives, they modify no expressed noun but function as nouns themselves: **amāns,** *a lover;* **sapiēns,** *a wise man, philosopher;* **venientēs,** *those coming.*

As *verbs,* participles have tense and voice; they may take direct objects or other constructions used with the particular verb; and they may be modified by an adverb or an adverbial phrase:

Patrem in casā videntēs, puella et puer ad eum cucurrērunt, *seeing their father in the house, the boy and girl ran up to him.*

In Latin as in English, the tense of a participle, it should be carefully noted, is not absolute but is relative to that of the main verb. For example, the action of a present participle is contemporaneous with the action of the verb of its clause, no matter whether that verb is in a present, a past, or a future tense; in the preceding sample you can see that it was at some time in the past that the children first saw and then ran toward their father (seeing him, i.e., when they saw him, they ran up to him). A similar situation obtains for the perfect and future participles, as can be seen in the following table:

1. Present participle = action *contemporaneous* with that of the verb (the same time).

2. Perfect participle = action *prior* to that of the verb (time before).

3. Future participle = action *subsequent* to that of the verb (time after).

Graecī nautae, videntēs Polyphēmum, timent, timuērunt, timēbunt.
The Greek sailors, seeing Polyphemus, are afraid, were afraid, will be afraid.

Graecī nautae, vīsī ā Polyphēmō, timent, timuērunt, timēbunt.
The Greek sailors, (having been) seen by P., are afraid, were afraid, will be afraid.

Graecī nautae, vīsūrī Polyphēmum, timent, timuērunt, timēbunt.
The Greek sailors, about to see Polyphemus, are afraid, were afraid, will be afraid.

TRANSLATING PARTICIPIAL PHRASES AS CLAUSES

Participial phrases are used much more frequently in Latin than in English, which prefers clauses with regular finite verbs. In translating from Latin to idiomatic English, therefore, it is often preferable to transform a participial phrase (especially if it sounds stilted in English) into a subordinate clause.

In doing so you need to consider 1) the relationship between the action in the phrase and the action in the clause to which it is attached, so that you can then choose an appropriate subordinating conjunction (especially "when," "since," or "although"), and 2) the relativity of participial tenses, so that you can then transform the participle into the appropriate verb tense.

Thus the example given earlier, **patrem in casā videntēs, puella et puer ad eum cucurrērunt,** can be translated *seeing their father in the house, the girl and boy ran up to him* or, more idiomatically, *when they saw their father in the house, the girl and boy ran up to him.* Likewise **Graecī nautae, vīsī ā Polyphēmō, timuērunt** is better translated *when they had been seen* [time prior to main verb] *by Polyphemus, the Greek sailors were afraid* than the more literal *having been seen by Polyphemus, the Greek sailors were afraid.* Consider these further examples:

Māter, fīlium amāns, auxilium dat, *since she loves her son* [lit., *loving her son*], *the mother gives him assistance.*

Pater, fīliam vīsūrus, casam parābat, *since he was about to see his daughter, the father was preparing the house.*

Puella, in casam veniēns, gaudēbat, *when she came into the house* [lit., *coming into the house*], *the girl was happy.*

VOCABULARY

arx, árcis, f., *citadel, stronghold*

dux, dúcis, m., *leader, guide; commander, general* (duke, ducal, ducat, duchess, duchy, doge; cp. **dūcō**)

équus, -ī, m., *horse* (equestrian, equine; cp. **equa, -ae,** *mare*)

hásta, -ae, f., *spear* (hastate)

ínsula, -ae, f., *island* (insular, insularity, insulate, isolate, isolation, peninsula)

lítus, lítoris, n., *shore, coast* (littoral)

míles, mílitis, m., *soldier* (military, militaristic, militate, militant, militia)

ōrátor, ōrātóris, m., *orator, speaker* (oratory, oratorio; cp. **ōrō,** Ch. 36, **ōrātiō,** Ch. 38)

sacérdōs, sacerdótis, m., *priest* (sacerdotal; cp. **sacer,** *sacred*)

áliquis, áliquid (gen. **alicuíus,** dat. **álicui,** etc.; cp. decl. of **quis, quid;** nom. and acc. neut. pl. are **áliqua**), indef. pron., *someone, somebody, something*

quísquis, quídquid (**quis** repeated; cases other than nom. rare), indef. pron., *whoever, whatever*

magnánimus, -a, -um, *great-hearted, brave, magnanimous* (magnanimity)

úmquam, adv., in questions or negative clauses, *ever, at any time* (cp. **numquam**)

édúcō (1), *to bring up, educate* (education, educator, educable; do not confuse with **ēdúcō**, *to lead out*)

gaúdeō, gaudére, gāvísus sum, *to be glad, rejoice* (gaudeamus; cp. **gaudium, -íī,** *joy,* as in **Latīna est gaudium!**)

osténdō, osténdere, osténdī, osténtum, *to exhibit, show, display* (ostentation, ostentatious, ostensible, ostensive; cp. **tendō,** *stretch, extend*)

pétō, pétere, petívī, petítum, *to seek, aim at, beg, beseech* (appetite, compete, competent, impetuous, petition, petulant, repeat; cp. **perpetuus**)

prémō, prémere, préssī, préssum, *to press; press hard, pursue;* **-primō** in compounds as seen in **opprimō** below (compress, depress, express, impress, imprint, print, repress, reprimand, suppress)

ópprimō, -prímere, -préssī, -préssum, *to suppress, overwhelm, overpower, check* (oppress, oppression, oppressive, oppressor)

vértō, vértere, vértī, vérsum, *to turn; change;* so **āvértō,** *turn away, avert,* **revertō,** *turn back,* etc. (adverse, advertise, avert, averse, convert, controversy, divers, diverse, divorce, invert, obverse, pervert, revert, subvert, subversive, transverse, verse, version, animadvert)

PRACTICE AND REVIEW

1. Aliquid numquam ante audītum cernō.
2. Illum ōrātōrem in mediō senātū iterum petentem fīnem bellōrum ac scelerum nōn adiūvistis.
3. Certī frūctūs pācis ab territō vulgō atque senātū cupiēbantur.
4. Quī vir magnanimus aliās gentēs gravī metū servitūtis līberābit?
5. Nēmō fidem neglegēns timōre umquam carēbit.
6. Illa fēmina fortūnāta haec cōnsilia contrā eōs malōs quondam aluit et salūtis commūnis causā semper labōrābat.
7. Illam gentem Latīnam oppressūrī et dīvitiās raptūrī, omnēs virōs magnae probitātis premere ac dēlēre prōtinus coepērunt.
8. Tollēturne fāma huius medicī istīs versibus novīs?
9. At vīta illīus modī aequī aliquid iūcundī atque fēlīcis continet.
10. Quō diē ex igne et ferrō atque morte certā ēreptus es?
11. We gave many things to nations lacking hope.
12. Those ten men, (when) called, will come again with great eagerness.
13. Through the window they saw the second old man running out of his neighbor's house and away from the city.
14. He himself was overpowered by uncertain fear because he desired neither truth nor liberty.

SENTENTIAE ANTĪQUAE

1. Vīvēs meīs praesidiīs oppressus. (Cicero.—**praesidium, -iī,** *guard.*)
2. Illī autem, tendentēs manūs dextrās, salūtem petēbant. (Livy.—**tendō, -ere,** *to stretch, extend.*)
3. Tantalus sitiēns flūmina ab ōre fugientia tangere dēsīderābat. (Horace.—**sitīre,** *to be thirsty.*)
4. Signa rērum futūrārum mundō ā dīs ostenduntur. (Cicero.)
5. Graecia capta asperum victōrem cēpit. (Horace.—**victor, -tōris,** here = Rome.)
6. Atticus Cicerōnī ex patriā fugientī multam pecūniam dedit. (Nepos.—**Atticus,** a friend of Cicero.)
7. Sī mihi eum ēducandum committēs, studia eius fōrmāre ab īnfantiā incipiam. (Quintilian.—**fōrmāre.**—**īnfantia, -ae.**)
8. Saepe stilum verte, bonum libellum scrīptūrus. (Horace.—**stilum vertere,** *to invert the stilus* = to use the eraser.)
9. Cūra ōrātōris dictūrī eōs audītūrōs dēlectat. (Quintilian.)
10. Mortī Sōcratis semper illacrimō, legēns Platōnem. (Cicero.—**Sōcratēs, -cratis.**—**illacrīmāre,** *to weep over.*—**Platō, -tōnis.**)
11. Memoria vītae bene āctae multōrumque bene factōrum iūcunda est. (Cicero.)
12. Quī timēns vīvet, līber nōn erit umquam. (Horace.—**quī,** as often, = **is quī.**)
13. Nōn is est miser quī iussus aliquid facit, sed is quī invītus facit. (Seneca.—**invītus, -a, -um,** *unwilling;* the adj. here has adverbial force, as it commonly does in Latin.)
14. Verbum semel ēmissum volat irrevocābile. (Horace.—**semel,** adv., *once.*—**ē-mittere.**—**volāre,** *to fly.*—**irrevocābilis, -e.**)

LAOCOON SPEAKS OUT AGAINST THE TROJAN HORSE

Oppressī bellō longō et ā deīs aversī, ducēs Graecōrum, iam post decem annōs, magnum equum ligneum arte Minervae faciunt. Uterum multīs mīlitibus complent, equum in lītore relinquunt, et ultrā īnsulam proximam nāvigant. Trōiānī nūllās cōpiās aut nāvēs vident; omnis Trōia gaudet; panduntur portae. Dē equō, autem, Trōiānī sunt incertī. Aliī eum in urbem dūcī cupiunt; aliī eum Graecās īnsidiās appellant. Prīmus ibi ante omnēs, dē arce currēns, Lāocoōn, sacerdōs Trōiānus, haec verba dīcit: "Ō miserī cīvēs, nōn estis sānī! Quid cōgitātis? Nōnne intellegitis Graecōs et īnsidiās eōrum? Aut inveniētis in istō equō multōs mīlitēs ācrēs, aut equus est machina bellī, facta contrā nōs, ventūra in urbem, vīsūra casās nostrās et populum. Aut aliquid latet. Equō nē crēdite, Trōiānī: quidquid id est, timeō Danaōs et dōna gerentēs!" Dīxit, et potentem hastam magnīs vīribus manūs sinistrae in uterum equī iēcit; stetit illa, tremēns.

(Virgil, *Aeneid* 2.13–52; prose adaptation.—**ligneus, -a, -um,** *wooden, of wood.*—Minerva, goddess of war and protectress of the Greeks.—**uterus, -ī.**—**complēre,** *to fill up, make pregnant.*—**proximus, -a, -um,** *nearby.*—**Trōiānus, -a, -um,** *Trojan.*—**pandō, -ere,** *to open.*—**Lāocoōn, -ontis,** m.—**Nōnne** introduces a question anticipating an affirmative answer, *Don't you . . . ?*—**machina, -ae.**—**vīsūra,** here *to spy on.*—**latēre,** *to be hidden, be concealed.*—**equō,** dat. with **crēdite** (see Ch. 35).—**nē = nōn.**—**Danaōs = Graecōs.**—**et** (with **gerentēs**) = **etiam.**—**tremō, -ere,** *to tremble, shake, vibrate.*—To be continued. . . .)

Trojan horse with Greek soldiers
Relief from neck of an amphora, Mykonos, 7th century B.C.
Archaeological Museum, Mykonos, Greece

ETYMOLOGY

In the readings
2. tend, tent, tense, attend, contend, distend, extend, extent, extensive, intend, intent, intense, portend, pretend, subtend, superintendent; cp. **ostendō** in the vocabulary. 3. tantalize, Gk. derivative. 8. stilus, style. 10. lachrymose. 14. volatile, volley. "Laocoon": uterine.—complete, completion, complement, complementary.—proximity, approximate.—expand, expansive.—machine, machinery, machination.—latent.—tremor, tremulous, tremulant, tremble, tremendous.

LATĪNA EST GAUDIUM—ET ŪTILIS!

Salvēte! This chapter's Vocab. suggests a couple of literary titles from ancient Rome: among Cicero's dozens of books was a rhetorical treatise titled **Dē Ōrātōre,** and one of Plautus' most popular plays was the **Mīles Glōriōsus,** usually translated *The Braggart Soldier.* Then there's the medieval student song with the famous line (quite apt for college Latin students) **gaudeāmus, igitur, iuvenēs dum sumus,** *so let us rejoice, while we are young!*

From **vertere** is **verte** for *turn the page* and **versō** for the left-hand page in a book (i.e., the side you see when you have just *turned* the page); printers call the the right-hand page the **rectō.**

And from the reading passage: the expression "a Trojan horse" is used of any person, group, or device that tries to subvert a government or any organization from within. Also from the Trojan saga and Virgil's story of Aeneas' sojourn in Carthage is the famous quotation **dux fēmina factī,** *a woman (was) leader of the action!* **Gaudēte atque valēte!**

Athena (Minerva) constructing the Trojan horse
Red-figure Greek kylix, the Sabouroff Painter, 470–460 B.C.
Museo Archeologico, Florence, Italy

24

Ablative Absolute; Passive Periphrastic; Dative of Agent

The participles which you learned in the last chapter were employed by the Romans in two very common constructions introduced below, the "ablative absolute" and the "passive periphrastic."

ABLATIVE ABSOLUTE

The ablative absolute is a type of participial phrase generally consisting of a noun (or pronoun) and a modifying participle in the ablative case; somewhat loosely connected to the rest of the sentence (hence the term, from **absolūtum,** *loosened from, separated*) and usually set off by commas, the phrase describes some general circumstances under which the action of the sentence occurs.

Rōmā vīsā, virī gaudēbant, *Rome having been seen, the men rejoiced.*

As typified by this example, the ablative absolute always is self-contained, i.e., the participle and the noun it modifies are both in the same phrase and the noun of the ablative absolute phrase is not referred to at all in the attached clause. In other types of participial phrases (such as those seen in

Ch. 23), the participles modify some noun or pronoun in the attached clause; compare the following example, which has an ordinary participial phrase, with the previous example:

Rōmam videntēs, virī gaudēbant, *seeing Rome, the men rejoiced.*

In this instance the participle modifies the subject of the main clause, and so an ablative absolute cannot be used.

Like other participial phrases, the ablative absolute can be translated quite literally, as in **Rōmā vīsā,** (*with*) *Rome having been seen.* Often, however, it is better style to transform the phrase to a clause, converting the participle to a verb in the appropriate tense, treating the ablative noun as its subject, and supplying the most logical conjunction (usually "when," "since," or "although"), as explained in the last chapter; thus, a more idiomatic translation of **Rōmā vīsā, virī gaudēbant** would be *when Rome was (had been) seen, the men rejoiced.* Compare the following additional examples:

Hīs rēbus audītīs, coepit timēre.
   These things having been heard, he began to be afraid.

Or in much better English:
   When (since, after, etc., depending on the context) these things had been heard, he began . . .
   When (since, after, etc.) he had heard these things, he began . . .

Eō imperium tenente, ēventum timeō.
   With him holding the power,
   Since he holds the power,
   When he holds the power, ⎫ *I fear the outcome.*
   If he holds the power,
   Although he holds the power. ⎭

In the ablative absolute, the ablative noun/pronoun regularly comes first, the participle last; when the phrase contains additional words, like the direct object of the participle in the preceding example, they are usually enclosed within the noun/participle "frame."

As seen in the following examples, even two nouns, or a noun and an adjective, can function as an ablative absolute, with the present participle of **sum** (lacking in classical Latin) to be understood:

Caesare duce, nihil timēbimus.
   Caesar being the commander,
   Under Caesar's command, ⎫ *we shall fear nothing.*
   With Caesar in command,
   Since (when, if, etc.) Caesar is the commander, ⎭

Caesare incertō, bellum timēbāmus.

Since Caesar was uncertain (with Caesar uncertain), we were afraid of war.

THE PASSIVE PERIPHRASTIC CONJUGATION: GERUNDIVE + *Sum*

Despite its horrendous name, the passive periphrastic conjugation is simply a passive verb form consisting of the gerundive (i.e., the future passive participle) along with a form of **sum.**[1] The gerundive, as a predicate adjective, agrees with the subject of **sum** in gender, number, and case, e.g., **haec fēmina laudanda est,** *this woman is to be praised.*

The gerundive often conveys an idea of necessary, obligatory, or appropriate action, rather than simple futurity, and this is the case in the passive periphrastic construction. Hence **id faciendum est** means not simply *this is about to be done,* but rather *this has to be done;* **hic liber cum cūrā legendus erit,** *this book will have to be (must be) read with care.*

Just as Latin uses the auxiliary **sum** in its various tenses in this construction, English commonly uses the expressions "has to be," "had to be," "will have to be"; "should," "ought," and "must" are other auxiliaries commonly used in translating the passive periphrastic (cp. **dēbeō,** which, as you have already learned, is also used to indicate obligatory action).

THE DATIVE OF AGENT

Instead of the ablative of agent, the dative of agent is used with the passive periphrastic. A literal translation of the passive periphrastic + dative of agent generally sounds awkward, and so it is often best to transform such a clause into an active construction; consider the following examples:

Hic liber mihi cum cūrā legendus erit, *this book will have to be read by me with care* or (better) *I will have to (ought to, must, should) read this book with care.*

---

[1] The word "periphrasis" (adj. "periphrastic") comes from the Gk. equivalent of Lat. **circumlocūtiō,** *a roundabout way of speaking,* and simply refers to the form's construction from a participle plus **sum** as an auxiliary (even "did sing" in Eng. is a periphrastic for "sang"); the entire perfect passive system is similarly "periphrastic," consisting of **sum** + the perfect passive participle rather than the gerundive (be careful not to confuse the two: the pass. periphrastic will always contain an **-nd-** gerundive).

Illa fēmina omnibus laudanda est, *that woman should be praised by all* or *everyone should praise that woman.*

Pāx ducibus nostrīs petenda erat, *peace had to be sought by our leaders* or *our leaders had to seek peace.*

VOCABULARY

Carthágō, Cartháginis, f., *Carthage* (a city in North Africa)

fábula, -ae, f., *story, tale; play* (fable, fabulous, confabulate; cp. **fāma**)

imperátor, imperātóris, m., *general, commander-in-chief, emperor* (cp. **parō, imperium, imperō,** Ch. 35)

impérium, -iī, n., *power to command, supreme power, authority, command, control* (imperial, imperialism, imperious, empire)

perfúgium, -iī, n., *refuge, shelter* (cp. **fugiō**)

sérvus, -ī, m., and **sérva, -ae,** f., *slave* (serf, servant, servile, service; cp. **serviō,** Ch. 35)

sōlácium, -iī, n., *comfort, relief* (solace, consolation, inconsolable)

vúlnus, vúlneris, n., *wound* (vulnerable, invulnerable)

re- or **red-,** prefix, *again, back* (recede, receive, remit, repeat, repel, revert)

ut, conj. + indic., *as, just as, when*

pósteā, adv., *afterwards* (cp. **post**)

accípiō, -cípere, -cḗpī, -céptum, *to take* (to one's self), *receive, accept* (cp. **capiō**)

excípiō, -cípere, -cḗpī, -céptum, *to take out, except; take, receive, capture* (exception, exceptionable)

recípiō, -cípere, -cḗpī, -céptum, *to take back, regain; admit, receive* (recipe, R$_x$, receipt, recipient, receptacle, reception)

péllō, péllere, pépulī, púlsum, *to strike, push; drive out, banish* (compel, compulsion, compulsory, dispel, expel, impel, propel, repel, pelt, pulsate, pulse)

expéllō, -péllere, -pulī, -púlsum, *to drive out, expel, banish* (expulsion)

nárrō (1), *to tell, report, narrate* (narration, narrative, narrator)

quaérō, quaérere, quaesívī, quaesítum, *to seek, look for, strive for, ask, inquire, inquire into* (acquire, conquer, exquisite, inquire, inquest, inquisition, perquisite, query, quest, question, request, require)

rídeō, rīdḗre, rísī, rísum, *to laugh, laugh at* (deride, derisive, ridicule, ridiculous, risibilities; cf. **rīdiculus,** Ch. 30, **subrīdeō,** Ch. 35)

PRACTICE AND REVIEW

1. Igne vīsō, omnēs virī et uxōrēs territae sunt et ultrā urbem ad lītus īnsulae nāvigāvērunt, ubi perfugium inventum est.

2. Populō metū oppressō, iste imperātor nōbīs ex urbe pellendus est.

3. Ōrātor, signō ā sacerdōte datō, eō diē revēnit et nunc tōtus populus Latīnus gaudet.
4. Gēns Rōmāna versūs illīus scrīptōris magnā laude quondam recēpit.
5. Laudēs atque dōna huius modī ab ōrātōribus dēsīderābantur.
6. Imperiō acceptō, dux magnanimus fidem suam reī pūblicae ostendit.
7. Aliquis eōs quīnque equōs ex igne ēripī posteā iusserat.
8. Cernisne omnia quae tibi scienda sunt?
9. Ille, ab arce urbis reveniēns, ab istīs hominibus premī coepit.
10. Cupiō tangere manum illīus mīlitis quī metū caruit atque gravia scelera contrā rem pūblicam oppressit.
11. Iste dux prōtinus expulsus est, ut imperium excipiēbat.
12. Illae servae, autem, perfugium sōlāciumque ab amīcīs quaerēbant.
13. Cornū audītō, ille mīles, incertus cōnsiliī, cōpiās ad mediam īnsulam vertit.
14. When the common danger had been averted, two of our sons and all our daughters came back from Asia.
15. Our hopes must not be destroyed by those three evil men.
16. Since the people of all nations are seeking peace, all leaders must conquer the passion for (= of) power. (Use an ablative absolute and a passive periphrastic.)
17. The leader, having been driven out by both the free men and the slaves, could not regain his command.

SENTENTIAE ANTĪQUAE

1. Carthāgō dēlenda est. (Cato.)
2. Asiā victā, dux Rōmānus fēlīx multōs servōs in Italiam mīsit. (Pliny the Elder.)
3. Omnibus ferrō mīlitis perterritīs, quisque sē servāre cupiēbat. (Caesar.)
4. Quidquid dīcendum est, līberē dīcam. (Cicero.—**līberē,** adv. of **līber.**)
5. Haec omnia vulnera bellī tibi nunc sānanda sunt. (Cicero.—**sānāre,** *to heal.*)
6. Nec tumultum nec hastam mīlitis nec mortem violentam timēbō, Augustō terrās tenente. (Horace.—**tumultus -ūs,** *disturbance, civil war.*—**violentus, -a, -um.**—**Augustus, -ī.**)
7. Tarquiniō expulsō, nōmen rēgis audīre nōn poterat populus Rōmānus. (Cicero.)
8. Ad ūtilitātem vītae omnia cōnsilia factaque nōbīs regenda sunt. (Tacitus.—**ūtilitās, -tātis,** *benefit, advantage.*)

DĒ CUPIDITĀTE

Homō stultus, "Ō cīvēs, cīvēs," inquit, "pecūnia ante omnia quaerenda est; virtūs et probitās post pecūniam."

Pecūniae autem cupiditās fugienda est. Fugienda etiam est cupiditās glōriae; ēripit enim lībertātem. Neque imperia semper petenda sunt neque semper accipienda; etiam dēpōnenda nōn numquam.

(Horace, *Epistulae* 1.1.53, and Cicero, *Dē Officiīs* 1.20.68.—**dēpōnō, -ere,** *to put down, resign.*)

Caelō receptus propter virtūtem, Herculēs multōs deōs salūtāvit; sed Plūtō veniente, quī Fortūnae est fīlius, āvertit oculōs. Tum, causā quaesītā, "Ōdī," inquit, "illum, quod malīs amīcus est atque omnia corrumpit lucrī causā."

(Phaedrus, *Fābulae* 4.12.—**Herculēs, -lis.**—**salūtāre,** *to greet.*—**Plūtus, -ī,** god of wealth.—**Fortūnae,** here personified.—**corrumpō, -ere,** *to corrupt.*—**lucrum, -ī,** *gain, profit.*)

Heracles (Hercules) fighting the Nemean lion, one of his 12 labors
Attic black-figure kalpis, Early 5th century B.C.
Kunsthistorisches Museum, Vienna, Austria

THE SATIRIST'S MODUS OPERANDI

Rīdēns saturās meās percurram, et cūr nōn? Quid vetat mē rīdentem dīcere vērum, ut puerīs ēducandīs saepe dant crūstula magistrī? Quaerō rēs gravēs iūcundō lūdō et, nōminibus fictīs, dē multīs culpīs vitiīsque nārrō. Sed quid rīdēs? Mūtātō nōmine, dē tē fābula nārrātur!

(Horace, *Sermōnēs* 1.1.23–27, 69–70; prose adaptation.—**per + currō.**—**vetāre,** *to forbid.*—**puerīs . . . magistrī,** the order of the nouns is varied for effect: indirect obj., direct obj., subject.—**crūstulum, -ī,** *cookie, pastry.*—**fingō, -ere, fīnxī, fictum,** *to form, invent, make up.*)

ETYMOLOGY

In the readings

6. tumultuous.—"Violent" is clearly based on **vīs.**—Originally the Romans, counting March as the first month of the year, named the fifth month **Quīntīlis** (**quīntus,** *fifth*), but Julius Caesar renamed it **Iūlius** (July) because he was born in July. Subsequently, when the Roman Senate gave Octavian, Caesar's heir, the title of "Augustus" (the august, the revered one), the Senate also changed the name of the sixth month (**Sextīlis**) to **Augustus** (August). "**Dē Cupiditāte**": Herculean—salute; cp. **salvēre, salūs.**—plutocrat, a word of Gk. origin.—lucre, lucrative.—"The Satirist": veto.—crust.—fiction, fictitious, fictive.

LATĪNA EST GAUDIUM—ET ŪTILIS!

Salvēte, amīcae amīcīque! Quid agitis hodiē? Bet you didn't know that R$_x$ and "recipe" came from the same word (see **recipiō** in the Vocab.), but now, thanks to Latin, you do! There are countless derivatives from the **capiō** family, as you have seen already; and from **excipere** there are some "exceptionally" familiar phrases: **exceptiō probat regulam,** *the exception proves the rule,* and **exceptīs excipiendīs,** *with all the necessary exceptions* (lit., *with things excepted that should be excepted:* recognize the gerundive?). And, by analogy with this last, what are the idiomatic and the literal meanings of the very common phrase **mūtātīs mūtandīs?** (If you can't figure that out, it's in your Webster's, along with hundreds of other Latin phrases, mottoes, words, and abbreviations in current Eng. usage!)

Some other gerundives that pop up in Eng.: **agenda** (*things to be done*), **corrigenda** (*things to be corrected,* i.e., an **errāta** list), and even the passive periphrastics **dē gustibus nōn disputandum est,** sometimes shortened simply to **dē gustibus** (*you can't argue about taste*), and **quod erat dēmōnstrandum** (which we've seen before), abbreviated **Q.E.D.** at the end of a mathematical proof.

Servus, also in the new Vocab., gives us one of the Pope's titles, **servus servōrum deī** (another is **pontifex,** the name of an ancient Roman priestly office, which may originally have meant *bridge-builder*—because priests bridge the gap between men and gods?); and **quaere** is used in Eng. as a note to request further information. **Nunc est satis: valēte atque semper rīdēte!**

25

Infinitives; Indirect Statement

INFINITIVES

Having surveyed the forms and uses of the verbal adjectives known as participles in the last two chapters, we turn now to the common verbal noun known as the infinitive (e.g., **amāre,** *to love*—two other verbal nouns, the supine and the gerund, are introduced in Chs. 38–39). Most transitive verbs have six infinitives, the present, future, and perfect, active and passive, though the future passive is rare[1]; intransitive verbs usually lack the passive. You are already familiar with the present active and passive infinitives, whose forms vary with each of the four conjugations; the perfect and future infinitives are all formed according to the following patterns, regardless of conjugation:

	Active	Passive
Pres.	**-āre, -ēre, -ere, -īre**[2]	**-ārī, -ērī, -ī, -īrī**
Perf.	perfect stem + **-isse**	perf. pass. participle + **esse**
Fut.	fut. act. participle + **esse**	[supine in **-um** + **īrī**][3]

[1] In other words, there are active and passive infinitives for each of the three basic time frames, past, present, and future; contrast participles, which lack present passive and perfect active forms.

[2] Actually, the ending of the present active infinitive is **-re,** which is added to the present stem; but for purposes of distinction it is convenient to include here the stem vowel as well.

[3] The future passive infinitive is given in brackets here because it is not a common form and does not occur in this book. The Romans preferred a substitute expression like **fore ut** + subjunctive (result clause). The supine in **-um** has the same spelling as that of the perf. pass. part. in the nom. neut. sg.

INFINITIVES OF agō, agere, ēgī, āctum, *to lead*

	Active	**Passive**
Pres.	ágere, *to lead*	ágī, *to be led*
Perf.	ēgísse, *to have led*	áctus, -a, -um[4] ésse, *to have been led*
Fut.	āctū́rus, -a, -um[4] ésse, *to be about to lead, to be going to lead*	áctum írī, *to be about to be led, to be going to be led*

The literal translations of the six infinitives given above are conventional; in actual use (especially in indirect statement, as explained below) the perfect and particularly the future infinitives are rarely translated literally.

The infinitives of the other model verbs are as follows:

Active

Pres.	laudā́re	monḗre	audī́re	cápere
Perf.	laudāvísse	monuísse	audīvísse	cēpísse
Fut.	laudātū́rus, -a, -um, ésse	monitū́rus, -a, -um, ésse	audītū́rus, -a, -um, ésse	captū́rus, -a, -um, ésse

Passive

Pres.	laudā́rī	monḗrī	audī́rī	cápī
Perf.	laudā́tus, -a, -um, ésse	mónitus, -a, -um, ésse	audī́tus, -a, -um, ésse	cáptus, -a, -um, ésse
Fut.	laudā́tum írī	mónitum írī	audī́tum írī	cáptum írī

USAGE

As a verbal noun, an infinitive can function in a variety of ways. We have seen its use as a subject (**errāre est humānum,** *to err is human*) and as a complement with such verbs as **possum** and **dēbeō** (**discēdere nunc possunt,** *they can leave now*—Ch. 6), and the infinitive, with its own accusative subject, can also serve as a direct object (**iussit eōs venīre,** *he ordered them to come:* see S.S., p. 445). One of the commonest uses of the infinitive, however, is in a construction known as "indirect statement."

---

[4] The participles are regarded as predicate adjectives and so are made to agree with the subject of **esse.**

INFINITIVE IN INDIRECT STATEMENT WITH ACCUSATIVE SUBJECT

An indirect statement simply reports indirectly (i.e., not in direct quotation) what someone has said, thought, felt, etc. The following is a *direct* statement, made by a teacher:

Julia is a good student.

Here the teacher's comment is *directly* reported or quoted:

"Julia is a good student," says the teacher.
The teacher said, "Julia is a good student."

Latin also uses direct quotations with certain verbs of speaking, etc., including **inquit** (Ch. 22 Vocab.):

"Iūlia," magister inquit, "est discipula bona."

Often, however, both Latin and English will report someone's remarks (or thoughts or feelings) indirectly. In English we regularly put such indirect statements into a subordinate clause introduced by *that:*

The teacher says that Julia is a good student.
The teacher said that Julia was a good student.

Latin, on the other hand, uses no introductory word for *that* and employs an infinitive phrase with an accusative subject, instead of a clause:

Magister dīcit Iūliam esse discipulam bonam.
Magister dīxit Iūliam esse discipulam bonam.

This indirect statement construction is regularly employed in Latin after verbs of "speech," "mental activity," or "sense perception" (i.e., saying, thinking, knowing, perceiving, feeling, seeing, hearing, etc.: see the list of Latin verbs following the Vocab.). English uses a similar objective case + infinitive construction after a few verbs of this type (e.g., "the teacher considers *her to be* a good student"), but in classical Latin this pattern is always followed and the accusative subject is always expressed, even when it is the same as the subject of the verb of *saying,* etc. (in which case the subject is ordinarily a reflexive pronoun):

Iūlia putat sē esse bonam discipulam, *Julia thinks that she (herself) is a good student.*

Recognizing indirect statements is easy: look for the main verb of speech, mental activity, or sense perception with an accusative + infinitive phrase following. The greater challenge is in translation, since you must nearly always supply *that* and convert the infinitive phrase into a regular clause, as in the above examples, where literal translations (e.g., *the teacher says Julia to be a good student* or *Julia thinks herself to be a good student*) would not produce idiomatic English. After supplying *that* and translating the accusative subject as if it were a nominative, you must then transform the infinitive into a regular finite verb *in the correct tense,* noting that tenses of the infinitive, like those of the participle, are relative not absolute.

INFINITIVE TENSES IN INDIRECT STATEMENT

Study carefully the *tenses* in the following groups of sentences.

1. Dīcunt— *They say*	A. eum **iuvāre** eam.	*that he is helping her.*
	B. eum **iūvisse** eam.	*that he helped her.*
	C. eum **iūtūrum esse** eam.	*that he will help her.*

2. Dīxērunt— *They said*	A. eum **iuvāre** eam.	*that he was helping her.*
	B. eum **iūvisse** eam.	*that he had helped her.*
	C. eum **iūtūrum esse** eam.	*that he would help her.*

3. Dīcent— *They will say*	A. eum **iuvāre** eam.	*that he is helping her.*
	B. eum **iūvisse** eam.	*that he helped her.*
	C. eum **iūtūrum esse** eam.	*that he will help her.*

You probably noticed that after any tense of the main verb (*dīcunt, dīxērunt, dīcent*) the present, the perfect, or the future tense of the infinitive may be used. This fact shows that the tenses of the infinitive are not absolute but are relative.

To put it another way, *regardless of the tense of the main verb:*

1. the *present infinitive* indicates the *same time as* that of the main verb (= contemporaneous infinitive).

2. the *perfect infinitive* indicates *time before* that of the main verb (= prior infinitive).

3. the *future infinitive* indicates *time after* that of the main verb (= subsequent infinitive).

Here are some further examples; note carefully the translation of tenses, the use of reflexives, the agreement of participial endings with the accusative subjects, and the use in one instance of the passive periphrastic infinitive (gerundive + **esse,** to indicate obligatory action).

Gāius dīcit **sē** iūvisse eam,
*Gaius **says** that he (Gaius) **helped** her.*

Gāius dīxit **eum** iūvisse eam,
*Gaius **said** that he (e.g., Marcus) **had helped** her.*

Gāius dīcit litterās ā sē scrīptās esse,
*G. **says** that the letter **was written** by him (Gaius).*

Gāius dīcit litterās tibi scrībendās esse,
*G. **says** that the letter **ought to be written** by you (or that you ought to write the letter).*

Discipulī putant sē linguam Latīnam amātūrōs esse,
*the (male) students **think** that they **will love** the Latin language.*

Magistra scīvit discipulās Latīnam amātūrās esse,
*the (female) teacher **knew** that the (female) students **would love** Latin.*

VOCABULARY

língua, -ae, f., *tongue; language* (linguist, linguistics, bilingual, lingo, linguine: see **Latīna Est Gaudium,** Ch. 14)

férōx, gen. **ferócis,** *fierce, savage* (ferocious, ferocity; cp. **ferus, -ī,** *beast*)

fidélis, fidéle, *faithful, loyal* (fidelity, infidelity, infidel; cp. **fidēs**)

géminus, -a, -um, *twin* (geminate, gemination, Gemini)

sápiēns, gen. **sapiéntis,** as adj., *wise, judicious;* as noun, *a wise man, philosopher* (homo sapiens, sapience, insipience, sapid, insipid, verbum sapienti, savant, sage; cp. **sapientia, sapiō,** Ch. 35)

últimus, -a, -um, *farthest, extreme; last, final* (ultimate, ultimatum, penultimate, antepenult)

déhinc, adv., *then, next*

hīc, adv., *here*

áit, áiunt, *he says, they say, assert,* commonly used in connection with proverbs and anecdotes (adage)

crédō, crédere, crédidī, créditum + acc. or (Ch. 35) dat., *to believe, trust* (credence, credentials, credible, incredible, credulity, credulous, creed, credibility, credo, credit, creditable, accreditation, miscreant, grant)

iáceō, iacére, iácuī, *to lie; lie prostrate; lie dead* (adjacent, adjacency, interjacent, subjacent, gist, joist; do not confuse with **iaciō, iacere**)

négō (1), *to deny, say that . . . not* (negate, negative, abnegate, renegade, renege, denial, runagate)

néscīō, nescíre, nescívī, nescítum, *not to know, be ignorant* (nice; cp. **sciō**)

núntiō (1), *to announce, report, relate* (denounce, enunciate, pronounce, renounce, nuncio; cp. **prōnūntiō, nūntius, -ī,** *messenger*)

patefáciō, -fácere, -fécī, -fáctum, *to make open, open; disclose, expose*

pútō (1), *to reckon, suppose, judge, think, imagine* (compute, count, account, depute, dispute, impute, putative, repute, amputate)

spḗrō (1), *to hope for, hope,* regularly + fut. inf. in ind. state. (despair, desperado, desperate, desperation, prosper; cp. **spēs.**)

suscípiō, -cípere, -cḗpī, -céptum (sub-capiō), *to undertake* (susceptible, susceptibility)

LIST OF VERBS CAPABLE OF INTRODUCING INDIRECT STATEMENT[5]

1. *saying:* dḯcō, négō, áit, nū́ntiō, prōnū́ntiō, nárrō, scrī́bō, dóceō, osténdō, dēmṓnstrō, móneō, pétō
2. *knowing:* scíō, néscíō, intéllegō, memóriā téneō, díscō
3. *thinking:* cérnō, cṓgitō, crḗdō, hábeō, pútō, spḗrō
4. *perceiving and feeling:* aúdiō, vídeō, séntiō, gaúdeō

PRACTICE AND REVIEW

1. "Quisque," inquit, "semper putat suās rēs esse magnās."
2. Posteā audīvimus servōs dōnōrum causā labōrāvisse, ut mīlitēs fidēlēs herī narrāverant.
3. Vīcīnī nostrī vim ignis magnā virtūte dehinc āvertērunt, quod laudem atque dōna cupīvērunt.
4. Hoc signum perīculī tōtam gentem nostram tanget, nisi hostem ex urbe excipere ac ab Italiā pellere poterimus.
5. Duce ferōcī Carthāginis expulsō, spēs fidēsque virōrum magnanimōrum rem pūblicam continēbunt.
6. Cūr iūcundus Horātius culpās hūmānās in saturīs semper ostendēbat atque rīdēbat?
7. Crēdimus fidem antīquam omnibus gentibus iterum alendam esse.
8. Dux, ad senātum missus, imperium accēpit et imperātor factus est.
9. Rēs pūblica, ut āit, libellīs huius modī tollī potest.
10. Aliquī negant hostēs victōs servitūte umquam opprimendōs esse.
11. Crēdunt magistram sapientem vēritātem patefactūram esse.
12. Quisquis vēritātem recipiet bene ēducābitur.
13. We thought that your sisters were writing the letter.
14. They will show that the letter was written by the brave slavegirl.
15. He said that the letter had never been written.
16. We hope that the judge's wife will write those two letters tomorrow.

SENTENTIAE ANTĪQUAE

1. Id factum esse tum nōn negāvit. (Terence.)
2. Hīs rēbus prōnūntiātīs, igitur, eum esse hostem scīvistī. (Cicero.)

---

[5] Others to be introduced later are **respondeō,** *answer;* **cognōscō,** *learn, know;* **arbitror,** *think;* **opīnor,** *think, suppose;* **prōmittō,** *promise;* **dēcernō,** *decide;* **doleō,** *grieve.*

3. Eum ab hostibus exspectārī nunc sentīs. (Cicero.)

4. Vīdī eōs in urbe remānsisse et nōbīscum esse. (Cicero.)

5. Itaque aeternum bellum cum malīs cīvibus ā mē susceptum esse cernō. (Cicero.)

6. Idem crēdō tibi faciendum esse. (Cicero.)

7. Tē enim esse fidēlem mihi sciēbam. (Terence.)

8. Hostibus sē in cīvitātem vertentibus, senātus Cincinnātō nūntiāvit eum factum esse dictātōrem. (Cicero.—**Cincinnātus, -ī.—dictātor, -tōris.**)

9. Dīcō tē, Pyrrhe, Rōmānōs posse vincere. (Ennius.—**Pyrrhus, -ī.**)

10. Dīc, hospes, Spartae tē nōs hīc iacentēs vīdisse, patriae fidēlēs. (Cicero; epigram on the Spartans who died at Thermopylae.—**hospes, -pitis,** m., *stranger.*—**Spartae,** *to Sparta.*)

11. Sōcratēs putābat sē esse cīvem tōtīus mundī. (Cicero.)

12. Illī magistrī negant quemquam virum esse bonum nisi sapientem. (Cicero.—**quisquam, quidquam,** *anyone, anything; any.*)

13. Negāvī, autem, mortem timendam esse. (Cicero.)

14. Crēdō deōs immortālēs sparsisse spīritūs in corpora hūmāna. (Cicero.—**spargō, -ere, sparsī, sparsum,** *to scatter, sow.*)

15. Adulēscēns spērat sē diū vīctūrum esse; senex potest dīcere sē diū vīxisse. (Cicero.—Do not confuse **vīctūrum,** from **vīvō,** with **victūrum,** from **vincō**).

16. Āiunt enim multum legendum esse, nōn multa. (*Pliny.)

THE DEATH OF LAOCOON . . . AND TROY

Hīc alius magnus timor (Ō fābula misera!) animōs caecōs nostrōs terret. Lāocoōn, sacerdōs Neptūnī fortūnā factus, ācrem taurum ad āram in lītore mactābat. Tum geminī serpentēs potentēs, mare prementēs, ab īnsulā ad lītora currunt. Iamque agrōs tenēbant et, oculīs igne ardentibus, ōra linguīs sībilīs lambēbant.

Nōs omnēs fugimus; illī viā certā Lāocoonta fīliōsque eius petunt. Prīmum parva corpora duōrum puerōrum capiunt et lacerant necantque dēvōrantque. Tum patrem fortem, ad fīliōs miserōs currentem, rapiunt et magnīs spīrīs tenent et superant. Nec sē ā vulneribus dēfendere nec fugere potest, et ipse, ut taurus saucius ad āram, clāmōrēs horrendōs ad caelum tollit. Eōdem tempore serpentēs fugiunt, petuntque perfugium in arce Minervae ācris.

Quod Lāocoōn in equum Minervae hastam iēcerat, nōs putāvimus eum errāvisse et poenās dedisse; vēritātem acerbam nescīvimus. Portās patefacimus et admittimus istum equum in urbem; atque puerī puellaeque—Ō patria, Ō dī magnī, Ō Trōia!—eum tangere gaudent. Et quoque gaudēmus nōs miserī, quibus ille diēs fuit ultimus ac quibus numquam erit ūllum sōlācium.

(Virgil, *Aeneid* 2.199–249; prose adaptation.—**Lāocoōn, -ontis,** m.—**Neptūnus,** god of the sea, took the side of the Greeks in the Trojan war.—**taurus, -ī,** *bull.*—**āra, -ae,** *altar.*—**mactāre,** *to sacrifice, sacrificially slaughter.*—**serpēns, -pentis,** m.—**ardēre,** *to blaze.*—**sībilus, -a, -um,** *hissing.*—**lambō, -ere,** *to lick.*—**Lāo-coonta,** Gk. acc.—**prīmum,** adv. of **prīmus.**—**lacerāre,** *to tear to pieces, mangle.*—**dēvōrāre,** *to devour.*—**spīra, -ae,** *coil.*—**saucius, -a, -um,** *wounded.*—**clāmor, -mōris,** *shout, scream.*—**horrendus, -a, -um.**)

The Laocoon group
Roman copy, perhaps after Agesander, Athenodorus, and Polydorus of Rhodes
1st century B.C., Vatican Museums, Vatican State

ETYMOLOGY

In the readings   8. propinquity.—"Cincinnati," both the organization composed originally of the officers who served under George Washington and also the city named after the organization. 9. Pyrrhus, the Greek general, defeated the Romans twice, but the victories cost him almost as many men as they cost the Romans; hence the term "Pyrrhic victory." 14. aspersion, disperse, intersperse, sparse. "Laocoon": toreador.—serpent, serpentine; "herpes" is cognate.—lambent.—lacerate, laceration.—voracious.—spire, spiral.—clamor, clamorous; cp. **clāmāre, dēclāmāre, exclāmāre.**—horrendous.

LATĪNA EST GAUDIUM—ET ŪTILIS!

Quid agitis hodiē, amīcī et amīcae? Also from **iacēre** in the new Vocab. is the phrase **hīc iacet,** *here lies . . . ,* often inscribed on tombstones (sometimes spelled **hic jacet** and mistaken to mean *a country boy's sportcoat!*). And here are some other well-known mottoes and phrases: **dum spīrō, spērō,** *while I breathe, I hope* (South Carolina's state motto—the verb **spīrāre** is related to **spīritus,** Ch. 20, and gives us "conspire," "expire," "inspire," "perspire," "respiratory," "transpire," etc.); **crēde Deō,** *trust in God* (for **crēdere** + dat., see Ch. 35); and It. **lingua franca,** lit. *Frankish language,* used of any hybrid language that is employed for communication among different cultures. **Spīrāte, spērāte, rīdēte, atque valēte!**

Trojan horse fresco from the House of Menander
Pompeii, mid- to late 1st century A.D.
Museo Archeologico Nazionale, Naples, Italy

26

Comparison of Adjectives; Declension of Comparatives; Ablative of Comparison

COMPARISON OF ADJECTIVES

The adjective forms you have learned thus far indicate a basic characteristic (a quality or quantity) associated with the modified noun, e.g., **vir beātus,** *a happy man.* This is called the "positive degree" of the adjective.

In Latin, as in English, an adjective may be "compared" in order to indicate whether a person or thing being described has a greater degree of a particular characteristic than some other person(s) or thing(s), or more than is usual or customary. When comparing a person/thing with just one other, the "comparative degree" is used: **vir beātior,** *the happier man.* When comparing a person/thing with two or more others, the "superlative degree" is employed: **vir beātissimus,** *the happiest man.*

FORMATION OF THE COMPARATIVE AND THE SUPERLATIVE

The form of the positive degree is learned from the vocabulary. The forms of the comparative and the superlative of regular adjectives are ordinarily made on the *base* of the positive, which is identified, as you know, by dropping the ending of the genitive singular.[1]

---

[1] Occasionally an adjective is compared by adding **magis** (*more*) and **maximē** (*most*) to the positive. This is regular in adjectives like **idōneus, -a, -um** (*suitable*) where a vowel precedes the endings: **magis idōneus, maximē idōneus.**

Comparative: base of positive + **-ior** (m. & f.), **-ius** (n.); **-iōris,** gen.
Superlative: base of positive + **-issimus, -issima, -issimum**

Positive	Comparative	Superlative
cárus, -a, -um (*dear*)	cárior, -ius (*dearer*)	cāríssimus, -a, -um (*dearest*)
lóngus, -a, -um (*long*)	lóngior, -ius (*longer*)	longíssimus, -a, -um (*longest*)
fórtis, -e (*brave*)	fórtior, -ius (*braver*)	fortíssimus, -a, -um (*bravest*)
fēlīx, *gen.* fēlícis (*happy*)	fēlícior, -ius (*happier*)	fēlīcíssimus, -a, -um (*happiest*)
pótēns, *gen.* poténtis (*powerful*)	poténtior, -ius (*more powerful*)	potentíssimus, -a, -um (*most powerful*)
sápiēns, *gen.* sapiéntis (*wise*)	sapiéntior, -ius (*wiser*)	sapientíssimus, -a, -um (*wisest*)

DECLENSION OF COMPARATIVES

The declension of superlatives quite simply follows the pattern of **magnus, -a, -um.** Comparatives, however, are two-ending adjectives of the third declension, but they follow the *consonant declension;* and so they constitute the chief exception to the rule that adjectives of the third declension belong to the **i**-stem declension (i.e., comparatives do *not* have the **-ī** abl. sg., **-ium** gen. pl., or **-ia** neut. nom./acc. pl. endings that characterize other third declension adjectives, as seen in Ch. 16). Memorize the following paradigm, taking special note of the endings given in bold.

	Singular M. & F.	N.	Plural M. & F.	N.
Nom.	fórtior	fórtius	fortiórēs	fortióra
Gen.	fortióris	fortióris	fortiórum	fortiórum
Dat.	fortiórī	fortiórī	fortióribus	fortióribus
Acc.	fortiórem	fórtius	fortiórēs	fortióra
Abl.	fortióre	fortióre	fortióribus	fortióribus

USAGE AND TRANSLATION

Comparative degree adjectives are commonly translated with *more* or the suffix *-er* and superlatives with *most* or *-est,* depending on the context and English idiom, e.g.: **fēmina sapientior,** *the wiser woman;* **urbs antīquior,** *a more ancient city;* **tempus incertissimum,** *a most uncertain time;* **lūx clāris-sima,** *the brightest light.* Though there is no direct connection between the forms, it may be helpful for mnemonic purposes to associate the Latin comparative marker **-ōr-** with English *more/-er* and the superlative marker **-ss-** with English *most/-est.*

The comparative sometimes has the force of *rather,* indicating a greater degree of some quality than usual (**lūx clārior,** *a rather bright light*), or *too,* indicating a greater degree than desirable (**vīta eius erat brevior,** *his/her life was too short*). The superlative is sometimes translated with *very,* especially when comparing a person/thing to what is usual or ideal: **vīta eius erat bre-vissima,** *his/her life was very short.*

Quam WITH THE COMPARATIVE AND SUPERLATIVE

When **quam** *follows a comparative* degree adjective it functions as a co-ordinating conjunction meaning *than,* linking two items that are being compared; the same case or construction follows **quam** as precedes:

Hī librī sunt clāriōrēs quam illī, *these books are more famous than those.*

Dīcit hōs librōs esse clāriōrēs quam illōs, *he says that these books are more famous than those.*

When **quam** *precedes* a *superlative,* it functions adverbially and indicates that the person/thing modified has the greatest possible degree of a particular quality:

Amīcus meus erat vir quam iūcundissimus, *my friend was the pleasantest man possible* or *as pleasant as can be.*

ABLATIVE OF COMPARISON

When the first element to be compared was in the nominative or accusative case, **quam** was often omitted and the second element followed in the ablative case, the so-called "ablative of comparison" (which should be added to your now extensive list of ablative case uses).

Cōnsilia tua sunt clāriōra lūce, *your plans are clearer than light.*
(Cp. **cōnsilia tua sunt clāriōra quam lūx,** which means the same.)

Quis in Italiā erat clārior Cicerōne? *Who in Italy was more famous than Cicero?*

Vīdī paucōs fēlīciōrēs patre tuō, *I have seen few men happier than your father.*

VOCABULARY

cḗna, -ae, f., *dinner* (cenacle)

fórum, -ī, n., *marketplace, forum* (forensic)

lēx, lḗgis, f., *law, statute;* cp. **iūs,** which emphasizes *right, justice* (legal, legislator, legitimate, loyal, colleague, college, privilege)

līmen, līminis, n., *threshold* (liminality, subliminal, eliminate, preliminary)

lūx, lū́cis, f., *light* (lucid, elucidate, translucent, lucubration, illustrate, illuminate)

mḗnsa, -ae, f., *table; dining; dish, course;* **mḗnsa secū́nda,** *dessert* (the constellation Mensa)

nox, nóctis, f., *night* (nocturnal, nocturne, equinox, noctiluca, noctuid; cp. **pernoctō,** Ch. 39)

sómnus, -ī, m., *sleep* (somnambulate, somnambulism, somnambulist, somniferous, somniloquist, somnolent, insomnia, Sominex)

quī́dam, quaédam, quíddam (pron.) or **quóddam** (adj.), indef. pron. and adj.; as pron., *a certain one or thing, someone, something;* as adj., *a certain, some* (gen. **cuiúsdam,** dat. **cuídam,** etc.)

pudī́cus, -a, -um, *modest, chaste* (impudent, pudency, pudendum; cp. **pudī́citia,** *modesty, chastity*)

supérbus, -a, -um, *arrogant, overbearing, haughty, proud* (superb; cp. **superāre**)

trī́stis, trī́ste, *sad, sorrowful; joyless, grim, severe* (cp. **trīstitia,** *sorrow*)

túrpis, túrpe, *ugly; shameful, base, disgraceful* (turpitude)

urbā́nus, -a, -um, *of the city, urban; urbane, elegant* (urbanity, urbanization, suburban, suburbanite; cp. **urbs**)

prae, prep. + abl., *in front of, before* (frequent as a prefix, e.g., **praepōnere,** *to put before, prefer;* sometimes intensifying, e.g., **praeclārus, -a, -um,** *especially famous, remarkable;* precede, prepare, preposition; cp. **praeter,** Ch. 40)

quam, adv. and conj. after comparatives, *than;* with superlatives, *as . . . as possible:* **quam fortissimus,** *as brave as possible* (cp. **quam,** *how,* Ch. 16, and do not confuse with the rel. pron. fem. acc. sg.)

tántum, adv., *only*

invī́tō (1), *to entertain, invite, summon* (invitation, vie)

PRACTICE AND REVIEW

1. Ille dux nescīvit sē imperium prōtinus susceptūrum esse.
2. "Quīdam," inquit, "imperium quondam petēbant et līberōs virōs opprimere cupiēbant."
3. Eōdem diē decem mīlia hostium ab duce fidēlissimō āversa ac pulsa sunt; multī mīlitēs vulnera recēperant et in agrīs iacēbant.

4. Morte tyrannī ferōcis nūntiātā, quisque sē ad ōrātōrem potentissimum magnā spē vertit.
5. Rīdēns, scrīptor illīus fābulae sapiēns aliquid iūcundius dehinc nārrāvit.
6. Hīs rēbus audītīs, adulēscentēs geminī propter pecūniae cupiditātem studium litterārum relinquent.
7. Rēgīna fortissima Carthāginis posteā ostendit fidem semper esse sibi cāriōrem dīvitiīs.
8. Negāvit sē umquam vīdisse servam fidēliōrem quam hanc.
9. Iūcundior modus vītae hominibus nunc quaerendus est.
10. Crēdimus illōs vīgintī līberōs virōs fēmināsque vītam quam iūcundissimam agere.
11. Imperātor centum mīlitēs fortissimōs prae sē herī mīsit.
12. Lūx in illā casā nōn fuit clārissima, quod familia paucās fenestrās patefēcerat.
13. Amīcōs trīstēs excēpit, ad mēnsam invītāvit, et eīs perfugium ac sōlācium hīc dedit.
14. What is sweeter than a very pleasant life?
15. Certain men, however, say that death is sweeter than life.
16. When these three very sure signs had been reported, we sought advice and comfort from the most powerful leader.
17. In that story the author says that all men seek as happy lives as possible.
18. This light is always brighter than the other.

SENTENTIAE ANTĪQUAE

1. Senectūs est loquācior. (Cicero.—**loquāx,** gen. **loquācis,** *garrulous.*)
2. Tua cōnsilia omnia nōbīs clāriōra sunt quam lūx. (Cicero.)
3. Quaedam remedia graviōra sunt quam ipsa perīcula. (Seneca.)
4. Eō diē virōs fortissimōs atque amantissimōs reī pūblicae ad mē vocāvī. (Cicero.—**amāns reī pūblicae,** i.e., *patriotic.*)
5. Quī imperia libēns accēpit, partem acerbissimam servitūtis vītat. (Seneca.—**libēns,** gen. **libentis,** *willing;* here, as is often the case, the adj. has adverbial force.)
6. Iūcundissima dōna, ut āiunt, semper sunt ea quae auctor ipse cāra facit. (Ovid.)
7. Beātus sapiēnsque vir forum vītat et superba līmina potentiōrum cīvium. (Horace.)
8. Quid est turpius quam ab aliquō illūdī? (Cicero.—**illūdō, -ere,** *to deceive.*)
9. Quid enim est stultius quam incerta prō certīs habēre, falsa prō vērīs? (*Cicero.—**falsus, -a, -um.***)

10. Saepe mihi dīcis, cārissime amīce: "Scrībe aliquid magnum; dēsidiō-
    sissimus homō es." (Martial.—**dēsidiōsus, -a, -um,** *lazy.*)
11. Verba currunt; at manus notāriī est vēlōcior illīs; nōn lingua mea,
    sed manus eius, labōrem perfēcit. (Martial.—**notārius, -iī,** *stenogra-*
    pher.—**vēlōx,** gen. **vēlōcis,** *swift.*—**perficiō, -ere, -fēcī, -fectum,** *to*
    complete.)
12. Multī putant rēs bellicās graviōrēs esse quam rēs urbānās; sed haec
    sententia mūtanda est, nam multae rēs urbānae sunt graviōrēs
    clāriōrēsque quam bellicae. (Cicero.—**bellicus, -a, -um,** adj. of
    bellum.)
13. Invītātus ad cēnam, manū sinistrā lintea neglegentiōrum sustulistī.
    Hoc salsum esse putās? Rēs sordidissima est! Itaque mihi linteum
    remitte. (Catullus.—**linteum, -ī,** *linen, napkin.*—**neglegēns,** gen. **neg-**
    legentis, *careless.*—**salsus, -a, -um,** *salty; witty.*—**sordidus, -a, -um,**
    dirty, mean.)

THE NATIONS OF GAUL

Gallia est omnis dīvīsa in partēs trēs, quārum ūnam incolunt Belgae,
aliam Aquītānī, tertiam quī ipsōrum linguā Celtae, nostrā Gallī appellantur.
Hī omnēs linguā, īnstitūtīs, lēgibus inter sē differunt. Gallōs ab Aquītānīs
Garumna flūmen, ā Belgīs Matrona et Sequana dīvidit. Hōrum omnium
fortissimī sunt Belgae.

(*Caesar, *Bellum Gallicum* 1.1.—The places and peoples mentioned: Gaul, the
Belgae, the Aquitani, the Celts or Gauls, and the rivers Garonne, Marne, and
Seine.—**dīvidō, -ere, -vīsī, -vīsum,** *to divide, separate.*—**incolō, -ere,** *to inhabit;*
Belgae, Aquītānī, and [eī] **quī** are all subjects of this verb.—**ipsōrum linguā** =
linguā suā.—**nostrā,** sc. **linguā.**—**īnstitūtum, -ī,** *custom, institution.*—**differō.**)

Julius Caesar
Museo Pio Clementino, Vatican Museums, Vatican State

THE GOOD LIFE

Haec sunt, amīce iūcundissime, quae vītam faciunt beātiōrem: rēs nōn facta labōre sed ā patre relicta, ager fēlīx, parvum forī et satis ōtiī, mēns aequa, vīrēs et corpus sānum, sapientia, amīcī vērī, sine arte mēnsa, nox nōn ebria sed solūta cūrīs, nōn trīstis torus et tamen pudīcus, somnus facilis. Dēsīderā tantum quod habēs, cupe nihil; nōlī timēre ultimum diem aut spērāre.

(Martial 10.47; prose adaptation.—**rēs**, here *property, wealth.*—**ā patre relicta,** i.e., inherited.—**forī**, gen. of the whole with **parvum.**—**sine arte,** i.e., simple, modest.—**ebrius, -a, -um,** *drunken.*—**solvō, -ere, solvī, solūtum,** *to loosen, free (from).*—**torus, -ī,** *bed.*—**nōlī** is used with the inf. for a negative command, *do not . . . .*)

Funeral banquet, Etruscan fresco
Tomb of the Leopards, early 5th century B.C.
Tarquinia, Italy

ETYMOLOGY

In Sp. the comparative degree of an adjective is regularly formed by putting **más** (*more*) before the adjective: **más caro, más alto.** This **más** comes from the **magis** mentioned in n. 1. Sp. and It. both retain some vestiges of the Lat. superlative ending **-issimus.** Forms with this ending, however, are not the normal superlative forms, but are used to convey the intensive idea of *very, exceedingly.*

Latin	Italian	Spanish	
cārissimus	carissimo	carisimo	*very dear*
clārissimus	chiarissimo	clarisimo	*very clear*
altissimus	altissimo	altisimo	*very high*

In the readings

1. loquacious, loquacity. 8. illusion, illusive, illusory. 11. notary, note. 13. lint.—From **salsus** through Fr. come "sauce," "saucer," "saucy," "sausage." "Gaul": divide, division.—institute.—differ, differential, differentiate. "The Good Life": inebriated.—solve, absolve, absolution, dissolve, resolve, solution, resolution, ablative absolute.

LATĪNA EST GAUDIUM—ET ŪTILIS!

Salvēte! Here are some more familiar mottoes, phrases, famous quotations, and etymological tidbits **ex vocābulāriō huius capitis** (**vocābulārium** is medieval Lat. for *vocabulary,* a list of "what you call things," words that is, from **vocāre**): **auctor ignōtus** means *author unknown,* i.e., "anonymous"; **cēna Dominī** is the *Lord's Supper;* **dūra lēx sed lēx,** *a harsh law, but the law nevertheless;* **lēx nōn scrīpta,** *customary law* (as opposed to **lēx scrīpta**—what are the lit. meanings?—you can also figure out **lēx locī**); then there's Ovid's admonition to loners, **trīstis eris sī sōlus eris,** and the hope of one of Plautus' characters for **lēx eadem uxōrī et virō;** a legal decree of **ā mēnsā et torō,** *from table and bed* (**torus, -ī**), is a separation prohibiting husband and wife from cohabiting.

Knowing the noun **lūx** and the related verb **lūceō, lūcēre,** *to shine brightly,* can shed some light on these items: **lūx et vēritās** is the motto of Yale University, **lūx et lēx** is the motto of the University of North Carolina at Chapel Hill, pellucid explanations are perfectly clear (**per + lūc-**), translucent materials let the light shine through, and Lux soap will make you shine like light! **Lūcēte, discipulae discipulīque, et valēte!**

27

Special and Irregular Comparison of Adjectives

ADJECTIVES HAVING PECULIAR FORMS IN THE SUPERLATIVE

Two groups of adjectives, which are otherwise regular, have peculiar forms in the superlative:

I. Six adjectives ending in **-lis** form the superlative by adding **-limus, -lima, -limum** to the *base.*

Positive	Comparative	Superlative
fácilis, -e (*easy*)	facílior, -ius (*easier*)	facíl-limus, -a, -um (*easiest*)
diffícilis, -e (*difficult*)	difficílior, -ius (*more difficult*)	difficíllimus, -a, -um (*most difficult*)
símilis, -e (*like*)	simílior, -ius (*more l.*)	simíllimus, -a, -um (*most l.*)

Dissimilis (*unlike, dissimilar*), **gracilis** (*slender, thin*), and **humilis** (*low, humble*) follow this same pattern; all other **-lis** adjectives have regular superlatives (e.g., **fidēlissimus, ūtilissimus,** etc.).

II. Any adjective which has a masculine in **-er,** regardless of the declension, forms the superlative by adding **-rimus** directly to this masculine **-er,** *not* to the base; note that the comparatives of **-er** adjectives are formed regularly, by adding **-ior, -ius** to the base (which, as you know, in some cases retains the -e- and sometimes drops it).

Positive	Comparative	Superlative
líber, -bera, -berum *(free)*	lībérior, -ius *(freer)*	lībér-rimus, -a, -um *(freest)*
púlcher, -chra, -chrum *(beautiful)*	púlchrior, -ius *(more beautiful)*	pulchérrimus, -a, -um *(most beautiful)*
ácer, ácris, ácre *(keen)*	ácrior, ácrius *(keener)*	ācérrimus, -a, -um *(keenest)*

ADJECTIVES OF IRREGULAR COMPARISON

More important from the consideration of frequency of appearance are a few adjectives which are so irregular in their comparison that the only solution to the difficulty is memorization. However, English derivatives from the irregular forms greatly aid the memorization (see the Etymology section below). A list of the most useful of these adjectives follows.[1]

Positive	Comparative	Superlative
bónus, -a, -um *(good)*	mélior, -ius *(better)*	óptimus, -a, -um *(best)*
mágnus, -a, -um *(great)*	máior, -ius *(greater)*	máximus, -a, -um *(greatest)*
málus, -a, -um *(bad)*	péior, -ius *(worse)*	péssimus, -a, -um *(worst)*
múltus, -a, -um *(much)*	——, plūs *(more)*	plúrimus, -a, -um *(most)*
párvus, -a, -um *(small)*	mínor, mínus *(smaller)*	mínimus, -a, -um *(smallest)*
(prae, prō)[2] *(in front of, before)*	príor, -íus *(former)*	prīmus, -a, -um *(first)*
súperus, -a, -um *(that above)*	supérior, -ius *(higher)*	{ súmmus, -a, -um *(highest, furthest)* suprêmus, -a, -um *(highest, last)*

[1] Others less important for this book are:
   exterus, -a, -um *(foreign)*, **exterior, -ius** *(outer)*, **extrēmus, -a, -um** *(outermost)*
   ī̆nferus, -a, -um *(below)*, **ī̆nferior, -ius** *(lower)*, **ī̆nfimus, -a, -um** *(lowest)*
   (prope, near), **propior, -ius** *(nearer)*, **proximus, -a, -um** *(nearest)*

[2] There is no positive degree adj. corresponding to **prior** and **prīmus,** since those words, by the very definition of "priority" and "primacy," imply comparison with one or more persons or things; the prepositions **prae** and **prō,** however, are related.

DECLENSION OF Plūs

None of the irregular forms offers any declensional difficulty except **plūs.** In the plural **plūs** functions as an adjective (e.g., **plūrēs amīcī**), but has mixed **i**-stem and consonant-stem forms (**-ium** in the genitive plural but **-a,** not **-ia,** in the neuter nominative and accusative); in the singular it functions not as an adjective at all, but as a neuter noun which is commonly followed by a genitive of the whole (e.g., **plūs pecūniae,** *more money,* lit. *more of money*—see Ch. 15).

	Singular M. & F.	N.	Plural M. & F.	N.
Nom.	——	plūs	plŭrēs	plŭra
Gen.	——	plŭris	plŭrium	plŭrium
Dat.	——	——	plŭribus	plŭribus
Acc.	——	plūs	plŭrēs	plŭra
Abl.	——	plŭre	plŭribus	plŭribus

VOCABULARY

dēlectátiō, dēlectātiốnis, f., *delight, pleasure, enjoyment* (delectation, delectable, delicious, dilettante; cp. **dēlectō, dēlicia,** *delight*)

népōs, nepótis, m., *grandson, descendant* (nephew, nepotism, niece)

sōl, sólis, m., *sun* (solar, solarium, solstice, parasol)

dīligēns, gen. **dīligéntis,** *diligent, careful* (diligence, diligently)

dissímilis, dissímile, *unlike, different* (dissimilar, dissimilarity, dissemble)

grácilis, grácile, *slender, thin* (gracile)

húmilis, húmile, *lowly, humble* (humility, humiliate, humiliation; cp. **humus,** Ch. 37)

máior, máius, comp. adj., *greater; older;* **maiốrēs, maiốrum,** m. pl., *ancestors* (i.e., *the older ones;* major, majority, etc.—see Etymology below).

prímus, -a, -um, *first, foremost, chief, principal* (primary, primate, prime, primeval, primer, premier, primitive, prim, primo-geniture, prima facie, primordial, primrose)

quot, indecl. adj., *how many, as many as* (quota, quotation, quote, quotient)

símilis, símile, + gen. or dat., *similar (to), like, resembling* (similarly, simile, assimilate, dissimilar, dissimilarity, simulate, dissimulate, verisimilitude, assemble, resemble, simultaneous; cp. same)

súperus, -a, -um, *above, upper;* **súperī, -ốrum,** m. pl., *the gods* (superior, etc.; cp. **superō** and see Etymology below)

útilis, útile, *useful, advantageous* (what Latin is to YOU!—utility, from **ūtilitās, -tātis;** utilitarian, utilization, utilize; cp. **ūtor,** Ch. 34)

All the irregular adjectival forms given above in this lesson.

pṓnō, pṓnere, pósuī, pósitum, *to put, place, set* (See Etymology at end of chapter.)

prṓbō (1), *to approve, recommend; test* (probe, probate, probation, probative, probable, probably, probability, approbation, proof, prove, approve, approval, disprove, improve, reprove, reprobate; cp. **probitās**)

PRACTICE AND REVIEW

1. Quisque cupit quam pulcherrima atque ūtilissima dōna dare.
2. Quīdam turpēs habent plūrima sed etiam plūra petunt.
3. Ille ōrātor, ab tyrannō superbissimō expulsus, ducem iūcundiōrem et lēgēs aequiōrēs dehinc quaesīvit.
4. Summum imperium optimīs virīs semper petendum est.
5. Senex nepōtibus trīstibus casam patefēcit et eōs trāns līmen invītāvit.
6. Ostendit hostēs ultimum signum lūce clārissimā illā nocte dedisse.
7. Iste tyrannus pessimus negāvit sē virōs līberōs umquam oppressisse.
8. Fidēlissimus servus plūs cēnae ad mēnsam accipiēbat quam trēs peiōrēs.
9. Āiunt hunc auctōrem vītam humillimam hīc agere.
10. Cūr dī superī oculōs ā rēbus hūmānīs eō tempore āvertērunt?
11. Habēsne pecūniam et rēs tuās prae rē pūblicā?
12. Sōlem post paucās nūbēs gracillimās in caelō hodiē vidēre possumus.
13. Some believe that very large cities are worse than very small ones.
14. In return for the three rather small gifts, the young man gave even more and prettier ones to his very sad mother.
15. Those very large mountains were higher than these.

SENTENTIAE ANTĪQUAE

1. Trahit mē nova vīs: videō meliōra probōque, sed peiōra tantum faciō et nesciō cūr. (Ovid.)
2. Quaedam carmina sunt bona; plūra sunt mala. (Martial.)
3. Optimum est. Nihil melius, nihil pulchrius hōc vīdī. (Terence.)
4. Spērō tē et hunc nātālem et plūrimōs aliōs quam fēlīcissimōs āctūrum esse. (Pliny.—**nātālis [diēs]**, *birthday.*)
5. Quoniam cōnsilium et ratiō sunt in senibus, maiōrēs nostrī summum concilium appellāvērunt senātum. (Cicero.—**concilium, -iī,** *council.*)
6. Plūs operae studiīque in rēbus domesticīs nōbīs nunc pōnendum est etiam quam in rēbus mīlitāribus. (Cicero.—**opera, -ae,** *work, effort.*—**domesticus, -a, -um.**—**mīlitāris, -e.**)
7. Neque enim perīculum in rē pūblicā fuit gravius umquam neque ōtium maius. (Cicero.)
8. Sumus sapientiōrēs illīs, quod nōs nātūram esse optimam ducem

scīmus. (Cicero.—**optimam,** f. by attraction to the gender of **nā-tūram.**)

9. Nātūra minimum petit; nātūrae autem sē sapiēns accommodat. (*Seneca.—**accommodāre,** *to adapt.*)
10. Maximum remedium īrae mora est. (*Seneca.)
11. Quī animum vincit et īram continet, eum cum summīs virīs nōn com-parō sed eum esse simillimum deō dīcō. (Cicero.—**comparāre,** *to compare.*)
12. Dionȳsius, tyrannus urbis pulcherrimae, erat vir summae in vīctū temperantiae et in omnibus rēbus dīligentissimus et ācerrimus. Īdem tamen erat ferōx ac iniūstus. Quā ex rē, sī vērum dīcimus, vidēbātur miserrimus. (Cicero.—Dionysius, ruler of Syracuse in the 4th cen. B.C.—**vīctus, -ūs,** *mode of life.*—**temperantia, -ae.**—**in-iūstus, -a, -um,** *unjust.*—**Quā ex rē = Ex illā rē.**)
13. Nisi superōs vertere possum, Acheronta movēbō. (Virgil.—**Ache-ronta,** Gk. acc., *Acheron,* a river in the underworld, here by meton-ymy *the land of the dead.*)

ALLEY CAT

Caelī, Lesbia nostra, Lesbia illa,
illa Lesbia, quam Catullus ūnam
plūs quam sē atque suōs amāvit omnēs,
nunc in quadriviīs et angiportīs
5 glūbit magnanimī Remī nepōtēs.

(*Catullus 58; meter: hendecasyllabic.—Caelius, a rival of Catullus for Lesbia's favors.—**quadrivium, -iī,** *crossroads.*—**angiportum, -ī,** *alley.*—**glūbō, -ere,** *to peel* (*back*), *strip* (*off*); used of stripping the bark off trees or the skin off an animal, here in an obscene sense.—**Remus,** brother of Romulus, legendary founders of Rome.)

THANKS A LOT, TULLY!

Dīsertissime Rōmulī nepōtum,
quot sunt quotque fuēre, Marce Tullī,
quotque post aliīs erunt in annīs,
grātiās tibi maximās Catullus
5 agit, pessimus omnium poēta,
tantō pessimus omnium poēta
quantō tū optimus omnium patrōnus.

(*Catullus 49; meter: hendecasyllabic. The poet sends thanks to the orator and statesman, Marcus Tullius Cicero; whether or not the tone is ironic is a matter debated by scholars.—**dīsertus, -a, -um,** *eloquent, learned.*—**fuēre** = **fuērunt,** see p. 77.—**post** = **posteā.**—**tantō . . . quantō,** *just as much . . . as.*—**tū,** sc. **es.**)

AN UNCLE'S LOVE FOR HIS NEPHEW AND ADOPTED SON

Adulēscēns est cārior mihi quam ego ipse! Atque hic nōn est fīlius meus sed ex frātre meō. Studia frātris iam diū sunt dissimillima meīs. Ego vītam urbānam ēgī et ōtium petīvī et, id quod quīdam fortūnātius putant, uxōrem numquam habuī. Ille, autem, haec omnia fēcit: nōn in forō sed in agrīs vītam ēgit, parvum pecūniae accēpit, uxōrem pudīcam dūxit, duōs fīliōs habuit. Ex illō ego hunc maiōrem adoptāvī mihi, ēdūxī ā parvō puerō, amāvī prō meō. In eō adulēscente est dēlectātiō mea; sōlum id est cārum mihi.

(Terence, *Adelphoe* 39–49.—**dūxit,** *he married.*—**adoptāre.**—**ēdūxī,** *I raised.*)

ETYMOLOGY

In many instances the irregular comparison of a Latin adjective can easily be remembered by English derivatives:

bonus
    melior: ameliorate
    optimus: optimist, optimum, optimal

magnus
    maior: major, majority, mayor
    maximus: maximum

malus
    peior: pejorative
    pessimus: pessimist

multus
    plūs: plus, plural, plurality, nonplus

parvus
    minor: minor, minority, minus, minute, minuet, minister, minstrel
    minimus: minimum, minimize

(prō)
    prior: prior, priority
    prīmus: prime, primacy, primary, primeval, primitive

superus
    superior: superior, superiority
    summus: summit, sum, consummate
    suprēmus: supreme, supremacy

Lat. **plūs** is the parent of Fr. **plus** and It. **più,** words which are placed before adjectives to form the comparative degree in those Romance languages. If the definite article is then added to these comparatives, it converts them into superlatives.

Latin	French	Italian
longior	plus long	più lungo
longissimus	le plus long	il più lungo
cārior	plus cher	più caro
cārissimus	le plus cher	il più caro

From **pōnō** come innumerable derivatives: apposite, apposition, component, composite, compost, compound, deponent, deposit, deposition, depot, exponent, exposition, expound, imposition, impost, impostor, juxtaposition, opponent, opposite, positive, post, postpone, preposition, proposition, propound, repository, supposition, transposition.

However, note that "pose" and its compounds derive, not from **pōnō** as one would think, but from the late Latin **pausāre,** which stems from Gk. **pausis,** *a pause,* and **pauein,** *to stop.* In Fr. this **pausāre** became **poser,** which took the place of **pōnō** in compounds. Consequently, the forms given above under **pōnō** are not etymologically related to the following words despite their appearance: compose, depose, expose, impose, oppose, propose, repose, suppose, transpose.

In the readings

4. natal, prenatal, postnatal, Natalie. 5. council (vs. **cōnsilium,** *counsel*), conciliate, conciliatory. 6. opera, operetta.—domesticate, etc.; cp. **domus.**—military, cp. **mīles.** 9. accommodate, accommodation. 11. comparative, incomparable. 12. victual, victualer, vittles.—temperance, intemperance.—injustice. "An Uncle's Love": adopt, adoption.

LATĪNA EST GAUDIUM—ET ŪTILIS!

Salvē! Quid agis hodiē? Spīrasne? Spērāsne? Rīdēsne? Valēsne? Sī tū valēs, ego valeō! And here are some more **rēs Latīnae** to give you a **mēns sāna:** First, an old Latin maxim which you should now be able to read, **sapiēns nihil affīrmat quod nōn probat.** Likewise this quote from Horace (*Epistulae* 1.1.106), **sapiēns ūnō minor est Iove,** and the motto of the Jesuit order, **ad maiōrem glōriam Deī.** Now, **quid est tempestās? Pluitne? Estne frīgida? Nimbōsa?** Well, it really won't matter, if you remember this proverb: **sōl lūcet omnibus!** (Remember **lūcēre** from last chapter?) Birds of a feather flock together and, according to another old Latin proverb, **similis in similī gaudet.**

Here are some more from the irregular comparatives and superlatives you've just learned: **meliōrēs priōrēs,** freely, *the better have priority;* **maximā cum laude** and **summā cum laude** (what you should have on your next diploma, **sī es dīligēns in studiō Latīnae!**); **peior bellō est timor ipse bellī** (note the abl. of comparison); **ē plūribus ūnum,** motto of the United States, *one from several,* i.e., one union from many states; **prīmus inter parēs,** *first among equals;* **prīmā faciē,** *at first sight;* and, finally, **summum bonum,** *the highest good,* which can come from studying Latin, of course: **valē!**

28

Subjunctive Mood; Present Subjunctive; Jussive and Purpose Clauses

THE SUBJUNCTIVE MOOD

You will recall from Ch. 1 that "mood" (from Lat. **modus**) is the "manner" of expressing a verbal action or state of being. Thus far we have encountered verbs in two of the three Latin moods, the indicative and the imperative. As you know, an imperative (from **imperāre,** *to command*) emphatically commands someone to undertake an action that is not yet going on, while indicatives (from **indicāre,** *to point out*) "indicate" real actions, i.e., actions that have in fact occurred (or have definitely not occurred) in the past, that are occurring (or are definitely not occurring) in the present, or that fairly definitely will (or will not) occur in the future.

In contrast to the indicative, the mood of actuality and factuality, the subjunctive is in general (though not always) the mood of potential, tentative, hypothetical, ideal, or even unreal action. An example in English is, "If the other student were here, he would be taking notes"; in this conditional sentence, which imagines actions that are contrary to the actual facts, English employs the auxiliaries "were" and "would" to indicate that the action described is only ideal. Among the other auxiliaries used in English to describe potential or hypothetical actions are "may," "might," "should," "would," "may have," "would have," etc.

Latin employs the subjunctive much more frequently than English, in a wide variety of clause types, and it uses special subjunctive verb forms rather than auxiliaries. There are two tasks involved in mastering the subjunctive: first, learning the new forms, which is a relatively simple matter; second, learning to recognize and translate the various subjunctive clause types, which is also quite easily done, if your approach is systematic.

SUBJUNCTIVE TENSES

There are only four tenses in the subjunctive mood. The present subjunctive is introduced in this chapter and has rules for formation that vary slightly for each of the four conjugations; rules for forming the imperfect (Ch. 29), perfect, and pluperfect (Ch. 30) are the same for all four conjugations, and even for irregular verbs.

SUBJUNCTIVE CLAUSES

In this and subsequent chapters you will be introduced to a series of subjunctive clause types: the jussive subjunctive and purpose clauses (Ch. 28), result clauses (29), indirect questions (30), **cum** clauses (31), proviso clauses (32), conditions (33, with three distinct subjunctive types), jussive noun clauses (36), relative clauses of characteristic (38), and fear clauses (40). You should catalog these clause types in your notebook or computer file and systematically learn three details for each: (1) its definition, (2) how to recognize it in a Latin sentence, and (3) how to translate it into English.

CONJUGATION OF THE PRESENT SUBJUNCTIVE

1. laúdem	móneam	ágam	aúdiam	cápiam
2. laúdēs	móneās	ágās	aúdiās	cápiās
3. laúdet	móneat	ágat	aúdiat	cápiat
1. laudḗmus	moneámus	agámus	audiámus	capiámus
2. laudḗtis	moneātis	agātis	audiātis	capiātis
3. laúdent	móneant	ágant	aúdiant	cápiant

Note that in the first conjugation the characteristic stem vowel changes from **-ā-** in the present indicative to **-ē-** in the present subjunctive. In the other conjugations **-ā-** is consistently the sign of the present subjunctive, but with variations in the handling of the actual stem vowel (shortened in the second, replaced in the third, altered to short **-i-** in the fourth/third **-iō**); the sentence "we **fear a liar**" will help you remember that the actual vowels preceding the personal endings are **-ē-, -eā-, -ā-,** and **-iā-** for the first, second, third, and fourth/third **-iō** conjugations, respectively.

Note that a subjunctive may be mistaken for an indicative, if you neglect to recognize a verb's conjugation (e.g., cp. **agat** with **amat,** and **amet** with **monet**), so remember your vocabulary.

The present passive subjunctive naturally follows the pattern of the active except that passive endings are used.

laúder, laudéris (and remember the alternate **-re** ending, Ch. 18), laudétur; laudémur, laudéminī, laudéntur

mónear, moneáris, moneátur; moneámur, moneáminī, moneántur

ágar, agáris, agátur; agámur, agáminī, agántur

aúdiar, audiáris, audiátur; audiámur, audiáminī, audiántur

cápiar, capiáris, capiátur; capiámur, capiáminī, capiántur

TRANSLATION

While *may* is sometimes used to translate the present subjunctive (e.g., in purpose clauses), the translation of all subjunctive tenses, in fact, varies with the type of clause, as you will see when each is introduced.

THE JUSSIVE SUBJUNCTIVE

As the term "subjunctive" (from **subiungere,** *to subjoin, subordinate*) suggests, the subjunctive was used chiefly in subordinate (or dependent) clauses. However, the subjunctive was also employed in certain types of main, or independent, clauses. The "jussive" subjunctive (from **iubēre,** *to order*) is among the most important of these independent uses, and the only one formally introduced in this book. As the term implies, the jussive expresses a command or exhortation, especially in the first or third person, singular or plural (the imperative is generally used for the second person); **nē** is employed for negative commands. The clause type is easily recognized, since the sentence's main verb (and often its only verb) is subjunctive; while *may* and *should* can sometimes be employed in translating the jussive subjunctive (particularly with the second person: **semper spērēs,** *you should always hope*), *let* is the English auxiliary most often used, followed by the subject noun or pronoun (in the objective case, i.e., *me, us, him, her, it, them*).

Cōgitem nunc dē hāc rē, et tum nōn errābō, *let me now think about this matter, and then I will not make a mistake.*

Discipulus discat aut discēdat, *let the student either learn or leave.*

Doceāmus magnā cum dēlectātiōne linguam Latīnam, *let us teach the Latin language with great delight.*

Nē id faciāmus, *let us not do this.*

Audeant illī virī et fēminae esse fortēs, *let those men and women dare to be brave.*

PURPOSE CLAUSES

A purpose clause is a subordinate clause indicating the purpose or objective of the action in the main clause; e.g., "we study Latin *so that we may learn more about ancient Rome*" or "we study Latin *to improve our English.*" As seen in this second example, English often employs an infinitive to express purpose, but that use of the infinitive is rare in Latin prose (though not unusual in verse). Instead Latin most commonly employed a subjunctive clause introduced by **ut** or, for a negative purpose, **nē**; the auxiliary *may* (as in the first English example above) is frequently used in translating the present tense in a purpose clause, but often we can translate with an infinitive (if the subject of the purpose clause is the same as that of the main clause). Study carefully the following Latin sentences and the several acceptable translations:

Hoc dīcit **ut** eōs **iuvet.**
He says this to help them.
  in order to help them.
  that he may help them.
  so that he may help them.
  in order that he may help them.

The first two translation options given above are more colloquial, the others more formal.

Discēdit **nē** id **audiat.**
He leaves in order not to hear this.
  so that he may not hear this.

Cum cūrā docet **ut** discipulī bene **discant.**
He teaches with care so (that) his students may learn well.

Hoc facit **nē capiātur.**
He does this in order not to be captured.

Librōs legimus **ut** multa **discāmus.**
We read books (in order) to learn many things.

Bonōs librōs nōbīs dent **nē** malōs **legāmus.**
Let them give us good books so that we may not read bad ones.

You should have no difficulty recognizing a purpose clause: look for a subordinate clause, introduced by **ut** or **nē,** ending with a subjunctive verb, and answering the question "why?" or "for what purpose?"

VOCABULARY

árma, -ṓrum, n. pl., *arms, weapons* (armor, army, armament, armada, armature, armistice, armadillo, alarm, disarmament, gendarme)

cúrsus, -ūs, m., *running, race; course* (courser, cursor, cursory, cursive, concourse, discourse, recourse, precursor, excursion; cp. **currō**)

lū́na, -ae, f., *moon* (lunar, lunacy, lunate, lunatic, lunation, interlunar)

occā́siō, occāsiónis, f., *occasion, opportunity* (occasional; cp. **occidō**, Ch. 31)

pá̄rēns, paréntis, m./f., *parent* (parentage, parental, parenting; cp. **pariō, parere,** to give birth to)

stélla, -ae, f., *star, planet* (stellar, constellation, interstellar)

vésper, vésperis or **vésperī,** m., *evening; evening star* (vesper, vesperal, vespertine)

mórtuus, -a, -um, *dead* (mortuary; cp. **mors, mortālis, immortālis,** and, Ch. 34, **morior**)

prínceps, gen. **príncipis,** *chief, foremost;* m./f. noun, *leader, emperor* (prince, principal, principality; cp. **prīmus, prīncipium**)

ut, conj. + subj., *in order that, so that, that, in order to, so as to, to;* + indic., *as, when*

nē, adv. and conj. with subjunctives of command and purpose, *not; in order that . . . not, that . . . not, in order not to*

cé̄dō, cé̄dere, céssī, céssum, *to go, withdraw; yield to, grant, submit* (accede, access, accession, antecedent, ancestor, cede, concede, deceased, exceed, intercede, precede, proceed, recede, secede, succeed; cp. **discē̄dō**)

dé̄dicō (1), *to dedicate* (dedication, dedicatory, rededication)

égeō, egé̄re, éguī + abl. or gen., *to need, lack, want* (indigence, indigent; do not confuse with **ē̄gī,** from **agō**)

éxpleō, -plé̄re, -plé̄vī, -plé̄tum, *to fill, fill up, complete* (expletive, expletory, deplete, replete; cp. **plē̄nus, pleō,** *to fill*)

praéstō, -stá̄re, -stitī, -stitum, *to excel; exhibit, show, offer, supply, furnish*

táceō, tacé̄re, tácuī, tácitum, *to be silent, leave unmentioned* (tacit, taciturn, taciturnity, reticence, reticent)

PRACTICE AND REVIEW

1. Auctor sapiēns et dīligēns turpia vītet et bona probet.
2. Itaque prō patriā etiam maiōra meliōraque nunc faciāmus.
3. Nepōs tuus ā mēnsā discēdat nē ista verba acerba audiat.
4. Nē imperātor superbus crēdat sē esse fēlīciōrem quam virum humillimum.
5. Quisque petit quam fēlīcissimum et urbānissimum modum vītae.
6. Quīdam dēlectātiōnēs et beneficia aliīs praestant ut beneficia similia recipiant.
7. Multī medicī lūcem sōlis fuisse prīmum remedium putant.
8. Imperium ducī potentiōrī dabunt ut hostēs ācerrimōs āvertat.

9. Hīs verbīs trīstibus nūntiātīs, pars hostium duōs prīncipēs suōs relīquit.

10. Maiōrēs putābant deōs superōs habēre corpora hūmāna pulcherrima et fortissima.

11. Uxor pudīca eius haec decem ūtilissima tum probāvit.

12. Let him not think that those dissimilar laws are worse than the others (translate with and without **quam**).

13. They will send only twenty men to do this very easy thing in the
forum.

14. They said: "Let us call the arrogant emperor a most illustrious man
in order not to be expelled from the country."

15. Therefore, let them not order this very wise and very good woman
to depart from the dinner.

SENTENTIAE ANTĪQUAE

1. Ratiō dūcat, nōn fortūna. (*Livy.)

2. Arma togae cēdant. (Cicero.—**toga, -ae,** the garment of peace and
civil, in contrast to military, activity.)

3. Ex urbe nunc discēde nē metū et armīs opprimar. (Cicero.)

4. Nunc ūna rēs mihi prōtinus est facienda ut maximum ōtium et sōlācium habeam. (Terence.)

5. Rapiāmus, amīcī, occāsiōnem dē diē. (*Horace.)

6. Corpus enim somnō et multīs aliīs rēbus eget ut valeat; animus ipse
sē alit. (Seneca.)

7. Quī beneficium dedit, taceat; nārret quī accēpit. (*Seneca.)

8. Dē mortuīs nihil nisi bonum dīcāmus. (Diogenes Laertius.)

9. Parēns ipse nec habeat vitia nec toleret. (Quintilian.)

10. In hāc rē ratiō habenda est ut monitiō acerbitāte careat. (Cicero.—
monitiō, -ōnis, *admonition.*—**acerbitās, -tātis,** noun of **acerbus.**)

11. Fēminae ad lūdōs semper veniunt ut videant—et ut ipsae videantur. (Ovid.)

12. Arma virumque canō quī prīmus ā lītoribus Trōiae ad Italiam vēnit.
(Virgil.—**canō, -ere,** *to sing about.*)

PLEASE REMOVE MY NAME FROM YOUR MAILING LIST!

Cūr nōn mitto meōs tibi, Pontiliāne, libellōs?
Nē mihi tū mittās, Pontiliāne, tuōs.

(*Martial 7.3; meter: elegiac couplet. Roman poets, just like American writers,
would often exchange copies of their works with one another; but Pontilianus'
poems are not Martial's cup of tea!—**mitto:** final **-ō** was often shortened in Latin
verse.—**Pontiliānus, -ī.**—**Nē . . . mittās,** not jussive, but purpose, following the
implied statement, "I don't send mine to you. . . .")

TO HAVE FRIENDS ONE MUST BE FRIENDLY

Ut praestem Pyladēn, aliquis mihi praestet Orestēn.
Hoc nōn fit verbīs, Mārce; ut amēris, amā.

(*Martial 6.11.9–10; meter: elegiac couplet. Orestes and Pylades were a classic pair of very devoted friends; Martial cannot play the role of Pylades unless someone proves a real Orestes to him.—**Pyladēn** and **Orestēn** are Greek acc. sg. forms.—**fit,** *is accomplished.*)

Pylades and Orestes Brought as Victims before Iphigenia
Benjamin West, 1766, Tate Gallery, London, Great Britain

THE DAYS OF THE WEEK

Diēs dictī sunt ā deīs quōrum nōmina Rōmānī quibusdam stēllīs dēdicāvērunt. Primum enim diem ā Sōle appellāvērunt, quī prīnceps est omnium stēllārum ut īdem diēs est prae omnibus diēbus aliīs. Secundum diem ā Lūnā appellāvērunt, quae ex Sōle lūcem accēpit. Tertium ab stēllā Mārtis, quae vesper appellātur. Quārtum ab stēllā Mercuriī. Quīntum ab stēllā Iovis. Sextum ā Veneris stēllā, quam Lūciferum appellāvērunt, quae inter omnēs stēllās plūrimum lūcis habet. Septimum ab stēllā Sāturnī, quae dīcitur cursum suum trīgintā annīs explēre. Apud Hebraeōs autem diēs prīmus dīcitur ūnus diēs sabbatī, quī in linguā nostrā diēs dominicus est, quem pāgānī Sōlī dēdicāvērunt. Sabbatum autem septimus diēs ā dominicō est, quem pāgānī Sāturnō dēdicāvērunt.

(Isidore of Seville, *Orīginēs* 5.30, 7th cen.—**Mārs, Mārtis.**—**Mercurius, -ī.**—**Iuppiter, Iovis.**—**Venus, Veneris.**—**Lūciferus, -ī,** *Lucifer, light-bringer.*—**Sāturnus, -ī.**—**trīgintā,** *30.*—**Hebraeus, -ī,** *Hebrew.*—**sabbatum, -ī,** *the Sabbath;* **ūnus diēs sabbatī,** i.e., *the first day after the Sabbath.*—**dominicus, -a, -um,** *of the Lord, the Lord's.*—**pāgānus, -ī,** *rustic, peasant;* here, *pagan.*)

ETYMOLOGY

"Alarm" derives ultimately from It. **all'arme** (*to arms*), which stands for **ad illa arma.**

From **cessō** (1), an intensive form of **cēdō:** cease, cessation, incessant.

The **-ā-** which is consistently found in the present subjunctive of all conjugations except the first in Latin is similarly found in the present subjunctive of all conjugations except the first in both Italian and Spanish. And Spanish even has the characteristic **-ē-** of the Latin in the present subjunctive of the first conjugation.

In the readings

"Days of the Week": martial.—mercury, mercurial.—Jovian, by Jove! jovial.—Venusian, venereal, venery.—lucifer, luciferase, luciferin, luciferous.—Saturnian, Saturday, saturnine.—Dominic, Dominica, Dominican, dominical; cp. **dominus/domina.**—paganism, paganize.

LATĪNA EST GAUDIUM—ET ŪTILIS!

Salvēte! Here are some nuggets from the new Vocab.: teachers and guardians can serve **in locō parentis; mortuī nōn mordent,** "dead men tell no tales" (lit., *the dead don't bite!*); **occāsiō fūrem facit,** *opportunity makes a thief;* those who know about Watergate will now recognize the etymology of the "expletives deleted" (four-letter words that "fill out" the sentences of vulgar and illiterate folk!); an **ēditiō prīnceps** is a *first edition;* **tacet,** a musical notation calling for a vocalist or instrumentalist to be silent; related to **cursus** is **curriculum,** *running, course, course of action,* hence a résumé provides your **curriculum vītae;** and the motto of New York University (**fīliō meō grātiās!**), a good one for Latin students, is **perstāre et praestāre,** *to persevere and to excel.*

Now let's focus on jussives: first off, I hope that all my students in Wyoming recognized **arma togae cēdant** as their state motto; another motto, with this new verb **cēdere** and an imperative rather than a jussive, is Virgil's **nē cēde malīs,** *yield not to evils;* Vegetius, an ancient military analyst, has advised us, **quī dēsīderat pācem, praeparet bellum;** and I'm certain all the *Star Wars* fans can decipher this: **sit vīs tēcum!**

Before bidding you farewell, friends, let me point out that the jussive subjunctive, common in the first and third person, is sometimes used in the second as well, in lieu of an imperative, and translated with *should* or *may;* an example is seen in this anonymous proverb, which makes the same point as the Pylades reading above: **ut amīcum habeās, sīs amīcus,** *in order to have a friend, you should be a friend.* By the way, I call first person plural jussives the "salad subjunctives" (remember VENI, VIDI, VEGI?) because they always contain "let us": GROAN!! On that punny note lettuce juss say goodbye: **amīcī amīcaeque meae, semper valeātis!**

29

Imperfect Subjunctive; Present and Imperfect Subjunctive of Sum and Possum; Result Clauses

THE IMPERFECT SUBJUNCTIVE

The imperfect subjunctive is perhaps the easiest of all the subjunctive tenses to recognize and form. For all verbs it is in effect simply the present active infinitive + the present system personal endings, active and passive, with the **-ē-** long (except, as usual, before final **-m, -r,** and **-t,** and both final and medial **-nt/-nt-**). Sample forms are given in the following paradigms; for complete conjugations, see the Appendix (p. 453–54).

1. laudā́re-m	laudā́re-r	ágerer	audī́rem	cáperem
2. laudā́rē-s	laudā́rē-ris	ageréris	audī́rēs	cáperēs
3. laudā́re-t	laudā́rḗ-tur	agerétur	audī́ret	cáperet
1. laudārḗ-mus	laudārḗ-mur	agerḗmur	audīrḗmus	caperḗmus
2. laudārḗ-tis	laudārḗ-minī	agerḗminī	audīrḗtis	caperḗtis
3. laudā́re-nt	laudārḗ-ntur	ageréntur	audī́rent	cáperent

PRESENT AND IMPERFECT SUBJUNCTIVE OF *Sum* AND *Possum*

The present subjunctives of **sum** and **possum** are irregular (though they do follow a consistent pattern) and must be memorized. The imperfect subjunctives, however, follow the rule given above.

Present Subjunctive		Imperfect Subjunctive	
1. sim	póssim	éssem	póssem
2. sīs	póssīs	éssēs	póssēs
3. sit	póssit	ésset	pósset
1. sīmus	possímus	essémus	possémus
2. sītis	possítis	essétis	possétis
3. sint	póssint	éssent	póssent

Particular care should be taken to distinguish between the forms of the present and the imperfect subjunctive of **possum.**

USE AND TRANSLATION OF THE IMPERFECT SUBJUNCTIVE

The imperfect subjunctive is used in a variety of clause types, including purpose and result clauses, when the main verb is a past tense. As for all subjunctives, the translation depends upon the type of clause, but auxiliaries sometimes used with the imperfect include *were, would,* and, in purpose clauses, *might* (vs. *may* for the present tense). Study these sample sentences containing purpose clauses:

Hoc dīcit **ut** eōs **iuvet.**
He says this (in order) to help them.
    *so that he **may** help them.*

Hoc dīxit (dīcēbat) **ut** eōs **iuvāret.**
He said (kept saying) this (in order) to help them.
    *so that he **might** help them.*

Hoc facit **nē** urbs **capiātur.**
*He does this so that the city **may** not be captured.*

Hoc fēcit (faciēbat) **nē** urbs **caperētur.**
*He did (was doing) this so that the city **might** not be captured.*

Remember that in order to master the subjunctive (notice the purpose clause?!) you must 1) learn a definition for each clause type, 2) know how to recognize each, and 3) know the proper translation for the subjunctive verb in each type. Keep these three points in mind—*definition, recognition, translation*—as you proceed to the following discussion of result clauses and to the subsequent chapters in this book.

RESULT CLAUSES

A result clause is a subordinate clause that shows the result of the action in the main clause; the purpose clause answers the question *"why* is (was) it being done?"*, while the result clause answers the question "what is (was) the *outcome?"* Examples in English are: "it is raining so hard *that the streets are flooding"* and "she studied Latin so diligently *that she knew it like a Roman."* Notice that English introduces such clauses with "that" and uses the indicative mood, generally with *no auxiliary* (i.e., neither *may* nor *might).*

Latin result clauses begin with **ut** and contain (usually at the end) a subjunctive verb. The result clause can be easily recognized, and distinguished from a purpose clause, by the sense and context and also by the fact that the main clause usually contains an adverb (**ita, tam, sīc,** *so*) or adjective (**tantus,** *so much, so great*) indicating degree and signaling that a result clause is to follow. Moreover, if the clause describes a negative result, it will contain some negative word such as **nōn, nihil, nēmō, numquam** or **nūllus** (vs. a negative purpose clause, which is introduced by **nē**). Analyze carefully the following examples, and note that in the result clauses (vs. the purpose clauses) the subjunctive verb is regularly translated *as an indicative,* without an auxiliary (*may* or *might* are used only in those instances where a potential or ideal result, rather than an actual result, is being described):

Tanta fēcit **ut** urbem **servāret,** *he did* **such great** *things* **that he saved** *the city.* (Result)

Haec fēcit **ut** urbem **servāret,** *he did these things* **that he might save** *the city.* (Purpose)

Tam strēnuē labōrat **ut** multa **perficiat,** *he works* **so** *energetically* **that he accomplishes** *many things.* (Result)

Strēnuē labōrat **ut** multa **perficiat,** *he works energetically* **so that** *he* **may accomplish** *many things.* (Purpose)

Hoc **tantā** benevolentiā dīxit **ut** eōs **nōn offenderet,** *he said this with* **such great** *kindness* **that he did not offend** *them.* (Result)

Hoc magnā benevolentiā dīxit **nē** eōs **offenderet,** *he said this with great kindness* **in order that** *he* **might not offend** *them.* (Purpose)

Saltus erat angustus, **ut** paucī Graecī multōs mīlitēs prohibēre **possent,** *the pass was narrow,* **so that** *a few Greeks* **were able** *to stop many soldiers.* (Result)

In this last example you will notice that there is no "signal word" such as **ita** or **tam** in the main clause, but it is clear from the context that the **ut** clause indicates the *result* of the pass's narrowness (the pass was clearly not designed by nature with the purpose of obstructing Persians, but it was so narrow that the Persians were in fact obstructed by it).

VOCABULARY

fátum, -ī, n., *fate; death* (fatal, fatalism, fatality, fateful, fairy; cp. **fábula, fāma,** and **for,** Ch. 40)

ingénium, -iī, n., *nature, innate talent* (ingenuity, genius, genial, congenial; cp. **genus, gens, gignō,** *to create, give birth to*)

moénia, moénium, n. pl., *walls of a city* (munitions, ammunition; cp. **mūniō,** *to fortify*)

náta, -ae, f., *daughter* (prenatal, postnatal, Natalie; cp. **nātūra, nātālis,** *of birth, natal,* **nāscor,** Ch. 34)

ósculum, -ī, n., *kiss* (osculate, osculation, osculant, oscular, osculatory)

sídus, síderis, n., *constellation, star* (sidereal, consider, desire)

dígnus, -a, -um + abl., *worthy, worthy of* (dignify, dignity from **dignitās,** Ch. 38, indignation from **indignātiō,** deign, disdain, dainty)

dū́rus, -a, -um, *hard, harsh, rough, stern, unfeeling, hardy, difficult* (dour, durable, duration, during, duress, endure, obdurate)

tántus, -a, -um, *so large, so great, of such a size* (tantamount)

dénique, adv., *at last, finally, lastly*

íta, adv. used with adjs., vbs., and advs., *so, thus*

quídem, postpositive adv., *indeed, certainly, at least, even;* **nē . . . quídem,** *not . . . even*

sīc, adv. most commonly with verbs, *so, thus* (sic)

tam, adv. with adjs. and advs., *so, to such a degree;* **tam . . . quam,** *so . . . as;* **tamquam,** *as it were, as if, so to speak*

vérō, adv., *in truth, indeed, to be sure, however* (very, verily, etc.; cp. **vérus, vēritās**)

cóndō, -dere, -didī, -ditum, *to put together* or *into, store; found, establish* (= **con-** + **dō, dare;** condiment, abscond, recondite, sconce)

conténdō, -téndere, -téndī, -téntum, *to strive, struggle, contend; hasten* (contender, contentious; cp. **tendō,** *to stretch, extend*)

móliō, mollíre, mollívī, mollítum, *to soften; make calm* or *less hostile* (mollescent, mollify, mollusk, emollient; cp. **mollis,** *soft, mild*)

púgnō (1), *to fight* (pugnacious, impugn, pugilist, pugilism; cp. **oppugnō,** Ch. 39)

respóndeō, -spondére, -spóndī, -spónsum, *to answer* (respond, response, responsive, responsibility, correspond)

súrgō, súrgere, surréxī, surréctum, *to get up, arise* (surge, resurgent, resurrection, insurgent, insurrection, source, resource)

PRACTICE AND REVIEW

1. Prīnceps arma meliōra in manibus mīlitum posuit, ut hostēs terrērent.
2. Hostēs quidem negāvērunt sē arma dissimilia habēre.
3. Pars mīlitum lūcem diēī vītāvit nē hīc vidērentur.
4. Sōlem prīmam lūcem caelī superī, lūnam prīmam lūcem vesperī, et stēllās oculōs noctis appellābant.
5. Illī adulēscentēs sapientiae dēnique cēdant ut fēlīciōrēs hīs sint.
6. Sapientēs putant beneficia esse potentiōra quam verba acerba et turpia.
7. Quīdam magister verba tam dūra discipulīs dīxit ut discēderent.
8. Respondērunt auctōrem hōrum novem remediōrum esse medicam potentissimam.
9. Nihil vērō tam facile est ut sine labōre id facere possīmus.
10. Prō labōre studiōque patria nostra nōbīs plūrimās occāsiōnēs bonās praestat.
11. Parentēs plūrima ōscula dedērunt nātae gracilī, in quā maximam dēlectātiōnem semper inveniēbant.
12. The words of the philosopher were very difficult, so that those listening were unable to learn them.
13. The two women wished to understand these things so that they might not live base lives.
14. Those four wives were so pleasant that they received very many kindnesses.
15. He said that the writer's third poem was so beautiful that it delighted the minds of thousands of citizens.

SENTENTIAE ANTĪQUAE

1. Omnia vincit Amor; et nōs cēdāmus Amōrī. (Virgil.)
2. Urbem clārissimam condidī; mea moenia vīdī; explēvī cursum quem Fāta dederant. (Virgil.)
3. Ita dūrus erās ut neque amōre neque precibus mollīrī possēs. (Terence.—**prex, precis,** f., *prayer.*)
4. Nēmō quidem tam ferōx est ut nōn mollīrī possit, cultūrā datā. (Horace.—**cultūra, -ae.**)
5. Difficile est saturam nōn scrībere; nam quis est tam patiēns malae urbis ut sē teneat? (Juvenal.—**patiēns,** gen. **patientis,** *tolerant of.*)
6. Fuit quondam in hāc rē pūblicā tanta virtūs ut virī fortēs cīvem perniciōsum ācriōribus poenīs quam acerbissimum hostem reprimerent. (Cicero.—**perniciōsus, -a, -um,** *pernicious.*—**re-primō,** cp. **opprimō.**)
7. Ita praeclāra est recuperātiō lībertātis ut nē mors quidem in hāc rē sit fugienda. (Cicero.—**recuperātiō, -ōnis,** *recovery.*)

8. Nē ratiōnēs meōrum perīculōrum ūtilitātem reī pūblicae vincant. (Cicero.—**ūtilitās, -tātis,** *advantage;* cp. **ūtilis.**)

9. Eō tempore Athēniēnsēs tantam virtūtem praestitērunt ut decemplicem numerum hostium superārent, et hōs sīc perterruērunt ut in Asiam refugerent. (Nepos.—**Athēniēnsēs, -ium,** *Athenians.*—**decemplex, -icis,** *tenfold.*—**per-terreō.**)

10. Ōrātor exemplum dignum petat ab Dēmosthene illō, in quō tantum studium tantusque labor fuisse dīcuntur ut impedīmenta nātūrae dīligentiā industriāque superāret. (Cicero.—**exemplum, -ī,** *example.*—**Dēmosthenēs, -thenis,** a famous Greek orator.—**impedīmentum, -ī.**—**dīligentia, -ae.**—**industria, -ae.**)

Demosthenes
Vatican Museums, Vatican State

11. Praecepta tua sint brevia ut cito mentēs discipulōrum ea discant teneantque memoriā fidēlī. (Horace.—**praeceptum, -ī,** *precept.*)

12. Nihil tam difficile est ut nōn possit studiō invēstīgārī. (Terence.—**invēstīgāre,** *to track down, investigate.*)

13. Bellum autem ita suscipiātur ut nihil nisi pāx quaesīta esse videātur. (Cicero.)

14. Tanta est vīs probitātis ut eam etiam in hoste dīligāmus. (Cicero.)

HOW MANY KISSES ARE ENOUGH?

Quaeris, Lesbia, quot bāsia tua sint mihi satis? Tam multa bāsia quam magnus numerus Libyssae harēnae aut quam sīdera multa quae, ubi tacet nox, furtīvōs amōrēs hominum vident—tam bāsia multa (nēmō numerum scīre potest) sunt satis Catullō īnsānō!

(Catullus 7; prose adaptation.—**quot . . . sint,** *how many . . . are* (an indirect question; see Ch. 30)—**Libyssae,** *Libyan, African.*—**harēna, -ae,** *sand,* here = *the grains of sand.*—**furtīvus, -a, -um,** *stolen, secret.*—**īnsānus, -a, -um.**)

THE NERVOUSNESS OF EVEN A GREAT ORATOR

Ego dehinc ut respondērem surrēxī. Quā sollicitūdine animī surgēbam—dī immortālēs—et quō timōre! Semper quidem magnō cum metū incipiō dīcere. Quotiēnscumque dīcō, mihi videor in iūdicium venīre nōn sōlum ingeniī sed etiam virtūtis atque officiī. Tum vērō ita sum per-turbātus ut omnia timērem. Dēnique mē collēgī et sīc pugnāvī, sīc omnī ratiōne contendī ut nēmō mē neglēxisse illam causam putāret.

(Cicero, *Prō Cluentiō* 51.—**sollicitūdō, -dinis,** f., *anxiety.*—**quotiēnscumque,** adv., *whenever.*—The genitives **ingeniī, virtūtis,** and **officiī** all modify **iūdicium.**—**per-turbāre,** *to disturb, confuse.*—**colligō, -ere, -lēgī, -lēctum,** *to gather, collect, control.*)

YOU'RE ALL JUST WONDERFUL!

Nē laudet dignōs, laudat Callistratus omnēs:
    cui malus est nēmō, quis bonus esse potest?

(*Martial 12.80; meter: elegiac couplet.—**dignōs,** i.e., *only the deserving.*—**Callistratus,** a Greek name, meant to suggest perhaps a former slave.—**quis ... potest,** supply **eī,** antecedent of **cui,** *to a man to whom.*)

ETYMOLOGY

The adverbial ending **-mente** or **-ment** which is so characteristic of Romance languages derives from Lat. **mente** (abl. of **mēns**) used originally as an abl. of manner but now reduced to an adverbial suffix. The following examples are based on Latin adjectives which have already appeared in the vocabularies.

Latin Words	It. Adverb	Sp. Adverb	Fr. Adverb
dūrā mente	duramente	duramente	durement
clārā mente	chiaramente	claramente	clairement
sōlā mente	solamente	solamente	seulement
certā mente	certamente	certamente	certainement
dulcī mente	dolcemente	dulcemente	doucement
brevī mente	brevemente	brevemente	brèvement
facilī mente	facilmente	fácilmente	facilement

Lat. **sīc** is the parent of It. **sì,** Sp. **sí,** and Fr. **si** meaning *yes.*

In the readings

3. precatory, precarious, pray, prayer. 5. patient. 10. exemplar, exemplary, exemplify. 12. vestige, vestigial. "Nervousness": solicitous, solicitude.—perturbation.—collection. "Kisses": arena.—furtive.—insanity.

LATĪNA EST GAUDIUM—ET ŪTILIS!

Salvē! Long-time *Tonight Show* fans will know why I call result clauses "Johnny Carson clauses": during his monologue, Johnny began many an anecdote with the likes of "I saw this fellow the other night who was *so funny . . .* ". Ed McMahon (or some bloke from the audience) then chimes in, "*How* funny *was* he, Johnny?" and Johnny replies, always with a result clause, "Why, he was *so* funny *that . . . !*"

Sunt multae dēlectātiōnēs in novō vocābulāriō nostrō: e.g., there's Virginia's state motto, **sīc semper tyrannīs,** *thus always to tyrants* (death, i.e.!); and **ingenium,** which really means *something inborn,* like a Roman man's **genius** (his inborn guardian spirit, counterpart to the woman's **iūnō,** magnified and deified in the goddess Juno); the connection of **moenia** and **mūnīre** reminds us that fortification walls were the ancients' best munitions, and there's the old proverb **praemonitus, praemūnītus,** *forewarned (is) forearmed;* **sīc** is an editor's annotation, meaning *thus (it was written),* and used to identify an error or peculiarity in a text being quoted.

And here's a brief "kissertation" on the nicest word in this new list: **ōsculum** was the native word for *kiss* (vs. **bāsium,** which the poet Catullus seems to have introduced into the language from the north); it is actually the diminutive of **ōs, ōris** (Ch. 14) and so means literally *little mouth* (which perhaps proves the Romans "puckered up" when they smooched!). Catullus, by the way, loved to invent words, and one was **bāsiātiō,** *kissification* or *smooch-making* ("smooch," by the way, is not Latinate, alas, but Germanic and related to "smack," as in "to smack one's lips," which one might do before enjoying either a kiss or a slice of toast with "Smucker's"!). **Rīdēte et valēte!**

Reconstruction of the Roman Forum, Soprintendenza alle Antichita, Rome, Italy

30

Perfect and Pluperfect Subjunctive; Indirect Questions; Sequence of Tenses

PERFECT AND PLUPERFECT SUBJUNCTIVE

Perfect system subjunctives, like perfect system indicatives, all follow the same basic rules of formation, regardless of the conjugation to which they belong. For the perfect subjunctive active, add **-erī-** + the personal endings to the perfect stem (shortening the **-i-** before **-m, -t,** and **-nt**); for the pluperfect active, add **-issē-** + the personal endings to the perfect stem (shortening the **-e-** before **-m,** etc.). For the passives, substitute the subjunctives **sim** and **essem** for the equivalent indicatives **sum** and **eram.**

The forms of **laudō** are shown below; those for the other model verbs (which follow the very same pattern) are provided in the Appendix.

PERFECT SUBJUNCTIVE ACTIVE

Sg. laudắv-erim, laudắverīs, laudắverit
Pl. laudāverímus, laudāverítis, laudắverint

Note that these forms are identical to those of the future perfect indicative except for the first person singular and the long **-ī-** in certain of the subjunctive forms; the identical forms can be distinguished as indicative or subjunctive by sentence context.

PLUPERFECT SUBJUNCTIVE ACTIVE

Sg.   laudāv-íssem, laudāvíssēs, laudāvísset
Pl.   laudāvissḗmus, laudāvissḗtis, laudāvíssent

Note that these forms resemble the perfect active infinitive, **laudāvisse,** +
the endings (with the **-ē-** long except before **-m,** etc.; cp. the imperfect subjunctive, which resembles the present active infinitive + endings).

PERFECT SUBJUNCTIVE PASSIVE

Sg.   laudā́tus, -a, -um sim, laudā́tus sīs, laudā́tus sit
Pl.   laudā́tī, -ae, -a sī́mus, laudā́tī sī́tis, laudā́tī sint

PLUPERFECT SUBJUNCTIVE PASSIVE

Sg.   laudā́tus, -a, -um éssem, laudā́tus éssēs, laudā́tus ésset
Pl.   laudā́tī, -ae, -a essḗmus, laudā́tī essḗtis, laudā́tī éssent

TRANSLATION AND USAGE

As with the present and imperfect subjunctives, the perfect and pluperfect are employed in a variety of clauses (in accordance with the sequence
of tenses discussed below) and with a variety of translations. Just as *may*
and *might/would* are *sometimes* used in translating the present and imperfect,
respectively, so *may have* and *might have/would have* are *sometimes* employed
with the perfect and pluperfect; likewise, they are often translated as simple
indicatives: the best procedure is to learn the rules for translation of each
clause type.

SYNOPSIS

You have now learned to conjugate a verb fully in all of its finite forms;
following is a complete third person singular synopsis of **agō, agere, ḗgī,**
āctum (cp. Ch. 21):

Indicative Mood

	Pres.	Fut.	Impf.	Perf.	Fut.Perf.	Plupf.
Act.	ágit	áget	agḗbat	ḗgit	ḗgerit	ḗgerat
Pass.	ágitur	agḗtur	agēbā́tur	áctus	áctus	áctus
				est	érit	érat

Subjunctive Mood

	Pres.	Fut.	Impf.	Perf.	Fut.Perf.	Plupf.
Act.	ágat	——	ágeret	ḗgerit	——	ēgísset
Pass.	agátur	——	agerḗtur	áctus	——	áctus
				sit		ésset

INDIRECT QUESTIONS

An indirect question is a subordinate clause which reports some question indirectly, i.e., not via a direct quotation (e.g., "they asked what Gaius was doing" vs. "they asked, 'What is Gaius doing?'"); as such, it is comparable in conception to an indirect statement, which reports indirectly, not a question, but some affirmative statement (see Ch. 25). The indirect question, however, uses a subjunctive verb (not an infinitive) and is easily distinguished from other subjunctive clause types since it is introduced by some interrogative word such as **quis/quid, quī/quae/quod** (i.e., the interrogative adjective), **quam, quandō, cūr, ubi, unde, uter, utrum . . . an** (*whether . . . or*), **-ne** (attached to the clause's first word, = *whether*), etc.; moreover, the verb in the main clause is ordinarily a verb of speech, mental activity, or sense perception (including many of the same verbs that introduce indirect statements: see the list in Ch. 25).

The subjunctive verb in an indirect question is usually translated as though it were an indicative in the same tense (i.e., *without* any auxiliary such as *may* or *might*). Compare the first three examples below, which are direct questions, with the next three, which contain indirect questions:

Quid Gāius facit?	*What is Gaius doing?*
Quid Gāius fēcit?	*What did Gaius do?*
Quid Gāius faciet?	*What will Gaius do?*
Rogant quid Gāius faciat.	*They ask what Gaius is doing.*
Rogant quid Gāius fēcerit.	*They ask what Gaius did.*
Rogant quid Gāius factūrus sit.	*They ask what Gaius will do* (lit., *is about to do*).

Factūrus sit in this last example is a form sometimes called the "future active periphrastic"; in the absence of an actual future subjunctive, this combination of a form of **sum** + the future active participle (cp. the passive periphrastic, consisting of **sum** + the future passive participle, in Ch. 24) was occasionally employed in order to indicate future time unambiguously in certain types of clauses (including the indirect question). In this last example, if the main verb were a past tense, then (in accordance with the rules for sequence of tenses) the sentence would be **rogāvērunt quid Gaius factūrus esset,** *they asked what Gaius would do (was about to do, was going to do).*

SEQUENCE OF TENSES

As in English, so also in Latin, there is a logical sequence of tenses as the speaker or writer proceeds from a main clause to a subordinate clause.

The rule in Latin is simple: a "primary" tense of the indicative must be followed by a primary tense of the subjunctive, and a "historical" (or "secondary") indicative tense must be followed by a historical subjunctive tense, as illustrated in the following chart.

It may be helpful to note at this point that the so-called primary tenses of the indicative, the present and future, both indicate *incomplete* actions (i.e., actions now going on, in the present, or only to be begun in the future), while the historical tenses, as the term implies, refer to past actions.

Group	Main Verb	Subordinate Subjunctive
Primary	Pres. or Fut.	Present (= action *at same time* or *after*) Perfect (= action *before*)
Historical	Past Tenses	Imperfect (= action *at same time* or *after*) Pluperfect (= action *before*)

After a primary main verb the *present* subjunctive indicates action occurring *at the same time* as that of the main verb or *after* that of the main verb. The *perfect* subjunctive indicates action which occurred *before* that of the main verb.

Similarly after a historical main verb the *imperfect* subjunctive indicates action occurring *at the same time* as that of the main verb or *after* that of the main verb. The *pluperfect* subjunctive indicates action which occurred *before* that of the main verb.[1]

These rules for the sequence of tenses operate in purpose clauses, result clauses, indirect questions, and similar constructions to be introduced in subsequent chapters; analyze carefully the sequencing in each of the following examples:

Id **facit** (faciet) ut mē iuvet, *he does (will do) it to help me.*
Id **fēcit** (faciēbat) ut mē iuvāret, *he did (kept doing) it to help me.*

Tam dūrus **est** ut eum vītem, *he is so harsh that I avoid him.*
Tam dūrus **fuit** (erat) ut eum vītārem, *he was so harsh that I avoided him.*

Rogant, rogābunt—*They ask, will ask*
    quid faciat, *what he is doing.*

---

[1] There are two common and quite logical exceptions to the rules for sequence of tenses: a historical present main verb (i.e., a present tense used for the vivid narration of past events) will often take a historical sequence subjunctive, and a perfect tense main verb, when focussing on the present consequences of the past action, may be followed by a primary sequence subjunctive (see P.R. 8 below). Note, too, that since purpose and result clauses logically describe actions that *follow* (actually or potentially) the actions of the main verb, they do not ordinarily contain perfect or pluperfect tense verbs, which indicate *prior* action (though the perfect subjunctive was sometimes used as a *historical* tense in a result clause).

quid fēcerit, *what he did.*

quid factūrus sit, *what he will do.*

Rogāvērunt, rogābant—*They asked, kept asking*

quid faceret, *what he was doing.*

quid fēcisset, *what he had done.*

quid factūrus esset, *what he would do.*

VOCABULARY

hónor, honóris, m., *honor, esteem; public office* (honorable, honorary, honorific, dishonor, honest)

céterī, -ae, -a, pl., *the remaining, the rest, the other, all the others;* cp. **alius,** *another, other* (etc. = et cetera)

quántus, -a, -um, *how large, how great, how much* (quantify, quantity, quantitative, quantum; cp. **tantus**); **tántus . . . quántus,** *just as much (many) . . . as*

rīdículus, -a, -um, *laughable, ridiculous* (ridicule, etc.; cp. **rīdeō, subrīdeō,** Ch. 35)

vívus, -a, -um, *alive, living* (vivid, vivify, convivial; cp. **vīvō, vīta**)

fúrtim, adv., *stealthily, secretly* (furtively, ferret; cp. **fūrtīvus, -a, -um,** *secret, furtive;* **fūr, fūris,** m./f., *thief*)

mox, adv., *soon*

prímō, adv., *at first, at the beginning* (cp. **prīmus, -a, -um**)

repénte, adv., *suddenly*

únde, adv., *whence, from what* or *which place, from which, from whom*

útrum . . . an, conj., *whether . . . or*

bíbō, bíbere, bíbī, *to drink* (bib, bibulous, imbibe, wine-bibber, beverage)

cognóscō, -nóscere, -nóvī, -nitum, *to become acquainted with, learn, recognize;* in perfect tenses, *know* (cognizance, cognizant, cognition, connoisseur, incognito, reconnaissance, reconnoiter; cp. **nōscō, nōscere, nōvī, nōtum,** noble, notice, notify, notion, notorious, and **recognōscō,** Ch. 38)

comprehéndō, -héndere, -héndī, -hénsum, *to grasp, seize, arrest; comprehend, understand* (comprehensive, comprehensible, incomprehensible)

cōnsúmō, -súmere, -súmpsī, -súmptum, *to consume, use up* (consumer, consumption, assume, assumption, presume, presumable, presumption, presumptive, presumptuous, resume, resumption; cp. **sūmō,** *to take*)

dúbitō (1), *to doubt, hesitate* (dubious, dubitable, dubitative, doubtful, doubtless, indubitable, undoubtedly)

expónō, -pónere, -pósuī, -pósitum, *to set forth, explain, expose* (exponent, exposition, expository, expound)

mínuō, minúere, mínuī, minútum, *to lessen, diminish* (cp. **minor, minus,**

minimus; diminish, diminuendo, diminution, diminutive, minuet, minute, minutiae, menu, mince)

rógō (1), *to ask* (interrogate, abrogate, arrogant, derogatory, prerogative, surrogate)

PRACTICE AND REVIEW

1. Rogāvit ubi illae duae discipulae dignae haec didicissent.
2. Vidēbit quanta fuerit vīs illōrum verbōrum fēlīcium.
3. Hās īnsidiās repente exposuit nē rēs pūblica opprimerētur.
4. Hī taceant et trēs cēterī expellantur nē occāsiōnem similem habeant.
5. Ita dūrus erat ut beneficia uxōris comprehendere nōn posset.
6. Cēterī quidem nesciēbant quam ācris esset mēns nātae eōrum.
7. Dēnique prīnceps cognōscet cūr potentior pars mīlitum nōs vītet.
8. Iam cognōvī cūr clāra facta vērō nōn sint facillima.
9. Quīdam auctōrēs appellābant arma optimum remedium malōrum.
10. Mortuīs haec arma mox dēdicēmus nē honōre egeant.
11. Fātō duce, Rōmulus Remusque Rōmam condidērunt; et, Remō necātō, moenia urbis novae cito surrēxērunt.
12. Tell me in what lands liberty is found.
13. We did not know where the sword had finally been put.
14. He does not understand the first words of the little book which they wrote about the constellations.
15. They asked why you could not learn what the rest had done.
16. Let all men now seek better things than money or supreme power so that their souls may be happier.

SENTENTIAE ANTĪQUAE

1. Nunc vidētis quantum scelus contrā rem pūblicam et lēgēs nostrās vōbīs prōnūntiātum sit. (Cicero.)
2. Quam dulcis sit lībertās vōbīs prōtinus dīcam. (Phaedrus.)
3. Rogābat dēnique cūr umquam ex urbe cessissent. (Horace.)
4. Nunc sciō quid sit amor. (*Virgil.)
5. Videāmus uter hīc in mediō forō plūs scrībere possit. (Horace.)
6. Multī dubitābant quid optimum esset. (*Cicero.)
7. Incipiam expōnere unde nātūra omnēs rēs creet alatque. (Lucretius.)
8. Dulce est vidēre quibus malīs ipse careās. (Lucretius.)
9. Auctōrem Trōiānī bellī relēgī, quī dīcit quid sit pulchrum, quid turpe, quid ūtile, quid nōn. (Horace.—**Trōiānus, -a, -um,** *Trojan.*)
10. Doctōs rogābis quā ratiōne bene agere cursum vītae possīs, utrum virtūtem doctrīna paret an nātūra ingeniumque dent, quid minuat cūrās, quid tē amīcum tibi faciat. (Horace.—**doctrīna, -ae,** *teaching.*)
11. Istī autem rogant tantum quid habeās, nōn cūr et unde. (Seneca.)

12. Errat, quī fīnem vēsānī quaerit amōris: vērus amor nūllum nōvit habēre modum. (*Propertius.—**vēsānus, -a, -um,** *insane.*)
13. Sed tempus est iam mē discēdere ut cicūtam bibam, et vōs discēdere ut vītam agātis. Utrum autem sit melius, dī immortālēs sciunt; hominem quidem nēminem scīre crēdō. (Cicero.—Socrates' parting words to the jury which had condemned him to death.—**cicūta, -ae,** *hemlock.*—**nēmō homō,** *no human being.*)

The Death of Socrates, Charles Alphonse Dufresnoy, 17th century
Galleria Palatina, Palazzo Pitti, Florence, Italy

EVIDENCE AND CONFESSION

Sit dēnique scrīptum in fronte ūnīus cuiusque quid dē rē pūblicā sentiat; nam rem pūblicam labōribus cōnsiliīsque meīs ex igne atque ferrō ēreptam esse vidētis. Haec iam expōnam breviter ut scīre possītis quā ratiōne comprehēnsa sint. Semper prōvīdī quō modō in tantīs īnsidiīs salvī esse possēmus. Omnēs diēs cōnsūmpsī ut vidērem quid coniūrātī āctūrī essent. Dēnique litterās intercipere potuī quae ad Catilīnam ā Lentulō aliīsque coniūrātīs missae erant. Tum, coniūrātīs comprehēnsīs et senātū convocātō, contendī in senātum, ostendī litterās Lentulō, quaesīvī cognōsceretne signum. Dīxit sē cognōscere; sed prīmō dubitāvit et negāvit sē dē hīs rēbus respōnsūrum esse. Mox autem ostendit quanta esset vīs cōnscientiae; nam repente mollītus est

atque omnem rem nārrāvit. Tum cēterī coniūrātī sīc fūrtim inter sē aspiciēbant ut nōn ab aliīs indicārī sed indicāre sē ipsī vidērentur.

(Cicero, excerpts from the first and third Catilinarian orations—Cicero finally
succeeded in forcing Catiline to leave Rome, but his henchmen remained and
Cicero still lacked the tangible evidence he needed to convict them in court; in
this passage he shows how he finally obtained not only that evidence but even a
confession. See the readings in Chs. 11 and 14, "Cicero Urges Catiline's Departure" in Ch. 20, and the continuation, "Testimony Against the Conspirators,"
in Ch. 36.—**frōns, frontis**, f., *brow, face.*—**breviter**, adv. of **brevis.**—**prō-videō**, *to
fore-see, give attention to.*—**intercipiō, -ere, -cēpī, -ceptum.**—**cōnscientia, -ae**,
conscience.—**inter sē aspiciō, -ere**, *to glance at each other.*—**indicāre**, *to accuse.*)

A COVERED DISH DINNER!

Mēnsās, Ōle, bonās pōnis, sed pōnis opertās.
Rīdiculum est: possum sīc ego habēre bonās.

(*Martial 10.54; meter: elegiac couplet.—Olus, another of Martial's
"friends."—**opertus, -a, -um**, *concealed, covered.*—**ego**, i.e., even a poor fellow
like me.)

Cocks fighting in front of a mensa
Mosaic from Pompeii, detail
Museo Archeologico Nazionale, Naples, Italy

A LEGACY-HUNTER'S WISH

Nīl mihi dās vīvus; dīcis post fāta datūrum:
sī nōn es stultus, scīs, Maro, quid cupiam!

(*Martial 11.67; meter: elegiac couplet.—**nīl** = **nihil.**—**fāta**, poetic pl. for sg. =
mortem.—**datūrum** = **tē datūrum esse.**—Maro, another of Martial's fictitious
[?] addressees.)

NOTE ON A COPY OF CATULLUS' CARMINA

Tantum magna suō dēbet Vērōna Catullō
quantum parva suō Mantua Vergiliō.

(*Martial 14.195; meter: elegiac couplet. Verona and Mantua were the birthplaces of Catullus and Virgil respectively; see the Introd.—Note the interlocked word order within each verse and the neatly parallel structure between the two verses.)

ETYMOLOGY

The "dubitative" (or "deliberative") subjunctive is another of the independent subjunctives. On the basis of **dubitō** you should have a good sense of the idea conveyed by this subjunctive; e.g., **quid faciat?** *what is he to do* (*I wonder*)?

Further derivatives from the basic **prehendō,** *seize,* are: apprehend, apprentice, apprise, imprison, prehensile, prison, prize, reprehend, reprisal, surprise.

In the readings

"Evidence": front, frontal, affront, confront, effrontery, frontier, frontispiece.—provide, providence, provision, improvident, improvise, improvisation.—interception.—conscientious, conscious, inconscionable.—aspect.

LATĪNA EST GAUDIUM—ET ŪTILIS!

Salvēte, amīcī! This chapter's **vocābulārium novum** brings a veritable **cēna verbōrum** for your **mēnsa Latīna;** let's start with the main course: the **cursus honōrum,** a familiar phrase in Eng., was the traditional course of political office-holding in Rome; ordinarily one served first as **quaestor** (a treasury official), then as **praetor** (judge), and only later as **cōnsul.** The consulship was something like our presidency, but the term was one year, and there were two consuls, each with veto power over the other (Cicero, as you recall, was one of the consuls in 63 B.C., when he uncovered the Catilinarian conspiracy).

Now for the **mēnsa secunda,** Lat. for *dessert:* first, an old proverb that will serve you near as well as **carpe diem: occāsiōnem cognōsce!** And here's another that may save you from temptation to even the slightest of crimes: **nēmō repente fuit turpissimus,** *no one was ever suddenly most vicious* (Juvenal 2.83: the satirist meant that even the worst criminals attained that status through the gradual accumulation of guilty acts). An honorary degree is granted **honōris causā; honōrēs mūtant mōrēs** is an ancient truism; from **cēterī,** besides **et cētera/etc.,** is **cētera dēsunt,** *the rest is lacking,* an editorial notation for missing sections of a text; from **quantus** comes a large quantity of phrases, one of which should be sufficient here, **quantum satis,** *as much as suffices* (if you are not satisfied, see Chs. 32 and 35; and when day is done you can shout **mox nox, in rem,** *soon ('twill be) night, (let's get down) to business.* **Valēte!**

31

Cum Clauses; Ferō

Cum CLAUSES

You are already quite familiar with the use of **cum** as a preposition. **Cum** can also serve as a conjunction, meaning *when, since,* or *although* and introducing a subordinate clause.

Sometimes the verb in a **cum** clause is indicative, especially when describing the precise time of an action. In these so-called "**cum** temporal clauses," **cum** is translated *when* (or *while*); **tum** is occasionally found in the main clause, and **cum . . . tum** together may be translated *not only . . . but also:*

Cum eum vidēbis, eum cognōscēs, *when you (will) see him* [i.e., at that very moment], *you will recognize him.*

Cum vincimus, tum pācem spērās, *when (while) we are winning, you are (at the same time) hoping for peace.*

Cum ad illum locum vēnerant, tum amīcōs contulerant, *when they had come to that place, they had brought their friends* or *not only had they come to that place, but they had also brought their friends.*

Very often, however, the verb of the **cum** clause is in the subjunctive mood, especially when it describes either the general circumstances (rather than the exact time) when the main action occurred (often called a "**cum** circumstantial clause"), or explains the cause of the main action ("**cum** causal"), or describes a circumstance that might have obstructed the main action or is in some other way opposed to it ("**cum** adversative"):

Cum hoc fēcisset, ad tē fūgit.
When he had done this, he fled to you. (circumstantial)

Cum hoc scīret, potuit eōs iuvāre.
Since he knew this, he was able to help them. (causal)

Cum hoc scīret, tamen mīlitēs mīsit.
Although he knew this, nevertheless he sent the soldiers. (adversative)

Cum Gāium dīligerēmus, nōn poterāmus eum iuvāre.
Although we loved Gaius, we could not help him. (adversative)

Remember that when **cum** is followed immediately by a noun or pronoun in the ablative case, you should translate it *with.* When instead it introduces a subordinate clause, translate it *when, since, although,* etc. You should have little difficulty distinguishing among the four basic types of **cum** clauses: the temporal has its verb in the indicative, and the three subjunctive types can generally be recognized by analyzing the relationship between the actions in the main clause and the subordinate clause (note, too, that in the case of adversative clauses the adverb **tamen** often appears in the main clause). The verb in a **cum** clause, whatever its type, is regularly translated *as an indicative,* i.e., without an auxiliary such as *may* or *might.*

IRREGULAR *Ferō, ferre, tulī, lātum,*
to bear, carry

Ferō is one of a series of irregular verbs to be introduced in the closing chapters of this text (the others being **volō, nōlō, mālō, fīō,** and **eō**); they are all very commonly used and should be learned thoroughly.

The English verb "to bear" is cognate with Latin **ferō, ferre** and has generally the same basic and metaphorical meanings, *to carry* and *to endure.* In the present system **ferō** is simply a third conjugation verb, formed exactly like **agō** except that the stem vowel does not appear in a few places, including the infinitive **ferre.** The only irregular forms, all of them in the present tense (indicative, imperative, and infinitive), are highlighted below in bold; the imperfect subjunctive, while formed on the irregular infinitive **ferre,** nevertheless follows the usual pattern of present infinitive + endings. Remember that the singular imperative lacks the **-e,** just like **dīc, dūc,** and **fac** (Ch. 8).

Although **tulī** (originally **tetulī**) and **lātum** (originally ***tlātum**) derive ultimately from a different verb related to **tollō** (the Eng. hybrid "go, went, gone," e.g., is similarly composed from two different verbs through a common linguistic phenomenon known as "suppletion"), their conjugation follows the regular pattern and so should cause no difficulty.

Present Indicative

Active

1. férō
2. **fers** (cp. ágis)
3. **fert** (cp. ágit)

1. férimus
2. **fértis** (cp. ágitis)
3. férunt

Passive

féror
férris (ágeris)
fértur (ágitur)

férimur
feríminī
ferúntur

Present Imperative

Active

2. **fer** (áge), **férte** (ágite)

Infinitives

Active

Pres. **férre** (ágere)
Perf. tulísse
Fut. lātū́rus ésse

Passive

férrī (ágī)
lātus ésse
lātum írī

SYNOPSIS

The following third person singular synopsis, showing irregular forms in bold and taken together with the preceding summary, should provide a useful overview of the conjugation of **ferō;** for the complete conjugation, see the Appendix (p. 459–60)

Indicative Mood

	Pres.	Fut.	Impf.	Perf.	Fut.Perf.	Plupf.
Act.	**fert**	féret	ferḗbat	túlit	túlerit	túlerat
Pass.	**fértur**	ferḗtur	ferēbā́tur	lā́tus est	lā́tus érit	lā́tus érat

Subjunctive Mood

	Pres.	Fut.	Impf.	Perf.	Fut.Perf.	Plupf.
Act.	férat	—	**férret**	túlerit	—	tulísset
Pass.	ferā́tur	—	**ferrḗtur**	lā́tus sit	—	lā́tus ésset

VOCABULARY

as, ássis, m., *an as* (a small copper coin, roughly equivalent to a penny; ace)

auxílium, -iī, n., *aid, help* (auxiliary; cp. **augeō,** *to increase, augment*)

dígitus, -ī, m., *finger, toe* (digit, digital, digitalis, digitalize, digitate, digitize, prestidigitation; see **Latīna Est Gaudium,** Ch. 20)

elephántus, -ī, m. and f., *elephant* (elephantiasis, elephantine)

exsílium, -ií, n., *exile, banishment* (exilic)

invídia, -ae, f., *envy, jealousy, hatred* (invidious, invidiousness, envious; cp. **invideō** below)

rúmor, rūmóris, m., *rumor, gossip* (rumormonger)

vínum, -ī, n., *wine* (vine, vinegar, viniculture, viniferous, vintage, vinyl)

medíocris, medíocre, *ordinary, moderate, mediocre* (mediocrity; cp. **medius**)

cum, conj. + subj., *when, since, although;* conj. + indic., *when*

ápud, prep. + acc., *among, in the presence of, at the house of*

sémel, adv., *a single time, once, once and for all, simultaneously*

úsque, adv., *all the way, up (to), even (to), continuously, always*

dóleō, dolére, dóluī, dolitúrum, *to grieve, suffer; hurt, give pain* (doleful, dolor, dolorous, Dolores, condole, condolences, indolent, indolence; cp. **dolor,** Ch. 38)

dórmiō, dormíre, dormívī, dormítum, *to sleep* (dormitory, dormer, dormancy, dormant, dormouse)

férō, férre, túlī, látum, *to bear, carry, bring; suffer, endure, tolerate; say, report* (fertile, circumference, confer, defer, differ, infer, offer, prefer, proffer, refer, suffer, transfer; cp. bear)

ádferō, adférre, áttulī, allátum, *to bring to* (afferent)

cónferō, cōnférre, cóntulī, collátum, *to bring together, compare; confer, bestow;* **sē cōnférre,** *betake oneself, go* (conference, collation)

ófferō, offérre, óbtulī, oblátum, *to offer* (offertory, oblation)

réferō, reférre, réttulī, relátum, *to carry back, bring back; repeat, answer, report* (refer, reference, referent, referral, relate, relation, relative)

invídeō, -vidére, -vídī, -vísum, *to be envious;* + dat. (see Ch. 35), *to look at with envy, envy, be jealous of*

óccidō, -cídere, -cidī, -cásum, *to fall down; die; set* (occident, occidental, occasion, occasional; cp. **cadō, occāsiō**)

PRACTICE AND REVIEW

1. Iam vērō cognōvimus istās mentēs dūrās ferrum prō pāce offerre.
2. Nē nātae geminae discant verba tam acerba et tam dūra.
3. Cum hī decem virī ex moenibus semel discessissent, alia occāsiō pācis numquam oblāta est.
4. Tantum auxilium nōbīs referet ut nē ācerrimī quidem mīlitēs aut pugnāre aut hīc remanēre possint.
5. Rogābat cūr cēterae tantam fidem apud nōs praestārent et nōbīs tantam spem adferrent.
6. Cum patria nostra tanta beneficia offerat, tamen quīdam sē in īnsidiās fūrtim cōnferunt et contrā bonōs mox pugnābunt.
7. Dēnique audiāmus quantae sint hae īnsidiae ac quot coniūrātī contrā cīvitātem surgant.

8. Haec scelera repente exposuī nē alia et similia ferrētis.
9. Respondērunt plūrima arma ā mīlitibus ad lītus allāta esse et in nāvibus condita esse.
10. Cum parentēs essent vīvī, fēlīcēs erant; mortuī quoque sunt beātī.
11. Nesciō utrum trēs coniūrātī maneant an in exsilium contenderint.
12. Nōs cōnferāmus ad cēnam, meī amīcī, bibāmus multum vīnī, cōnsū-
    māmus noctem, atque omnēs cūrās nostrās minuāmus!
13. When the soldiers had been arrested, they soon offered us money.
14. Although life brings very difficult things, let us endure them all and
    dedicate ourselves to philosophy.
15. Since you know what help is being brought by our six friends, these
    evils can be endured with courage.
16. Although his eyes could not see the light of the sun, nevertheless
    that humble man used to do very many and very difficult things.

SENTENTIAE ANTĪQUAE

1. Potestne haec lūx esse tibi iūcunda, cum sciās hōs omnēs cōnsilia
   tua cognōvisse? (Cicero.)
2. Themistoclēs, cum Graeciam servitūte Persicā līberāvisset et propter
   invidiam in exsilium expulsus esset, ingrātae patriae iniūriam nōn
   tulit quam ferre dēbuit. (Cicero.—**Persicus, -a, -um.**—**ingrātus, -a,
   -um,** *ungrateful.*—**iniūria, -ae,** *injury.*)
3. Quae cum ita sint, Catilīna, cōnfer tē in exsilium. (Cicero.—**quae
   cum = et cum haec.**)
4. Ō nāvis, novī flūctūs bellī tē in mare referent! Ō quid agis? Unde erit
   ūllum perfugium? (Horace.—**nāvis,** *ship [of state].*—**flūctus, -ūs,**
   wave, billow.)
5. Cum rēs pūblica immortālis esse dēbeat, doleō eam salūtis egēre ac
   in vītā ūnīus mortālis cōnsistere. (Cicero.—**cōnsistō, -ere + in,** *to
   depend on.*)
6. Cum illum hominem esse servum nōvisset, eum comprehendere nōn
   dubitāvit. (Cicero.)
7. Ille comprehēnsus, cum prīmō impudenter respondēre coepisset, dēnique tamen nihil negāvit. (Cicero.—**impudenter,** adv.)
8. Milō dīcitur per stadium vēnisse cum bovem umerīs ferret. (Cicero.—**Milō, -lōnis,** m., a famous Greek athlete.—**stadium, -iī.**—**bōs,
   bovis,** m./f., *ox.*—**umerus, -ī,** *shoulder.*)
9. Quid vesper et somnus ferant, incertum est. (Livy.)
10. Ferte miserō tantum auxilium quantum potestis. (Terence.)
11. Hoc ūnum sciō: quod fāta ferunt, id ferēmus aequō animō.
    (Terence.)
12. Lēgum dēnique idcircō omnēs servī sumus, ut līberī esse possīmus.
    (*Cicero.—**idcircō,** adv., *for this reason.*)

GIVE ME A THOUSAND KISSES!

Vīvāmus, mea Lesbia, atque amēmus,
rūmōrēsque senum sevēriōrum
omnēs ūnius aestimēmus assis!
Sōlēs occidere et redīre possunt;
5   nōbīs cum semel occidit brevis lūx,
nox est perpetua ūna dormienda.
Dā mī bāsia mīlle, deinde centum;
dein mīlle altera, dein secunda centum;
deinde ūsque altera mīlle, deinde centum.
10   Dein, cum mīlia multa fēcerīmus—
conturbābimus illa, nē sciāmus,
aut nē quis malus invidēre possit,
cum tantum sciat esse bāsiōrum.

(*Catullus 5; an exhortation to love, and to ignore the grumbling of stern old men who envy the young and curse their passion.—**rūmōrēs,** with **omnēs;** adj. and noun were often widely separated in poetry, so it is especially important to take note of the endings.—**sevērus, -a, -um.**—**ūnius . . . assis,** gen. of value, *at one penny.*—**aestimāre,** *to value, estimate.*—**redīre,** *to return.*—**nōbīs,** dat. of reference [Ch. 38], here = **nostra,** with **brevis lūx.**—**mī = mihi.**—**dein = deinde.**—**conturbāre,** *to throw into confusion, mix up, jumble;* possibly an allusion to disturbing the counters on an abacus.—**nē sciāmus,** sc. **numerum;** if the number is unknown then, in a sense, it is limitless.—**quis,** here *someone.*—**invidēre,** with **malus,** means both *to envy* and *to cast an evil eye upon,* i.e., to hex.—**tantum,** with **bāsiōrum,** gen. of the whole, = *so many kisses.*)

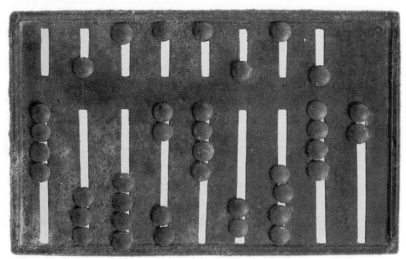

Small Roman abacus, Museo Nazionale Romano delle Terme, Rome, Italy

RINGO

Sēnōs Charīnus omnibus digitīs gerit
   nec nocte pōnit ānulōs
nec cum lavātur. Causa quae sit quaeritis?
   Dactyliothēcam nōn habet!

(*Martial 11.59; meter: iambic trimeter and dimeter.—Charinus, an ostentatious chap who liked to show off his rings.—**sēnī, -ae, -a,** *six each, six apiece,* here with **ānulōs,** *rings* [see **Latīna Est Gaudium,** Ch. 20]; what effect might the poet be hoping to achieve by so widely separating noun and adj.?—**pōnit** = **dēpōnit,** *put away.*—**lavāre,** *to bathe.*—**Causa ... quaeritis:** the usual order would be **quaeritisne quae sit causa.**—**dactyliothēca, -ae,** *a ring-box, jewelry chest.*)

Gold ring
Kunsthistorisches Museum, Vienna, Austria

FACĒTIAE (WITTICISMS)

Cum Cicerō apud Damasippum cēnāret et ille, mediocrī vīnō in mēnsā positō, dīceret, "Bibe hoc Falernum; hoc est vīnum quadrāgintā annōrum," Cicerō respondit, "Bene aetātem fert!"

(Macrobius, *Sāturnālia* 2.3.—**Falernum, -ī,** *Falernian wine,* actually a very famous wine, not a "mediocre" one.—**quadrāgintā,** indecl., *40.*)

Augustus, cum quīdam rīdiculus eī libellum trepidē adferret, et modo prōferret manum et modo retraheret, "Putās," inquit, "tē assem elephantō dare?"

(Macrobius, *Sāturnālia* 2.4.—**trepidē,** adv., *in confusion.*—**modo ... modo,** *now ... now.*—**re-trahō.**—**elephantō:** one thinks of a child offering a peanut to a circus elephant.)

ETYMOLOGY

In the readings

2. ingrate, ingratitude.—injurious. 4. fluctuate. 5. consist, consistent. 7. impudent, impudence. 8. bovine.—humerus, humeral. "Kisses": severe, severity, asseverate.—estimate, estimation, inestimable. "Ringo": annulus, annular eclipse, annulate, annulet (all spelled with *nn,* perhaps by analogy with **annus,** *year,* despite the classical **ānulus,** which—to get down to "fundamentals"—is actually the diminutive of **ānus,** *ring, circle, anus*). "**Facētiae**": trepidation.—retract, retraction.

LATĪNA EST GAUDIUM—ET ŪTILIS!

Iterum salvēte, doctae doctīque! Having made it this far, you've certainly earned that appellation, and, as a further reward, here are more tidbits **ex vocābuláriō novō huius capitis,** all focussed on that villainous Catiline: to start with, there's that famous **cum** temporal clause from Cicero's indictment of Catiline: **cum tacent, clāmant,** *when they are silent, they are shouting,* i.e., "by their silence they condemn you." Poor Catiline, perhaps he had too much to drink, **ūsque ad nauseam,** and spilled the beans, ignoring the warning, **in vīnō vēritās;** if only he had observed Horace's **aurea mediocritās,** *the golden mean,* he might have received **auxilium ab altō,** *help from on high,* but the gods, it appears, were against him. And so he soon met his end, **semel et simul,** *once and for all:* **valē, miser Catilīna, et vōs omnēs, amīcī vēritātis honōrisque, valeātis!**

32

Formation and Comparison of Adverbs; Volō, Mālō, Nōlō; Proviso Clauses

FORMATION AND COMPARISON OF ADVERBS

You are by now familiar with a wide range of Latin adverbs, words employed (as in English) to modify verbs, adjectives, or other adverbs. Many have their own peculiar forms and endings and must simply be memorized when first introduced in the vocabularies (often without benefit of English derivatives to aid in the memorization): among these are **cūr, etiam, ita, tam,** etc.

POSITIVE DEGREE

A great many adverbs, however, are formed directly from adjectives and are easily recognized. Many first/second declension adjectives form positive degree adverbs by adding **-ē** to the base:

lóng-ē	(*far;* longus, -a, -um)
líber-ē	(*freely;* līber, lībera, līberum)
púlchr-ē	(*beautifully;* pulcher, -chra, -chrum)

From adjectives of the third declension, adverbs are often formed by adding **-iter** to the base; if the base ends in **-nt-** only **-er** is added:

fórt-iter	(*bravely;* fortis, -e)
celér-iter	(*quickly,* celer, celeris, celere)
ácr-iter	(*keenly;* ācer, ācris, ācre)
fēlíc-iter	(*happily;* fēlīx, gen. fēlīcis)
sapiént-er	(*wisely;* sapiēns, gen. sapientis)

COMPARATIVE AND SUPERLATIVE DEGREE

Many Latin adverbs have comparative and superlative forms, just as they do in English, and their English translations correspond to those of comparative and superlative adjectives; e.g., positive degree "quickly"; comparative "more (rather, too) quickly"; superlative "most (very) quickly," etc.

The comparative degree of adverbs is with few exceptions the **-ius** form which you have already learned as the neuter of the comparative degree of the adjective.

The superlative degree of adverbs, being normally derived from the superlative degree of adjectives, regularly ends in **-ē** according to the rule given above for converting adjectives of the first and the second declensions into adverbs.

Quam WITH COMPARATIVE AND SUPERLATIVE ADVERBS

Quam is used with adverbs in essentially the same ways as with adjectives: **hic puer celerius cucurrit quam ille,** *this boy ran more quickly than that one;* **illa puella quam celerrimē cucurrit,** *that girl ran as quickly as possible.* The ablative of comparison is not ordinarily employed after comparative adverbs (except in poetry).

COMPARISON OF IRREGULAR ADVERBS

When the comparison of an adjective is irregular (see Ch. 27), the comparison of the adverb derived from it normally follows the basic irregularities of the adjective but, of course, has adverbial endings. Study carefully the following list of representative adverbs; those that do not follow the standard rules stated above for forming adverbs from adjectives are highlighted in bold (be prepared to point out how they do not conform). Note the alternate superlatives **prīmō,** which usually means *first (in time)* vs. **prīmum,** usually *first (in a series);* **quam prīmum,** however, has the idiomatic translation *as soon as possible.*

Positive	Comparative	Superlative
lóngē (*far*)	lóngius (*farther, too f.*)	longíssimē (*farthest, very f.*)
líberē (*freely*)	lībérius (*more f.*)	lībérrimē (*most, very f.*)
púlchrē (*beautifully*)	púlchrius (*more b.*)	pulchérrimē (*most b.*)
fórtiter (*bravely*)	fórtius (*more b.*)	fortíssimē (*most b.*)

celériter (*quickly*)   celérius (*more q.*)   celérrimē (*most q.*)
ácriter (*keenly*)   ácrius (*more k.*)   ācérrimē (*most k.*)
fēlíciter (*happily*)   fēlícius (*more h.*)   fēlīcíssimē (*most h.*)
sapiénter (*wisely*)   sapiéntius (*more w.*)   sapientíssimē (*most w.*)
fácile (*easily*)   facílius (*more e.*)   facíllimē (*most e.*)
béne (*well*)   mélius (*better*)   óptimē (*best*)
mále (*badly*)   peíus (*worse*)   péssimē (*worst*)
múltum (*much*)   plūs (*more,* quantity)   **plúrimum** (*most, very much*)
magnópere (*greatly*)   **mágis** (*more,* quality)   máximē (*most, especially*)
párum (*little, not very [much]*)   mínus (*less*)   mínimē (*least*)

(prō)   príus (*before, earlier*)   { **prímō** (*first, at first*) **prímum** (*in the first place*)

díū (*for a long time*)   **diútius** (*longer*)   **diūtíssimē** (*very long*)

IRREGULAR *Volō, velle, voluī,* to wish

Like **ferō,** introduced in the last chapter, **volō** is another extremely common third conjugation verb which, though regular for the most part, does have several irregular forms, including the present infinitive **velle.** Remember these points:

—**volō** has no passive forms at all, no future active infinitive or participle, and no imperatives;
—the perfect system is entirely regular;
—the only irregular forms are in the present indicative (which must be memorized) and the present subjunctive (which is comparable to **sim, sīs, sit**);
—the imperfect subjunctive resembles that of **ferō;** while formed from the irregular infinitive **velle,** it nevertheless follows the usual pattern of present infinitive + personal endings;
—**vol-** is the base in the present system indicatives, **vel-** in the subjunctives.

Pres. Ind.	Pres. Subj.	Impf. Subj.	Infinitives
1. vólō	vélim	véllem	*Pres.* vélle
2. vīs	vélīs	véllēs	*Perf.* voluísse
3. vult	vélit	véllet	*Fut.*———
1. vólumus	velímus	vellémus	**Participle**
2. vúltis	velítis	vellétis	*Pres.* vólēns
3. vólunt	vélint	véllent	

SYNOPSIS

The following third person singular synopsis, with irregular forms in bold, should provide a useful overview of the conjugation of **volō**; for the complete conjugation, see the Appendix (p. 458–59).

Indicative Mood

	Pres.	Fut.	Impf.	Perf.	Fut.Perf.	Plupf.
Act.	**vult**	vólet	volébat	vóluit	volúerit	volúerat

Subjunctive Mood

	Pres.	Fut.	Impf.	Perf.	Fut.Perf.	Plupf.
Act.	**vélit**	—	**véllet**	volúerit	—	voluísset

Nōlō AND Mālō

The compounds **nōlō, nōlle, nōluī** (**nē + volō**), *not to wish, to be unwilling,* and **mālō, mālle, māluī** (**magis + volō**), *to want (something) more* or *instead, prefer,* follow **volō** closely, but have long vowels in their stems (**nō-, mā-**) and some other striking peculiarities, especially in the present indicative.

PRESENT INDICATIVE OF Nōlō

Sg. nólō, nōn vīs, nōn vult **Pl.** nólumus, nōn vúltis, nólunt

PRESENT INDICATIVE OF Mālō

Sg. málō, mávīs, mávult **Pl.** málumus, māvúltis, málunt

The following synopses provide representative forms, again with irregular forms in bold, but you should see the Appendix (p. 458–59) for the full conjugation of these verbs.

Indicative Mood

	Pres.	Fut.	Impf.	Perf.	Fut.Perf.	Plupf.
Act.	**nōn vult**	nólet	nōlébat	nóluit	nōlúerit	nōlúerat

Subjunctive Mood

	Pres.	Fut.	Impf.	Perf.	Fut.Perf.	Plupf.
Act.	**nólit**	—	**nóllet**	nōlúerit	—	nōluísset

Indicative Mood

	Pres.	Fut.	Impf.	Perf.	Fut.Perf.	Plupf.
Act.	**mávult**	málet	mālébat	máluit	mālúerit	mālúerat

Subjunctive Mood

	Pres.	Fut.	Impf.	Perf.	Fut.Perf.	Plupf.
Act.	**málit**	—	**mállet**	mālúerit	—	māluísset

Nōlō AND NEGATIVE COMMANDS

While **volō** and **mālō** lack imperatives, **nōlō** has both singular and plural imperatives that were very commonly employed along with complementary infinitives to express negative commands:

Nōlī manēre, Catilīna, *do not remain, Catiline!*

Nōlīte discēdere, amīcī meī, *do not leave, my friends!*

PROVISO CLAUSES

The subjunctive is used in a subordinate clause introduced by **dummodo,** *provided that, so long as,* and certain other words that express a provisional circumstance or "proviso"; **nē** is used as the negative in such clauses.

Nōn timēbō, dummodo hīc remaneās, *I shall not be afraid, provided that you remain here.*

Erimus fēlīcēs, dummodo nē discēdās, *we shall be happy, so long as (provided that) you do not leave.*

Note that the verb in such clauses is simply translated as an indicative.

VOCABULARY

custódia, -ae, f., *protection, custody;* pl., *guards* (custodian, custodial)

exércitus, -ūs, m., *army* (exercise)

paupértās, paupertátis, f., *poverty, humble circumstances* (cp. **pauper** below)

díves, gen. **dívitis** or **dítis,** *rich,* (Dives)

pār, gen. **páris** + dat. (cp. Ch. 35), *equal, like* (par, pair, parity, peer, peerless, disparage, disparity, umpire, nonpareil)

paúper, gen. **paúperis,** *of small means, poor* (poverty, impoverished; cp. **paupertās**)

dúmmodo, conj. + subj., *provided that, so long as*

All adverbs given in the list above, p. 220–21.

málō, málle, máluī, *to want (something) more, instead; prefer*

nōlō, nólle, nóluī, *to not . . . wish, be unwilling* (nolo contendere, nol. pros.)

páteō, patére, pátuī, *to be open, lie open; be accessible; be evident* (patent, pātent, patency)

praébeō, -bére, -buī, -bitum, *to offer, provide*

prōmíttō, -míttere, -mísī, -míssum, *to send forth; promise* (promissory)

vólō, vélle, vóluī, *to wish, want, be willing, will* (volition, voluntary, involuntary, volunteer, volitive, voluptuous, benevolent, malevolent, nolens volens)

PRACTICE AND REVIEW

1. Prīmō illī trēs rīdiculī nē mediocria quidem perīcula fortiter ferre poterant et ūllum auxilium offerre nōlēbant.
2. Maximē rogāvimus quantum auxilium septem fēminae adferrent et utrum dubitārent an nōs mox adiūtūrae essent.
3. Dēnique armīs collātīs, imperātor prōmīsit decem mīlia mīlitum celerrimē discessūra esse, dummodo satis cōpiārum reciperent.
4. Paria beneficia, igitur, in omnēs dignōs cōnferre māvultis.
5. Haec mala melius expōnant nē dīvitiās minuant aut honōrēs suōs āmittant.
6. At volumus cognōscere cūr sīc invīderit et cūr verba eius tam dūra fuerint.
7. Cum cēterī hās īnsidiās cognōverint, vult in exsilium fūrtim ac quam celerrimē sē cōnferre ut rūmōrēs et invidiam vītet.
8. Multīne discipulī tantum studium ūsque praestant ut hās sententiās facillimē ūnō annō legere possint?
9. Cum dīvitiās āmīsisset et ūnum assem nōn habēret, tamen omnēs cīvēs ingenium mōrēsque eius maximē laudābant.
10. Plūra meliōraque lēgibus aequīs quam ferrō certē faciēmus.
11. Oculī tuī sunt pulchriōrēs sīderibus caelī, mea puella; es gracilis et bella, ac ōscula sunt dulciōra vīnō: amēmus sub lūce lūnae!
12. Iste hostis, in Italiam cum multīs elephantīs veniēns, prīmō pugnāre nōluit et plūrimōs diēs in montibus cōnsūmpsit.
13. Sī nepōs tē ad cēnam invītābit, mēnsam explēbit et tibi tantum vīnī offeret quantum vīs; nōlī, autem, nimium bibere.
14. Do you wish to live longer and better?
15. He wishes to speak as wisely as possible so that they may yield to him very quickly.
16. When these plans had been learned, we asked why he had been unwilling to prepare the army with the greatest possible care.
17. That man, who used to be very humble, now so keenly wishes to have wealth that he is willing to lose his two best friends.

SENTENTIAE ANTĪQUAE

1. Occāsiō nōn facile praebētur sed facile ac repente āmittitur. (Publilius Syrus.)
2. Nōbīscum vīvere iam diūtius nōn potes; nōlī remanēre; id nōn ferēmus. (Cicero.)
3. Vīs rēctē vīvere? Quis nōn? (*Horace.—**rēctus, -a, -um,** *straight, right.*)
4. Plūs nōvistī quid faciendum sit. (Terence.)
5. Mihi vērē dīxit quid vellet. (Terence.)

6. Parēs cum paribus facillimē congregantur. (*Cicero.—**congregāre,** *to gather into a flock.*)
7. Tē magis quam oculōs meōs amō. (Terence.)
8. Hominēs libenter id crēdunt quod volunt. (Caesar.—**libēns, -entis,** *willing.*)
9. Multa ēveniunt hominibus quae volunt et quae nōlunt. (Plautus.—**ēvenīre,** *to happen.*)
10. Cōnsiliō melius contendere atque vincere possumus quam īrā. (Publilius Syrus.)
11. Optimus quisque facere māvult quam dīcere. (Sallust.—**māvult quam = magis vult quam.**)
12. Omnēs sapientēs fēlīciter, perfectē, fortūnātē vīvunt. (Cicero.—**perfectus, -a, -um,** *complete.*)
13. Maximē eum laudant quī pecūniā nōn movētur. (Cicero.)
14. Sī vīs scīre quam nihil malī in paupertāte sit, cōnfer pauperem et dīvitem: pauper saepius et fidēlius rīdet. (Seneca.)
15. Magistrī puerīs crūstula dant ut prīma elementa discere velint. (Horace.—**crūstulum, -ī,** *cookie.*—**elementum, -ī.**)
16. Sī vīs mē flēre, dolendum est prīmum ipsī tibi. (*Horace.—**flēre,** to weep.)

THE CHARACTER OF CIMON

Cimōn celeriter ad summōs honōrēs pervēnit. Habēbat enim satis ēloquentiae, summam līberālitātem, magnam scientiam lēgum et reī mīlitāris, quod cum patre ā puerō in exercitibus fuerat. Itaque hic populum urbānum in suā potestāte facillimē tenuit et apud exercitum valuit plūrimum auctōritāte.

Cum ille occidisset, Athēniēnsēs dē eō diū doluērunt; nōn sōlum in bellō, autem, sed etiam in pāce eum graviter dēsīderāvērunt. Fuit enim vir tantae līberālitātis ut, cum multōs hortōs habēret, numquam in hīs custōdiās pōneret; nam hortōs līberrimē patēre voluit nē populus ab hīs frūctibus prohibērētur. Saepe autem, cum aliquem minus bene vestītum vidēret, eī suum amiculum dedit. Multōs locuplētāvit; multōs pauperēs vīvōs iūvit atque mortuōs suō sūmptū extulit. Sīc minimē mīrum est sī, propter mōrēs Cimōnis, vīta eius fuit sēcūra et mors eius fuit omnibus tam acerba quam mors cuiusdam ex familiā.

(Nepos, *Cimōn;* adapted excerpts.—**per-venīre.**—**ēloquentia, -ae.**—**līberālitās, -tātis.**—**mīlitāris, -e.**—**ā puerō,** *from his boyhood.*—**potestās, -tātis,** *power.*—**auctōritās, -tātis,** *authority;* the abl. tells in what respect.—**Athēniēnsēs,** *Athenians.*—**hortus, -ī,** garden,—**vestītus, -a, -um,** *clothed.*—**amiculum, -ī,** *cloak.*—**locuplētāre,** *to enrich.*—**sūmptus, -ūs,** *expense.*—**extulit: ef-ferō,** *bury.*—**mīrus, -a, -um,** *surprising.*—**sē-cūrus, -a, -um: sē-** means *without.*)

A VACATION . . . FROM YOU!

Quid mihi reddat ager quaeris, Line, Nōmentānus?
   Hoc mihi reddit ager: tē, Line, nōn videō!

(*Martial 2.38; meter: elegiac couplet.—**reddō, -ere,** *to give back, return (in profit).*—**Linus, -ī,** another of Martial's addressees.—**Nōmentānus, -a, -um,** *in Nomentum,* a town of Latium known for its wine industry.)

PLEASE . . . DON'T!

Nīl recitās et vīs, Māmerce, poēta vidērī.
   Quidquid vīs estō, dummodo nīl recitēs!

(*Martial 2.88; meter: elegiac couplet.—**nīl** = **nihil.**—**Māmercus, -ī.**—**estō,** fut. imper. of **esse,** *"Be . . . !"*)

ETYMOLOGY

In the readings   3. rectitude, rectify, direct, erect, correct; cp. right. 6. congregate, segregate, gregarious, aggregate. 9. event (=out-come), eventual. 12. perfect (= made or done thoroughly). "Cimon": vest, vestment, invest, divest.—sumptuous, sumptuary.—miraculous, admire. "Vacation": render, rendering, rendition.

LATĪNA EST GAUDIUM—ET ŪTILIS!

Salvēte! The modern Olympic games have as their motto three comparative adverbs, **citius, altius** (from **altus, -a, -um,** *high*), **fortius.** The new irregular verbs in this chapter, especially **volō** and **nōlō** are extremely common in Lat. and you'll find them, willy-nilly, all through English. You know very well, for example, the legal plea of **nōlō,** short for **nōlō contendere,** *I am unwilling to contest* (the accusation); there's also **nol. pros.** = **nōlle prōsequī,** *to be unwilling to pursue* (the matter), meaning to drop a lawsuit; **nōlēns, volēns,** *unwilling (or) willing,* i.e., whether or not one wishes, like "willy-nilly" (a contraction of "will ye, nill ye"); the abbreviation "d.v.," for **deō volente;** also **volō, nōn valeō,** *I am willing but not able;* **nōlī mē tangere,** a warning against tampering as well as Lat. for the jewel-weed flower or "touch-me-not"; **quantum vīs,** *as much as you wish* (which may be more than just **quantum satis,** Ch. 30!); **Deus vult,** the call to arms of the First Crusade; and **malō morī quam foedārī,** freely "death before dishonor" (lit., *I wish to die rather than to be dishonored:* for the deponent verb **morior,** see Ch. 34). Years ago some pundit wrote (demonstrating the importance of macrons), **mālō malō malō mālō,** *I'd rather be in an apple tree than a bad man in adversity;* the first **malō** is from **mālum, -ī,** *apple, fruit-tree,* which calls to mind Horace's characterization of a Roman **cēna,** from the hors d'oeuvres to the dessert, as **ab ovō**

(**ovum, -ī,** *egg*) **ūsque ad māla,** a phrase, very like the expression "from soup to nuts," that became proverbial for "from start to finish."

    Et cētera ex vocābulāriō novō: cēterīs pāribus, *all else being equal;* **custōdia** is related to **custōs, custōdis,** *guard,* and **custōdīre,** *to guard,* hence Juvenal's satiric query, **sed quis custōdiet ipsōs custōdēs; exercitus** is connected with **exerceō, exercēre,** *to practice, exercise,* and the noun **exercitātiō,** which gives us the proverb, most salutary for Latin students: **exercitātiō est optimus magister.** And so, **valēte, discipulī/ae, et exercēte, exercēte, exercēte!**

Banqueter with egg, Etruscan fresco
Tomb of the Lionesses, late 6th century B.C.
Tarquinia, Italy

33

Conditions

CONDITIONAL SENTENCES

Conditions are among the most common sentence types, others being "declarative," "interrogative," and "exclamatory." You have encountered numerous conditional sentences in your Latin readings already, and so you are aware that the basic sentence of this type consists of two clauses: 1) the "condition" (or "protasis," Gk. for *proposition* or *premise*), a subordinate clause usually introduced by **sī,** *if,* or **nisi,** *if not* or *unless,* and stating a hypothetical action or circumstance, and 2) the "conclusion" (or "apodosis," Gk. for *outcome* or *result*), the main clause, which expresses the anticipated outcome if the premise turns out to be true.

There are six basic conditional types; three have their verbs in the indicative, three in the subjunctive, and the reason is simple. While all conditional sentences, by their very nature, describe actions in the past, present, or future that are to one extent or another hypothetical, the indicative was employed in those where the condition was more likely to be realized, the subjunctive in those where the premise was either less likely to be realized or where both the condition and the conclusion were absolutely contrary to the actual facts of a situation. Study carefully the following summary, learning the names of each of the six conditional types, how to recognize them, and the standard formulae for translation.

INDICATIVE CONDITIONS

1. **Simple fact present:** Sī id facit, prūdēns est. *If he is doing this [and it is quite possible that he is], he is wise.* Present indicative in both clauses; translate verbs as present indicatives.

2. **Simple fact past:** Sī id fēcit, prūdēns fuit. *If he did this [and quite possibly he did], he was wise.* Past tense (perfect or imperfect) indicative in both clauses; translate verbs as past indicatives.

3. **Simple fact future** (sometimes called "future more vivid"): Sī id faciet, prūdēns erit. *If he does (will do) this [and quite possibly he will], he will be wise.* Future indicative in both clauses; translate the verb in the protasis as a *present* tense (here Eng. "if" + the present has a future sense), the verb in the conclusion as a future. (Occasionally the future perfect is used, in either or both clauses, with virtually the same sense as the future: see S.A. 8 and "B.Y.O.B." line 3, p. 231.)

SUBJUNCTIVE CONDITIONS

The indicative conditions deal with potential facts; the subjunctive conditions are ideal rather than factual, describing circumstances that are either, in the case of the "future less vivid," somewhat less likely to be realized or less vividly imagined or, in the case of the two "contrary to fact" types, opposite to what actually is happening or has happened in the past.

1. **Contrary to fact present:** Sī id faceret, prūdēns esset. *If he were doing this [but in fact he is not], he would be wise [but he is not].* Imperfect subjunctive in both clauses; translate with auxiliaries *were (. . . ing)* and *would (be).*

2. **Contrary to fact past:** Sī id fēcisset, prūdēns fuisset. *If he had done this [but he did not], he would have been wise [but he was not].* Pluperfect subjunctive in both clauses; translate with auxiliaries *had* and *would have.*

3. **Future less vivid** (sometimes called "should-would"): Sī id faciat, prūdēns sit. *If he should do this [and he may, or he may not], he would be wise.* Present subjunctive in both clauses; translate with auxiliaries *should* and *would.*

There are occasional variants on these six basic types, i.e., use of the imperative in the apodosis, "mixed conditions" with different tenses or moods in the protasis and apodosis, different introductory words (e.g., **dum**), etc., but those are easily dealt with in context.

FURTHER EXAMPLES

Classify each of the following conditions.

1. Sī hoc dīcet, errābit; *if he says this, he will be wrong.*
2. Sī hoc dīcit, errat; *if he says this, he is wrong.*
3. Sī hoc dīxisset, errāvisset; *if he had said this, he would have been wrong.*
4. Sī hoc dīcat, erret; *if he should say this, he would be wrong.*

5. Sī hoc dīxit, errāvit; *if he said this, he was wrong.*
6. Sī hoc dīceret, errāret; *if he were saying this, he would be wrong.*
7. Sī veniat, hoc videat; *if he should come, he would see this.*
8. Sī vēnit, hoc vīdit; *if he came, he saw this.*
9. Sī venīret, hoc vidēret; *if he were coming, he would see this.*
10. Sī veniet, hoc vidēbit; *if he comes, he will see this.*
11. Sī vēnisset, hoc vīdisset; *if he had come, he would have seen this.*

VOCABULARY

inítium, -iī, n., *beginning, commencement* (initial, initiate, initiation)

ops, ópis, f., *help, aid;* **ópēs, ópum,** pl., *power, resources, wealth* (opulent, opulence; cp. **cōpia,** from **con-** + **ops**)

philósophus, -ī, m., and **philósopha, -ae,** f., *philosopher* (philosophy, philosophical)

plēbs, plḗbis, f., *the common people, populace, plebeians* (plebs, plebe, plebeian, plebiscite)

sāl, sális, m., *salt; wit* (salad, salami, salary, salina, saline, salify, salimeter, salinometer, sauce, sausage)

spéculum, -ī, n., *mirror* (speculate, speculation; cp. **spectō,** Ch. 34)

quis, quid, after **sī, nisi, nē, num,** indef. pron., *anyone, anything, someone, something* (cp. **quis? quid? quisque, quisquis**)

cándidus, -a, -um, *shining, bright, white; beautiful* (candescent, candid, candidate, candor, incandescent, candle, chandelier)

mérus, -a, -um, *pure, undiluted* (mere, merely)

suávis, suáve, *sweet* (suave, suaveness, suavity, suasion, dissuade, persuasion; cp. **persuādeō,** Ch. 35)

-ve, conj. suffixed to a word = **aut** before the word (cp. **-que**), *or*

heu, interj., *ah!, alas!* (a sound of grief or pain)

súbitō, adv., *suddenly* (sudden, suddenness)

recū́sō (1), *to refuse* (recuse, recusant; cp. **causa**)

trā́dō, -dere, -didī, -ditum (**trāns** + **dō**), *to give over, surrender; hand down, transmit, teach* (tradition, traditional, traitor, treason)

PRACTICE AND REVIEW

1. Dummodo exercitus opem mox ferat, moenia urbis celeriter cōnservāre poterimus.
2. Cum cōnsilia hostium ab initiō cognōvissēs, prīmō tamen ūllum auxilium offerre aut etiam centum mīlitēs prōmittere nōluistī.
3. Sī dīvitiae et invidia nōs ab amōre et honōre ūsque prohibent, dīvitēsne vērē sumus?
4. Pauper quidem nōn erit pār cēterīs nisi scientiam ingeniumve habēbit; sī haec habeat, autem, multī magnopere invideant.
5. Nisi īnsidiae patērent, ferrum eius maximē timērēmus.

6. Sī quis rogābit quid nunc discās, refer tē artem nōn mediocrem sed ūtilissimam ac difficillimam discere.

7. Lēgēs ita scrībantur ut dīvitēs et plēbs—etiam pauper sine asse—sint parēs.

8. Sī custōdiae dūriōrēs fortiōrēsque ad casam tuam contendissent, heu, numquam tanta scelera suscēpissēs et hī omnēs nōn occidissent.

9. Illa fēmina sapientissima, cum id semel cognōvisset, ad eōs celerrimē sē contulit et omnēs opēs suās praebuit.

10. Dūrum exsilium tam ācrem mentem ūnō annō mollīre nōn poterit.

11. Propter omnēs rūmōrēs pessimōs (quī nōn erant vērī), nātae suāvēs eius magnopere dolēbant et dormīre nōn poterant.

12. If those philosophers should come soon, you would be happier.

13. If you had not answered very wisely, they would have hesitated to offer us peace.

14. If anyone does these three things well, he will live better.

15. If you were willing to read better books, you would most certainly learn more.

SENTENTIAE ANTĪQUAE

1. Sī vīs pācem, parā bellum. (Flavius Vegetius.—**parā,** *prepare for.*)

2. Arma sunt parvī pretiī, nisi vērō cōnsilium est in patriā. (Cicero.—**pretium, -iī,** *value.*)

3. Salūs omnium ūnā nocte certē āmissa esset, nisi illa sevēritās contrā istōs suscepta esset. (Cicero.—**sevēritās, -tātis.**)

4. Sī quid dē mē posse agī putābis, id agēs—sī tū ipse ab istō perīculō eris līber. (Cicero.)

5. Sī essem mihi cōnscius ūllīus culpae, aequō animō hoc malum ferrem. (Phaedrus.—**cōnscius, -a, -um,** *conscious.*)

6. Dīcis tē vērē mālle fortūnam et mōrēs antīquae plēbis; sed sī quis ad illa subitō tē agat, illum modum vītae recūsēs. (Horace.)

7. Minus saepe errēs, sī sciās quid nesciās. (Publilius Syrus.)

8. Dīcēs "heu" sī tē in speculō vīderis. (Horace.)

9. Nīl habet īnfēlīx paupertās dūrius in sē quam quod rīdiculōs hominēs facit. (*Juvenal.—**nīl** = **nihil.**—**quod,** *the fact that.*)

B.Y.O.B., etc., etc.

Cēnābis bene, mī Fabulle, apud mē
paucīs (sī tibi dī favent) diēbus—
sī tēcum attuleris bonam atque magnam
cēnam, nōn sine candidā puellā
5   et vīnō et sale et omnibus cachinnīs;
haec sī, inquam, attuleris, venuste noster,
cēnābis bene; nam tuī Catullī

plēnus sacculus est arāneārum.
Sed contrā accipiēs merōs amōrēs,
10   seu quid suāvius ēlegantiusve est:
nam unguentum dabo, quod meae puellae
dōnārunt Venerēs Cupīdinēsque;
quod tū cum olfaciēs, deōs rogābis,
tōtum ut tē faciant, Fabulle, nāsum.

(*Catullus 13; meter: hendecasyllabic. The poet invites a friend to dinner, but there's a hitch and a BIG surprise.—**favēre** + dat., *to be favorable toward, favor.*—**cachinna, -ae,** *laugh, laughter.*—**venustus, -a, -um,** *charming.*—**sacculus, -ī,** *money-bag, wallet.*—**arānea, -ae,** *spiderweb.*—**contrā,** here adv., *on the other hand, in return.*—**seu,** conj., *or.*—**ēlegāns,** gen. **ēlegantis.**—**unguentum, -ī,** *salve, perfume.*—**dabo:** remember that **-ō** was often shortened in verse.—**dōnārunt** = **dōnāvērunt,** from **dōnāre,** *to give.*—**Venus, -neris,** f., and **Cupīdō, -dinis,** m.; Venus and Cupid, pl. here to represent all the fostering powers of Love.—**quod . . . olfaciēs** = **cum tū id olfaciēs.**—**olfaciō, -ere,** *to smell.*—For formal discussion of the "jussive noun" clause **deōs rogābis . . . ut . . . faciant,** easily translated here, see Ch. 36.—**tōtum . . . nāsum,** from **nāsus, -ī,** *nose,* objective complement with **tē;** the wide separation of adj. and noun suggests the cartoon-like enormity of the imagined schnoz!)

THE RICH GET RICHER

Semper pauper eris, sī pauper es, Aemiliāne:
dantur opēs nūllī nunc nisi dīvitibus.

(*Martial 5.81.; meter: elegiac couplet.—**Aemiliānus, -ī.**)

ARISTOTLE, TUTOR OF ALEXANDER THE GREAT

An Philippus, rēx Macedonum, voluisset Alexandrō, fīliō suō, prīma elementa litterārum trādī ab Aristotele, summō eius aetātis philosophō, aut hic suscēpisset illud maximum officium, nisi initia studiōrum pertinēre ad summam sapientissimē crēdidisset?

(Quintilian, *Īnstitūtiōnēs Ōrātōriae* 1.1.23.—**an,** interrog. conj., *or, can it be that.*—**Macedonēs, -donum,** m./f. pl., *Macedonians.*—**Aristotelēs, -telis.**—**pertinēre ad,** *to relate to, affect.*—**summa, -ae,** *highest part, whole.*)

YOUR LOSS, MY GAIN!

Cum Quīntus Fabius Maximus magnō cōnsiliō Tarentum fortissimē recēpisset et Salīnātor (quī in arce fuerat, urbe āmissā) dīxisset, "Meā operā, Quīnte Fabī, Tarentum recēpistī," Fabius, mē audiente, "Certē," inquit rīdēns, "nam nisi tū urbem āmīsissēs, numquam eam recēpissem."

(Cicero, *Dē Senectūte* 4.11.—During the second Punic War, Tarentum revolted from the Romans to Hannibal, though the Romans under Marcus Livius

Salinator continued to hold the citadel throughout this period. In 209 B.C. the city was recaptured by Quintus Fabius Maximus.—**Tarentum -ī,** a famous city in southern Italy (which the Romans called Magna Graecia).—**meā operā,** *thanks to me.*)

ETYMOLOGY

In the readings 2. price, precious, prize, praise, appraise, appreciate, depreciate. 3. severe, persevere, perseverance, asseverate. 5. conscious, unconscious, conscience.

"B.Y.O.B.": favorite, disfavor.—cachinnate, cachinnation.—sack, satchel.—araneid.—elegance, elegantly.—unguent, unguentary.—donate, donation, donor.—olfaction, olfactory, olfactometer, olfactronics.—nasal, nasalize, nasalization; "nose," "nostril," and "nozzle" are cognate. "Aristotle": pertain, pertinent, pertinacity, purtenance, appertain, appurtenance, impertinent, impertinence.—sum, summary, summation.

LATĪNA EST GAUDIUM—ET ŪTILIS!

Salvēte! Here are some well known conditions: **sī nātūra negat, facit indignātiō versum,** *if nature denies* (i.e., if my talent is lacking), *indignation creates my verse* (so said the satirist Juvenal, who had plenty of both!); **sī fortūna iuvat; sī fēcistī, negā!** (a lawyer's advice); **sī Deus nōbīscum, quis contrā nōs** (the verbs are left out, but the meaning is clear); **sī post fāta venit glōria, nōn properō,** *if glory comes (only) after death, I'm in no hurry!* (Martial); **sī sīc omnēs,** freely, a wistful "if only everything were like this" (or does it really mean "all on the boat became ill"?!!).

Ex vocābulāriō novō quoque: well, to start "from the beginning," the phrase **ab initiō** is quite common in Eng.; those running for political office in Rome wore the **toga candida,** *white toga,* hence Eng. "candidate." The Romans called undiluted wine **merum** (which the bibulous merely imbibed!); **ope et cōnsiliō** is a good way to manage life. The expression "with a grain of salt" comes from Lat. **cum grānō salis**; **sāl Atticum** is dry *Athenian wit;* and "salary" is also from **sāl,** a package of which was part of a Roman soldier's pay (we "bring home the [salty] bacon," Romans brought home the salt!). Art is a **speculum vītae.** If you remember how to form adverbs from adjectives, then you can decipher the proverb **suāviter in modō, fortiter in rē,** a good mode for the Latin teacher; and if you read music, you may have seen **subitō,** a musical annotation meaning *quickly.*

Hope you enjoy these closing **miscellānea** (from **miscellāneus, -a, -um,** *varied, mixed*), and here's one reason why: **sī fīnis bonus est, tōtum bonum erit,** an old proverb, a "mixed condition," and familiar vocabulary, so I'll give you the free version, "All's well that ends well (including this chapter)!"": **et vōs omnēs, quoque valeātis!**

34

Deponent Verbs; Ablative with Special Deponents

DEPONENT VERBS

Latin has a number of commonly used "deponent verbs," verbs that have passive endings but active meanings. There are very few new forms to be learned in this chapter (only the imperatives); the most crucial matter is simply to recall *which verbs are deponent,* so that you remember to translate them in the active voice, and that can be managed through careful vocabulary study. There are a few exceptions to the rule of passive forms/active meanings, and those will also need to be carefully noted.

PRINCIPAL PARTS AND CONJUGATION

As you will see from the following examples, deponents regularly have only three principal parts, the passive equivalents of the first three principal parts of regular verbs (1. first pers. sg. pres. indic., 2. pres. infin., 3. first pers. sg. perf. indic.).

Present Indic.	Present Infin.	Perfect Indic.
hórtor, *I urge*	hortā́rī, *to urge*	hortā́tus (-a, -um) sum, *I urged*
fáteor, *I confess*	fatḗrī, *to confess*	fássus (-a, -um) sum, *I confessed*
séquor, *I follow*	séquī, *to follow*	secū́tus (-a, -um) sum, *I followed*
mṓlior, *I work at*	mōlī́rī, *to work at*	mōlī́tus (-a, -um) sum, *I worked at*
pátior, *I suffer*	pátī, *to suffer*	pássus (-a, -um) sum, *I suffered*

SAMPLE FORMS OF Hortor AND Sequor

Again, deponents are conjugated according to precisely the same rules as regular verbs in the passive voice; the following representative forms are provided for review, and full conjugations for each of the five examples given above are included in the Appendix (p. 455–57).

Indicative	**PRESENT**

1. hórtor, *I urge*   séquor, *I follow*
2. hortáris (-re), *you urge*   séqueris (-re), *you follow*
3. hortátur, *he urges*   séquitur, *he follows*

1. hortámur, *we urge*   séquimur, *we follow*
2. hortáminī, *you urge*   sequíminī, *you follow*
3. hortántur, *they urge*   sequúntur, *they follow*

IMPERFECT

1. hortábar, *I was urging*   sequébar, *I was following*
2. hortābáris (-re), *you were urging*   sequēbáris (-re), *you were following,*
etc.   etc.

FUTURE

1. hortábor, *I shall urge*   séquar, *I shall follow*
2. hortáberis (-re), *you will urge*   sequéris (-re), *you will follow*
3. hortábitur, *he will urge*   sequétur, *he will follow*
etc.   etc.

PERFECT

hortátus, -a, -um sum, *I urged*   secútus, -a, -um sum, *I followed*
etc.   etc.

PLUPERFECT

hortátus, -a, -um éram, *I had urged*   secútus, -a, -um éram, *I had followed*
etc.   etc.

FUTURE PERFECT

hortátus, -a, -um érō,   secútus, -a, -um érō,
    I shall have urged   *I shall have followed*
etc.   etc.

Subjunctive   **PRESENT**

hórter, hortéris, hortétur   séquar, sequáris, sequátur
etc.   etc.

IMPERFECT

hortā́rer, hortārḗris, hortārḗtur   séquerer, sequerḗris, sequerḗtur
etc.   etc.

PERFECT

hortā́tus, -a, -um sim, sīs, etc.   secū́tus, -a, -um sim, sīs, etc.

PLUPERFECT

hortā́tus, -a, -um éssem, etc.   secū́tus, -a, -um éssem, etc.

SYNOPSIS

The following third person singular synopsis of **fateor, fatērī, fassus sum** should provide a useful overview of the conjugation of deponents; remember that all the English equivalents are active, i.e., *he confesses, he will confess,* etc.

Indicative Mood

Pres.	Fut.	Impf.	Perf.	Fut. Perf.	Plupf.
fatḗtur	fatḗbitur	fatēbā́tur	fássus est	fássus érit	fássus érat

Subjunctive Mood

fateā́tur	——	fatērḗtur	fássus sit	——	fássus ésset

PARTICIPLES AND INFINITIVES

The participles and infinitives of typical deponent verbs are here given in full not because of any actually new forms but because of certain discrepancies in the general rule of passive forms with active meanings.

Participles

Pres. hórtāns, *urging*   séquēns, *following*
Perf. hortā́tus, -a, -um,   secū́tus, -a, -um,
    having urged   *having followed*
Fut. hortātū́rus, -a, -um,   secūtū́rus, -a, -um,
    about to urge   *about to follow*
Ger. hortándus, -a, -um,   sequéndus, -a, -um,
    to be urged   *to be followed*

Infinitives

Pres. hortā́rī, *to urge*   séquī, *to follow*
Perf. hortā́tus, -a, -um ésse,   secū́tus, -a, -um ésse,
    to have urged   *to have followed*

Fut. hortātū́rus, -a, -um ésse,   secūtū́rus, -a, -um ésse,
    to be about to urge   *to be about to follow*

Exceptions: Deponents have the same four participles that regular verbs have, but only three infinitives, one for each tense. Three of the participles and one of the infinitives present exceptions to the basic rule that deponents are passive in form but active in meaning:

1. Present and future participles: active forms with active meanings.
2. Gerundive (future passive participle): passive form with passive meaning.
3. Future infinitive: active form with active meaning.

Imperatives

The present imperative of deponent verbs would naturally have the forms of the present "passive" imperative. These forms have not been given before because they are found only in deponent verbs, but they are easy to learn.

1. The second person singular has the same spelling as that of the *alternate* second person singular of the present *indicative,* e.g., **sequere!** (Note that this is also the same form as the non-existent present active *infinitive:* be especially careful not to mistake this characteristic deponent imperative form for an infinitive.)

2. The second person plural imperative has the same spelling as that of the second person plural of the present indicative, e.g., **sequiminī!**

Take careful note of the following examples:

2. hortā́re, *urge!*   fatḗre, *confess!*   sḗquere   mōlī́re   pátere
2. hortā́minī, *urge!*   fatḗminī, *confess!*   sequī́minī   mōlī́minī   patī́minī

SEMI-DEPONENT VERBS

Semi-deponent ("half-deponent") is the name given to a few verbs which are normal in the present system but are deponent in the perfect system, as is clearly demonstrated by the principal parts. For example:

aúdeō, *I dare*   audḗre, *to dare*   aúsus sum, *I dared*
gaúdeō, *I rejoice*   gaudḗre, *to rejoice*   gāvī́sus sum, *I rejoiced*

ABLATIVE WITH SPECIAL DEPONENTS

The ablative of means is used idiomatically with a few deponent verbs, of which **ūtor** (and its compounds) is by far the most common (the others, **fruor,** *to enjoy,* **fungor,** *to perform,* **potior,** *to possess,* and **vēscor,** *to eat,* are not employed in this book, but you will likely encounter them in your later reading). **Ūtor,** *to use, enjoy,* is in fact a reflexive verb and means literally *to benefit oneself* by means of something.[1]

Ūtitur stilō,
> *he is benefiting himself by means of a pencil* (literally).
> *he is using a pencil* (idiomatically).

Nōn audent ūtī nāvibus, *they do not dare to use the ships.*
Nōn ausī sunt ūtī nāvibus, *they did not dare to use the ships.*

FURTHER EXAMPLES OF DEPONENT FORMS IN SENTENCES

1. Eum patientem haec mala hortātī sunt,
   they encouraged him (as he was) suffering these evils.
2. Eum passūrum haec mala hortātī sunt,
   they encouraged him (as he was) about to suffer these evils.
3. Is, haec mala passus, hortandus est,
   this man, having suffered these evils, ought to be encouraged.
4. Is haec mala fortiter patiētur,
   he will suffer these evils bravely.
5. Eum sequere et haec mōlīre,
   follow him and work at these things.
6. Eum sequī et haec mōlīrī nōn ausus es,
   you did not dare to follow him and work at these things.
7. Eum sequeris/sequēris,
   you are following/will follow him.
8. Eum hortēmur et sequāmur,
   let us encourage and follow him.
9. Cicerō Graecīs litterīs ūtēbātur,
   Cicero used to enjoy Greek literature.

VOCABULARY

ánima, -ae, f., *soul, spirit* (anima, animism, animatism, animation, animated, inanimate, etc.; cp. **animal, animus**)

remíssiō, remissiónis, f., *letting go, release; relaxation* (remiss, remission; from **re + mittō**)

vōx, vṓcis, f., *voice, word* (vocal, vocalic, vocalize, vociferous, vowel; vox angelica, vox humana, vox populi; cp. **vocō**)

advérsus, -a, -um, *opposite, adverse* (adversary, adversative, adversely, adversity; cp. **vertō**)

tális, tále, *such, of such a sort* (cp. **quālis,** *of what sort, what kind of*)

vae, interj., often + dat., *alas, woe to*

---

[1] Cp. Fr. **se servir de,** "to use," orig. "to serve oneself with."

árbitror, arbitrárī, arbitrắtus sum, *to judge, think* (arbiter, arbitress, arbitration, arbitrator, arbitrary, arbitrarily)

cốnor, cōnắrī, cōnắtus sum, *to try, attempt* (conation, conative)

créscō, créscere, crévī, crétum, *to increase* (crescent, crescendo, crescive, concrescence, concrete, decrease, excrescence, increment, accretion, accrue, crew, recruit)

ēgrédior, égredī, ēgréssus sum, *to go out* (aggression, congress, degrade, digress, egress, grade, gradient, gradual, graduate, ingredient, ingress, progress, regress, retrogress, transgress)

fáteor, fatḗrī, fássus sum, *to confess, admit* (confess, confession, profess, profession, professor; cp. **fắbula, fắma, fắtum,** also **for, fắrī, fắtus sum,** Ch. 40)

hórtor, hortắrī, hortắtus sum, *to encourage, urge* (hortatory, exhort, exhortation)

lóquor, lóquī, locútus sum, *to say, speak, tell* (loquacious, circumlocution, colloquial, elocution, eloquent, obloquy, soliloquy, ventriloquist)

mólior, mōlī́rī, mōlī́tus sum, *to work at, build, undertake, plan* (demolish, demolition; cp. **mṓlēs,** *a large mass, massive structure*)

mórior, mórī, mórtuus sum, fut. act. part. **moritū́rus,** *to die* (moribund, mortuary; cp. **mors, mortālis, immortālis**)

nắscor, nắscī, nắtus sum, *to be born; spring forth, arise* (agnate, cognate, innate, nascent, natal, nation, nature, naive; cp. **nắta, nātū́ra**)

pátior, pátī, pássus sum, *to suffer, endure; permit* (passion, passive, patient, compassion, compatible, incompatibility, impatient, impassioned, impassive, dispassionate)

proficī́scor, -ficī́scī, -féctus sum, *to set out, start* (profit and proficient from the related verb **prṓficiō,** *to make headway, gain results*)

rū́sticor, rūsticắrī, rūsticắtus sum, *to live in the country* (rusticate, rustic, rural, cp. **rū́sticus,** *rural,* **rūs,** Ch. 37)

sédeō, sedḗre, sḗdī, séssum, *to sit* (sedan, sedate, sedentary, sediment, sessile, session, assess, assiduous, president, siege, subsidy)

séquor, séquī, secútus sum, *to follow* (consequent, consecutive, sequence, sequel, subsequent; see Etymology below)

spéctō (1), *to look at, see* (spectate, spectator, spectacle, speculate, aspect, circumspect, inspect, prospect, respect, suspect; cp. **speculum**)

útor, útī, úsus sum + abl., *to use; enjoy, experience* (abuse, disuse, peruse, usual, usurp, usury, utensil, utilize, utility, utilitarian; cp. **útilis**)

PRACTICE AND REVIEW

1. Nisi quis plēbī opem celeriter referet auxiliumve prōmissum praebēbit, mīlia virōrum morientur.
2. Cum urbs plēna custōdiārum esset, nōn ausī estis suscipere scelera tam gravia quam voluerātis.

3. Dīc nunc cūr velīs tē ad istam dīvitem et candidam cōnferre. Vērē ac līberē loquere; nōlī recūsāre!

4. Dīvitiīs trāditīs, heu, illī philosophī eādem nocte subitō profectī sunt in exsilium, unde numquam ēgredī potuērunt.

5. Nē patiāmur hanc antīquissimam scientiam āmittī.

6. Fateor mē vīnō merō apud mē ūsūrum esse.

7. Ab initiō nōn comprehendistī quantus exercitus nōs sequerētur et quot elephantōs istī mīlitēs sēcum dūcerent.

8. Prīmō respondit sē nōlle sequī ducem mediocris virtūtis sapientiaeve, cum cīvitās in līmine bellī stāret.

9. Ex urbe subitō ēgressus, ferrō suō morī semel cōnātus est.

10. Cum Aristotelēs hortārētur hominēs ad virtūtem, tamen arbitrābātur virtūtem in hominibus nōn nāscī.

11. Māter paterque nunc rūsticantur ut ā labōribus remissiōne suāvī ūtantur.

12. Dā mihi, amābō tē, multum salis et vīnum aquamve, ut cēnā maximē ūtar.

13. They did not permit me to speak with him at that time.

14. We kept thinking (**arbitror**) that he would use the office more wisely.

15. If any one should use this water even once, he would die.

16. If those four soldiers had followed us, we would not have dared to put the weapons on the ships.

17. This dinner will be good, provided that you use salt.

SENTENTIAE ANTĪQUAE

1. Cēdāmus Phoebō et, monitī, meliōra sequāmur. (*Virgil.—Phoebus Apollo was god of prophecy.)

2. Nam nēmō sine vitiīs nāscitur; optimus ille est quī minima habet. (Horace.)

3. Mundus est commūnis urbs deōrum atque hominum; hī enim sōlī, ratiōne ūtentēs, iūre ac lēge vīvunt. (Cicero.)

4. Tardē sed graviter vir sapiēns īrāscitur. (*Publilius Syrus.—**tardus, -a, -um,** *slow, late.*—**īrāscor, īrāscī, īrātus sum,** *to become angry.*)

5. Quae cum ita sint, Catilīna, ēgredere ex urbe; patent portae; proficīscere; nōbīscum versārī iam diūtius nōn potes; id nōn feram, nōn patiar. (Cicero.—**Quae cum = Cum haec.**—**versor, versārī, versātus sum,** *to stay.*)

6. Cūra pecūniam crēscentem sequitur et dīves male dormit. (Horace.)

7. Sī in Britanniam profectus essēs, nēmō in illā tantā īnsulā iūre perītior fuisset. (Cicero.—**Britannia, -ae,** Britain.—**perītus, -a, -um** + abl., *skilled in.*)

8. Nisi laus nova nāscitur etiam vetus laus in incertō iacet ac saepe āmittitur. (Publilius Syrus.)—**vetus,** gen. **veteris,** *old.*)

9. Spērō autem mē secūtum esse in libellīs meīs tālem temperantiam ut nēmō bonus dē illīs querī possit. (Martial.—**temperantia, -ae.— queror, querī, questus sum,** *to complain.*)

10. Hōrae quidem et diēs et annī discēdunt; nec praeteritum tempus umquam revertitur, nec quid sequātur potest scīrī. (Cicero.—**praeteritus, -a, -um,** *past.*—**revertor, revertī, reversus sum,** *to return.*)

11. Nōvistī mōrēs mulierum: dum mōliuntur, dum cōnantur, dum in speculum spectant, annus lābitur. (Terence.—**mulier, -eris,** *woman.*—**lābor, lābī, lāpsus sum,** *to slip, glide.*)

12. Amīcitia rēs plūrimās continet; nōn aquā, nōn igne in plūribus locīs ūtimur quam amīcitiā. (Cicero.)

13. Homō stultus! Postquam dīvitiās habēre coepit, mortuus est! (Cicero.—**postquam,** conj., *after.*)

14. Ō passī graviōra, dabit deus hīs quoque fīnem. (*Virgil.—**Ō passī,** voc. pl., *O you who have . . . .*—**hīs** = **hīs rēbus gravibus.**)

CLAUDIUS' EXCREMENTAL EXPIRATION

Et ille quidem animam ēbulliit, et ex eō dēsiit vīvere vidērī. Exspīrāvit autem dum comoedōs audit, ut sciās mē nōn sine causā illōs timēre. Ultima vōx eius haec inter hominēs audīta est, cum maiōrem sonitum ēmisisset illā parte quā facilius loquēbātur: "Vae mē, putō, concacāvī." Quod an fēcerit, nesciō—omnia certē concacāvit!

(*Seneca, *Apocolocyntōsis* 4; a satirical farce on the emperor Claudius' death and deification.—**ēbulliō, -īre, ēbulliī,** *to bubble out,* + **animam,** comic for *he died.*—**ex eō,** sc. **tempore.**—**dēsinō, -sinere, -siī, -situm,** *to cease.*—**exspīrāre,** *to breathe out, die.*—**comoedus, -ī,** *comic actor.*—**sonitus, -ūs,** *sound.*—**ē** + **mittere.**—**illā parte,** sc. **ex,** i.e., his bottom.—**concacāre,** *to defecate upon.*—**quod** = **id.**—**an,** *whether,* introducing an ind. quest.)

The emperor Claudius
Louvre, Paris, France

AND VICE IS NOT NICE!

Mentītur quī tē vitiōsum, Zōile, dīcit:
    nōn vitiōsus homō es, Zōile, sed vitium!

(*Martial 11.92; meter: elegiac couplet.—**mentior, mentīrī, mentītus sum,** *to lie,*
deceive.—**vitiōsus,** adj. from **vitium.**—**tē vitiōsum,** sc. **esse,** and remember that
the verb **sum, esse** is often omitted in both prose and verse when it is readily
understood from the context.—**Zōilus,** a Greek name.)

PRETTY IS AS PRETTY DOES

Bella es, nōvimus, et puella, vērum est,
et dīves—quis enim potest negāre?
Sed cum tē nimium, Fabulla, laudās,
nec dīves neque bella nec puella es!

(*Martial 1.64; meter: hendecasyllabic.)

ON LESBIA'S HUSBAND

Ille mī pār esse deō vidētur,
ille, sī fās est, superāre dīvōs,
quī, sedēns adversus, identidem tē
        spectat et audit
5   dulce rīdentem, miserō quod omnīs
ēripit sēnsūs mihi: nam simul tē,
Lesbia, aspexī, nihil est super mī,
        [Lesbia, vōcis,]
lingua sed torpet, tenuis sub artūs
10   flamma dēmānat, sonitū suōpte
tintinant aurēs, gemināteguntur
        lūmina nocte.
Ōtium, Catulle, tibi molestum est;
ōtiō exsultās nimiumque gestīs;
15   ōtium et rēgēs prius et beātās
        perdidit urbēs.

(*Catullus 51; meter: Sapphic stanza.—**mī**= **mihi.**—**fās est,** *it is right.*—**dīvōs** =
deōs.—**identidem,** adv., *again and again.*—**dulce,** adv. of **dulcis.**—**miserō ...**
mihi, dat. of separation; the prose order would be **quod omnīs** (= **omnēs**) **sēnsūs**
mihi miserō ēripit.—**quod,** *a circumstance which;* the entire preceding clause is
the antecedent.—**simul,** adv., *as soon as.*—**aspexī** = **spectāvī.**—**nihil,** with **vōcis,**
gen. of the whole, *no voice;* **est super** = **superest,** *remains.*—**Lesbia, vōcis** is an
editorial suggestion for a verse missing in the manuscripts.—**torpēre,** *to grow*
numb.—**tenuis,** with **flamma,** from **tenuis, -e,** *thin, slender.*—**artus, -ūs,** *joint, limb*
(of the body).—**flamma, -ae,** *flame.*—**dēmānāre,** *to flow through.*—**sonitus, -ūs,**

sound.—**suōpte,** intensive for **suō.**—**tintināre,** *to ring.*—**tegō, -ere,** *to cover.*—**lūmen, -minis,** *light; eye.*—**molestus, -a, -um,** *troublesome.*—**exsultāre,** *to celebrate, exult* (*in*), + **ōtiō.**—**gestīre,** *to act without restraint, be elated* or *triumphant.*—**perdō, -ere, perdidī, perditum,** *to destroy.*)

ETYMOLOGY

"Sympathy" derives from Gk. **syn** (*with*) + **pathos** (*suffering*). What Latin-rooted word is the exact equivalent of "sympathy"?

Further words associated with **sequor:** execute, executive, executor, obsequious, prosecute, persecute, pursue, ensue, sue, suit, suite, sect, second. Related to **sequor,** besides **secundus,** is **socius** (*a follower, ally*), whence: social, society, associate, dissociate.

In the readings

4. irate, irascible, irascibility. 5. **Versārī** literally means *to turn* (*oneself*) *around:* versatile, converse, conversant, conversation. 8. veteran, inveterate. 9. intemperance.—querulous, quarrel. 10. preterit, preterition, praeteritio.—revert, reverse, reversible, reversion. "Claudius": ebullient.—expire, expiration, expiratory, expiry.—cp. **sonus, -ī,** *sound:* sonic, sonar, resonate. "Lesbia": divine.—aspect.—tenuous, tenuity.—flammable, inflame, inflammatory, inflammation.—tintinnabulation.—luminary, lumination, illuminate.—molest, molestation.—exultant, exultation.—perdition.

LATĪNA EST GAUDIUM—ET ŪTILIS!

Salvēte, meī discipulī discipulaeque! Quid agitis? (Spērō vōs valēre.) Now that you've begun to read more real, unadapted Latin literature (like the above selections from Martial, Seneca, and Catullus), you might appreciate the following remark: "Looking back on school, I really liked Latin. In my case, a little bit stuck: I ended up with a feeling for literature."—Paul McCartney. So, how much Latin is enough?—**quantum placeat,** *as much as gives one pleasure* (close to **quantum vīs,** Ch. 32, and more, one hopes, than **quantum satis,** Ch. 30!).

Here are some Latin phrases that are by no means moribund: first, an unfortunate (and fortunately overstated!) old proverb, **quem dī dīligunt, adulēscēns moritur;** a reminder of one's mortality is a **mementō morī,** freely "remember that you must die" (the **-tō** form is a relatively rare future imperative not formally introduced in this book but used not infrequently in ancient legal and religious texts); on sacrificing one's life for one's country, Horace wrote **dulce et decōrum** (from **decōrus, -a, -um,** *fitting, proper*) **est prō patriā morī;** another bleak proverb (but essential here, as it offers two deponents!) is the astronomer Manilius' dictum, **nascentēs morimur** (*even as we are*) *being born, we* (*begin to*) *die;* and then there is Seneca's version of "eat, drink, and be merry," complete with a passive periphrastic, **bibāmus, moriendum est,** and the words addressed to the emperor by gladiators entering the arena, **avē, Caesar: moritūrī tē salutāmus,** *hail, Caesar: we* (*who are*) *about to die salute you!* To any who have suffered, not death, but defeat, one might proclaim **vae, victīs,** *woe to the conquered,* a famous line from Livy's account of the Gallic sack of Rome in 390 B.C.

Well, enough morbidity. **Hīc sunt alia miscellānea ex vocābulāriō novō: vōx populī; vōx clamantis in dēsertō,** *the voice of one calling out in the wilderness* (from the gospel of Matthew); **crēscit amor nummī quantum ipsa pecūnia crēvit,** *love of the coin grows as much as one's wealth itself has grown* (Juvenal 14.139); **sedente animō,** *with a calm mind.* And here are some other deponents: Maryland's state motto is **crēscite et multiplicāminī** (can you figure that one out?); **loquitur** is a note in a dramatic text; and the legal phrase **rēs ipsa loquitur,** *the matter speaks for itself,* we have seen before, but now you understand the verb form. And how about this sequence: **seq.** is an abbreviation for **sequēns/sequentēs,** *the following,* once common in footnotes; a **nōn sequitur** is a remark that *does not follow* logically from a prior statement (a **sequitur,** of course, does!); **sequor nōn īnferior,** *I follow* (*but am*) *not inferior.* Will this exciting chapter have a sequel in the subsequent chapter? And, if not, what will be the consequences? Stay tuned . . . **et valēte!**

Gladiators in combat, detail of mosaic from Torrenova, 4th century A.D.
Galleria Borghese, Rome, Italy

35

Dative with Adjectives; Dative with Special Verbs; Dative with Compounds

The dative case is in general employed to indicate a person or thing that some act or circumstance applies to or refers to "indirectly," as opposed to the accusative, which indicates the more immediate recipient or object of an action. The indirect object, e.g., is the person/thing toward which a direct object is "referred" by the subject + verb: "I am giving the book [direct object] to you [indirect object]" = "I am giving the book, not just to anyone anywhere, but in your direction, i.e., to you." Even in the passive periphrastic construction, the dative of agent indicates the person for whom a certain action is obligatory. A number of other dative case usages are distinguished by grammarians, but most are simply variants on this basic notion of reference or direction.

DATIVE WITH ADJECTIVES

The dative with adjectives construction is one example which you have already encountered in your readings, though it has not yet been formally introduced. Simply stated, a noun in the dative case is employed with many Latin adjectives—particularly those indicating attitude, quality, or relation—to indicate the direction (literally or metaphorically) in which the adjective applies; such adjectives are normally followed by "to," "toward," or "for" in English (e.g., "friendly to/toward," "hostile to/toward," "suitable to/ for," "useful to," "similar to," "equal to," etc.).

Mors est similis **somnō,** *death is similar to sleep.*
Sciēbam tē **mihi** fidēlem esse, *I knew that you were loyal to me.*
Nōbīs est vir amīcus, *he is a man friendly toward us.*
Quisque **sibi** cārus est, *each one is dear to himself.*
Ille vidētur pār esse **deō,** *that man seems to be equal to a god.*

DATIVE WITH SPECIAL VERBS

Conceptually similar is the dative with special verbs construction. Many of these verbs (the most important of which are listed below) are actually intransitive and, like the adjectives that take the dative, indicate attitude or relationship, e.g., **nocēre,** *to be injurious to,* **parcō,** *to be lenient toward,* etc. Although these verbs are often translated into English as though they were transitive and the dative nouns they govern as though they were direct objects (e.g., **tibi parcit,** *he spares you;* lit., *he is lenient toward you*), the datives again indicate the person (or thing) toward whom the attitude or quality applies.

Although a common rule for the dative with special verbs lists those meaning *to favor, help, harm, please, displease, trust, distrust, believe, persuade, command, obey, serve, resist, envy, threaten, pardon,* and *spare,* the list is cumbersome and involves some important exceptions (including **iuvō,** *to help,* and **iubeō,** *to command, order,* which take accusative objects). The best procedure at this point in your study of the language is simply to understand the concept and then to learn some of the commonest Latin verbs that take this construction.

In memorizing the following list, note carefully that the more literal translation, given first for each verb, includes English *to* and thus reminds you of the required dative; note as well that each verb conveys some notion of *attitude toward* a person or thing, again suggesting a dative, as discussed above.

crēdō + dat., *entrust to; trust, believe* (**crēdō tibi,** *I believe you*)
ignōscō + dat., *grant pardon to; pardon, forgive* (**ignōscō virīs,** *I forgive the men*)
imperō + dat., *give orders to; command* (**imperō mīlitibus,** *I command the soldiers*)
noceō + dat., *do harm to; harm* (**noceō hostibus,** *I harm the enemy*)

nūbō + dat., *be married to; marry* (**nūbō illī virō,** *I am marrying that man*)
parcō + dat., *be lenient to; spare* (**parcō vōbīs,** *I spare you*)
pāreō + dat., *be obedient to; obey* (**pāreō ducī,** *I obey the leader*)
persuādeō + dat., *make sweet to; persuade* (**persuādeō mihi,** *I persuade myself*)
placeō + dat., *be pleasing to; please* (**placeō patrī,** *I please my father*)
serviō + dat., *be a slave to; serve* (**serviō patriae,** *I serve my* country)
studeō + dat., *direct one's zeal to; study* (**studeō litterīs,** *I study literature*)

Crēde amīcīs, *believe (trust) your friends.*
Ignōsce mihi, *pardon me (forgive me).*
Magistra discipulīs parcit, *the teacher spares (is lenient toward) her pupils.*
Hoc eīs nōn placet, *this does not please them.*
Nōn possum eī persuādēre, *I cannot persuade him.*
Variae rēs hominibus nocent, *various things harm men.*
Cicerō philosophiae studēbat, *Cicero used to study philosophy.*
Philosophiae servīre est lībertās, *to serve philosophy is liberty.*

Some of these verbs, it should be noted, can also take a direct object (e.g., **crēdō** takes a dative for a person believed, **mātrī crēdit,** *he believes his mother,* but an accusative for a thing, **id crēdit,** *he believes it*); and some, like **imperō** and **persuādeo,** take a noun clause as an object, as we shall see in the next chapter.

DATIVE WITH COMPOUND VERBS

A very similar dative usage occurs with certain verbs compounded with **ad, ante, con-** (=**cum**), **in, inter, ob, post, prae, prō, sub, super,** and sometimes **circum** and **re-** (in the sense of *against*). The dative is especially common when the meaning of a compound verb is significantly different from its simple form, whether transitive or intransitive; conversely, if the meaning of the compound is not essentially different from that of the simple verb, then the dative is ordinarily not employed:

Sequor eum, *I follow him.*
Obsequor eī, *I obey him.*
Sum amīcus eius, *I am his friend.*
Adsum amīcō, *I support my friend* (lit., *I am next to my friend,* i.e., at his side).
Vēnit ad nōs, *he came to us.*
Advēnit ad nōs, *he came to us.*

Often the dative appears to function essentially as a kind of object of the prepositional prefix, though the preposition would take another case if separate from the verb; thus **adsum amīcō** above and the following examples:

Aliīs praestant, *they surpass the others* (lit., *they stand before the others*).
Praeerat exercituī, *he was in charge of the army* (lit., *he was in front of/before the army*).

If the simple verb is transitive, then the compound may take an accusative as object of the root verb as well as a dative:

Praeposuī eum exercituī, *I put him in charge of the army* (lit., *I put him* [**posuī eum**] *in front of the army* [**prae- + exercituī**]).
Praeposuī pecūniam amīcitiae, *I preferred money to friendship* (lit., *I put money* [**posuī pecūniam**] *before friendship* [**prae- + amīcitiae**]).

Since there is such variability in the rules for dative with special verbs and with compounds, the best procedure is to *understand the concepts involved* and then, when encountering a dative in a sentence, to be aware of these possible functions; just as with the other cases, you should be maintaining a list of the dative uses you have learned (there have been five thus far) in your notebook or computer file, including definitions and representative examples.

VOCABULARY

aéstās, aestātis, f., *summer* (estival, estivate, estivation; cp. **aestus, -ūs,** *heat,* **aestuāre,** *to be hot, seethe, boil*)

iánua, -ae, f., *door* (janitor, Janus, January)

péctus, péctoris, n., *breast, heart* (pectoral, expectorate, parapet)

praémium, -iī, n. *reward, prize* (premium)

īrātus, -a, -um, *angry* (irate; cp. **īra, īrāscor,** *to be angry*)

antepōnō, -pónere, -pósuī, -pósitum, *to put before, prefer*

fóveō, fovḗre, fōvī, fōtum, *to comfort, nurture, cherish* (foment)

ignōscō, -nōscere, -nōvī, -nōtum + dat., *to grant pardon to, forgive*

ímperō (1) + dat., *to give orders to, command* (imperative, emperor; cp. **imperātor, imperium**)

míror, mīrārī, mīrātus sum, *to marvel at, admire, wonder* (admire, marvel, miracle, mirage, mirror; cp. **mīrābilis,** Ch. 38, **mīrāculum,** *a marvel*)

nóceō, nocḗre, nócuī, nócitum + dat., *to do harm to, harm, injure* (innocent, innocuous, noxious, nuisance, obnoxious; cp. **innocēns,** *blameless*)

nūbō, nūbere, nūpsī, nūptum, *to cover, veil;* + dat. (of a bride) *to be married to, marry* (nubile, connubial, nuptials; cp. **nūptiae,** *marriage*)

párcō, párcere, pepércī, parsūrum + dat., *to be lenient to, spare* (parsimonious, parsimony)

páreō, pārére, párui + dat., *to be obedient to, obey* (apparent, appear)

persuádeō, -suādére, -suásī, -suásum + dat., *to succeed in urging, persuade, convince* (assuage, dissuade, suasion, suave; cp. **suāvis**)

pláceō, placére, plácui, plácitum + dat., *to be pleasing to, please* (complacent, placable, implacable, placate, placid, plea, plead, pleasure, displease; cp. **placidus**, *kindly, agreeable, calm*)

sápiō, sápere, sapívī, *to have good taste; have good sense, be wise* (sapient, sapid, insipid, sage, savor; cp. **sapiēns, sapientia**)

sérviō, servíre, servívī, servítum + dat., *to be a slave to, serve* (service, disservice, subserve, subservient, servile, servility, deserve, desert = reward, dessert; cp. **servus, servitūs;** distinguish from **servāre**)

stúdeō, studére, stúdui + dat., *to direct one's zeal to, be eager for, study* (student; cp. **studium, studiōsus**, *eager, diligent, scholarly*)

subrídeō, -rīdére, -rísī, -rísum, *to smile (down) upon* (cp. **rīdeō, rīdiculus**)

PRACTICE AND REVIEW

1. Minerva, fīlia Iovis, nāta est plēna scientiae et ingeniī.
2. Custōdiae sī cum duce nostrō līberē loquantur et huic tyrannum trādere cōnentur, sine perīculō ex moeniīs urbis prōtinus ēgredī possint.
3. Pārēre lēgibus aequīs melius est quam tyrannō servīre.
4. Cum optimē honōribus ūsus esset et sibi cīvitātem semper antepōneret, etiam plēbs eī crēdēbat et nōn invidēbat.
5. Diū passa, māter vestra fēlīciter, sedēns apud amīcōs, mortua est.
6. Philosophī cōnsilium spectāvērunt et recūsāvērunt tālem rem suscipere mōlīrīve.
7. Cum dīves sīs atque dīvitiae crēscant, tamen opibus tuīs parcere vīs et nēminī assem offerēs.
8. Ab illā īnsulā repente profectus, eādem nocte ad patriam nāve advēnit; tum, quaerēns remissiōnem animae, diū rūsticābātur.
9. Hic mīles, cum imperātōrī vestrō nōn placēret, heu, illa praemia prōmissa āmīsit.
10. Nisi mōrēs parēs scientiae sunt—id nōbīs fatendum est—scientia nōbīs magnopere nocēre potest.
11. Magistra tum rogāvit duōs parvōs puerōs quot digitōs habērent.
12. Māter candida nātae cārissimae subrīdet, quam maximē fovet, et eī plūrima ōscula suāvia dat.
13. Why does he now wish to hurt his two friends?
14. If he does not spare the plebeians, alas, we shall never trust him.
15. Since you are studying Roman literature, you are serving a very difficult but a very great master.
16. If they were truly willing to please us, they would not be using their wealth thus against the state.

SENTENTIAE ANTĪQUAE

1. Nēmō līber est quī corporī servit. (Seneca.)
2. Imperium habēre vīs magnum? Imperā tibi! (Publilius Syrus.)
3. Bonīs nocet quisquis pepercit malīs. (*Id.)
4. Cum tū omnia pecūniae postpōnās, mīrāris sī nēmō tibi amōrem praestat? (Horace.—**post-pōnō.**)
5. Frūstrā aut pecūniae aut imperiīs aut opibus aut glōriae student; potius studeant virtūtī et honōrī et scientiae et alicui artī. (Cicero.—**frūstrā**, adv., *in vain.*—**potius**, adv., *rather.*)
6. Virtūtī melius quam Fortūnae crēdāmus; virtūs nōn nōvit calamitātī cēdere. (Publilius Syrus.—**calamitās, -tātis.**)
7. Et Deus āit: "Faciāmus hominem ad imāginem nostram et praesit piscibus maris bēstiīsque terrae." (*Genesis.*—**imāgō, -ginis,** f.—**prae-sum.**—**piscis, piscis,** m., *fish.*—**bēstia, -ae,** *beast.*)
8. Omnēs arbitrātī sunt tē dēbēre mihi parcere. (Cicero.)
9. Quid facere vellet, ostendit, et illī servō spē lībertātis magnīsque praemiīs persuāsit. (Caesar.)
10. Sī cui librī Cicerōnis placent, ille sciat sē prōfēcisse. (Quintilian.—**prōficiō = prō + faciō,** *to progress, benefit.*)
11. In urbe nostrā mihi contigit docērī quantum īrātus Achillēs Graecīs nocuisset. (Horace.—**contingō, -ere, -tigī, -tāctum,** *to touch closely, fall to the lot of.*)
12. Alicui rogantī melius quam iubentī pārēmus. (Publilius Syrus.)
13. Vīvite fortiter fortiaque pectora rēbus adversīs oppōnite. (Horace.—**oppōnō = ob + pōnō,** *to set against.*)
14. Nōn ignāra malī, miserīs succurrere discō. (*Virgil.—**ignārus, -a, -um,** *ignorant;* **ignāra** is fem. because it agrees with Dido, exiled queen, who speaks these words to shipwrecked Aeneas.—**succurrō = sub + currō,** *to help.*)
15. Ignōsce saepe alterī, numquam tibi. (Publilius Syrus.)
16. Quandō tē, deum meum, quaerō, vītam beātam quaerō; quaeram tē ut vīvat anima mea. (St. Augustine.)

OVID ASKS THE GODS TO INSPIRE HIS WORK

In nova fert animus mūtātās dīcere fōrmās
corpora: dī, coeptīs—nam vōs mūtāstis et illās—
adspīrāte meīs prīmāque ab orīgine mundī
ad mea perpetuum dēdūcite tempora carmen!

(*Ovid, *Metamorphōsēs* 1.1–4; meter: dactylic hexameter. Ovid's *Metamorphōsēs* was an epic that recounted hundreds of stories of miraculous transformations, from the creation of the universe right down into his own times; the challenge in translating this brief excerpt, as with much of Latin verse, is to connect the adjectives with the nouns they modify, so watch the endings!—**nova,** with **corpora.**—**fert,** *compels (me).*—**coeptīs . . . meīs,** dat. with the compound **adspīrāte,** *my beginnings,* i.e., *the inception of my work.*—**mūtāstis = mūtāvistis;** such contractions, with **v** and the following vowel dropped, are common in certain perfect tense forms.—**et = etiam.**—**illās,** sc. **fōrmās.**—**adspīrāre,** *to breathe upon, inspire.*—**orīgō, -ginis,** f.—Note the interlocked word order of **mea . . . tempora** and **perpetuum . . . carmen.**—**dē + dūcō.**)

SORRY, NOBODY'S HOME!

Nāsīca ad poētam Ennium vēnit. Cum ad iānuam Ennium quaesīvisset et serva respondisset eum in casā nōn esse, sēnsit illam dominī iussū id dīxisse et Ennium vērō esse in casā. Post paucōs diēs, cum Ennius ad Nāsīcam vēnisset et eum ad iānuam quaereret, Nāsīca ipse exclāmāvit sē in casā nōn esse. Tum Ennius "Quid?" inquit, "Ego nōn cognōscō vōcem tuam?" Hīc Nāsīca merō cum sale respondit: "Vae, homō es impudēns! Ego, cum tē quaererem, servae tuae crēdidī tē nōn in casā esse; nōnne tū mihi ipsī nunc crēdis?"

(Cicero, *Dē Ōrātōre* 2.276.—Publius Cornelius Scipio Nasica was a celebrated jurist.—Quintus Ennius, a famous early Roman poet.—**iussū,** *at the command of.*—**exclāmāre,** *to shout out.*—**impudēns,** gen. **impudentis.**)

"I DO." "I DON'T!"

Nūbere vīs Prīscō. Nōn mīror, Paula; sapīstī.
Dūcere tē nōn vult Prīscus: et ille sapit!

(*Martial 9.10; meter: elegiac couplet.—Priscus was an eligible bachelor, and probably a rich one; Paula was apparently not his type!—**sapīstī = sapīvistī;** see on **mūtāstis** above.—**dūcere,** i.e., **in mātrimōnium.**—**et** here, as often, = **etiam.**)

MARONILLA HAS A COUGH

Petit Gemellus nūptiās Marōnillae
et cupit et īnstat et precātur et dōnat.
Adeōne pulchra est? Immō, foedius nīl est.
Quid ergō in illā petitur et placet? Tussit!

(*Martial 1.10; meter: choliambic. Gemellus is a legacy-hunter, and Maronilla a rich old hag whose estate he hopes to inherit.—**nūptiae, -ārum,** f. pl., *marriage.*—**īnstāre,** *to press, insist.*—**precor, precārī, precātus sum,** *to beg, entreat.*—**dōnat = dat.**—**adeō = tam.**—**immō,** adv., *on the contrary.*—**foedius = turpius.**—**nīl = nihil.**—**ergō = igitur.**—**tussīre,** *to cough.*)

SUMMER VACATION

Ludī magister, parce simplicī turbae:

. . .

aestāte puerī sī valent, satis discunt.

(*Martial 10.62.1, 12; meter: choliambic.—**simplex**, gen. **simplicis**, here *youthful.*)

ETYMOLOGY

In the readings   4. postponement. 5. frustrate, frustration. 6. calamitous. 7. imagine, imagery.—Pisces, piscatory, piscatology, piscary.—bestial, bestiality, bestialize, beast, beastly. 10. proficient, proficiency. 11. contingent, contingency, contiguous, contiguity, contact, contagion, contagious. 13. opponent, opposite, opposition. 14. succor. "Ovid": aspire, aspiration, aspiratory.—original, originate. "Sorry": exclamation, exclamatory.—impudence. "Maronilla": nuptials; cp. **nūbō.**—instant, instance, instantly.—imprecation.—donate, donation.—tussive, pertussis. "Summer": simple, simpleton, simplex, simplicity, simplistic.

LATĪNA EST GAUDIUM—ET ŪTILIS!

Salvēte, discipulī discipulaeque! Or perhaps now that you have learned the meaning of **studēre** you should be termed **studentēs,** since it is clearly your zeal for learning that has brought you this far in your study of Latin! So, **studentēs,** here is your **praemium,** more delectables for your **cēna Latīna,** once more **ex novā grammaticā** (*grammar*) **atque vocābulāriō:** if you remember that verbs signifying "favor . . . etc." govern the dative, you can understand this first, fortuitously alliterative motto, **fortūna favet fortibus; favēte linguīs,** lit. *be favorable with your tongues,* was an expression used in Roman religious rituals meaning "to avoid any ill-omened words, keep silent"; **imperō** obviously gives us "imperative," but also the expression **dīvide** (from **dīvidere,** *to separate, divide*) **et imperā;** a **placet** is an affirmative vote, a **placitum** a judicial decision, and a "placebo" is an unmedicated preparation meant to humor a patient (what, literally, does the "medicine" promise to do?); secret meetings are held **iānuīs clausīs** (from **claudō, claudere, clausī, clausum,** *to close,* as in "recluse," "closet," etc.), but **iānuae mentis** are the ones studying Latin will help you to open (**aperiō, aperīre, aperuī, apertum** is *to open,* as in "aperture"). **Studēte Latīnae, aperīte mentēs, et semper valēte, studentēs!**

36

Jussive Noun Clauses; Fīō

JUSSIVE NOUN CLAUSES

The "jussive noun clause" may be regarded as a kind of indirect command. As in the case of indirect statements (Ch. 25) and indirect questions (Ch. 30), the actual command (or request, or entreaty, etc.) is not quoted verbatim, via an imperative or a jussive subjunctive (Ch. 28) in a main clause, but is reported indirectly in a subordinate clause, i.e., not "he ordered them, 'Do this!'" but "he ordered them to do this." In Latin such clauses are usually introduced by either **ut** or **nē** and employ a subjunctive verb (usually present or imperfect tense), whereas in English, and therefore in translation, we ordinarily employ a *present infinitive* with no introductory word and no auxiliary such as *may* or *might:*

1. Hoc facite, *do this* (imperative). Direct command.
2. Hoc faciant, *let them do this* (jussive subj.). Direct command.
3. Imperat vōbīs ut hoc faciātis, *he commands you to do this.*
4. Imperāvit eīs ut hoc facerent, *he commanded them to do this.*
5. Persuādet eīs ut hoc faciant, *he persuades them to do this.*
6. Petīvit ab eīs nē hoc facerent, *he begged (from) them not to do this.*
7. Monuit eōs nē hoc facerent, *he warned them not to do this.*
8. Hortātus est eōs ut hoc facerent, *he urged them to do this.*

These clauses are often confused with purpose clauses because in appearance they are identical, but a study of the examples given above reveals their essentially jussive nature. In contrast to purpose clauses, which function adverbially (answering the question "why?"), the jussive clauses under discussion function as noun objects of the main verbs which introduce them (answering the question "what . . . was ordered, requested, advised, etc.?"). The following list includes some of the more common verbs that can introduce jussive noun clauses and also indicates the case (dative, accusative, etc.) employed for the person being ordered or requested to act:

> hortor eum ut, *I urge him to* . . .
> imperō eī ut, *I order him to* . . .
> moneō eum ut, *I advise him to* . . .
> ōrō eum ut, *I beg him to* . . .
> persuādeō eī ut, *I persuade him to* . . . (or *I persuade him that* . . .)
> petō ab eō ut, *I beg* (*from*) *him to* . . .
> quaerō ab eō ut, *I request* (*from/of*) *him to* . . .
> rogō eum ut, *I ask him to* . . .

Volō, nōlō, and **mālō** (Ch. 32) sometimes introduce such clauses (e.g., **mālō ut,** *I prefer that* . . .), although they also commonly are followed by infinitives; **iubeō** nearly always takes the infinitive construction.

IRREGULAR Fīō, fierī, factus sum, to occur, happen; be done, be made

The common irregular verb **fīō, fierī,** meaning *to occur, happen,* was used by the Romans in place of the passive of the present system of **faciō** and so, although active in form, also has the passive meanings *to be done, be made.*[1] Conversely, its own perfect system was supplied by the perfect passive system of **faciō.**

In effect, then, we have a composite verb with the principal parts **fīō, fierī, factus sum** and with the range of related meanings *occur, happen, become, be made, be done.* In translating, when you see the active present system forms of **fīō** remember the passive force options *be done, be made,* and when you see the passive perfect system forms **factus est, factus erat, factus sit,** etc., remember the options *has become, had occurred,* etc.

The only new forms to be learned are those listed below; note that: the stem vowel **-ī-** is long in all places except **fit, fierī,** and the imperfect subjunctive; otherwise, the forms of the present, future, and imperfect indicative and the present subjunctive follow the pattern of **audiō;** the imperfect subjunctive follows a predictable pattern, given the infinitive **fierī.**

---

[1] This is true of the basic verb **faciō** (e.g., **fit** was used instead of **facitur** for *it is done, is made*); the practice with compounds varied, e.g., **perficitur,** *is completed,* but **calefit** instead of **calefacitur** for *is heated.*

Indicative			**Subjunctive**	
Pres.	**Impf.**	**Fut.**	**Pres.**	**Impf.**
1. fīō	fīēbam	fīam	fīam	fíerem
2. fīs	fīēbās	fīēs	fīās	fíerēs
3. fit	fīēbat	fīet	fīat	fíeret
1. fīmus	fīēbámus	fīḗmus	fīámus	fierḗmus
2. fītis	fīēbátis	fīḗtis	fīátis	fierḗtis
3. fīunt	fīēbant	fīent	fīant	fíerent

Infinitive	**Imperatives**	
fíerī	**Sg.** fī	**Pl.** fíte

Study carefully the following examples:

Hoc facit (faciet), *he is doing* or *making this* (*will do* or *make*).
Hoc fit (fīet), *this is done* or *made* (*will be done* or *made*).
Hoc faciat, *let him do* or *make this.*
Hoc fīat, *let this be done* or *made.*
Dīcunt eum hoc facere, *they say that he is doing this.*
Dīcunt hoc fierī, *they say that this is being done.*
Perīculum fit gravius, *the danger is becoming graver.*
Mox factī sunt fēlīces, *they soon became happy.*

VOCABULARY

cupído, cupídinis, f., *desire, passion* (cupidity, Cupid; cp. **cupiō, cupiditās, cupidus,** Ch. 39)

léctor, lēctóris, m., and **léctrīx, lēctrícis,** f., *reader* (lector; cp. **legō,** lectern, lection, lectionary, lecture)

vínculum, -ī, n., *bond, chain, fetter* (vinculum; cp. **vinciō,** *to bind*)

cōtídiē, adv., *daily, every day* (**quot + diēs;** cotidian)

fortásse, adv., *perhaps* (cp. **fortūna**)

accédō, -cédere, -céssī, -céssum, *to come* (*to*), *approach* (accede, access, accessible, accession, accessory; cp. **cēdō, discēdō**)

cárpō, cárpere, cárpsī, cárptum, *to harvest, pluck; seize* (carp at, excerpt, carpet, scarce; **carpe diem:** see **Latīna Est Gaudium,** Ch. 22)

cṓgō, cṓgere, coḗgī, coáctum (**cum + agō**), *to drive* or *bring together, force, compel* (cogent, coaction, coactive, coagulate; cp. **cōgitō**)

contémnō, -témnere, -témpsī, -témptum, *to despise, scorn* (contemn, contempt, contemptible, contemptuous)

contúndō, -túndere, -tudī, -tū́sum, *to beat, crush, bruise, destroy* (contuse, contusion; obtuse, from **obtundō,** *to beat, make blunt*)

cū́rō (1), *to care for, attend to; heal, cure; take care* (cure, curator, procure, proctor, accurate; cp. **cū́ra**)

dēcérnō, -cérnere, -crḗvī, -crḗtum, *to decide, settle, decree* (decretal, decretory)

éxigō, -ígere, -ḗgī, -ā́ctum (ex + agō), *to drive out, force out, exact; drive through, complete, perfect* (exactitude, exigent, exigency, exigible)

fī́ō, fī́erī, fáctus sum, *to occur, happen; become; be made, be done* (fiat)

obléctō (1), *to please, amuse, delight; pass time pleasantly* (cp. **dēlectō, dēlectātiō**)

ṓrō (1), *to speak, plead; beg, beseech, entreat, pray* (orator, oration, oracle, orison, adore, inexorable, peroration; cp. **ṓrātor, ṓrātiō,** Ch. 38)

récreō (1), *to restore, revive; refresh, cheer* (recreate, recreation)

requī́rō, -quī́rere, -quī́sī́vī, -quī́sī́tum, *to seek, ask for; miss, need, require* (requirement, requisite, requisition, prerequisite, request)

serḗnō (1), *to make clear, brighten; cheer up, soothe* (serene, serenity, serenade)

PRACTICE AND REVIEW

1. Poterāsne etiam centum virīs persuādēre ut viam virtūtis sine praemiīs sequerentur?
2. Haec fēmina vult ex urbe ēgredī et ad illam īnsulam proficīscī ut sine morā illī agricolae nūbat et semper rūsticētur.
3. Petēbant ā nōbīs ut etiam in adversīs rēbus huic ducī pārērēmus et servīrēmus.
4. Haec ab fēminīs facta sunt nē tantam occāsiōnem āmitterent.
5. Rogāmus tē ut honōre et opibus sapientius ūtāris et hōs quīnque amīcōs semper foveās.
6. Nisi quis hoc suscipere audēbit, nōlent nōbīs crēdere et fīent īrātī.
7. Rogāvit nōs cūr neque dīvitibus neque pauperibus placēre cōnātī essēmus.
8. Arbitrābātur tālem vītam nōn ex dīvitiīs sed ex animō plēnō virtūtis nāscī.
9. Scientiam et ingenium magis quam magnās dīvitiās mīrēmur.
10. Senātus ducī imperāvit nē hostibus victīs nocēret sed eīs parceret et remissiōnem poenae daret.
11. Ille ōrātor vulgum īrātissimum vōce potentī serēnāvit atque, ut omnibus subrīsit, eōs oblectāvit.
12. Ut parva puella per iānuam currēbat, subitō occidit et genua male contudit.
13. Dummodo sīs aequus hīs virīs, fīent tibi fidēlēs.
14. That summer they urged that this be done better.

15. Provided that this is done, they will beg us to spare him.
16. That teacher wants to persuade her twenty pupils to study more good literature.
17. Since his hope is becoming very small, let him confess that he commanded (use **imperō**) those two men not to do it.

SENTENTIAE ANTĪQUAE

1. Dīxitque Deus: "Fīat lūx." Et facta est lūx. (*Genesis.)
2. Fatendum est nihil dē nihilō posse fierī. (Lucretius.—**nihilō**, abl. of **nihilum, -ī, = nihil.**)
3. Magnae rēs nōn fīunt sine perīculō. (Terence.)
4. Hīs rēbus cognitīs, ille suōs hortātus est nē timērent. (Caesar.)
5. Omnia fīent quae fierī aequum est. (Terence.)
6. "Pater, ōrō tē ut mihi ignōscās." "Fīat." (Terence.)
7. Dum loquimur, fūgerit invida aetās: carpe diem! (*Horace.—**invidus, -a, -um,** *envious.*)
8. Carpāmus dulcia; post enim mortem cinis et fābula fīes. (Persius.—**cinis, -neris,** m., *ashes.*)
9. Ante senectūtem cūrāvī ut bene vīverem; in senectūte cūrō ut bene moriar. (Seneca.)
10. Solōn dīxit sē senem fierī cotīdiē aliquid addiscentem. (Cicero.—**Solōn, -lōnis.—ad-discō, -ere.**)
11. Caret pectus tuum inānī ambitiōne? Caret īrā et timōre mortis? Ignōscis amīcīs? Fīs lēnior et melior, accēdente senectūte? (Horace.—**inānis, -e,** *empty, vain.*—**ambitiō, -ōnis.—lēnis, -e,** *gentle, kind.*)
12. Hoc dūrum est; sed levius fit patientiā quidquid corrigere est nefās. (Horace.—**patientia, -ae.—corrigō, -ere.—est nefās,** *it is wrong, contrary to divine law.*)
13. Sapiāmus et cēdāmus! Leve fit onus quod bene fertur. (Ovid.—**onus, oneris,** n., *burden.*)
14. Ego vōs hortor ut amīcitiam omnibus rēbus hūmānīs antepōnātis—vae illīs quī nūllōs amīcōs habent! (Cicero.)
15. Petō ā vōbīs ut patiāminī mē dē studiīs hūmānitātis ac litterārum loquī. (Cicero.—**hūmānitās, -tātis,** *culture.*)

THE QUALITY OF MARTIAL'S BOOK

Sunt bona, sunt quaedam mediocria, sunt mala plūra
    quae legis hīc; aliter nōn fit, Avīte, liber.

(*Martial 1.16; meter, elegiac couplet.—**aliter,** adv., *otherwise.*—**Avītus, -ī,** a friend of the poet.)

I DON'T COOK FOR COOKS!

Lēctor et audītor nostrōs probat, Aule, libellōs,
    sed quīdam exāctōs esse poēta negat.
Nōn nimium cūrō, nam cēnae fercula nostrae
    mālim convīvīs quam placuisse cocīs!

(*Martial 9.81; meter: elegiac couplet.—**quīdam,** with **poēta.**—sc. **eōs,** = **li-bellōs,** as subject of the infin. in the indir. statement.—**ferculum, -ī,** *course [of a meal].*—**mālim,** potential subj., *I would prefer that.*—The prose order would be: **mālim fercula cēnae nostrae placuisse convīvīs quam cocīs.**—**quam,** i.e., **magis quam.**—**convīva, -ae,** m., dinner-guest.—**cocus, -ī,** *cook.*)

I LOVE HER . . . I LOVE HER NOT

Ōdī et amō! Quārē id faciam fortasse requīris.
    Nescio, sed fierī sentiō et excrucior.

(*Catullus 85; meter: elegiac couplet.—**excruciāre,** *to crucify, torment.*)

OH, I'D LOVE TO READ YOU MY POEMS . . . NOT!

Ut recitem tibi nostra rogās epigrammata. Nōlō—
    nōn audīre, Celer, sed recitāre cupis!

(*Martial 1.63; meter: elegiac couplet.—**epigramma, -matis,** n.)

WHO IS TRULY FREE?

Quis igitur vērō līber est? Tantum vir sapiēns, quī sibi imperat, quem neque fortūna adversa neque paupertās neque mors neque vincula terrent, quī potest cupīdinibus fortiter respondēre honōrēsque contemnere, cuius virtūs cōtīdiē crēscit, quī in sē ipsō tōtus est.

(Horace, *Sermōnēs* 2.7.83ff; prose adaptation.)

TESTIMONY AGAINST THE CONSPIRATORS

Senātum coēgī. Intrōdūxī Volturcium sine Gallīs. Fidem pūblicam eī dedī. Hortātus sum ut ea quae scīret sine timōre nūntiāret. Tum ille, cum sē ex magnō timōre recreāvisset, dīxit sē ab Lentulō habēre ad Catilīnam man-dāta ut auxiliō servōrum ūterētur et ad urbem quam prīmum cum exercitū accēderet. Intrōductī autem Gallī dīxērunt sibi litterās ad suam gentem ab Lentulō datās esse et hunc imperāvisse ut equitātum in Italiam quam prīmum mitterent. Dēnique, omnibus rēbus expositīs, senātus dēcrēvit ut coniūrātī, quī hās īnsidiās mōlītī essent, in custōdiam trāderentur.

(Cicero; in this adaptation from his third oration against Catiline, Cicero in-forms the Roman citizenry of the evidence against Catiline and the actions of the senate. See the earlier readings on Catiline in Chs. 11, 14, 20, and 30.—

intrō-dūcō, -ere.—Volturcius was a conspirator in Catiline's band.—**Gallus, -ī,** *a Gaul;* Lentulus, the leading conspirator at Rome in Catiline's absence, had been seeking to stir into rebellion against the Roman state the Gallic Allobroges, who had a delegation at Rome.—**scīret:** a subordinate clause that would ordinarily have an indicative verb often has instead a subjunctive when the clause occurs either within an indirect statement or, as here, within another subjunctive clause; in this latter instance the verb is often termed a "subjunctive by attraction."—**mandātum, -ī,** *order.*—**quam prīmum,** see Ch. 32.—**equitātus, -ūs,** *cavalry.*)

ETYMOLOGY

In the readings   8. cinerary, incinerator, incinerate. 11. inane, inanity.—ambition; **ambitiō** literally meant *a going around* by a candidate to individual citizens in quest of political support.—lenient, leniency, lenity. 12. correct, incorrigible. 13. onerous. 15. humanity, the humanities; cp. **homō, hūmānus.** "I Love Her": excruciate; cp. crux, crucial, from **crux, crucis,** f., *cross.* "I'd Love to Read": epigrammatic. "Testimony":—mandate, mandatory, command, countermand, demand, remand.—equitation.

LATĪNA EST GAUDIUM—ET ŪTILIS!

Salvēte, studentēs! Here are some **fīō** items: if you've found it easier to write a speech than a poem, you'll believe the old saying **nāscimur poētae, fīmus ōrātōrēs;** a fiat (*not* the car) is a magisterial command, *let it be done!* From Publilius Syrus (the source of many of this book's **sententiae**) comes **repente dīvēs nēmō factus est bonus** (like Juvenal's **nēmō repente fuit turpissimus,** Ch. 30); also the legal expression regarding "consenting adults," **volentī nōn fit iniūria,** *injury is not done to a willing person,* and **fīat ut petitur,** *let it be done as requested,* the phrase used for granting a legal petition.

Et cētera ex hōc vocābulāriō: an **accessit** (lit., *he/she approached, came close*) is a recognition for second place or honorable mention in a competition; **vinculum mātrimōniī** is *the bond of matrimony,* and **ā vinculō mātrimōniī** is legal Lat. for an annulment; **dē minimīs nōn cūrat lēx,** *the law does not concern itself with trivialities,* is another familiar legal maxim; there are numerous mottoes and familiar sayings from **ōrāre,** including **ōrāre et spērāre** and **ōrā et labōrā;** besides **carpe diem,** there is **carpent tua pōma nepōtēs,** *your descendants will harvest your fruits.* **Carpāmus omnēs diēs, lēctōrēs et lēctrīcēs!**

37

Conjugation of Eō; Constructions of Place and Time

IRREGULAR Eō, īre, iī, itum, to go

The irregular fourth conjugation verb **eō, īre, iī, itum,** *to go,* is fully conjugated below; the verb is as common in Latin as "go" is in English, and so the conjugation should be learned thoroughly.

INDICATIVE

Pres.	Impf.	Fut.	Perf.	Plupf.	Fut. Perf.
1. éō	íbam	íbō	íī	íeram	íerō
2. īs	íbās	íbis	ístī	íerās	íeris
3. it	íbat	íbit	íit	íerat	íerit
1. ímus	ībámus	íbimus	íimus	ierámus	iérimus
2. ítis	ībátis	íbitis	ístis	ierátis	iéritis
3. éunt	íbant	íbunt	iérunt	íerant	íerint

SUBJUNCTIVE

Pres.	Impf.	Perf.	Plupf.
1. éam	írem	íerim	íssem
2. éās	írēs	ierīs	íssēs
3. éat	íret	íerit	ísset

1. eámus	īrḗmus	ierímus	īssḗmus
2. eátis	īrḗtis	ierítis	īssḗtis
3. éant	írent	íerint	íssent

IMPERATIVES

Sg. ī   **Pl.** íte

PARTICIPLES (in common use)

Pres. íēns (eúntis, eúntī, etc.)   **Fut.** itū́rus, -a, -um

INFINITIVES   GERUND: eúndī

Pres. íre
Fut. itū́rus ésse
Perf. ísse

OBSERVATIONS ON Eō

In the present system of **eō** there are two major difficulties:

(1) The normal stem, **ī-,** as derived from the present infinitive, becomes **e-** before **a, o,** and **u;** e.g., **eō, eunt, eam.** Give particular attention to the present indicative and the present subjunctive above. A similar change from **ī-** to **e-** is seen in all forms of the present participle, except the nominative singular, and in the gerund (a form whose use is explained in Ch. 39).

(2) The future of this fourth conjugation verb has the tense sign and endings of a first or second conjugation verb.

The perfect system is formed regularly except that **ii-** before **s** usually contracts to **ī-;** e.g., **īstī, īsse.** Forms with **-v-,** such as **īvī,** are rare and do not appear in this book.

Only the active forms are here presented; the rare impersonal passive (e.g., **ītur, ībātur**) and the future and perfect passive participles (**eundum, itum**) do not appear in this book. Transitive compounds such as **adeō,** *to approach,* commonly have passive endings (e.g., **adeor, adībātur,** etc.), but those forms likewise are not employed in this book.

PLACE CONSTRUCTIONS

You have already learned how to use the proper prepositions and cases in the regular place constructions, but they are repeated here for review and for contrast with the special rules for the *names* of cities, towns, and small islands and for **domus, humus,** and **rūs.**

I. Regular constructions: prepositions + proper case.

(1) Place *where:* **in** or **sub** + ablative.

In illā urbe vīsus est, *he was seen in that city.*
Nihil sub sōle est novum, *there is nothing new under the sun.*

(2) Place *to which:* **in, ad,** or **sub** + accusative.

In illam urbem ībit, *he will go into that city.*
Sub hastam hostis occidit, *he fell under the enemy's spear.*

(3) Place *from which:* **ab, dē,** or **ex** + ablative.

Ex illā urbe iit, *he went out of that city.*

II. With the actual names of cities, towns, and small islands, as well as the three nouns **domus, humus,** and **rūs,** no prepositions were employed in Latin, though they usually must be supplied in English translation (cp., however, Eng. "he ran home" for "he ran *to his* home").

(1) For place *where* with these particular words a special case was used in Latin, the "locative." The locative is identical to the *genitive* for the singular of first and second declension nouns; elsewhere the locative is usually identical to the *ablative.*

Vīsus est Rōmae, Ephesī, Athēnīs, et Carthāgine.
He was seen at Rome, Ephesus, Athens, and Carthage.

(2) Place *to which:* accusative without a preposition.

Ībit Rōmam, Ephesum, Athēnās, et Carthāginem.
He will go to Rome, Ephesus, Athens, and Carthage.

(3) Place *from which:* ablative without a preposition.

Iit Rōmā, Ephesō, Athēnīs, et Carthāgine.
He went from Rome, Ephesus, Athens, and Carthage.

Domus, as seen in the vocabulary below, is a slightly irregular feminine noun, having some second declension endings and some fourth. In place constructions the commonest forms are as follows:

domī (locative), *at home*   Domī vīsus est, *he was seen at home.*
domum (acc.), *home* (= *to home*) Domum ībit, *he will go home.*
domō (abl.), *from home*   Domō iit, *he went from home.*

The locative of **humus,** a feminine second declension noun, follows the rule: **humī,** *on the ground.* The locative of **rūs** is either **rūrī** or **rūre,** *in the country.*

TIME CONSTRUCTIONS

(1) You are already familiar with the ablative of time *when* or *within which* (Ch. 15); no preposition is used in Latin, but in English translation you must supply *in, within, at, on,* etc., depending on the particular noun:

Eōdem diē iit, *he went on the same day.*
Paucīs hōrīs domum ībit, *he will go home in a few hours.*

(2) Newly introduced here is the accusative of *duration of time,* which indicates, not the time at or within which an action occurs, but *for how long a period of time* the action occurs. No preposition is employed in Latin; in English translation, the preposition *for* is sometimes used, sometimes omitted. The construction also commonly occurs with **nātus** to indicate a person's age.

Multōs annōs vīxit, *he lived (for) many years.*
Paucās hōrās domī manēbit, *he will stay at home (for) a few hours.*
Quīnque et vīgintī annōs nātus, imperātor factus est, *At the age of 25* (lit., *having been born for 25 years), he became commander.*

VOCABULARY

Athḗnae, -ā́rum, f. pl., *Athens* (cp. athenaeum)

dómus, -ūs (-ī), f., *house, home;* **dómī,** *at home;* **dómum,** *(to) home;* **dómō,** *from home* (domain, domicile, domestic, domesticate, dome, major-domo; cp. **dominus, domina,** Ch. 40)

húmus, -ī, f., *ground, earth; soil* (humus, exhume, inhume, inhumation, posthumous; cp. humiliate, humility, from **humilis, -e,** *on the earth, down-to-earth, humble*)

íter, itíneris, n., *journey; route, road* (itinerant, itinerary; cp. **eō** below)

rūs, rū́ris, n., *the country, countryside* (rustic, rusticity; cp. **rūsticor, rūsticus,** *rural*)

Syrācū́sae, -ā́rum, f. pl., *Syracuse*

ábsēns, gen. **abséntis,** *absent, away* (absence, absentee, absenteeism, in absentia; from **absum, abesse**)

grā́tus, -a, -um, *pleasing, agreeable; grateful* (grace, gracious, grateful, gratitude, gratify, gratis, gratuitous, gratuity, ingrate, ingratiate, agree, congratulate; cp. **grātiās agō**)

idṓneus, -a, -um, *suitable, fit, appropriate*

immṓtus, -a, -um, *unmoved; unchanged; unrelenting* (immotile; cp. **moveō**)

fórīs, adv., *out of doors, outside* (foreclose, foreign, forest, forfeit)

éō, íre, íī, ítum, *to go* (ambition, circuit, concomitant, exit, initial, initiate, initiative, obituary, perish, preterit, sedition, transient, transit, transition, transitive, transitory: many of these derive from the several compounds of **eō**, including the seven listed below)

ábeō, -íre, -iī, -itum, *to go away, depart, leave*

ádeō, -íre, -iī, -itum, *to go to, approach*

éxeō, -íre, -iī, -itum, *to go out, exit*

íneō, -íre, -iī, -itum, *to go in, enter*

óbeō, -íre, -iī, -itum, *to go up against, meet; die*

péreō, -íre, -iī, -itum, *to pass away, be destroyed, perish*

rédeō, -íre, -iī, -itum, *to go back, return*

interfíciō, -fícere, -fécī, -féctum, *to kill, murder*

lícet, licére, lícuit, impersonal,[1] *it is permitted, one may;* commonly with an infinitive as subject and a dative for the person permitted to act, e.g., **licet tibi abīre,** *you may leave,* lit., *it is permitted for you to leave* (license, licentious, illicit, leisure, viz. = **vidélicet,** sc. = **scílicet**)

peregrínor, peregrīnárī, peregrīnátus sum, *to travel abroad, wander* (peregrine, peregrinate, pilgrim, pilgrimage; from **per** + **ager**)

requiéscō, -quiéscere, -quiévī, -quiétum, *to rest* (requiescat, requiem)

sóleō, solére, sólitus sum, *to be accustomed* (insolent, obsolete)

PRACTICE AND REVIEW

1. Dehinc petet ā frātre meō et sorōre ut occāsiōnem carpant et in urbem quam celerrimē ineant.
2. Nisi domum hāc aestāte redīssēs, in longō itinere Athēnās fortasse peregrīnātī essēmus, et nōs ibi oblectāvissēmus.
3. Nē levēs quidem timōrēs ferre poterātis; rūrī, igitur, nōn in urbe semper vīvēbātis.
4. Haec locūtī, lēctōribus et lēctrīcibus persuādēbunt nē opēs cupīdinēsque praemiīs bonae vītae antepōnant.
5. Multōs annōs eōs cīvitātī servīre coēgit, sed animōs numquam contudit.
6. At nōs, ipsī multa mala passī, cōnātī sumus eīs īrātīs persuādēre ut servōs vinculīs līberārent et nē cui nocērent.
7. Sī quis vult aliōs iuvāre, cūret ut ad eōs adeat plēnus sapientiae.
8. Philosophī cōtīdiē requīrēbant utrum illī discipulī nātūrae pārērent.
9. Contemnāmus omnia perīcula, ea ex pectoribus exigāmus, et fateāmur haec difficillima Rōmae suscipienda esse.
10. Omnēs solent mīrārī ea pulcherrima quae Athēnīs vident.
11. Nisi māvīs morī, exī Syrācūsīs, sequere alium ducem, et accēde Athēnās.

---

[1] Impersonal verbs have only third person (and infinitive) forms because they have as their subject, not a person, but an infinitive phrase or a clause or an indefinite "it" or "one"; e.g., **licet abīre** lit. means *to leave is permitted,* though the idiomatic translation is *it is permissible to leave* or *one may leave.*

12. Fēmina candida ante speculum immōta stetit, sed sē spectāre recūsāvit et animōs recreāre nōn potuit.
13. Paucās hōras duodecim puerī puellaeque humī sedēbant, ut magistra, subrīdēns et eōs serēnāns, plūrimās fābulās nārrābat.
14. Sī sapiēs et tibi imperāre poteris, fīēs grātior iūstiorque, parcēs miserīs ac amīcōs fovēbis.
15. They commanded that this be done in Rome for three days.
16. Unless he goes to Syracuse within five days, his father's fear will become greater.
17. He thought that his brother would perhaps not go away from home that summer.
18. Nobody may speak freely in that country, as we all know.

SENTENTIAE ANTĪQUAE

1. Mortālia facta perībunt. (*Horace.)
2. Noctēs atque diēs patet ātrī iānua Dītis. (*Virgil.—**āter, ātra, ātrum,** *dark, gloomy.*—**Dīs, Dītis,** *Dis,* another name for Pluto, god of the dead.)
3. Annī eunt mōre modōque fluentis aquae. Numquam hōra quae praeteriit potest redīre; ūtāmur aetāte. (Ovid.—**praeterīre,** *to go by, pass.*)
4. Heu, obiī! Quid ego ēgī! Fīlius nōn rediit ā cēnā hāc nocte. (Terence.)
5. Frāter meus ōrat nē abeās domō. (Terence.)
6. Dīcit patrem ab urbe abīsse sed frātrem esse domī. (Terence.)
7. Tertiā hōrā forīs ībam Sacrā Viā, ut meus mōs est. (Horace.—**Sacrā Viā,** abl. of means or way by which; the Sacred Way was the main street through the Roman Forum.)

The Roman Forum with remains of the temple of Castor and Pollux in the foreground and beyond it the Sacra Via Rome, Italy

8. Dēnique Dāmoclēs, cum sīc beātus esse nōn posset, ōrāvit Dionȳsium tyrannum ut abīre ā cēnā licēret. (Cicero.)

9. Eō tempore, Syrācūsīs captīs, Mārcellus multa Rōmam mīsit; Syrācūsīs autem multa atque pulcherrima relīquit. (Cicero.)

10. Diēs multōs in eā nāve fuī; ita adversā tempestāte ūsī sumus. (Terence.)

11. Īram populī ferre nōn poterō, sī in exsilium ieris. (Cicero.)

12. Caesare interfectō, Brūtus Rōmā Athēnās fūgit. (Cicero.)

13. Ipse Rōmam redīrem, sī satis cōnsiliī dē hāc rē habērem. (Cicero.)

14. Nēmō est tam senex ut nōn putet sē ūnum annum posse vīvere. (Cicero.)

15. Dum nōs fāta sinunt, oculōs satiēmus amōre; nox tibi longa venit, nec reditūra diēs. (*Propertius.—**sinō, -ere,** *to allow.*—**reditūra,** sc. **est,** fut. act. periphrastic for **redībit; diēs** is sometimes fem.)

THANKS . . . BUT NO THANKS!

Candidius nihil est tē, Caeciliāne. Notāvī:
   sī quandō ex nostrīs disticha pauca legō,
prōtinus aut Mārsī recitās aut scrīpta Catullī.
   Hoc mihi dās, tamquam dēteriōra legās,
5   ut collāta magis placeant mea? Crēdimus istud:
   mālo tamen recitēs, Caeciliāne, tua!

(*Martial 2.71; meter: elegiac couplet.—**notāre,** *to note, notice.*—with **nostrīs,** sc. **libellīs.**—**disticha** (a Gk. acc. ending), *couplets, verses.*—Domitius Marsus, like Catullus, was a popular Latin poet.—**scrīptum, -ī,** *writing, written works.*—**hoc . . . dās,** i.e., as a favor.—**tamquam** here introduces an imagined comparison, something like a condition, hence the verb is subj.—**dēteriōra,** sc. **scrīpta,** *worse poetry.*—**collāta,** with **mea,** *compared, in comparison.*—**mālo [ut] recitēs;** the conj. is often omitted in a jussive noun clause.)

TRIMALCHIO'S EPITAPH

"Īnscrīptiō quoque vidē dīligenter sī haec satis idōnea tibi vidētur: 'C. Pompeius Trimalchiō Maecēnātiānus hīc requiēscit. Huic sēvirātus absentī dēcrētus est. Cum posset in omnibus decuriīs Rōmae esse, tamen nōluit. Pius, fortis, fidēlis, ex parvō crēvit; sestertium relīquit trecentiēs, nec umquam philosophum audīvit. Valē. Et tū.'" Haec ut dīxit Trimalchiō, flēre coepit ūbertim. Flēbat et Fortūnāta; flēbat et Habinnas; tōta dēnique familia, tamquam in fūnus rogāta, lāmentātiōne triclīnium implēvit.

(*Petronius, *Satyricon* 71–72; the boorish, nouveau-riche host Trimalchio asks his dinner-guests their opinion of his proposed epitaph.—**īnscrīptiō, -ōnis;** the more usual order would be **quoque vidē dīligenter sī haec īnscrīptiō. . . .**—**C. = Gaius.**—**Maecēnātiānus:** Trimalchio, an ex-slave, takes this name to associate himself with the famous Maecenas, a powerful and wealthy associate of Augustus.—**Huic . . . absentī,** i.e., in absentia from Rome.—**sēvirātus, -ūs,** *the post of sēvir Augustālis,* a member of the six-man commission that supervised the cult of the emperor.—**decūria, -ae,** *club;* these were groups of ten men organized for both business and social purposes.—**pius, -a, -um,** *devoted, dedicated.*—**ex parvō,** i.e., from humble beginnings.—**sestertium . . . trecentiēs,** *30 million sesterces,* a VERY hefty sum!—**nec . . . audīvit,** i.e., he "never even went to college!"—**Et tū,** sc. **valē;** epitaphs typically represented such "conversations": the deceased wishes the passerby *"Farewell,"* and the passerby, reading the inscription, replies, *"And you (likewise farewell)."*—**Haec ut** = Ut haec.—**flēre,** *to weep.*—**ūbertim,** adv., *profusely.*—**et** = **etiam.**—Fortunata ("Lucky") and Habinnas were Trimalchio's wife and a guest.—**fūnus, -neris,** n., *funeral.*—**lamentātiō, -ōnis.**—**triclīnium, -iī,** *dining room.*—**impleō, -plēre, -plēvī, -plētum,** *to fill.*)

MĀRCUS QUĪNTŌ FRĀTRĪ S.

Licinius, servus Aesōpī nostrī, Rōmā Athēnās fūgit. Is Athēnīs apud Patrōnem prō līberō virō fuit. Deinde in Asiam abiit. Posteā Platō, quīdam quī Athēnīs solet esse multum et quī tum Athēnīs fuerat cum Licinius Athēnās vēnisset, litterīs Aesōpī dē Liciniō acceptīs, hunc Ephesī comprehendit et in custōdiam trādidit. Petō ā tē, frāter, ut Ephesō exiēns servum Rōmam tēcum redūcās. Aesōpus enim ita īrāscitur propter servī scelus ut nihil eī grātius possit esse quam recuperātiō fugitīvī. Valē.

(Cicero, *Epistulae ad Quīntum Frātrem* 1.2.14; Marcus Cicero wrote this letter to his brother Quintus, who was at the time governor of Asia.—**S.** = **salūtem dīcit,** *says greetings.*—**Licinius, -ī.**—**Aesōpus, -ī,** the leading tragic actor of Rome.—**Patrō, -trōnis.**—**prō,** *as a.*—**Plato,** an Epicurean from Sardis.—**multum,** adv.—**Ephesus, -ī,** a city in Asia Minor.—**re-dūcō.**—**īrāscor, īrāscī, īrātus sum,** *to be angry;* cp. **īra** and **īrātus.**—**recuperātiō, -ōnis,** *recovery.*—**fugitīvus, -ī.**)

ETYMOLOGY

Vidēlicet, *namely,* derives from **vidēre licet,** lit., *it is permitted to see,* i.e., *it is plain to see.* In medieval manuscripts this long word was often contracted to **vi-et,** and one abbreviation for **et** resembled a **z;** hence the abbreviation **viz.** From another compound of **licet** is the much more common abbreviation **sc.** for **scīlicet,** *namely, clearly* (from **scīre licet,** *you may understand*), which we use as an instruction to supply some word or idea that has been omitted from a text but is readily understood (see the example above in the notes on "Trimalchio").

In the readings

7. Another famous street in Rome was **Via Lāta.** On the analogy of **Sacra Via** how is **Via Lāta** (**lātus, -a, -um,** *broad*) to be translated? "Thanks": note, notation, notary.—script; from the fourth principal part of **scrībō.**—deteriorate, deterioration.—collate, collation. "Trimalchio": funereal.—lament, lamentable. "**Mārcus**": irascible.—"Recover" and "recuperate" are cognates, both derived from **recuperāre,** *to regain.*)

LATĪNA EST GAUDIUM—ET ŪTILIS!

Salvēte! These familiar words and phrases from **eō** are certainly *going to* interest you (notice how colloquial Eng. employs "go" as an auxiliary verb to indicate futurity, and cp. Latin's use of **īrī** in those rare future passive infinitive forms): **exit** and **exeunt omnēs** are stage directions; to "perish" is to be "thoroughly gone" (from **per + eō**), i.e., to make one's final "exit" from life's stage, an exodus often marked by **obiit** on old tombstones or by the abbreviation **O.S.P.** for **obiit sine prōle** (*he/she died without offspring,* from **prōlēs, prōlis,** f., the source of "proletariate"); **pereant quī ante nōs nostra dīxērunt** is a proverbial curse on folks who had all our best ideas before we had them ourselves (!); **iter** (lit. *a going*) is related to **eō** and also to the adv. **obiter,** which gives us **obiter dictum,** something *said along the way* (or "in passing"), and likewise **obiter scrīptum;** Monty Python fans will recall the **Rōmānī, īte domum** routine from the "Life of Brian"; and finally **aut bibat aut abeat,** *let him either drink or go away,* is an old Roman toast and the motto of our local tavern!

Et cētera: grātus is related to **grātia,** *favor, kindness, gratitude, thanks,* as in **grātiās agere,** *to give thanks,* **Deī grātiā,** *by the grace of God,* and also Eng. "gratis," something done "for thanks" (**grātīs**), i.e., without a fee. **R.I.P.,** also found on tombstones (though not Trimalchio's!), stands for **requiēscat in pāce** (remember the jussive subj.?); **rūs in urbe,** a phrase from Martial, refers to a city park or garden or some other rustic setting or view that reminds one of the countryside. Well, enough for today: **nunc domum eāmus!**

38

Relative Clauses of Characteristic; Dative of Reference; Supines

RELATIVE CLAUSES OF CHARACTERISTIC

The type of relative clause you have encountered thus far provides some factual description of its antecedent, an actual person or thing, and thus has an indicative verb (Ch. 17); e.g., **hic est discipulus quī Latīnam amat,** *this is the student who loves Latin.* The "relative clause of characteristic," by contrast, describes some general quality of an antecedent that is itself either general, indefinite, interrogative, or negative, and accordingly has its verb in the subjunctive; e.g., *hic est discipulus quī Latīnam amet, this is a student* (or *the sort of student*) *who would love Latin.*

The relative clause of characteristic is easily recognized, since its verb is subjunctive and its antecedent is often obviously general, negative, etc. (typical examples are **sunt quī,** *there are people who;* **quis est quī,** *who is there who;* **nēmō est quī,** *there is no one who*); the auxiliary *would* is sometimes used in translating the subjunctive verb, and sometimes a phrase like *the sort of* or *the kind of* is employed in the main clause to make it clear that the antecedent is indefinite:

> Quis est quī huic crēdat, *who is there who trusts this man (of such a sort that he would trust this man)?*
> Nēmō erat quī hoc scīret, *there was no one who knew this.*
> Sunt quī hoc faciant, *there are some who do this (of such a sort as to do this).*

Is nōn est quī hoc faciat, *he is not a person who does (would do) this.*
Hic est liber quem omnēs legant, *this is the kind of book which all read*
    (*a book which all would read*).
Hic est liber quem omnēs legunt, *this is the book which all are reading*
    (= a fact, hence the indicative).

Some relative clauses have the force of result (e.g., S.A. 4 below), purpose (see "Give Me a Figgy Sprig!" below), causal, or adversative clauses (i.e., clauses otherwise generally introduced by **ut, cum,** etc.) and so also have their verbs in the subjunctive.

DATIVE OF REFERENCE OR INTEREST

The dative case is often used to indicate a person (or a thing) to whom some statement refers, or from whose perspective it is true, or to whom it is of special interest. This "dative of reference or interest" (which should be compared to the dative uses discussed in Ch. 35) can sometimes be translated with "to" or "for," but often some more elaborate phrase is required, depending upon the context, as you will see from the following examples; occasionally the function seems to be simply possessive (as in the second example below), but the intended force is generally more emotional.

Sī quis metuēns vīvet, līber **mihi** nōn erit umquam.
    If anyone lives in fear, he will not ever be free—as I see it (**mihi**) *or to
    my way of thinking.*
Caret **tibi** pectus inānī ambitiōne?
    Is your breast free from vain ambition—are you sure (**tibi**)?
Nūllīus culpae **mihi** cōnscius sum.
    In my own heart (**mihi**), *I am conscious of no fault.*
Claudia est sapiēns **multīs,** *to many people Claudia is wise.*

Remember to add the dative of reference or interest to your list of other dative case constructions (indirect object, dative of agent, dative with adjectives, dative with special verbs and compounds).

SUPINES

The "supine" is a defective fourth declension verbal noun, formed on the same stem as the perfect passive participle; only two forms were in common use, the accusative and ablative singular. The supines for our model verbs are: acc. **laudátum,** abl. **laudátū; mónitum, mónitū; áctum, áctū; audítum, audítū; cáptum, cáptū.**

The ablative is used with the neuter of certain adjectives to indicate in what respect a particular quality is applicable: e.g., **mīrábile dictū,** *amazing to say* (lit., *amazing in respect to saying*); **facile factū,** *easy to do.* The accusative (which must be carefully distinguished from the perfect passive participle) is used with verbs of motion to indicate purpose: e.g., **ībant Rōmam rogátum pecūniam,** *they were going to Rome to ask for money;* **persuásum amīcīs vēnērunt,** *they came to persuade their friends* (note that the supine can take a direct object, a dative, or any other construction the basic verb can govern).

VOCABULARY

árbor, árboris, f., *tree* (arbor, Arbor Day, arboraceous, arboreal, arboretum, arboriculture)

dígnitās, dignitátis, f., *merit, prestige, dignity* (indignity; cp. **dignus,** deign, dignify, indignant, indignation)

dólor, dolóris, m., *pain, grief* (doleful, dolorous, condole, condolences, indolent, indolence; cp. **doleō**)

ódium, -ī, n., *hatred* (odium, odious, annoy, ennui, noisome; cp. **ōdī**)

ópus, óperis, n., *a work, task; deed, accomplishment* (opus, opera, operate, operative, inoperative, operand, operose, co-operate, uncooperative, inure, hors d'oeuvre, maneuver, manure)

ōrátiō, ōrātiónis, f., *speech* (oration; cp. **ōrō, ōrātor**)

pēs, pédis, m., *lower leg, foot* (pedal, pedate, pedestal, pedestrian, pedicel, pedigree, piedmont, pawn, peon, pioneer, biped, quadruped, impede, impediment, expedite, expedition, expeditious; cp. **impediō** below)

sátor, satóris, m., *sower, planter; begetter, father; founder* (cp. **serō,** *to plant, sow;* serial, series, assert, desert, exert, insert)

fírmus, -a, -um, *firm, strong; reliable* (firmament, affirm, affirmation, affirmative, confirm, confirmation, farm, farmer)

īnfírmus, -a, -um, *not strong, weak, feeble* (infirm, infirmary, infirmity)

mīrábilis, mīrábile, *amazing, wondrous, remarkable* (mirabilia, admirable, marvel; cp. **mīror,** miracle, mirador, mirage, mirror)

prístinus, -a, -um, *ancient; former, previous* (pristine)

sublímis, sublíme, *elevated, lofty; heroic, noble* (sublimate, sublime, sublimity; not subliminal)

étsī, conj. with ind. or subj. according to rules for **sī,** *even if* (et -sī), *although*

érgā, prep. + acc., *toward*

libénter, adv., *with pleasure, gladly* (cp. the impersonal verb **libet,** *it pleases, is pleasing;* cognate with love)

impédiō, -pedíre, -pedívī, -pedítum, *to impede, hinder, prevent* (impediment, impedimenta, impedance, impeach; see **Lātina Est Gaudium**)

métuō, metúere, métuī, *to fear, dread; be afraid for* + dat. (cp. **metus,** meticulous)

quéror, quérī, quéstus sum, *to complain, lament* (querulous; cp. quarrel, from **querēla, -ae,** *complaint*)

recognóscō, -nóscere, -nóvī, -nitum, *to recognize, recollect* (recognition, recognizance, reconnaisance, reconnoitre; cp. **nōscō, cognōscō**)

suspéndō, -péndere, -péndī, -pénsum, *to hang up, suspend; interrupt* (suspense, suspension; cp. **pendere,** *to hang,* pendant, pendulum, expend)

véndō, véndere, véndidī, vénditum, *to sell* (vend, vendor)

PRACTICE AND REVIEW

1. Rēgī persuāsī ut sorōrī frātrīque tuō grātiōra praemia libenter daret.
2. Deinde, ab eā īnsulā nāve profecta, vīsum amīcōs Athēnās iniit.
3. Eum hortātī sumus ut ad Caesarem sine timōre accēdere cōnārētur.
4. Solitī sunt eī crēdere quī philosophiae servīret, virtūtem sequerētur, et cupīdinēs superāret.
5. Sapiēns nōs ōrat nē virīs sententiārum adversārum noceāmus.
6. In illīs terrīs nōn licet litterīs bonīs vērīsque studēre, ut sub tyrannō saepe fit; dēbēs, igitur, exīre et peregrīnārī.
7. Cūrēmus nē cīvitātem eīs trādāmus quī sē patriae antepōnant.
8. Sunt īnfirmī quī levia opera mīrentur et semper sibi ignōscant.
9. Iste dux, diū absēns, tam stultīs cōnsiliīs cīvitātī ūtēbātur ut mīlia cīvium adversa patī cōgerentur atque multī bonī perīrent.
10. Haec locūtus, fassus est illōs, quī odium immōtum ergā cīvitātem multōs annōs habēbant, Rōmae interfectōs esse.
11. Initium operis nōs saepe impedit.
12. Sator sublīmis hominum atque animālium omnibus nōbīs animās dedit; cum corpora obeant, animae numquam morientur.
13. Cum rūs rediimus, tum domī invēnimus—mīrābile vīsū!—plūrimōs amīcōs.
14. Cicero, who was the greatest Roman orator, was a consul who would obey the senate.
15. I shall persuade him to become better and to return to Rome, I assure you.
16. We begged them not to trust a man whom a tyrant pleased.
17. Wherefore, let that man who hesitates to defend our country depart to another land.

SENTENTIAE ANTĪQUAE

1. Sē omnēs Caesarī ad pedēs prōiēcērunt. (Caesar.—**prō-iaciō.**)
2. Hīc in nostrō numerō sunt quī lēgēs contemnant ac dē exitiō huius urbis cōtīdiē cōgitent. (Cicero.)

3. Quis est cui haec rēs pūblica atque possessiō lībertātis nōn sint cārae et dulcēs? (Id.—**possessiō, -ōnis.**)
4. Quae domus tam stabilis est, quae cīvitās tam fīrma est quae nōn odiīs, invidiā, atque īnsidiīs possit contundī? (Id.—**stabilis, -e.**—**quae . . . contundī;** here the characteristic clause has the force of result.)
5. Quārē, quid est quod tibi iam in hāc urbe placēre possit, in quā nēmō est quī tē nōn metuat? (Id.)
6. Quis enim aut eum dīligere potest quem metuat aut eum ā quō sē metuī putet? (Id.)
7. Tibi sōlī necēs multōrum cīvium impūnītae ac līberae fuērunt. (Id.— **nex, necis,** f., *murder.*—**impūnītus, -a, -um,** *unpunished.*)
8. Habētis autem eum cōnsulem quī exigere officium et pārēre vestrīs dēcrētīs nōn dubitet atque vōs dēfendere possit. (Id.—**dēcrētum, -ī,** *decree.*)
9. Ille mihi semper deus erit. (Virgil.)
10. Nūllus dolor est quem nōn longinquitās temporis minuat ac molliat. (*Cicero.—**longinquitās, -tātis,** *length.*)
11. Parāvisse dīvitiās fuit multīs hominibus nōn fīnis sed mūtātiō ma- lōrum. (Epicurus quoted by Seneca.—**mūtātiō, -ōnis,** *change.*)
12. Nihil est opere et manū factum quod tempus nōn cōnsūmat. (Cicero.)
13. Vīribus corporis dēficientibus, vigor tamen animī dūrāvit illī ad vītae fīnem. (Pliny.—**dēficiō, -ere,** *to fail.*—**vigor, -gōris.**—**dūrāre,** *to last.*)
14. Nunc est bibendum; nunc pede līberō pulsanda tellus. (*Horace; from his ode celebrating the death of the Egyptian queen Cleopa- tra.—sc. **nōbīs** as dat. of agent with both pass. periphrastics.—**pul- sāre,** *to strike, beat;* with **pulsanda,** sc. **est,** *should be struck,* i.e., *danced upon.*—**tellūs, -lūris,** f., = **terra.**)

NOTE ON A BOOK BY LUCAN

Sunt quīdam quī mē dīcant nōn esse poētam;
    sed quī mē vēndit bibliopōla putat.

(*Martial 14.194; meter: elegiac couplet. In this note from a gift copy of Lucan's poetry, the author is himself imagined as speaking.—**bibliopōla, -ae,** m., *book- dealer,* antecedent of **quī.**)

TWO EXAMPLES OF ROMAN WIT

Oh, Give Me a Figgy Sprig!

Cum quīdam, querēns, dīxisset uxōrem suam dē fīcū suspendisse sē, amī- cus illīus "Amābō tē," inquit, "dā mihi ex istā arbore surculōs quōs seram!"

(Cicero, *Dē Ōrātōre* 2.278.—**fīcus, -ūs,** f., *fig tree;* nouns for trees are usually feminine.—**surculus, -ī,** *shoot, sprig.*—**quōs** = **ut eōs,** rel. clause of purpose.— **serō, -ere,** *to plant, sow.*)

The Most Pitiful Speech I've Ever Heard!

Cum quīdam ōrātor sē misericordiam ōrātiōne fortasse mōvisse putāret, rogāvit Catulum vidērēturne misericordiam mōvisse. "Ac magnam quidem, mihi," inquit, "putō enim nēminem esse tam dūrum cui ōrātiō tua nōn vīsa sit digna misericordiā!"

(Cicero, *Dē Ōrātōre* 2.278.—**misericordia, -ae,** *pity;* an important objective for the ancient orator, and one for which he was trained, was to arouse the audience's emotions.—**Catulus, -ī.**—**vidērēturne:** the **-ne,** *whether,* signals an ind. quest.—**magnam,** sc. **misericordiam mōvistī!**—**cui** = **ut eī,** rel. clause of result.)

TWO LETTERS TO CICERO

Gn. Magnus Prōcōnsul Salūtem Dīcit Cicerōnī Imperātōrī

Sī valēs, bene est. Tuās litterās libenter lēgī; recognōvī enim tuam prīstinam virtūtem etiam in salūte commūnī. Cōnsulēs ad eum exercitum vēnērunt quem in Āpūliā habuī. Magnopere tē hortor ut occāsiōnem carpās et tē ad nōs cōnferās, ut commūnī cōnsiliō reī publicae miserae opem atque auxilium ferāmus. Moneō ut Rōmā exeās, viā Appiā iter faciās, et quam celerrimē Brundisium veniās.

Caesar Imperātor Salūtem Dīcit Cicerōnī Imperātōrī

Cum Brundisium celerius adeam atque sim in itinere, exercitū iam praemissō, dēbeō tamen ad tē scrībere et grātiās idōneās tibi agere, etsī hoc fēcī saepe et saepius factūrus videor; ita dignus es. Imprīmīs, quoniam crēdō mē celeriter ad urbem ventūrum esse, ā tē petō ut tē ibi videam ut tuō cōnsiliō, dignitāte, ope ūtī possim. Festīnātiōnī meae brevitātīque litterārum ignōscēs; cētera ex Furniō cognōscēs.

(Cicero, *Epistulae ad Atticum* 8.11 and 9.6; in these letters, two of hundreds that survive from Cicero's correspondence, both Gnaeus Pompeius Magnus, "Pompey the Great," and Julius Caesar bid for the statesman's support in the civil war that followed Caesar's crossing of the Rubicon in 49 B.C.—**prōcōnsul, -sulis,** *proconsul, governor* (of a province).—**salūte commūnī,** here *the public welfare.*—Apulia was a district in south Italy.—**viā Appiā,** abl. of route, a common construction; the Via Appia, built in the 4th century B.C., was the highway leading south from Rome and, ultimately, to Brundisium, the port of departure for Greece.—**prae-mittō, -ere.**—**imprīmīs,** adv., *especially.*—**festīnātiō, -ōnis,** *haste, rush.*—**brevitās, -tātis.**—**Furnius,** the name of an associate.)

ASK ME IF I CARE

Nīl nimium studeō, Caesar, tibi velle placēre,
    nec scīre utrum sīs albus an āter homō!

(*Catullus 93; meter: elegiac couplet.—**nīl** = **nōn.**—**albus, -a, -um,** *white.*—**āter, ātra, ātrum,** *black.*)

ETYMOLOGY

The use of **opus** in the titles of musical works is well known; e.g., Beethoven's "Symphony No. 5 in C Minor, Opus 67." "Opera," on the other hand, comes to us through Italian from **opera, -ae,** *effort, pains, work,* which clearly has the same root as **opus.** Finally, we have the term **magnum opus,** which is most commonly used in the literary field.

A few Romance derivatives follow:

Latin	Italian	Spanish	French
dolor	dolore	dolor	douleur
odium	odio	odio	odieux (odiōsus)
pēs, pedis	piede	pie	pied

In the readings
1. project, projection. 4. stable (adj.), stability, stabilize. 7. internecine; cp. **necāre.**—impunity, punitive. 13. deficient, deficiency, defect, defective, defection. 14. pulse, pulsate, pulsar. "Note": bibliopole, bibliopolist; cp. bibliography, bibliophile (all Gk. in origin). "Hang Her": ficus.—surculose. "Pity": misericord; cp. **miser.** "Two Letters": festinate, festination.—brevity; cp. **brevis.** "Ask Me": alb, alba, Alba Longa, Alban, albedo, albescent, albinism, albino, albugeneous, album, albumen, albumin.—atrabilious.

LATĪNA EST GAUDIUM—ET ŪTILIS!

Salvēte! Have you noticed that we like to **ad lib.** in this section of each chapter? **Ad libitum,** *at one's pleasure,* is connected with **libenter,** which is how Latin should be both taught and learned: *gladly!* So, **libenter carpite diem et hās rēs novās:** first, note that **impediō** is from **in + pēs;** when you're "impeded," you've got something *on your feet* (like "fetters," from the same base as "foot"), so perhaps you should consult a podiatrist (**pod-** is the Gk. cognate of Lat. **ped-**) and ask him to "expedite" your treatment (**expedīre** is essentially "to de-fetter," the opposite of **impedīre;** cp. "implicate" and "explicate" from **implicāre/explicāre**); otherwise, just give up your pedestrian ways and start pedaling. **Odium** means *rivalry* as well as *hatred;* guess who the rivals are in **odium medicum, odium scholasticum,** and **odium theologicum?** And speaking of odious types, the emperor Tiberius (A.D. 14–37) is said to have remarked of his subjects, **ōderint dum metuant,** *let them hate (me), so long as they fear me!* The abbreviation **op. cit.** is from **opere citātō,** *in the work cited;* and **opera omnia** are an author's *complete works.* An old legal prescript provides that **vendēns eandem rem duōbus est falsārius** (*fraudulent*); such a swindle would be **īnfrā dignitātem,** *beneath one's dignity,* so remember the familiar admonition **caveat ēmptor,** *let the buyer beware!* **Iterum tempus fūgit: valeātis, amīcī et amīcae!**

39

Gerund and Gerundive

THE GERUNDIVE

You are already familiar with the gerundive, or future passive participle, a verbal adjective formed with the endings **-ndus, -nda, -ndum** (Ch. 23). Besides functioning occasionally as a simple adjective (**liber legendus,** *a book to be read*), the gerundive is commonly employed in the passive periphrastic conjugation (Ch. 24: **hic liber legendus est,** *this book should be read*); some further uses are examined in this chapter.

THE GERUND

The "gerund" is a verbal *noun* formed like the gerundive, except that it has only four forms, the neuter singular of the genitive, dative, accusative, and ablative. These forms are identical to the corresponding cases of the gerundive, but are *active* in meaning and correspond to the English gerund in "-ing" (**legendī,** *of reading,* as in **magnum amōrem legendī habet,** *he has a great love of reading*).

DECLENSION OF THE GERUND

Following are the complete gerund declensions for some representative Latin verbs:

Gen.   laudándī   dūcéndī   sequéndī   audiéndī
                  (of praising, leading, following, hearing)

Dat.	laudándō	dūcéndō	sequéndō	audiéndō
	(*to*/*for praising,* etc.)			
Acc.	laudándum	dūcéndum	sequéndum	audiéndum
	(*praising,* etc.)			
Abl.	laudándō	dūcéndō	sequéndō	audiéndō
	(*by praising,* etc.)			

Since the gerund is a verbal noun, it can be modified as a verb and used as a noun in the various cases. Having no nominative case, however, the gerund was not used as a subject, a function performed instead by the infinitive, another of Latin's verbal nouns (i.e., Latin could say **errāre est humānum,** *to err is human,* but not *erring is human*); likewise the accusative was ordinarily employed as an object of **ad** and certain other prepositions, not as a direct object (a function again performed by the infinitive, e.g., **iussit eōs venīre,** *he ordered them to come:* see Appendix, p. 445). The following sentences illustrate typical uses of the gerund in its four cases:

studium **vīvendī** cum amīcīs, *fondness of (for) living with friends.*
Operam dat **vīvendō** bene, *he gives attention to living well.*
Athēnās iit ad **vīvendum** bene, *he went to Athens to live well.*
Fēlīciōrēs fīmus **vīvendō** bene, *we become happier by living well.*

DIFFERENCES BETWEEN GERUND AND GERUNDIVE

Remember these distinctions between gerund and gerundive: 1) the gerund*ive* is a verbal adjec*tive* (**liber legendus,** *a book to be read*), the gerund a verbal noun (**amor legendī,** *love of reading*); 2) as an adjective, the gerundive has a full set of masculine, feminine, and neuter endings, both singular and plural, for all cases, whereas the gerund has only neuter singular forms and only in the genitive, dative, accusative, and ablative, i.e., a total of only four forms altogether; 3) the gerundive is passive in meaning, the gerund active.

GERUND AND GERUNDIVE PHRASES

As a verbal noun, the gerund may take the case construction required by its verb:

studium legendī librōs, *fondness of reading books.*
Discimus legendō librōs, *we learn by reading books.*

In actual practice, however, when the gerund would be followed by a noun in the accusative as a direct object, the Romans preferred to put this noun in the case in which the gerund would otherwise appear and to use the gerundive in agreement with the noun. The translation is the same no matter which construction is used, since English idiom requires the gerund construction rather than the unidiomatic gerundive. In the examples which follow, those marked A are what we should expect on the basis of English idiom; those marked B are the regular gerundive phrases which the Romans actually preferred:

A. studium legendī librōs (acceptable)
B. studium librōrum legendōrum (preferred)
 fondness of reading books (not *fondness of books to be read,* which is unidiomatic)

A. Operam dat legendō librōs.
B. Operam dat librīs legendīs.
 He gives attention to reading books.

A. Discimus legendō librōs.
B. Discimus librīs legendīs.
 We learn by reading books.

A. Hoc locūtus est dē legendō librōs.
B. Hoc locūtus est dē librīs legendīs.
 He said this about reading books.

Quite common was the use of **ad** + an accusative gerundive (or gerund) phrase and postpositive **causā** + a genitive phrase to indicate *purpose:*

A. Vēnit ad legendum librōs.
B. Vēnit ad librōs legendōs.
 He came to read books.

A. Ōtium petit legendī librōs causā.
B. Ōtium petit librōrum legendōrum causā.
 He seeks leisure for the sake of reading books.

Remember that purpose can be expressed in Latin, not only with gerundive/gerund phrases, but also with **ut/nē** + the subjunctive and, after a main verb of motion, the accusative supine: **venit ut hōs librōs legat** and **venit hōs librōs lēctum** both mean *he is coming to read these books.*

VOCABULARY

 aedifícium, -iī, n., *building, structure* (edification, edifice, edify, aedile)
 iniū́ria, -ae, f., *injustice, injury, wrong* (injurious; cp. **iū́dex, iū́dicium, iūs, iū́stus,** Ch. 40)
 mú̄lier, mulíeris, f., *woman* (muliebrity)
 tránsitus, -ūs, m., *passing over, transit; transition* (cp. **tránseō** below)
 véntus, -ī, m., *wind* (vent, ventilate, ventilation, ventilator)
 cúpidus, -a, -um, *desirous, eager, fond;* + gen., *desirous of, eager for* (cp. **cupiō, cupiditās, cupī́dō**)

līberális, līberále, *of, relating to a free person; worthy of a free man, decent, liberal; generous* (liberal arts, liberality; cp. **līber, līberō**)

necésse, indecl. adj. used as nom. or acc., *necessary, inevitable* (necessitate, necessitous, unnecessary; cp. **cēdō**)

vétus, gen. **véteris,** *old* (veteran, inveterate, veterinary, veterinarian)

quási, adv. or conj., *as if, as it were* (quasi; = **quam** + **sī**)

ámbulō (1), *to walk* (amble, ambulance, ambulate, ambulatory, perambulate, preamble, somnambulist)

expérior, -perírī, -pértus sum, *to try, test; experience* (experiment, expert, inexpert, inexperience; cp. **perīculum**)

lībō (1), *to pour a libation of, on; pour ritually; sip; touch gently* (libation)

opórtet, oportére, opórtuit, impers., *it is proper, right, necessary*

oppúgnō (1), *to fight against, attack, assault, assail* (oppugn; cp. **pugnō**)

órnō (1), *to equip, furnish, adorn* (adornment, ornate, ornament, ornamental, ornamentation, suborn, subornation)

pernóctō (1), *to spend* or *occupy the night* (nocturnal, nocturne; cp. **nox**)

tránseō, -íre, -íī, -itum, *to go across, cross; pass over, ignore* (transit, transition, transitive, intransitive, transitory, trance)

PRACTICE AND REVIEW

1. Caesar eōs cōtīdiē ōrābat nē fāta adversa metuerent.
2. Etsī hoc fīat, illī mīlitēs urbem oppugnātum fortasse accēdant et multī cīvēs obeant.
3. Sī licēbit, septem diēbus domum ībimus ad nostrōs amīcōs videndōs.
4. Amīcus līberālissimus noster, quōcum pernoctābāmus, dīs vīnum ante cēnam lībāvit, et deinde mēnsam ōrnāvit.
5. Cōnsul, vir maximae dignitātis, ōtium cōnsūmpsit in operibus sublīmibus scrībendīs.
6. Sunt autem quī dolōrum vītandōrum causā, ut āiunt, semper levia opera faciant, labōrem contemnant, et dē officiīs querantur.
7. In rē pūblicā gerendā istī nōn dubitant praemia grāta sibi requīrere, officia suspendere, atque honōrem suum vēndere.
8. Lēctrīx doctissima mox surget ad tria carmina recitanda, quae omnēs audītōrēs oblectābunt atque animōs serēnābunt.
9. Nēmō est cui iniūria placeat, ut nōs omnēs recognōscimus.
10. Nisi vincula patī ac sub pedibus tyrannōrum humī contundī volumus, lībertātī semper studeāmus et eam numquam impediāmus.
11. Pauca opera mihi sedendō fīunt, multa agendō et experiendō.
12. Illa mulier mīrābilis frūctūs amōris libenter carpsit et virō grātissimō nūpsit.

13. They are going to Rome to talk about conquering the Greeks.
14. By remaining at Rome he persuaded them to become braver.
15. Who is there who has hope of doing great works without pain?
16. We urged the consul to serve the state and preserve our dignity by attacking these injustices.

SENTENTIAE ANTĪQUAE

1. Coniūrātiōnem nāscentem nōn crēdendō corrōborāvērunt. (*Cicero.—**coniūrātiō, -ōnis,** *conspiracy.*—**corrōborāre,** *to strengthen.*)
2. Malī dēsinant īnsidiās reī pūblicae cōnsulīque parāre et ignēs ad īnflammandam urbem. (Cicero.—**dēsinō, -ere,** *to cease.*—**īnflammāre,** *to set on fire.*)
3. Multī autem propter glōriae cupiditātem sunt cupidī bellōrum gerendōrum. (Cicero.)
4. Veterem iniūriam ferendō invītāmus novam. (Publilius Syrus.)
5. Cūrēmus nē poena maior sit quam culpa; prohibenda autem maximē est īra in pūniendō. (Cicero.—**pūnīre,** *to punish.*)
6. Syrācūsīs captīs, Mārcellus aedificiīs omnibus sīc pepercit—mīrābile dictū—quasi ad ea dēfendenda, nōn oppugnanda vēnisset. (Cicero.)
7. Rēgulus laudandus est in cōnservandō iūre iūrandō. (*Cicero.— Regulus, prisoner of the Carthaginians, swore to them that he would return to Carthage after a mission to Rome.—**iūs iūrandum, iūris iūrandī,** n., *oath.*)
8. In ōrātiōne meā dīcam dē mōribus firmīs Sēstiī et dē studiō cōnservandae salūtis commūnis. (Cicero.—**Sēstius, -iī.**)
9. Trānsitus ad senectūtem nōs āvocat ā rēbus gerendīs et corpus facit īnfirmius. (Cicero.)
10. Cum recreandae vōcis īnfirmae causā necesse esset mihi ambulāre, hās litterās dictāvī forīs ambulāns. (Cicero.—**dictāre,** *to dictate.*)
11. Semper metuendō sapiēns vītat malum. (Publilius Syrus.)
12. Haec virtūs ex prōvidendō est appellāta prūdentia. (Cicero.—**prōvidēre.**—**prūdentia = prō-videntia.**)
13. Fāma vīrēs acquīrit eundō. (Virgil.—**acquīrō,** from **ad-quaerō,** *to acquire.*)
14. Hae vicissitūdinēs fortūnae, etsī nōbīs iūcundae in experiendō nōn fuērunt, in legendō tamen erunt iūcundae. Recordātiō enim praeteritī dolōris dēlectātiōnem nōbīs habet. (Cicero.—**vicissitūdō, -dinis.**—**recordātiō, -ōnis,** *recollection.*—**praeteritus, -a, -um,** *past.*)

PROMISES, PROMISES!

Nūllī sē dīcit mulier mea nūbere mālle
  quam mihi, nōn sī sē Iuppiter ipse petat.
Dīcit: sed mulier cupidō quod dīcit amantī,
  in ventō et rapidā scrībere oportet aquā.

(*Catullus 70; meter: elegiac couplet.—**Nūllī** and **mihi** are both dat. with **nūbere**, and **quam** = **magis quam;** the prose order would be **mulier mea dīcit sē nūllī quam mihi nūbere mālle.**—**amantī,** *lover.*—Note the separation of adj. from noun in **cupidō . . . amantī** and **rapidā . . . aquā,** a common feature of Latin verse used here to emphasize the nouns that are delayed; the prose order: **sed quod mulier amantī cupidō dīcit.**—**rapidus, -a, -um.**)

PAETE, NŌN DOLET

Casta suō gladium cum trāderet Arria Paetō,
  quem dē vīsceribus strīnxerat ipsa suīs,
"Sī qua fidēs, vulnus quod fēcī nōn dolet," inquit,
  "sed quod tū faciēs, hoc mihi, Paete, dolet."

(*Martial 1.13; meter: elegiac couplet.—Caecina Paetus was compelled to commit suicide in 42 A.D., because of the role he had played in a conspiracy against the emperor Claudius; his courageous and devoted wife Arria, choosing to die with him, stabbed herself before passing the sword to her husband and assuring him that the pain of the wound itself would be slight. See below, L.I. 39.—The prose order of the first verse would be: **Cum Arria casta Paetō suō gladium trāderet.**—**castus, -a, -um,** *loyal, chaste.*—**gladius, -ī,** *sword.*—**vīscera, -cerum,** n. pl., *vital organs, abdomen.*—**stringō, -ere, strīnxī, strictum,** *to draw tight, tie; pull, draw out.*—**sī qua [=quae,** indef.**] fidēs,** i.e., *if you have any faith in me, if you will trust me.*)

HANNIBAL AND THE BEGINNINGS OF THE SECOND PUNIC WAR

Hannibal, fīlius Hamilcaris, Carthāgine nātus est. In adulēscentiā prīstinum odium patris ergā Rōmānōs sīc firmē cōnservāvit ut numquam id dēpōneret. Cum patre exiit Carthāgine et in Hispāniam longō itinere profectus est; et post multōs annōs, Hamilcare interfectō, exercitus eī imperium trādidit. Sīc Hannibal, quīnque et vīgintī annōs nātus, imperātor factus est. Tribus annīs nōn requiēvit, sed omnēs gentēs Hispāniae superāvit et trēs exercitūs maximōs parāvit. Ex hīs ūnum in Āfricam mīsit, alterum cum frātre in Hispāniā relīquit, tertium in Italiam sēcum dūxit.

Ad Alpēs adiit, quās nēmō umquam ante eum cum exercitū trānsierat. Populōs cōnantēs prohibēre eum trānsitū necāvit; loca patefēcit; et cum multīs elephantīs mīlitibusque in Italiam iniit. In hōc itinere tam gravī morbō oculōrum adfectus est ut posteā numquam dextrō oculō bene ūtī posset. Multōs ducēs, tamen, exercitūsque Rōmānōs vīcit, et propter illum imperātōrem mīlia mīlitum Rōmānōrum periērunt.

(Nepos, *Hannibal,* excerpts; see L.A. 8.—Hannibal, general who led the Carthaginians against the Romans in the Second Punic War, 218–02 B.C.—**Hamilcar, -caris.**—**dē** + **pōnō.**—**Hispānia, -ae,** *Spain.*—**Āfrica, -ae.**—**Alpēs, Alpium,** f. pl., *the Alps.*—**adficiō, -ere, -fēcī, -fectum,** *to affect, afflict, weaken.*)

The Oath of Hannibal, Johann Heinrich Schoenfeld, 17th century
Germanisches Nationalmuseum, Nuremberg, German

ETYMOLOGY

The terms "gerund" and "gerundive" derive ultimately from the stem **gerund-** (= **gerend-**) of **gerō.** The gerund indicates "doing" (action); the gerundive indicates what is "to be done."

In late Latin the ablative of the gerund was used with increasing frequency as the equivalent of a present participle. From this usage derive the Italian and the Spanish present participles, which end in **-ndo** and are invariable.

Latin Gerund	It. Participle	Sp. Participle
dandō	dando	dando
faciendō	facendo	haciendo
dīcendō	dicendo	diciendo
pōnendō	ponendo	poniendo
scrībendō	scrivendo	escribiendo

In the readings   1. conjuration; cp. **coniūrātī.**—corroborate, corroborate; cp. **rōbur, rō-boris,** n., *hard wood, oak.* 2. inflammation, inflammatory. 5. punitive, impunity; cp. **poena.** 10. dictator. 14. In **re-cord-ātiō** you see the stem of **cor, cordis,** *heart.* This shows that formerly the heart was regarded not only as the seat of the emotions but also as the mind and the seat of the memory, a belief reflected in our own phrase "learn by heart." Cp. record, accord, concord, discord, cordial, cordate, courage. Eng. "heart" is cognate with Lat. **cord-.** "Promises": rapid, rapids, rapidity; cp. **rapiō.** "Paete": chaste, chasten, chastity, chastise.—gladiator, gladiatorial, gladiola, gladiolus.—viscera, visceral, eviscerate.—stringency, stringendo, stringent, astringent, strict, constrict, restrict. "Hannibal": deponent, depose, deposit, deposition.—affect, affection.

LATĪNA EST GAUDIUM—ET ŪTILIS!

Salvēte, discipulī discipulaeque; haec sunt discenda: Cato's definition of an orator, as quoted by the 1st cen. A.D. educator Quintilian (*Īnstitūtiōnēs Ōrātōriae* 12.1.1), is quite well known, and you can easily translate it now that you've studied gerunds (and with the explanation that **perītus, -a, -um** + gen. = *experienced in*): **ōrātor est vir bonus dīcendī perītus.** Here are some more familiar items with gerunds and gerundives: New Mexico's state motto, **crēscit eundō** (review Ch. 37, if you have trouble with that one!); **docendō discimus; spectēmur agendō,** *let us be judged by what we do* (lit., *by our doing*); **modus vīvendī** and **modus operandī** ("m.o." to you detective show buffs!); **onus probandī,** *the burden of proof* (lit., *of proving*); then, of course, there are these many "things to be done": **agenda, addenda, corrigenda, referendum.**

Et duo cētera ex vocābulāriō novō: iniūria nōn excūsat iniūriam, (*one*) *injury does not excuse* (*another*) *injury,* is an old legal tenet, and **expertō crēdite** is still good advice. **Habēte fēlīcem modum vīvendī, studentēs, et valēte!**

40

-Ne, Num, and Nōnne in Direct Questions; Fear Clauses; Genitive and Ablative of Description

-Ne, Num, AND Nōnne IN DIRECT QUESTIONS

As we have already seen, a Roman could ask a direct question in a variety of ways, by beginning a sentence with an interrogative pronoun (**quis, quid**) or such other interrogatives as **ubi** or **cūr,** or by suffixing **-ne** to the first word of the sentence (often the verb, or some other word on which the question hinged). But "leading questions" can also be asked in Latin: if the speaker expected "yes" as an answer, the question was introduced with **nōnne** (a construction already encountered, though not formally discussed); if a negative reply was anticipated, **num** was the introductory word.

Quis venit? *Who is coming?*
Cūr venit? *Why is he coming?*
Venitne? *Is he coming?*
Nōnne venit? *He is coming, isn't he?* or *Isn't he coming?*
Num venit? *He isn't coming, is he?*
Scrīpsistīne illās litterās? *Did you write that letter?*

Nōnne illās litterās scrīpsistī? *You wrote that letter, didn't you?* or *Didn't you write that letter?*

Num illās litterās scrīpsistī? *You didn't write that letter, did you?*

FEAR CLAUSES

Verbs denoting fear or apprehension often take subjunctive noun clauses introduced by **nē** (*that*) or **ut** (*that . . . not;* occasionally **nē nōn** was employed instead of **ut**); the conjunctions are just the opposite of what might be expected, because in origin the clauses they introduced were essentially independent jussive clauses (i.e., **timeō nē abeās,** *I fear that you may go away,* = **Timeō. Nē abeās!,** *I'm afraid—Don't go away!*). Auxiliaries commonly employed in translating include *will* or *may* (in primary sequence) and *would* or *might* (in secondary sequence), as indicated in the following examples:

Timeō nē id crēdant, *I fear that they will (may) believe this.*

Vereor ut id crēdant, *I am afraid that they will (may) not believe this.*

Timuērunt nē amīcōs amitterent, *they feared that they might (would) lose their friends.*

Metuistī ut mulierēs ex casā exīssent, *you were afraid that the women had not left the house.*

GENITIVE AND ABLATIVE OF DESCRIPTION

A noun in either the ablative or genitive case plus a modifying adjective may be employed to modify another noun; both the ablative of description and the genitive of description (already encountered in the readings) might describe a noun by indicating its character, quality, or size, although the ablative usage was especially common in describing physical traits. Like adjectives, these descriptive phrases usually follow the nouns they modify.

fēmina **magnae sapientiae,** *a woman of great intellect*

pāx in hominibus **bonae voluntātis,** *peace among men of good will*

cōnsilium **eius modī,** *a plan of this kind*

Dīligō hominem **antīquā virtūte,** *I esteem a man of old-fashioned morality.*

mīles **fīrmā manū,** *the soldier with the strong hand*

Es **mōribus bonīs,** *you are a person of good character.*

VOCABULARY

aes, aéris, n., *bronze* (era; cp. **aerārium, -ī,** *treasury;* **aereus, -a, -um,** *made of bronze*)

dóminus, -ī, m., *master (of a household), lord,* and **dómina, -ae,** f., *mistress, lady* (dominate, dominant, domineer, dominion, domain, domino, domine, don, dungeon, belladonna, madonna, dame, damsel, danger; cp. **domus**)

lácrima, -ae, f., *tear* (lacrimal, lacrimation)

mḗta, -ae, f., *turning point, goal; limit, boundary*

monuméntum, -ī, n., *monument* (monumental, monumentalize; cp. **moneō**)

nā́sus, -ī, m., *nose* (nasal, nasalize, nasogastric; cp. nostril, nozzle)

sáxum, -ī, n., *rock, stone* (saxatile, saxifrage, saxicolous; cp. **secō,** *to cut, saw,* saxon)

vúltus, -ūs, m., *countenance, face*

iū́stus, -a, -um, *just, right* (justice, injustice, unjust, justify, justification, adjust, adjustment, readjust; cp. **iūs, iūdex, iniūria**)

tot, indecl. adj., *so many* (cp. **quot; totidem,** indecl. adj., *the same number;* **totiēns,** adv., *that number of times, so often*)

praéter, prep. + acc., *besides, except; beyond, past* (preterit, preterition, pretermit, preternatural; cp. **prae**)

nṓnne, interrog. adv. which introduces questions expecting the answer "yes."

num, interrog. adv.: (1) introduces direct questions which expect the answer "no"; (2) introduces indirect questions and means *whether.*

omnī́nō, adv., *wholly, entirely, altogether* (cp. **omnis**)

postrḗmum, adv., *after all, finally; for the last time* (cp. **post**)

quīn, adv., *indeed, in fact*

éxplicō (1), *unfold; explain; spread out, deploy* (explicate, inexplicable; implicate, implication, from **implicō,** *to enfold, interweave*)

fatī́gō (1), *to weary, tire out* (fatigue, indefatigable)

for, fā́rī, fā́tus sum, *to speak* (*prophetically*), *talk, foretell* (affable, ineffable, infant, infantry, preface; cp. **fābula, fāma, fātum**)

opī́nor, opīnā́rī, opīnā́tus sum, *to suppose* (opine, opinion)

repériō, reperī́re, répperī, repértum, *to find, discover, learn; get* (repertoire, repertory; cp. **parēns** and **pariō,** *to give birth to*)

véreor, verḗrī, véritus sum, *to show reverence for, respect; be afraid of, fear* (revere, reverend, reverent, reverential, irreverent)

PRACTICE AND REVIEW

1. Nōnne Rōmulus, sator huius urbis, fuit vir mīrābilis virtūtis et fideī pristinae?

2. At postrēmum vereor, heu, ut ā virīs parvae sapientiae hoc studium vetus intellegī possit.

3. Nōn oportet nōs trānsīre haec līberālia hūmānaque studia, nam praemia eōrum certē sunt maxima.

4. Dignitās illīus ōrātiōnis fuit omnīnō idōnea occāsiōnī.

5. Equī eius, cum fatīgātī essent et ventus esset eīs adversus, ad mētam tamen quam celerrimē currēbant.

6. Vir corpore īnfīrmō id nōn facere poterat.

7. Etsī trēs fīliī sunt cupidī magnōrum operum faciendōrum, eīs nōn licet domō abīre.

8. Domina fīrma acerbē querēbātur plūrimōs servōs fuisse absentēs— vae illīs miserīs!

9. Mīrābile rogātū, num istam mulierem amās, mī amīce?

10. Nōnne timent nē et Rōmae et rūrī magnī tumultūs sint?

11. Num ōpīnāris tot hominēs iūstōs omnīnō errāre?

12. Recognōvistīne, ut illa aedificia vīsum ambulābās, mulierem sub arbore humī requiēscentem?

13. I am afraid, in my heart, that few things can be accomplished now even by trying.

14. You do not hesitate to say this, do you?

15. They supposed that, after all, he was a man of very little faith.

16. You do recognize how great the danger is, do you not?

SENTENTIAE ANTĪQUAE

1. Quattuor causās reperiō cūr senectūs misera videātur. Videāmus quam iūsta quaeque eārum sit. (Cicero.)

2. Verērī videntur ut habeam satis praesidī. (*Cicero.—**praesidium, -iī,** *guard*).

3. Necesse est enim sit alterum dē duōbus: aut mors sēnsūs omnīnō aufert aut animus in alium locum morte abit. Sī mors somnō similis est sēnsūsque exstinguuntur, dī bonī, quid lucrī est morī! (Cicero.— **necesse est** may be followed by the subjunctive.—**aufert = ab-fert.— exstinguō, -ere.—lucrum, -ī,** *gain, profit.*)

4. Aetās semper trānsitum et aliquid novī adfert. (Terence.)

5. Nōnne ūnum exemplum luxuriae aut cupiditātis multum malī facit? (Seneca.—**luxuria, -ae.**)

6. Mīror tot mīlia virōrum tam puerīliter identidem cupere currentēs equōs vidēre. (Pliny.—**puerīliter,** adv., based on **puer,** *childishly.—* **identidem,** adv., *again and again.*—**currentēs,** i.e., in the races.)

7. Nōnne vidēs etiam guttās, in saxa cadendō, pertundere illa saxa? (Lucretius.—**gutta, -ae,** *drop [of water].*—**pertundō, -ere,** *to bore a hole through, erode.*)

8. Metuō nē id cōnsilī cēperīmus quod nōn facile explicāre possīmus. (*Cicero.—**cōnsilī**, gen. of the whole with **id.**)

9. Antōnius, ūnus ex inimīcīs et vir minimae clēmentiae, iussit Cicerōnem interficī et caput eius inter duās manūs in Rōstrīs pōnī. (Livy.—**inimīcus, -ī**, from **in** + **amīcus**, *personal enemy.*—**Rōstra, -ōrum**, *the Rostra*, the speaker's stand in the Roman Forum.)

10. Omnēs quī habent aliquid nōn sōlum sapientiae sed etiam sānitātis volunt hanc rem pūblicam salvam esse. (*Cicero.—**sānitās, -tātis.**)

11. Salvē, nec minimō puella nāsō nec bellō pede nec nigrīs ocellīs nec longīs digitīs nec ōre siccō! (*Catullus.—**niger, nigra, nigrum**, *black, dark.*—**ocellus**, diminutive of **oculus.**—**siccus, -a, -um**, *dry.*)

12. Homō sum; nihil hūmānī aliēnum ā mē putō. (Terence.—**aliēnus, -a, -um** + **ab** = *foreign to.*)

13. Amīcus animum amīcī ita cum suō miscet quasi facit ūnum ex duōbus. (Cicero.)

14. Sex diēbus fēcit Dominus caelum et terram et mare et omnia quae in eīs sunt, et requiēvit diē septimō. (Exodus.)

15. Mīsit legātum Valerium Procillum, summā virtūte et hūmānitāte adulēscentem. (Caesar.—**legātus, -ī**, *ambassador.*—Valerius Procillus.—**hūmānitās, -tātis.**)

16. Num negāre audēs? Quid tacēs? Convincam, sī negās; videō enim esse hīc in senātū quōsdam quī tēcum ūnā fuērunt. Ō dī immortālēs! (*Cicero.—**quid**, here = *why?*—**con** + **vincō**, *to prove wrong, convict;* sc. **tē.**—**ūnā**, adv., *together, in concert.*)

17. Nunc timeō nē nihil tibi praeter lacrimās queam reddere. (*Cicero—**queam** = **possim.**—**reddō, -dere**, *to give back, return.*)

JUPITER PROPHESIES TO VENUS THE FUTURE GLORY OF ROME

Ollī subrīdēns hominum sator atque deōrum
255 vultū, quō caelum tempestātēsque serēnat,
ōscula lībāvit nātae, dehinc tālia fātur:
"Parce metū, Cytherēa; manent immōta tuōrum
fāta tibī. Cernēs urbem et prōmissa Lavīnī
moenia sublīmemque ferēs ad sīdera caelī
260 magnanimum Aenēan; neque mē sententia vertit.
     . . .
263 Bellum ingēns geret Italiā populōsque ferōcīs
contundet mōrēsque virīs et moenia pōnet.
     . . .
Rōmulus excipiet gentem et Māvortia condet
moenia Rōmānōsque suō dē nōmine dīcet.
Hīs ego nec mētās rērum nec tempora pōnō:
imperium sine fīne dedī. Quīn aspera Iūnō,
280 quae mare nunc terrāsque metū caelumque fatīgat,

cōnsilia in melius referet, mēcumque fovēbit
Rōmānōs, rērum dominōs gentemque togātam."

(*Virgil, *Aeneid* 1.254ff; meter: dactylic hexameter.—**Ollī** = **illī,** here Venus, who has come to her father Jupiter to ask whether his intentions have changed toward her son, the Trojan prince Aeneas, or if he is still destined to found a new Trojan nation in Italy.—**vultū,** abl. of means with **subrīdēns.**—**ōscula lībāvit,** i.e., he kissed her in ritual fashion.—**nātae,** ind. obj.—**dēhinc,** scanned here as a monosyllable.—**metū,** an alternate form of the dat. **metuī.**—**Cytherēa, -ae,** *the Cytherean,* i.e., Venus, so-called for the Aegean island of Cythera, which was sacred to her.—**immōta,** pred. adj., after **manent.**—**tuōrum,** i.e., Aeneas and his Trojan followers.—**Lavīnium, -iī,** *Lavinium,* the town Aeneas was destined to found in Latium, near the future city of Rome.—**sublīmem,** in the predicate with **Aenēan** (a Gk. acc. form), *you will carry Aeneas on high.*—**neque . . . vertit,** i.e., *I have not changed my mind;* but what is the literal translation?—**geret . . . pōnet:** Aeneas is subject of all three verbs.—**Ītaliā,** sc. **in;** prepositions usual in prose were commonly omitted in verse.—**ferōcīs** = **ferōcēs,** acc. pl.—Through a device known as zeugma, **pōnet** has different senses with its two objects, *institute* with **mōrēs** and *build* with **moenia.**—**Māvortius, -a, -um,** *of Mars,* so-called because of the legend that Mars was father of Romulus, Rome's first king.—**rērum,** *of their affairs,* i.e., *for their empire.*—**tempora,** *time limits.*—**cōnsilia . . . referet,** i.e., *will change her attitude for the better;* Juno had sided with the Greeks in the Trojan war and had continued to resist Aeneas' mission.—**togātus, -a, -um,** *togaed, toga-clad.*)

*Virgil between two Muses
Mosaic, early 3rd century A.D.
Musée National du Bardo
Tunis, Tunisia*

THE VALUE OF LITERATURE

Sī ex hīs studiīs dēlectātiō sōla peterētur, tamen, ut opīnor, hanc animī remissiōnem hūmānissimam ac līberālissimam iūdicārētis. Nam cēterae neque temporum sunt neque aetātum omnium neque locōrum; at haec studia adulēscentiam alunt, senectūtem oblectant, rēs secundās ōrnant, adversīs perfugium ac sōlācium praebent, dēlectant domī, nōn impediunt forīs, pernoctant nōbīscum, peregrīnantur, rūsticantur.

(*Cicero, *Prō Archiā* 7.16.—**hanc,** sc. **esse.**—**iūdicāre,** *to judge, consider.*—**cēterae,** sc. **remissiōnēs.**—take **omnium** with all three descriptive genitives, **temporum, aetātum,** and **locōrum.**)

A MONUMENT MORE LASTING THAN BRONZE

Exēgī monumentum aere perennius.

. . .

Nōn omnis moriar, multaque pars meī
vītābit Libitīnam.

(*Horace, *Odes* 3.30.1, 6–7; meter: first Asclepiadean. See L.I. 28.—**perennis, -e,** *lasting [throughout the years].*—**multa,** here = **magna.**—**Libitīna, -ae,** *goddess of funerals; death.*)

ETYMOLOGY

In the readings   2. presidium, preside, president, presidency. 3. extinguish, extinct.—lucre, lucrative. 6. puerile, puerility. 7. "gtt.," medical abbreviation for "drops." 9. inimical, enemy. 11. denigrate, desiccate. 12. **Aliēnus** literally means *belonging to another* (**alius**): alien, alienate, alienation, inalienable. 15. legate, legation, delegate.—humanity, humanities, humanitarian; cp. **hūmānus, homō.** 16. convince, convict, conviction. "Jupiter": Connected with **for, fārī, fātus sum** is the noun **fātum;** what Jupiter has prophecied is one's "fate." "Value of Literature": adjudicate. "A Monument": "perennials" are outdoor plants that survive *through the years,* i.e., from one year to the next; and Latin, dear friends, is a perennial language!

LATĪNA EST GAUDIUM—ET ŪTILIS!

Salvēte postrēmum, discipulī et discipulae! Here are some **rēs novae ex hōc capite ultimō: dominus illūminātiō mea,** *the Lord is my light,* is the motto of Oxford University; **lacrima Christī** is a well known Lat. phrase for *the tear of Christ* (and also the name of a sweet Italian wine). An oft quoted line from Virgil's *Aeneid* comes as the hero Aeneas, shipwrecked in North Africa, gazes upon a Carthaginian mural that depicts the suffering of both his own people and the Greeks in the Trojan war: **hīc etiam . . . sunt lacrimae rērum et mentem mortālia tangunt.** The Latin works better than a literal English translation (which you can now easily provide for yourself), but a free rendering would be: *even here there are tears for the ways of the world, and man's mortality touches the heart.*

Not to be so lacrimose (or "lachrymose," an alternate spelling), let's move to some more upbeat items: remember how to make masculine agent nouns from verbs?—e.g., from **reperiō** is **repertor,** *discover.* Well, the feminine agentive suffix is **-trīx, -trīcis** (cp. Eng. "aviator" and "aviatrix," and **lēctor/lēctrīx,** which we've seen before), hence this proverb: **paupertās omnium artium repertrīx,** something like our "necessity is the mother of invention" (but what is the literal meaning?). **Vultus est index animī,** *the face is an indication of the soul,* it has often been said. And speaking of faces, to "stick your nose up in the air" and to "look down your nose" on someone are not wholly modern idioms for viewing others critically or with disdain; the Neronian satirist Persius says of his predecessor Horace, in a brilliant and not wholly complimentary metaphor, that he *hung the people from his well-blown nose* (**excussō populum suspendere nāsō**). **Nāsō,** by the way, was the "nickname" or **cognōmen** of the Augustan poet Ovid: the Romans often gave their children names that focussed on physical or mental traits and they were frequently passed on from generation to generation (our friend Marcus Tullius, **mīrābile dictū,** was stuck with the name **Cicerō,** *garbanzo bean,* because of a peculiar growth on an ancestor's nose!).

May your love of Latin be **aere perennius: rīdēte, gaudēte, carpite omnēs diēs vestrōs, atque postrēmum, lēctōrēs et lēctrīcēs dulcēs, valēte!**

Locī Antīquī

Although these passages chosen from ancient authors have been adapted to meet the linguistic experience of first-year students, they have been edited as little as possible; the language and the thoughts are those of the ancient writers. In the case of poetry, one or more verses have been omitted from each excerpt but the verses actually presented here have not been altered. In the case of a prose passage, some words or sentences may have been omitted or the wording has been somewhat simplified at one point or another.

Students should find the perusal of these varied **Locī Antīquī** interesting per se and should also find satisfaction and a sense of accomplishment in being able to translate passages of such maturity at their stage of Latin study. Words appearing here that have not been introduced in the 40 chapter vocabularies are glossed at their first one or two occurrences, and especially important words are listed in the "Vocabulary" following the glosses to each passage; most are also included in the Latin-English Vocabulary at the end of the book for easy reference.

1. DISILLUSIONMENT

> Miser Catulle, dēsinās[1] ineptīre,[2]
> et quod vidēs perīsse perditum[3] dūcās.
> Fulsēre[4] quondam candidī tibī sōlēs,
> cum ventitābās[5] quō[6] puella dūcēbat,
> 5 amāta nōbīs quantum amābitur nūlla.

1

METER: choliambic.

[1] **dēsinō, -ere, -siī, -situm,** cease (**dēsinās** = *juss. subj.* for **dēsine**)

[2] **ineptiō** (4), play the fool

[3] **perdō, -ere, -didī, -ditum,** destroy, lose

[4] **fulgeō, -ēre, fulsī,** shine (**fulsēre** = **fulsērunt**)

[5] **ventitō** (1), *frequentative form of* **veniō,** come often

[6] **quō,** *adv.,* whither, where

Fulsēre vērē candidī tibī sōlēs.

Nunc iam illa nōn vult; tū quoque, impotēns,[7] nōlī;

nec quae fugit sectāre[8] nec miser vīve,

sed obstinātā[9] mente perfer,[10] obdūrā.[11]

10   Valē, puella, iam Catullus obdūrat,

nec tē requīret nec rogābit invītam[12];

at tū dolēbis, cum rogāberis nūlla.

Scelesta, vae tē! Quae tibī manet vīta![13]

Quis nunc tē adībit? Cui vidēberis bella?

15   Quem nunc amābis? Cuius esse dīcēris?

At tū, Catulle, dēstinātus obdūrā. (**Catullus** 8)

2. HOW DEMOSTHENES OVERCAME HIS HANDICAPS

Ōrātor imitētur[1] illum cui summa vīs dīcendī concēditur,[2] Dē-
mosthenem, in quō tantum studium fuisse dīcitur ut impedīmenta[3] nātūrae
dīligentiā[4] industriāque[5] superāret. Nam cum ita balbus[6] esset ut illīus ipsīus
artis[7] cui studēret prīmam litteram nōn posset dīcere, perfēcit[8] meditandō[9]
5   ut nēmō plānius[10] loquerētur. Deinde, cum spīritus eius esset angustior,[11]
spīritū continendō multum perfēcit in dīcendō; et coniectīs[12] in ōs calculīs,[13]
summā vōce versūs multōs ūnō spīritū prōnūntiāre cōnsuēscēbat[14]; neque id
faciēbat stāns ūnō in locō sed ambulāns. (**Cicero,** *Dē Ōrātōre* 1.61.260–61)

3. THE TYRANT CAN TRUST NO ONE

Multōs annōs tyrannus Syrācūsānōrum[1] fuit Dionȳsius. Pulcherrimam
urbem servitūte oppressam tenuit. At ā bonīs auctōribus cognōvimus eum
fuisse hominem summae temperantiae[2] in vīctū[3] et in rēbus gerendīs ācrem
et industrium,[4] eundem tamen malum et iniūstum.[5] Quārē, omnibus virīs
5   bene vēritātem quaerentibus hunc vidērī miserrimum necesse est, nam

---

[7] **im-potēns,** *gen.* **-entis,** powerless, weak, hopelessly
in love

[8] **sectāre,** *imper. of* **sector** (1), follow eagerly, pursue;
word order: **sectāre (eam) quae fugit**

[9] **obstinātus, -a, -um,** firm

[10] **per-ferō,** endure

[11] **obdūrō** (1), *vb. of adj.* **dūrus**

[12] **invītus, -a, -um,** unwilling

[13] *see notes on excerpt in Ch. 19.*

VOCABULARY: **perdō, quō, invītus.**

2

[1] **imitor, -ārī, -ātus sum**

[2] **con-cēdō**

[3] **impedīmentum, -ī**

[4] **dīligentia, -ae**

[5] **industria, -ae**

[6] **balbus, -a, -um,** stuttering

[7] **illīus . . . artis,** *i.e., rhetoric*

[8] **per-ficiō,** do thoroughly, bring about, accomplish

[9] **meditor** (1), practice

[10] **plānius,** *comp. of adv.* **plānē**

[11] **angustus, -a, -um,** narrow, short

[12] **con-iciō (iaciō)**

[13] **calculus, -ī,** pebble

[14] **cōnsuēscō, -ere, -suēvī, -suētum,** become accustomed

VOCABULARY: **concēdō, perficiō, angustus, coniciō,
cōnsuēscō.**

3

[1] **Syrācūsānī, -ōrum,** Syracusans

[2] **temperantia, -ae**

[3] **vīctus, -ūs,** mode of life

[4] **industrius, -a, -um**

[5] **in-iūstus, -a, -um**

nēminī crēdere audēbat. Itaque propter iniūstam cupiditātem dominātūs[6] quasi in carcerem[7] ipse sē inclūserat.[8] Quīn etiam,[9] nē tōnsōrī[10] collum[11] committeret, fīliās suās artem tōnsōriam docuit.[12] Ita hae virginēs tondē-bant[13] barbam[14] et capillum[15] patris. Et tamen ab hīs ipsīs, cum iam essent
10 adultae,[16] ferrum remōvit, eīsque imperāvit ut carbōnibus[17] barbam et capil-lum sibi adūrerent.[18] (**Cicero,** *Tusculānae Disputātiōnēs* 5.20.57–58)

4. THE SWORD OF DAMOCLES

Hic tyrannus ipse dēmōnstrāvit quam beātus esset. Nam cum quīdam ex eius assentātōribus,[1] Dāmoclēs,[2] commemorāret[3] cōpiās eius, maiestātem[4] dominātūs, rērum abundantiam,[5] negāretque quemquam[6] umquam beāti-ōrem fuisse, Dionȳsius "Vīsne igitur," inquit, "Ō Dāmocle, ipse hanc vītam
5 dēgustāre[7] et fortūnam meam experīrī?" Cum ille sē cupere dīxisset, homi-nem in aureō[8] lectō[9] collocārī[10] iussit mēnsāsque ōrnāvit argentō[11] aurōque.[12] Tum puerōs bellōs iussit cēnam exquīsītissimam[13] īnferre. Fortūnātus sibi Dāmoclēs vidēbātur. Eōdem autem tempore Dionȳsius gladium suprā[14] ca-put eius saetā equīnā[15] dēmittī[16] iussit. Dāmoclēs, cum gladium vīdisset, ti-
10 mēns ōrāvit tyrannum ut eī abīre licēret, quod iam "beātus" nōllet esse. Satisne Dionȳsius vidētur dēmōnstrāvisse nihil esse eī beātum cui semper aliquī[17] metus impendeat?[18] (**Cicero,** *Tusculānae Disputātiōnēs* 5.20.61–62)

5. DERIVATION OF "PHILOSOPHUS" AND SUBJECTS OF PHILOSOPHY

Eī quī studia in contemplātiōne[1] rērum pōnēbant "sapientēs" appellā-bantur, et id nōmen ūsque ad Pȳthagorae[2] aetātem mānāvit.[3] Hunc aiunt doctē et cōpiōsē[4] quaedam cum Leonte[5] disputāvisse[6]; et Leōn, cum illīus

[6] **dominātus, -ūs,** absolute rule or power
[7] **carcer, -eris,** *m.,* prison
[8] **inclūdō, -ere, -clūsī, -clūsum,** shut in
[9] **quīn etiam,** moreover
[10] **tōnsor, -ōris,** *m.,* barber
[11] **collum, -ī,** neck
[12] **doceō** *may take two objects.*
[13] **tondeō, -ēre, totondī, tōnsum,** shear, clip
[14] **barba, -ae,** beard
[15] **capillus, -ī,** hair
[16] **adultus, -a, -um**
[17] **carbō, -ōnis,** *m.,* glowing coal
[18] **adūrō, -ere, -ussī, -ustum,** singe
VOCABULARY: **temperantia, iniūstus, inclūdō.**

4

[1] **assentātor, -ōris,** *m.,* flatterer, "yes-man"
[2] **Dāmoclēs, -is,** *m.*
[3] **commemorō** (1), mention, recount
[4] **maiestās, -tātis,** *f.,* greatness
[5] **abundantia, -ae**
[6] **quisquam, quidquam,** anyone, anything

[7] **dēgustō** (1), taste, try
[8] **aureus, -a, -um,** golden
[9] **lectus, -ī,** couch
[10] **col-locō,** place
[11] **argentum, -ī,** silver
[12] **aurum, -ī,** gold
[13] **exquīsītus, -a, -um: ex-quaesītus**
[14] **suprā,** *adv. and prep.* + *acc.,* above
[15] **saetā equīnā,** by a horsehair
[16] **dēmittō,** let down
[17] **aliquī, -qua, -quod,** *adj. of* **aliquis**
[18] **impendeō, -ēre,** hang over, threaten
VOCABULARY: **quisquam, collocō, aurum, suprā.**

5

[1] **contemplātiō, -ōnis,** *f.*
[2] **Pȳthagorās, -ae,** *m.*
[3] **mānō** (1), flow, extend
[4] **cōpiōsē,** *adv.,* fully
[5] **Leōn, -ontis,** *m.,* ruler of Phlius
[6] **disputō** (1), discuss

ingenium et ēloquentiam[7] admīrātus esset,[8] quaesīvit ex eō quā arte maximē
5   ūterētur. At ille dīxit sē artem nūllam scīre sed esse philosophum. Tum Leōn,
admīrātus novum nōmen, quaesīvit quī essent philosophī. Pȳthagorās respondit multōs hominēs glōriae aut pecūniae servīre sed paucōs quōsdam
esse quī cētera prō nihilō[9] habērent sed nātūram rērum cognōscere cuperent;
hōs sē appellāre "studiōsōs[10] sapientiae," id est enim "philosophōs."[11] Sīc
10   Pȳthagorās huius nōminis inventor[12] fuit.

Ab antīquā philosophiā ūsque ad Sōcratem[13] philosophī numerōs et
sīdera tractābant[14] et unde omnia orīrentur[15] et quō[16] discēderent. Sōcratēs
autem prīmus philosophiam dēvocāvit ē caelō et in urbibus hominibusque
collocāvit et coēgit eam dē vītā et mōribus rēbusque bonīs et malīs quaerere.
(**Cicero,** *Tusculānae Disputātiōnēs* 5.3.8–9; 5.4.10)

6. CICERO ON THE VALUE AND THE NATURE OF FRIENDSHIP

Ego vōs hortor ut amīcitiam omnibus rēbus hūmānīs antepōnātis. Sentiō equidem,[1] exceptā[2] sapientiā, nihil melius hominī ā deīs immortālibus
datum esse. Dīvitiās aliī antepōnunt; aliī, salūtem; aliī, potestātem[3]; aliī,
honōrēs; multī, etiam voluptātēs. Illa autem incerta sunt, posita nōn tam
5   in cōnsiliīs nostrīs quam in fortūnae vicissitūdinibus.[4] Quī autem in virtūte
summum bonum pōnunt, bene illī quidem faciunt; sed ex ipsā virtūte amīcitia nāscitur nec sine virtūte amīcitia esse potest.

Dēnique cēterae rēs, quae petuntur, opportūnae[5] sunt rēbus singulīs[6]:
dīvitiae, ut eīs ūtāris; honōrēs, ut laudēris; salūs, ut dolōre careās et rēbus
10   corporis ūtāris. Amīcitia rēs plūrimās continet; nūllō locō exclūditur[7]; numquam intempestīva,[8] numquam molesta[9] est. Itaque nōn aquā, nōn igne in
locīs plūribus ūtimur quam amīcitiā; nam amīcitia secundās rēs clāriōrēs
facit et adversās rēs leviōrēs.

Quis est quī velit in omnium rērum abundantiā ita[10] vīvere ut neque dīligat
15   quemquam[11] neque ipse ab ūllō dīligātur? Haec enim est tyrannōrum vīta,
in quā nūlla fidēs, nūlla cāritās,[12] nūlla benevolentia[13] potest esse; omnia
semper metuuntur, nūllus locus est amīcitiae. Quis enim aut eum dīligat[14]
quem metuat aut eum ā quō sē metuī putet? Multī autem sī cecidērunt, ut

[7] **ēloquentia, -ae**
[8] **admīror** (1), wonder at, admire
[9] **nihilum, -ī,** = nihil
[10] **studiōsus, -a, -um,** fond of
[11] **philosophus:** *Greek* **philos,** fond of, + **sophia,** wisdom
[12] **inventor, -ōris,** *m., cp.* **inveniō**
[13] **Sōcratēs, -is**
[14] **tractō** (1), handle, investigate, treat
[15] **orior, -īrī, ortus sum,** arise, proceed, originate
[16] **quō,** *adv.,* where
VOCABULARY: **admīror, orior, quō.**
6
[1] **equidem,** *adv.,* indeed

[2] **excipiō, -ere, -cēpī, -ceptum,** except
[3] **potestās, -tātis,** *f.,* power
[4] **vicissitūdō, -inis,** *f.*
[5] **opportūnus, -a, -um,** suitable
[6] **singulus, -a, -um,** single, separate
[7] **exclūdō, -ere, -clūsī, -clūsum**
[8] **intempestīvus, -a, -um,** unseasonable
[9] **molestus, -a, -um,** troublesome
[10] **abundantia, -ae**
[11] **quemquam,** *L. A.* 4, n. 6
[12] **cāritās, -tātis,** *f.,* affection
[13] **bene-volentia, -ae,** goodwill
[14] **dīligat,** *deliberative subj.,* would esteem

saepe fit, tum intellegunt quam inopēs[15] amīcōrum fuerint. Quid vērō stul-
20   tius quam cētera parāre quae parantur pecūniā sed amīcōs nōn parāre, optimam et pulcherrimam quasi supellectilem[16] vītae?

Quisque ipse sē dīligit nōn ut aliam mercēdem[17] ā sē ipse petat sed quod
per sē quisque sibi cārus est. Nisi idem in amīcitiam trānsferētur,[18] vērus
amīcus numquam reperiētur. Amīcus enim est is quī est tamquam alter īdem.
25   Ipse sē dīligit et alterum quaerit cuius animum ita cum suō misceat ut faciat
ūnum ex duōbus. Quid enim dulcius quam habēre quīcum[19] audeās sīc loquī
ut tēcum? (**Cicero,** *Dē Amīcitiā,* excerpts from Chs. 5, 6, 15, 21)

7. CICERO ON WAR

Quaedam officia sunt servanda etiam adversus[1] eōs ā quibus iniūriam
accēpimus. Atque in rē pūblicā maximē cōnservanda sunt iūra bellī. Nam
sunt duo genera dēcertandī[2]: ūnum per disputātiōnem,[3] alterum per vim.
Illud est proprium[4] hominis, hoc bēluārum[5]; sed bellum vī gerendum est sī
5   disputātiōne ūtī nōn licet. Quārē suscipienda quidem bella sunt ut sine in-
iūriā in pāce vīvāmus; post autem victōriam eī cōnservandī sunt quī nōn
crūdēlēs,[6] nōn dūrī in bellō fuērunt, ut maiōrēs nostrī Sabīnōs[7] in cīvitātem
etiam accēpērunt. At Carthāginem omnīnō sustulērunt; etiam Corinthum
sustulērunt—quod nōn approbō[8]; sed crēdō eōs hoc fēcisse nē locus ipse ad
10   bellum faciendum hortārī posset. Meā quidem sententiā,[9] pāx quae nihil
īnsidiārum habeat semper quaerenda est. Ac aequitās[10] bellī fētiālī[11] iūre populī Rōmānī perscrīpta est.[12] Quārē potest intellegī nūllum bellum esse iūs-
tum nisi quod aut rēbus repetītīs[13] gerātur aut ante dēnūntiātum sit.[14]

Nūllum bellum dēbet suscipī ā cīvitāte optimā nisi aut prō fidē aut prō
15   salūte. Illa bella sunt iniūsta quae sine causā sunt suscepta. Nam extrā[15]
ulcīscendī[16] aut prōpulsandōrum[17] hostium causam nūllum bellum cum aequitāte gerī potest. Noster autem populus sociīs[18] dēfendendīs terrārum[19]

---

[15] **inops, -opis,** bereft of
[16] **supellex, -lectilis,** *f.,* furniture
[17] **mercēs, -ēdis,** *f.,* pay, reward
[18] **trāns-ferō,** transfer, direct
[19] **habēre quīcum = habēre eum cum quō**
VOCABULARY: **equidem, potestās, trānsferō.**

7

[1] **adversus,** *prep. + acc.,* toward
[2] **dēcertō** (1), fight (to a decision)
[3] **disputātiō, -ōnis,** *f.,* discussion
[4] **proprius, -a, -um,** characteristic of
[5] **bēlua, -ae,** wild beast
[6] **crūdēlis, -e,** cruel
[7] **Sabīnī, -ōrum**

[8] **approbō** (1), approve
[9] **sententiā:** *abl. here expressing accordance*
[10] **aequitās, -tātis,** *f.,* fairness, justice
[11] **fētiālis, -e,** fetial, *referring to a college of priests who were concerned with treaties and the ritual of declaring war*
[12] **per-scrībō,** write out, place on record
[13] **re-petō,** seek again
[14] **dēnūntiō** (1), declare officially
[15] **extrā,** *prep. + acc.,* beyond
[16] **ulcīscor, -ī, ultus sum,** avenge, punish
[17] **prōpulsō** (1), repel
[18] **socius, -iī,** ally
[19] **terrārum:** *depends on* **potītus est**

omnium potītus est.[20] (**Cicero,** *Dē Officiīs* 1.11.34–36 and *Dē Rē Pūblicā* 3.23.34–35)

8. HANNIBAL; THE SECOND PUNIC WAR

Hannibal,[1] fīlius Hamilcaris,[2] Carthāgine nātus est. Odium patris ergā Rōmānōs sīc cōnservāvit ut numquam id dēpōneret.[3] Nam post bellum Pūnicum,[4] cum ex patriā in exsilium expulsus esset, nōn relīquit studium bellī Rōmānīs īnferendī.[5] Quārē, cum in Syriam[6] vēnisset, Antiochō[7] rēgī haec
5 locūtus est ut hunc quoque ad bellum cum Rōmānīs indūcere[8] posset:

"Mē novem annōs nātō, pater meus Hamilcar, in Hispāniam[9] imperātor proficīscēns Carthāgine, sacrificium[10] dīs fēcit. Eōdem tempore quaesīvit ā mē vellemne sēcum proficīscī. Cum id libenter audīvissem et ab eō petere coepissem nē dubitāret mē dūcere, tum ille 'Faciam,' inquit, 'sī mihi fidem
10 quam quaerō dederis.' Tum mē ad āram[11] dūxit et mē iūrāre[12] iussit mē numquam in amīcitiā cum Rōmānīs futūrum esse. Id iūs iūrandum[13] patrī datum ūsque ad hanc aetātem ita cōnservāvī ut nēmō sit quī plūs odiī ergā Rōmānōs habeat."

Hāc igitur aetāte Hannibal cum patre in Hispāniam profectus est. Post
15 multōs annōs, Hamilcare et Hasdrubale[14] interfectīs, exercitus eī imperium trādidit. Sīc Hannibal, quīnque et vīgintī annōs nātus, imperātor factus est. Tribus annīs omnēs gentēs Hispāniae superāvit et trēs exercitūs maximōs parāvit. Ex hīs ūnum in Āfricam[15] mīsit, alterum cum frātre in Hispāniā relīquit, tertium in Italiam sēcum dūxit.
20 Ad Alpēs[16] vēnit, quās nēmō umquam ante eum cum exercitū trānsierat. Alpicōs[17] cōnantēs prohibēre eum trānsitū occīdit[18]; loca patefēcit; itinera mūnīvit[19]; effēcit[20] ut[21] elephantus īre posset quā[22] anteā[23] ūnus homō vix[24] poterat rēpere.[25] Sīc in Italiam pervēnit et, Scīpiōne[26] superātō, Etrūriam[27]

---

[20] **potior, -īrī, potītus sum,** + *gen. (or abl.)*, get possession of
VOCABULARY: **dēcertō, proprius, crūdēlis, potior.**

8

[1] **Hannibal, -alis,** *m., illustrious general who led the Carthaginian forces against the Romans in the Second Punic (= Carthaginian) War, 218–202* B.C.
[2] **Hamilcar, -aris,** *m.*
[3] **dē-pōnō**
[4] **Pūnicus, -a, -um**
[5] **bellum īn-ferō,** make war on
[6] **Syria, -ae**
[7] **Antiochus, -ī**
[8] **in-dūcō**
[9] **Hispānia, -ae,** Spain
[10] **sacrificium, -iī**
[11] **āra, -ae,** altar

[12] **iūrō** (1), swear
[13] **iūs iūrandum, iūris iūrandī,** *n.,* oath
[14] **Hasdrubal, -alis,** *m., next in command after Hamilcar*
[15] **Āfrica, -ae**
[16] **Alpēs, -ium,** *f. pl.,* the Alps
[17] **Alpicī, -ōrum,** men of the Alps
[18] **occīdō, -ere, -cīdī, -cīsum,** cut down
[19] **mūniō** (4), fortify, build
[20] **efficiō,** bring it about, cause
[21] **ut . . . posset:** *noun cl. of result, obj. of* **effēcit**
[22] **quā,** *adv.,* where
[23] **anteā,** *adv.,* before, formerly
[24] **vix,** *adv.,* scarcely
[25] **rēpō, -ere, rēpsī, rēptum,** crawl
[26] **Scīpiō, -ōnis,** *m., father of the Scipio mentioned below*
[27] **Etrūria, -ae,** *district north of Rome, Tuscany*

petīvit. Hōc in itinere tam gravī morbō[28] oculōrum adfectus est[29] ut posteā
25 numquam dextrō oculō bene ūterētur.

Multōs ducēs exercitūsque Rōmānōs superāvit; longum est omnia proelia[30] ēnumerāre.[31] Post Cannēnsem[32] autem pugnam nēmō eī in aciē[33] in
Italiā restitit.[34] Cum autem P. Scīpiō tandem[35] in Āfricam invāsisset,[36] Hannibal, ad patriam dēfendendam revocātus, Zamae[37] victus est. Sīc post tot
30 annōs Rōmānī sē perīculō Pūnicō līberāvērunt. (**Nepos**, *Hannibal,* excerpts)

9. AUTOBIOGRAPHICAL NOTES BY HORACE

Nūlla fors[1] mihi tē, Maecēnās,[2] obtulit: optimus Vergilius et post hunc
Varius[3] dīxērunt quid essem. Ut ad tē vēnī, singultim[4] pauca locūtus (nam
pudor[5] prohibēbat plūra profārī[6]), ego nōn dīxī mē clārō patre nātum esse
sed narrāvī quod eram. Respondēs,[7] ut tuus mōs est, pauca. Abeō et post
5 nōnum mēnsem[8] mē revocās iubēsque esse in amīcōrum numerō. Hoc magnum esse dūcō, quod[9] placuī tibi, quī bonōs ā turpibus sēcernis[10] nōn patre
clārō sed vītā et pectore pūrō.[11]

Atquī[12] sī mea nātūra est mendōsa[13] vitiīs mediocribus ac paucīs sed
aliōquī[14] rēcta,[15] sī neque avāritiam neque sordēs[16] quisquam[17] mihi obiciet,[18]
10 sī pūrus sum et īnsōns[19] (ut mē laudem!) et vīvō cārus amīcīs, causa fuit
pater meus. Hic enim, cum pauper in parvō agrō esset, tamen nōluit mē
puerum in lūdum Flāviī[20] mittere sed ausus est mē Rōmam ferre ad artēs
discendās quās senātōrēs[21] suōs filiōs docent. Ipse mihi paedagōgus[22] incor-
ruptissimus[23] erat. Mē līberum servāvit nōn sōlum ab omnī factō sed etiam
15 ab turpī opprobriō.[24] Quārē laus illī ā mē dēbētur et grātia[25] magna.

---

[28] **morbus, -ī,** disease
[29] **adficiō,** afflict
[30] **proelium, -iī,** battle
[31] **ēnumerō** (1)
[32] **Cannēnsis pugna,** battle at Cannae, *where in 216* B.C.
Hannibal cut the Roman army to shreds
[33] **aciēs, -ēī,** battle line
[34] **resistō, -ere, -stitī,** + *dat.,* resist
[35] **tandem,** *adv.,* at last, finally
[36] **invādō, -ere, -vāsī, -vāsum,** go into, invade
[37] **Zama, -ae,** *city south of Carthage in North Africa*
VOCABULARY: **occīdō, efficiō, quā, anteā, vix, proelium, tandem.**

9

[1] **fors, fortis,** *f.,* chance, accident
[2] **Maecēnās, -ātis,** *m., Augustus' unofficial prime minister and Horace's patron*
[3] **Varius, -iī,** *an epic poet*
[4] **singultim,** *adv.,* stammeringly
[5] **pudor, -ōris,** *m.,* bashfulness, modesty
[6] **profor** (1), speak out

[7] **respondēs, abeō, revocās, iubēs:** *in vivid narration the
pres. tense was often used by the Romans with the
force of the perf. This is called the "historical pres."*
[8] **mēnsis, -is,** *m.,* month
[9] **quod,** the fact that
[10] **sēcernō, -ere, -crēvī, -crētum,** separate
[11] **pūrus, -a, -um**
[12] **atquī,** *conj.,* and yet
[13] **mendōsus, -a, -um,** faulty
[14] **aliōquī,** *adv.,* otherwise
[15] **rēctus, -a, -um,** straight, right
[16] **sordēs, -ium,** *f. pl.,* filth
[17] **quisquam,** anyone
[18] **ob-iciō,** cast in one's teeth
[19] **īnsōns,** *gen.* -ontis, guiltless
[20] **Flāvius, -iī,** *teacher in Horace's small home town of
Venusia*
[21] **senātor, -ōris,** *m.*
[22] **paedagōgus, -ī,** *slave who attended a boy at school*
[23] **in-corruptus, -a, -um,** uncorrupted
[24] **opprobrium, -iī,** reproach
[25] **grātia, -ae,** gratitude

Sīc Rōmae nūtrītus sum[26] atque doctus sum quantum[27] īrātus Achillēs Graecīs nocuisset. Deinde bonae Athēnae mihi plūs artis adiēcērunt,[28] scīlicet[29] ut vellem rēctum ā curvō[30] distinguere[31] atque inter silvās[32] Acadēmī[33] quaerere vēritātem. Sed dūra tempora mē illō locō grātō ēmōvērunt et ae-

20 stus[34] cīvīlis[35] bellī mē tulit in arma Brūtī.[36] Tum post bellum Philippēnse[37] dīmissus sum[38] et audāx[39] paupertās mē humilem et pauperem coēgit versūs facere. (**Horace,** *Saturae* 1.6 and *Epistulae* 2.2; excerpts in prose form)

10. HORACE LONGS FOR THE SIMPLE, PEACEFUL COUNTRY LIFE ON HIS SABINE FARM

Ō rūs, quandō tē aspiciam?[1] Quandō mihi licēbit nunc librīs veterum auctōrum, nunc somnō et ōtiō ūtī sine cūrīs sollicitae[2] vītae? Ō noctēs cēnaeque deōrum! Sermō[3] oritur[4] nōn dē vīllīs[5] et domibus aliēnīs[6]; sed id quaerimus quod magis ad nōs pertinet[7] et nescīre malum est: utrum dīvitiīs

5 an virtūte hominēs fīant beātī; quid nōs ad amīcitiam trahat, ūsus[8] an rēctum[9]; et quae sit nātūra bonī[10] et quid sit summum bonum.

Inter haec Cervius[11] fābulam narrat. Mūs[12] rūsticus,[13] impulsus[14] ab urbānō mūre, domō rūsticā ad urbem abiit ut, dūrā vītā relictā, in rēbus iūcundīs cum illō vīveret beātus. Mox, autem, multa perīcula urbāna expertus,

10 rūsticus "Haec vīta," inquit, "nōn est mihi necessāria.[15] Valē; mihi silva cavusque[16] tūtus[17] ab īnsidiīs placēbit." (**Horace,** *Saturae* 2.6, excerpts in prose form)

11. WHY NO LETTERS?

C.[1] Plīnius Fabiō[2] Suō S.[3]

Mihi nūllās epistulās[4] mittis. "Nihil est," inquis, "quod scrībam." At hoc ipsum scrībe: nihil esse quod scrībās; vel[5] illa verba sōla ā quibus maiōrēs nostrī incipere solēbant: "Sī valēs, bene est; ego valeō." Hoc mihi sufficit[6]; est enim maximum. Mē lūdere[7] putās? Sēriō[8] petō. Fac ut sciam quid agās.
5 Valē. (**Pliny,** *Epistulae* 1.11)

12. WHAT PLINY THINKS OF THE RACES

C. Plīnius Calvisiō[1] Suō S.

Hoc omne tempus inter tabellās[2] ac libellōs iūcundissimā quiēte[3] cōnsūmpsī. "Quemadmodum,[4]" inquis, "in urbe potuistī?" Circēnsēs[5] erant quō genere spectāculī[6] nē levissimē quidem teneor. Nihil novum, nihil varium,[7] nihil quod semel spectāvisse nōn sufficiat. Quārē mīror tot mīlia virōrum
5 tam puerīliter[8] identidem[9] cupere currentēs equōs vidēre. Valē. (**Pliny,** *Epistulae* 9.6)

13. PLINY ENDOWS A SCHOOL

Nūper cum Cōmī[1] fuī, vēnit ad mē salūtandum[2] fīlius amīcī cuiusdam. Huic ego "Studēs?" inquam. Respondit: "Etiam." "Ubi?" "Mediolānī.[3]" "Cūr nōn hīc?" Et pater eius, quī ipse puerum ad mē addūxerat, respondit: "Quod nūllōs magistrōs hīc habēmus." Huic aliīsque patribus quī audiēbant
5 ego: "Quārē nūllōs?" inquam. "Nam ubi iūcundius līberī[4] vestrī discere possunt quam hīc in urbe vestrā et sub oculīs patrum? Atque ego, quī nōndum[5] līberōs habeō, prō rē pūblicā nostrā quasi prō parente tertiam partem eius pecūniae dabō quam cōnferre vōbīs placēbit. Nihil enim melius praestāre līberīs vestrīs, nihil grātius patriae potestis." (**Pliny,** *Epistulae* 4.13)

11
[1] **C.** = Gāius
[2] **Fabius, -iī**
[3] **S.** = salūtem (dīcit)
[4] **epistula, -ae,** letter
[5] **vel,** or, *an optional alternative;* **aut** *means* or *without any option*
[6] **sufficiō,** suffice, be sufficient
[7] **lūdō, -ere, lūsī, lūsum,** play, jest
[8] **sēriō,** *adv.,* seriously
VOCABULARY: **vel, sufficiō.**
12
[1] **Calvisius, -ī**
[2] **tabella, -ae,** writing pad
[3] **quiēs, -ētis,** *f.,* quiet

[4] **quem-ad-modum,** *adv.,* how
[5] **Circēnsēs (lūdī),** games, *races in the Circus Maximus*
[6] **spectāculum, -ī**
[7] **varius, -a, -um,** different
[8] **puerīliter,** *adv., based on* **puer**
[9] **identidem,** *adv.,* repeatedly
VOCABULARY: **quiēs, quemadmodum, varius.**
13
[1] **Cōmum, -ī,** Como, *Pliny's birthplace in N. Italy*
[2] **salūtō** (1), greet
[3] **Mediolānum, -ī,** Milan
[4] **līberī, -ōrum,** children
[5] **nōndum,** *adv.,* not yet
VOCABULARY: **līberī, nōndum.**

14. LARGE GIFTS—YES, BUT ONLY BAIT

"Mūnera[1] magna tamen mīsit." Sed mīsit in hāmō[2];
et piscātōrem[3] piscis[4] amāre potest? (**Martial** 6.63.5–6)

15. THE LORD'S PRAYER

Et cum ōrātis nōn eritis sīcut[1] hypocritae,[2] quī amant in synagōgīs[3] et in angulīs[4] plateārum[5] stantēs ōrāre ut videantur ab hominibus: āmēn[6] dīcō vōbīs, recēpērunt mercēdem[7] suam. Tū autem cum ōrābis, intrā[8] in cubiculum[9] tuum et, clausō[10] ōstiō[11] tuō, ōrā Patrem tuum in abscondito[12]; et Pater
5   tuus quī videt in abscondito reddet[13] tibi. . . . Sīc ergō[14] vōs ōrābitis: Pater noster quī es in caelīs, sānctificētur[15] nōmen tuum; adveniat rēgnum[16] tuum; fīat voluntās[17] tua sīcut in caelō et[18] in terrā. Pānem[19] nostrum supersubstantiālem[20] dā nōbīs hodiē, et dīmitte[21] nōbīs dēbita[22] nostra, sīcut et nōs dīmittimus dēbitōribus[23] nostrīs; et nē indūcās nōs in temptātiōnem[24]: sed līberā
10   nōs ā malō. (*Vulgate, Matthew* 6.5–6, 9–13)

16. CAEDMON'S ANGLO-SAXON VERSES
AND THE DIFFICULTIES OF TRANSLATION

Cum Caedmon[1] corpus somnō dedisset, angelus[2] Dominī eī dormientī "Caedmon," inquit, "cantā[3] mihi prīncipium creātūrārum.[4]" Et statim[5] coepit cantāre in laudem Deī creātōris[6] versūs quōs numquam audīverat, quōrum hic est sēnsus: "Nunc laudāre dēbēmus auctōrem rēgnī[7] caelestis,[8] po-

14

METER: elegiac couplet.
[1] **mūnus, mūneris,** *n.,* gift
[2] **hāmus, -ī,** hook
[3] **piscātor, -ōris,** *m.,* fisherman
[4] **piscis, -is,** *m.,* fish
VOCABULARY: **mūnus.**

15

[1] **sīcut,** *adv. and conj.,* just as
[2] **hypocrita, -ae,** *m.,* hypocrite
[3] **synagōga, -ae,** synagogue
[4] **angulus, -ī,** corner
[5] **platea, -ae,** street
[6] **āmēn,** *adv.,* truly, verily
[7] **mercēs, -ēdis,** *f.,* wages, reward
[8] **intrō** (1), enter
[9] **cubiculum, -ī,** bedroom, room
[10] **claudō, -ere, clausī, clausum,** close
[11] **ōstium, -iī,** door
[12] **in abscondito,** in (a) secret (place)
[13] **red-dō, -dere, -didī, -ditum,** give back, answer, requite
[14] **ergō,** *adv.,* therefore

[15] **sānctificō** (1), treat as holy
[16] **rēgnum, -ī,** kingdom
[17] **voluntās, -tātis,** *f.,* will, wish
[18] **et,** also
[19] **pānis, -is,** *m.,* bread
[20] **supersubstantiālis, -e,** necessary to the support of life
[21] **dī-mittō,** send away, dismiss
[22] **dēbitum, -ī,** that which is owing, debt (*figuratively*) = sin
[23] **dēbitor, -ōris,** *m.,* one who owes something, one who has not yet fulfilled his duty
[24] **temptātiō, -ōnis,** *f.*
VOCABULARY: **sīcut, claudō, reddō, ergō, rēgnum, voluntās.**

16

[1] **Caedmon,** *Anglo-Saxon poet of the 7th cen.*
[2] **angelus, -ī,** angel
[3] **cantō** (1), sing
[4] **creātūra, -ae,** creature
[5] **statim,** *adv.,* immediately
[6] **creātor, -ōris,** *m.*
[7] **rēgnum, -ī,** kingdom
[8] **caelestis, -e,** *adj. of* **caelum**

5 testātem[9] creatōris et cōnsilium illīus, facta Patris glōriae, quī, omnipotēns[10]
   custōs[11] hūmānī generis, fīliīs hominum caelum et terram creāvit." Hic est
   sēnsus, nōn autem ōrdō[12] ipse verbōrum quae dormiēns ille cantāvit; neque
   enim possunt carmina, quamvīs[13] optimē composita,[14] ex aliā in aliam linguam ad verbum[15] sine dētrīmentō[16] suī decōris[17] ac dignitātis trānsferrī.[18]
   (**Bede,** *Historia Ecclēsiastica Gentis Anglōrum* 4.24; 8th cen.)

17. WHO WILL PUT THE BELL ON THE CAT'S NECK?

Mūrēs[1] iniērunt cōnsilium quō modō sē ā cattō[2] dēfendere possent et
quaedam sapientior quam cēterae āit: "Ligētur[3] campāna[4] in collō[5] cattī. Sīc
poterimus eum eiusque īnsidiās vītāre." Placuit omnibus hoc cōnsilium, sed
alia mūs "Quis igitur," inquit, "est inter nōs tam audāx[6] ut campānam in
5 collō cattī ligāre audeat?" Respondit ūna mūs: "Certē nōn ego." Respondit
alia: "Certē nōn ego audeō prō tōtō mundō cattō ipsī appropinquāre.[7]" Et
idem cēterae dīxērunt.

Sīc saepe hominēs, cum quendam āmovendum esse arbitrantur et contrā
eum insurgere[8] volunt, inter sē dīcunt: "Quis appōnet sē contrā eum? Quis
10 accūsābit[9] eum?" Tum omnēs, sibi timentēs, dīcunt: "Nōn ego certē! Nec
ego!" Sīc illum vīvere patiuntur. (**Odo de Cerinton,** *Narrātiōnēs,* 12th cen.)

18. THE DEVIL AND A THIRTEENTH-CENTURY SCHOOLBOY

In illā ecclēsiā[1] erat scholāris[2] parvus. Cum hic diē quādam[3] versūs compōnere ex eā māteriā[4] ā magistrō datā nōn posset et trīstis sedēret, diabolus[5]
in fōrmā hominis vēnit. Cum dīxisset: "Quid est, puer? Cūr sīc trīstis sedēs?"
respondit puer: "Magistrum meum timeō quod versūs compōnere nōn pos-
5 sum dē themate[6] quod ab eō recēpī." Et ille: "Vīsne mihi servīre sī ego versūs
tibi compōnam?" Puer, nōn intellegēns quod[7] ille esset diabolus, respondit:
"Etiam, domine, parātus sum facere quidquid iusseris—dummodo versūs

[9] **potestās, -tātis,** *f.,* power
[10] **omni-potēns**
[11] **custōs, -tōdis,** *m.,* guardian
[12] **ōrdō, -inis,** *m.,* order
[13] **quamvīs,** *adv. and conj.,* although
[14] **com-pōnō,** put together, compose
[15] **ad verbum,** to a word, literally
[16] **dētrīmentum, -ī,** loss
[17] **decor, -ōris,** *m.,* beauty
[18] **trāns-ferō**
VOCABULARY: **statim, rēgnum, potestās, custōs,
ōrdō, compōnō.**

17

[1] **mūs, mūris,** *m./f.,* mouse
[2] **cattus, -ī** (*late Lat. for* **fēles, -is**), cat
[3] **ligō** (1), bind
[4] **campāna, -ae** (*late Lat. for* **tintinnābulum**), bell

[5] **collum, -ī,** neck
[6] **audāx, -ācis,** daring, bold
[7] **appropinquō** (1), + *dat.,* approach
[8] **īnsurgō, -ere, -surrēxī, -surrēctum,** rise up
[9] **accūsō** (1)
VOCABULARY: **audāx, appropinquō.**

18

[1] **ecclēsia, -ae,** church
[2] **scholāris, -is,** *m.,* scholar
[3] **diē quādam: diēs** *is sometimes f., especially when referring to a specific day.*
[4] **māteria, -ae,** material
[5] **diabolus, -ī,** devil
[6] **thema, -atis,** *n.,* theme, subject
[7] **quod,** that, *introducing an ind. state., common in Medieval Lat.*

habeam et verbera[8] vītem." Tum, versibus statim[9] dictātīs,[10] diabolus abiit. Cum puer autem hōs versūs magistrō suō dedisset, hic, excellentiam[11] ver-

10 suum mīrātus, timuit, dūcēns scientiam in illīs dīvīnam,[12] nōn hūmānam. Et ait: "Dīc mihi, quis tibi hōs versūs dictāvit?" Prīmum puer respondit: "Ego, magister!" Magistrō autem nōn crēdente et verbum interrogātiōnis[13] saepius repetente, puer omnia tandem[14] cōnfessus est.[15] Tum magister "Fīlī," inquit, "ille versificātor[16] fuit diabolus. Cārissime, semper illum sēductōrem[17] et eius

15 opera cavē.[18]" Et puer diabolum eiusque opera relīquit. (**Caesar of Heisterbach,** *Mīrācula* 2.14; 13th cen.)

---

[8] **verbera, -um,** *n.,* blows, a beating
[9] **statim,** *adv.,* immediately
[10] **dictō** (1), dictate
[11] **excellentia, -ae**
[12] **dīvīnus, -a, -um; dīvīnam** *is pred. acc.*
[13] **interrogātiō, -ōnis,** *f.*

[14] **tandem,** *adv.,* at last
[15] **cōnfiteor, -ērī, -fessus sum**
[16] **versificātor, -ōris,** *m.,* versifier
[17] **sēductor, -ōris,** *m.,* seducer
[18] **caveō, -ēre, cāvī, cautum,** beware, avoid
VOCABULARY: **statim, tandem, cōnfiteor, caveō.**

Locī Immūtātī

The *Locī Immūtātī* are offered for those who may finish all the *Locī Antīquī* and wish to try their wits on some unaltered classical Latin.

These passages are straight Latin, unchanged except for omissions, which have been regularly indicated by three dots. Naturally this genuinely literary material had to be rather heavily annotated, but more in the matter of vocabulary than in other respects. As in the case of the *Locī Antīquī,* words appearing here that have not been introduced in the regular chapter vocabularies are glossed at their first one or two occurrences, and most are also included in the Latin-English Vocabulary at the end of the book for easy reference. New grammatical principles have been treated as they occur, either by a brief statement in the notes or by reference to the Appendix.

1. A DEDICATION

> Cui dōnō[1] lepidum[2] novum libellum
> āridō[3] modo[4] pūmice[5] expolītum[6]?
> Cornēlī,[7] tibi, namque[8] tū solēbās
> meās esse aliquid putāre nūgās,[9]
> 5   iam tum cum ausus es ūnus Ītalōrum[10]

1

METER: Phalaecean, or hendecasyllabic.
[1] **dōnō** (1), (=**dō**), present, dedicate
[2] **lepidus, -a, -um,** pleasant, neat
[3] **āridus, -a, -um,** dry, arid
[4] **modo,** *adv.,* just now
[5] **pūmex, -icis,** *m.,* pumice stone. *The ends of a volume were smoothed with pumice.*

[6] **expoliō** (4), smooth, polish
[7] *Cornelius Nepos, biographer and historian;* see Introd.
[8] *strong form of* **nam** = for (indeed, surely)
[9] **nūgae, -ārum,** trifles, nonsense
[10] **Ītalī, -ōrum,** the Italians; *initial* **i-** *long here for meter. This work, now lost, was apparently less annalistic than most histories by Romans.*

omne aevum[11] tribus explicāre[12] chartīs,[13]
doctīs—Iuppiter!—et labōriōsīs.[14]
Quārē habē tibi quidquid hoc libellī[15]
quālecumque,[15] quod, Ō patrōna[16] virgō,
10   plūs ūnō maneat[17] perenne[18] saeclō.[19]

(Catullus 1)

2. HOW MANY KISSES[1]

Quaeris quot mihi bāsiātiōnēs[2]
tuae, Lesbia, sint satis superque.[3]
Quam magnus numerus Libyssae[4] harēnae[5]
laserpīciferīs[6] iacet Cyrēnīs,[7]

. . .

5   aut quam sīdera multa, cum tacet nox,
fūrtīvōs[8] hominum vident amōrēs,
tam tē[9] bāsia multa bāsiāre[10]
vēsānō[11] satis et super Catullō est.

(Catullus 7.1–4, 7–10)

3. DEATH OF A PET SPARROW

Lūgēte,[1] Ō Venerēs[2] Cupīdinēsque[3]
et quantum est hominum[4] venustiōrum[5]!
Passer[6] mortuus est meae puellae,
passer, dēliciae[7] meae puellae,

---

[11] **aevum, -ī,** time
[12] **explicō** (1), unfold, explain
[13] **charta, -ae,** leaf of (papyrus) paper; *here* = volume
[14] **labōriōsus, -a, -um,** laborious
[15] **libellī,** *gen. of whole; lit.* whatever kind of book this is of whatsoever sort; *i.e.,* this book such as it is. **quāliscumque, quālecumque,** of whatever sort *or* kind
[16] **patrōna, -ae,** protectress; protectress maiden (**virgō**) = Muse
[17] let *or* may it remain
[18] **perennis, -e,** lasting, perennial
[19] **saeclum,** *syncopated form of* **saeculum, -ī,** age, century

2

METER: Phalaecean.
[1] *This poem is obviously a companion piece to Catullus 5 (see ch. 31).*
[2] **bāsiātiō, -ōnis,** *f.,* kiss
[3] and to spare, and more
[4] **Libyssus, -a, -um,** Libyan
[5] **harēna, -ae,** sand (*cp.* arena)

[6] **laserpīcifer, -a, -um,** bearing laserpicium, *a medicinal plant*
[7] **Cȳrēnae, -ārum,** Cyrene, *city of North Africa; short* **y** *here for meter.*
[8] **fūrtīvus, -a, -um,** stealthy, furtive (**fūr,** thief)
[9] *subject of* **bāsiāre**
[10] **bāsiō** (1), to kiss kisses = to give kisses; **bāsiāre** *is subject of* **est satis.**
[11] **vēsānus, -a, -um,** mad, insane

3

METER: Phalaecean.
[1] **lūgeō, -ēre, lūxī, lūctum,** mourn, grieve
[2] **Venus, -eris,** *f.,* Venus; *here pl. as* **Cupīdinēs** *is.*
[3] **Cupīdō, -inis,** *m.,* Cupid, *often in the pl. as is Greek Eros and as we see in art.*
[4] *gen. of whole with* **quantum:** how much of people there is = all the people there are
[5] **venustus, -a, -um,** charming, graceful; **venustiōrum** = more charming (*than ordinary men*)
[6] **passer, -eris,** *m.,* sparrow (*a bird which, incidentally, was sacred to Venus*)
[7] **dēliciae, -ārum,** delight, darling, pet

5   quem plūs illa oculīs suīs amābat.
       Nam mellītus[8] erat, suamque nōrat[9]
       ipsam[10] tam bene quam puella mātrem;
       nec sēsē[11] ā gremiō[12] illius movēbat,
       sed circumsiliēns[13] modo hūc[14] modo illūc[15]
10   ad sōlam dominam ūsque pīpiābat.[16]
       Quī[17] nunc it per iter tenebricōsum[18]
       illūc unde negant redīre quemquam.[19]
       At vōbīs male sit, malae tenebrae[20]
       Orcī,[21] quae omnia bella dēvorātis;[22]
15   tam bellum mihi[23] passerem abstulistis.[24]
       Ō factum male! Iō[25] miselle[26] passer!
       Tuā nunc operā[27] meae puellae
       flendō[28] turgidulī[29] rubent[30] ocellī.[31]
       (Catullus 3)

4. FRĀTER AVĒ, ATQUE VALĒ[1]

       Multās per gentēs et multa per aequora[2] vectus[3]
       adveniō hās miserās, frāter, ad īnferiās,[4]
       ut tē postrēmō[5] dōnārem[6] mūnere[7] mortis
       et mūtam[8] nēquīquam[9] adloquerer[10] cinerem,[11]

---

[8] **mellītus, -a, -um,** sweet as honey
[9] *contracted form* = **nōverat** (*from* **nōscō**)
[10] **suam . . . ipsam,** its very own (mistress)
[11] **sēsē** = **sē** (*acc.*)
[12] **gremium, -iī,** lap
[13] **circumsiliō** (4), jump around
[14] **hūc,** *adv.,* hither, to this place
[15] **illūc,** *adv.,* thither, to that place
[16] **pīpiō** (1), chirp
[17] **quī** = **et hic,** *conjunctive use of the rel. at the beginning of a sent.*
[18] **tenebricōsus, -a, -um,** dark, gloomy
[19] *L.A. 4 n. 6.*
[20] **tenebrae, -ārum,** darkness
[21] **Orcus, -ī,** Orcus, the underworld
[22] **dēvorō** (1), devour, consume
[23] *dative of separation*
[24] **auferō, auferre, abstulī, ablātum,** take away
[25] **iō,** *exclamation of pain,* oh!, *or of joy,* hurrah!
[26] **misellus, -a, -um,** *diminutive of* **miser,** wretched, poor, unhappy; *a colloquial word*
[27] **tuā operā,** thanks to you: **opera, -ae,** work, pains, effort
[28] **fleō, -ēre, flēvī, flētum,** weep
[29] **turgidulus, -a, -um,** (somewhat) swollen
[30] **rubeō, -ēre,** be red

[31] **ocellus, -ī,** *diminutive* of **oculus**

4

METER: elegiac couplet.
[1] *Catullus journeyed to Bithynia on the staff of Memmius, the governor, apparently for two prime reasons. He undoubtedly wanted to get away from Rome in order to regain his equilibrium and fortitude after his final break with the notorious Lesbia. The present poem shows that he also deeply desired to carry out the final funeral rites for his dearly beloved brother, who had died in a foreign land far from his loved ones.*
[2] **aequor, -oris,** *n.,* flat surface, the sea
[3] **vehō, -ere, vexī, vectum,** carry
[4] **īnferiae, -ārum,** offerings in honor of the dead
[5] **postrēmus, -a, -um,** last
[6] **dōnō** (1), present you with; *cp. the idiom in L.I. 1 line 1.*
[7] **mūnus, -eris,** *n.,* service, gift
[8] **mūtus, -a, -um,** mute, silent
[9] **nēquīquam,** *adv.,* in vain
[10] **ad-loquor,** address
[11] **cinis, -eris,** *m. but occasionally f. as here,* ashes (*cp. incinerator*)

5   quandoquidem[12] fortūna mihī[13] tētē[14] abstulit[15] ipsum,
      heu miser indignē[16] frāter adempte[17] mihī.
    Nunc tamen intereā[18] haec,[19] prīscō[20] quae mōre parentum
      trādita sunt trīstī mūnere ad īnferiās,
    accipe frāternō[21] multum[22] mānantia[23] flētū,[24]
10   atque in perpetuum,[25] frāter, avē[26] atque valē.

           (Catullus 101)

5. VITRIOLIC DENUNCIATION[1] OF THE LEADER OF A CONSPIRACY AGAINST THE ROMAN STATE

    Quō ūsque[2] tandem abūtēre,[3] Catilīna, patientiā nostrā? Quam diū etiam furor[4] iste tuus nōs ēlūdet[5]? Quem ad fīnem sēsē[6] effrēnāta[7] iactābit[8] audācia[9]? Nihilne[10] tē nocturnum[11] praesidium[12] Palātī,[13] nihil urbis vigiliae,[14] nihil timor populī, nihil concursus[15] bonōrum omnium, nihil hic mūnītissi-
5 mus[16] habendī senātūs locus, nihil hōrum ōra[17] vultūsque mōvērunt? Patēre tua cōnsilia nōn sentīs? Cōnstrictam[18] iam omnium hōrum scientiā tenērī coniūrātiōnem[19] tuam nōn vidēs? Quid proximā,[20] quid superiōre[21] nocte ēgerīs, ubi fuerīs, quōs convocāverīs,[22] quid cōnsilī cēperīs, quem nostrum[23] ignōrāre[24] arbitrāris?

---

[12] **quandoquidem,** *conj.,* since
[13] *dat. of separation. Final* **-ī** *is long here because of meter.*
[14] = **tē**
[15] *L.I. 3 n. 24*
[16] **indignē,** *adv.,* undeservedly
[17] **adimō, -ere, -ēmī, -ēmptum,** take away; **adēmpte,** *voc. agreeing with* **frāter**
[18] **intereā,** *adv.,* meanwhile
[19] *n. acc. pl., obj. of* **accipe**
[20] **prīscus, -a, -um,** ancient
[21] **frāternus, -a, -um,** fraternal, of a brother, a brother's
[22] **multum,** *adv. with* **mānantia**
[23] **mānō** (1), flow, drip with; **mānantia** *modifies* **haec** *in line 7.*
[24] **flētus, -ūs,** weeping, tears
[25] **in perpetuum,** forever
[26] **avē** = **salvē**

5

[1] *For the general situation of this speech see the introductory note to the reading passage in Ch. 30. Since Cicero as yet lacked evidence that would stand in court, this speech is a magnificent example of bluff; but it worked to the extent of forcing Catiline (though not the other leaders of the conspiracy) to leave Rome for his army encamped at Fie-*

sole near Florence.
[2] **ūsque,** *adv.,* how far
[3] = **abūtēris; ab-ūtor** + abl., abuse
[4] **furor, -ōris,** *m.,* madness
[5] **ēlūdō, -ere, -lūsī, -lūsum,** mock, elude
[6] **quem ad fīnem** = **ad quem fīnem; sēsē** = **sē**
[7] **effrēnātus, -a, -um,** unbridled; *cp.* **frēnum,** bridle, *and the frenum of the upper lip*
[8] **iactō** (1), *frequentative form of* **iaciō,** toss about, vaunt
[9] **audācia, -ae,** boldness, audacity
[10] **nihil** = *strong* **nōn;** not at all
[11] **nocturnus, -a, -um,** *adj. of* **nox**
[12] **praesidium, -ī,** guard
[13] **Palātium, -ī,** the Palatine hill. *From the sumptuous dwellings on the Palatine comes our word "palace."*
[14] **vigilia, -ae,** watch; *pl.,* watchmen, sentinels
[15] **concursus, -ūs,** gathering
[16] **mūnītus, -a, -um,** fortified
[17] *here* = expression
[18] **cōnstringō, -ere, -strīnxī, -strictum,** bind, curb
[19] **coniūrātiō, -ōnis,** *f.,* conspiracy (a swearing together)
[20] **proximus, -a, -um,** nearest, last (*sc.* **nocte**)
[21] **superiōre** (*sc.* **nocte**) = the night before
[22] **con-vocō**
[23] *gen. of* **nōs** (*Ch. 11*)
[24] **ignōrō** (1), be ignorant, not know

10   Ō tempora[25]! Ō mōrēs! Senātus haec intellegit, cōnsul videt; hic tamen vīvit. Vīvit? Immō[26] vērō[27] etiam in senātum venit, fit pūblicī cōnsilī particeps,[28] notat[29] et dēsignat[30] oculīs ad caedem[31] ūnum quemque nostrum. Nōs, autem, fortēs virī, satis facere reī pūblicae vidēmur sī istīus furōrem ac tēla[32] vītāmus. Ad mortem tē, Catilīna, dūcī iussū[33] cōnsulis iam prīdem[34]

15   oportēbat, in tē cōnferrī pestem[35] quam tū in nōs māchināris[36] . . .

Habēmus senātūs cōnsultum[37] in tē, Catilīna, vehemēns[38] et grave. Nōn deest[39] reī pūblicae cōnsilium, neque auctōritās[40] huius ōrdinis[41]; nōs, nōs, dīcō apertē,[42] cōnsulēs dēsumus . . . At nōs vīcēsimum[43] iam diem patimur hebēscere[44] aciem[45] hōrum auctōritātis. Habēmus enim eius modī[46] senātūs

20   cōnsultum, . . . quō ex[47] senātūs cōnsultō cōnfestim[48] tē interfectum esse, Catilīna, convēnit.[49] Vīvis, et vīvis nōn ad dēpōnendam,[50] sed ad cōnfirmandam[51] audāciam. Cupiō, patrēs cōnscrīptī,[52] mē esse clēmentem[53]; cupiō in tantīs reī pūblicae perīculīs mē nōn dissolūtum[54] vidērī, sed iam mē ipse inertiae[55] nēquitiaeque[56] condemnō.[57]

25   Castra[58] sunt in Italiā contrā populum Rōmānum in Etrūriae[59] faucibus[60] collocāta[61]; crēscit in diēs singulōs[62] hostium numerus; eōrum autem castrōrum imperātōrem ducemque hostium intrā[63] moenia atque adeō[64] in senātū vidēmus, intestīnam[65] aliquam cotīdiē perniciem[66] reī pūblicae mōlientem[67] . . .

30   Quae[68] cum ita sint, Catilīna, perge[69] quō[70] coepistī. Ēgredere[71] ali-

---

[25] *The acc. was used in exclamatory expressions.*

[26] **immō,** *adv.,* on the contrary; nay more

[27] **vērō,** *adv.,* in fact

[28] **particeps, -cipis,** *m.,* participant

[29] **notō** (1), mark out, note

[30] **dēsignō** (1), mark out, designate, choose

[31] **caedēs, -is,** *f.,* slaughter

[32] **tēlum, -ī,** weapon

[33] **iussū,** *chiefly in abl.,* by *or* at the command of

[34] **iam prīdem,** *adv.,* long ago

[35] **pestis, -is,** *f.,* plague, destruction

[36] **māchinor** (1), contrive (*cp. "machine"*); **in nōs, in** + *acc. sometimes means* against (**contrā**)

[37] **cōnsultum, -ī,** decree

[38] **vehemēns,** *gen.* **-entis,** emphatic, vehement

[39] **dē + sum,** be wanting, fail + *dat.*

[40] **auctōritās, -tātis,** *f.,* authority

[41] **ōrdō, -dinis,** *m.,* class, order

[42] *adv.,* openly

[43] **vīcēsimus, -a, -um,** twentieth

[44] **hebēscō, -ere,** grow dull

[45] **aciēs, -ēī,** sharp edge

[46] **eius modī,** of this sort; *modifies* **cōnsultum**

[47] *here* = in accordance with; *with* **quō . . . cōnsultō**

[48] **cōnfestim,** *adv.,* at once

[49] **convenit, -īre, -vēnit,** *impers.,* it is fitting

[50] **dē + pōnō,** put aside

[51] **cōnfirmō** (1), strengthen

[52] **patrēs cōnscrīptī,** senators

[53] **clēmēns,** *gen.* **-entis,** merciful, gentle

[54] **dissolūtus, -a, -um,** lax

[55] **inertia, -ae,** inactivity; *example of gen. of thing charged:* "I condemn myself *on a charge of inactivity,* find myself guilty of inactivity."

[56] **nēquitia, -ae,** worthlessness; *gen. of charge*

[57] **condemnō** (1), find guilty, condemn

[58] **castra, -ōrum,** a camp (*n. pl. form but sg. meaning*)

[59] **Etrūria, -ae,** Etruria

[60] **faucēs, -ium,** *f. pl.,* jaws, narrow pass

[61] **collocō** (1), to position

[62] **in diēs singulōs,** from day to day

[63] **intrā,** *prep.* + *acc.,* within

[64] **adeō,** *adv.,* so even

[65] **intestīnus, -a, -um,** internal

[66] **perniciēs, -ēī,** slaughter, destruction

[67] **mōlientem** *modifies* **ducem** *and has* **perniciem** *as its obj.*

[68] = **et haec,** *conjunctive use of the rel. pron.*

[69] **pergō, -ere, -rēxī, -rēctum,** proceed, continue

[70] **quō,** *adv.,* where. *A few lines before these words Cicero said:* **cōnfirmāstī** (you asserted) **tē ipsum iam esse exitūrum** (*from* **ex-eō**).

[71] **ēgredior, -ī, -gressus sum,** go out, depart. *What is the form of* **ēgredere**?

quandō[72] ex urbe; patent portae; proficīscere. Nimium diū tē imperātōrem tua illa Mānliāna[73] castra dēsīderant. Ēdūc tēcum etiam omnēs tuōs; sī minus,[74] quam plūrimōs; pūrgā[75] urbem. Magnō mē metū līberāveris dum modo inter mē atque tē mūrus[76] intersit.[77] Nōbīscum versārī[78] iam diūtius

35 nōn potes; nōn feram, nōn patiar, nōn sinam[79] . . .

Quamquam[80] nōn nūllī[81] sunt in hōc ōrdine quī aut ea quae imminent[82] nōn videant, aut ea quae vident dissimulent[83]; quī[84] spem Catilīnae mollibus[85] sententiīs aluērunt coniūrātiōnemque nāscentem nōn crēdendō corrōborāvērunt[86]; quōrum[87] auctōritātem secūtī,[88] multī nōn sōlum improbī,[89]

40 vērum[90] etiam imperītī,[91] sī in hunc animadvertissem,[92] crūdēliter[93] et rēgiē[94] factum esse[95] dīcerent. Nunc intellegō, sī iste, quō intendit,[96] in Mānliāna castra pervēnerit,[97] nēminem tam stultum fore[98] quī nōn videat coniūrātiōnem esse factam, nēminem tam improbum quī nōn fateātur.

Hōc autem ūnō interfectō, intellegō hanc reī pūblicae pestem paulīsper[99]

45 reprimī,[100] nōn in perpetuum[101] comprimī[102] posse. Quod sī[103] sē ēiēcerit,[104] sēcumque suōs[105] ēdūxerit, et eōdem[106] cēterōs undique[107] collēctōs[108] naufragōs[109] adgregārit,[110] exstinguētur[111] atque dēlēbitur nōn modo haec tam adulta[112] reī pūblicae pestis, vērum etiam stirps[113] ac sēmen[114] malōrum omnium . . . Quod sī[103] ex tantō latrōciniō[115] iste ūnus tollētur, vidēbimur fortasse ad[116] breve quoddam tempus cūrā et metū esse relevātī;[117] perīculum

50 autem residēbit[118] . . .

---

[72] **quandō,** *adv.,* at some time, at last
[73] *Manlius was in charge of Catiline's army at Fiesole.*
[74] **minus = nōn omnēs**
[75] **pūrgō** (1), cleanse
[76] **mūrus, -ī,** wall
[77] **inter-sum**
[78] **versor** (1), dwell, remain
[79] **sinō, -ere, sīvī, situm,** allow
[80] **quamquam,** *conj.,* and yet
[81] **nōn nūllī,** not none = some, several
[82] **immineō, -ēre,** overhang, threaten
[83] **dissimulō** (1), conceal
[84] **quī = et hī**
[85] **mollis, -e,** soft, weak
[86] **corrōborō** (1), strengthen; *cp. corroborate*
[87] **quōrum = et eōrum**
[88] **secūtī,** *participle going with* **multī**
[89] **improbus, -a, -um,** wicked, depraved
[90] **vērum etiam = sed etiam**
[91] **imperītus, -a, -um,** inexperienced
[92] **animadvertō, -ere, -vertī, -versum,** notice; *with* **in** + *acc.* = inflict punishment on. *This is a mixed condition of what general category?*
[93] **crūdēliter,** *adv. of* **crūdēlis**
[94] **rēgiē,** *adv.,* in the fashion of a king, tyrannically
[95] *Sc.* **id** *as subject.*
[96] **intendō, -ere, -tendī, -tēnsum,** intend; *parenthetical cl.*

[97] **per-veniō ad** *or* **in** + *acc.,* arrive at, reach; **pervēnerit** = *perf. subj. for a fut. perf. indic. in a more vivid condition. For the subj. in a subordinate cl. in ind. state., see App.*
[98] **fore = futūrus, -a, -um, esse**
[99] **paulīsper,** *adv.,* for a little while
[100] **re-primō,** press back, check
[101] **= semper**
[102] **comprimō, -ere, -pressī, -pressum,** suppress
[103] **quod sī,** but if
[104] *fut. perf. ind. What kind of condition?*
[105] **suōs (virōs)**
[106] **eōdem,** *adv.,* to the same place
[107] **undique,** *adv.,* from all sides
[108] **colligō, -ligere, -lēgī, -lēctum,** gather together
[109] **naufragus, -ī,** (shipwrecked) ruined man
[110] **adgregō** (1), gather; **adgregārit = adgregāverit**
[111] **exstinguō, -ere, -stīnxī, -stīnctum,** extinguish
[112] **adultus, -a, -um,** mature
[113] **stirps, stirpis,** *f.,* stem, stock
[114] **sēmen, -inis,** *n.,* seed
[115] **latrōcinium, -iī,** brigandage; band of brigands
[116] *here* = for
[117] **relevō** (1), relieve
[118] **re-sideō** (= **sedeō**), **-ēre, -sēdī, -sessum,** (sit down), remain

Quārē sēcēdant[119] improbī; sēcernant[120] sē ā bonīs; ūnum in locum congregentur[121]; mūrō dēnique (id quod saepe iam dīxī) sēcernantur ā nōbīs; dēsinant[122] īnsidiārī[123] domī suae[124] cōnsulī, circumstāre[125] tribūnal[126] prae-
55 tōris urbānī,[127] obsidēre[128] cum gladiīs cūriam,[129] malleolōs[130] et facēs[131] ad īnflammandam[132] urbem comparāre[133]; sit dēnique īnscrīptum[134] in fronte[135] ūnīus cuiusque quid dē rē pūblicā sentiat. Polliceor[136] hoc vōbīs, patrēs cōnscrīptī,[52] tantam in nōbīs cōnsulibus fore[98] dīligentiam,[137] tantam in vōbīs auctōritātem,[40] tantam in equitibus[138] Rōmānīs virtūtem, tantam in omnibus
60 bonīs cōnsēnsiōnem,[139] ut Catilīnae profectiōne[140] omnia patefacta, illūstrāta,[141] oppressa, vindicāta[142] esse videātis.

Hīsce[143] ōminibus,[144] Catilīna, cum summā reī pūblicae salūte,[145] cum tuā peste ac perniciē,[146] cumque eōrum exitiō quī sē tēcum omnī scelere parricīdiōque[147] iūnxērunt, proficīscere ad impium[148] bellum ac nefārium.[149]
65 Tū, Iuppiter, quī eīsdem[150] quibus haec urbs auspiciīs ā Rōmulō[151] es cōnstitūtus,[152] quem Statōrem[153] huius urbis atque imperiī vērē nōminā-mus,[154] hunc et huius sociōs ā tuīs cēterīsque templīs,[155] ā tēctīs[156] urbis ac moenibus, ā vītā fortūnīsque cīvium arcēbis,[157] et hominēs bonōrum inimī-cōs,[158] hostēs patriae, latrōnēs[159] Italiae, scelerum foedere[160] inter sē ac ne-

[119] **sē-cēdō** (sē = apart, away). *Why subj.?*
[120] **sēcernō, -ere, -crēvī, -cretum,** separate
[121] **congregō** (1), gather together
[122] **dēsinō, -ere, -sīvī, -situm,** cease
[123] **īnsidior** (1), plot against + *dat.*
[124] **domī suae,** *loc.* Catiline had tried to have Cicero assassinated.
[125] **circum-stō, -āre, -stetī,** stand around, surround
[126] **tribūnal, -ālis,** *n.*
[127] **praetor urbānus,** *judicial magistrate who had charge of civil cases between Roman citizens*
[128] **obsideō, -ere, -sēdī, -sessum,** besiege, beset
[129] **cūria, -ae,** senate house
[130] **malleolus, -ī,** firebrand
[131] **fax, facis,** *f.,* torch
[132] **īnflammō** (1), set on fire
[133] = **parāre**
[134] **in-scrībō**
[135] **frōns, frontis,** *f.,* forehead
[136] **polliceor, -ērī, -licitus sum,** promise
[137] **dīligentia, -ae**
[138] **eques, equitis,** *m.,* horseman, knight. *Here the equi-tēs are the wealthy business class in Rome.*
[139] **cōnsēnsiō, -ōnis,** *f.,* agreement, harmony
[140] **profectiō, -ōnis,** *f.,* departure; *cp.* **profiscīscor**
[141] **illūstrō** (1), bring to light
[142] **vindicō** (1), avenge, punish

[143] **hīs-ce** = **hīs** + *intensive enclitic* **-ce;** *abl. case with* **ōminibus**
[144] **ōmen, ōminis,** *n.,* omen: with these omens *or* with these words which I have uttered as omens, *abl. of attendant circumstance without* **cum.**
[145] **cum . . . salūte (peste, exitiō)** *abl. of attendant circumstance with* **cum,** *here indicating the result:* to the safety of state, to your own destruction. . . .
[146] **perniciēs, -ēī,** disaster, calamity
[147] **parricīdium, -iī,** murder
[148] **impius, -a, -um,** wicked, disloyal
[149] **nefārius, -a, -um,** infamous, nefarious
[150] **eīsdem auspiciīs quibus haec urbs (cōnstitūta est); auspicia, -ōrum,** auspices
[151] **Rōmulus, -ī,** *the founder of Rome*
[152] **cōnstituō, -ere, -stituī, -stitūtum,** establish
[153] **Stator, -ōris,** *m.,* the Stayer (of flight), the Supporter, Jupiter Stator
[154] **nōminō** (1), name, call (*cp.* **nōmen**)
[155] **templum, -ī,** temple
[156] **tēctum, -ī,** roof, house
[157] **arceō, -ēre, -uī,** ward off
[158] **inimīcus, -ī,** personal enemy; **inimīcōs, hostēs,** *etc. are in apposition with* **hominēs.**
[159] **latrō, -ōnis,** *m.,* robber, bandit
[160] **foedus, -eris,** *n.,* treaty, bond

70 fāriā societāte[161] coniūnctōs,[162] aeternīs[163] suppliciīs[164] vīvōs mortuōsque
mactābis.[165]

(**Cicero,** *In Catilīnam Ōrātiō I,* excerpts)

6. THE ARREST AND TRIAL OF THE CONSPIRATORS[1]

Rem pūblicam, Quirītēs,[2] vītamque[3] omnium vestrum, bona,[4] fortūnās,
coniugēs[5] līberōsque[6] vestrōs, atque hoc domicilium[7] clārissimī imperī, for-
tūnātissimam pulcherrimamque urbem, hodiernō[8] diē deōrum immortālium
summō ergā vōs amōre, labōribus, cōnsiliīs, perīculīs meīs, ē flammā[9] atque
5 ferrō ac paene[10] ex faucibus[11] fātī ēreptam et vōbīs cōnservātam ac restitū-
tam[12] vidētis[13] . . . Quae[14] quoniam in senātū illūstrāta, patefacta, comperta[15]
sunt per mē, vōbīs iam expōnam breviter, Quirītēs, ut[16] et[17] quanta[18] et quā
ratiōne investīgāta[19] et comprehēnsa sint, vōs, quī ignōrātis et exspectātis,
scīre possītis.

10 Prīncipiō, ut[20] Catilīna paucīs ante diēbus[21] ērūpit[22] ex urbe, cum sceleris
suī sociōs, huiusce[23] nefāriī bellī ācerrimōs ducēs, Rōmae relīquisset, semper
vigilāvī[24] et prōvīdī,[25] Quirītēs, quem ad modum[26] in tantīs et tam ab-
sconditīs[27] īnsidiīs salvī esse possēmus. Nam tum cum ex urbe Catilīnam
ēiciēbam (nōn enim iam vereor huius verbī invidiam, cum illa[28] magis[29] sit

---

[161] **societās, -tātis,** *f.,* fellowship, alliance (*cp.* **socius**)
[162] **con** (together) + **iungō: coniūnctōs** *modifies* **latrōnēs,** *etc.*
[163] **aeternus, -a, -um,** eternal
[164] **supplicium, -iī,** punishment
[165] **mactō** (1), punish, pursue. *The basic structure of the
sent. is this:* **Tū (quī . . . es cōnstitūtus, quem
. . . nōmināmus) hunc et sociōs ā templīs . . .
fortūnīsque cīvium arcebis; et hominēs (inimīcōs
. . . coniūnctōs) suppliciīs vīvōs mortuōsque
mactābis.**

6

[1] *Cicero here tells how, shortly after his first speech
against Catiline, he secured the written evidence
necessary for the trial and conviction of the conspirators.*
[2] fellow-citizens, *an old word of uncertain origin*
[3] *The Romans regularly used the sg. even when referring
to a number of people; we use the pl., "lives."*
[4] *n. pl.,* good things = goods
[5] **coniūnx, -iugis,** *f.,* wife (*cp.* **coniungō**)
[6] **līberī, -ōrum,** children
[7] **domicilium, -iī,** home (*cp.* **domus**)
[8] **hodiernus diēs,** this day, today (*cp.* **hodiē**)

[9] **flamma, -ae,** flame
[10] **paene,** *adv.,* almost
[11] **faucēs, -ium,** *f. pl.,* jaws; a narrow passage
[12] **restituō, -ere, -stituī, -stitūtum,** restore
[13] *The outline of the sent. is this:* **Rem pūblicam (. . .
urbem) amōre deōrum(. . . perīculīs meīs) ē
flammā (. . . faucibus fātī) ēreptam (. . . restitū-
tam) vidētis.**
[14] *conjunctive use of the rel.; n. nom. pl.*
[15] **comperiō, -īre, -perī, -pertum,** find out
[16] introduces **possītis**
[17] **et . . . et**
[18] *nom. n. pl., subject of* **comprehēnsa sint**
[19] **investīgō** (1), track out, investigate
[20] **ut** + *ind., here* = ever since
[21] before by a few days (*abl. of degree of difference, see
S.S.*) = a few days ago; *actually some three
weeks before*
[22] **ērumpō, -ere, -rūpī, -ruptum,** burst forth
[23] **huius** + **ce,** an intensifying suffix
[24] **vigilō** (1), watch, be vigilant
[25] **prō-videō,** foresee, make provision
[26] **quem ad modum,** how
[27] **absconditus, -a, -um,** hidden
[28] **illa (invidia)**
[29] *compar. of* **magnopere**

15   timenda, quod[30] vīvus exierit)—sed tum cum[31] illum extermināri[32] volēbam,
      aut[33] reliquam[34] coniūrātōrum manum simul[35] exitūram[36] aut eōs quī restitis-
      sent[37] īnfīrmōs sine illō ac dēbilēs[38] fore[39] putābam. Atque ego, ut vīdī, quōs
      maximō furōre et scelere esse īnflammātōs sciēbam, eōs nōbīscum esse et
      Rōmae remānsisse, in eō[40] omnēs diēs noctēsque cōnsūmpsī ut quid agerent,
20   quid mōlīrentur, sentīrem ac vidērem . . . Itaque, ut comperī lēgātōs[41] Al-
      lobrogum[42] bellī Trānsalpīnī[43] et tumultūs[44] Gallicī[45] excitandī[46] causā, ā
      P. Lentulō[47] esse sollicitātōs,[48] eōsque in Galliam[49] ad suōs cīvēs eōdemque
      itinere cum litterīs mandātīsque[50] ad Catilīnam esse missōs, comitemque[51]
      eīs adiūnctum esse[52] T. Volturcium,[53] atque huic esse ad Catilīnam datās
25   litterās, facultātem[54] mihi oblātam putāvī ut—quod[55] erat difficillimum
      quodque ego semper optābam[56] ab dīs immortālibus—tōta rēs nōn sōlum ā
      mē sed etiam ā senātū et ā vōbis manifestō[57] dēprehenderētur.[58]

      Itaque hesternō[59] diē L. Flaccum et C. Pomptīnum praetōrēs,[60] fortissi-
      mōs atque amantissimōs[61] reī pūblicae[62] virōs, ad mē vocāvī, rem exposuī,
30   quid fierī[63] placēret ostendī. Illī autem, quī omnia dē rē pūblicā praeclāra[64]
      atque ēgregia[65] sentīrent,[66] sine recūsātiōne[67] ac sine ūllā morā negōtium[68]
      suscēpērunt et, cum advesperāsceret,[69] occultē[70] ad pontem[71] Mulvium per-

---

[30] *This cl. is a noun cl. in apposition with* **illa** (**invidia**).
The perf. subj. (**exierit**) *is used in informal ind.
state. indicating what people may say:* he went out
alive (**vīvus**).

[31] **tum cum,** *mere repetition of* **tum cum** *above as Cicero
starts the sent. over again.*

[32] **exterminō** (1), banish (**ex + terminus,** boundary)

[33] **aut . . . exitūram (esse) aut . . . fore putābam**

[34] **reliquus, -a, -um,** remaining, the rest of

[35] **simul,** *adv.,* at the same time

[36] **ex-eō; exitūram (esse)**

[37] **restō, -āre, -stitī,** stay behind, remain

[38] **dēbilis, -e,** helpless, weak

[39] = **futūrōs esse**

[40] **in eō ut sentīrem et vidērem quid . . . mōlīrentur:** in
this that I might see . . . ; *the ut-cl. of purpose is
in apposition with* **eō.**

[41] **lēgātus, -ī,** ambassador

[42] **Allobrogēs, -um,** *m. pl.,* the Allobroges, *a Gallic tribe
whose ambassadors had come to Rome to make
complaints about certain Roman magistrates.*

[43] **Trānsalpīnus, -a, -um,** Transalpine

[44] **tumultus, -ūs,** *m.,* uprising

[45] **Gallicus, -a, -um,** Gallic

[46] **excitō** (1), excite, arouse

[47] *Publius Lentulus after having been consul in 71 B.C.
was removed from the Senate on grounds of moral
turpitude. He was now one of the leading conspirators and at the same time he was holding the office
of praetor.*

[48] **sollicitō** (1), stir up

[49] **Gallia, -ae,** Gaul

[50] **mandātum, -ī,** order, instruction

[51] **comes, -itis,** *m.,* companion

[52] **ad-iungō**

[53] **Titus Volturcius,** *an errand-boy for Lentulus*

[54] **facultās, -tātis,** *f.,* opportunity

[55] **quod,** a thing which. *The antecedent of* **quod** *is the
general idea in the* **ut**-*cl.*

[56] **optō** (1), desire

[57] **manifestō,** *adv.,* clearly

[58] **dēprehendō** (cp. **comprehendō**), detect, comprehend

[59] **hesternō diē,** yesterday

[60] *Though praetors were judicial magistrates, they did
possess the imperium by which they could command troops.*

[61] most loving of the state = very patriotic

[62] *obj. gen.; see App.*

[63] **fierī,** *subject of* **placēret** (it was pleasing) *used imper-
sonally*

[64] **praeclārus, -a, -um,** noble

[65] **ēgregius, -a, -um,** excellent, distinguished

[66] *subj. in a characteristic cl.*

[67] **recūsātiō, -ōnis,** *f.,* refusal

[68] **negōtium, -iī,** business, matter

[69] **advesperāscit, -ere, -perāvit,** *impers. inceptive,* it is ap-
proaching evening (*cp.* vespers)

[70] **occultē,** *adv.,* secretly

[71] **pōns, pontis,** *m.,* bridge; *the Mulvian bridge across
the Tiber near Rome*

vēnērunt atque ibi in proximīs vīllīs[72] ita bipertītō[73] fuērunt ut Tiberis[74] inter eōs et pōns interesset.[75] Eōdem[76] autem et ipsī sine cuiusquam suspīciōne[77] 35 multōs fortēs virōs ēdūxerant, et ego ex praefectūrā[78] Reātīnā[79] complūrēs[80] dēlēctōs[81] adulēscentēs, quōrum operā[82] ūtor assiduē[83] in rē pūblicā, praesidiō[84] cum gladiīs mīseram. Interim,[85] tertiā ferē[86] vigiliā[87] exāctā, cum iam pontem Mulvium magnō comitātū[88] lēgātī Allobrogum ingredī[89] inciperent ūnāque[90] Volturcius, fit in eōs impetus[91]; ēdūcuntur[92] et ab illīs gladiī et ā 40 nostrīs.[93] Rēs praetōribus erat nōta sōlīs, ignōrābātur ā cēterīs. Tum interventū[94] Pomptīnī atque Flaccī pugna[95] sēdātur.[96] Litterae, quaecumque[97] erant in eō comitātū, integrīs[98] signīs praetōribus trāduntur; ipsī, comprehēnsī, ad mē, cum iam dīlūcēsceret,[99] dēdūcuntur. Atque hōrum omnium scelerum improbissimum[100] māchinātōrem,[101] Cimbrum Gabīnium,[102] 45 statim[103] ad mē nihildum[104] suspicantem,[105] vocāvī. Deinde item[106] arcessītus est[107] L. Statilius, et post eum C. Cethēgus. Tardissimē[108] autem Lentulus vēnit . . .

Senātum frequentem[109] celeriter, ut vīdistis, coēgī. Atque intereā[110] statim admonitū[111] Allobrogum C. Sulpicium praetōrem, fortem virum, mīsī 50 quī ex aedibus[112] Cethēgī, sī quid tēlōrum[113] esset, efferret[114]; ex quibus[115] ille maximum sīcārum[116] numerum et gladiōrum extulit.[117]

Intrōdūxī[118] Volturcium sine Gallīs; fidem pūblicam[119] iussū[120] senātūs

---

[72] **vīlla, -ae,** country house
[73] **bipertītō,** *adv.,* in two divisions
[74] **Tiberis, -is,** *m.,* the Tiber
[75] **inter-sum,** be between
[76] **eōdem,** *adv.,* to the same place
[77] **suspīciō, -ōnis,** *f.,* suspicion
[78] **praefectūra, -ae,** prefecture, *a city of the Roman allies governed by a Roman prefect*
[79] **Reātīnus, -a, -um,** of Reate, *a Sabine town about forty miles from Rome.*
[80] **complūrēs, -a,** *pl. adj.,* very many
[81] **dēligō, -ere, -lēgī, -lēctum,** choose, select
[82] **opera, -ae,** help; *why abl.?*
[83] **assiduē,** *adv.,* constantly
[84] **praesidiō,** as a guard, *dat. of purpose (S.S.)*
[85] **interim,** *adv.,* meanwhile
[86] **ferē,** *adv.,* about, almost; *usually follows the word it modifies*
[87] **vigilia, -ae,** watch. *The night was divided into four watches.*
[88] **comitātus, -ūs,** company, retinue. *The abl. of accompaniment may be used without* **cum** *in military expressions.*
[89] **ingredior, -gredī, -gressus sum,** enter on
[90] and together with (them)
[91] **impetus, -ūs,** attack
[92] **ēdūcuntur . . . gladiī,** swords were drawn
[93] **nostrīs (virīs)**
[94] **interventus, -ūs,** intervention

[95] **pugna, -ae,** fight
[96] **sēdō (1),** settle, stop (*not to be confused with* **sedeō,** sit)
[97] **quīcumque, quaecumque, quodcumque,** whoever, whatever
[98] **integer, -gra, -grum,** untouched, whole
[99] **dīlūcēscit, -ere, -lūxit,** it grows light, dawn comes
[100] **improbus, -a, -um,** wicked
[101] **māchinātor, -ōris,** *m.,* contriver, plotter
[102] **Cimber Gabīnius**
[103] **statim,** *adv.,* immediately
[104] **nihil-dum,** nothing yet
[105] **suspicor (1),** suspect
[106] **item,** *adv.,* likewise
[107] **arcessō, -ere, -īvī, -ītum,** summon
[108] **tardē,** *adv.,* slowly
[109] **frequēns,** *gen.* -entis, crowded, full
[110] **intereā,** *adv.,* meanwhile
[111] **admonitus, -ūs,** warning, suggestion
[112] **aedēs, -ium,** *f. pl.,* house
[113] **tēlum, -ī,** weapon; **tēlōrum** *is gen. of whole with* **quid:** anything of weapons = any weapons
[114] *rel. cl. of purp.:* **quī** = **ut is**
[115] *Antecedent is* **aedibus.**
[116] **sīca, -ae,** dagger
[117] **efferō: ex-ferō**
[118] **intrō-dūcō** = *Eng.* introduce
[119] promise of protection in the name of the state
[120] **iussus, -ūs,** command

dedī; hortātus sum ut ea quae scīret sine timōre indicāret.[121] Tum ille dīxit,
cum vix[122] sē ex magnō timōre recreāsset,[123] ā P. Lentulō sē habēre ad Catilī-
55 nam mandāta et litterās ut servōrum praesidiō ūterētur,[124] ut ad urbem quam
prīmum[125] cum exercitū accēderet; id[126] autem eō cōnsiliō ut,[127] cum urbem
ex[128] omnibus partibus, quem ad modum[129] discrīptum distribūtumque
erat,[130] incendissent[131] caedemque[132] īnfīnītam[133] cīvium fēcissent, praestō[134]
esset ille[135] quī et fugientēs exciperet[136] et sē cum hīs urbānīs ducibus con-
60 iungeret.[137]

Intrōductī autem Gallī iūs iūrandum[138] sibi et litterās ab Lentulō, Cethēgō, Statiliō ad suam gentem datās esse dīxērunt atque ita sibi ab hīs et ā
L. Cassiō esse praescrīptum[139] ut equitātum[140] in Italiam quam prīmum mitterent[141] . . .

65 Ac nē longum sit,[142] Quirītēs, tabellās[143] prōferrī[144] iussimus quae ā quōque dīcēbantur datae.[145] Prīmum ostendimus Cethēgō signum; cognōvit.
Nōs līnum[146] incīdimus[147]; lēgimus. Erat scrīptum ipsīus[148] manū Allobrogum
senātuī et populō sēsē[149] quae eōrum lēgātīs cōnfīrmāsset[150] factūrum esse;
ōrāre ut item illī facerent quae sibi eōrum lēgātī recēpissent. Tum Cethēgus
70 (quī paulō[151] ante aliquid tamen dē gladiīs ac sīcīs, quae apud ipsum erant

---

[121] **indīcō** (1), indicate, make known
[122] **vix**, *adv.*, hardly
[123] *The perf. endings in* **-āvi-, -ēvi-, -ōvi-** *often contract to* **-ā-, -ē-, -ō-,** *respectively. So here* **recreāvisset** *has contracted to* **recreāsset**. *Perfs. in* **-īvi-** *may lose the* **v** *but the two resultant vowels rarely contract to* **ī** *except before* **ss** *and* **st: audīverat, audierat; audīvisse, audīsse; quaesīssent**
[124] *jussive noun cl. with* **mandāta et litterās**
[125] **quam prīmum,** as soon as possible
[126] (that he should do) this (**id**) with this plan (in mind) that . . .
[127] *The rest of the sentence can be outlined thus:* **ut (cum . . . partibus [quem ad modum . . . distribūtum erat] incendissent et . . . fēcissent) praestō esset ille (quī et . . . exciperet et . . . coniungeret)**
[128] *here* in
[129] **quem ad modum,** as
[130] *impers. pass. vbs.:* as had been marked out and as-signed
[131] **incendō, -ere, -cendī, -cēnsum,** set fire to
[132] **caedēs, -is,** *f.,* slaughter
[133] **īnfīnītus, -a, -um,** unlimited
[134] **praestō,** *adv.,* on hand, ready
[135] **ille** = Catiline
[136] **ex-cipiō,** pick up, capture
[137] **con + iungō.** *Why are* **exciperet** *and* **coniungeret** *in the subj.?*
[138] **iūs, iūrandum, iūris iūrandī,** *n.,* oath

[139] **prae-scrībō,** order, direct; **esse praescrīptum,** *impers. pass.* (it had been commanded to themselves, **sibi**) *but translate as personal:* they had been di-rected.
[140] **equitātus, -ūs,** cavalry
[141] *jussive noun cl. depending on* **esse praescrīptum**
[142] to be brief
[143] **tabella, -ae,** tablet: *very shallow trays, not unlike the modern slate, filled with wax on which writing was done with a sharp-pointed stilus. Two of these closed face to face, tied together with a string, and sealed with wax and the impression of a signet ring, were the equivalent of a modern letter in an en-velope.*
[144] **prō-ferō**
[145] **datae** (esse); **datae** *is nom. f. pl. to agree with* **quae** (tabellae), *the subject of* **dīcēbantur.**
[146] **līnum, -ī,** string
[147] **incīdō, -ere, -cīdī, -cīsum,** cut
[148] (**Cethēgī**) **ipsīus:** *emphatic because letters were often written by an amanuensis, a slave to whom the let-ter was dictated.*
[149] **sēsē** = **sē** (*i.e., Cethegus*), *subject of* **factūrum esse** *and also of* **ōrāre**
[150] **cōnfīrmō** (1), assert, declare; *subj. in ind. state. (see S.S.)*
[151] a little before (before by a little), *abl. of degree of difference (see S.S.)*

dēprehēnsa,[152] respondisset dīxissetque[153] sē semper bonōrum ferrāmen-
tōrum[154] studiōsum[155] fuisse) recitātīs litterīs dēbilitātus[156] atque abiectus[157]
cōnscientiā,[158] repente conticuit.[159]

Intrōductus est Statilius; cognōvit et signum et manum suam. Recitātae
75 sunt tabellae in eandem ferē sententiam; cōnfessus est.

Tum ostendī tabellās Lentulō, et quaesīvī cognōsceretne signum. Ad-
nuit[160] . . . Leguntur eādem ratiōne ad senātum Allobrogum populumque
litterae. Sī quid dē hīs rēbus dīcere vellet,[161] fēcī potestātem.[162] Atque ille
prīmō quidem negāvit. Post[163] autem aliquantō,[164] tōtō iam indiciō[165]
80 expositō atque ēditō,[166] surrēxit; quaesīvit ā Gallīs quid sibi esset cum eīs,
quam ob rem[167] domum suam vēnissent, itemque ā Volturciō. Quī cum illī
breviter cōnstanterque[168] respondissent per quem ad eum quotiēnsque[169]
vēnissent, quaesīssentque[170] ab eō nihilne sēcum[171] esset dē fātīs Sibyllīnīs[172]
locūtus, tum ille subitō, scelere dēmēns,[173] quanta cōnscientiae vīs esset os-
85 tendit. Nam cum id posset īnfitiārī,[174] repente praeter opīniōnem[175] omnium
cōnfessus est . . .

Gabīnius deinde intrōductus, cum prīmō impudenter[176] respondēre coepisset, ad extrēmum[177] nihil ex eīs[178] quae Gallī īnsimulābant[179] negāvit.

Ac mihi[180] quidem, Quirītēs, cum[181] illa[182] certissima vīsa sunt argūmenta
90 atque indicia sceleris, tabellae, signa, manūs, dēnique ūnīus cuiusque cōnfessiō,[183] tum multō[184] certiōra illa, color,[185] oculī, vultūs, taciturnitās.[186] Sīc

---

[152] **dēprehendō, -ere, -hendī, -hēnsum,** seize

[153] **respondisset dīxissetque,** *subjs. in rel. cl. of charac-teristic, which have the force of a concessive cl.* (= *although*)

[154] **ferrāmentum, -ī,** weapon

[155] **studiōsus, -a, -um,** fond of (*i.e., he was a collector.*)

[156] **dēbilitō** (1), weaken

[157] **abiectus, -a, -um,** downcast

[158] **cōnscientia, -ae,** knowledge, conscience

[159] **conticēscō, -ere, -ticuī,** become silent

[160] **adnuō, -ere, -nuī,** nod assent

[161] **vellet,** *subj. because it is a subordinate cl. in an im-plied ind. state. for Cicero's original words:* **sī quid . . . dīcere vīs**

[162] **potestās, -tātis,** *f.,* power, opportunity

[163] = **posteā**

[164] **aliquantō,** *abl. of degree of difference* (by somewhat) *equivalent to an adv.:* somewhat, a little

[165] **indicium, -iī,** evidence, information

[166] **ē-dō, -ere, -didī, -ditum,** give forth, publish

[167] **quam ob rem** = **quārē**

[168] **constanter,** *adv.,* consistently, steadily

[169] **quotiēns,** *adv.,* how often

[170] *contracted form, n. 122 above*

[171] **sēcum:** *an ind. reflexive referring to the subject of*

quaesīssent; *translate* to them.

[172] **fāta Sibyllīna,** *a collection of ancient prophecies for which the Romans had very high respect. By these Lentulus had sought to prove to the Allobroges that he was destined to hold the regnum and imperium at Rome.*

[173] **dē-mēns,** *gen.* **-mentis,** out of one's mind

[174] **īnfitior** (1), deny

[175] **opīniō, -ōnis,** *f.,* expectation

[176] **impudenter,** *adv.,* impudently

[177] **ad extrēmum,** at the last, finally

[178] **eīs** = *n. pl.,* those things

[179] **īnsimulō** (1), charge

[180] *depends on* **vīsa sunt**

[181] **cum . . . tum,** not only . . . but also (*cp.* **nōn sōlum . . . sed etiam**)

[182] **illa argūmenta atque indicia** (*i.e.,* tabellae . . . con-fessiō) **certissima vīsa sunt**

[183] **cōnfessiō, -ōnis,** *f.* = *Eng.*

[184] *lit.* more certain by much. *What kind of abl. is* **multō?** (*see S.S.*)

[185] **color . . . taciturnitās,** *in apposition with* **illa,** *which is nom. n. pl.* **color, -ōris,** *m.,* = *Eng.*

[186] **taciturnitās, -tātis,** *f.,* silence (*cp.* taciturn)

enim obstupuerant,[187] sīc terram intuēbantur,[188] sīc fūrtim nōn numquam
inter sēsē aspiciēbant ut nōn iam ab aliīs indicārī[189] sed indicāre sē ipsī vidērentur.

95   Indiciīs expositīs atque ēditīs, Quirītēs, senātum cōnsuluī[190] dē summā
rē pūblicā[191] quid fierī placēret. Dictae sunt ā prīncipibus ācerrimae ac fortissimae sententiae, quās senātus sine ūllā varietāte[192] est secūtus . . .

         Quibus prō tantīs rēbus, Quirītēs, nūllum ego ā vōbīs praemium virtūtis,
nūllum īnsigne[193] honōris, nūllum monumentum laudis postulō[194] praeter-
100 quam[195] huius diēī memoriam sempiternam[196] . . .

         Vōs, Quirītēs, quoniam iam est nox, venerātī[197] Iovem illum custōdem
huius urbis ac vestrum, in vestra tēcta[198] discēdite; et ea, quamquam[199] iam
est perīculum dēpulsum,[200] tamen aequē ac[201] priōre nocte custōdiīs
vigiliīsque dēfendite. Id nē vōbīs diūtius faciendum sit atque ut in perpetuā
105 pāce esse possītis prōvidēbō. (**Cicero,** *In Catilīnam Ōrātiō III,* excerpts)

DĒ VĪTĀ ET MORTE (7–9)

7. SOCRATES' "EITHER-OR" BELIEF[1]

         Quae est igitur eius ōrātiō quā[2] facit eum Platō ūsum apud iūdicēs iam
morte multātum[3]?

         "Magna mē," inquit "spēs tenet iūdicēs, bene mihi ēvenīre[4] quod mittar[5]
ad mortem. Necesse[6] est enim sit[7] alterum dē duōbus, ut aut[8] sēnsūs omnīnō
5   omnēs mors auferat aut in alium quendam locum ex hīs locīs morte mi-
grētur.[9] Quam ob rem,[10] sīve[11] sēnsus exstinguitur morsque eī somnō similis
est quī nōn numquam etiam sine vīsīs[12] somniōrum[13] plācātissimam[14] quiē-

---

[187] **obstupēscō, -ere, -stupuī,** become stupefied, be
    thunderstruck
[188] **intueor, -ērī, -tuitus sum,** look at
[189] **indicō** (1), accuse (*cp.* **indicium,** *n. 165 above*)
[190] **cōnsulō, -ere, -suluī, -sultum,** consult, ask advice of
[191] highest interest of the state
[192] **varietās, -tātis,** *f.,* variation
[193] **īnsigne, -is,** *n.,* sign, symbol
[194] **postulō** (1), request, demand
[195] except
[196] **sempiternus, -a, -um,** eternal
[197] **veneror** (1), worship
[198] **tēctum, -ī,** roof; house
[199] **quamquam,** *conj.,* although
[200] **dēpellō,** drive off, avert
[201] equally as = just as

7

[1] *As part of his demonstration that death is not an evil,*
Cicero cites Socrates' views as given in Plato's

"Apology," Socrates' defense of his life before the
jury that finally condemned him to death.
[2] **quā . . . ūsum,** which Plato represents him as using;
    quā, *abl. with the participle* **ūsum**
[3] **multō,** (1), punish, sentence
[4] **ē-veniō,** turn out; *impers. inf. in ind. state.*
[5] *subordinate cl. in ind. state.*
[6] **necesse,** *indecl. adj.,* (it is) necessary
[7] *Supply* **ut** *before* **sit:** that there be one of two possi-
    bilities, *with the* **ut . . . migrētur** *cl. in apposition*
    with **duōbus**
[8] **aut . . . aut**
[9] **migrō** (1), depart, migrate; **migrātur** *as impers. pass.,*
    one departs
[10] = **quārē**
[11] = **sī**
[12] **vīsum, -ī,** vision
[13] **somnium, -iī,** dream
[14] **plācātus, -a, -um,** peaceful

tem adfert, dī bonī, quid lucrī est ēmorī[15]! Aut quam multī diēs reperīrī possunt quī tālī noctī antepōnantur? Cui sī similis futūra est[16] perpetuitās[17]
10   omnis cōnsequentis[18] temporis, quis[19] mē beātior?

"Sin[20] vēra[21] sunt quae dīcuntur, migrātiōnem[22] esse mortem in eās ōrās[23] quās quī[24] ē vītā excessērunt[25] incolunt,[26] id multō[27] iam beātius est . . . Haec peregrīnātiō[28] mediocris vōbīs vidērī potest? Ut vērō colloquī[29] cum Orpheō, Mūsaeō,[30] Homērō, Hēsiodō[31] liceat, quantī[32] tandem aestimātis[33]? . . . Nec
15   enim cuiquam[34] bonō malī[35] quicquam ēvenīre potest nec vīvō nec mortuō[36] . . .

"Sed tempus est iam hinc[37] abīre mē, ut moriar, vōs, ut vītam agātis. Utrum autem sit melius, dī immortālēs sciunt; hominem quidem scīre arbitror nēminem."[38] (**Cicero,** *Tusculānae Disputātiōnēs* 1.40.97–1.41.99, excerpts)

8. A MORE POSITIVE VIEW ABOUT IMMORTALITY[1]

Artior[2] quam solēbāt[3] somnus (mē) complexus est[4] . . . (et) Āfricānus sē ostendit eā fōrmā[5] quae mihi ex imāgine[6] eius quam ex ipsō erat nōtior.[7] Quem ubi agnōvī,[8] equidem cohorruī[9], . . . quaesīvī tamen vīveretne ipse et Paulus[10] pater et aliī quōs nōs exstīnctōs[11] arbitrārēmur.

5   "Immō vērō," inquit, "hī vīvunt quī ē corporum vinclīs tamquam ē car-

---

[15] **ē-morior,** die (off)
[16] **futūra est,** is going to be
[17] **perpetuitās, -tātis,** *f.,* perpetuity
[18] **cōn-sequor**
[19] **quis (est)**
[20] **sīn,** *conj.,* but if
[21] **(ea) sunt vēra**
[22] **migrātiō, -ōnis,** *f.,* the noun of **migrō,** *n. 9 above*
[23] **ōra, -ae,** shore, region
[24] **(eī) quī**
[25] **ex-cēdō** = **discēdō**
[26] **incolō, -ere, -uī,** inhabit
[27] *abl. of degree of difference (S.S.)*
[28] **peregrīnātiō, -ōnis,** *f.,* travel abroad
[29] **col-loquor,** talk with, converse (*cp.* colloquial)
[30] *Orpheus and Musaeus were famous poets and musicians before the time of Homer*
[31] *Hesiod, a Greek epic poet chronologically next after Homer.*
[32] **quantī (pretiī),** of how much (value), *gen. of indef. value.* **quantī . . . aestimātis,** how valuable, pray, do you estimate this is?
[33] **aestimō** (1), estimate, value
[34] **quisquam, quidquam (quicquam),** anyone, anything; **cuiquam** *modified by* **bonō:** to any good man
[35] **malī** (*gen.*) *depends on* **quicquam:** anything of evil =

any evil
[36] **vīvō** *and* **mortuō** *modify* **cuiquam bonō.**
[37] **hinc,** *adv.,* from this place
[38] **hominem . . . nēminem,** no man

8

[1] *In these excerpts Scipio Africanus Minor (the Younger, hero of the Third Punic War in 146 B.C.) tells how the deceased Scipio Africanus Maior (the Elder, hero of the Second Punic War who defeated Hannibal in 202 B.C.) appeared to him in a dream and discoursed on the nature of life here and hereafter.*
[2] **artus, -a, -um,** deep (sleep); narrow
[3] **solēbat (esse)**
[4] **complector, -ī, -plexus sum,** embrace
[5] *abl. of description*
[6] **imāgō, -inis,** *f.,* image; *here* = portrait mask of an ancestor. *The* **imāginēs** *of a Roman patrician's ancestors were displayed in the atrium of the house.*
[7] **nōtus, -a, -um,** known, familiar
[8] **agnōscō** (*cp.* **cognōscō**), recognize
[9] **cohorrēscō, -ere, -horruī,** shudder
[10] **L. Aemilius Paulus,** *father of Africanus Minor*
[11] **exstīnctōs (esse): exstinguō**

cere[12] ēvolāvērunt[13]; vestra vērō quae dīcitur vīta mors est. Quīn[14] tū aspicis ad tē venientem Paulum patrem?"

Quem ut vīdī, equidem vim[15] lacrimārum prōfūdī. Ille autem mē complexus[4] atque ōsculāns[16] flēre[17] prohibēbat. Atque ego ut prīmum[18] flētū[19]
10   repressō[20] loquī posse coepī, "Quaesō,[21]" inquam, "pater sānctissime[22] atque optime, quoniam haec est vīta, ut Āfricānum audiō dīcere, quid moror[23] in terrīs? Quīn[24] hūc[25] ad vōs venīre properō[26]?

"Nōn est ita,[27]" inquit ille. "Nisi enim deus is,[28] cuius hoc templum[29] est omne quod cōnspicis,[30] istīs tē corporis custōdiīs līberāverit, hūc tibi aditus[31]
15   patēre nōn potest. Hominēs enim sunt hāc lēge[32] generātī,[33] quī tuērentur[34] illum globum[35] quem in hōc templō medium vidēs, quae terra dīcitur, iīsque[36] animus datus est ex illīs sempiternīs ignibus quae sīdera et stēllās vocātis . . . Quārē et tibi, Pūblī,[37] et piīs omnibus retinendus[38] est animus in custōdiā corporis, nec iniussū[39] eius ā quō ille[40] est vōbīs datus ex hominum vītā mi-
20   grandum est, nē mūnus[41] hūmānum adsignātum[42] ā deō dēfūgisse[43] videā-minī . . . Iūstitiam[44] cole[45] et pietātem,[46] quae cum sit magna[47] in parentibus et propinquīs,[48] tum[49] in patriā maxima est. Ea vīta via est in caelum et in hunc coetum[50] eōrum quī iam vīxērunt et corpore laxātī[51] illum incolunt locum . . . quem vōs, ut ā Graīs accēpistis, orbem lacteum,[52] nuncupātis.[53]"
. . .

---

[12] **carcer, -eris,** *n.,* prison
[13] **ē-volō** (1), fly away; *not to be confused with* **volō, velle**
[14] **quīn aspicis:** why, don't you see?
[15] **vim** = **cōpiam**
[16] **ōsculor** (1), kiss
[17] **fleō, -ēre, flēvī, flētum,** weep
[18] **ut prīmum,** as soon as
[19] **flētus, -ūs,** *noun of* **fleō,** *n. 17 above*
[20] **re-primō** (**premō**)
[21] **quaesō, -ere,** *commonly exclamatory:* I beg you!, pray tell!, please
[22] **sānctus, -a, -um,** holy
[23] **moror** (1), delay, wait
[24] why not?
[25] **hūc,** *adv.,* to this place, here
[26] **properō** (1), hasten
[27] = that is not the way
[28] *order* = **is deus**
[29] **templum, -ī,** sacred area, temple
[30] **cuius . . . cōnspicis:** whose this temple is *or* to whom belongs this temple—everything which you behold. *Apparently, as he says* **hoc templum,** *he makes a sweeping gesture with his arm to indicate the universe and then adds* **omne quod cōnspicis** *to make this even clearer.* **cōnspiciō** = **aspiciō**
[31] **aditus, -ūs,** approach, entrance
[32] *abl. of accordance:* in accordance with this law, on this condition

[33] **generō** (1), create
[34] **tueor, -ērī, tūtus sum,** watch, protect. *Why subj.?*
[35] **globus, -ī,** sphere, globe
[36] *i.e.,* **hominibus**
[37] **Pūblius,** praenomen (*first name*) *of Africanus Minor*
[38] **re-tineō,** retain, preserve
[39] **iniussū,** *abl. as adv.,* without the command (of); *cp.* **iussū**
[40] **ille** (**animus**)
[41] **mūnus, -eris,** *n.,* duty, service
[42] **adsignō** (1), assign
[43] **dē-fugiō,** flee from, avoid
[44] **iūstitia, -ae,** justice (*cp.* **iūstus**)
[45] **colō, -ere, -uī, cultum,** cultivate, cherish
[46] **pietās, -tātis,** *f.,* loyalty, devotion
[47] important
[48] **propinquus, -ī,** relative
[49] *here* = surely
[50] **coetus, -ūs,** gathering, company
[51] **laxō** (1), set free
[52] **orbis** (**-is**) **lacteus** (**-ī**), *m.,* the Milky Way (orb), *which Cicero here says is a term received from the Greeks* (**ut ā Graīs,** *i.e.* **Graecīs, accēpistis**), *who called it* **galaxias kyklos** (= **lacteus orbis**); *cp. our word* galaxy.
[53] **nuncupō** (1) = **appellō**

25   Et ille, "Tū vērō . . . sīc habētō[54] nōn esse tē mortālem, sed corpus hoc[55]; nec enim tuīs[56] es quem fōrma ista dēclārat,[57] sed mēns cuiusque is est quisque, nōn ea figūra[58] quae digitō dēmōnstrārī potest. Deum tē igitur scītō[59] esse; sīquidem[60] deus est quī viget,[61] quī sentit, quī meminit,[62] quī prōvidet, quī tam regit et moderātur[63] et movet id corpus cui praepositus

30   est[64] quam[65] hunc mundum ille prīnceps deus."[66] (**Cicero,** excerpts from *Somnium Scīpiōnis* 2ff. = *Dē Rē Pūblicā* 6.10 ff.*)

9. ON CONTEMPT OF DEATH[1]

Sed quid[2] ducēs et prīncipēs nōminem[3] cum legiōnēs[4] scrībat Catō[5] saepe alacrēs[6] in eum locum profectās[7] unde reditūrās sē nōn arbitrārentur? Parī animō Lacedaemoniī[8] in Thermopylīs[9] occidērunt, in quōs[10] Simōnidēs:

Dīc, hospes,[11] Spartae[12] nōs tē[13] hīc vīdisse iacentīs,[14]

5   dum sānctīs patriae lēgibus obsequimur.[15]

Virōs commemorō.[16] Quālis[17] tandem Lacaena? Quae, cum fīlium in proelium mīsisset et interfectum[18] audīsset, "Idcircō,[19]" inquit, "genueram[20] ut esset quī[21] prō patriā mortem nōn dubitāret occumbere.[22]"

. . . Admoneor[23] ut aliquid etiam dē humātiōne[24] et sepultūrā[25] dīcen-

10   dum[26] exīstimem[27] . . . Sōcratēs, rogātus ā Critōne[28] quem ad modum sepelīrī[29] vellet, "Multam vērō," inquit, "operam,[30] amīcī, frūstrā[31] cōnsūmpsī.

---

[54] **habētō,** *fut. imper.,* you shall consider; consider
[55] **sc. esse mortāle**
[56] **tuīs,** to your (friends), *dat. depending on* **dēclārat**
[57] **dēclārō** (1) = *Eng.*
[58] = **fōrma**
[59] **scītō,** *another fut. imper.,* you shall know; know
[60] **sīquidem,** *conj.,* since
[61] **vigeō -ēre, -uī** be strong, be active
[62] **meminī, meminisse,** *defective, found only in perf. system,* remember
[63] **moderor** (1), control
[64] **prae-pōnō,** put in charge of
[65] as
[66] *From the preceding cl. sc.* **regit,** *etc. as vbs.*

9

[1] *If death is such a great evil, how can the following attitudes be explained?*
[2] **quid,** *as adv.,* why? (= **cūr**?)
[3] **nōminō** (1), name, mention (*cp.* **nōmen**)
[4] **legiō, -ōnis,** *f.,* legion
[5] **Catō, -ōnis,** *m.,* Cato, *the famous censor, who wrote a now-lost history of Rome called the Origines.*
[6] **alacer, -cris, -cre,** eager, happy. *We should use an adv. instead of a predicate adj.:* eagerly
[7] **profectās** (**esse**); **reditūrās** (**esse**)

[8] **Lacedaemoniī, -ōrum,** *m.,* Spartans
[9] **Thermopylae, -ārum;** *480* B.C.
[10] on whom Simonides (wrote); *Simonides a sixth-century Greek poet famous especially for his poems and epigrams in the elegiac couplet.*
[11] **hospes, -itis,** *m.,* stranger
[12] **Sparta, -ae,** *f.,* **Spartae,** *dat. depending on* **dīc**
[13] **tē vīdisse nōs**
[14] = **iacentēs**
[15] **ob-sequor** + *dat.,* obey
[16] **commemorō** (1), call to mind mention (*cp.* **memoria**)
[17] What kind of person, then, was the Spartan woman? **quālis, -e,** what kind of
[18] (**eum**) **interfectum** (**esse**)
[19] **idcircō,** *adv.,* for that reason
[20] **gignō, -ere, genuī, genitum,** beget (*cp.* generate), bear
[21] (the kind of person) who
[22] **occumbō, -ere, -cubuī, -cubitum,** meet
[23] **ad-moneō** = **moneō,** remind
[24] **humātiō, -ōnis,** *f.* burial (*cp.* **humus,** earth)
[25] **sepultūra, -ae,** funeral (*cp.* sepulchre)
[26] **dīcendum** (**esse**)
[27] **exīstimō** (1), think
[28] **Critō, -ōnis,** *m.,* Crito, *a friend of Socrates*
[29] **sepeliō, -īre, -īvī, -pultum,** bury
[30] **opera, -ae,** effort, pains
[31] **frūstrā,** *adv.,* in vain (*cp.* frustrate)

Critōnī enim nostrō nōn persuāsī mē hinc āvolātūrum,[32] neque meī[33] quicquam relictūrum[34] . . . Sed, mihi crēde, (Critō), nēmō mē vestrum,[35] cum hinc excesserō,[36] cōnsequētur.[37] . . .

15   Dūrior Diogenēs[38] Cynicus prōicī[39] sē iussit inhumātum.[40] Tum amīcī, "Volucribusne[41] et ferīs[42]?" "Minimē[43] vērō," inquit; "sed bacillum[44] propter[45] mē, quō abigam,[46] pōnitōte.[47]" "Quī[48] poteris?" illī; "nōn enim sentiēs." "Quid igitur mihi ferārum laniātus[49] oberit[50] nihil sentientī[51]?" (**Cicero**, *Tusculānae Disputātiōnēs* 1.42.101–43.104, excerpts)

10. LITERATURE: ITS VALUE AND DELIGHT[1]

Quaerēs ā nōbīs, Grattī, cūr tantō opere[2] hōc homine dēlectēmur.[3] Quia[4] suppeditat[5] nōbīs ubi[6] et animus ex hōc forēnsī[7] strepitū[8] reficiātur[9] et aurēs convīciō[10] dēfessae[11] conquiēscant[12] . . . Quārē quis tandem mē reprehendat,[13] aut quis mihi iūre[14] suscēnseat,[15] sī,[16] quantum[17] cēterīs ad suās rēs 5   obeundās[18] quantum ad fēstōs[19] diēs lūdōrum celebrandōs,[20] quantum ad

---

[32] **ā-volō** (1); **avolātūrum** (**esse**), *inf. in ind. state. with* **persuāsī**

[33] **meī,** *gen. of* **ego,** *depending on* **quicquam.**

[34] **relictūrum** (**esse**)

[35] *gen. of* **vōs**

[36] **ex-cēdō,** *cp.* **discēdō**

[37] **cōnsequor, -ī, -secūtus sum,** overtake, catch

[38] *Diogenes, the Cynic philosopher, famed for his asceticism and independence*

[39] **prō-iciō** (**iaciō**), throw out

[40] **inhumātus, -a, -um,** unburied

[41] **volucris, -is,** *f.,* bird

[42] **fera, -ae,** wild beast; *dat. with* **prōicī** *understood*

[43] **minimē,** *adv.,* no, not at all

[44] **bacillum, -ī,** staff (*cp.* **bacillus,** *a New Latin form*)

[45] *here* = near

[46] **abigō, -ere, -ēgī, -āctum,** drive away; *sc.* **volucrēs et ferās.** *Why subj.?*

[47] *fut. imperative* = you shall put

[48] **quī,** *adv.,* how?

[49] **laniātus, -ūs,** lacerating

[50] **obsum, -esse, -fuī, -futūrus,** be against, hurt. *Why does* **oberit** *have the dat.* **mihi***?*

[51] **sentientī** *modifies* **mihi** *and has* **nihil** *as its obj.*

10

[1] *In the course of a speech defending the citizenship of the poet Archias against the charges of a certain Grattius, Cicero pronounced one of the world's finest encomiums on the inestimable value and delight of literature.*

[2] **tantō opere,** so greatly (*cp.* **magnopere**)

[3] **homine,** *the poet Archias.*

[4] **quia,** *conj.,* because

[5] **suppeditō** (1), supply

[6] the means by which

[7] **forēnsis, -e,** of the forum. *By Cicero's time the Forum was primarily the political and legal center of Rome.*

[8] **strepitus, -ūs,** din

[9] **re-ficiō,** refresh, revive

[10] **convīcium, -ī,** wrangling

[11] **dēfessus, -a, -um,** exhausted

[12] **conquiēscō, -ere, -quiēvī, -quiētum,** find rest

[13] **reprehendō, -ere, -hendī, -hēnsum,** censure; **reprehendat,** *deliberative, or dubitative, subj. The deliberative subj. is used in questions implying doubt, indignation, or impossibility.* **Quis mē reprehendat:** who is to blame me (I wonder)?

[14] **iūre** = **cum iūre,** *abl. of manner that has virtually become an adv.:* rightly

[15] **suscēnseō, -ēre, -uī,** be incensed, + *dat.*

[16] **sī** *introduces* **sūmpserō.** *The only real difficulty with this complex cl. is the involvement of the* **quantum** *cls. Although these cls. should be read and understood in the order in which they stand, the following outline may prove a welcome guide.* **Quis mē reprehendat . . . sī ego tantum temporum ad haec studia sūmpserō quantum temporum cēterīs ad suās rēs (fēstōs diēs, voluptātēs,** *etc.***) concēditur, quantum temporum aliī tribuunt convīviīs (alveolō pilae)?**

[17] **quantum** (**temporum**)

[18] **ob-eō,** attend to

[19] **fēstus, -a, -um,** festive

[20] **celebrō** (1), celebrate

aliās voluptātēs et ad ipsam requiem[21] animī et corporis concēditur[22] temporum, quantum aliī tribuunt[23] tempestīvīs[24] convīviīs,[25] quantum dēnique alveolō,[26] quantum pilae,[27] tantum[28] mihi egomet[29] ad haec studia recolenda[30] sūmpserō[31]? Atque hoc ideō[32] mihi concēdendum est magis quod ex
10 hīs studiīs haec quoque crēscit ōrātiō et facultās,[33] quae, quantacumque[34] est in mē, numquam amīcōrum perīculīs dēfuit[35] . . .

Plēnī omnēs sunt librī, plēnae sapientium vōcēs, plēna exemplōrum[36] vetustās[37]; quae iacērent in tenebrīs[38] omnia, nisi litterārum lūmen[39] accēderet. Quam multās nōbīs imāginēs[40]—nōn sōlum ad intuendum,[41]
15 vērum[42] etiam ad imitandum[43]—fortissimōrum virōrum expressās[44] scrīptōrēs et Graecī et Latīnī reliquērunt! Quās ego mihi semper in administrandā[45] rē pūblicā prōpōnēns[46] animum et mentem meam ipsā cōgitātiōne[47] hominum excellentium[48] cōnfōrmābam.[49]

Quaeret quispiam,[50] "Quid? illī ipsī summī virī quōrum virtūtēs litterīs
20 prōditae sunt,[51] istāne doctrīnā[52] quam tū effers[53] laudibus ērudītī fuērunt[54]?" Difficile est hoc dē omnibus cōnfīrmāre,[55] sed tamen est certum quid respondeam . . . : saepius ad laudem atque virtūtem nātūram sine doctrīnā quam sine nātūrā valuisse[56] doctrīnam. Atque īdem[57] ego contendō,[58] cum ad nātūram eximiam[59] et illūstrem[60] accesserit[61] ratiō quaedam cōnfōrmātiōque[62]
25 doctrīnae, tum illud nesciō quid[63] praeclārum ac singulāre[64] solēre exsistere[65] . . .

---

[21] **requiēs, -ētis,** *acc.* **requiētem** *or* **requiem,** rest
[22] **concēdō,** grant, concede
[23] **tribuō, -ere, -uī, -ūtum,** allot
[24] **tempestīvus, -a, -um,** timely; here = early, *beginning in the afternoon so as to be conveniently prolonged.*
[25] **convīvium, -iī,** banquet
[26] **alveolus, -ī,** gaming board
[27] **pila, -ae,** ball (*cp.* pill)
[28] **tantum (temporum) . . . quantum,** as much . . . as
[29] **ego-met,** *an emphatic form of* **ego**
[30] **re-colō, -ere, -uī, -cultum,** renew
[31] **sūmō, -ere, sūmpsī, sūmptum,** take
[32] **ideō,** *adv.,* for this reason, therefore
[33] **facultās, -tātis,** *f.,* skill. *Combine with* **ōrātiō** *and translate:* this oratorical skill.
[34] **quantuscumque, -acumque, -umcumque,** however great
[35] **dē-sum,** be lacking
[36] **exemplum, -ī,** example; **exemplōrum** *also goes with* **plēnī** *and* **plēnae.**
[37] **vetustās, -tātis,** *f.,* antiquity
[38] **tenebrae, -ārum,** darkness
[39] **lūmen, -inis,** *n.,* light
[40] **imāgō, -ginis,** *f.,* portrait, picture
[41] **intueor,** gaze on, contemplate
[42] **vērum,** *conj.,* but
[43] **imitor** (1), imitate

[44] **ex-primō (premō),** describe, portray
[45] **administrō** (1), manage
[46] **prō-pōnō,** put forward, set before; **prōpōnēns** *has* **quās** *as direct obj. and* **mihi** *as indirect obj.*
[47] **cōgitātiō, -ōnis,** *f.,* thought; *cp.* **cōgitō**
[48] **excellēns,** *gen.* **-entis,** superior, remarkable
[49] **cōnfōrmō** (1), mold
[50] **quispiam, quaepiam, quidpiam,** someone
[51] **prōdō, -ere, -didī, -ditum,** transmit, reveal
[52] **doctrīna, -ae,** instruction
[53] **efferō, -ferre, extulī, ēlātum,** lift up, extol
[54] **ērudiō** (4), educate, train
[55] **cōnfīrmō** (1), assert
[56] **valuisse ad laudem,** to be powerful toward praise = to have led to praise; *inf. in ind. state.*
[57] **idem ego,** I the same person = I also
[58] maintain
[59] **eximius, -a, -um,** extraordinary
[60] **illustris, -e,** noble, brilliant
[61] **accēdō** *here* = be added
[62] **cōnfōrmātiō, -ōnis,** *f.,* molding, shaping
[63] **nesciō quis, nesciō quid,** *indef. pron., lit.* I know not who/what = some (uncertain) person *or* thing; *the* **nesciō** *remains unchanged in this phrase.*
[64] **singulāris, -e,** unique, extraordinary
[65] **exsistō, -ere, -stitī,** arise, appear, exist

Quod sī nōn hic tantus frūctus ostenderētur, et sī ex hīs studiīs dēlectātiō sōla peterētur, tamen, ut opīnor, hanc animī remissiōnem hūmānissimam ac līberālissimam iūdicārētis. Nam cēterae[66] neque temporum[67] sunt neque
30   aetātum omnium neque locōrum; at haec studia adulēscentiam alunt, senectūtem oblectant, rēs secundās ōrnant, adversīs perfugium ac sōlācium praebent, dēlectant domī, nōn impediunt forīs, pernoctant nōbīscum, peregrīnantur, rūsticantur. (**Cicero,** *Prō Archiā* 6.12–7.16, excerpts).

ANECDOTES FROM CICERO (11–15)

11. DEATH OF A PUPPY (EXAMPLE OF AN OMEN)

L. Paulus[1] cōnsul iterum, cum eī[2] bellum[3] ut cum rēge Perse[4] gereret[5] obtigisset,[6] ut eā ipsā diē domum ad vesperum rediit, fīliolam[7] suam Tertiam,[8] quae tum erat admodum[9] parva, ōsculāns[10] animadvertit[11] trīsticulam.[12] "Quid est,[13]" inquit, "mea Tertia? Quid[14] trīstis es?" "Mī pater," inquit,
5   inquit, "Persa[15] periit." Tum ille artius[16] puellam complexus,[17] "Accipiō," inquit, "mea fīlia, ōmen.[18]" Erat autem mortuus catellus[19] eō nōmine. (**Cicero,** *Dē Dīvīnātiōne* 1.46.103)

12. TOO CONSCIENTIOUS (AN EXAMPLE OF IRONY)

Est huic fīnitimum[1] dissimulātiōnī[2] cum honestō[3] verbō vitiōsa[4] rēs appellātur: ut cum Āfricānus cēnsor[5] tribū[6] movēbat eum centuriōnem[7] quī in

---

[66] **cēterae (remissiōnēs** or **dēlectātiōnēs)**
[67] *gen. of possession used in predicate = predicate gen.; sc.* **omnium** *with each gen.:* the other delights do not belong to all times . . .

11

[1] *L. Aemilius Paulus Macedonicus was the father of Scipio Africanus Minor. As consul in 168 B.C. he brought the war with Macedonia to a successful conclusion by the defeat of the Macedonian King, Perseus. This explains why, before setting out against Perseus, he interpreted the chance words* **Persa periit** *as a favorable omen. The Romans believed seriously in the importance of omens.*
[2] *dat. with* **obtigisset**
[3] *obj. of* **gereret**
[4] **Perseus, -eī; Perse** *abl.*
[5] **ut . . . gereret,** *noun cl. subject of* **obtigisset**
[6] **obtingō, -ere, -tigī,** touch, fall to one's lot
[7] **fīli (a)** *with the diminutive ending* **-ola,** little daughter
[8] **Tertia,** *a name meaning* third. *The Romans often used ordinal numerals as names, though commonly without strict regard to the number of children they had; e.g.,* **Secundus, Quīntus, Sextus, Decimus.**
[9] **admodum,** *adv.,* very

[10] **ōsculor** (1), kiss
[11] **anim-ad-vertō,** turn the mind to, notice, observe
[12] **trīsticulus, -a, -um,** rather sad, *diminutive of* **tristis**
[13] What is it? What is the matter?
[14] **quid = cūr**
[15] **Persa,** *the name of her pet*
[16] **artius,** *adv.,* closely
[17] **complector, -ī, -plexus sum,** embrace
[18] **ōmen, -inis,** *n.,* omen, sign; *i.e., the omen of his victory over Perseus*
[19] **catellus, -ī,** puppy

12

[1] **fīnitimus, -a, -um,** neighboring; akin to: **est fīnitinum,** it is akin to
[2] **dissimulātiō, -ōnis,** *f.,* irony
[3] **honestus, -a, -um,** honorable, fine
[4] **vitiōsus, -a, -um,** faulty, bad
[5] **cēnsor, -ōris,** *m.,* censor, *Roman magistrate among whose duties was the assigning of citizens to their proper rank according to their property and service and the removal of names from the census rolls when citizens proved unworthy of citizenship.*
[6] **tribus, -ūs,** *f.,* tribe, *a political division of the Roman people*
[7] **centuriō, -ōnis,** *m.,* centurion

Paulī pugnā[8] nōn adfuerat,[9] cum ille sē custōdiae causā dīceret in castrīs[10] remānsisse quaereretque cūr ab eō notārētur[11]: "Nōn amō," inquit, "nimium
5 dīligentēs." (**Cicero,** *Dē Ōrātōre* 2.67.272)

13. QUAM MULTA NŌN DĒSĪDERŌ!

Sōcratēs, in pompā[1] cum magna vīs[2] aurī[3] argentīque[4] ferrētur, "Quam multa nōn dēsīderō!" inquit.

Xenocratēs,[5] cum lēgātī ab Alexandrō[6] quīnquāgintā[7] eī talenta[8] attulissent (quae erat pecūnia temporibus illīs, Athēnīs praesertim,[9] maxima), ab-
5 dūxit lēgātōs ad cēnam in Acadēmīam[10]; iīs apposuit[11] tantum quod satis esset, nūllō apparātū.[12] Cum postrīdiē[13] rogārent eum cui numerārī[14] iubēret, "Quid? Vōs hesternā,[15]" inquit, "cēnulā[16] nōn intellēxistis mē pecūniā nōn egēre?" Quōs cum trīstiōrēs vīdisset, trīgintā[17] minās[18] accēpit nē aspernārī[19] rēgis līberālitātem[20] vidērētur.
10 At vērō Diogenēs[21] līberius,[22] ut[23] Cynicus, Alexandrō rogantī ut dīceret sī quid opus[24] esset: "Nunc quidem paululum,[25]" inquit, "ā sōle.[26]" Offēcerat[27] vidēlicet[28] aprīcantī.[29] (**Cicero,** *Tusculānae Disputātiōnēs* 5.32.91–92)

14. WHAT MAKES A GOOD APPETITE

Dārēus[1] in fugā[2] cum aquam turbidam[3] et cadāveribus[4] inquinātam[5] bibisset, negāvit umquam sē bibisse iūcundius. Numquam vidēlicet sitiēns[6]

---

[8] **pugna, -ae,** battle
[9] **ad-sum,** be present
[10] **castra, -ōrum,** camp
[11] **notō** (1), mark, *here with the* **nota cēnsōria** *placed opposite a citizen's name to indicate his removal from the citizen list in disgrace.*

13
[1] **pompa, -ae,** parade
[2] **vīs** here = quantity (*cp.* **cōpia**)
[3] **aurum, -ī,** gold
[4] **argentum, -ī,** silver
[5] **Xenocratēs, -is,** *pupil of Plato and later head of the Academy*
[6] **Alexander, -drī**
[7] *indecl. adj.,* fifty
[8] **talentum, -ī,** a talent, a large sum of money
[9] **praesertim,** *adv.,* especially
[10] **Acadēmīa, -ae,** the Academy, *a gymnasium in a grove just outside of Athens. Here Plato established his school, which might be called the first European university.*
[11] **ap-pōnō,** place near, serve
[12] **apparātus, -ūs,** equipment, splendor
[13] **postrīdiē,** *adv.,* on the next day
[14] **numerō** (1), count, pay out; *sc.* **pecūniam** *as subject of* **numerārī**

[15] **hesternus, -a, -um,** of yesterday
[16] **cēnula, -ae,** diminutive of **cēna**
[17] *indecl. adj.,* thirty
[18] **mina, -ae,** a Greek coin
[19] **aspernor** (1), spurn, despise
[20] **līberālitās, -tātis,** *f.,* generosity
[21] *L.I. 9 n. 38*
[22] **līberius,** *adv.,* freely, boldly
[23] as a Cynic, being a Cynic
[24] **opus** (*indecl.*) **est,** is necessary: if he needed anything
[25] **paululum,** *adv.,* a little
[26] *i.e.,* you are blocking my sunlight
[27] **officiō, -ere, -fēcī, -fectum** + *dat.,* be in the way, obstruct
[28] **vidē-licet,** *adv.* (you may see), clearly, evidently
[29] **aprīcor** (1), sun oneself

14

[1] *Darius III, defeated by Alexander the Great in 331* B.C. *The spelling* **Dārīus** *reflects later Greek pronunciation.*
[2] **fuga, -ae,** flight
[3] **turbidus, -a, -um,** turbid, roiled
[4] **cadāver, -eris,** *n.,* corpse (*cp.* cadaverous)
[5] **inquinātus, -a, -um,** polluted
[6] **sitiō** (4), be thirsty

biberat. Nec ēsuriēns[7] Ptolemaeus[8] ēderat,[9] cui cum peragrantī[10] Aegyptum,[11] comitibus[12] nōn cōnsecūtīs[13] cibārius[14] in casā pānis datus esset, nihil
5   vīsum est illō pāne iūcundius. Sōcratem ferunt,[15] cum ūsque ad vesperum
contentius[16] ambulāret quaesītumque esset[17] ex eō quārē id faceret, respondisse sē, quō[18] melius cēnāret, obsōnāre[19] ambulandō famem.[20]

Quid? Vīctum[21] Lacedaemoniōrum in philitiīs[22] nōnne vidēmus? Ubi[23]
cum tyrannus cēnāvisset Dionȳsius, negāvit sē iūre[24] illō nigrō quod cēnae[25]
10   caput erat dēlectātum.[26] Tum is quī illa coxerat,[27] "Minimē mīrum[28]; condīmenta[29] enim dēfuērunt.[30]" "Quae tandem?" inquit ille. "Labor in vēnātū,[31] sūdor,[32] cursus ad Eurōtam,[33] famēs, sitis.[34] Hīs enim rēbus Lacedaemoniōrum epulae[35] condiuntur.[36]"

Cōnfer sūdantēs,[37] ructantēs,[38] refertōs[39] epulīs tamquam opīmōs
15   bovēs.[40] Tum intellegēs quī voluptātem maximē sequantur, eōs minimē cōnsequī[41]; iūcunditātemque[42] vīctūs[43] esse in dēsīderiō,[44] nōn in satietāte.[45] (**Cicero**, *Tusculānae Disputātiōnēs* 5.34.97–98 and 100, excerpts)

15. THEMISTOCLES; FAME AND EXPEDIENCY

Themistoclēs fertur[1] Serīphiō[2] cuidam in iūrgiō[3] respondisse, cum ille
dīxisset nōn eum suā sed patriae glōriā splendōrem[4] assecūtum[5]: "Nec her-

---

[7] **ēsuriō** (4), be hungry
[8] *Which Egyptian king of this name is unknown.*
[9] **edō, -ere, ēdī, ēsum,** eat (*cp.* edible)
[10] **per-agrō** (1), wander through
[11] **Aegyptus, -ī,** *f.,* Egypt
[12] **comes, -itis,** *m.,* companion
[13] **cōn-sequor**
[14] **cibārius ... pānis,** ordinary (coarse) bread; **pānis, -is,** *m.*
[15] **ferō** *here* = report, say
[16] **contentē,** strenuously, *adv. from* **contendō,** struggle
[17] it had been asked of him, he had been asked
[18] **quō,** *regularly used instead of* **ut** *to introduce a purp. containing a compar.*
[19] **obsōnō** (1), buy provisions, *here* = provide (an appetite)
[20] **famēs, -is,** *f.,* hunger
[21] **vīctus, -ūs,** living, mode of living, food
[22] **philitia, -ōrum,** public meals (*for Spartan citizens of military age*)
[23] **ubi** = *among the Lacedaemonians*
[24] **iūs, iūris,** *n.,* soup
[25] *dat. of purp.* (*S.S.*)
[26] **dēlectātum** (**esse**)
[27] **coquō, -ere, coxī, coctum,** cook (*cp.* concoct)
[28] **mīrus, -a, -um,** wonderful, surprising
[29] **condīmentum, -ī,** seasoning, condiment

[30] **dē-sum,** be lacking
[31] **vēnātus, -ūs,** hunting
[32] **sūdor, -ōris,** *m.,* sweat
[33] at the Eurotas (**Eurōtās, -ae,** *m., river on which Sparta was located*)
[34] **sitis, -is,** *f.,* thirst
[35] **epulae, -ārum,** banquet
[36] **condiō** (4), season, spice
[37] **sūdō** (1), sweat
[38] **ructō** (1), belch
[39] **refertus, -a, -um,** stuffed, crammed, + *abl.*
[40] **opīmus, -a, -um,** fertile, fat; **bōs, bovis,** *m.,* ox
[41] **cōn-sequor,** follow up, gain
[42] **iūcunditās, -tātis,** *f.,* pleasure, charm
[43] *n. 21 above; here* = food
[44] **dēsīderium, -ī,** desire
[45] **satietās, -tātis,** *f.,* abundance, satisfy

15

(*For more about Themistocles and Aristides see selections 19 and 20 below.*)
[1] is said, is reported
[2] **Serīphius, -ī,** *inhabitant of Seriphos, a small island in the Aegean Sea.*
[3] **iūrgium, -ī,** quarrel
[4] **splendor, -ōris,** *m.,* distinction, honor
[5] **as-sequor** = **ad-sequor,** gain, attain

cule,[6]" inquit, "sī ego Serīphius essem, nec tū, sī Athēniēnsis[7] essēs, clārus umquam fuissēs." (**Cicero**, *Dē Senectūte,* 3.8)

5   Themistoclēs, post victōriam eius bellī quod cum Persīs[8] fuit, dīxit in cōntiōne[9] sē habēre cōnsilium reī pūblicae salūtāre,[10] sed id scīrī nōn opus esse.[11] Postulāvit[12] ut aliquem populus daret quīcum[13] commūnicāret.[14] Datus est Aristīdēs. Huic[15] ille (dīxit) classem[16] Lacedaemoniōrum, quae subducta esset[17] ad Gythēum,[18] clam[19] incendī[20] posse, quō factō frangī[21] Lace-
10 daemoniōrum opēs necesse esset.[22] Quod Aristīdēs cum audīsset, in cōntiōnem magnā exspectātiōne[23] vēnit dīxitque perūtile[24] esse cōnsilium quod Themistoclēs adferret, sed minimē honestum. Itaque Athēniēnsēs, quod honestum nōn esset, id nē ūtile quidem putāvērunt, tōtamque eam rem, quam nē audierant quidem, auctōre Aristīde[25] repudiāvērunt.[26] (**Cicero**, *Dē Officiīs* 3.11.48–49)

16. GET THE TUSCULAN COUNTRY HOUSE READY[1]

Tullius[2] S.D.[3] Terentiae[4] Suae

In Tusculānum[5] nōs ventūrōs[6] putāmus aut Nōnīs[7] aut postrīdiē.[8] Ibi ut[9] sint omnia parāta. Plūrēs[10] enim fortasse[11] nōbīscum erunt et, ut arbitror, diūtius ibi commorābimur.[12] Lābrum[13] sī in balneō[14] nōn est, ut[15] sit; item[16]
5 cētera quae sunt ad vīctum et ad valētūdinem[17] necessāria.[18] Valē. Kal. Oct.[19] dē Venusīnō.[20] (**Cicero**, *Epistulae ad Familiārēs* 14.20)

16

[6] **hercule,** *a mild oath,* by Hercules
[7] **Athēniēnsis, -e,** Athenian
[8] **Persae, -ārum,** *m.,* the Persians
[9] **cōntiō, -ōnis,** *f.,* assembly
[10] **salūtāris, -e,** salutary, advantageous; *modifies* **cōnsilium**
[11] **opus est,** it is necessary
[12] **postulō** (1), demand, request
[13] **quīcum, quī** = *old abl. form* + **cum,** with whom
[14] **commūnicō** (1), communicate, share
[15] **huic** = *the last mentioned, Aristides*
[16] **classis, -is,** *f.,* fleet
[17] **sub-dūcō,** beach; *subj. because subordinate cl. in ind. state. (see S.S.). Because of their shallow draft and small size, ancient ships were more often beached than anchored.*
[18] **Gythēum, -ī,** *the port of Sparta*
[19] **clam,** *adv.,* secretly
[20] **incendō, -ere, -cendī, -cēnsum,** set on fire, burn
[21] **frangō, -ere, frēgī, frāctum,** break, crush
[22] **necesse** (*indecl. adj.*) **est,** it is necessary
[23] **exspectātiō, -ōnis,** *f.,* expectation, *abl. of attendant circumstance*
[24] **per-ūtilis, -e,** very useful, advantageous
[25] **auctōre Aristīde,** *abl. abs.*
[26] **repudiō** (1), reject

[1] *A homely little letter which serves as an antidote to Cicero's usually lofty concerns.*
[2] (**Mārcus**) **Tullius** (**Cicerō**)
[3] **salūtem dīcit**
[4] **Terentia, -ae,** wife of Cicero
[5] **Tusculānum, -ī,** Tusculan estate (**praedium**) *southeast of Rome in Latium*
[6] **ventūrōs (esse)**
[7] **Nōnae, -ārum,** the Nones *were the seventh day in March, May, July, October; the fifth day in other months.*
[8] **postrīdiē,** *adv.,* the day after
[9] (**cūrā**) **ut,** take care that
[10] **plūrēs,** several people
[11] **fortasse,** *adv.,* perhaps
[12] **com-moror** (1), remain
[13] **lābrum, -ī,** a wash basin or a bath
[14] **balneum, -ī,** bathroom
[15] (**cūrā**) **ut**
[16] **item,** *adv.,* likewise
[17] **valētūdō, -inis,** *f.,* health
[18] **necessārius, -a, -um** = *Eng.*
[19] **Kalendīs Octōbribus,** on the Kalends of October = October 1st
[20] *Sent from his estate at Venusia, in Apulia. The year is said to be 47* B.C.

17. LIVY ON THE DEATH OF CICERO[1]

M. Cicerō sub adventum[2] triumvirōrum[3] cesserat urbe . . . Prīmō in Tusculānum[4] fūgit; inde trānsversīs[5] itineribus in Formiānum,[6] ut ab Caiētā[7] nāvem cōnscēnsūrus,[8] proficīscitur. Unde aliquotiēns[9] in altum[10] provectum,[11] cum modo ventī adversī rettulissent, modo ipse iactātiōnem[12] nā-

5 vis . . . patī nōn posset, taedium[13] tandem eum et fugae[14] et vītae cēpit, regressusque[15] ad superiōrem vīllam . . . "Moriar," inquit, "in patriā saepe servātā." Satis cōnstat[16] servōs fortiter fidēliterque parātōs fuisse ad dīmicandum,[17] ipsum dēpōnī lectīcam[18] et quiētōs[19] patī quod sors[20] inīqua[21] cōgeret iussisse. Prōminentī[22] ex lectīcā praebentīque immōtam cervīcem[23] caput

10 praecīsum est.[24]

Manūs quoque, scrīpsisse in Antōnium aliquid exprobrantēs,[25] praecīdērunt. Ita relātum caput ad Antōnium, iussūque eius inter duās manūs in Rōstrīs positum,[26] ubi ille cōnsul, ubi saepe cōnsulāris,[27] ubi eō ipsō annō adversus[28] Antōnium . . . (quanta nūlla umquam hūmāna vōx[29]!) cum ad-

15 mīrātiōne[30] ēloquentiae[31] audītus fuerat. Vix attollentēs[32] prae lacrimīs oculōs, hominēs intuērī[33] trucīdāta[34] membra[35] eius poterant. Vīxit trēs et sexāgintā[36] annōs . . . Vir magnus, ācer, memorābilis[37] fuit, et in cuius laudēs persequendās[38] Cicerōne laudātōre opus[39] fuerit.[40] (**Livy** 120.50)

17

[1] *In 43* B.C.

[2] **adventus, -ūs,** arrival

[3] **triumvirī, -ōrum,** commission of three men, *the second triumvirate composed of Antony, Octavian, and Lepidus*

[4] his Tusculan villa

[5] **trānsversus, -a, -um,** transverse, crosswise

[6] **Formiānum, -ī,** estate near Formiae, *which was nearly 100 miles south of Rome on the Appian Way near the sea*

[7] **Caiēta, -ae,** *a sea-coast town not far from Formiae*

[8] as he was going to board ship (**cōnscendō, -ere, -scendī, -scēnsum,** ascend)

[9] **aliquotiēns,** *adv.,* several times

[10] **altum, -ī,** the deep, the sea

[11] **prō-vehō, -ere, -vexī, -vectum,** carry forward; **provectum** (having sailed out) *goes with* **eum** *below*

[12] **iactātiō, -ōnis,** *f.,* tossing

[13] **taedium, -iī,** weariness, disgust

[14] **fuga, -ae,** flight; **fugae** *depends on* **taedium**

[15] **regredior, -ī, -gressus sum,** go back

[16] **cōnstat,** it is agreed

[17] **dīmicō** (1), fight (to the finish)

[18] **lectīca, -ae,** litter

[19] (**eōs**) **quiētōs,** them quiet, *subject of* **patī;** *but we say:* them quietly. (**quiētus, -a, -um**)

[20] **sors, sortis,** *f.,* lot

[21] **inīquus, -a, -um,** unfavorable, unjust (**in-aequus**)

[22] **prōmineō, -ēre, -uī,** jut out, step forth: (**eī**) **prōminentī,** for him stepping forth = as he stepped forth, *dat. of ref. or interest*

[23] **cervīx, -vīcis,** *f.,* neck

[24] **praecīdō, -ere, -cīdī, cīsum (prae-caedō,** cut), cut off—*by the soldiers whom Antony had sent to execute Cicero in reprisal for Cicero's "Philippics" denouncing Antony. Such were the horrors of the proscriptions.*

[25] **exprobrō** (1), reproach, charge: (**militēs**), **exprobrantēs (manūs) scrīpsisse aliquid, manūs praecīdērunt**

[26] **positum,** *sc.* est

[27] **cōnsulāris, -is,** *m.,* ex-consul

[28] **adversus,** *prep. + acc.,* against

[29] **quanta . . . vōx (fuerat),** how great no voice had been = greater than any voice had been

[30] **admīrātiō, -ōnis,** *f. = Eng.*

[31] **ēloquentia, -ae,** *f.;* **ēloquentiae,** *obj. gen. (S.S.)*

[32] **attollō, -ere,** raise, lift

[33] **intueor, -ērī, -tuitus sum,** look at

[34] **trucīdō** (1), cut to pieces, butcher

[35] **membrum, -ī,** member (of the body), limb

[36] *indecl. adj.,* sixty

[37] **memorābilis, -e,** remarkable, memorable

[38] **per-sequor,** follow up, set forth

[39] **opus est** + *abl.* = there is need of (Cicero)

[40] **fuerit,** *perf. subj., potential subj.,* there would be need of

18. MILTIADES AND THE BATTLE OF MARATHON[1]

Eīsdem temporibus Persārum rēx Dārēus, ex Asiā in Eurōpam[2] exercitū trāiectō,[3] Scythīs[4] bellum īnferre[5] dēcrēvit. Pontem fēcit in Histrō[6] flūmine, quā[7] cōpiās trādūceret.[8] Eius pontis, dum ipse abesset,[9] custōdēs[10] relīquit prīncipēs quōs sēcum ex Iōniā et Aeolide[11] dūxerat; quibus singulārum[12] ur-
5   bium perpetua dederat imperia. Sīc enim facillimē putāvit sē[13] Graecā lin-
guā loquentēs[14] quī Asiam incolerent[15] sub suā retentūrum[16] potestāte, sī amīcīs suīs oppida[17] tuenda[18] trādidisset.[19] In hōc[20] fuit tum numerō Miltiadēs.[21] Hic, cum crēbrī[22] adferrent nūntiī[23] male rem gerere Dārēum pre-
mīque ā Scythīs, hortātus est pontis custōdēs nē ā Fortūnā[24] datam occāsiō-
10   nem līberandae Graeciae dīmitterent.[25]

Nam sī cum eīs cōpiīs, quās sēcum trānsportārat,[26] interīsset Dārēus, nōn sōlum Eurōpam fore[27] tūtam,[28] sed etiam eōs quī Asiam incolerent Graecī genere[29] līberōs ā Persārum futūrōs dominātiōne[30] et perīculō. Id facile efficī[31] posse;[32] ponte enim rescissō[33] rēgem vel[34] hostium ferrō vel ino-
15   piā[35] paucīs diēbus interitūrum. Ad hoc cōnsilium cum plērīque[36] ac-

18

[1] *490 B.C., the first major battle of the Persian wars and one of the most illustrious victories in the apparently unending conflict between democracies and autocracies (despotisms): the relatively few Athenians, practically alone, against the hordes of the Persian autocracy.*

[2] **Eurōpa, -ae,** Europe

[3] **trāiciō, -ere, -iēcī, -iectus,** transfer

[4] **Scythae, -ārum,** *m.,* the Scythians, *a nomadic people of southeastern Europe;* **Scythīs,** *dat. with compound vbs.*

[5] **bellum īn-ferō (-ferre, -tulī, -lātus),** make war upon, + *dat.*

[6] **Hister, -trī,** the Danube

[7] **quā,** *rel. adv. instead of rel. pron.,* where, by which, *referring to* **pontem**

[8] **trā (= trāns)-dūcō.** *Why the subj. in the rel. cl.?*

[9] **ab-sum,** be away, be absent; **abesset,** *subj. of implied ind. state., the thought in his mind being:*"while I shall be away"

[10] as guards

[11] Ionia and Aeolis, *Greek sections of Asia Minor*

[12] **singulī, -ae, -a** (*pl.*), separate, one each

[13] **sē,** *acc., subject of* **retentūrum** (**esse**)

[14] the Greek-speaking peoples, *obj. of* **retentūrum**

[15] **incolō, -ere, -uī,** inhabit

[16] **retentūrum** (**esse**); **re-tineō**

[17] **oppidum, -ī,** town; *occasionally* city

[18] **tuenda,** (the towns) to be protected = the protection of the towns (**tueor, -ērī, tūtus sum,** look at, protect)

[19] *fut. more vivid condition in ind. state.:* **eōs retinēbō sī amīcīs oppida trādiderō.**

[20] **hōc** *modifies* **numerō.** *Note carefully that a characteristic of Nepos' style is the fondness for separating modifiers from the words which they modify. Be sure to match up such separated words accurately according to the rules of agreement.*

[21] **Miltiadēs, -is,** *m.,* Miltiades, *Athenian general, hero of Marathon, who many years before the Battle of Marathon had been sent by the Athenians to rule over the Thracian Chersonesus, a peninsula west of the Hellespont.*

[22] **crēber, -bra, -brum,** numerous

[23] **nūntius, -iī,** messenger

[24] **Fortūna** *is here regarded as a person* (*deity*). *Why is* **ā** *used?*

[25] **dī-mittō,** let go, lose

[26] **trānsportō** (1), transport, take across; **trāns-portārat = trānsportāverat**

[27] *ind. state. depending on the idea of saying in* **hortātus est** *of the preceding sent.; direct form:* **sī Dārēus interierit, Eurōpa erit tūta. inter-eō,** perish

[28] **tūtus, -a, -um**

[29] *abl. of specification (S.S.),* Greek in race *or* by race

[30] **dominātiō, -ōnis,** *f. = Eng.*

[31] **ef-ficiō,** accomplish

[32] *still ind. state.*

[33] **rescindō, -ere, rescidī, rescissum,** cut down

[34] **vel . . . vel,** either . . . or

[35] **inopia, -ae,** need, privation

[36] **plērīque, -ōrumque,** most people, very many (**plē-rusque, -aque, -umque,** the greater part, very many)

cēderent, Histiaeus[37] Mīlēsius . . . [dīxit] adeō[38] sē abhorrēre[39] ā cēterōrum
cōnsiliō ut nihil putet ipsīs ūtilius quam cōnfirmārī[40] rēgnum[41] Persārum.
Huius cum sententiam plūrimī essent secūtī, Miltiadēs . . . Chersonēsum relīquit ac rūrsus[42] Athēnās dēmigrāvit.[43] Cuius[44] ratiō etsī nōn valuit, tamen
20 magnopere est laudanda cum amīcior omnium libertātī quam suae fuerit
dominātiōnī.

Dārēus autem, cum ex Eurōpā in Asiam redīsset, hortantibus amīcīs ut
Graeciam redigeret[45] in suam potestātem, classem quīngentārum[46] nāvium
comparāvit[47] eīque[48] Dātim praefēcit[49] et Artaphernem,[50] eīsque ducenta[51]
25 (mīlia) peditum,[52] decem equitum[53] mīlia dedit—causam interserēns[54] sē
hostem esse Athēniēnsibus quod eōrum auxiliō Iōnes[55] Sardīs[56] expugnās-
sent[57] suaque[58] praesidia interfēcissent. Illī praefectī[59] rēgiī,[60] classe ad Euboeam[61] appulsā[62] celeriter Eretriam[63] cēpērunt, omnēsque eius gentis cīvēs
abreptōs[64] in Asiam ad rēgem mīsērunt. Inde[65] ad Atticam[66] accessērunt ac
30 suās cōpiās in campum[67] Marathōna[68] dēdūxērunt. Is abest ab oppidō circiter[69] mīlia passuum[70] decem.

Hōc tumultū[71] Athēniēnsēs tam propinquō[72] tamque magnō permōtī[73]
auxilium nūsquam[74] nisi ā Lacedaemoniīs petīvērunt Phīdippumque,[75] cur-
sōrem eius generis quī hēmerodromoe[76] vocantur, Lacedaemonem[77] mīsē-

---

[37] **Histiaeus, -ī,** *tyrant of Miletus in Asia Minor*
[38] **adeō,** *adv.,* so, to such a degree
[39] **ab-horreō, -ēre, -uī,** shrink from, be averse to
[40] **cōnfirmō** (1), strengthen
[41] *subject of* **cōnfirmārī**
[42] **rūrsus,** *adv.,* again
[43] **dēmigrō** (1), depart (*cp.* migrate)
[44] *conjunctive use of rel.*
[45] **redigō, -ere, -ēgī, -āctum,** reduce
[46] **quīngentī, -ae, -a,** 500
[47] **comparāvit** *here = strong form of* **parāvit**
[48] **eī** (= **classī**), *dat. with compounds*
[49] **prae-ficiō,** + *dat.,* put in charge *or* command of
[50] **Dātis, -tidis,** *acc.* **Dātim,** Datis, *a general;* **Arta-phernēs, -is,** Artaphernes, *nephew of Darius*
[51] **ducentī, -ae, -a,** 200
[52] **pedes, -itis,** *m.,* foot-soldier
[53] **eques, -itis,** *m.,* horseman
[54] **interserō, -ere,** allege
[55] **Iōnes, -um,** *m.,* the Ionians, *a Greek people inhabiting the central western coast of Asia Minor;* **-es,** *Greek ending*
[56] **Sardēs, -ium,** *acc.* **Sardīs,** Sardis, *capital of the Persian province of Lydia in western Asia Minor*
[57] **expugnō** (1), take by storm
[58] **sua,** *refers to Sardis*
[59] **praefectus, -ī,** commander, deputy
[60] **rēgius, -a, -um,** royal
[61] **Euboea, -ae,** Euboea, *a large island off the eastern*

shore of central Greece
[62] **appellō, -ere, -pulī, -pulsum,** drive, bring to land
[63] **Eretria, -ae,** Eretria, *a city of the western central coast of Euboea*
[64] **ab-ripiō = ēripiō; abreptōs . . . mīsērunt,** they carried away and sent to
[65] **inde,** *adv.,* from that place
[66] **Attica, -ae,** Attica, *district in central Greece of which the capital was Athens (somewhat unusually called an* **oppidum** *in the next sentence)*
[67] **campus, -ī,** field, plain
[68] **Marathōn, -ōnis,** *acc.* **-ōna,** *f.,* Marathon
[69] **circiter,** *adv.,* about
[70] **passus, -ūs,** pace (ca. 5′); **mīlia passuum,** thousands of paces = miles
[71] **tumultus, -ūs,** disturbance, uprising
[72] **propinquus, -a, -um,** near, neighboring
[73] **per-moveō,** move thoroughly, trouble
[74] **nūsquam,** *adv.,* nowhere
[75] **Phīdippus, -ī,** Phidippus, *an Athenian courier* (**cursor, -ōris,** *m.,* runner)
[76] **hēmerodromus, -ī** (**-dromoe,** *Gk. nom. pl.*), day runner (*Gk. word*), professional runner. *Herodotus says that Phidippus (or Phidippides) covered the 140 miles between Athens and Sparta in two days.* **Quī** *agrees with* **hēmerodromoe** *rather than* **generis** *since a rel. pron. agrees with a pred. noun rather than with the antecedent.*
[77] **Lacedaemōn, -onis,** *f.,* Lacedaemonia, Sparta

35 runt ut nūntiāret quam celerrimō opus esse[78] auxiliō. Domī autem creant[79]
decem praetōrēs,[80] quī exercituī praeessent,[81] in eīs Miltiadem; inter quōs
magna fuit contentiō[82] utrum moenibus sē dēfenderent an obviam[83] īrent
hostibus aciēque[84] dēcernerent. Ūnus[85] Miltiadēs maximē nītēbātur[86] ut
prīmō tempore castra fierent[87] . . .

40   Hōc tempore nūlla cīvitās Athēniēnsibus auxiliō[88] fuit praeter Plataeēnsēs;[89] ea mīlle mīsit mīlitum.[90] Itaque hōrum adventū[91] decem mīlia armā-
tōrum[92] complēta sunt,[93] quae manus mīrābilī[94] flagrābat[95] pugnandī cupiditāte; quō[96] factum est[97] ut plūs quam collēgae[98] Miltiadēs valēret.[99]

     Eius ergō auctōritāte impulsī[100] Athēniēnsēs cōpiās ex urbe ēdūxērunt
45 locōque[101] idōneō castra fēcērunt. Dein[102] posterō[103] diē sub montis rādīci-
bus[104] aciē regiōne[105] īnstrūctā[106] nōn apertissimā[107]—namque[108] arborēs
multīs locīs erant rārae[109]—proelium commīsērunt[110] hōc cōnsiliō ut et mon-
tium altitūdine[111] tegerentur[112] et arborum tractū[113] equitātus[114] hostium im-
pedīrētur, nē multitūdine[115] clauderentur.[116] Dātis, etsī nōn aequum locum[117]
50 vidēbat suīs, tamen frētus[118] numerō cōpiārum suārum cōnflīgere[119] cupiēbat,
eōque[120] magis quod, priusquam[121] Lacedaemoniī subsidiō[122] venīrent, dīmi-
cāre ūtile arbitrābātur.

---

[78] **opus est** + *abl.* (*of means*), there is need of, *an impers.
construction in which* **opus** *remains indecl.;* **opus
esse,** *inf. in ind. state. with* **auxiliō** *in abl.*
[79] **creant,** *historical pres.*
[80] **praetor, -ōris,** *m., called* **stratēgoi,** generals, *by the
Athenians*
[81] **prae-sum** + *dat.,* be in charge of; *why subj.?*
[82] **contentiō, -ōnis,** *f.,* controversy
[83] **obviam** (*adv.*) **īre** + *dat.,* go to meet
[84] **aciēs, -ēī,** line of battle
[85] alone, *i.e., of the ten generals*
[86] **nītor, -ī, nīxus sum,** strive labor
[87] that a camp should be made = to take the field
[88] *dat. of purp.* (*S. S.*)
[89] **Plataeēnsēs, -ium,** *m. pl.,* the men of Plataea, *a city
in Boeotia just over the border from Attica*
[90] **mīlle** here = *a noun with gen. of whole* **mīlitum.** *This
is regular with* **mīlia** *but uncommon with* **mīlle.**
[91] **adventus, -ūs,** approach
[92] **armātī, -ōrum,** armed men
[93] **compleō, -ēre, -plēvī, -plētum,** fill out, complete
[94] **mīrābilis, -e,** wonderful, extraordinary; *modifies* **cupiditāte**
[95] **flagrō** (1), burn, be excited
[96] because of which = and because of this
[97] it happened that
[98] **collēga, -ae,** *m.,* colleague
[99] **plūs . . . valēret,** he had power more than = he had

more power or influence than, he prevailed over.
valēret, *why subj.?*
[100] **impellō, -ere, -pulī, -pulsum,** impel
[101] **locō,** *place where, no prep. necessary with* **locō**
[102] **dein** = **deinde**
[103] **posterus, -a, -um,** next following
[104] **rādīx, -īcis,** *f.,* root, base
[105] **regiō, -ōnis,** *f.,* region
[106] **īnstruō, -ere, -strūxī, -strūctum,** draw up (battle line)
[107] *interlocked word order:* **aciē īnstrūctā** (*in*) **regiōne nōn
apertissimā; apertus, -a, -um,** open
[108] **namque,** *conj., more emphatic form of* **nam**
[109] **rārus, -a, -um,** scattered: there were scattered trees
[110] **proelium committere,** join battle
[111] **altitūdō, -inis,** *f.,* height
[112] **tegō, -ere, tēxī, tēctum,** cover, protect
[113] **tractus, -ūs,** dragging
[114] **equitātus, -ūs,** cavalry
[115] **multitūdō, -inis,** *f.,* large number
[116] **claudō,** *here* enclose, surround
[117] **locum (esse) nōn aequum suīs**
[118] **frētus, -a, -um,** + *abl.,* relying on
[119] **cōnflīgō, -ere, -flīxī, -flīctum,** fight (*cp.* conflict)
[120] **eō,** *adv.,* on that account
[121] **priusquam** *and* **antequam,** before, + *indic. denote an
actual fact;* + *subj. denote anticipation as here:*
before they could come
[122] *dat.*

Itaque in aciem peditum centum (mīlia), equitum decem mīlia prōdūxit proeliumque commīsit. In quō[123] tantō[124] plūs[125] virtūte valuērunt Athēni-
55 ēnsēs ut decemplicem[126] numerum hostium prōflīgārint,[127] adeōque eōs per- terruērunt ut Persae nōn castra sed nāvēs petierint. Quā pugnā nihil adhūc[128] exsistit[129] nōbilius[130]; nūlla enim umquam tam exigua[131] manus tantās opēs prōstrāvit.[132] (**Nepos,** *Miltiadēs* 3–5, excerpts)

19. THEMISTOCLES AND THE BATTLE OF SALAMIS[1]

Themistoclēs[2] ad (bellum Corcȳraeum[3]) gerendum praetor ā populō fac- tus, nōn sōlum praesentī[4] bellō sed etiam reliquō[5] tempore ferōciōrem red- didit cīvitātem. Nam cum pecūnia pūblica, quae ex metallīs[6] redībat, largītī- ōne[7] magistrātuum[8] quotannīs[9] interīret,[10] ille persuāsit populō ut eā
5 pecūniā classis centum nāvium aedificārētur.[11] Quā[12] celeriter effectā, prīmum Corcȳraeōs frēgit,[13] deinde maritimōs praedōnēs[14] cōnsectandō[15] mare tūtum reddidit. In quō[16] . . . perītissimōs[17] bellī nāvālis[18] fēcit Athēni- ēnsēs. Id quantae salūtī[19] fuerit ūniversae[20] Graeciae, bellō cognitum est Per- sicō.[21] Nam cum Xerxēs[22] et marī et terrā[23] bellum ūniversae īnferret Eurō-
10 pae, cum tantīs cōpiīs eam invāsit[24] quantās neque ante nec posteā habuit quisquam. Huius enim classis mīlle et ducentārum nāvium longārum[25] fuit,

---

[123] **in quō (proeliō)**
[124] *abl. of degree of difference (S.S.)*
[125] they were strong by so much more (strength) in re- spect to courage = they were so much more pow- erful in the matter of courage
[126] **decemplex,** *gen.* **-plicis,** tenfold
[127] **prōflīgō** (1), overthrow; **prōflīgārint** = **-gāverint.** *Why subj.?*
[128] **ad-hūc,** *adv.,* thus far, hitherto
[129] **exsistō, -ere, -stitī,** arise, exist, be
[130] **nōbilis, -e,** famous
[131] **exiguus, -a, -um,** small, scanty. "Never did so many owe so much to so few."
[132] **prōsternō, -ere, -strāvī, -strātum,** overthrow, throw down

19

[1] *480* B.C. *The Battle of Salamis was the naval counter- part of Marathon, except that this time Athens had the help of Sparta.*
[2] **Themistoclēs, -is,** *or* **-ī,** Themistocles, *a talented Athenian politician.*
[3] **Corcȳraeus, -a, -um,** Corcyraen; *Corcyra, a large is- land off the northwest coast of Greece. Actually Nepos is in error about Themistocles' command in the Corcyraean affair but he is correct about the tremendous importance of Themistocles' big-navy policy.*

[4] **praesēns,** *gen.* **-entis,** present
[5] **reliquus, -a, -um,** remaining, rest of
[6] **metallum, -ī,** a mine, *silver mines at Laurium in Attica south of Athens*
[7] **largītiō, -ōnis,** *f.,* generosity, liberality
[8] **magistrātus, -ūs,** civil office; civil officer, magistrate
[9] **quotannīs,** *adv.,* annually
[10] **inter-eō,** be lost, perish (*cp.* **pereō**): **interīret,** *subj. in- troduced by* **cum;** *the subject is* **pecūnia.**
[11] **aedificō** (1), build (*cp.* edifice)
[12] **quā (classe)**
[13] **frangō, -ere, frēgī, frāctum,** break, overcome
[14] **maritimus** (**-a, -um** = *Eng.; cp.* **mare**) **praedō (-ōnis,** *m.,* robber) = pirate; *obj. of* **cōnsectandō**
[15] **cōnsector** (1), pursue, hound (*cp.* **cōnsequor**)
[16] in (doing) which
[17] **perītus, -a, -um,** + *gen.,* skilled in; *obj. complement*
[18] **nāvālis, -e;** *cp.* **nāvis**
[19] **quantae salūtī,** dat. of purp. with a dat. of ref., **Graeciae** (*S.S.*)
[20] **ūniversus, -a, -um,** entire, whole, as a whole
[21] **Persicus, -a, -um,** Persian; *the Second Persian War*
[22] **Xerxēs, -is** or **-ī,** *m.,* Xerxes, *son of Darius and king of the Persians, 485–465* B.C.
[23] **marī et terrā** (*or* **terrā marīque**) *abl. of place where, without a prep., regular in this formula*
[24] **invādō, -ere, -vāsī, -vāsum,** move against, invade
[25] **nāvium longārum,** of 1,200 men-of-war; his fleet was of 1,200 ships = his fleet consisted of . . .

quam duo mīlia onerāriārum[26] sequēbantur. Terrestris[27] autem exercitus sep-
tingenta[28] (mīlia) peditum, equitum quadringenta[29] mīlia fuērunt.[30]

Cuius dē adventū[31] cum fāma in Graeciam esset perlāta[32] et maximē
15 Athēniēnsēs petī dīcerentur propter pugnam Marathōniam, mīsērunt
Delphōs[33] cōnsultum[34] quidnam[35] facerent[36] dē rēbus suīs. Dēlīberantibus[37]
Pȳthia[38] respondit ut moenibus līgneīs[39] sē mūnīrent.[40] Id respōnsum[41] quō[42]
valēret cum intellegeret nēmō, Themistoclēs persuāsit cōnsilium esse[43] Apol-
linis ut in nāvēs sē suaque[44] cōnferrent: eum[45] enim ā deō significārī[46] mūrum
20 ligneum. Tālī cōnsiliō probātō, addunt[47] ad superiōrēs (nāvēs) totidem[48]
nāvēs trirēmēs,[49] suaque omnia quae movērī poterant partim[50] Salamīna,[51]
partim Troezēna[52] dēportant.[53] Arcem[54] sacerdōtibus paucīsque maiōribus
nātū[55] ad sacra[56] prōcūranda[57] trādunt; reliquum[5] oppidum relinquunt.

Huius[58] cōnsilium plērīsque cīvitātibus[59] displicēbat[60] et in terrā dīmi-
25 cārī[61] magis placēbat. Itaque missī sunt dēlēctī[62] cum Leōnidā,[63] Lacedaemoniōrum rēge, quī Thermopylās[64] occupārent[65] longiusque barbarōs[66] prō-

---

[26] **onerāria, -ae (nāvis)**, transport
[27] **terrestris exercitus,** land army
[28] **septingentī, -ae, -a,** seven hundred
[29] **quadringentī, -ae, -a,** four hundred
[30] *Though the subject,* **exercitus,** *is sg.,* **fuērunt** *is pl. according to the idea of plurality which precedes it.*
[31] **adventus, -ūs,** approach, arrival
[32] **per-ferō**
[33] *acc. of place to which. At Delphi was the famous oracle of Apollo.*
[34] *acc. supine of* **cōnsulō** *to express purp.* = *to consult*
[35] **quisnam, quidnam,** who *or* what in the world
[36] *both ind. quest. and deliberative subj.*
[37] **dēlīberō (1),** deliberate; **(eīs) dēlīberantibus,** *dat.*
[38] **Pȳthia, -ae,** the Pythian priestess, *who gave the response of Apollo*
[39] **ligneus, -a, -um,** wooden
[40] **mūniō (4),** fortify, defend
[41] **respōnsum, -ī,** *the noun of* **respondeō,** *subject of* **valēret**
[42] **quō** *(adv.)* **valēret,** *lit.* in what direction this was strong or valid = in what way this applied *or* what this meant
[43] **esse.** *The inf. shows that this is ind. state. with* **persuādeō** *and not the more common jussive noun cl. introduced by* **ut:** he persuaded (them) that it was the advice of Apollo that they should betake . . .
[44] **sua,** their things = their possessions
[45] **eum mūrum ligneum,** that wooden wall (= the ships)
[46] **significō (1),** signify, mean; **significārī,** *ind. state, depending on a vb. of saying understood*
[47] **ad-dō, -dere, -didī, -ditum,** add

[48] **totidem,** *indecl. adj.,* just as many
[49] **trirēmis, -e,** having three banks of oars
[50] **partim,** *adv.,* partly
[51] **Salamīs, -īnis,** *acc.* **Salamīna,** *f.,* Salamis, *island on west coast of Attica; acc. of place to which (islands as well as cities and towns)*
[52] **Troezēn, -ēnis,** *acc.* Troezēna, *f.,* Troezen, *southeastern part of Argolis, across the Saronic Gulf from Athens.*
[53] **dēportō (1),** carry off
[54] *the acropolis of the city of Athens.*
[55] **maiōrēs nātū,** those greater in respect to birth = old men, elders
[56] **sacer, -cra, -crum,** sacred; **sacra,** *n. pl.* sacred vessels, *or* rites
[57] **prōcūrō (1),** take care of
[58] *i.e.,* Themistocles'
[59] **plērīsque cīvitātibus,** *i.e.,* the allies of the Athenians; *dat. with* **displicēbat**
[60] **dis-placeō**
[61] **dīmicārī,** *impers. pass., lit.* that it be fought, *but translate* that the war be fought. *The inf.* **dīmicārī** is subject of **placēbat.**
[62] **dēlēctus, -a, -um,** chosen, picked; chosen men
[63] **Leōnidās, -ae,** *m.,* Leonidas
[64] **Thermopylae, -ārum,** Thermopylae, *a mountain pass near the southern border of Thessaly*
[65] **occupō (1),** seize
[66] **barbarus, -a, -um,** foreign, uncivilized, barbarian *(commonly applied by a kind of ethnocentrism to those not of the Greek and Roman civilization)*

gredī nōn paterentur. Iī vim hostium nōn sustinuērunt,[67] eōque locō omnēs interiērunt.[10]

At classis commūnis Graeciae trecentārum[68] nāvium, in quā ducentae[68]
30   erant Athēniēnsium,[69] prīmum apud Artemīsium[70] inter Euboeam continen-
temque[71] terram cum classiāriīs[72] rēgiīs[73] cōnflīxit.[74] Angustiās[75] enim Themistoclēs quaerēbat, nē multitūdine[76] circumīrētur.[77] Hinc etsī parī proeliō[78]
discesserant, tamen eōdem locō nōn sunt ausī manēre, quod erat perīculum
nē,[79] sī pars nāvium adversāriōrum[80] Euboeam superāsset,[81] ancipitī[82] pre-
35   merentur perīculō. Quō[83] factum est ut[84] ab Artemīsiō discēderent et exadversum[85] Athēnās apud Salamīna classem suam cōnstituerent.[86]

At Xerxēs, Thermopylīs expugnātīs, prōtinus accessit astū,[87] idque,
nūllīs dēfendentibus, interfectīs sacerdōtibus quōs in arce invēnerat, incen-
diō[88] dēlēvit. Cuius flammā perterritī[89] classiāriī cum manēre nōn audērent
40   et plūrimī hortārentur ut domōs[90] suās discēderent moenibusque sē dēfenderent, Themistoclēs ūnus restitit[91] et ūniversōs parēs esse posse[92] aiēbat,[93]
dispersōs[94] testābātur[95] peritūrōs; idque Eurybiadī,[96] rēgī Lacedaemoniōrum, quī tum summae[97] imperiī praeerat,[98] fore[99] adfīrmābat.[100]

Quem cum minus quam vellet movēret, noctū[101] dē servīs suīs[102] quem
45   habuit[103] fidēlissimum ad rēgem mīsit ut eī nūntiāret suīs verbīs[104] adversā-

---

[67] **sustineō, -ēre, -tinuī, -tentum,** sustain; *the subject is* **iī** (= **eī**).

[68] *See App. under Numerals (cardinals 200 and 300);* **ducentae (nāvēs)**

[69] *predicate gen. of possession:* were of the Athenians = belonged to the Athenians

[70] **apud Artemīsium,** near Artemisium, *promontory at northern tip of Euboea*

[71] **continēns terra, continentis terrae,** the mainland

[72] **classiārius, -iī,** a marine (*lit.* a soldier of the fleet)

[73] **rēgius, -a, -um,** royal

[74] **cōnflīgō, -ere, -flīxī, -flīctum,** to fight

[75] **angustiae, -ārum,** narrow place

[76] **multitūdō, -inis,** *f.,* large number, multitude

[77] **circum-eō,** surround

[78] **parī proeliō,** the battle was a draw

[79] **nē** = lest, *similar to the construction after verbs of fearing*

[80] **adversārius, -a, -um,** hostile; **adversārius, -iī,** opponent, enemy

[81] *a simple fut. condition in a* **nē-** *cl. The original thought was* **sī pars superāverit, . . . premēmur;** *the fut. perf. indic.* **superāverit** *becomes plupf. subj.* **superāsset.**

[82] **anceps,** *gen.* **ancipitis,** two-headed, double

[83] **quō** = **quārē**

[84] *result cl., subject of* **factum est:** = the result was that

[85] **exadversum,** *prep.* + *acc.,* opposite

[86] **cōnstituō, -ere, -stituī, -stitūtum,** draw up, establish

[87] **astū,** *n. indecl.,* the city (= Athens), *obj. of* **accessit**

[88] **incendium, -iī,** burning, fire. *The marks of this fire can still be seen on some of the marble pieces later built into the wall of the Acropolis.*

[89] **per-terreō**

[90] *place to which without a prep. as in the sg.* **domum**

[91] **resistō, -ere, -stitī,** make a stand, resist

[92] **ūniversōs . . . posse,** all together (united) they could be equal (*to the Persians*)

[93] *impf. of* **ait**

[94] **di-spergō, -ere, -spersī, -spersum,** scatter

[95] **testor** (1), testify, declare

[96] **Eurybiadēs, -is,** *m.,* Eurybiades; **Eurybiadī** *depends on* **adfīrmābat.**

[97] **summa, -ae,** highest place

[98] **summae imperiī** (*gen. of whole*) **praeerat,** he was in charge of the highest part of the command = he was commander-in-chief

[99] *Subject of* **fore** (= **futūrum esse**) *is* **id.**

[100] **adfīrmō** (1), assert, declare

[101] **noctū,** *adv.,* at night

[102] **(illum) dē servīs suīs,** that one of his slaves

[103] considered

[104] in his (Themistocles') own words, *i.e.,* in his own name

riōs eius[105] in fugā[106] esse; quī[107] sī discessissent,[108] maiōre cum labōre . . . (eum) bellum cōnfectūrum, cum singulōs[109] cōnsectārī cōgerētur; quōs sī statim aggrederētur,[110] brevī (tempore) ūniversōs oppressūrum . . . Hāc rē audītā barbarus, nihil dolī[111] subesse[112] crēdēns, postrīdiē aliēnissimō[113] sibi
50 locō, contrā[114] opportūnissimō[115] hostibus, adeō angusto marī[116] cōnflīxit ut eius multitūdō nāvium explicārī nōn potuerit[117] . . . Victus ergō est magis etiam cōnsiliō Themistoclī quam armīs Graeciae . . . Sīc ūnīus virī prū-dentiā[118] Graecia līberāta est Eurōpaeque succubuit[119] Asia.

Haec (est) altera victōria quae cum Marathōniō possit comparārī tro-
55 paeō.[120] Nam parī modō apud Salamīna parvō numerō nāvium maxima post hominum memoriam classis est dēvicta.[121] (**Nepos,** *Themistoclēs* 2–4, ex-cerpts)

20. ARISTIDES THE JUST

Aristīdēs,[1] Lȳsimachī[2] fīlius, Athēniēnsis, aequālis[3] ferē fuit Themistoclī[4] atque cum eō dē prīncipātū[5] contendit . . . In hīs autem cognitum est quantō[6] antistāret[7] ēloquentia innocentiae.[8] Quamquam enim adeō ex-cellēbat[9] Aristīdēs abstinentiā[10] ut ūnus post hominum memoriam . . . cog-
5 nōmine[11] "Iūstus" sit appellātus, tamen ā Themistocle collabefactus[12] tes-tulā[13] illā[14] exsiliō[15] decem annōrum[16] multātus est.[17]

---

[105] **adversāriōs** (= **hostēs**) **eius** (= **rēgis**)
[106] **fuga, -ae,** flight
[107] **quī** = **et eī**
[108] **sī discessissent . . . (eum) bellum cōnfectūrum (esse),** *another simple fut. condition in ind. state.:* **sī dis-cesserint** (*fut. perf.*), **tū bellum cōnficiēs . . . ; cōn-ficiō, -ere, -fēcī, -fectum,** finish, accomplish.
[109] one at a time
[110] **aggredior, -gredī, -gressus sum,** attack
[111] **dolus, -ī,** deceit, trick. *What kind of gen.* is **dolī**?
[112] **sub-sum,** be under, be concealed
[113] **aliēnus, -a, -um,** foreign, unfavorable
[114] **contrā,** *adv.,* on the contrary
[115] **opportūnus, -a, -um,** advantageous, *referring to* **locō**
[116] *abl. of place where without a prep.*
[117] *The perf. subj. is not uncommon in result cl. in histor-ical sequence.*
[118] **prūdentia, -ae,** foresight, discretion
[119] **succumbō, -ere, -cubuī,** submit, succumb
[120] **Marathōniō tropaeō,** trophy *or* victory at Marathon
[121] **dē-vincō,** conquer completely

20

[1] **Aristīdēs, -is,** *m.,* Aristides, *Athenian statesman and general*
[2] **Lȳsimachus, -ī,** Lysimachus

[3] **aequālis, -is,** *m.,* an equal in age, a contemporary
[4] **Themistoclī,** *here gen. of possession*
[5] **prīncipātus, -ūs,** first place, leadership
[6] *abl. of degree of difference (S.S.) depending on the idea of comparison in* **antistāret:** how much
[7] **anti-stō, -āre, -stetī,** stand before = excel
[8] **innocentia, -ae,** harmlessness; integrity. *Why dat.?*
[9] **excellō, -ere, -uī, -celsum,** excel; **excellēbat:** *note that* **quamquam** (although) *is used with the indic.*
[10] **abstinentia, -ae,** self-restraint, *especially in matters involving public funds,* uprightness; **abstinentiā,** *abl. of specification (S.S.).*
[11] **cognōmen, -minis,** *n., here* = epithet, apellative. *Of the three regular Roman names (***praenōmen, nō-men, cognōmen***) the* **cognōmen** (*cp.* **cognōscō**) *seems to have originated as a kind of nickname.*
[12] **collabefīō, -fierī, -factus sum,** be overthrown, be ruined
[13] **testula, -ae,** little potsherd; ostracism; **testulā** *abl. of accordance or perhaps means. Look up the inter-esting history of ostracism, a political safety valve against tyranny.*
[14] **illā,** *in the unusual position of following its noun* = that famous
[15] **exsiliō,** *abl. of penalty* (= *a form of abl. of means*)
[16] **decem annōrum,** *gen. of description*
[17] **multō** (1), punish

Quī quidem cum intellegeret reprimī[18] concitātam[19] multitūdinem nōn posse, cēdēnsque animadvertisset quendam scrībentem ut patriā pellerētur,[20] quaesīsse ab eō[21] dīcitur quārē id faceret aut quid Aristīdēs commīsisset cūr[22]

10 tantā poenā dignus dūcerētur. Cui ille respondit sē ignōrāre[23] Aristīdēn, sed sibi nōn placēre[24] quod tam cupidē labōrāsset ut praeter cēterōs "Iūstus" appellārētur. Hic decem annōrum lēgitimam[25] poenam nōn pertulit. Nam postquam[26] Xerxēs in Graeciam dēscendit,[27] sextō ferē annō quam[28] erat expulsus, populī scītō[29] in patriam restitūtus est.[30]

15 Interfuit[31] autem pugnae nāvālī apud Salamīna quae facta est priusquam[32] poenā līberārētur. Īdem[33] praetor fuit Athēniēnsium apud Plataeās[34] in proeliō quō fūsus[35] (est) barbarōrum exercitus Mardoniusque[36] interfectus est . . . Huius aequitāte[37] factum est,[38] cum in commūnī classe esset Graeciae simul cum Pausaniā[39] (quō duce[40] Mardonius erat fugātus[41]), ut summa im-

20 periī[42] maritimī ab Lacedaemoniīs trānsferrētur ad Athēniēnsēs; namque ante id tempus et marī et terrā ducēs erant Lacedaemoniī. Tum autem et intemperantiā[43] Pausaniae et iūstitiā factum est Aristīdis ut omnēs ferē cīvitātēs Graeciae ad Athēniēnsium societātem[44] sē applicārent[45] et adversus barbarōs hōs ducēs dēligerent[46] sibi.

25 Quōs[47] quō[48] facilius repellerent,[49] sī forte[50] bellum renovāre[51] cōnārentur, ad classēs aedificandās exercitūsque comparandōs[52] quantum pecūniae quaeque[53] cīvitās daret, Aristīdēs dēlēctus est quī cōnstitueret,[54] eiusque

---

[18] **re-primō, -ere, -pressī, -pressum,** press back, check
[19] **concitō** (1), arouse, excite
[20] *jussive noun cl.,* writing that he should be driven out
[21] **eō,** *i.e., the* **quendam** *above*
[22] (what he had committed) that
[23] **ignōrō** (1), not know, be unacquainted with
[24] **sibi nōn placēre** (*impers.*), it was not pleasing to him = he was displeased (because . . .)
[25] **lēgitimus, -a, -um,** fixed by law, legal
[26] **postquam,** *conj.* + *perf. ind.,* after
[27] **dēscendō, -ere, -scendī, -scēnsum,** descend, march on
[28] **quam** = **postquam; post** *sometimes omitted after an ordinal number in the abl. of time construction*
[29] **scītum, -ī,** decree (*cp. plebiscite*)
[30] **restituō, -ere, -stituī, -stitūtum,** restore
[31] **inter-sum** + *dat.,* be present at, take part in
[32] **priusquam** + *subj.*
[33] the same man = he also
[34] **Plataeae, -ārum,** Plataea
[35] **fundō, -ere, fūdī, fūsum,** pour out, rout
[36] **Mardonius, -iī,** Mardonius, *Persian general under Xerxes in command of the "barbarians"*
[37] **aequitās, -tātis,** *f.,* equity, fairness; **aequitāte,** *abl. of cause* (*S.S.*)
[38] **factum est . . . ut summa imperiī trānsferrētur,** it happened that the chief command was transferred;

ut . . . trānsferrētur, *noun cl. of result used as subject of* **factum est**
[39] **Pausaniās, -ae,** *m.,* Pausanias, *a Spartan, victor over the Persians at Plataea in 479* B.C. *but a person whose selfish ambition was too great to permit his continuing long as commander-in-chief of the united Greek forces*
[40] *abl. abs.*
[41] **fugō** (1), put to flight, rout; *not to be confused with* **fugiō**
[42] *L.I. 19 n. 97–98*
[43] **intemperantia, -ae,** intemperance, arrogance
[44] **societās, -tātis,** *f.,* confederacy, alliance
[45] **applicō** (1), attach
[46] **dēligō, -ere, -lēgī, -lēctum** = **legō**
[47] = **barbarōs**
[48] *L.I. 14 n. 18*
[49] **re-pellō**
[50] **forte,** *adv.,* by chance
[51] *If* **novus** *is new, what must the vb.* **re-novō** (1) *mean?*
[52] *Both gerundive phrases belong in the* **quantum** *cl.*
[53] **quaeque cīvitās: quaeque,** *f. adj. form of* **quisque**
[54] **cōnstituō, -ere, -stituī, -stitūtum,** establish, decide; **quī cōnstitueret,** *rel. cl. of purp., which has as its obj. the* **quantum . . . daret** *cl.*

arbitriō[55] quadringēna[56] et sexāgēna talenta quotannīs Dēlum[57] sunt conlāta; id enim commūne aerārium[58] esse voluērunt. Quae omnis pecūnia posterō[59]

30 tempore Athēnās trānslāta est. Hic quā[60] fuerit[61] abstinentiā, nūllum est certius indicium[62] quam quod,[63] cum tantīs rēbus praefuisset,[64] in tantā paupertāte dēcessit,[65] ut quī[66] efferrētur vix relīquerit. Quō[67] factum est ut fīliae eius pūblicē[68] alerentur et dē commūnī aerāriō dōtibus[69] datīs collocārentur.[70] (**Nepos**, *Aristīdēs,* excerpts)

21. TIMOLEON[1]

Diōne[2] Syrācūsīs interfectō, Dionȳsius[3] rūrsus Syrācūsārum potītus est.[4] Cuius adversāriī opem ā Corinthiīs[5] petiērunt ducemque, quō in bellō ūterentur, postulārunt. Hūc Tīmoleōn[6] missus incrēdibilī[7] fēlīcitāte[8] Dionȳsium tōtā Siciliā dēpulit.[9] Cum (eum) interficere posset, nōluit, tūtōque[10] ut Co-

5 rinthum[11] pervenīret effēcit,[12] quod utrōrumque[13] Dionȳsiōrum opibus Corinthiī saepe adiūtī fuerant . . . eamque praeclāram victōriam dūcēbat in quā plūs esset clēmentiae quam crūdēlitātis[14] . . .

Quibus rēbus cōnfectīs,[15] cum propter diūturnitātem[16] bellī nōn sōlum regiōnēs[17] sed etiam urbēs dēsertās[18] vidēret, conquīsīvit[19] . . . colōnōs.[20]

10 Cīvibus veteribus sua[21] restituit, novīs[22] bellō vacuēfactās[23] possessiōnēs[24]

[55] **arbitrium, -ī,** judgment, decision; **arbitriō,** *what kind of abl.?*

[56] **quadringēna et sexāgēna** (*distributive numerals*) **talenta quotannīs,** 460 talents each year

[57] **Dēlos, -ī,** *f.,* Delos, *small island in the center of the Cyclades in the Aegean*

[58] **aerārium, -iī,** treasury

[59] **posterus, -a, -um,** coming after (post), later

[60] **quā abstinentiā,** *abl. of description,* of what integrity he was = how great was his integrity

[61] *perf. subj., ind. quest. depending on* **indicium**

[62] **indicium, -iī,** indication, proof

[63] the fact that

[64] **prae-sum** + *dat.,* be in charge of

[65] **dē-cēdō,** depart, die

[66] **quī** = *old form of abl.:* with **efferrētur** = by which he might be buried = enough to bury him

[67] **quō,** *adv.,* wherefore

[68] **pūblicē,** *adv.,* at public expense

[69] **dōs, dōtis,** *f.,* dowry

[70] **collocō** (1), place, settle in marriage

21

[1] *Timoleon, who came from a noble family at Corinth, was a great champion of liberty against tyranny. By 334* B.C. *he was in Sicily fighting the Carthaginians, expelling tyrants, and establishing democracies.*

[2] **Diōn, Diōnis,** *m.,* Dion, *relative and friend of the tyrant Dionysius the Elder. With the aid of Plato he*

tried—but in vain—to give a noble pattern to the life of Dionysius the Younger, who followed his father in tyranny. After finally exiling Dionysius the Younger from Syracuse, he himself ruled tyrannically and was assassinated in 353 B.C.

[3] **Dionȳsius, -iī,** Dionysius the Younger

[4] **potior** + *gen. or abl.*

[5] **Corinthiī, -ōrum,** Corinthians

[6] **Tīmoleōn, -ontis,** *m.,* Timoleon

[7] **incrēdibilis, -e,** incredible

[8] **fēlīcitās, -tātis,** *f.,* happiness, good fortune

[9] **dē-pellō**

[10] **tūtō,** *adv.,* safely

[11] **Corinthus, -ī,** *f.,* Corinth, *on the Isthmus of Corinth*

[12] *L. A. 8 n. 20–21*

[13] **uterque, utraque, utrumque,** each; *here* = both

[14] **crūdēlitās, -tātis,** *f.,* cruelty

[15] *These words refer not only to the expulsion of Dionysius, but also to a great victory over the Carthaginians in Sicily as recounted in the omitted passages.*

[16] **diūturnitās, -tātis,** *f.,* long duration

[17] **regiō, -ōnis,** *f.,* region; *here* = country districts

[18] **dēsertus, -a, -um,** deserted

[19] **con-quīrō, -ere, -quīsīvī, -quīsītum (quaerō),** seek out, gather together

[20] **colōnus, -ī,** settler, colonist

[21] **sua,** *n. pl.*

[22] **novīs (colōnīs)**

[23] **vacuē-faciō,** make empty

[24] **possessiō, -ōnis,** *f.,* possession, property

dīvīsit[25]; urbium moenia disiecta[26] fānaque[27] dētēcta[28] refēcit[29]; cīvitātibus lēgēs lībertātemque reddidit . . . Cum tantīs esset opibus[30] ut etiam invītīs[31] imperāre posset, tantum[32] autem amōrem habēret omnium Siculōrum[33] ut nūllō recūsante rēgnum obtinēre[34] licēret, māluit sē dīligī quam metuī.

15   Itaque, cum prīmum[35] potuit, imperium dēposuit ac prīvātus[36] Syrācūsīs . . . vīxit. Neque vērō id imperītē[37] fēcit, nam quod cēterī rēgēs imperiō potuērunt, hic benevolentiā[38] tenuit . . .

Hic cum aetāte iam prōvectus esset,[39] sine ūllō morbō lūmina[40] oculōrum āmīsit. Quam calamitātem[41] ita moderātē[42] tulit ut . . . (nēmō) eum
20   querentem audierit[43] . . . Nihil umquam neque īnsolēns[44] neque glōriōsum[45] ex ōre eius exiit. Quī quidem, cum suās laudēs audīret praedicārī,[46] numquam aliud dīxit quam[47] sē in eā rē maximē dīs agere grātiās . . . quod, cum Siciliam recreāre cōnstituissent, tum sē potissimum[48] ducem esse voluissent. Nihil enim rērum hūmānārum sine deōrum nūmine[49] gerī putābat . . .

25   Proelia maxima nātālī[50] suō diē fēcit omnia; quō factum est ut[51] eius diem nātālem fēstum[52] habēret ūniversa Sicilia . . .

Cum quīdam Dēmaenetus[53] in cōntiōne[54] populī dē rēbus gestīs[55] eius dētrahere[56] coepisset ac nōnnūlla inveherētur[57] in Timoleonta, dīxit nunc dēmum[58] sē vōtī esse damnātum[59]; namque hoc ā dīs immortālibus semper
30   precātum[60] ut tālem lībertātem restitueret Syrācūsānīs in quā cuivīs[61] licēret dē quō vellet impūne[62] dīcere.[63]

---

[25] **dīvidō, -ere, dīvīsī, dīvīsum,** divide, distribute
[26] **dis-iciō,** throw apart, scatter
[27] **fānum, -ī,** shrine, temple (cp. profane, fanatic, fan = devotee)
[28] **dē-tegō, -ere, -tēxī, -tēctum,** unroof, uncover (cp. detect)
[29] **re-ficiō**
[30] **tantīs . . . opibus:** abl. of description
[31] **(Siculīs) etiam invītīs,** (the Sicilians) even against their will
[32] **tantum . . . licēret: cum,** although, introduces this cl. as well as the preceding one.
[33] **Siculī, -ōrum,** the Sicilians
[34] **obtineō, -ēre, -tinuī, -tentum,** occupy, hold
[35] **cum prīmum,** as soon as
[36] **prīvātus, -ī,** private citizen; as a private citizen, he . . .
[37] **imperītē,** adv., unskillfully, ignorantly
[38] **benevolentia, -ae,** good-will, kindness
[39] **prō-vehō, -ere, -vexī, -vectum,** carry forward
[40] **lūmen, -minis,** n., light; sight
[41] **calamitās, -tātis,** f., misfortune
[42] **moderātē,** adv., with moderation
[43] perf. subj. in historical sequence
[44] **īnsolēns,** gen. -entis, arrogant, insolent
[45] **glōriōsus, -a, -um,** here = boastful
[46] **praedicō** (1), declare, relate
[47] **aliud quam,** other than
[48] **potissimum,** adv., especially, above all
[49] **nūmen, -minis,** n., divine power, command
[50] **nātālis diēs, nātālis diēī,** m., birthday
[51] **quō . . . ut,** L.I. 20 n. 38, 67
[52] **fēstus, -a, -um,** festive
[53] **Dēmaenetus, -ī,** Demaenetus, an enemy of Timoleon
[54] **cōntiō, -ōnis,** f., assembly
[55] **rēs gestae, rērum gestārum** (lit. things done), exploits, deeds
[56] **dē-trahō,** detract, disparage
[57] **nōnnūlla** is n. acc. pl.—**invehor, -ī, -vectus sum** (deponent form of **in-vehō**), + in + acc., make an attack on, inveigh against: **nōnnūlla inveherētur in,** he made some attacks on
[58] **dēmum,** adv., at last
[59] **damnō** (1) + gen., condemn on the charge of; **vōtī damnārī,** to be condemned to pay a vow = to have a vow or prayer granted
[60] **precor** (1), beseech
[61] dat. of **quī-vīs, quae-vīs, quid-vīs (quod-vīs),** indef., anyone at all, anything at all
[62] **impūne,** adv., with impunity
[63] **dīcere,** subject of **licēret**

Hic cum diem suprēmum obīsset, pūblicē[64] ā Syrācūsānīs in gymnasiō,[65]
quod Tīmoleontēum[66] appellātur, tōtā celebrante[67] Siciliā, sepultus est.[68]
(**Nepos**, *Tīmoleōn* 2–5, excerpts)

22. HORACE'S "CARPE DIEM"

Tū nē quaesierīs[1]—scīre nefās[2]—quem mihi, quem[3] tibi
fīnem dī dederint, Leuconoē,[4] nec Babylōniōs
temptārīs[5] numerōs.[6] Ut melius,[7] quidquid erit, patī.

. . .

Spem longam[8] resecēs.[9] Dum loquimur, fūgerit invida[10]
5   aetās. Carpe diem, quam minimum[11] crēdula[12] posterō.[13]
(**Horace**, *Odes* 1.11, excerpts)

23. INTEGER VĪTAE

Integer[1] vītae scelerisque pūrus[2]
nōn eget Maurīs[3] iaculīs[4] neque arcū[5]
nec venēnātīs[6] gravidā[7] sagittīs,[8]
    Fusce,[9] pharetrā.[10]

. . .

---

[64] **pūblicē,** *adv. of* **pūblicus**
[65] **gymnasium, -iī,** gymnasium, *which in Gk. had a much broader meaning than it does in Eng.*
[66] **Tīmoleontēum,** the Timoleonteum (gymnasium)
[67] **celebrō** (1), celebrate
[68] **sepeliō, -īre, -pelīvī, -pultum,** bury

22

METER: Greater Asclepiad.
[1] **nē quaesierīs** (= **quaesīverīs**): **nē** + *perf. subj.* = *a colloquial prohibition (negative command),* do not seek
[2] **nefās,** *n., indecl.,* wrong, sin; **nefās (est),** it is wrong
[3] **quem . . . quem,** *modifies* **fīnem**
[4] **Leuconoē, -es,** *f.,* Leuconoë, *a Gk. name*
[5] **temptō** (1), try; **temptārīs** = **temptāverīs,** *another neg. command*
[6] **numerōs,** *calculations employed by astrologers in casting horoscopes; "Babylonian" because astrology was associated with the East. With the decay of belief in the old-time religion in Rome during the first cen.* B.C., *astrology and superstitions prospered. Apparently Leuconoë had visited a fortune teller.*
[7] **ut melius (est),** how (much) better it is
[8] *i.e., projected too far into the future*

[9] **resecō, -āre, -secuī, -sectum,** cut off, prune back; **resecēs,** *poetic use of the pres. subj.* (*jussive*) *for the pres. imper.*
[10] **invidus, -a, -um,** envious
[11] **minimum,** *adv.* = **minimē**
[12] **crēdulus, -a, -um,** believing in, trusting + *dat.;* **crēdula,** *nom. f. sg. agreeing with the subject of* **carpe,** *i.e.* **Leuconoē**
[13] **posterō (diēī),** *dat.*

23

METER: Sapphic stanza.
[1] **integer, -gra, -grum,** untouched, blameless; (**vir**) **integer vītae** (*poetic gen. of specification*), the person blameless in his life
[2] **pūrus, -a, -um,** pure, free from; **sceleris,** *poetic gen. of separation or specification*
[3] **Maurus, -a, -um,** Moorish (= Mauritanian)
[4] **iaculum, -ī,** missile, javelin (*cp.* **iaciō**)
[5] **arcus, -ūs,** bow
[6] **venēnātus, -a, -um,** poisonous, dipped in poison
[7] **gravidus, -a, -um,** laden (with); *cp.* **gravis**
[8] **sagitta, -ae,** arrow
[9] **Fuscus, -ī,** Fuscus, *a literary man and a close, sometimes waggish, friend of Horace*
[10] **pharetra, -ae,** quiver

5   Namque mē silvā lupus[11] in Sabīnā[12]
    dum meam cantō[13] Lalagēn[14] et ultrā
    terminum[15] cūrīs vagor[16] expedītīs[17]
        fūgit[18] inermem.[19]

    . . .

    Pōne mē pigrīs[20] ubi nūlla campīs
10   arbor aestīvā[21] recreātur aurā,[22]
    quod[23] latus mundī nebulae[24] malusque[25]
        Iuppiter urget[26];
    pōne sub currū[27] nimium propinquī
    sōlis in terrā domibus negāta:
15   dulce[28] rīdentem Lalagēn amābō
        dulce loquentem.
              (Horace, *Odes* 1.22.1–4, 9–12, 17–24)

24. AUREA MEDIOCRITĀS—THE GOLDEN MEAN

    Rēctius[1] vīvēs, Licinī,[2] neque altum[3]
    semper urgendō[4] neque, dum procellās[5]
    cautus[6] horrēscis,[7] nimium premendō
        lītus[8] inīquum.[9]

[11] **lupus, -ī,** wolf

[12] **Sabīnus, -a, -um,** Sabine; *cp. L. A. 10*

[13] **cantō** (1), sing about; **dum** + *historical pres. to denote continued action in past time:* while I was singing about

[14] **Lalagē, -ēs,** *acc.* **Lalagēn** (*Gk. noun*), *f.,* Lalage, *name of a girl—a most mellifluous name!*

[15] **terminus, -ī,** boundary (*cp. terminus, term, terminate*)

[16] **vagor** (1), wander, ramble (*cp. vagary, vagabond*)

[17] **expediō** (4), disentangle, set free; **cūrīs expedītīs,** *abl. abs.*

[18] *Note the interlocked word order of this stanza, which is so characteristic of Lat. poetry:* **mē** (*obj. of* **fūgit**) *at the beginning modified by* **inermem** *at the end;* **silvā in Sabīnā,** *place where phrase interrupted by* **lupus** *subject of* **fūgit;** *all this separated from the main vb. by a double* **dum** *cl.*

[19] **inermis, -e,** unarmed; *cp.* **integer vītae ... nōn eget iaculīs.**

[20] **piger, -gra, -grum,** lazy, sluggish, torpid (*because frozen*), *modifying* **campīs** (campus, -ī, field) *in a place-where phrase without a prep.* (*the omission of a prep. is common in poetry*). *The order of the thought is:* **pōne mē (in) pigrīs campīs ubi ...**

[21] **aestīvus, -a, -um,** summer (*cp.* **aestās**)

[22] **aura, -ae,** breeze

[23] = (or put me) **in eō latere mundī quod ... ; latus, -eris,** *n.,* side, region

[24] **nebula, -ae,** mist, fog

[25] **malus** = inclement, *because Jupiter is here god of the weather*

[26] **urgeō, -ēre, ursī,** urge, press, oppress

[27] **currus, -ūs,** chariot

[28] **dulce,** *poetic for* **dulciter.** *These exquisitely mellifluous last lines somewhat onomatopoetically suggest the dulcet timbre of Lalage's voice and laugh.*

24

METER: Sapphic stanza.

[1] **rēctius,** *adv.,* rightly, well, suitably

[2] **Licinī,** *voc. of* Licinius, *a person who seems to have been wanting in the virtue of moderation*

[3] the deep (sea)

[4] *i.e.,* heading out to the deep

[5] **procella, -ae,** storm, gale

[6] **cautus, -a, -um,** cautious, circumspect; *with* **dum ... horrēscis,** while you in your caution ...

[7] **horrēscō, -ere, horruī,** begin to shudder at, begin to dread

[8] **altum** and **lītus** = *extremes*

[9] **inīquus, -a, -um,** unequal; *here* = treacherous

5   Auream[10] quisquis mediocritātem[11]
       dīligit, tūtus[12] caret obsolētī[13]
       sordibus[14] tēctī, caret invidendā[15]
         sōbrius[16] aulā.[17]
       Saepius ventīs agitātur[18] ingēns

10   pīnus[19] et celsae[20] graviōre cāsū[21]
       dēcidunt[22] turrēs[23] feriuntque[24] summōs
         fulgura[25] montēs.
       Spērat[26] īnfestīs,[27] metuit secundīs[28]
       alteram[29] sortem[30] bene praeparātum[31]

15   pectus.[32] Īnfōrmēs[33] hiemēs[34] redūcit
       Iuppiter[35]; īdem[36]
       summovet.[37] Nōn, sī male[38] nunc, et ōlim[39]
       sīc erit: quondam[40] citharā[41] tacentem
       suscitat[42] Mūsam,[43] neque semper arcum

20   tendit[44] Apollō.[45]
       Rēbus angustīs[46] animōsus[47] atque

---

[10] **aureus, -a, -um,** golden

[11] **mediocritās, -tātis,** *f.,* moderation, the mean between extremes. *Note that Horace does not say that "mediocrity" is golden! The idea of* (**aurea**) **mediocritās** *was common in Gk. ethical thought, and Aristotle made it a cardinal virtue in his "Ethics."*

[12] **tūtus caret,** secure (*in his philosophy of the "golden mean"*) he is free from . . .

[13] **obsolētus, -a, -um,** worn out, dilapidated

[14] **sordēs, -ium,** *f. pl.,* dirt, filth; **sordibus,** *what kind of abl.?*

[15] **invidendā,** sure to be envied

[16] **sōbrius, -a, -um,** sober-minded, moderate, in his sobriety

[17] **aula, -ae,** palace

[18] **agitō** (1), agitate, toss

[19] **pīnus, -ī,** *f.,* pine

[20] **celsus, -a, -um,** high, lofty

[21] **cāsus, -ūs,** fall, destruction

[22] **dēcidō, -ere, -cidī,** fall down (*cp.* **cadō**)

[23] **turris, -is,** *f.,* tower

[24] **feriō** (4), strike

[25] **fulgur, -uris,** *n.,* lightning, thunderbolt

[26] anticipates, expects

[27] **īnfestus, -a, -um,** unsafe, dangerous, adverse; **īnfestīs** (**rēbus**) *dat., lit.:* for his adverse circumstances (= in adversity) he anticipates the other (= the opposite) fortune (**sortem**)

[28] **secundīs** (**rēbus**) *balances* **īnfestīs:** for his favorable circumstances (= in prosperity) he apprehends the opposite fortune.

[29] **alter,** the other of two; *here* = the opposite

[30] **sors, sortis,** *f.,* lot, fortune; **sortem,** *obj. of* **spērat** *and* **metuit**

[31] **prae-parō** (1), make ready in advance, prepare: well prepared (*by the philosophy of life which Horace is here enunciating*)

[32] *subject of* **spērat** *and* **metuit**

[33] **īnfōrmis, -e,** shapeless, hideous, horrid

[34] **hiems, hiemis,** *f.,* stormy weather, winter

[35] Jupiter *as god of sky and weather*

[36] **īdem,** the same god = he also

[37] **sum-moveō,** remove, drive away, *sc.* **hiemēs**

[38] **male (est),** it is bad, things are bad

[39] **et ōlim,** also in the future

[40] *here* = sometimes

[41] **cithara, -ae,** lyre

[42] **suscitō** (1), arouse; **suscitat,** *subject is* **Apollō**

[43] **Mūsa, -ae,** a Muse

[44] **tendō, -ere, tetendī, tēnsum,** stretch

[45] **Apollō, -inis,** *m.,* Apollo, *god of the sun, prophecy, poetry, and music; also god of archery, pestilence, and medicine. Apollo has two aspects: happy and constructive* (**Mūsam**); *unhappy and destructive* (**arcum**).

[46] **rēbus angustīs,** *abl. abs.,* when things are narrow (= **difficilis**), *i.e.,* in adversity

[47] **anim-ōsus, -a, -um** (**-ōsus,** *suffix* = full of), spirited

fortis appārē[48]; sapienter[49] īdem[50]
contrahēs[51] ventō nimium secundō
   turgida[52] vēla.[53]

(**Horace,** *Odes* 2.10)

25. LĀBUNTUR ANNĪ

Ēheu![1] fugācēs,[2] Postume, Postume,
lābuntur[3] annī; nec pietās[4] moram
   rūgīs[5] et īnstantī[6] senectae[7]
      adferet indomitaeque[8] mortī.

   . . .

5   Frūstrā[9] cruentō[10] Mārte[11] carēbimus
   frāctīsque[12] raucī[13] flūctibus[14] Hadriae[15];
      frūstrā[9] per autumnōs[16] nocentem
         corporibus[17] metuēmus Austrum.[18]
   Vīsendus[19] āter[20] flūmine languidō[21]
10   Cōcȳtos[22] errāns et Danaī genus[23]
      īnfāme[24] damnātusque[25] longī
         Sīsyphus[26] Aeolidēs[27] labōris.[28]

---

[48] **appāreō, -ēre, -uī, -itum,** show one's self; **appārē,** *analyze the form carefully.*
[49] *here = if you are wise*
[50] *see n. 36 above*
[51] **con-trahō,** draw in, shorten
[52] **turgidus, -a, -um,** swollen
[53] **vēlum, -ī,** sail

25

METER: Alcaic stanza.
[1] **ēheu,** *cp.* **heu.** *This sigh is emphasized by the repetition of Postumus' name.*
[2] **fugāx,** *gen.* **-ācis,** fleeting
[3] **lābor, -ī, lāpsus sum,** slip, glide
[4] **pietās, -tātis,** *f.,* loyalty, devotion, piety
[5] **rūga, -ae,** wrinkle (*cp. corrugated*)
[6] **īnstāns,** *gen.* **-antis,** pressing, urgent
[7] **senecta, -ae = senectūs**
[8] **indomitus, -a, -um,** untamable, invincible
[9] **frūstrā,** *adv.,* in vain. *What is the significance of its emphatic position?*
[10] **cruentus, -a, -um,** bloody
[11] **Mārs, Mārtis,** *m.,* Mars, *god of war;* **Mārte,** *what abl.?*
[12] **frangō, -ere, frēgī, frāctum,** break
[13] **raucus, -a, -um,** hoarse, noisy

[14] **flūctus, -ūs,** wave; **frāctīs flūctibus,** broken waves = breakers
[15] **Hadria, -ae,** *m.,* Adriatic Sea
[16] **autumnus, -ī,** autumn, *unhealthy part of the year because of the Sirocco*
[17] *depends on* **nocentem**
[18] **auster, -trī,** the south wind, *the Sirocco blowing from the Sahara*
[19] **vīsō, -ere, vīsī, vīsum,** visit; **vīsendus (est)**
[20] **āter, ātra, ātrum,** dark, *modifying* **Cōcȳtos**
[21] **languidus, -a, -um,** sluggish, weak
[22] **Cōcȳtos, -ī,** *m.,* Cocytus, the river of wailing, *one of the rivers surrounding Hades;* **Cōcȳtos,** *Gk. nom.*
[23] **Danaī genus,** *the offspring of* **Danaüs,** *whose 49 daughters murdered their husbands and in Hades were punished by having to pour water eternally into a sieve*
[24] **īnfāmis, -e,** infamous
[25] **damnō** (1) condemn
[26] **Sīsyphus, -ī,** Sisyphus, *who was condemned eternally to roll up a hill a stone which rolled down again—an exquisite nightmare*
[27] **Aeolidēs, -ae,** *m.,* son of Aeolus
[28] *After vbs. of accusing, condemning, and acquitting the gen. can be used to express the charge or the penalty involved.*

Linquenda[29] tellūs[30] et domus et placēns
uxor, neque hārum, quās colis, arborum
15   tē praeter invīsās[31] cupressōs[32]
ūlla[33] brevem dominum[34] sequētur.
(**Horace,** *Odes* 2.14.1–4, 13–24)

26. A SENSE OF BALANCE IN LIFE

Vīvitur[1] parvō bene cui[2] paternum[3]
splendet[4] in mēnsā tenuī[5] salīnum,
nec levēs[6] somnōs timor aut cupīdō
sordidus[7] aufert.[8]
5   Quid[9] brevī fortēs[10] iaculāmur[11] aevō
multa? Quid[12] terrās aliō calentēs
sōle mūtāmus? Patriae quis exsul[13]
sē quoque fūgit?[14]
Scandit[15] aerātās[16] vitiōsa nāvēs
10   cūra nec turmās[17] equitum relinquit,
ōcior[18] cervīs[19] et agente nimbōs[20]
ōcior Eurō.[21]

---

[29] **linquenda (est),** *balancing* **vīsendus** in contrast; **lin-quō = relinquō**

[30] **tellūs, -ūris,** *f.,* earth, land

[31] **invīsus, -a, -um,** hated, hateful

[32] **cupressus, -ī,** *f.,* cypress (tree); **invīsās** *because they were used at funerals and were planted near tombs*

[33] **neque ūlla hārum arborum,** nor any = and none . . .

[34] **brevem dominum,** *in apposition with* **tē; brevem,** *implying that life is brief*

26

METER: Sapphic stanza.

[1] **vīvitur parvō bene (ab eō) cui,** it is lived on little well by him for whom: **vīvitur,** *impers. pass.* = he lives well on little (*i.e., not in abject poverty and not in the lap of luxury*).

[2] **cui,** *dat. of ref. but most easily translated by* whose

[3] **paternum salīnum (salīnum, -ī),** paternal salt-cellar; *the long list of words derived from* **sāl** *provides some idea of the importance of salt and the salt-cellar.*

[4] **splendeō, -ēre,** shine

[5] **tenuis, -e,** plain, simple

[6] **levis, -e,** *here* = gentle

[7] **sordidus, -a, -um,** sordid (*cp.* **sordēs** *L.I. 24 n. 14*); **cupīdō** *is m. in Horace.*

[8] **auferō (ab-ferō)**

[9] = **cūr**

[10] **fortēs (virī) brevī aevō (aevum, -ī,** time, life)

[11] **iaculor (1),** aim at

[12] **Quid . . . mūtāmus,** *lit.* why do we exchange lands warmed by another sun? *The expression is poetic and in part illogical but the sense is clear:* why do we exchange our lands for those warmed by another sun? "The pasture is always greener . . ."

[13] **exsul, exsulis,** *m.,* exile; *with* **patriae quis,** who an exile of (from) his native land

[14] **fūgit,** *perf.,* has ever fled

[15] **scandō, -ere, scandī, scānsum,** climb up

[16] **aerātus, -a, -um,** fitted with bronze, *probably referring to the bronze beaks of the men-of-war* (**longae nāvēs**), *which were faster than the ordinary ships—though even these cannot outstrip anxiety.*

[17] **turma, -ae,** a troop of cavalry (**equitum,** *L.I. 18 n. 53*). *A person cannot ride fast enough to escape care.*

[18] **ōcior, -ius,** *adj. in compar. degree,* swifter, *agreeing with* **cūra**

[19] **cervus, -ī,** stag

[20] **nimbus, -ī,** rain cloud

[21] **Eurus, -ī,** wind (from the southeast)

Laetus[22] in praesēns[23] animus quod ultrā est
ōderit[24] cūrāre et amāra[25] lentō[26]
15   temperet[27] rīsū[28]: nihil est ab omnī
parte[29] beātum.

(Horace, *Odes* 2.16.13–28)

27. DIĒS FĒSTUS

Hic diēs[1] vērē mihi fēstus ātrās
eximet[2] cūrās: ego nec tumultum
nec morī per vim metuam tenente
Caesare[3] terrās.
5   Ī, pete unguentum,[4] puer,[5] et corōnās,[6]
et cadum[7] Mārsī[8] memorem[9] duellī,
Spartacum[10] sī quā[11] potuit vagantem
fallere[12] testa.[13]

(Horace, *Odes* 3.14.13–20)

28. A MONUMENT MORE LASTING THAN BRONZE

Exēgī monumentum aere perennius[1]
rēgālīque[2] sitū[3] pȳramidum[4] altius,[5]
quod nōn imber[6] edāx,[7] nōn Aquilō[8] impotēns[9]
possit dīruere[10] aut innumerābilis[11]

[22] **laetus, -a, -um,** happy, joyful
[23] **praesēns,** *gen.* **-entis,** present; **in praesēns (tempus)**
for the present (*cp. the* **carpe diem** *philosophy*)
[24] **ōderit,** *perf. subj., jussive,* let (the **laetus animus**) refuse to (hate to) be anxious about (**cūrāre**)
[25] **amārus, -a, -um,** bitter, disagreeable; **amāra,** *n. pl.*
[26] **lentus, -a, -um,** pliant, tenacious, slow, lingering;
here = tolerant, quiet
[27] **temperō** (1), control, temper
[28] **rīsus, -ūs,** laughter (*cp.* **rīdeō**)
[29] **ab omnī parte,** from every part = in every respect,
completely

27

METER: Sapphic stanza.
[1] **Hic diēs,** *referring to Augustus' return from the cam-
paign of 27–25* B.C. *in Spain*
[2] **eximō, -ere, -ēmī, -ēmptum,** take away
[3] Caesar = Augustus. *When C. Octavius was adopted
by his great-uncle, C. Iulius Caesar, his name became C. Iulius Caesar Octavianus, to which the
senate added the title of Augustus in 27* B.C.
[4] **unguentum, -ī,** ointment, perfume
[5] **puer** = slave; *cp. Fr.* **garçon**
[6] **corōna, -ae,** crown, wreath
[7] **cadus, -ī,** wine jar

[8] **Mārsus, -a, -um,** Marsian; **duellum** = *old form of* **bellum: Mārsī duellī,** *of the Marsian, or Social, War
of 91–88* B.C., *by which the* **sociī** (*allies*) *of Rome
in Italy gained full citizenship; i.e., a 65-year-old
wine*
[9] **memor,** *gen.* **-oris,** mindful
[10] **Spartacus, -ī,** Spartacus, *the gladiator who led the
slaves in revolt against Rome, 73–71* B.C.
[11] **quā,** *adv.,* anywhere *or* in any way
[12] **fallō, -ere, fefellī, falsum,** deceive, escape the notice
of
[13] **testa, -ae,** jug

28

METER: Lesser Asclepiad.
[1] **perennis, -e,** lasting (throughout the year)
[2] **rēgālis, -e,** royal
[3] **situs, -ūs,** site, situation; *here* = structure
[4] **pȳramis, -idis,** *f.,* pyramid
[5] **altus, -a, -um,** high; **altius** *agrees with* **monumentum.**
[6] **imber, -bris,** *m.,* storm
[7] **edāx,** *gen.* **edacis,** greedy, destructive
[8] **aquilō, -ōnis,** *m.,* north wind
[9] **impotēns,** *gen.* **-ntis,** powerless (*to injure my monument*)
[10] **dīruō, -ere, -ruī, -rutum,** raze, destroy
[11] **in-numerābilis, -e** = *Eng.*

5   annōrum seriēs[12] et fuga temporum.
     Nōn omnis moriar, multaque pars meī
     vītābit Libitīnam[13] . . .
                     (Horace, *Odes* 3.30.1–7)

29. THE OTHER PERSON'S FAULTS AND OUR OWN

Pērās[1] imposuit[2] Iuppiter nōbīs duās:
propriīs[3] replētam[4] vitiīs post tergum[5] dedit,[6]
aliēnīs[7] ante pectus[8] suspendit[9] gravem.
Hāc rē vidēre nostra mala nōn possumus;
5   aliī simul[10] dēlinquunt,[11] cēnsōrēs[12] sumus.
                (Phaedrus, *Fābulae* 4.10)

30. SOUR GRAPES

Famē[1] coācta vulpēs[2] altā in vīneā[3]
ūvam[4] appetēbat,[5] summīs saliēns[6] vīribus.
Quam[7] tangere ut nōn potuit, discēdēns ait:
"Nōndum mātūra[8] est; nōlō acerbam sūmere.[9]"
5   Quī facere[10] quae nōn possunt verbīs ēlevant,[11]
     adscrībere[12] hoc dēbēbunt exemplum sibī.
                 (Phaedrus, *Fābulae* 4.3)

31. THE FOX AND THE TRAGIC MASK

Persōnam[1] tragicam[2] forte[3] vulpēs vīderat.
"Ō quanta speciēs,[4]" inquit, "cerebrum[5] nōn habet!"

---

[12] **seriēs, -ēī,** succession
[13] **Libitīna, -ae,** Libitina, *goddess of funerals;* death

29

METER: Iambic trimeter.
   Phaedrus: freedman of Augustus, who made extensive use of Aesop's fables.
[1] **pēra, -ae,** wallet
[2] **im-pōnō,** + *dat.,* put on
[3] **proprius, -a, -um,** one's own, *here* = our own
[4] **repleō, -ēre, -plēvī, -plētum,** fill; **(pēram) replētam**
[5] **tergum, -ī,** back
[6] **dedit,** *here* = put
[7] **aliēnus, -a, -um,** belonging to another; **aliēnīs (vitiīs),** *abl. with* **gravem**
[8] *sc.* **nostrum**
[9] **(alteram pēram) gravem . . . suspendit**
[10] **simul = simul ac,** as soon as
[11] **dēlinquō, -ere, -līquī, -lictum,** fail, commit a crime
[12] **cēnsor, -ōris,** *m.,* censor; censurer, severe judge

30

METER: Iambic trimeter.

[1] **famēs, -is,** *abl.* **-e,** appetite, hunger
[2] **vulpēs, -is,** *f.,* fox
[3] **vīnea, -ae,** vineyard
[4] **ūva, -ae,** bunch of grapes
[5] **ap-petō (= ad-petō),** reach toward, desire (*cp. appetite*); **appetēbat,** *note the force of the impf.*
[6] **saliō, -īre, -uī, saltum,** jump
[7] **quam = ūvam**
[8] **mātūrus, -a, -um,** ripe
[9] **sūmō, -ere, sūmpsī, sūmptum,** take
[10] *compl. inf. with* **possunt**
[11] **ēlevō (1),** disparage, weaken
[12] **ad-scrībō,** assign

31

METER: Iambic trimeter.
[1] **persōna, -ae,** mask *worn by actors*
[2] **tragicus, -a, -um,** tragic
[3] **forte,** *adv.,* by chance
[4] **speciēs, -ēī,** appearance, form
[5] **cerebrum, -ī,** brain

Hoc illīs dictum est quibus honōrem et glōriam
Fortūna tribuit,[6] sēnsum commūnem abstulit.
(**Phaedrus**, *Fābulae* 1.7)

32. THE STAG AT THE SPRING

Ad fontem[1] cervus, cum bibisset, restitit,[2]
et in liquōre[3] vīdit effigiem[4] suam.
Ibi dum rāmōsa[5] mīrāns[6] laudat cornua,
crūrumque[7] nimiam[8] tenuitātem[9] vituperat,[10]
5   vēnantum[11] subitō vōcibus conterritus,[12]
per campum fugere coepit, et cursū levī
canēs[13] ēlūsit.[14] Silva tum excēpit ferum,[15]
in quā retentīs[16] impedītus cornibus,
lacerārī[17] coepit morsibus[18] saevīs[19] canum.
10   Tunc moriēns vōcem hanc ēdidisse[20] dīcitur:
"Ō mē īnfēlīcem[21]! quī nunc dēmum[22] intellegō
ūtilia mihi quam[23] fuerint quae[24] dēspexeram,[25]
et quae laudāram,[26] quantum lūctūs[27] habuerint."
(**Phaedrus**, *Fābulae* 1.12)

33. THE FOX GETS THE RAVEN'S CHEESE

Quī sē laudārī gaudet verbīs subdolīs,[1]
ferē dat poenās turpī paenitentiā.[2]
Cum dē fenestrā corvus[3] raptum cāseum[4]
comēsse[5] vellet, celsā residēns[6] arbore,

---

[6] **tribuō, -ere, -uī, -ūtum,** allot, assign, give

32

METER: Iambic trimeter.
[1] **fōns, fontis,** *m.,* spring
[2] **restō, -āre, restitī,** remain (standing)
[3] **liquor, -ōris,** *m.,* liquid
[4] **effigiēs, -ēī,** image, likeness
[5] **rāmōsus, -a, -um,** branching
[6] **mīror (1),** marvel at, wonder
[7] **crūs, crūris,** *n.,* leg
[8] **nimius, -a, -um,** excessive
[9] **tenuitās, -tātis,** *f.,* thinness
[10] **vituperō (1),** blame, find fault with
[11] **vēnor (1),** hunt; **vēnantum,** *gen. pl. of pres. part.*
[12] **con-territus**
[13] **canis, -is,** *m./f.,* dog
[14] **ēlūdō, -ere, -lūsī, -lūsum,** evade
[15] **ferus, -ī,** wild animal
[16] **re-tentus, -a, -um,** held back, held fast

[17] **lacerō (1),** tear to pieces (*cp.* lacerate)
[18] **morsus, -ūs,** bite
[19] **saevus, -a, -um,** fierce, savage
[20] **ēdō, -ere, -didī, -ditum,** give out, utter
[21] **mē īnfēlīcem,** *acc. of exclamation.*
[22] **dēmum,** *adv.,* at last
[23] **ūtilia . . . quam = quam ūtilia**
[24] **(ea,** those things**) quae**
[25] **dēspiciō, -ere, -spexī, -spectum,** look down on, despise
[26] **= laudāveram**
[27] **lūctus, -ūs,** grief, sorrow

33

METER: Iambic trimeter.
[1] **subdolus, -a, -um,** deceitful
[2] **paenitentia, -ae,** repentance
[3] **corvus, -ī,** raven
[4] **cāseus, -ī,** cheese
[5] **comedō, comedere** *or* **comēsse, -ēdī, -ēsum,** eat up
[6] **resideō, -ēre, -sēdī, -sessum,** sit, be sitting

5   hunc vīdit vulpēs; deinde sīc coepit loquī:
       "Ō quī tuārum, corve, pennārum[7] est nitor[8]!
       Quantum decōris[9] corpore et vultū geris![10]
       Sī vōcem habērēs, nūlla prior[11] āles[12] foret." [13]
       At ille stultus, dum vult vōcem ostendere,
10   ēmīsit[14] ōre cāseum, quem celeriter
       dolōsa[15] vulpēs avidīs[16] rapuit dentibus.[17]
                        (Phaedrus, *Fābulae* 1.13.1–10)

34. THE ASS AND THE OLD SHEPHERD

       In prīncipātū[1] commūtandō[2] cīvium
       nīl praeter dominī nōmen mūtant pauperēs.
       Id esse vērum parva haec fābella[3] indicat.
       Asellum[4] in prātō[5] timidus[6] pāscēbat[7] senex.
5   Is, hostium clamōre[8] subitō[9] territus,
       suādēbat[10] asinō fugere nē possent capī.
       At ille lentus:[11] "Quaesō,[12] num bīnās[13] mihī
       clītellās[14] impositūrum[15] victōrem[16] putās?"
       Senex negāvit. "Ergō quid rēfert meā[17]
10   cui serviam clītellās dum portem[18] meās?"
                        (Phaedrus, *Fābulae* 1.15)

35. THE TWO MULES AND THE ROBBERS

       Mūlī[1] gravātī[2] sarcinīs[3] ībant duō.
       Ūnus ferēbat fiscōs[4] cum pecūniā;

[7] **penna, -ae,** feather
[8] **nitor, -ōris,** *m.,* brightness, beauty; **quī est nitor,** what (= how great) is the beauty
[9] **decor, decōris,** *m.,* grace, beauty
[10] you bear, *i.e.,* have in your body and face; **(in) corpore,** *preps. often omitted in poetry*
[11] **prior,** *predicate adj. after* **foret,** better, finer
[12] **āles, ālitis,** *f.,* bird
[13] **foret = esset**
[14] **ē-mittō**
[15] **dolōsus, -a, -um,** crafty, cunning
[16] **avidus, -a, -um,** greedy, eager
[17] **dēns, dentis,** *m.,* tooth

34

METER: Iambic trimeter.
[1] **prīncipātus, -ūs,** rule, dominion
[2] **com-mūtō** (1), change
[3] **fābella, -ae,** fable
[4] **asellus, -ī,** a little ass, *diminutive of* **asinus, -ī,** an ass (*verse 6*)
[5] **prātum, -ī,** meadow

[6] **timidus, -a, -um,** timid
[7] **pāscō, -ere, pāvī, pāstum,** pasture
[8] **clāmor, -ōris,** *m.,* shouting
[9] **subitus, -a, -um,** sudden
[10] **suādeō, -ēre, suāsī, suāsum,** urge
[11] **lentus, -a, -um,** slow, motionless, apathetic
[12] **quaesō, -ere,** beg, beseech, = **quaerō**
[13] **bīnās clītellās,** two pairs of panniers (*i.e., instead of the present single pair*); **bīnī, -ae, -a,** *distributive numeral used with a regularly pl. noun*
[14] **clītellae, -ārum,** a pair of panniers, baskets
[15] **im-pōnō = in + pōnō**
[16] **victor, -ōris =** *Eng.*
[17] what difference does it make to me, *highly idiomatic*
[18] **portō** (1), bear, carry

35

METER: Iambic trimeter.
[1] **mūlus, -ī,** mule
[2] **gravō** (1), load, burden
[3] **sarcina, -ae,** bundle, pack
[4] **fiscus, -ī,** basket

alter tumentēs[5] multō saccōs[6] hordeō.[7]
Ille onere[8] dīves, celsā cervīce[9] ēminēns[10]
5   clārumque collō[11] iactāns[12] tintinnābulum[13];
comes[14] quiētō[15] sequitur et placidō[16] gradū.[17]
Subitō latrōnēs[18] ex īnsidiīs advolant,[19]
interque caedem ferrō mūlum lancinant[20];
dīripiunt[21] nummōs,[22] neglegunt vīle[23] hordeum.
10   Spoliātus[24] igitur cāsūs[25] cum flēret suōs,
"Equidem," inquit alter, "mē contemptum gaudeō.
Nam nihil āmīsī, nec sum laesus[26] vulnere."
Hōc argūmentō tūta est hominum tenuitās[27];
magnae perīclō[28] sunt opēs obnoxiae.[29]
(**Phaedrus**, *Fābulae* 2.7)

36. DELIGHTS OF THE COUNTRY

C.[1] PLĪNIUS CALPURNIŌ MACRŌ[2] SUŌ S.[1]

Bene est[3] mihi quia[4] tibi est bene. Habēs uxōrem tēcum, habēs fīlium; frueris[5] marī, fontibus, viridibus,[6] agrō, vīllā amoenissimā.[7] Neque enim dubitō esse amoenissimam,[8] in quā sē composuerat[9] homō[10] fēlīcior antequam[11] "fēlīcissimus" fieret. Ego in Tuscīs[12] et vēnor[13] et studeō, quae[14] inter-

[5] **tumeō, -ēre,** swell, be swollen
[6] **saccus, -ī,** sack
[7] **hordeum, -ī,** barley
[8] **onus, -eris,** *n.,* burden, load
[9] **cervīx, -vīcis,** *f.,* neck
[10] **ēmineō, -ēre, -minuī,** stand out, be conspicuous
[11] **collum, -ī,** neck
[12] **iactō** (1), toss
[13] **tintinnābulum, -ī,** bell, *a delightfully onomatopoetic word*
[14] **comes, comitis,** *m./f.,* companion
[15] **quiētus, -a, -um,** quiet
[16] **placidus, -a, -um,** placid, gentle
[17] **gradus, -ūs,** step
[18] **latrō, -ōnis,** *m.,* bandit, robber
[19] **advolō** (1), fly, hasten
[20] **lancinō** (1), mangle
[21] **dīripiō, -ere, -ripuī, -reptum,** plunder
[22] **nummus, -ī,** currency, money
[23] **vīlis, -e,** cheap
[24] **spoliō** (1), rob
[25] **cāsus, -ūs,** accident
[26] **laedō, -ere, laesī, laesum,** injure
[27] **tenuitās, -tātis,** *f.,* poverty
[28] **perīclum, -ī,** *early Lat. form, used instead of* **perīculum** *in classical Lat. poetry whenever it was metrically convenient*

[29] **obnoxius, -a, -um,** subject to, exposed to
36
[1] *L.A. 11 n. 1 and 3*
[2] **Calpurnius Macer**
[3] *it is*
[4] **quia,** *conj.,* because
[5] **fruor, -ī, frūctus sum** + *abl.,* enjoy (*cp.* **frūctus, -ūs**)
[6] **viridis, -e,** green; **viridia,** *gen.* **viridium,** *n. pl. as a noun,* green things, greenery
[7] **amoenus, -a, -um,** pleasant
[8] **amoenissimam,** *agreeing with* **vīllam** *understood as subject of* **esse**
[9] **sē compōnere,** to compose oneself, to rest
[10] the man, *apparently referring to a former owner who had been happier (*fēlīcior*) on this estate as an ordinary person (*homō*) before he could realize his ambition of becoming "most happy" (*fēlīcissimus*), i.e., before he could achieve some very high position which did not give him supreme happiness after all.*
[11] **antequam** + *subj.*
[12] *lit.* in the Tuscans = on my Tuscan estate
[13] **vēnor** (1), hunt
[14] **quae,** *n. pl. referring to* **vēnor** *and* **studeō** *as antecedents*

5   dum[15] alternīs,[16] interdum simul[17] faciō; nec tamen adhūc[18] possum prōnūntiāre utrum sit difficilius capere aliquid an scrībere. Valē. (**Pliny,** *Epistulae* 5.18)

37. C. PLĪNIUS CANĪNIŌ[1] SUŌ S.

Studēs an[2] piscāris[3] an vēnāris an simul omnia? Possunt enim omnia
simul fierī ad Lārium[4] nostrum. Nam lacus[5] piscem,[6] ferās[7] silvae quibus
lacus cingitur,[8] studia altissimus iste sēcessus[9] adfatim[10] suggerunt.[11] Sed
sīve[12] omnia simul sīve aliquid facis, nōn possum dīcere "invideō"; angor[13]
5   tamen . . . Numquamne hōs artissimōs laqueōs[14] . . . abrumpam?[15] Numquam, putō. Nam veteribus negōtiīs[16] nova accrēscunt,[17] nec tamen priōra
peraguntur[18]; tot nexibus,[19] tot quasi catēnīs[20] maius in diēs[21] occupā-
tiōnum[22] agmen[23] extenditur.[24] Valē. (**Pliny,** *Epistulae* 2.8, excerpts)

38. HAPPY MARRIED LIFE

C. PLĪNIUS GEMINŌ SUŌ S.

Grave vulnus Macrinus noster accēpit: āmīsit[1] uxōrem singulāris[2] exemplī . . . Vīxit cum hāc trīgintā novem annīs[3] sine iūrgiō,[4] sine offēnsā.[5]
Quam illa reverentiam[6] marītō[7] suō praestitit, cum ipsa summam merērē-
tur![8] Quot quantāsque virtūtēs ex dīversīs[9] aetātibus sūmptās collēgit et mis-
5   cuit! Habet quidem Macrinus grande[10] sōlācium, quod tantum bonum tam
diū tenuit; sed hinc[11] magis exacerbātur[12] quod āmīsit. Nam fruendīs volup-

[15] **interdum,** *adv.,* sometimes, at times
[16] **alternīs,** *adv.,* alternately, by turns
[17] **simul,** *adv.,* at the same time, simultaneously. *In an-other letter (1.6), Pliny tells how he combined hunting and studying in one operation.*
[18] **adhūc,** *adv.,* thus far, till now

37

[1] *Pliny and Caninius were fellow townsmen from Comum (Como) at the south end of beautiful Lake Larius (Como) in northern Italy.*
[2] **an** *in questions,* or
[3] **piscor** (1), to fish
[4] **Lārius, -iī,** Lake Larius (now Lake Como)
[5] **lacus, -ūs,** lake
[6] **piscis, -is,** *m.,* fish
[7] **fera** (*sc.* **bēstia**), **-ae,** wild animal
[8] **cingō, -ere, cīnxī, cīnctum,** surround, gird
[9] **sēcessus, -ūs,** retreat, summer place
[10] **adfatim,** *adv.,* sufficiently, abundantly
[11] **sug-gerō, -ere, -gessī, -gestum,** furnish, afford, supply
[12] **sīve . . . sīve, (sī-ve),** if . . . or if, whether . . . or
[13] **angō, -ere,** torment
[14] **artus, -a, -um,** close, narrow; **laqueus, -ī,** noose, cord
[15] **ab-rumpō, -ere, -rūpī, -ruptum,** break off, sever. *Pliny is tied up in Rome.*

[16] **negōtium, -iī,** business; duty
[17] **accrēscō, -ere, -crēvī, -crētum,** increase; **nova (negō-tia) accrēscunt (veteribus negōtiīs)** new duties in-crease by . . . *or* are added to . . .
[18] **per-agō,** complete
[19] **nexus, -ūs,** coils, obligations
[20] **catēna, -ae,** chain
[21] **in diēs,** from day to day
[22] **occupātiō, -ōnis,** *f.,* occupation, employment
[23] **agmen, -minis,** *n.,* line of march, column
[24] **ex-tendō, -ere, -tendī, -tentum,** extend, increase

38

[1] he lost (*not* sent away)
[2] **singulāris, -e,** extraordinary
[3] *The abl. is sometimes used instead of the acc. to ex-press the idea of extent of time.*
[4] **iūrgium, -iī,** quarrel
[5] **offēnsa, -ae,** hatred, affront
[6] **reverentia, -ae,** respect
[7] **marītus, -ī,** husband
[8] **mereor, -ērī, meritus sum,** deserve
[9] **dīversus, -a, -um,** diverse, different
[10] **grandis, -e,** great
[11] **hinc** *here* = from this cause
[12] **exacerbō** (1), exasperate; embitter

tātibus crēscit carendī dolor. Erō ergō suspēnsus[13] prō homine amīcissimō dum[14] admittere[15] āvocāmenta[16] et cicātrīcem[17] patī possit, quam nihil aequē ac[18] necessitās[19] ipsa et diēs[20] longa et satietās[21] dolōris indūcit.[22] Valē. (**Pliny,** *Epistulae* 8.5, excerpts)

39. FAITHFUL IN SICKNESS AND IN DEATH

C. PLĪNIUS NEPŌTĪ SUŌ S.

(. . . Fannia[1]) neptis[2] Arriae[3] illīus[4] quae marītō[5] et sōlācium mortis et exemplum fuit. Multa referēbat[6] aviae[7] suae nōn minōra hōc,[8] sed obscūri- ōra,[9] quae tibi exīstimō tam mīrābilia legentī[10] fore[11] quam mihi audientī fuērunt.

5   Aegrōtābat[12] Caecīna Paetus, marītus eius, aegrōtābat et fīlius, uterque mortiferē,[13] ut vidēbātur. Fīlius dēcessit[14] eximiā[15] pulchritūdine,[16] parī verē- cundiā,[17] et parentibus nōn minus ob[18] alia cārus quam quod fīlius erat. Huic illa ita fūnus[19] parāvit . . . ut ignōrāret marītus. Quīn immō,[20] quo- tiēns[21] cubiculum[22] eius intrāret,[23] vīvere fīlium atque etiam commodiōrem[24]

10   esse simulābat[25]; ac persaepe[26] interrogantī[27] quid ageret puer respondēbat, "Bene quiēvit,[28] libenter cibum[29] sūmpsit." Deinde, cum diū cohibitae[30] lacri-

---

[13] **suspēnsus, -a, -um,** in suspense, anxious

[14] **dum,** *conj.,* until, *used with the subj. to imply inten- tion or expectancy*

[15] **ad-mittō,** admit, receive

[16] **āvocāmentum, -ī,** diversion

[17] **cicātrīx, -trīcis,** *f.,* scar, *which implies healing*

[18] **aequē ac,** equally as, quite so well as

[19] **necessitās (-tātis,** *f.*) **ipsa,** necessity itself, sheer ne- cessity

[20] *here* = time

[21] **satietās, -tātis,** *f.,* satiety

[22] **in-dūcō,** bring on, induce

39

[1] **Fannia (est)**

[2] **neptis, -is,** *f.,* granddaughter

[3] **Arria, -ae,** Arria (Maior), *brave wife of Caecina Pae- tus. When, because of his part in a conspiracy against the emperor Claudius, he had to commit suicide in 42 A.D., Arria committed suicide with him, actually setting him an example as indicated at the end of the letter.* (*Cp.* **"Paete, Nōn Dolet,"** *ch. 39*).

[4] **ille,** the famous, *when immediately following its noun*

[5] **marītō,** *dat.*

[6] **referēbat,** *subject* = Fannia, *who related these epi- sodes during a conversation with Pliny on the pre- ceding day.*

[7] **avia, -ae,** grandmother; **aviae,** *gen. case*

[8] **hōc,** *abl. of comparison, referring to the rel. cl. of the preceding sent.*

[9] **obscūrus, -a, -um,** obscure, unknown

[10] **legentī,** to be construed with **tibi**

[11] **fore = futūra esse,** *fut. inf. in ind. state. depending on* **exīstimō** (1), think

[12] **aegrōtō** (1), be sick

[13] **mortiferē,** *adv.* (**mors-ferō**), fatally

[14] **dē-cēdō,** go away, die (*cp.* deceased)

[15] **eximius, -a, -um,** extraordinary

[16] **pulchritūdō, -dinis,** *f.,* beauty; **eximiā pulchritūdine,** *abl.* describing **fīlius** *but more easily translated if we supply a word like* **puer: fīlius dēcessit—(puer) eximiā pulchritūdine,** *etc.*

[17] **verecūndia, -ae,** modesty

[18] **ob,** *prep.* + *acc.,* on account of; toward

[19] **fūnus, -eris,** *n.,* funeral

[20] **quīn immō,** why, on the contrary

[21] **quotiēns,** *adv.,* as often as

[22] **cubiculum, -ī,** bedroom

[23] **intrō** (1), enter; **intrāret:** *in Silver Lat. the impf. subj. of customary action is often found in place of the indic.*

[24] **commodus, -a, -um,** suitable, satisfactory; *here* = better

[25] **simulō** (1) pretend

[26] **per-saepe,** *adv.,* very often

[27] **interrogō** (1), ask, inquire (*cp.* **rogō**); (**marītō**) **in- terrogantī**

[28] **quiēscō, -ere, -ēvī, -ētus,** rest, be quiet

[29] **cibus, -ī,** food

[30] **cohibeō, -ere, -uī, -itum,** hold together, hold back, re- strain

mae vincerent prōrumperentque,[31] ēgrediēbātur; tunc sē dolōrī dabat. Sati-
āta, siccīs[32] oculīs, compositō vultū redībat, tamquam orbitātem[33] forīs relīquisset.[34] Praeclārum quidem illud[35] eiusdem: ferrum stringere,[36]
15   perfodere[37] pectus, extrahere[38] pugiōnem,[39] porrigere[40] marītō, addere[41] vōcem immortālem ac paene[42] dīvīnam,[43] "Paete, nōn dolet." . . . Valē. (**Pliny,**
Epistulae 3.16, excerpts)

40. A SWEET, BRAVE GIRL

C. PLĪNIUS MARCELLĪNŌ SUŌ S.

Trīstissimus haec tibi scrībō, Fundānī nostrī fīliā minōre dēfūnctā,[1] quā
puellā[2] nihil umquam fēstīvius,[3] amābilius,[4] nec longiōre vītā . . . dignius
vīdī. Nōndum annōs trēdecim implēverat,[5] et iam illī[6] anīlis[7] prūdentia, mātrōnālis[8] gravitās[9] erat, et tamen suāvitās[10] puellāris[11] . . . Ut[12] illa patris cer-
5   vīcibus[13] inhaerēbat[14]! Ut nōs, amīcōs paternōs,[15] et amanter[16] et modestē[17]
complectēbātur![18] Ut nūtrīcēs,[19] ut paedagōgōs,[20] ut praeceptōrēs[21] prō suō
quemque officiō dīligēbat! Quam studiōsē,[22] quam intelligenter[23] lēctitā-
bat[24]! . . .

Quā illa temperantiā,[25] quā patientiā, quā etiam cōnstantiā[26] novissi-
10   mam valētūdinem[27] tulit! Medicīs obsequēbātur;[28] sorōrem, patrem adhortā-
bātur[29]; ipsamque sē dēstitūtam[30] corporis vīribus vigōre[31] animī susti-

[31] **prōrumpō, -ere, -rūpī, -ruptum,** burst forth
[32] **siccus, -a, -um,** dry; **siccīs oculīs** *abl. abs.*
[33] **orbitās, -tātis,** *f.,* bereavement, loss
[34] *What kind of condition in the* **tamquam** *cl.?*
[35] that deed; *sc.* **fuit**
[36] **stringō, -ere, -strīnxī, strictus,** draw; **stringere,** *inf. in apposition with* **illud**
[37] **perfodiō, -ere, -fōdī, -fossum,** pierce (*lit.* dig through)
[38] **ex-trahō**
[39] **pugiō, -ōnis,** *m.,* dagger
[40] **porrigō, -ere, -rēxī, -rēctum,** hold out, extend
[41] **ad-dō, -ere, -didī, -ditum,** add
[42] **paene,** *adv.,* almost
[43] **dīvīnus, -a, -um** = *Eng.*

40

[1] **dēfungor, -ī, -fūnctus sum,** finish *or* complete life, die. *The family tomb was discovered near Rome in 1880 and in it a cinerary urn with the inscription:* **Dīs mānibus Miniciae Mārcellae, Fundānī fīliae. Vīxit annīs XII, mēnsibus XI, diēbus VII:** To the divine shades of Minicia Marcella . . . (*The abbreviations in the inscription have been expanded.*)
[2] **puellā,** *abl. of comparison*
[3] **fēstīvus, -a, -um,** pleasant, agreeable
[4] **amābilis, -e,** lovable, lovely
[5] **impleō, -ēre, -plēvī, -plētum,** fill up, complete
[6] *dat. of possession* (*S.S.*)

[7] **anīlis, -e,** of an old woman
[8] **mātrōnālis, -e,** of a matron, matronly
[9] **gravitās, -tātis,** *f.,* seriousness, dignity
[10] **suāvitās, -tātis,** *f.,* sweetness
[11] **puellāris, -e,** girlish
[12] how
[13] **cervīx, -īcis,** *f., usually pl.* (**cervīcēs**) *as here,* neck
[14] **inhaereō, -ēre, -haesī, -haesum,** cling
[15] **paternus, -a, -um,** paternal, of a father
[16] **amanter,** *adv. of* **amāns**
[17] **modestē,** *adv.,* modestly
[18] **complector, -ī, -plexus sum,** hold in the arms, embrace
[19] **nūtrīx, -īcis,** *f.,* nurse
[20] **paedagōgus, -ī,** tutor (*slave who escorted children*)
[21] **praeceptor, -ōris,** *m.,* teacher (*in a school, not a private tutor*)
[22] **studiōsē,** *adv. of* **studiōsus,** full of **studium**
[23] **intellegenter,** *adv. of* **intelligēns**
[24] **lēctitō** (1), read (eagerly)
[25] **temperantia, -ae,** self-control
[26] **cōnstantia, -ae,** firmness
[27] **valētūdō, -dinis,** *f., here* = bad health, illness
[28] **ob** + **sequor,** obey
[29] **adhortor** = **hortor**
[30] **dēstituō, -ere, -stituī, -stitūtum,** desert, abandon
[31] **vigor, -ōris,** *m.,* vigor; **vigōre,** *abl. of means with* **sustinēbat**

nēbat.[32] Dūrāvit[33] hic[34] illī ūsque ad extrēmum,[35] nec aut spatiō[36] valētūdinis aut metū mortis īnfrāctus est[37] . . . Ō trīste plānē[38] acerbumque fūnus[39] . . . Iam dēstināta erat[40] ēgregiō[41] iuvenī,[42] iam ēlēctus[43] nūptiārum[44] diēs, iam nōs vocātī. Quod gaudium quō maerōre[45] mūtātum est!

15

Nōn possum exprimere[46] verbīs quantum animō vulnus accēperim cum audīvī Fundānum ipsum praecipientem,[47] quod[48] in vestēs,[49] margarīta,[50] gemmās[51] fuerat ērogātūrus,[52] hoc in tūs[53] et unguenta et odōrēs[54] impende- rētur[55] . . . Sī quās ad eum dē dolōre tam iūstō litterās mittēs, mementō[56] adhibēre[57] sōlācium . . . molle[58] et hūmānum. (**Pliny,** *Epistulae* 5.16, ex- cerpts)

20

41. PLINY'S CONCERN ABOUT A SICK FREEDMAN

C. PLĪNIUS VALERIŌ PAULĪNŌ SUŌ S.

Videō quam molliter[1] tuōs[2] habeās[3]; quō simplicius[4] tibi cōnfitēbor quā indulgentiā[5] meōs tractem.[6] Quod sī essem nātūrā asperior et dūrior, fran- geret mē tamen īnfīrmitās[7] lībertī[8] meī Zōsimī,[9] cui tantō maior hūmānitās[10] exhibenda[11] est, quantō nunc illā magis eget. Homō probus,[12] officiōsus,[13] litterātus[14]; et ars quidem eius et quasi īnscrīptiō[15]—cōmoedus . . . Ūtitur et

5

---

[32] **(puella) sustinēbat sē ipsam**
[33] **dūrō** (1), endure
[34] **hic (vigor animī)**
[35] **extrēmum, -ī = fīnis**
[36] **spatium, -iī,** space, duration
[37] **īnfringō, -ere, -frēgī, -frāctum,** break
[38] **plānē,** *adv.,* clearly
[39] *here =* **mors**
[40] **dēstinō** (1), bind, engage
[41] **ēgregius, -a, -um,** excellent, distinguished
[42] **iuvenis, -is,** *m.,* young man
[43] **ē-ligō = legō**
[44] **nūptiae, -ārum,** wedding
[45] **maeror, -ōris,** *m.,* grief
[46] **ex-primō (=** **premō),** express
[47] **praecipiō, -ere, -cēpī, -ceptum,** direct
[48] *The antecedent is* **hoc** *in the following line.*
[49] **vestis, -is,** *f.,* garment, clothes
[50] **margarītum, -ī,** pearl
[51] **gemma, -ae,** jewel
[52] **ērogō** (1), *pay out, spend;* **fuerat ērogātūrus** (*act. peri- phrastic*), he had been about to spend, had in- tended to spend (*on clothes, jewels, etc., for the wedding*)
[53] **tūs, tūris,** *n.,* incense
[54] **odor, -ōris,** *m.,* perfume
[55] **impendō, -ere, -pendī, -pēnsum,** expend; **impenderē- tur,** *subj. in a jussive noun cl.*
[56] **meminī, meminisse,** *defective vb.,* remember; **me- mentō,** *fut. imper.,* remember

[57] **adhibeō, -ere, -hibuī, -hibitum,** use, furnish
[58] **mollis, -e,** soft, gentle

41

[1] **molliter,** *adv. of* **mollis**
[2] **tuōs (servōs et lībertōs);** *so* **meōs** *below*
[3] treat
[4] **simpliciter,** *adv.,* frankly, candidly; **quō simplicius** by which (*degree of difference*) more frankly = the more frankly
[5] **indulgentia, -ae,** kindness
[6] **tractō** (1), handle, treat
[7] **īnfīrmitās, -tātis,** *f.,* illness, weakness
[8] **lībertus, -ī,** freedman (*a slave who had somehow se- cured his freedom*) in contrast to a **līber vir** (*one who was born free*). A freedman commonly re- mained closely attached to his former master.
[9] **Zōsimus, -ī,** Zosimus, apparently a Greek
[10] **hūmānitās, -tātis,** *f.,* kindness
[11] **ex-hibeō,** show, exhibit
[12] **probus, -a, -um,** honorable, fine
[13] **officiōsus, -a, -um,** obliging, courteous
[14] **litterātus, -a, -um,** well-educated; *Greek slaves espe- cially were often well educated.*
[15] **īnscrīptiō, -ōnis,** *f., here =* label, *a placard hung around a slave's neck in the slave market to indicate his special abilities.*—**cōmoedus, -ī,** comic actor, *often a slave trained to read at dinners scenes from famous comedies. Although this was Zosimus' spe- cialty, we find him in the next two sents. surpris- ingly versatile and talented.*

citharā perītē.[16] Īdem tam commodē[17] ōrātiōnēs et historiās[18] et carmina legit ut hoc sōlum didicisse videātur.

Haec tibi sēdulō[19] exposuī quō magis scīrēs quam multa ūnus mihi et quam iūcunda ministeria[20] praestāret. Accēdit longa iam cāritās[21] hominis,
10 quam ipsa perīcula auxērunt[22] . . . Ante aliquot[23] annōs,[24] dum intentē instanterque[25] prōnūntiat, sanguinem[26] reiēcit[27]; atque ob hoc in Aegyptum[28] missus ā mē, post longam peregrīnātiōnem[29] cōnfīrmātus[30] rediit nūper. Deinde . . . veteris īnfīrmitātis[31] tussiculā[32] admonitus,[33] rūrsus sanguinem reddidit.[34]

15 Quā ex causā dēstināvī[35] eum mittere in praedia[36] tua quae Forō Iūliī[37] possidēs.[38] Audīvī enim tē referentem esse ibi āera[39] salūbrem[40] et lac[41] eius modī cūrātiōnibus[42] accommodātissimum.[43] Rogō ergō scrībās[44] tuīs[45] ut illī vīlla, ut domus[46] pateat . . . Valē. (**Pliny,** *Epistulae* 5.19, excerpts)

ON BEHALF OF A PENITENT FREEDMAN (42–43)

42. C. PLĪNIUS SABĪNIĀNŌ SUŌ S.

Lībertus tuus, cui suscēnsēre[1] tē dīxerās, vēnit ad mē . . . Flēvit multum, multum rogāvit, multum etiam tacuit; in summā,[2] fēcit mihi fidem paenitentiae.[3] Vērē crēdō ēmendātum[4] quia dēlīquisse[5] sē sentit. Īrāsceris, sciō; et īrāsceris meritō,[6] id quoque sciō; sed tunc praecipua[7] mānsuētūdinis[8] laus
5 cum īrae causa iūstissima est. Amāstī[9] hominem et, spērō, amābis; interim[10]

[16] **perītē,** *adv.,* skillfully
[17] **commodē,** *adv.,* fitly, satisfactorily
[18] **historia, -ae** = *Eng.*
[19] **sēdulō,** *adv.,* carefully
[20] **ministerium, -iī,** service
[21] **cāritās, -tātis,** *f.,* dearness, affection (*cp.* **cārus**)
[22] **augeō, -ēre, auxī, auctum,** increase
[23] **aliquot,** *indecl. adj.,* several, some
[24] **ante . . . annōs,** several years ago
[25] earnestly and emphatically
[26] **sanguis, -inis,** *m.,* blood
[27] **re-iciō,** reject, spit out
[28] **Aegyptus, -ī,** *f.,* Egypt
[29] **peregrīnātiō, -ōnis,** *f.,* travel *or* sojourn abroad
[30] **cōnfīrmō** (1), strengthen
[31] **īnfīrmitās, -tātis,** *f.,* weakness, sickness
[32] **tussicula, -ae,** slight cough
[33] **ad-monitus** = **monitus**
[34] **reddidit** = **reiēcit**
[35] **dēstinō** (1), intend, resolve
[36] **praedium, -iī,** country seat
[37] **Forum Iūliī, Forī Iūliī,** Forum of Julius, *modern* Fréjus, *a coastal town of southern France;* **Forō,** *place where*
[38] **possideō, -ēre, -sēdī, -sessum,** possess, own

[39] **āēr, āeris,** *m.,* air; **āera** = *Gk. acc. sg.*
[40] **salūbris, -e,** healthful; *still so regarded*
[41] **lac, lactis,** *n.,* milk; *i.e., for the milk cure*
[42] **cūrātiō, -ōnis,** *f.,* cure
[43] **accommodātus, -a, -um,** suited
[44] **(ut) scrībās:** ut *is sometimes omitted in such cls.*
[45] **tuīs,** your servants
[46] **ut vīlla (pateat), ut domus pateat:** *i.e., he is to have access to the great house itself as well as to the estate.*

42

[1] **suscēnseō, -ēre, -cēnsuī, -cēnsum,** + *dat.,* be angry with
[2] **summa, -ae,** sum
[3] **paenitentia, -ae,** repentance
[4] **ēmendō** (1), correct; (**eum**) **ēmendātum (esse)**
[5] **dēlinquō, -ere, -līquī, -lictum,** fail (in duty), commit a crime
[6] **meritō,** *adv.,* rightly (with merit)
[7] **praecipuus, -a, -um,** special; *sc.* **est**
[8] **mānsuētūdō, -inis,** *f.,* gentleness, mildness
[9] *contracted form* = **amāvistī**
[10] **interim,** *adv.,* meanwhile (*cp.* **intereā**)

sufficit[11] ut exōrārī[12] tē sinās[13] . . . Nē torserīs[14] illum, nē torserīs etiam tē; torquēris[15] enim, cum tam lēnis[16] īrāsceris. Vereor nē videar nōn rogāre sed cōgere, sī precibus[17] eius meās iūnxerō. Iungam tamen tantō plēnius[18] et effūsius,[19] quantō[20] ipsum[21] ācrius sevēriusque[22] corripuī[23] . . . Valē. (**Pliny**, *Epistulae* 9.21, excerpts)

43. C. PLĪNIUS SABĪNIĀNŌ SUŌ S.

Bene fēcistī[1] quod lībertum[2] aliquandō[3] tibi cārum redūcentibus[4] epistulīs[5] meīs in domum,[6] in animum recēpistī. Iuvābit hoc tē, mē certē iuvat; prīmum,[7] quod tē tam tractābilem[8] videō ut in īrā regī possīs; deinde, quod tantum mihi tribuis[9] ut vel[10] auctōritātī meae pāreās vel precibus indulgeās.[11]
5   Igitur laudō et grātiās agō . . . Valē. (**Pliny**, *Epistulae* 9.24, excerpts)

44. SELECTION OF A TEACHER

C. PLĪNIUS MAURICŌ SUŌ S.

Quid ā tē mihi iūcundius potuit iniungī[1] quam ut praeceptōrem frātris tuī līberīs quaererem? Nam beneficiō[2] tuō in scholam[3] redeō et illam dulcissimam aetātem quasi resūmō.[4] Sedeō inter iuvenēs, ut solēbam, atque etiam experior quantum apud illōs auctōritātis[5] ex studiīs habeam. Nam prox-
5   imē[6] frequentī[7] audītōriō[8] inter sē cōram[9] multīs ōrdinis[10] nostrī clārē[11]

---

[11] **sufficit,** *subject =* **ut**-*cl.*
[12] **ex-ōrō,** *stronger form of* **ōrō**
[13] **sinō, -ere, sīvī, situm,** allow, permit
[14] **torqueō, -ēre, torsī, tortum,** twist, torture; **nē torserīs,** *L.I. 22 n. 1*
[15] **torquēris,** you are tormented = you torment yourself (*reflexive use of the pass.*)
[16] **lēnis, -e,** gentle, kind; *agreeing with subject of* **īrāsceris:** you, such a gentle person
[17] **prex, precis,** *f.,* prayer
[18] **plēnē,** *adv. of* **plēnus**
[19] **effūsē,** *adv.,* profusely, unrestrainedly
[20] **tantō . . . quantō,** the more . . . the more, *abl. of degree of difference (S.S.)*
[21] (**lībertum**) **ipsum**
[22] **sevērē,** *adv.,* seriously, severely
[23] **cor-ripiō, -ere, -ripuī, -reptum,** seize, accuse, blame

43

[1] you did well because = thank you for
[2] **lībertum,** *in thought, the obj. of both* **redūcentibus** *and* **recēpistī**
[3] **aliquandō,** *adv.,* once

[4] **re-dūcō**
[5] **epistulīs,** *here pl. of a single letter* (*the preceding one*) *on the analogy of* **litterae, -ārum**
[6] *Both prepositional phrases, connected by* **et** *understood, depend on* **recēpistī**
[7] **prīmum,** *adv.,* first
[8] **tractābilis, -ē,** tractable, compliant
[9] **tribuō, -ere, -buī, -būtum,** attribute, ascribe
[10] **vel . . . vel,** either . . . or
[11] **indulgeō, -ēre, -dulsī, -dultum,** yield to, gratify

44

[1] **in-iungō,** enjoin, impose
[2] **beneficiō tuō,** thanks to you
[3] **schola, -ae,** school
[4] **re-sūmō, -ere, -sūmpsī, -sūmptum,** resume
[5] *gen. with* **quantum**
[6] **proximē,** *adv.,* very recently
[7] **frequēns,** *gen.* **-entis,** crowded
[8] **audītōrium, -iī,** lecture room, school; **audītōriō,** *place where without a prep.*
[9] **cōram,** *prep. + abl.,* in the presence of
[10] *i.e., the senatorial order*
[11] **clārē** (*adv. of* **clārus**), *here =* loudly

loquēbantur: intrāvī, conticuērunt[12]; quod[13] nōn referrem, nisi ad illōrum magis laudem quam ad meam pertinēret[14] . . . Cum omnēs quī profitentur[15] audierō, quid dē quōque sentiam scrībam efficiamque,[16] quantum tamen epistulā cōnsequī[17] poterō, ut ipse omnēs audīsse videāris. Dēbeō enim tibi, dēbeō memoriae frātris tuī hanc fidem, hoc studium, praesertim[18] super[19] tantā rē. Nam quid magis interest vestrā[20] quam ut līberī . . . dignī illō patre, tē patruō[21] reperiantur? . . . Valē. (**Pliny**, *Epistulae* 2.8 excerpts)

45. THE OLD BOY DYED HIS HAIR

Mentīris[1] iuvenem tīnctīs,[2] Laetīne,[3] capillīs,[4]
   tam subitō corvus quī modo cycnus[5] erās.
Nōn omnēs fallis[6]; scit tē Prōserpina[7] cānum[8]:
   persōnam capitī dētrahet[9] illa[10] tuō.
   (**Martial** 3.43)

46. WHAT'S IN A NAME?

Cinnam,[1] Cinname,[2] tē iubēs vocārī.
Nōn est hic, rogo, Cinna, barbarismus[3]?
Tū sī Fūrius[4] ante dictus essēs,
Fūr[5] istā ratiōne dīcerēris.
   (**Martial** 6.17)

---

[12] **conticēscō, -ere, -ticuī,** become silent
[13] **quod,** *having as antecedent the whole preceding idea*
[14] **pertineō, -ēre, -uī, -tentum,** pertain to
[15] **profiteor, -ērī, -fessus sum,** teach, *a late meaning of the word*
[16] **efficiō . . . ut,** *L.A. 8 n. 20–21*
[17] **cōn-sequor,** accomplish
[18] **praesertim,** *adv.,* especially
[19] **super,** *prep. + abl.,* about
[20] **interest vestrā,** interests you (*highly idiomatic*)
[21] **patruus, -ī,** (paternal) uncle; **tē patruō** *is in the same construction as* **illō patre.**

45

METER: Elegiac couplet.
[1] **mentior, -īrī, -ītus sum,** lie, declare falsely, *here =* imitate
[2] **tingō, -ere, tīnxī, tīnctus,** wet, dye
[3] **Laetīnus, -ī,** Laetinus
[4] **capillī, -ōrum,** hair
[5] **cycnus, -ī,** swan

[6] **nōn ōmnēs (fallis)** *seems to imply that the hair dyes were good enough to deceive at least some people.*
[7] **Prōserpina, -ae,** Proserpina, *goddess of the underworld, and so of death*
[8] **cānus, -a, -um,** gray; **tē (esse) cānum**
[9] **dē-trahō**
[10] **illa** = Proserpina

46

METER: Hendecasyllabic.
[1] **Cinna, -ae,** *m.,* Cinna, *a famous Roman name*
[2] **Cinnamus, -ī,** Cinnamus, *a slave name meaning "cinnamon." The Romans often gave such names to slaves. Cinnamus, now a freedman, wanted to change his name to a Roman one for obvious reasons.*
[3] **barbarismus, -ī,** a barbarism, an impropriety of speech
[4] **Fūrius, -ī,** Furius, *an old Roman name*
[5] **Fūr,** *from* **fūr, fūris,** *m.,* thief; *cp.* **fūrtīvus**

47. FAKE TEARS

Āmissum[1] nōn flet cum sōla est Gellia[2] patrem;
    sī quis adest, iussae[3] prōsiliunt[4] lacrimae.
Nōn lūget[5] quisquis laudārī, Gellia, quaerit;
    ille dolet vērē quī sine teste[6] dolet.

        (**Martial** 1.33)

48. EVEN THOUGH YOU DO INVITE ME—I'LL COME!

Quod convīvāris[1] sine mē tam saepe, Luperce,[2]
    invēnī noceam quā ratiōne tibi.
Īrāscor: licet[3] ūsque vocēs mittāsque[4] rogēsque—
    "Quid faciēs?" inquis. Quid faciam? Veniam!

        (**Martial** 6.51)

49. PRO-*CRAS*-TINATION

Crās tē vīctūrum,[1] crās dīcis, Postume,[2] semper.
    Dīc mihi, crās istud,[3] Postume, quando venit?
Quam longē est crās istud? ubi est? aut unde petendum[4]?
    Numquid[5] apud Parthōs Armeniōsque[6] latet[7]?
5   Iam crās istud habet Priamī[8] vel Nestoris[9] annōs.
    Crās istud quantī[10] dīc mihi possit emī[11]?
Crās vīvēs? Hodiē iam vīvere, Postume, sērum[12] est.
    Ille sapit quisquis, Postume, vīxit herī.

        (**Martial** 5.58)

47

METER: Elegiac couplet.
[1] **āmissum patrem**
[2] **Gellia, -ae,** Gellia
[3] at her bidding; *how literally?*
[4] **prōsiliō** (4), leap forth
[5] **lūgeō, -ēre, lūxī, lūctum,** mourn
[6] **testis, -is,** *m.,* witness

48

METER: Elegiac couplet.
[1] **convīvor** (1), to feast
[2] **Lupercus, -ī,** Lupercus
[3] **licet ūsque (ut) vocēs** (it is even permitted that you call), you may even invite me, *or* even though you invite me
[4] *i.e., send a slave as a special messenger*

49

METER: Elegiac couplet.
[1] **vīctūrum,** *sc.* **esse**
[2] *No doubt Martial intended to have us think of Horace's Postumus in L.I. 25 above.*
[3] **crās istud,** that "tomorrow" of yours, *subj. of* **venit**
[4] **petendum (est)**
[5] **numquid latet,** it does not lie hidden, does it?
[6] among the Parthians and Armenians, *i.e., at land's end in the East*
[7] **lateō, -ēre, -uī,** lie hidden
[8] **Priamus, -ī,** Priam, *aged king of Troy*
[9] **Nestōr, -oris,** Nestor, *Greek leader famed for his years and wisdom*
[10] **quantī,** *gen. of indef. value:* at what price, for how much can that tomorrow be bought
[11] **emō, -ere, ēmī, ēmptum,** buy
[12] **sērus, -a, -um,** late; **sērum,** *pred. adj. in n.* to agree with **hodiē vīvere,** *which is subject of* **est**

50. ISSA

Issa[1] est passere[2] nēquior[3] Catullī:
Issa est pūrior ōsculō columbae;[4]
Issa est blandior[5] omnibus puellīs;
Issa est cārior Indicīs[6] lapillīs[7];
5   Issa est dēliciae[8] catella[9] Pūblī.[10]

Hanc tū, sī queritur,[11] loquī putābis.
Sentit trīstitiamque[12] gaudiumque.
. . .
Hanc nē lūx rapiat suprēma[13] tōtam,
pictā[14] Pūblius exprimit[15] tabellā
10   in quā tam similem vidēbis Issam[16]
ut sit tam similis sibī nec[17] ipsa.
Issam dēnique pōne cum tabellā:
aut utramque putābis esse vēram
aut utramque putābis esse pictam.

(**Martial** 1.109)

50

METER: Hendecasyllabic.

[1] **Issa,** *colloquial and affectionate form for* **Ipsa** *and here used as the name of a pet dog*
[2] **passer Catullī,** *see L.I. 3*
[3] **nēquam,** *indecl. adj.; compar.* **nēquior, -ius,** worthless, good for nothing, mischievous
[4] **columba, -ae,** dove
[5] **blandus, -a, -um,** flattering, caressing, coaxing
[6] **Indicus, -a, -um,** of India
[7] **lapillus, -ī,** precious stone, gem

[8] *see L.I. 3*
[9] **catella, -ae,** little dog
[10] **Pūblī = Pūbliī,** *gen. sg. of* **Pūblius**
[11] *here* = whimper
[12] **trīstitia, -ae,** sadness
[13] **lūx (diēs) suprēma = mors**
[14] **pingō, -ere, pīnxī, pictum,** paint; **pictā tabellā,** by a painted tablet = in a painting
[15] **exprimō, -ere, -pressī, pressum,** express, portray
[16] **tam similem . . . Issam:** an Issa (*of the painting*) so similar (*to the real Issa*)
[17] **nec** *here* = not even

Optional Self-Tutorial Exercises

These optional exercises have been included in the hope of enriching the potential of this book for its various types of users.

1. **Repetītiō est māter memoriae.** In language study the value of repetition is indisputable. To the already large amount of repetition achieved in the regular chapters these exercises add even more of this practice. The phrases and sentences have deliberately been made simple so that the immediate points in forms and syntax may stand out strikingly. The words are purposely limited to those of the formal lesson vocabularies, which obviously should be memorized before turning to these tutorial exercises. As a result of their very nature and purpose, such sentences can make no claim to inspiration. Some hints of the worthwhile reading matter for which one studies Latin are to be found in the *Sententiae Antīquae* and the reading passages from the ancient authors, which are the heart of this book; but if one wants additional repetitious drill by which to establish linguistic reflexes, one can find it here in these self-tutorial exercises. As has been suggested elsewhere, be sure always to read aloud every Latin word and sentence—carefully, for such a practice enables one to learn through the ear as well as the eye and can provide many of the benefits of a language laboratory.

2. To students enrolled in a regular Latin course these exercises with their keys can prove valuable for review and self-testing and can be helpful in preparation for examinations.

3. Also to the private individual who wishes to learn or review Latin independently, these exercises are certain to be valuable, since they can be used as self-tests which can be corrected via the key. Likewise, completing

these practice exercises with benefit of key will provide greater confidence in tackling the regular exercises of the book.

4. All students can test themselves in simple Latin composition by translating the English sentences of the key back into Latin and checking this work via the corresponding Latin sentences of the exercises.

5. In the translations ordinarily only one of the various meanings of a word given in the vocabulary will be used in any specific instance. If at times the translations are somewhat formal, the reason is that they can in this way follow the Latin more closely; and certainly these particular sentences are intended to provide practice in understanding Latin rather than practice in literary expression. Polished literary expression in translation is most desirable and should be practiced in connection with the other exercises in this book.

6. The answer keys have been placed by themselves after the exercises to facilitate self-testing and so that the exercises may be used for practice in class when the instructor wishes. It hardly need be added that the surest way to test oneself is to write out the answers before turning to the key.

7. Finally, let it be emphasized once again that for maximum value you must say aloud all the Latin words, phrases, and sentences, and that you must have studied the text of each lesson carefully through the vocabulary before turning to these exercises.

EXERCISES FOR CHAPTER 1

1. Give the English pronouns equivalent to each of the following Latin personal endings: (1) -t, (2) -mus, (3) -ō, (4) -nt, (5) -s, (6) -tis.
2. Name the following forms and translate each: (1) monēre, (2) vidēre, (3) valēre, (4) dēbēre.
3. Name the following forms and translate each: (1) vocāre, (2) servāre, (3) dare, (4) cōgitāre, (5) laudāre, (6) amāre, (7) errāre.
4. Name the following forms and translate each: (1) vocā, (2) servā, (3) dā, (4) cōgitā, (5) laudā, (6) amā, (7) monē, (8) vidē, (9) valē.
5. Name the following forms and translate each: (1) vocāte, (2) servāte, (3) date, (4) cōgitāte, (5) laudāte, (6) amāte, (7) monēte, (8) vidēte, (9) valēte.
6. Translate the following words: (1) vocat, (2) cōgitāmus, (3) amant, (4) dēbēs, (5) videt, (6) vident, (7) dēbēmus, (8) valēs, (9) errātis, (10) vidēmus, (11) amat, (12) vidētis, (13) errās, (14) dant, (15) servāmus, (16) dat, (17) amant, (18) vidēs.

7. Monent mē sī errō. 8. Monet mē sī errant. 9. Monēte mē sī errat. 10. Dēbēs monēre mē. 11. Dēbētis servāre mē. 12. Nōn dēbent laudāre mē. 13. "Quid dat?" "Saepe nihil dat." 14. Mē saepe vocant et (*and*) monent. 15. Nihil videō. Quid vidēs? 16. Mē laudā sī nōn errō, amābō tē.

17. Sī valētis, valēmus. 18. Sī valet, valeō. 19. Sī mē amat, dēbet mē laudāre. 20. Cōnservāte mē. 21. Nōn dēbeō errāre. 22. Quid dēbēmus laudāre? 23. Videt; cōgitat; monet.

EXERCISES FOR CHAPTER 2

1. Give the Latin for the definite article "the" and the indefinite article "a."
2. Name the Latin case for each of the following constructions or ideas: (1) direct object of a verb; (2) possession; (3) subject of a verb; (4) means; (5) direct address; (6) indirect object of a verb.
3. Name the case, number, and syntactical usage indicated by each of the following endings of the first declension: (1) -ās; (2) -a; (3) -am; (4) -ae (pl.).
4. Name the case(s) and number indicated by the following endings, and wherever possible name the English preposition(s) which can be associated with them: (1) -ārum; (2) -ā; (3) -ae; (4) -īs.
5. Translate the following nouns and state the syntactical usage of each as indicated by its ending: (1) puellam; (2) puella; (3) puellās; (4) puellae (plural form); (5) patriās; (6) patriam; (7) patria; (8) patriae (pl.); (9) pecūniam; (10) pecūnia; (11) poenās; (12) poenam.
6. Translate the following nouns in accordance with their case endings: (1) puellae (sg.); (2) puellārum; (3) Ō patria; (4) patriae (sg.); (5) pecūniā; (6) pecūniae (sg.); (7) poenīs; (8) poenā; (9) poenārum.
7. Given the following nominative singular forms, write the Latin forms requested in each instance: (1) **multa pecūnia** in the genitive and the accusative singular; (2) **magna fāma** in dat. and abl. sg.; (3) **vīta mea** in gen. sg. and nom. pl.; (4) **fortūna tua** in acc. sg. and pl.; (5) **magna patria** in gen. sg. and pl.; (6) **fortūna mea** in abl. sg. and pl.; (7) **magna poena** in dat. sg. and pl.; (8) **multa philosophia** in dat. and abl. pl.
8. Translate each of the following phrases into Latin according to the case either named or indicated by the English preposition in each instance: (1) by much money; (2) of many girls; (3) to/for my country; (4) great life (as direct object of a verb); (5) by your penalties; (6) many countries (subject of a verb); (7) to/for many girls; (8) of my life; (9) O fortune; (10) girl's; (11) girls'; (12) girls (direct address); (13) the girls (direct object of a verb); (14) the girls (subject of a verb).

9. Valē, patria mea. 10. Fortūna puellae est magna. 11. Puella fortūnam patriae tuae laudat. 12. Ō puella, patriam tuam servā. 13. Multae puellae pecūniam amant. 14. Puellae nihil datis. 15. Pecūniam puellae videt. 16. Pecūniam puellārum nōn vidēs. 17. Monēre puellās dēbēmus. 18. Laudāre puellam dēbent. 19. Vīta multīs puellīs fortūnam dat. 20. Vītam meam pecūniā tuā cōnservās. 21. Fāma est nihil sine fortūnā.

22. Vītam sine pecūniā nōn amātis.   23. Sine fāmā et fortūnā patria nōn valet.   24. Īram puellārum laudāre nōn dēbēs.   25. Vītam sine poenīs amāmus.   26. Sine philosophiā nōn valēmus.   27. Quid est vīta sine philosophiā?

EXERCISES FOR CHAPTER 3

1. Name the case, number, and syntactical usage indicated by each of the following endings of masculines of the 2nd declension: (1) -um; (2) -ī (pl.); (3) -us; (4) -ōs; (5) -e.

2. Name the case(s) and number of the following endings, and name the English preposition which can be associated with each: (1) -ō; (2) -ōrum; (3) -ī (sg.); (4) -īs.

3. Translate the following nouns and state the syntactical usage of each as indicated by its ending: (1) fīliōs; (2) fīliī (pl.); (3) fīlium; (4) populum; (5) popule; (6) populus; (7) vir; (8) virōs; (9) virī (pl.); (10) virum; (11) amīce; (12) amīcī (pl.); (13) amīcōs; (14) amīcum.

4. Translate the following in accordance with their case endings: (1) fīliōrum meōrum; (2) fīliō meō; (3) populī Rōmānī (sg.); (4) populō Rōmānō; (5) virīs; (6) virī (sg.); (7) virōrum; (8) amīcōrum paucōrum; (9) amīcīs paucīs; (10) amīcō meō; (11) amīcī meī (sg.); (12) multīs puerīs.

5. Given the following nom. sg. forms, write the Latin forms requested in each instance: (1) **populus Rōmānus** in gen. and abl. sg.; (2) **magnus vir** in acc. and abl. pl.; (3) **puer meus** in dat. and abl. pl.; (4) **magnus numerus** in dat. and abl. sg.; (5) **magnus vir** in voc. sg. and pl.; (6) **fīlius meus** in gen. sg. and pl.

6. Translate the following phrases into Latin according to the case named or indicated by the English preposition in each instance: (1) of many boys; (2) to/for the Roman people; (3) my sons (object of verb); (4) O my sons; (5) a great number (obj. of verb); (6) by the great number; (7) O great man; (8) to/for many boys; (9) the great man (subj. of verb); (10) of the Roman people.

7. Valē, mī amīce.   8. Populus Rōmānus sapientiam fīliī tuī laudat.   9. Ō vir magne, populum Rōmānum servā.   10. Numerus populī Rōmānī est magnus.   11. Multī puerī puellās amant.   12. Fīliō meō nihil datis.   13. Virōs in agrō videō.   14. Amīcum fīliī meī vidēs.   15. Amīcum fīliōrum tuōrum nōn videt.   16. Dēbēmus fīliōs meōs monēre.   17. Dēbent fīlium tuum laudāre.   18. Vīta paucīs virīs fāmam dat.   19. Mē in numerō amīcōrum tuōrum habēs.   20. Virī magnī paucōs amīcōs saepe habent.   21. Amīcus meus semper cōgitat.   22. Fīlius magnī virī nōn semper est magnus vir.   23. Sapientiam magnōrum virōrum nōn semper vidēmus.   24. Philosophiam, sapientiam magnōrum virōrum, laudāre dēbētis.

EXERCISES FOR CHAPTER 4

1. A 2nd-declension neuter has the same forms as the regular 2nd-declension masculine except in three instances. Name these three instances and give their neuter endings.
2. Name the case(s), number, and syntactical usage indicated by each of the following endings of the 2nd-declension neuter nouns: (1) -a; (2) -um.
3. Name the case(s) and number of the following 2nd-declension neuter endings and name the English preposition(s) which can be associated with each: (1) -ō; (2) -ōrum; (3) -ī; (4) -īs.
4. Translate the following neuter nouns and state the syntactical usage of each as indicated by its ending: (1) bella; (2) bellum; (3) officium; (4) officia; (5) perīcula.
5. Translate the following phrases in accordance with their case endings: (1) bellōrum malōrum; (2) bellō malō; (3) bellī malī; (4) bellīs malīs; (5) officiī magnī; (6) officiīs magnīs; (7) perīculō parvō.
6. Given the following nom. sg. forms, write the Latin forms requested in each instance: (1) **bellum parvum** in nom. and acc. pl.; (2) **ōtium bonum** in acc. sg. and pl.; (3) **perīculum magnum** in gen. sg. and pl.; (4) **officium vērum** in acc. and abl. sg.
7. Translate the following phrases into Latin in accordance with the case named or indicated by the English preposition in each instance: (1) O evil war; (2) to/for great duty; (3) by the great danger; (4) good leisure (object of verb); (5) by many wars; (6) of good leisure; (7) by the dangers of many wars; (8) small wars (subject of verb); (9) small wars (obj. of verb); (10) O foolish wars; (11) the small war (subj.)

8. Ōtium est bonum.   9. Multa bella ōtium nōn cōnservant.   10. Perīculum est magnum.   11. In magnō perīculō sumus.   12. Et ōtium perīcula saepe habet.   13. Vīta nōn est sine multīs perīculīs.   14. Bonī virī ōtium amant.   15. Stultus vir perīcula bellī laudat.   16. Ōtium bellō saepe nōn cōnservā-mus.   17. Populus Rōmānus ōtium bonum nōn semper habet.   18. Patriam et ōtium bellīs parvīs saepe servant.   19. Multae puellae sunt bellae.   20. Vērī amīcī sunt paucī.   21. Amīcus meus est vir magnī officiī.   22. Offi-cia magistrī sunt multa et magna.   23. Vir parvī ōtiī es.   24. Virī magnae cūrae estis.   25. Sine morā cūram officiō dare dēbēmus.   26. Sine oculīs vīta est nihil.

EXERCISES FOR CHAPTER 5

1. Identify the *personal* endings of the future and imperfect tenses of the first two conjugations.
2. Are these the same as the endings of the present tense? If not, point out the differences.

3. Identify the future and imperfect tense signs in the first two conjugations.

4. How, in effect, can the following verb endings be translated: (1) -bāmus; (2) -bit; (3) -bitis; (4) -bō; (5) -bunt; (6) -bat?

5. When an adjective of the 1st and 2nd declensions has the masculine ending in -*er,* how can you tell whether the *e* survives in the other forms or is lost?

6. How do English words like *liberty, pulchritude,* and *nostrum* help with the declension of Latin adjectives?

7. Translate the following forms: (1) manēbant; (2) manēbit; (3) manēbimus; (4) dabam; (5) dabitis; (6) dabit; (7) vidēbis; (8) vidēbimus; (9) vocābant; (10) vocābis; (11) habēbis; (12) habēbant.

8. Translate into Latin: (1) we shall give; (2) you (sg.) were remaining; (3) they will see; (4) we shall call; (5) he was calling; (6) you (pl.) will see; (7) I shall see; (8) they were saving; (9) we shall have; (10) we were having; (11) he will have; (12) he has.

9. Magister noster mē laudat et tē crās laudābit. 10. Līberī virī perīcula nostra superābant. 11. Fīliī nostrī puellās pulchrās amant. 12. Amīcus noster in numerō stultōrum nōn remanēbit. 13. Culpās multās habēbāmus et semper habēbimus. 14. Perīcula magna animōs nostrōs nōn superant. 15. Pulchra patria nostra est lībera. 16. Līberī virī estis; patriam pulchram habēbitis. 17. Magistrī līberī officiō cūram dabant. 18. Malōs igitur in patriā nostrā superābimus. 19. Sī īram tuam superābis, tē superābis. 20. Propter nostrōs animōs multī sunt līberī. 21. Tē, Ō patria lībera, semper amābāmus et semper amābimus. 22. Sapientiam pecūniā nōn cōnservābitis. 23. Habetne animus tuus satis sapientiae?

EXERCISES FOR CHAPTER 6

1. What connection can be traced between the spelling of *complementary* in the term *complementary infinitive* and the syntactical principle?

2. In the verb **sum** and its compounds what do the following personal endings mean: (1) -mus; (2) -nt; (3) -s; (4) -t; (5) -ō; (6) -m; (7) -tis?

3. If the verb **possum** is composed of **pot** + **sum,** where among the various forms is the **t** changed to **s** and where does it remain unchanged?

4. Translate the following random forms: (1) erat; (2) poterat; (3) erit; (4) poterit; (5) sumus; (6) possumus; (7) poterāmus; (8) poterimus; (9) poteram; (10) eram; (11) erō; (12) poterō; (13) erunt; (14) poterunt; (15) poterant; (16) esse; (17) posse.

5. Translate into Latin: (1) we are; (2) we were; (3) we shall be; (4) we shall be able; (5) he is able; (6) he will be able; (7) he was able; (8) to be able; (9) they were able; (10) they are able; (11) they will be able; (12) they are; (13) to be; (14) I was able.

6. Patria vestra erat lībera.   7. Poteram esse tyrannus.   8. Amīcus vester erit tyrannus.   9. Ubi tyrannus est, ibi virī nōn possunt esse līberī.   10. In patriā nostrā herī nōn poterat remanēre.   11. Tyrannī multa vitia semper habēbunt.   12. Tyrannōs superāre nōn poterāmus.   13. Tyrannum nostrum superāre dēbēmus.   14. Tyrannus bonōs superāre poterat; sed ibi remanēre nōn poterit.   15. Poteritis perīcula tyrannī vidēre.   16. Vitia tyrannōrum tolerāre nōn possumus.   17. Īnsidiās tyrannī nōn tolerābās.   18. Ōtium in patriā vestrā nōn potest esse perpetuum.   19. Dēbēs virōs līberōs dē tyrannīs monēre.   20. Magister vester librōs pulchrōs semper amābat.   21. Librī bonī vērīque poterant patriam cōnservāre.   22. Librīs bonīs patriam vestram cōnservāre poteritis.   23. Tyrannī sapientiam bonōrum librōrum superāre nōn poterunt.   24. Malī librōs bonōs nōn possunt tolerāre.

EXERCISES FOR CHAPTER 7

1. In the 3rd declension do the case endings of feminine nouns differ from those of masculine nouns as they do in the 1st and 2nd declensions already learned?
2. Do neuter nouns of the 3rd declension have any case endings which are identical with those of neuter nouns of the 2nd declension? If so, name them.
3. Name the gender(s) and case(s) indicated by each of the following endings in the 3rd declension: (1) -ēs; (2) -a; (3) -em.
4. Name the case(s) and number of the following 3rd-declensional endings: (1) -ibus; (2) -ī; (3) -e; (4) -em; (5) -um; (6) -is; (7) -ēs.
5. To indicate the gender of the following nouns give the proper nominative singular form of **magnus, -a, -um** with each: (1) tempus; (2) virtūs; (3) labor;   (4) cīvitās;   (5) mōs;   (6) pāx;   (7) rēx;   (8) corpus;   (9) vēritās; (10) amor.
6. Translate the following phrases in accordance with their case endings wherever possible; where they are nominative or accusative so state: (1) labōre multō; (2) labōrī multō; (3) labōris multī; (4) labōrēs multī; (5) pācis perpetuae; (6) pāce perpetuā; (7) pācī perpetuae; (8) cīvitātum parvārum; (9) cīvitātem parvam; (10) cīvitātēs parvās; (11) cīvitātēs parvae;   (12) cīvitāte parvā;   (13) tempora mala;   (14) tempus malum; (15) temporī malō;   (16) temporum malōrum;   (17) temporis malī; (18) mōrī tuō; (19) mōre tuō; (20) mōris tuī; (21) mōrēs tuī; (22) mōrēs tuōs; (23) mōrum tuōrum.
7. Translate the following phrases into Latin in accordance with the case named or indicated by the English preposition: (1) to/for great virtue; (2) great virtue (subject); (3) great virtues (object of verb); (4) of great virtues; (5) with great courage; (6) our time (obj. of verb); (7) our times (subj.); (8) our times (obj.); (9) to/for our times; (10) to/for our time; (11) of our time; (12) of our times; (13) my love (obj.); (14) my loves

(obj.); (15) to/for my love; (16) by my love; (17) of my love; (18) of my loves.

8. Meum tempus ōtiō est parvum. 9. Virtūs tua est magna. 10. Pecūnia est nihil sine mōribus bonīs. 11. Virtūtēs hominum multōrum sunt magnae. 12. Mōrēs hominis bonī erunt bonī. 13. Hominī litterās dabunt. 14. Hominēs multōs in cīvitāte magnā vidēre poterāmus. 15. Magnum amōrem pecūniae in multīs hominibus vīdēbāmus. 16. Paucī hominēs virtūtī cūram dant. 17. Cīvitās nostra pācem hominibus multīs dabit. 18. Pāx nōn potest esse perpetua. 19. Sine bonā pāce cīvitātēs temporum nostrōrum nōn valēbunt. 20. Post multa bella tempora sunt mala. 21. In multīs cīvitātibus terrīsque pāx nōn poterat valēre. 22. Sine magnō labōre homō nihil habēbit. 23. Virgō pulchra amīcōs mōrum bonōrum amat. 24. Hominēs magnae virtūtis tyrannōs superāre audēbant. 25. Amor patriae in cīvitāte nostrā valēbat.

EXERCISES FOR CHAPTER 8

1. (1) In the 3d conjugation what tense is indicated by the stem vowel **e**? (2) Can you think of some mnemonic device to help you remember this important point?
2. (1) In the 3d conjugation what tense is indicated by the vowels **i, ō, u**? (2) What mnemonic device may help here?
3. State the person, number, and tense indicated by the following 3d conjugation endings: (1) -imus; (2) -ēs; (3) -unt; (4) -et; (5) -itis; (6) -ēmus; (7) -ō; (8) -ent; (9) -it; (10) -ētis; (11) -is; (12) -am; (13) -ēbant.
4. What form of the verb does each of the following endings indicate: (1) -e; (2) -ere; (3) -ite?
5. Given the verbs **mittō, mittere,** *send;* **agō, agere,** *do;* **scrībō, scrībere,** *write,* translate each of the following forms according to its ending: (1) mittēbant; (2) mittit; (3) mittunt; (4) mittam; (5) mitte; (6) mittimus; (7) mittēbātis; (8) mittis; (9) mittite; (10) mittitis; (11) mittet; (12) mittēmus; (13) agit; (14) agent; (15) agunt; (16) agētis; (17) agēbāmus; (18) agam; (19) agēmus; (20) agis; (21) agitis; (22) scrībet; (23) scrībunt; (24) scrībam; (25) scrībēbam; (26) scrībitis; (27) scrībēmus; (28) scrībit; (29) scrībis; (30) scrībent; (31) scrībe.
6. Given **pōnō, pōnere,** *put,* translate the following phrases into Latin: (1) they were putting; (2) we shall put; (3) put (imperative sg.); (4) he puts; (5) they will put; (6) I shall put; (7) you (sg.) were putting; (8) you (pl.) will put; (9) put (imper. pl.); (10) we put; (11) you (pl.) are putting; (12) he will put.

7. Quid agunt? Quid agētis? 8. Hominem ad mē dūcēbant. 9. Dūc hominem ad mē, et hominī grātiās agam. 10. Dum tyrannus cōpiās dūcit, possumus nihil agere. 11. Litterās ad virginem scrībit. 12. Librum magnum

scrībēbās. 13. Librōs bonōs scrībēs. 14. Librōs dē pāce scrībēmus. 15. Cōpiamne librōrum bonōrum habētis? 16. Magister multōs puerōs docet. 17. Puerī magistrō grātiās nōn agunt. 18. Paucī cīvitātī nostrae grātiās agēbant. 19. Tyrannus magnās cōpiās ex cīvitāte nostrā dūcet. 20. Magna cōpia pecūniae hominēs ad sapientiam nōn dūcit. 21. Librīne bonī multōs ad ratiōnem dūcent? 22. Dūcimusne saepe hominēs ad ratiōnem? 23. Ratiō hominēs ad bonam vītam dūcere potest. 24. Agitisne bonam vītam? 25. Amīcō bonō grātiās semper agite.

EXERCISES FOR CHAPTER 9

1. Explain the term *demonstrative* pronoun and adjective.
2. Translate each of the following according to case(s) and number, indicating also the gender(s) in each instance:

(1) illī	(10) illīs	(19) huius	(28) ūnā
(2) illa	(11) illō	(20) hunc	(29) tōtī
(3) illīus	(12) illārum	(21) hōs	(30) tōtīus
(4) ille	(13) hōc	(22) huic	(31) tōta
(5) illā	(14) hoc	(23) hōrum	(32) tōtum
(6) illud	(15) haec	(24) hās	(33) nūllīus
(7) illōrum	(16) hae	(25) hīs	(34) nūllī
(8) illae	(17) hāc	(26) ūnīus	(35) nūlla
(9) illōs	(18) hanc	(27) ūnī	(36) nūllōs

3. How can the presence of a noun be helpful in determining the form of a modifying demonstrative?
4. Translate the following phrases into Latin in the declensional forms indicated:

(1) this girl (nom.)	(16) to/for that boy alone
(2) these girls (nom.)	(17) to/for that girl alone
(3) these times (acc. pl.)	(18) of that girl alone
(4) to/for this time	(19) of tyrants alone
(5) to/for this boy	(20) the whole state (acc.)
(6) of this time	(21) of the whole country
(7) of that time	(22) to/for the whole country
(8) by this book	(23) of no reason
(9) by that book	(24) no reason (acc.)
(10) that girl (nom.)	(25) no girls (nom.)
(11) those times (nom.)	(26) to/for no book
(12) those times (acc.)	(27) no books (acc.)
(13) that time (nom.)	(28) to/for one state
(14) to/for this state alone	(29) to/for one girl
(15) of this state alone	(30) of one time

(31) of one war

(32) to/for the other book

(33) by another book

5. Hī tōtam cīvitātem dūcent (dūcunt, dūcēbant). 6. Ille haec in illā terrā vidēbit (videt, vidēbat). 7. In illō librō illa dē hōc homine scrībet (scrībam, scrībēbam). 8. Ūnus vir istās cōpiās in hanc terram dūcit (dūcet). 9. Magister haec alterī puerō dat. 10. Hunc librum dē aliō bellō scrībimus (scrībēmus). 11. Tōta patria huic sōlī grātiās agit (aget, agēbat). 12. Tōtam cūram illī cōnsiliō nunc dant. 13. Amīcus huius hanc cīvitātem illō cōnsiliō cōnservābit. 14. Alter amīcus tōtam vītam in aliā terrā aget. 15. Hic vir sōlus mē dē vitiīs huius tyrannī monēre poterat. 16. Nūllās cōpiās in alterā terrā habēbātis. 17. Illī sōlī nūlla perīcula in hōc cōnsiliō vident. 18. Nōn sōlum mōrēs sed etiam īnsidiās illīus laudāre audēs. 19. Propter īnsidiās enim ūnīus hominis haec cīvitās nōn valēbat.

EXERCISES FOR CHAPTER 10

1. Name the conjugation indicated by each of the following endings: (1) -ere; (2) -ēre; (3) -īre; (4) -āre.

2. State the person, number, and tense indicated by the following endings from the 4th conjugation and the **-iō** 3d: (1) -iunt; (2) -iēs; (3) -īs; (4) -iēbāmus; (5) -īmus; (6) -ī; (7) -iētis; (8) -īte; (9) -ītis; (10) -iō; (11) -it; (12) -e; (13) -iēbās.

3. State three points at which **-iō** verbs of the 3d conjugation differ from verbs of the 4th conjugation.

4. Translate the following in accordance with their specific forms:

(1) veniet	(6) audiētis	(11) venīre	(16) faciunt
(2) venit	(7) audītis	(12) facit	(17) facis
(3) veniunt	(8) venīte	(13) faciet	(18) faciam
(4) venient	(9) veniēs	(14) faciēmus	(19) faciēs
(5) audīs	(10) venī	(15) facimus	(20) facere

5. Given **sentiō, sentīre,** *feel,* and **iaciō, iacere,** *throw,* translate the following phrases into Latin:

(1) I shall feel	(8) feel (imper. sg.)	(15) throw (imper. sg.)
(2) we shall feel	(9) he will feel	(16) you (pl.) are throwing
(3) he feels	(10) we feel	(17) we shall throw
(4) you (pl.) feel	(11) he is throwing	(18) throw (imper. pl.)
(5) they will feel	(12) he will throw	(19) to throw
(6) they do feel	(13) I shall throw	(20) you (sg.) are throwing
(7) to feel	(14) we are throwing	

6. Ex hāc terrā fugiēbāmus. 7. Cum fīliā tuā fuge. 8. In illum locum fugient. 9. Tempus fugit; hōrae fugiunt; senectūs venit. 10. Venīte cum

amīcīs vestrīs. 11. In patriam vestram veniēbant. 12. Ō vir magne, in cīvitātem nostram venī. 13. Fīliam tuam in illā cīvitāte inveniēs. 14. Parvam pecūniam in viīs invenīre possunt. 15. Tyrannus viam in hanc cīvitātem invenit. 16. Illōs cum amīcīs ibi capiētis. 17. Ad tē cum magnīs cōpiīs venīmus. 18. Invenietne multam fāmam glōriamque ibi? 19. Iste bellum semper faciēbat. 20. Istī hominēs pācem nōn facient. 21. Multī hominēs illa faciunt sed haec nōn faciunt. 22. Officium nostrum facimus et faciēmus. 23. Magnam cōpiam librōrum faciam. 24. Puerī cum illō virō bonō vīvēbant. 25. In librīs virōrum antīquōrum multam philosophiam et sapientiam inveniētis.

EXERCISES FOR CHAPTER 11

1. Name the nominative singular and plural of the following:
   (1) 3d personal pronoun; (2) 1st per. pron.; (3) 2nd per. pron.
2. Translate the following pronouns in accordance with case(s) and number; where a form is nom. or acc. so specify.
   (1) vōbīs; (2) nōbīs; (3) nōs; (4) vōs; (5) tuī; (6) meī; (7) mihi; (8) tibi; (9) tē; (10) mē.
3. Translate the following third-person pronouns in accordance with their gender(s), number(s), and case(s): (1) eōs; (2) eās; (3) eōrum; (4) eārum; (5) eius; (6) eā; (7) ea; (8) eō; (9) eī; (10) eīs; (11) eae; (12) id.
4. Give the Latin for the following:

(1) his	(10) to her	(19) it (neut. acc.)
(2) her (possess.)	(11) by/w./fr. her	(20) you (emphatic nom. pl.)
(3) their (masc.)	(12) by/w.fr. him	(21) you (emphatic nom. sg.)
(4) their (fem.)	(13) to/for you (pl.)	(22) you (acc. pl.)
(5) them (fem.)	(14) to/for you (sg.)	(23) us
(6) them (masc.)	(15) they (masc.)	(24) we
(7) them (neut.)	(16) they (neut.)	(25) to/for us
(8) its	(17) they (fem.)	(26) I (emphatic form)
(9) to him	(18) to/for it	(27) to/for me

5. Hī tibi id dabunt. 6. Ego vōbīs id dabam. 7. Vōs eīs id dōnum dabitis. 8. Eī idem dabō. 9. Nōs eī ea dabimus. 10. Ille mihi id dabit. 11. Vōbīs librōs eius dabimus. 12. Nōbīs librōs eōrum dabis. 13. Pecūniam eōrum tibi dabimus. 14. Pecūniam eius mihi dabunt. 15. Eōs librōs ad eam mittēmus. 16. Librum eius ad tē mittam. 17. Ille autem pecūniam eōrum ad nōs mittēbat. 18. Eās cum eā mittimus. 19. Eum cum eīs mittō. 20. Eōs cum amīcīs eius mittēmus. 21. Tū mē cum amīcō eōrum mittēs. 22. Vōs mēcum ad amīcum eius mittēbant. 23. Nōs tēcum in terram eōrum mittit. 24. Eās nōbīscum ad amīcōs eōrum mittent. 25. Eum vōbīscum ad amīcōs eōrum mittam. 26. Tē cum eō ad mē mittent.

EXERCISES FOR CHAPTER 12

1. Name the principal parts of a Latin verb in their regular sequence.
2. Give the principal parts of **mittō,** labeling and translating each one.
3. What is the major difference between the perfect and imperfect tenses?
4. You must be able to tell from what verb any specific verb form comes. Practice on the following list by naming the first principal part of each of the verbs in the list.

(1) mīsērunt	(6) āctum	(11) remānserant	(16) dīxērunt
(2) laudāveram	(7) est	(12) scrīpsimus	(17) erat
(3) vincēbāmus	(8) dedimus	(13) fuit	(18) vīxī
(4) dictum	(9) futūrum	(14) fēcit	(19) faciēbās
(5) fēcistī	(10) ēgimus	(15) fugere	(20) vīsum

5. Translate the following endings of the perfect system according to person, number, and tense in each instance, using these conventions: **-ī** = I (perfect) . . . ; **-eram** = I had . . . ; **-erō** = I shall have . . . ; (1) -istis; (2) -it; (3) -ērunt; (4) -istī; (5) -imus; (6) -erat; (7) -erimus; (8) -erāmus; (9) -erās; (10) -erint; (11) -erant; (12) -erit; (13) -erātis.

6. Translate the following in accordance with the person, number, and tense of each:

(1) vidēbant	(10) vīxistī	(19) fugit	(28) remānsimus
(2) vīderant	(11) vīxērunt	(20) fūgit	(29) remānserāmus
(3) vīdistī	(12) vincet	(21) fugiunt	(30) vēnit
(4) fēcit	(13) vīcit	(22) fūgērunt	(31) venit
(5) faciēbat	(14) vīcimus	(23) servāvit	(32) veniēbātis
(6) fēcerāmus	(15) vincimus	(24) servāvērunt	(33) vēnistis
(7) fēcimus	(16) dedistī	(25) servāvistis	(34) vēnērunt
(8) faciēmus	(17) dederātis	(26) servāverat	(35) veniunt
(9) fēcērunt	(18) dedimus	(27) servāverit	(36) vēnerant

7. Illī fūgerant (fugient; fugiunt; fugiēbant; fūgērunt). 8. Hī remānsērunt (remanent; remanēbunt; remanēbant; remānserant). 9. Rēx Asiam vīcerat (vincit; vīcit; vincet). 10. Rēgēs Asiam vīcērunt (vincent; vincunt; vīcerant). 11. Rēgēs Asiam habuērunt (habent; habēbunt; habuerant). 12. Caesar in eandem terram vēnerat (vēnit; venit; veniet). 13. Caesar eadem dīxit (dīcit; dīxerat; dīcet). 14. Vōs nōbīs pācem dedistis (dabitis; dabātis; dederātis). 15. Tū litterās ad eam mīsistī (mittēs; mittis; mīserās). 16. Eōs in eādem viā vīdimus (vidēmus; vīderāmus). 17. Diū vīxerat (vīxit; vīvet). 18. Id bene fēcerās (faciēs; fēcistī; facis). 19. Cīvitātem eōrum (eius) servāvī (servābō; servābam; servāveram). 20. Eum in eōdem locō invēnērunt (invēnerant; invenient). 21. Deus hominibus lībertātem dederat (dedit; dat; dabit). 22. Mihi grātiās ēgērunt (agent; agēbant; ēgerant; agunt). 23. Vōs fuistis (erātis; estis; eritis; fuerātis) virī līberī.

EXERCISES FOR CHAPTER 13

1. State the essential nature of reflexive pronouns, showing how, as a logical consequence, they differ from other pronouns.
2. Explain why the declension of reflexive pronouns begins with the genitive rather than with the nominative.
3. In what reflexive pronouns is the spelling the same as that of the corresponding simple pronoun?
4. Translate the following reflexive forms in accordance with their case(s) and number(s): (1) mihi; (2) tē; (3) nōbīs; (4) sibi; (5) vōs; (6) sē; (7) vōbīs.
5. Explain why the singular of **suus** can mean *their own* as well as *his own,* and the plural can mean *his own* as well as *their own.*
6. Explain why **eōrum** always means *their* and **eius** always means *his* (*her, its*) regardless of whether the nouns on which they depend are singular or plural.
7. Although **sē** and **ipse** can both be translated into English by *himself,* explain the basic difference between the Latin words.

8. Caesar eōs servāvit. 9. Caesar eum servābat. 10. Caesar sē servāvit. 11. Rōmānī sē servāvērunt. 12. Rōmānī eōs servāvērunt. 13. Rōmānī eum servāvērunt. 14. Caesar amīcum suum servāvit. 15. Caesar amīcōs suōs servāvit. 16. Caesar amīcum eius servāvit. 17. Caesar amīcōs eius servāvit. 18. Caesar amīcum eōrum servāvit. 19. Caesar amīcōs eōrum servāvit. 20. Rōmānī amīcum suum servāvērunt. 21. Rōmānī amīcōs suōs servāvērunt. 22. Rōmānī amīcum eōrum servāvērunt. 23. Rōmānī amīcōs eōrum servāvērunt. 24. Rōmānī amīcum eius servāvērunt. 25. Rōmānī amīcōs eius servāvērunt. 26. Caesar ipse eum servāvit. 27. Caesar ipse sē servāvit. 28. Caesarem ipsum servāvērunt. 29. Amīcum Caesaris ipsīus servābant. 30. Amīcum Rōmānōrum ipsōrum servāvērunt. 31. Amīcus Caesaris ipsīus sē servāvit. 32. Amīcī Caesaris ipsīus sē servāvērunt. 33. Amīcus Caesaris ipsīus eum servāvit. 34. Ipsī amīcī Caesaris eum servāvērunt. 35. Nōs nōn servāvērunt. 36. Nōs servāvimus. 37. Rōmānōs ipsōs servāvimus. 38. Rōmānī ipsī tē nōn servāvērunt. 39. Tū tē servāvistī. 40. Tū Rōmānōs ipsōs servāvistī. 41. Mihi nihil dabat. 42. Mihi nihil dedī. 43. Sibi nihil dedit. 44. Sibi nihil dedērunt. 45. Eīs nihil dedērunt. 46. Eī nihil dedērunt. 47. Mē vīcī. 48. Mē vīcērunt. 49. Īram eōrum vīcērunt. 50. Īram suam vīcērunt. 51. Īram suam vīcit. 52. Fīliōs suōs vīcit. 53. Fīliōs suōs vīcērunt.

EXERCISES FOR CHAPTER 14

1. In what specific case ending of all **i**-stem nouns does the characteristic **i** appear?
2. What are the other **i**-stem peculiarities of neuters in **-e, -al,** and **-ar?**

3. Translate each of the following according to its case(s) and number; when a form is nom. or acc. label it as such.

(1) arte	(9) corporum	(17) rēgum	(25) virōs
(2) artium	(10) partis	(18) rēgī	(26) virī
(3) artēs	(11) partibus	(19) nōmina	(27) vīrēs
(4) marī	(12) partium	(20) animālia	(28) virīs
(5) maribus	(13) urbe	(21) animālī	(29) vīs
(6) mare	(14) urbī	(22) animālis	(30) vim
(7) maria	(15) urbium	(23) animālium	(31) vīribus
(8) corpora	(16) urbēs	(24) vīrium	(32) vī

4. Of the forms in #3 above, list those which are **i-** stem forms.

5. Translate the following phrases into Latin:

(1) by/w./fr. great force	(8) many seas (nom.)
(2) great man (acc.)	(9) by/w./fr. a great sea
(3) of great strength	(10) a great sea (acc.)
(4) to/for great force	(11) great force (acc.)
(5) of many citizens	(12) of many men (vir)
(6) by/w./fr. a good citizen	(13) by/w./fr. great strength
(7) to/for many citizens	(14) great strength (acc.)

6. What kind of idea is expressed by each of the following ablatives? (1) cum rēge; (2) oculīs meīs; (3) cum cūrā; (4) labōre meō.

7. Translate each of the following verb forms and name the verb from which each comes: (1) cucurrērunt; (2) currēbāmus; (3) cucurristī; (4) trāxerāmus; (5) trahet; (6) trahunt; (7) gerēbat; (8) gerit; (9) gerunt; (10) gerēmus; (11) tenent; (12) tenēbunt; (13) tenuērunt; (14) tenuimus.

8. Multa bella cum Rōmānīs gessit. 9. Cīvitātem magnā cum sapientiā gerēbant. 10. Ipse cīvitātem vī cōpiārum tenuit. 11. Illa animālia multōs hominēs in mare trāxērunt. 12. Hoc magnā cum arte dīxistī. 13. Cum cūrā trāns urbem cucurrimus. 14. Magnā cum parte cīvium ad nōs veniēbat. 15. Iūra cīvium vī vincet. 16. Eum ad mortem trāns terram eius trāxistis. 17. Nōs cum cīvibus multārum urbium iungēmus. 18. Rēgī ipsī hās litterās cum virtūte scrīpsit. 19. Vīs illōrum marium erat magna. 20. Artem Graecōrum oculīs meīs vīdī. 21. Sententiās multās pulchrāsque ex virīs antīquīs trāximus.

22. Name the type of ablative found in each of the following sentences above: 8, 9, 10, 12, 13, 14, 15, 17, 18, 20.

EXERCISES FOR CHAPTER 15

1. State the difference between cardinal and ordinal numerals.
2. What cardinals are declined?
3. What ordinals are declined?

4. State the form or possible forms of each of the following: (1) duōbus; (2) mīlle; (3) tria; (4) duo; (5) quīnque; (6) mīlia; (7) decem; (8) duābus; (9) centum; (10) trium; (11) vīgintī; (12) octō.
5. Why is the genitive of the whole so called?
6. What construction did the Romans use after cardinal numerals?
7. Translate each of the following phrases.

(1) ūnus cīvis	(9) centum ex cīvibus
(2) decem cīvēs	(10) mīlle cīvēs
(3) pars cīvium	(11) tria mīlia cīvium
(4) trēs cīvēs	(12) quid novī
(5) trēs ex sex cīvibus	(13) multum laudis
(6) quīnque ex cīvibus	(14) satis pecūniae
(7) quīnque cīvēs	(15) nihil aquae
(8) centum cīvēs	

8. When the Romans put a word of time in the ablative case without a preposition, what kind of ideas did they express?
9. Study the ablatives in the following sentences. Then translate the sentences and name the type of ablative found in each one.

(1) Cum amīcīs veniēbat.	(4) Paucīs hōrīs librum scrīpsit.
(2) Ūnā hōrā veniet.	(5) Illō tempore librum scrīpsit.
(3) Eōdem tempore vēnit.	(6) Cum cūrā librum scrībēbat.

10. Illō tempore sōlō illa tria perīcula timuit; sed mortem semper timēbat.
11. Istī duo rēgēs pecūniam inter mīlia cīvium iaciēbant.   12. Iste ūnus tyrannus sē semper laudābat.   13. Cīvēs illārum quīnque urbium lībertātem exspectābant.   14. Urbem duābus hōrīs sapientiā suā cōnservāvērunt.
15. In urbem cum tribus ex amīcīs meīs veniēbam.   16. Bella magna cum virtūte gerēbātis.   17. Itaque centum Rōmānī mīlle Graecōs vīcērunt.
18. Patrēs fīliōs suōs saepe timēbant—et nunc multum timōris habent.
19. Vīdistīne duōs patrēs nostrōs eō tempore?   20. Ubi satis lībertātis invē-nistis?   21. Tribus hōrīs vēnērunt, et idem nōbīs dīcēbat.   22. Parvum argū-mentī intellegēbam.   23. Nūllam partem vītārum nostrārum mūtāvimus.
24. Cīvitās nostra lībertātem et iūra cīvium cōnservābat.   25. Rōmānī mō-rēs temporum antīquōrum laudābant.   26. Duo patrēs quattuor ex fīliīs mīsērunt.   27. Decem virī satis sapientiae et multum virtūtis habuērunt.
28. Quid novī, mī amīce?

EXERCISES FOR CHAPTER 16

1. If one has carefully learned the declension of **cīvis** and **mare** one can easily decline the 3d-declension adjective **fortis, forte** with the exception of one form. What is that form?

2. (1) Adjectives of the 3d declension may be classified as adjectives of 3 endings, 2 endings, or 1 ending. Which type is by far the most common? (2) In what one case do adjectives of 1 and 3 endings differ from those of 2 endings?

3. Cite and label three endings in which adjectives of the 3d declension show themselves to be **i**-stems.

4. Of the endings of the 3d-declension adjectives none is likely to cause recognition difficulty except perhaps the ablative singular. What is the normal ending of the ablative singular in all genders?

5. Can 3d-declension adjectives be used with nouns of the 1st or the 2nd declension?

6. Translate the following phrases in accordance with their case(s) and number. When they are nom. or acc., so indicate.

(1) dulcī puellae	(8) omnia nōmina	(15) beātō hominī
(2) dulcī puellā	(9) omnia maria	(16) omnī marī
(3) dulcī mātre	(10) omnī parte	(17) omnī bonae artī
(4) dulcī mātrī	(11) omnium partium	(18) omnī bonā arte
(5) beātae mātrī	(12) omnium rēgum	(19) omnis bonae artis
(6) beātā mātre	(13) omnium bellōrum	(20) vī celerī
(7) omnia bella	(14) beātō homine	

7. Aetās longa saepe est difficilis. 8. Aetās difficilis potest esse beāta. 9. Quam brevis erat dulcis vīta eius! 10. Memoria dulcis aetātis mīlia hominum adiuvat. 11. Librum brevem centum hōrīs scrīpsistī. 12. In omnī marī haec duo animālia potentia inveniēbāmus. 13. In omnī terrā multa mīlia virōrum fortium vidēbitis. 14. Celer rūmor (celeris fāma) per omnem terram cucurrit. 15. Illud bellum breve erat difficile. 16. Omnia perīcula sex hōrīs superāvimus. 17. Tyrannus potēns patriam eōrum vī celerī vincet. 18. Brevī tempore omnia iūra cīvium mūtābit. 19. Difficilem artem lībertātis dulcis nōn intellēxērunt, nam parvum sapientiae habuērunt. 20. Hominēs officia difficilia in omnibus terrīs timent.

EXERCISES FOR CHAPTER 17

1. Define the terms "antecedent" and "relative pronoun."

2. (1) What determines the *case* of the Latin relative pronoun? (2) What determines the *gender* and the *number* of the relative pronoun?

3. State in what ways a relative agrees with its antecedent.

4. Name (1) the English relative pronoun which refers to persons and (2) the one which refers to anything else. (3) Since in Latin the one relative pronoun serves both purposes, what two English meanings does it have?

5. Translate the following in accordance with their case(s) and number(s).

When a form is nom. or acc., so indicate if the translation does not make the point clear.

(1) cui	(4) cuius	(7) quā	(10) quās
(2) quōs	(5) quibus	(8) quī	(11) quōrum
(3) quae	(6) quod	(9) quem	(12) quam

6. Cīvem laudāvērunt quem mīserātis. 7. Decem cīvēs laudāvērunt quōs mīserātis. 8. Cīvem laudāvērunt quī patriam servāverat. 9. Centum cīvēs laudāvērunt quī patriam servāverant. 10. Cīvem laudāvērunt cuius fīlius patriam servāverat. 11. Cīvēs laudāvērunt quōrum septem fīliī patriam servāverant. 12. Cīvem laudāvērunt cui patriam commīserant. 13. Multōs ex cīvibus laudāvērunt quibus patriam commīserant. 14. Cīvem laudāvērunt quōcum vēnerant. 15. Cīvēs laudāvērunt quibuscum vēnerant. 16. Cum cīve vēnit cui vītam suam commīserat. 17. Tyrannī iūra cīvium dēlent quōs capiunt. 18. Tyrannus urbem dēlēvit ex quā mīlia cīvium fūgerant. 19. Tyrannus urbem dēlēvit in quam illī novem cīvēs fūgerant. 20. Tyrannus urbēs dēlēvit ex quibus cīvēs fūgerant. 21. Tyrannus urbēs dēlēvit in quās cīvēs fūgerant. 22. Perīculum superāvit quod timuimus. 23. Perīcula superāvit quae timuimus. 24. Puellīs quās laudābat librōs dedit. 25. Vir cuius fīliam amās in urbem veniēbat. 26. Virō cuius fīliam amās vītam suam commīsit. 27. Mātrem adiuvābat, quae multum virtūtis habuit. 28. Mātribus quae multōs fīliōs habuērunt rēx pecūniam dabat.

EXERCISES FOR CHAPTER 18

1. Define the term "passive voice" by explaining the etymology of "passive."
2. What is the difference between the ablative of means and the ablative of agent in both meaning and construction?
3. (1) What one letter occurs in 5 of the 6 passive personal endings and can thus be regarded as the peculiar sign of the passive?
   (2) Does this characteristically passive letter occur in any of the corresponding active personal endings?
4. Give the English pronoun by which each of the following passive endings can be translated: (1) -mur; (2) -tur; (3) -r; (4) -ntur; (5) -ris; (6) -minī.
5. (1) Name the tense signs of the imperfect and the future in the passive voice of the 1st and 2nd conjugations.
   (2) Are these the same as the tense signs in the active voice?
6. If -bar can be translated "I was being . . ." and -bor, "I shall be . . . ," translate each of the following: (1) -bimur; (2) -bāminī; (3) -bātur; (4) -beris; (5) -buntur; (6) -bāmur; (7) -bitur; (8) -bāris; (9) -biminī; (10) -bantur.

7. Mē terrent; ab eīs terreor; vī eōrum terreor. 8. Tyrannus hanc urbem dē-

lēbat. 9. Haec urbs ā tyrannō dēlēbātur; īnsidiīs dēlēbitur. 10. Ab amīcīs movēbātur; cōnsiliīs eōrum movēbātur. 11. Vīribus hominum nōn dēlēmur, sed possumus īnsidiīs dēlērī. 12. Nōn bellō dēlēbiminī, sed amōre ōtiī et cōnsiliīs hominum malōrum. 13. Tū ipse nōn mūtāris, sed nōmen tuum mūtātur. 14. Mīlia hominum amōre pecūniae tenentur. 15. Aliī ab tyrannīs tenēbantur. 16. Paucī amōre vēritātis amīcitiaeque tenēbuntur. 17. Puer ab amīcīs cōnservābitur. 18. Librī huius generis puerīs ā magistrō dabantur. 19. Lībertās populō ab rēge tertiō brevī tempore dabitur. 20. Patria nostra ā cīvibus fortibus etiam nunc servārī potest. 21. Fortūnā aliōrum monērī dēbēmus. 22. Cōnsiliīs istīus tyrannī quī trāns mare vīvit terrēmur; sed lībertātem amāmus et bellum magnā cum virtūte gerēmus. 23. Ab amīcīs potentibus adiuvābimur. 24. Omnēs virōs nostrōs laudāmus, quī virtūte et vēritāte moventur, nōn amōre suī.

EXERCISES FOR CHAPTER 19

1. Name the two basic verbal elements (1) of which the perfect passive indicative of all verbs is composed, and (2) of which the pluperfect passive indicative is composed.
2. In translation how does (1) **vir missus est** differ from **vir mittitur,** and (2) **vir missus erat,** from **vir mittēbātur?**
3. What is the use of the interrogative pronoun?
4. In what forms does the interrogative pronoun differ conspicuously in spelling from the relative?
5. By what two syntactical criteria can the interrogative pronoun be distinguished from the relative even when both have the same spelling?
6. Translate the following in accordance with their forms:

(1) movētur	(6) dēlēbantur	(11) tenēbāmur
(2) mōtus est	(7) dēlētī sunt	(12) mūtātus erat
(3) mōtum erat	(8) tenēmur	(13) mūtātus est
(4) movēbātur	(9) tentī sumus	(14) mūtātur
(5) dēlētī erant	(10) tentī erāmus	(15) mūtābātur

7. Translate the following forms of the interrogative pronoun: (1) cuius?; (2) quem?; (3) quī?; (4) quid?; (5) quōrum?; (6) cui?; (7) quās?; (8) quis?; (9) quae?

8. Ā quō liber parātus est (parātus erat, parābātur)? 9. Magister ā quō liber parātus est labōre superātur. 10. Cui liber datus est (dabātur, datus erat)? 11. Quī puer servātus est? 12. Puerum quī servātus est ego ipse vīdī. 13. Cuius duo fīliī servātī sunt? 14. Senem cuius fīliī servātī sunt numquam vīdī. 15. Quis missus est? 16. Ā cīve quī missus erat pāx et lībertās laudātae sunt. 17. Quī missī sunt? 18. Ā decem cīvibus quī missī erant amīcitia laudāta est. 19. Quōs in urbe vīdistī? 20. Ubi sunt trēs novī amīcī quōs in

urbe vīdistī?   21. Quae ā tē ibi inventa sunt?   22. Ubi sunt tria corpora quae ā tē ibi inventa sunt?   23. Ā quibus hoc dictum est?   24. Quibus hoc dictum est?   25. Octō hominēs miserī quibus haec dicta sunt ex urbe fūgērunt. 26. Quōrum fīliī ab eō laudātī sunt?   27. Patrēs quōrum fīliī laudātī sunt eī grātiās agent.   28. Quid vōs terret?   29. Quod perīculum vōs terret?   30. At perīculum quod vōs terret ā cīvibus fortibus victum est.

EXERCISES FOR CHAPTER 20

1. Indicate the force of the following masculine and feminine endings of the 4th declension: (1) -um; (2) -uum; (3) -ū; (4) -us; (5) -ūs; (6) -uī.
2. Translate the following nouns in accordance with their case forms:

(1) manuī	(6) frūctibus	(11) senātūs (sg.)
(2) manus	(7) frūctum	(12) senātuī
(3) manuum	(8) frūctūs	(13) senātus
(4) manū	(9) frūctuum	(14) senātū
(5) manūs	(10) frūctū	

3. (1) What gender predominates in the 4th declension?
   (2) Name the noun which is the most common exception to this rule.
4. (1) Explain the difference of idea between the ablative of place from which and the ablative of separation.
   (2) Which of the two is regular with verbs of freeing, lacking, and depriving?
   (3) Which of the two is regular with verbs of motion?
5. State any differences of construction between them.

6. Quis ad nōs eō tempore vēnit?   7. Senex magnae fāmae ex patriā suā ad senātum nostrum fūgit.   8. Quid novī ab eō dictum est?   9. Hoc ab illō virō dictum est: "Lībertāte carēmus."   10. Nōs servitūte et gravī metū līberāte. 11. Cōpiae nostrae bellum longum contrā ācrēs manūs tyrannī gessērunt. 12. Illae manūs ācrēs quās tyrannus contrā nōs illā ex terrā mīsit ā nōbīs victae sunt.   13. Post haec cīvēs quī tyrannum timuērunt ex patriā suā in cīvitātem nostram ductī sunt.   14. Eōs sceleribus istīus tyrannī līberāvimus. 15. Nunc omnī metū carent.   16. Fīliī eōrum bonōs librōs in lūdīs nostrīs cum studiō legunt.   17. Itaque mīlle versūs manibus suīs scrīpsērunt. 18. Hī centum versūs nōbīs grātiās magnās agunt.   19. In hīs versibus senātus populusque Rōmānus laudantur.   20. Nam illī miserī nunc frūctūs pācis et multum lībertātis sine metū habent.   21. Quoniam aliōs adiūvimus, etiam nōs ipsī frūctum magnum habēmus.   22. Virī bonī cōpiā hōrum frūctuum numquam carēbunt.   23. Aetāte nostrā multī hominēs vītam in metū et servitūte agunt.   24. Dēbēmus illōs miserōs metū līberāre. 25. Nam quis potest beātus esse sī aliī hominēs frūctibus pācis lībertātisque carent?

26. What idea is expressed by each of the following ablatives, respectively? tempore (6), patriā (7), eō (8), virō (9), metū (10), nōbīs (12), patriā (13), sceleribus (14), metū (15), studiō (16), manibus (17), cōpiā (22), aetāte (23), metū (24).

EXERCISES FOR CHAPTER 21

1. Give the passive personal endings of the present and future tenses.
2. Repeat *aloud* the present and future passive of the model verbs **agō, audiō,** and **capiō.**
3. How can the present passive infinitive be distinguished from the active in the 1st, 2nd, and 4th conjugations? Illustrate by changing the following active infinitives into passive ones: (1) sentīre; (2) movēre; (3) servāre; (4) scīre; (5) tenēre. Translate each.
4. What is exceptional about the form of the present passive infinitive of the 3d conjugation? Illustrate by changing the following active infinitives into passive ones: (1) mittere; (2) iacere; (3) tangere; (4) trahere. Translate each.
5. Translate each of the following in accordance with its form:

(1) mittar	(7) rapitur	(13) raperis	(19) tangēminī
(2) mitteris	(8) rapiētur	(14) rapiēris	(20) sciēris
(3) mittēris	(9) rapī	(15) tanguntur	(21) scīris
(4) mittī	(10) rapimur	(16) tangentur	(22) sciētur
(5) mittuntur	(11) rapientur	(17) tangī	(23) scītur
(6) mittor	(12) rapiuntur	(18) tangeris	(24) scīrī

6. Quis mittitur (mittētur, mittēbātur, missus est)? 7. Ā quō hae litterae mittentur (missae sunt, mittuntur)? 8. Cuius manū illae litterae scrīptae sunt (scrībentur)? 9. Quid dictum est (dīcēbātur, dīcētur, dīcitur)? 10. "Quis rapiētur?" "Tū rapiēris." 11. "Quī rapientur?" "Vōs rapiēminī." 12. Diū neglegēris/neglegēminī (neglēctus es/neglēctī estis). 13. Post multās hōrās līberātī sumus (līberābimur). 14. Cīvitātis causā eum rapī iussērunt. 15. Lībertātis causā cīvitās nostra ab alterō virō gerī dēbet. 16. Animus eius pecūniā tangī nōn poterat. 17. Amor patriae in omnī animō sentiēbātur (sentiētur, sentītur, sēnsus est). 18. Amōre patriae cum aliīs cīvibus iungimur (iungēbāmur, iungēmur). 19. Amīcitia nōn semper intellegitur, sed sentītur. 20. Sapientia et vēritās in illīs duōbus hominibus nōn invenientur (inveniuntur, inventae sunt). 21. Sapientia etiam multā pecūniā nōn parātur (parābitur, parāta est). 22. Vēritās saepe nōn scītur (sciētur, scīta est), quod studium eius est difficile. 23. Nōn sine magnō labōre vēritās inveniētur (inventa est, potest invenīrī). 24. Aliī studiō pecūniae atque laudis trahuntur; nōs dēbēmus amōre vēritātis sapientiaeque trahī.

EXERCISES FOR CHAPTER 22

1. As **u** is characteristic of the 4th declension, what vowel is characteristic of the 5th declension?

2. List the case endings of the 5th declension which are enough like the corresponding endings of the 3rd declension that they can be immediately recognized without difficulty.

3. (1) What is the gender of most nouns of the 5th declension?
   (2) Name the chief exception.

4. Translate each of the following in accordance with its case(s) and number(s). Where a form is nom. or acc., so state.

(1) speī	(6) fidē	(11) diēbus	(16) reī
(2) spērum	(7) fidem	(12) rem	(17) ignium
(3) spem	(8) fideī	(13) rērum	(18) ignem
(4) spēbus	(9) diērum	(14) rē	(19) ignibus
(5) spēs	(10) diēs	(15) rēbus	(20) ignēs

5. Name the type of adverbial idea in each of the following, and then translate the sentence.

(1) In urbe remānsit.	(4) Cum eīs vēnit.	(7) Illud igne factum est.
(2) Ūnā hōrā veniet.	(5) Ex urbe vēnit.	(8) Id ab eīs factum est.
(3) Eō tempore vēnit.	(6) Igne carent.	(9) Id cum fidē factum est.

6. Concerning each of the following adverbial ideas, state whether in Latin the ablative alone expresses the idea, or whether the Romans used a preposition with the ablative, or whether a preposition was sometimes used and sometimes not. Base your answers on the rules learned thus far.

(1) personal agent	(5) means
(2) accompaniment	(6) manner
(3) separation	(7) place from which
(4) place where	(8) time when or within when

7. Eō tempore lībertātem illōrum decem cīvium cum fidē cōnservāvit.
8. Rem pūblicam magnā cum cūrā gessit.   9. Rēs pūblica magnā cūrā ab eō gesta est.   10. Multae rēs bonae in mediā urbe vīsae sunt.   11. Eō diē multās rēs cum spē parāvērunt.   12. Ignem ex manibus puerī ēripuimus.
13. Quīnque diēbus Cicerō rem pūblicam ē perīculō ēripiet.   14. Duās rēs pūblicās metū līberāvistī.   15. Terra hominēs frūctibus bonīs alit.   16. Incertās spēs eōrum virtūte suā aluit.   17. Hāc aetāte spēs nostrae ā hīs tribus tyrannīs tolluntur.   18. Septem ex amīcīs nostrīs ex illā rē pūblicā magnō cum metū vēnērunt.   19. Tōta gēns in fīnēs huius reī pūblicae magnā cum manū amīcōrum ūnō diē vēnit.   20. Nōn omnēs virī līberī audent sē cum hāc rē pūblicā iungere.   21. Sī illī fidē carent, nūlla spēs est amīcitiae et pācis.

22. Bona fidēs et amor huius reī pūblicae possunt nōs cōnservāre. 23. Tōtam vītam huic reī pūblicae dedistī.

24. What idea is expressed by each of the following ablatives? (The numbers
refer to the sentences.) (7) tempore, fidē; (8) cūrā; (9) cūrā; (10) urbe;
(11) diē, spē; (13) diēbus, perīculō; (14) metū; (15) frūctibus; (16) virtūte; (17) aetāte, tyrannīs; (18) rē pūblicā, metū; (19) manū, diē;
(21) fidē.

EXERCISES FOR CHAPTER 23

1. State what Latin participle is indicated by each of the following endings
and give the English suffix or phrase which can be used as an approximate equivalent in each instance: (1) -tus; (2) -ns; (3) -sūrus; (4) -ntem;
(5) -tūrus; (6) -ndus; (7) -sus; (8) -ntēs; (9) -sī; (10) -tīs. Such forms
should be practiced aloud until you have an immediate linguistic reflex
to each one. These reflexes can be tested in the following exercise.

2. Translate the following participles in accordance with their tense and
voice.

(1) futūrus	(7) versus	(13) faciendus	(19) datī
(2) pressūrus	(8) versūrus	(14) rapientēs	(20) datūrōs
(3) premēns	(9) dictus	(15) raptūrōs	(21) dantem
(4) pressus	(10) dīcēns	(16) cupīta	(22) mōtus
(5) premendus	(11) dictūrus	(17) cupientēs	(23) moventem
(6) vertēns	(12) factus	(18) dandum	(24) mōtūrī

3. Translate the following participles or participial phrases into Latin in
their nom. sg. masc. form.

(1) (having been) seen	(10) (having been) conquered
(2) seeing	(11) about to conquer
(3) about to see	(12) conquering
(4) to be written	(13) about to join
(5) about to write	(14) joining
(6) (having been) written	(15) (having been) dragged
(7) sending	(16) dragging
(8) (having been) sent	(17) about to throw
(9) about to send	(18) (having been) thrown

4. Captus nihil dīxit. 5. Servitūte līberātus, vītam iūcundam aget. 6. Dōna
dantibus grātiās ēgit. 7. Aliquem dōna petentem nōn amō. 8. Hominī
multam pecūniam cupientī pauca dōna sōla dabat. 9. Ad lūdum tuum
fīlium meum docendum mīsī. 10. Iste, aliam gentem victūrus, magistrōs
librōsque dēlēre cupiēbat. 11. Hīs īnsidiīs territī, vītam miseram vīvēmus.
12. Diū oppressī, sē contrā opprimentem tyrannum vertere coepērunt.

13. Illī quattuor virī miserī, ā tyrannō vīsī, trāns fīnem cucurrērunt.   14. Ōrātor, tyrannum timēns, iūcunda semper dīcēbat.   15. Aliquem nōs timentem timēmus.   16. Hī vincentēs omnia iūra cīvium victōrum tollent.   17. Ille miser fugitūrus cōnsilium trium amīcōrum petēbat.   18. Senex, ab duōbus ex amīcīs monitus, ad nōs fūgit.   19. Ipse, ā sene secundō adiūtus, pecūniā carentibus multās rēs dabat.   20. Quis, hīs perīculīs līberātus, deīs grātiās nōn dabit?   21. Iūnctī vōbīscum, rem pūblicam cōnservābimus.   22. Fidem habentibus nihil est incertum.

EXERCISES FOR CHAPTER 24

1. (1) What are the two essential parts of a regular ablative absolute in Latin?
   (2) Can the noun or pronoun of an ablative absolute also appear as the subject or the object of the verb?
2. (1) Explain the term "absolute."
   (2) Guided by the examples in Chapter 24, p. 156, tell what punctuation usually indicates an ablative absolute, and show how this harmonizes with the term "absolute."
3. Should the ablative absolute always be translated literally? Explain.
4. Name five subordinating conjunctions in English which may be used to translate the ablative absolute depending on the requirements of the context.
5. State whether the Romans would have regarded any or all of the following sentences as incorrect, and explain why. (Examples in Chapter 24 will help you.)
   (1) Urbe captā, Caesar eam dēlēvit.
   (2) Caesar, urbem captus, eam dēlēvit.
   (3) Caesar urbem captam dēlēvit.
   (4) Urbe captā, Caesar multās gentēs dēlēvit.
6. (1) What idea is expressed by the **-ndus** participle (gerundive) **+ sum?**
   (2) Explain the agreement of the **-ndus, -nda, -ndum** participle.
   (3) What Latin verb + the infinitive expresses a similar idea?
7. (1) Explain the syntax of **mihi** in the following sentence: Cīvitās mihi cōnservanda est.
   (2) Fill out the blank in the following sentence with the Latin for "by me" and explain the construction: Cīvitās—cōnservāta est.

8. Hīs duōbus virīs imperium tenentibus, rēs pūblica valēbit.   9. Hāc fāmā narrātā, dux urbem sine morā relīquit.   10. Omnī cupiditāte pecūniae glōriaeque ex animō expulsā, ille dux sē vīcit.   11. Omnis cupiditās rērum malārum nōbīs vincenda est sī bonam vītam agere cupimus.   12. Cīvibus patriam amantibus, possumus habēre magnās spēs.   13. Omnēs cīvēs istum tyrannum timēbant, quī expellendus erat.   14. Tyrannō superātō, cīvēs

lībertātem et iūra recēpērunt.   15. At tyrannō expulsō, alius tyrannus imperium saepe accipit.   16. Quis imperium accipiēns adiuvāre cīvitātem sōlam,
nōn sē, cupit?   17. Multīs gentibus victīs, tōtum mundum tenēre cupīvistī.
18. Servitūs omnis generis per tōtum mundum opprimenda est.   19. Sī rēs
pūblica nostra valet, nihil tibi timendum est.   20. Patria nostra cuique adiuvanda est quī nostrum modum vītae amat.   21. Omnia igitur iūra cīvibus
magnā cūrā cōnservanda sunt.   22. Officiīs ā cīvibus relictīs, rēs pūblica in
magnō perīculō erit.   23. Hīs rēbus gravibus dictīs, ōrātor ā nōbīs laudātus
est.   24. Vēritās et virtūs omnibus virīs semper quaerendae sunt.   25. Vēritāte et virtūte quaesītīs, rēs pūblica cōnservāta est.

26. From the above sentences list:
 A. 10 instances of the ablative absolute.
 B. 7 instances of the **-ndus sum** construction (passive periphrastic).
 C. 5 instances of the dative of agent.
 D. 2 instances of the ablative of agent.

EXERCISES FOR CHAPTER 25

 1. Review the present active and passive infinitives of all four conjugations.
 2. If **-tūrus (-sūrus)** marks the future active participle, what form logically
    is **-tūrus (-sūrus) esse?**
 3. If **-tus (-sus)** marks the perfect passive participle, what form logically is
    -tus (-sus) esse?
 4. With what do the participial elements of the above infinitives (the **-tūrus,
    -tūra, -tūrum** and the **-tus, -a, -um**) agree?
 5. To what English verb phrase is the Latin ending **-isse** equivalent? Repeat
    this sufficiently so that when you see **-isse** your linguistic reflex automati-
    cally and instantly gives you the proper tense and voice of the infinitive.
 6. Now try your reflexes by translating the following forms in accordance
    with their tense and voice.

(1) mōvisse	(11) sustulisse	(21) quaesītum esse
(2) mōtus esse	(12) trāxisse	(22) expulsum esse
(3) mōtūrus esse	(13) tetigisse	(23) relictōs esse
(4) movērī	(14) amāvisse	(24) data esse
(5) dīcī	(15) vīcisse	(25) datūra esse
(6) scīrī	(16) vīxisse	(26) versūrum esse
(7) servārī	(17) trāctōs esse	(27) pressūrōs esse
(8) rapī	(18) vīsam esse	(28) raptūrōs esse
(9) mittī	(19) raptum esse	(29) iussūrum esse
(10) crēdidisse	(20) missōs esse	(30) tāctūrōs esse

 7. Explain the difference between a direct and an indirect statement.
 8. Indicate what verbs in the following list may introduce an indirect state-
    ment and give their meanings.

(1) mittō	(7) videō	(13) audiō	(19) ostendō
(2) nūntiō	(8) nesciō	(14) sentiō	(20) spērō
(3) rīdeō	(9) parō	(15) agō	(21) iungō
(4) intellegō	(10) crēdō	(16) scrībō	(22) putō
(5) accipiō	(11) terreō	(17) audeō	(23) amō
(6) cupiō	(12) neglegō	(18) gerō	(24) negō

9. In what four main categories can we list most verbs which introduce indirect statements?

10. In English the indirect statement most often appears as a "that" clause, though an infinitive with subject accusative is sometimes used ("I believe that he is brave"; "I believe him to be brave"). What is the form of the indirect statement in classical Latin?

11. In what case did the Romans put the subject of an infinitive?

12. In Latin indirect statement does the tense of the infinitive depend on the tense of the verb of saying? In other words, must a present infinitive be used only with a present main verb, a perfect only with a perfect main verb, etc.?

13. What time relative to that of the main verb does each of the following infinitive tenses indicate: (1) perfect; (2) future; (3) present?

14. Sciō tē hoc fēcisse (factūrum esse, facere).   15. Scīvī tē hoc fēcisse (factūrum esse, facere).   16. Crēdidimus eōs ventūrōs esse (vēnisse, venīre).   17. Crēdimus eōs ventūrōs esse (vēnisse, venīre).   18. Crās audiet (A) eōs venīre (i.e., crās); (B) eōs vēnisse (e.g., herī); (C) eōs ventūrōs esse (e.g., paucīs diēbus).   19. Hodiē audit (A) eōs venīre (hodiē); (B) eōs vēnisse (herī); (C) eōs ventūrōs esse (mox, *soon*).   20. Herī audīvit (A) eōs venīre (herī); (B) eōs vēnisse (e.g., prīdiē, *the day before yesterday*); (C) eōs ventūrōs (paucīs diēbus).   21. Spērant vōs eum vīsūrōs esse.   22. Sciō hoc ā tē factum esse.   23. Nescīvī illa ab eō facta esse.   24. Negāvērunt urbem ab hostibus capī (captam esse).   25. Scītis illōs esse (futūrōs esse, fuisse) semper fidēlēs.   26. Scīvistis illōs esse (futūrōs esse, fuisse) semper fidēlēs.   27. Putābant tyrannum sibi expellendum esse.   28. Crēdimus pācem omnibus ducibus quaerendam esse.   29. Dīcit pācem ab decem ducibus quaerī (quaesītam esse).   30. Dīxit duōs ducēs pācem quaesītūrōs esse (quaerere, quaesīvisse).   31. Hostēs spērant sē omnēs rēs pūblicās victūrōs esse.   32. Bene sciō mē multa nescīre; nēmō enim potest omnia scīre.

33. All infinitives except one in the above sentences are infinitives in indirect statement. Name that one exception.

34. Explain the syntax of the following words by stating in each instance (A) the form and (B) the reason for the form: (14) tē; fēcisse; (16) eōs; (17) ventūrōs esse; (21) eum; (22) hoc; (23) eō; (24) hostibus; (25) fidēlēs; (27) sibi; (28) pācem; ducibus; (29) ducibus; (30) pācem; (31) rēs pūblicās.

EXERCISES FOR CHAPTER 26

1. (1) In the comparison of adjectives, to what English ending does the Latin **-ior** correspond?

    (2) What mnemonic aid can be found in their superficial similarity?

2. (1) To what English adjectival ending does **-issimus** correspond?

    (2) Can any mnemonic device be found here?

3. (1) To what part of an adjective are **-ior** and **-issimus** normally added?

    (2) Illustrate by adding these endings to the following adjectives: **turpis; vēlōx,** gen. **vēlōcis,** *swift;* **prūdēns,** gen. **prūdentis,** *prudent.*

4. If **acerbus** means *harsh* give (1) three possible forces of the comparative **acerbior** and (2) two possible forces of the superlative **acerbissimus.**

5. Give the meaning of **quam** (1) with the comparative degree (e.g., hic erat acerbior quam ille) and (2) with the superlative (e.g., hic erat quam acerbissimus).

6. What case follows **quam,** *than?*

7. (1) Do most adjectives of the third declension have consonant stems or **i**-stems?

    (2) Do comparatives have consonant stems or **i**-stems?

8. Nūntiāvērunt ducem quam fortissimum vēnisse. 9. Lūce clārissimā ab quattuor virīs vīsā, cōpiae fortissimae contrā hostēs missae sunt. 10. Istō homine turpissimō expulsō, senātus cīvibus fidēliōribus dōna dedit. 11. Beātiōrēs cīvēs prō cīvibus miseriōribus haec dulcia faciēbant. 12. Hic auctor est clārior quam ille. 13. Quīdam dīxērunt hunc auctōrem esse clāriōrem quam illum. 14. Librōs sapientiōrum auctōrum legite, sī vītam sapientissimam agere cupitis. 15. Sex auctōrēs quōrum librōs lēgī sunt acerbiōrēs. 16. Quibusdam librīs sapientissimīs lēctīs, illa vitia turpiōra vītāvimus. 17. Hic vir, quī turpia vitia sua superāvit, fortior est quam dux fortissimus. 18. Quis est vir fēlīcissimus? Is quī vītam sapientissimam agit fēlīcior est quam tyrannus potentissimus. 19. Remedium vitiōrum vestrōrum vidētur difficilius. 20. Ille dux putāvit patriam esse sibi cāriōrem quam vītam. 21. Manus adulēscentium quam fidēlissimōrum senātuī quaerenda est.

EXERCISES FOR CHAPTER 27

1. (1) What is peculiar about the comparison of adjectives in which the masculine of the positive degree ends in **-er?**

    (2) Does this hold for adjectives of any declension or only for those of the 1st and 2nd declension?

2. (1) What is peculiar about the comparison of **facilis?**

    (2) Do all adjectives in **-lis** follow this rule? Be specific.

3. Some of the most common adjectives are the most irregular in their comparison. To illustrate how helpful English can be in learning these

irregular forms, write each of the following Latin words on a separate line:

parvus, malus, bonus, (prō), magnus, superus, multus;

and then, choosing from the following list, write opposite each of them the English words which suggest the comparative and the superlative respectively:

pessimist, prime, minus, ameliorate, summit, maximum, supreme, optimist, plus, superior, pejorative, prior, major, minimum.

4. Translate the following:

(1) bellum minus	(13) fidēs minima	(25) plūrēs labōrēs
(2) bellum pessimum	(14) mare minus	(26) ducēs optimī
(3) bellum maius	(15) in marī minōre	(27) ducēs maiōrēs
(4) bella priōra	(16) maria maiōra	(28) ducēs meliōrēs
(5) liber simillimus	(17) frūctūs optimī	(29) dōna minima
(6) liber difficilior	(18) frūctus peior	(30) dōna plūra
(7) puer minimus	(19) hominēs ācerrimī	(31) dōna prīma
(8) puer melior	(20) hominēs ācriōrēs	(32) plūs laudis
(9) puella pulcherrima	(21) hominēs plūrēs	(33) plūrēs laudēs
(10) puella pulchrior	(22) labor difficillimus	(34) cīvēs pessimī
(11) puellae plūrimae	(23) labor suprēmus	(35) cīvēs meliōrēs
(12) fidēs maior	(24) plūs labōris	(36) cīvēs līberrimī

5. Facillima saepe nōn sunt optima. 6. Difficilia saepe sunt maxima. 7. Meliōra studia sunt difficiliōra. 8. Pessimī auctōrēs librōs plūrimōs scrībunt. 9. Hī librī peiōrēs sunt quam librī auctōrum meliōrum. 10. Puer minor maius dōnum accēpit. 11. Illa rēs pūblica minima maximās spēs habuit. 12. Plūrēs virī crēdunt hoc bellum esse peius quam prīmum bellum. 13. Dux melior cum cōpiīs maiōribus veniet. 14. Ācrēs ducēs ācriōrēs cōpiās ācerrimōrum hostium saepe laudābant. 15. Tyrannō pessimō expulsō, cīvēs ducem meliōrem et sapientiōrem quaesivērunt. 16. Meliōrī ducī maius imperium et plūs pecūniae dedērunt. 17. Cīvēs urbium minōrum nōn sunt meliōrēs quam eī urbium maximārum. 18. Nōs nōn meliōrēs sumus quam plūrimī virī priōrum aetātum. 19. Maiōrēs nostrī Apollinem (Apollō, acc.) deum sōlis appellābant.

EXERCISES FOR CHAPTER 28

1. What does the subjunctive usually indicate in Latin—a fact or something other than a fact?
2. Is the subjunctive more or less common in Latin than it is in English?
3. What vowel is the sign of the present subjunctive (1) in the first conjugation and (2) in the other conjugations?
4. When the verb of the *main clause* is in the subjunctive, what is the force of this subjunctive?

5. What idea is expressed by the subjunctive in a *subordinate clause* introduced by **ut** or **nē?**

6. In this chapter when **nē** is used with a *main verb* in the subjunctive, what kind of subjunctive is it?

7. Did the Roman prose-writers of the classical period use the infinitive to express purpose as we do in English?

8. Whenever in the following list a form is subjunctive, so label it, indicating also its person and number. The indicative forms are to be translated in accordance with their person, number, and tense.

(1) mittet	(11) audiēmur	(21) līberēminī
(2) mittat	(12) audiāmur	(22) līberābiminī
(3) mittit	(13) audīmur	(23) dēlentur
(4) det	(14) ēripiās	(24) dēleantur
(5) dat	(15) ēripis	(25) vincēris
(6) crēdant	(16) ēripiēs	(26) vinceris
(7) crēdunt	(17) sciuntur	(27) vincāris
(8) crēdent	(18) scientur	(28) dīcimus
(9) movent	(19) sciantur	(29) dīcēmus
(10) moveant	(20) līberāminī	(30) dīcāmus

9. Ille dux veniat. Eum exspectāmus. 10. Cīvēs turpēs ex rē pūblicā discēdant ut in pāce vīvāmus. 11. Sī illī duo amīcōs cupiunt, vēra beneficia faciant. 12. Beneficia aliīs praestat ut amētur. 13. Haec verba fēlīcia vōbīs dīcō nē discēdātis. 14. Patriae causā haec difficillima faciāmus. 15. Illīs miserīs plūs pecūniae date nē armīs contrā hostēs careant. 16. Putat eōs id factūrōs esse ut īram meam vītent. 17. Arma parēmus nē lībertās nostra tollātur. 18. Armīsne sōlīs lībertās nostra ē perīculō ēripiētur? 19. Nē sapientēs librōs difficiliōrēs scrībant. 20. Satis sapientiae enim ā librīs difficiliōribus nōn accipiēmus. 21. Meliōra et maiōra faciat nē vītam miserrimam agat. 22. Haec illī auctōrī clārissimō nārrā ut in librō eius scrībantur. 23. Vēritātem semper quaerāmus, sine quā maximī animī nōn possunt esse fēlīcēs.

24. Explain the syntax of the following words (i.e., copy the words each on a new line, state the form, and give the reason for that form): (9) veniat; (10) discēdant, vīvāmus; (11) faciant; (12) praestat, amētur; (13) discēdātis; (14) faciāmus; (15) date, armīs, careant; (16) eōs, factūrōs esse, vītent; (17) parēmus, tollātur; (18) armīs, ēripiētur; (19) scrībant; (20) accipiēmus; (21) faciat, agat; (22) nārrā, scrībantur; (23) quaerāmus.

EXERCISES FOR CHAPTER 29

1. What is the easy rule for the recognition and the formation of the imperfect subjunctive active and passive?

2. Does this rule apply to such irregular verbs as **sum** and **possum?**
3. The indicatives in the following list are to be translated according to their forms. The subjunctives are to be so labeled, with indication also of their tense, person, and number.

(1) vocāret	(11) dīcat	(21) possīmus
(2) invenīrent	(12) dīcet	(22) essent
(3) vidērēmus	(13) dīcit	(23) accipiās
(4) dīcerem	(14) sint	(24) accipiēs
(5) ēriperēs	(15) posset	(25) acciperēs
(6) servet	(16) possit	(26) expellēminī
(7) servārētis	(17) discēderent	(27) expellerēminī
(8) videat	(18) discēdent	(28) expellāminī
(9) inveniēs	(19) discēdant	(29) movērentur
(10) inveniās	(20) dēmus	(30) moventur

4. How can the idea of result be expressed in Latin?
5. How can result clauses be distinguished from purpose clauses?
6. When and where is the imperfect subjunctive used?

7. Optimōs librōs tantā cum cūrā lēgērunt ut multum sapientiae discerent.
8. Bonōs librōs cum cūrā legēbāmus ut sapientiam discerēmus. 9. Optimī librī discipulīs legendī sunt ut vēritātem et mōrēs bonōs discant. 10. Sapientissimī auctōrēs plūrēs librōs scrībant ut omnēs gentēs adiuvāre possint. 11. Animī plūrimōrum hominum tam stultī sunt ut discere nōn cupiant. 12. At multae mentēs ita ācrēs sunt ut bene discere possint. 13. Quīdam magistrī discipulōs tantā cum arte docēbant ut ipsī discipulī quidem discere cuperent. 14. Imperium istīus tyrannī tantum erat ut senātus eum expellere nōn posset. 15. Omnēs cīvēs sē patriae dent nē hostēs lībertātem tollant. 16. Caesar tam ācer dux erat ut hostēs mīlitēs Rōmānōs nōn vincerent. 17. Dūcimusne aliās gentēs tantā cum sapientiā et virtūte ut lībertās cōnservētur? 18. Tanta beneficia faciēbātis ut omnēs vōs amārent. 19. Tam dūrus erat ut nēmō eum amāret. 20. Mīlia cīvium ex eā terrā fugiēbant nē ā tyrannō opprimerentur. 21. Lībertātem sīc amāvērunt ut numquam ab hostibus vincerentur.

22. Explain the syntax of the following words: (7) discerent; (8) discerēmus; (9) discant; (10) scrībant, possint; (11) cupiant; (12) possint; (13) cuperent; (14) posset; (15) dent, tollant; (16) vincerent; (17) cōnservētur; (18) amārent; (19) amāret; (20) opprimerentur; (21) vincerentur.

EXERCISES FOR CHAPTER 30

1. As the form of the imperfect subjunctive active is the present active infinitive plus personal endings, how can the pluperfect subjunctive active be easily recognized?

2. As the pluperfect indicative passive is the perfect passive particle + **eram** (i.e., the imperfect indicative of **sum**), what parallel rule holds for the pluperfect subjunctive passive?

3. If **positus est** is the perfect indicative passive, what most naturally is **positus sit?**

4. What forms of the active indicative do the forms of the perfect subjunctive active resemble in most instances?

5. State the tense, voice, person, and number of each of the following subjunctives:

(1) ponerētur	(5) posuerint	(9) darent	(13) dedissēs
(2) posuissem	(6) ponerēmus	(10) datī essēmus	(14) darētur
(3) positī sint	(7) posuissētis	(11) det	(15) dederīmus
(4) ponāmur	(8) positus esset	(12) datus sīs	(16) dedissent

6. (1) Name the primary tenses of the indicative.
(2) Name the primary tenses of the subjunctive.
(3) Name the historical tenses of the indicative.
(4) Name the historical tenses of the subjunctive.

7. (1) What time does the present subjunctive indicate relative to that of a primary main verb?
(2) What time does the imperfect subjunctive indicate relative to that of a historical main verb?
(3) What time does the perfect subjunctive indicate relative to that of a primary main verb?
(4) What time does the pluperfect subjunctive indicate relative to that of a secondary main verb?

8. Ubi dux est (fuit)? 9. Rogant ubi dux sit (fuerit). 10. Rogābant ubi dux esset (fuisset). 11. Rogābunt ubi dux sit (fuerit). 12. Nesciō ubi pecūnia posita sit. 13. Scīsne ubi pecūnia ponātur? 14. Scīvērunt ubi pecūnia ponerētur. 15. Nescīvit ubi pecūnia posita esset. 16. Vōbīs dīcēmus cūr mīles hoc fēcerit (faciat). 17. Mihi dīxērunt cūr mīles hoc fēcisset (faceret). 18. Dīc mihi quis vēnerit (veniat). 19. Ōrātor rogāvit cūr cēterī cīvēs haec cōnsilia nōn cognōvissent. 20. Ducī nūntiāvimus cēterōs mīlitēs in illam terram fugere (fūgisse). 21. Ducī nūntiāvimus in quam terram cēterī mīlitēs fugerent (fūgissent). 22. Audīvimus cīvēs tam fidēlēs esse ut rem pūblicam cōnservārent. 23. Audīvimus quid cīvēs fēcissent ut rem pūblicam cōnservārent. 24. Quaerēbant quōrum in rē pūblicā pāx invenīrī posset. 25. Cognōvimus pācem in patriā eōrum nōn inventam esse. 26. Illī stultī semper rogant quid sit melius quam imperium aut pecūnia. 27. Nōs quidem putāmus pecūniam ipsam nōn esse malam; sed crēdimus vēritātem et lībertātem et amīcitiam esse meliōrēs et maiōrēs. 28. Haec cupimus ut vītam pulchriōrem agāmus; nam pecūnia sōla et imperium possunt hominēs dūrōs facere,

ut fēlīcēs nōn sint.   29. Dēnique omnia expōnat ut iam comprehendātis quanta scelera contrā rem pūblicam commissa sint.

30. Explain the syntax of the following: (15) posita esset; (16) fēcerit; (17) fēcisset; (18) vēnerit; (20) fugere; (21) fugerent; (22) esse, cōnservārent; (23) fēcissent, cōnservārent; (24) posset; (25) inventam esse; (26) sit; (27) esse; (28) agāmus, sint; (29) expōnat, comprehendātis, commissa sint.

EXERCISES FOR CHAPTER 31

1. Name the three possible meanings of **cum** + the subjunctive.
2. When **tamen** follows a **cum**-clause, what does **cum** regularly mean?
3. (1) To what conjugation does **ferō** belong?
   (2) State the irregularity which the following forms of **ferō** have in common: ferre, fers, fert, fertis, ferris, fertur.
4. In the following list label the subjunctives and translate the rest according to their forms.

(1) ferat	(6) ferunt	(11) fertis	(16) tulisse
(2) fert	(7) ferent	(12) ferēris	(17) lātūrus esse
(3) ferret	(8) ferant	(13) ferris	(18) ferendus
(4) feret	(9) fertur	(14) fer	(19) lātus esse
(5) ferre	(10) ferte	(15) ferrī	(20) tulisset

5. Cum hoc dīxissēmus, illī vīgintī respondērunt sē pācem aequam oblātūrōs esse.   6. Cum sē in aliam terram contulisset, tamen amīcōs novōs invēnit.   7. Cum amīcitiam nōbīs offerant, eīs auxilium offerēmus.   8. Cum perīculum magnum esset, omnēs cōpiās et arma brevī tempore contulērunt. 9. Quid tū fers? Quid ille fert? Dīc mihi cūr haec dōna offerantur.   10. Cum exposuisset quid peteret, negāvistī tantum auxilium posse offerrī. 11. Cum dōna iūcunda tulissent, potuī tamen īnsidiās eōrum cognōscere. 12. Cum cōnsilia tua nunc comprehendāmus, īnsidiās tuās nōn ferēmus. 13. Tanta mala nōn ferenda sunt. Cōnfer tē in exsilium.   14. Dēnique hī centum cīvēs reī pūblicae auxilium ferant.   15. Putābam eōs vīnum nāvibus lātūrōs esse.   16. Cum mīlitēs nostrī hostēs vīcissent, tamen eīs multa beneficia obtulērunt.   17. Cum cognōvisset quanta beneficia cēterī trēs offerrent, ipse aequa beneficia obtulit.   18. Cīvibus miserīs gentium parvārum satis auxiliī dēbēmus offerre.   19. Cum cōnsul haec verba dīxisset, senātus respondit pecūniam ad hanc rem collātam esse.

20. Explain the syntax of the following words: (5) dīxissēmus, oblātūrōs esse; (6) contulisset; (7) offerant; (8) esset; (9) offerantur; (10) exposuisset, peteret; (11) tulissent; (12) comprehendāmus; (13) cōnfer; (14) ferant; (15) nāvibus, lātūrōs esse; (16) vīcissent; (17) offerrent; (19) dīxisset.

EXERCISES FOR CHAPTER 32

1. What is the regular positive ending (1) of adverbs made from adjectives of the first and the second declensions and (2) of adverbs made from adjectives of the third declension?

2. In English what adverbial ending is equivalent to the Latin adverbial **-ē** or **-iter?**

3. Do all Latin adverbs of the positive degree end in **-ē** or **-iter?**

4. (1) What is the ending of the comparative degree of an adverb in Latin? (2) With what form of the adjective is this identical? (3) In English how is the comparative degree of the adverb usually formed?

5. How does the base of the superlative degree of a Latin adverb compare with that of the corresponding adjective?

6. Translate each of the following adverbs in two ways: (1) līberius; (2) līberrimē.

7. Translate each of the following adverbs in accordance with its form.

(1) iūcundē	(6) breviter	(11) minimē	(16) minus
(2) iūcundius	(7) celerrimē	(12) magis	(17) facile
(3) iūcundissimē	(8) peius	(13) diūtius	(18) maximē
(4) melius	(9) fidēlius	(14) male	(19) gravissimē
(5) fidēlissimē	(10) facilius	(15) miserius	(20) celerius

8. (1) What is the stem of **volō** in the indicative? (2) What is the stem of **volō** in the present and the imperfect subjunctive?

9. To what other irregular verb is **volō** similar in the present subjunctive?

10. Label the subjunctives in the following list and translate the other forms.

(1) volēs	(7) māllēmus	(13) voluisse	(19) voluistī
(2) velīs	(8) voluissēs	(14) volunt	(20) vellet
(3) vīs	(9) volam	(15) voluimus	(21) nōlunt
(4) vellēs	(10) volēbant	(16) velle	(22) nōllet
(5) māvult	(11) volet	(17) voluerat	(23) mālit
(6) velīmus	(12) vultis	(18) voluērunt	(24) nōlet

11. Quīdam mālunt crēdere omnēs esse parēs. 12. Quīdam negant mentēs quidem omnium hominum esse parēs. 13. Hī dīvitiās celerrimē invēnērunt; illī diūtissimē erunt pauperēs. 14. Hic plūrimōs honōrēs quam facillimē accipere vult. 15. Nōlīte hanc scientiam āmittere. 16. Cīvēs ipsī rem pūblicam melius gessērunt quam ille dux. 17. Ibi terra est aequior et plūs patet. 18. Nōs ā scientiā prohibēre nōlent virī līberī; sed tyrannī maximē sīc volunt. 19. Tyrannus cīvēs suōs ita male opprimēbat ut semper līberī esse vellent. 20. Plūrima dōna līberrimē offeret ut exercitus istum tyrannum adiuvāre velit. 21. Cum auxilium offerre minimē vellent, nōluimus eīs beneficia

multa praestāre.   22. Cum hostēs contrā nōs celeriter veniant, volumus nostrōs ad arma quam celerrimē vocāre.   23. Cum lībertātem lēgēsque cōn-servāre vērē vellent, tamen scelera tyrannī diūtissimē ferenda erant. 24. Māvult haec sapientius facere nē hanc quidem occasiōnem āmittat. 25. Nōlī discēdere, mī amīce.

EXERCISES FOR CHAPTER 33

1. (1) What form of the verb is found in both clauses of a future less vivid condition?
   (2) Explain why this construction is called "less vivid" as compared with the simple future (or "future more vivid")
2. (1) Name the specific type of condition (A) that has the imperfect sub-junctive in both clauses and (B) that has the pluperfect subjunctive in both clauses.
   (2) In each of these conditions which part of the sentence is essentially the same in both Latin and English?
3. What is the regular negative of the conditional clause in Latin?
4. What type of Latin condition is translated by "should . . . would" and hence can be called a "should-would condition"?
5. What is the meaning of **quis, quid** after **sī, nisi, nē,** and **num?**

6. Sī ratiō dūcit, fēlīx es.   7. Sī ratiō dūcet, fēlīx eris.   8. Sī ratiō dūcat, fēlīx sīs.   9. Sī ratiō dūceret, fēlīx essēs.   10. Sī ratiō dūxisset, fēlīx fuissēs.   11. Sī pecūniam amās, sapientiā carēs.   12. Sī pecūniam amābis, sapientiā carēbis. 13. Sī pecūniam amēs, sapientiā careās.   14. Sī pecūniam amārēs, sapientiā carērēs.   15. Sī pecūniam amāvissēs, sapientiā caruissēs.   16. Sī vēritātem quaerimus, scientiam invenīmus.   17. Sī vēritātem quaerēmus, scientiam in-veniēmus.   18. Sī vēritātem quaerāmus, scientiam inveniāmus.   19. Sī vēri-tātem quaererēmus, scientiam invenīrēmus.   20. Sī vēritātem quaesīvis-sēmus, scientiam invēnissēmus.   21. Nisi īram vītābis, duōs amīcōs āmittētis.   22. Nisi īram vītāvissētis, quīnque amīcōs āmīsissētis.   23. Nisi īram vītētis, multōs amīcōs āmittātis.   24. Nisi īram vītārētis, multōs amīcōs āmitterētis.   25. Nisi īram vītātis, multōs amīcōs āmittitis.   26. Nisi īram vītāvistis, multōs amīcōs āmīsistis.   27. Sī quis bonōs mōrēs habet, eum lau-dāmus.   28. Sī quis bonōs mōrēs habuisset, eum laudāvissēmus.   29. Sī quis bonōs mōrēs habeat, eum laudēmus.   30. Sī quis bonōs mōrēs habuit, eum laudāvimus (laudābāmus).   31. Sī quis bonōs mōrēs habēret, eum laudārē-mus.   32. Sī quis bonōs mōrēs habēbit, eum laudābimus.   33. Sī istī vincent, discēdēmus.   34. Sī istī vincant, discēdāmus.   35. Sī istī vīcissent, discessis-sēmus.   36. Sī librōs bene lēgissēs, melius scrīpsissēs.   37. Sī librōs bene legēs, melius scrībēs.   38. Sī librōs bene legās, melius scrībās.

39. Name in sequence the types of conditions found in sentences 6–10 and 21–26.

EXERCISES FOR CHAPTER 34

1. State the chief peculiarity of deponent verbs.
2. Write a synopsis of the following verbs in the 6 tenses of the indicative and the 4 tenses of the subjunctive as indicated:
   (1) **cōnor** in the 1st person plural.
   (2) **loquor** in the 3d person singular.
3. (1) Write, label, and translate all the participles of **patior.**
   (2) Write, label, and translate all the infinitives of **patior.**
4. Using the proper form of **illud cōnsilium** fill in the following blanks to complete the idea suggested by the English sentence in each instance.
   (1) He will not follow that plan: nōn sequētur _____.
   (2) He will not use that plan: nōn utētur _____.
   (3) He will not permit that plan: nōn patiētur _____.
5. Explain the proper form of **illud cōnsilium** in #4 (2) above.
6. Name the *active forms* found in deponent verbs.
7. Give the imperative forms of (1) **cōnor** and (2) **loquor,** and translate each one.
8. Translate the following participles: (1) locūtus; (2) mortuus; (3) cōnātus; (4) passus; (5) secūtus; (6) ēgressus; (7) profectus.
9. In the following list label any subjunctive forms and translate the rest:

(1) ūtētur	(6) ūsus esset	(11) patī	(16) patitur
(2) ūtātur	(7) ūsūrum esse	(12) passī sunt	(17) patiēmur
(3) ūtitur	(8) patiēris	(13) passum esse	(18) arbitrētur
(4) ūterētur	(9) pateris	(14) patientēs	(19) arbitrārētur
(5) ūsus	(10) patere	(15) patiātur	(20) patiendum est

10. Arbitrātur haec mala patienda esse. 11. Cōnābimur haec mala patī. 12. Nisi morī vīs, patere haec mala. 13. Maxima mala passus, homō miser mortuus est. 14. Tyrannus arbitrātus est eōs duōs haec mala diū passūrōs esse. 15. Cum tria bella passī essent, istum tyrannum in exsilium expellere ausī sunt. 16. Sī hunc ducem novum sequēminī, lībertāte et ōtiō ūtēminī. 17. Hīs verbīs dictīs, eum sequī ausī sumus. 18. Haec verba locūtī, profectī sumus nē in eō locō miserō morerēmur. 19. Cum vōs cōnsiliō malō ūsōs esse arbitrārētur, tamen vōbīscum līberē locūtus est. 20. Sī quis vīnō eius generis ūtī audeat, celeriter moriātur. 21. Eōdem diē fīlius eius nātus est et mortuus est. 22. Omnibus opibus nostrīs ūtāmur ut patria nostra servētur. 23. Cum in aliam terram proficīscī cōnārētur, ā mīlitibus captus est. 24. Arbitrābar eum ex urbe cum decem amīcīs ēgressūrum esse. 25. Eā nocte profectus, Caesar ad quandam īnsulam clārissimam vēnit. 26. Sī meliōribus librīs ūsī essent, plūra didicissent. 27. Sī multōs amīcōs habēre vīs, nōlī esse superbus.

28. Name the type of condition found above in each of the following sentences: 12, 16, 20, 26.

29. Explain the syntax of the following: (14) passūrōs esse; (17) verbīs; (18) locūtī, morerēmur; (19) cōnsiliō, arbitrārētur; (21) diē; (22) ūtāmur; (25) nocte; (26) librīs.

EXERCISES FOR CHAPTER 35

1. A certain number of verbs, which in English apparently take a direct object, in Latin take a dative. In lieu of a good rule to cover such verbs, what procedures can prove helpful?

2. Some other verbs also, when compounded with certain prepositions, may take a dative.
(1) What is the concept that underlies this?
(2) Do all compound verbs take the dative?

3. Copy each of the following verbs on a new line; after it write that one of the three forms **eī, eum, eō** which is in the case required by the verb; and then translate the whole expression, using the pronoun to mean "him" generally and "it" where necessary.

(1) cognōscunt	(7) patiuntur	(13) superant	(19) persuādent
(2) ignōscunt	(8) invenient	(14) crēdunt	(20) ūtuntur
(3) serviunt	(9) nocent	(15) carent	(21) pellunt
(4) servant	(10) iuvant	(16) student	(22) parcunt
(5) parāvī	(11) placent	(17) hortantur	(23) imperant
(6) pāruī	(12) iaciunt	(18) sequuntur	(24) iubent

4. Ducem servāvit. 5. Ducī servīvit. 6. Servī aliīs hominibus serviunt. 7. Virī fortēs aliōs servant. 8. Ille servus fīliō meō servīvit et eum servāvit. 9. Sī quis sibi sōlī serviet, rem publicam numquam servābit. 10. Sī quis hunc labōrem suscēpisset, mīlle virōs servāvisset. 11. Deī mihi ignōscent; vōs, ō cīvēs, tōtī exercituī ignōscite. 12. Sī Deum nōbīs ignōscere volumus, nōs dēbēmus aliīs hominibus ignōscere. 13. Mihi nunc nōn crēdunt, neque umquam duōbus fīliīs meīs crēdere volent. 14. Illī amīcī sunt mihi cārissimī. 15. Cum bonā fidē carērēs, tibi crēdere nōn poterant. 16. Huic ducī pāreāmus ut nōbīs parcat et urbem servet. 17. Nisi Caesar cīvibus placēbit, vītae eius nōn parcent. 18. Litterīs Latīnīs studeō, quae mihi placent etiam sī amīcīs meīs persuadēre nōn possum. 19. Vēritātī et sapientiae semper studeāmus et pāreāmus. 20. Optimīs rēbus semper studēte sī vērē esse fēlīcēs vultis. 21. Hīs rēbus studentēs, et librīs et vītā ūtāmur. 22. Vir bonus nēminī nocēre vult: omnibus parcit, omnēs iuvat. 23. Praemia mea sunt simillima tuīs.

24. Explain the syntax of the following: (5) ducī; (8) eum; (9) sibi; (11) exercituī; (12) hominibus; (13) fīliīs; (14) mihi; (15) fidē; (16) ducī, pāreāmus, servet; (17) cīvibus, vītae; (18) litterīs, amīcīs; (21) rēbus, librīs, ūtāmur; (22) omnibus; (23) tuīs.

EXERCISES FOR CHAPTER 36

1. We have already learned how the Romans expressed indirect statements (Chapter 25) and indirect questions (Chapter 30). Now after a verb having the connotation of command, how did the Romans express an indirect command?

2. List some common Latin verbs which can take an indirect command.

3. In the following list label the subjunctives and translate the other forms.

(1) fīet	(6) fīunt	(10) fierent	(14) fierem
(2) fit	(7) fīēbant	(11) fīmus	(15) fīant
(3) fīat	(8) fīēs	(12) fīent	(16) faciendus
(4) fieret	(9) factus esse	(13) fīs	(17) fīāmus
(5) fierī			

4. Dīxit eōs litterīs Latīnīs studēre. 5. Dīxit cūr litterīs Latīnīs studērent. 6. Dīxit ut litterīs Latīnīs studērent. 7. Ab eīs quaesīvimus cūr philosophiae Graecae studērent. 8. Quaerisne ut nātūram omnium rērum cognōscāmus? 9. Tē moneō ut hīs sapientibus parcās. 10. Mīlitēs monuit nē eīs pācem petentibus nocērent. 11. Nōbīs imperābit nē hostibus crēdāmus. 12. Tibi imperāvit ut ducī pārērēs. 13. Tē rogō cūr hoc fēcerīs. 14. Tē rogō ut hoc faciās. 15. Ā tē petō ut pāx fīat. 16. Ā mē petēbant nē bellum facerem. 17. Eum ōrāvī nē rēgī turpī pārēret. 18. Vōs ōrāmus ut discipulī ācerrimī fīātis. 19. Nōlī esse similis istī tyrannō dūrō. 20. Caesar cūrāvit ut imperium suum maximum in cīvitāte fieret. 21. Ōrātor nōs hortātus est ut līberae patriae nostrae cum studiō servīrēmus. 22. Nōbīs persuāsit ut aequīs lēgibus semper ūterēmur. 23. Cōnāmur ducī persuādēre nē artibus et lēgibus patriae noceat. 24. Tyrannus imperat ut pecūnia fīat; et pecūnia fit. At ille stultus nōn sentit hanc pecūniam sine bonā fidē futūram esse nihil. 25. Plūrēs quidem discipulōs hortēmur ut linguae Latīnae studeant.

26. Explain the syntax of the following: (4) studēre; (5) studērent; (6) studērent; (7) studērent; (8) cognōscāmus; (9) parcās; (10) eīs, pācem; (11) hostibus; (13) fēcerīs; (14) faciās; (16) facerem; (18) fīātis; (22) lēgibus; (23) lēgibus; (24) futūram esse; (25) hortēmur.

EXERCISES FOR CHAPTER 37

1. (1) Name the tenses and moods in which the stem of **īre** is changed to **e** before **a, o,** and **u.**

(2) Otherwise, what is the stem of **eō** in the indicative, subjunctive, imperative, and infinitives?

2. State the nominative singular and the nominative plural of the present participle of **eō.**

3. Write a synopsis of **eō** in the 2nd singular and the 3d plural indicative and subjunctive active.

4. In the following list label the subjunctives and translate the other forms.

(1) iimus	(7) itūrus esse	(13) iī	(19) euntēs
(2) īmus	(8) euntem	(14) ībat	(20) ībō
(3) īrēmus	(9) iērunt	(15) ierant	(21) iit
(4) ībimus	(10) eunt	(16) ierim	(22) ībāmus
(5) īssēmus	(11) eant	(17) īret	(23) īsset
(6) eāmus	(12) ībunt	(18) īsse	(24) eat

5. State how the Romans regularly expressed the following place concepts and translate the English example into Latin:
   (1) place from which: from (out of) that land.
   (2) place where: in that land; on that island.
   (3) place to which: into (to) that land.

6. State the general rules for these place constructions when the name of a city is involved.

7. Define the locative case, and state the nature of the locative forms.

8. State how the Romans expressed each of the following time concepts and translate the English example:
   (1) time when: on the same day.
   (2) time how long: for many days.
   (3) time within which: in one day.

9. What is peculiar about the principal parts of **licet?** Explain. Translate into Latin "You may go."

10. Translate each of the following words or phrases in accordance with the principles of this chapter.

(1) ūnum diem	(7) paucīs diēbus	(13) domum
(2) ūnō diē	(8) eādem nocte	(14) Athēnīs
(3) illō diē	(9) multōs diēs	(15) domī
(4) Rōmā	(10) in nāvem	(16) Athēnās
(5) Rōmae	(11) in nāve	(17) domō
(6) Rōmam	(12) ex nāve	(18) paucās hōrās

11. Paucīs hōrīs Rōmam ībimus. 12. Nōs ad urbem īmus; illī domum eunt.
13. Ut saepe fassī sumus, tibi nōn licet Rōmā Athēnās īre. 14. Cūr domō tam celeriter abīstī? 15. Rōmam veniunt ut cum frātre meō Athēnās eant.
16. Nōlīte abīre Rōmā. 17. Frātre tuō Rōmae interfectō, hortābāmur tē ut Athēnās redīrēs. 18. Sī in fīnēs hostium hōc tempore eat, paucīs hōrīs pereat. 19. Negāvit sē velle in istā terrā multōs diēs remanēre. 20. Dīxistī tē domum Athēnīs ūnā hōrā reditūrum esse. 21. Ā tē petō ut ex nāve ad īnsulam brevī tempore redeās. 22. Eīs diēbus solitī sumus Athēnīs esse. 23. Sī amīcīs eius Rōmae nocuissent, Rōmam brevissimō tempore redīsset.

24. Cum frāter meus domī remanēret, ego tamen in novās terrās domō abiī.
25. Rōmānī, sī quid malī loquī volēbant, saepe dīcēbant: "Abī in malam rem." 26. Eīs persuādet ut Latīnae studeant.

27. Explain the syntax of the following words: (11) hōrīs, Rōmam; (12) domum; (13) Rōmā, Athēnās, īre; (14) domō; (15) Rōmam; (17) frātre; (18) tempore, eat, hōrīs; (19) velle, diēs; (20) domum, Athēnīs, hōrā, reditūrum esse; (21) tempore, redeās; (22) diēbus, Athēnīs; (23) amīcīs, Rōmae, redīsset; (24) domī, terrās, domō; (26) studeant.

EXERCISES FOR CHAPTER 38

1. What does a relative clause with the indicative tell about the antecedent?
2. What does a relative clause with the subjunctive tell about its antecedent, and what is the nature of the antecedent?
3. What is the basic difference between the dative of indirect object and the dative of reference?
4. How are supines formed and what are their functions?

5. Amīcus meus quī cōnsulem dēfendit ipse erat vir clārissimus. 6. At nēmō erat quī istum hominem turpem dēfenderet. 7. Quid est quod virī plūs metuant quam tyrannum? 8. Quis est quī inter lībertātem et imperium tyrannī dubitet? 9. Rōmae antīquae erant quī pecūniam plūs quam rem pūblicam amārent. 10. Abeat ā patriā iste homō malus quī odium omnium cīvium bonōrum passus est. 11. Catilīna (= Catiline), quī tantās īnsidiās contrā rem pūblicam fēcerat, ex urbe ā Cicerōne expulsus est. 12. Istī ducī in exsilium abeuntī quae vīta potest esse iūcunda? 13. Quis est quī tantum dolōrem ferre possit? 14. Nisi quis iūcundus bonusque erit, vītam vērē fēlīcem mihi nōn vīvet. 15. Cōnsulī nōn crēdent quī opera turpia faciat. 16. Nōlī crēdere eī quī sit acerbus amīcīs. 17. Cicerō erat cōnsul quī rem pūblicam salūtī suae antepōneret. 18. Scīvērunt quārē cōnsulem tam fortem sequī vellēmus. 19. Nihil sciō quod mihi facilius esse possit. 20. Ducem quaerō quem omnēs laudent. 21. Rōmam ībant rogātum lībertātem. 22. Rōmānī, quī decem rēs pūblicās Graecās exercitibus suīs cēperant, ipsī—mīrābile dictū—Graecīs artibus captī sunt! 23. Virīs antīquīs nihil erat quod melius esset quam virtūs et sapientia. 24. Nihil metuendum est quod animō nocēre nōn possit.

25. Analyze the relative clauses in the following pair of sentences, showing how they differ in their force: 5 and 6.
26. Explain the syntax of the following words: (7) metuant; (8) dubitet; (9) Rōmae, amārent; (10) abeat, passus est; (11) fēcerat; (12) ducī, potest; (13) possit; (14) erit, mihi; (15) cōnsulī; (16) amīcīs; (17) salūtī, antepōneret; (18) vellēmus; (19) mihi, possit; (21) rogātum; (22) cēperant, dictū; (23) virīs; (24) animō, possit.

EXERCISES FOR CHAPTER 39

1. (1) Define the term *gerund.*
   (2) What is the ending of the gerund in English?
   (3) How is the gerund declined in Latin?
   (4) As a noun, what is the syntax of the gerund in Latin?
   (5) What serves in place of the nominative of the gerund in Latin?
2. (1) What part of speech is the Latin gerundive?
   (2) What mnemonic device may help you to remember this?
   (3) As an adjective, what is the syntax of the gerundive?
   (4) How is the gerundive declined?
   (5) How can the gerundive be distinguished from the gerund in Latin usage (though not in English translation)?
3. (1) How is the Latin gerund to be translated?
   (2) How is the gerundive in agreement with its noun to be translated?
   (3) For example, translate:
       (A) Discimus legendō cum cūrā (gerund).
       (B) Discimus librīs legendīs cum cūrā (gerundive).

4. Experiendō discimus.   5. Ad discendum vēnērunt.   6. Sē discendō dedit.
7. Discendī causā ad lūdum tuum vēnērunt.   8. Puer cupidus discendī ad lūdum iit.   9. Metus moriendī eum terrēbat.   10. Spēs vīvendī post mortem multōs hortātur.   11. Cōgitandō eōs superāvit.   12. Sē dedit—

(1) glōriae quaerendae.	(9) iniūriīs oppugnandīs.
(2) bellō gerendō.	(10) librīs scrībendīs.
(3) pecūniae faciendae.	(11) librīs legendīs.
(4) imperiō accipiendō.	(12) philosophiae discendae.
(5) cīvitātibus delendīs.	(13) litterīs Latīnīs discendīs.
(6) huic ducī sequendō.	(14) vēritātī intellegendae.
(7) patriae servandae.	(15) sapientiae quaerendae.
(8) pācī petendae.	(16) hominibus adiuvandīs.

13. Rōmam vēnit—

(1) ad hoc opus suscipiendum.	(5) huius operis suscipiendī causā.
(2) ad lūdōs Rōmānōs videndōs.	(6) philosophiae discendae causā.
(3) ad aedificia vetera videnda.	(7) novōrum librōrum legendōrum causā.
(4) ad pācem petendam.	(8) lūdōs vīsum.

14. Librum scrīpsit—

(1) dē dolōre ferendō.	(5) dē bellō gerendō.
(2) dē metū superandō.	(6) dē lībertāte dēfendendā.
(3) dē bonā vītā vīvendā.	(7) dē hostibus vincendīs.
(4) dē rē pūblicā gerendā.	(8) dē dōnīs dandīs.

15. Sapientiōrēs fīmus—

(1) Latīnīs litterīs legendīs. (4) metū vincendō.
(2) philosophiā discendā.   (5) vēritāte sequendā.
(3) vītā experiendā.

16. Nōs ipsōs adiuvāmus—

(1) bonīs librīs semper legendīs. (3) auxiliō offerendō.
(2) virīs miserīs metū liberandīs. (4) aliīs adiuvandīs.

17. Multum tempus cōnsūmpsit—

(1) in cōgitandō (loquendō, currendō). (4) in exercitū parandō.
(2) in hīs operibus faciendīs.   (5) in cōpiīs parandīs.
(3) in viā inveniendā.

18. Tempus huic librō sōlī scrībendō habuit.

EXERCISES FOR CHAPTER 40

1. Explain the essential differences involved in introducing questions with **-ne, nōnne,** and **num.**
2. What word is used to introduce a positive fear clause? a negative fear clause? Can you explain why this is the opposite of what one might expect?
3. In order for a noun to function as either a descriptive genitive or a descriptive ablative, what condition must be met?

4. Magnopere vereor ut imperātor nōbīs satis auxiliī mittat. 5. Fuit fēmina maximā virtūte et fidē atque simillima mātrī. 6. Nōlī timēre nē omnēs virī et fēminae magnōrum animōrum Rōmā discēdant. 7. Id quidem est facile dictū sed difficile factū! 8. Parentibus placitum domum vēnērunt. 9. Nōnne vīs audīre aliquid bonī? 10. Vīsne habēre multum sapientiae? Studē Latīnae! 11. Imperāvit tribus mīlitibus ut pācem petītum Rōmam adīrent. 12. Num dubitās hoc dīcere, mī amīce? 13. Tū mē hortāris ut sim animō magnō et spem salūtis habeam, sed timeō nē sim īnfīrmior. 14. Ego dīvitiās sapientiae antepōnō. Nōn enim arbitror hominēs vītam fēlīcem sine cōpiā pecūniae reperīre posse. 15. Plūrimī autem virī dīvitēs multum metūs sentiunt. 16. Pauperēs saepe sunt fēlīciōrēs et minus metūs habent. 17. Pecūnia ipsa nōn est mala: sed rēs mentis animīque plūs opis ad fēliciter vīvendum offerunt. 18. Novem ex ducibus nōs hortātī sunt ut plūs auxiliī praestārēmus. 19. Quīnque ex custōdiīs interfectīs, pater meus cum duōbus ex fīliīs et cum magnō numerō amīcōrum in illam terram līberam fūgit. 20. Numquam satis ōtiī habēbit; at aliquid ōtiī melius est quam nihil. 21. Nostrīs temporibus omnēs plūs metūs et minus speī habēmus. 22. Magna fidēs et virtūs omnibus virīs reperiendae sunt.

Key to Exercises

KEY FOR CHAPTER 1

1. (1) he, she, it; (2) we; (3) I; (4) they; (5) you (sg.); (6) you (pl.)
2. The forms are present active infinitives of the 2nd conjugation. (1) to advise/warn; (2) to see; (3) to be strong; (4) to owe.
3. The forms are present active infinitives of the 1st conjugation. (1) to call; (2) to save; (3) to give; (4) to think; (5) to praise; (6) to love; (7) to err.
4. The forms are present active imperatives 2nd person singular of the 1st or the 2nd conjugations. (1) call; (2) save; (3) give; (4) think; (5) praise; (6) love; (7) advise/warn; (8) see; (9) be strong/good-bye.
5. The forms are present active imperatives 2nd person plural of the 1st or the 2nd conjugations. (1) call; (2) save; (3) give; (4) think; (5) praise; (6) love; (7) advise/warn; (8) see; (9) be strong/good-bye.
6. (1) he/she/it calls, is calling, does call; (2) we think; (3) they love; (4) you (sg.) owe/ought; (5) he sees; (6) they see; (7) we owe/ought; (8) you (sg.) are strong; (9) you (pl.) err/are mistaken; (10) we see; (11) he/she/it loves; (12) you (pl.) see; (13) you (sg.) err; (14) they give; (15) we save; (16) he gives; (17) they love; (18) you (sg.) see.

7. They warn me if I err. 8. He warns me if they err. 9. Warn me if he errs. 10. You (sg.) ought to warn me. 11. You (pl.) ought to save me. 12. They ought not to praise me. 13. "What does he give?" "He often gives nothing." 14. They often call me and advise me. 15. I see nothing. What do you see? 16. Praise me, please, if I do not make a mistake. 17. If you (pl.) are well, we are well. 18. If he is well, I am well. 19. If he (she) loves me, he (she) ought to praise me. 20. Save me. 21. I ought not to err. 22. What ought we to praise? 23. He sees; he ponders; he advises.

KEY FOR CHAPTER 2

1. In classical Latin there was no regular definite or indefinite article. The words *the* and *a* have to be added in the English translation according to the sense of

a Latin passage. Thus **puella** may mean *the girl* or *a girl,* and **puellae** may mean *the girls* or *girls* according to the Latin context. Often in an isolated sentence *the* and *a* can be used interchangeably, or perhaps no article at all need be used.

2. (1) acc. case; (2) gen. case; (3) nom. case; (4) abl.; (5) voc.; (6) dat.

3. (1) acc. pl. as direct object of a verb; (2) nom. sg. as subject of a verb or voc. sg. for direct address; (3) acc. sg. as direct object; (4) nom. pl. subject, or voc. for direct address.

4. (1) gen. pl., of; (2) abl. sg., by/with/from, etc.; (3) gen. sg., of; dat. sg., to/for; nom. pl.; voc. pl.; (4) dat. pl., to/for; abl. pl., by/with/from, etc.

5. (1) girl, direct obj. of verb; (2) girl, subject or vocative; (3) girls, object; (4) girls, subj. or voc.; (5) countries, obj.; (6) country, obj.; (7) country, subj. or voc.; (8) countries, subj. or voc.; (9) money, obj.; (10) money, subj. or voc.; (11) penalties, obj.; (12) penalty, obj.

6. (1) of the girl, girl's, or to/for the girl; (2) of the girls, girls'; (3) O fatherland; (4) of or to/for the fatherland; (5) by/with, etc., money; (6) of or to/for money; (7) to/for or by/with, etc., penalties; (8) by/with etc., a penalty; (9) of penalties.

7. (1) multae pecūniae, multam pecūniam; (2) magnae fāmae, magnā fāmā; (3) vītae meae, vītae meae; (4) fortūnam tuam, fortūnās tuās; (5) magnae patriae, magnārum patriārum; (6) fortūnā meā, fortūnīs meīs; (7) magnae poenae, magnīs poenīs; (8) multīs philosophiīs, multīs philosophiīs.

8. (1) multā pecūniā; (2) multārum puellārum; (3) meae patriae; (4) magnam vītam; (5) tuīs poenīs; (6) multae patriae; (7) multīs puellīs; (8) meae vītae; (9) Ō fortūna; (10) puellae; (11) puellārum; (12) puellae; (13) puellās; (14) puellae.

9. Farewell (goodbye), my native land.   10. The fortune of the girl (the girl's fortune) is great.   11. The girl is praising the fortune of your (sg.) country.   12. O girl, save your country.   13. Many girls love money.   14. You (pl.) are giving nothing to the girl, *or* you give nothing to a girl.   15. He sees the money of the girl, *or* the girl's money.   16. You (sg.) do not see the girls' money.   17. We ought to warn the girls.   18. They ought to praise the girl.   19. Life gives (good) fortune to many girls.   20. You (sg.) are saving my life by *or* with your money.   21. Fame is nothing without fortune.   22. You (pl.) do not like life without money.   23. A country is not strong without fame and fortune.   24. You (sg.) ought not to praise the anger of the girls.   25. We like a life without punishments.   26. We are not strong without philosophy.   27. What is life without philosophy?

KEY FOR CHAPTER 3

1. (1) acc. sg., obj.; (2) nom. pl. as subj., voc. pl. for direct address; (3) nom. sg., subj.; (4) acc. pl. obj.; (5) voc. sg., direct address.

2. (1) dat. sg., to/for; abl. sg., by/with, etc.; (2) gen. pl., of; (3) gen. sg., of; (4) dat. pl., to/for; abl. pl., by/with, etc.

3. (1) sons, obj.; (2) sons, subj. or direct address; (3) son, obj.; (4) people, obj.; (5) people, direct address; (6) people, subj.; (7) man, subj. or direct address; (8) men, obj.; (9) men, subj. or direct address; (10) man, obj.; (11) friend, direct address; (12) friends, subj. or direct address; (13) friends, obj.; (14) friend, obj.

4. (1) of my sons; (2) to/for my son, by/with, etc., my son; (3) of the Roman people; (4) to/for the Roman people, by/with, etc., the Roman people; (5) to/for the men,

by/with, etc., the men; (6) of the man; (7) of the men; (8) of a few friends; (9) to/
for or by/with, etc., a few friends; (10) to/for or by/with, etc., my friend; (11) of
my friend; (12) to/for or by/with, etc., many boys.

5. (1) populī Rōmānī, populō Rōmānō; (2) magnōs virōs, magnīs virīs; (3) puerīs
meīs, puerīs meīs; (4) magnō numerō, magnō numerō; (5) magne vir, magnī virī;
(6) fīliī meī, fīliōrum meōrum.

6. (1) multōrum puerōrum; (2) populō Rōmānō; (3) fīliōs meōs; (4) Ō fīliī meī;
(5) magnum numerum; (6) magnō numerō; (7) Ō vir magne; (8) multīs puerīs;
(9) vir magnus; (10) populī Rōmānī.

7. Good-bye, my friend.   8. The Roman people praise your (sg.) son's wisdom.
9. O great man, save the Roman people.   10. The number of the Roman people is
great.   11. Many boys love girls.   12. You (pl.) are giving nothing to my son.   13. I
see men in the field.   14. You (sg.) see the friend of my son.   15. He does not see
your (sg.) sons' friend.   16. We ought to warn my sons.   17. They ought to praise
your (sg.) son.   18. Life gives fame to few men.   19. You (sg.) consider me in the
number (circle) of your friends.   20. Great men often have few friends.   21. My
friend is always thinking.   22. The son of a great man is not always a great man.
23. We do not always see (understand) the wisdom of great men.   24. You (pl.)
ought to praise philosophy, the wisdom of great men.

KEY FOR CHAPTER 4

1. Nom. sg. in **-um;** nom. and acc. pl. in **-a.** Actually the vocative should also be
added here; but henceforth, since aside from the singular of 2nd-declension masculines in **-us** the vocatives follow the rule of having the same form as the nominative, little specific mention is made of the vocative.

2. (1) nom. pl. as subject; acc. pl. as obj.; (2) nom. sg. as subj.; acc. sg. as obj.

3. (1) dat. sg., to/for; abl. sg., by/with, etc.; (2) gen. pl., of; (3) gen. sg., of; (4) dat.
pl., to/for; abl. pl., by/with, etc.

4. (1) wars, subj. or obj.; (2) war, subj. or obj.; (3) duty, subj. or obj.; (4) duties,
subj. or obj.; (5) dangers, subj. or obj. Of course any of these forms could also
be vocative.

5. (1) of evil wars; (2) to/for evil war, by/with, etc., evil war; (3) of evil war; (4) to/
for evil wars, by/with, etc., evil wars; (5) of great duty or service; (6) to/for great
duties, by/with, etc., great duties; (7) to/for small danger, by/with, etc., small
danger.

6. (1) bella parva, bella parva; (2) ōtium bonum, ōtia bona; (3) perīculī magnī, perīculōrum magnōrum; (4) officium vērum, officiō vērō.

7. (1) Ō bellum malum; (2) officiō magnō; (3) perīculō magnō; (4) ōtium bonum;
(5) multīs bellīs; (6) ōtiī bonī; (7) perīculīs multōrum bellōrum; (8) bella parva;
(9) bella parva; (10) Ō bella stulta; (11) bellum parvum.

8. Peace (leisure) is good.   9. Many wars do not preserve peace.   10. The danger is
great.   11. We are in great danger.   12. And leisure often has dangers.   13. Life is
not without many dangers.   14. Good men love peace.   15. The foolish man praises
the dangers of war.   16. Often we do not preserve the peace by war.   17. The Roman people do not always have good peace.   18. They often save the fatherland and

peace by small wars. 19. Many girls are pretty. 20. True friends are few. 21. My friend is a man of great service. 22. The duties of a teacher are many and great. 23. You (sg.) are a man of little leisure. 24. You (pl.) are men of great care. 25. We ought to give attention to duty without delay. 26. Life is nothing without eyes.

KEY FOR CHAPTER 5

1. future: **-ō, -s, -t, -mus, -tis, -nt;** imperfect: **-m, -s, -t, -mus, -tis, -nt.**
2. They are the same in the future, but the imperfect has **-m** instead of **-ō** in the first pers. sg.
3. future: **-bi-** (**-b-** in 1st pers. sg.; **-bu-** in 3d pers. pl.); imperfect: **-bā-** (with the **-a-** shortened before **-m, -t,** and **-nt**).
4. (1) we were; (2) he will; (3) you (pl.) will; (4) I shall; (5) they will; (6) he was.
5. By learning the vocabulary form of the adjective: **līber, lībera, līberum, pulcher, pulchra, pulchrum;** and often by learning English derivatives.
6. They show whether the **e** of a masculine in **-er** survives throughout the rest of the paradigm; liberty, **līber, lībera, līberum;** pulchritude, **pulcher, pulchra, pulchrum.**
7. (1) they were remaining, remained; (2) he will remain; (3) we shall remain; (4) I was giving, I gave; (5) you (pl.) will give; (6) he will give; (7) you (sg.) will see; (8) we shall see; (9) they were calling, called; (10) you (sg.) will call; (11) you (sg.) will have; (12) they were having, had.
8. (1) dabimus; (2) manēbās; (3) vidēbunt; (4) vocābimus; (5) vocābat; (6) vidēbitis; (7) vidēbō; (8) servābant; (9) habēbimus; (10) habēbāmus; (11) habēbit; (12) habet.

9. Our teacher praises me and he will praise you tomorrow (sg.). 10. Free men were overcoming our dangers. 11. Our sons love pretty girls. 12. Our friend will not stay in the company (number) of fools. 13. We used to have many faults and always shall have. 14. Great dangers do not overcome our courage. 15. Our beautiful country is free. 16. You (pl.) are free men; you will have a beautiful country. 17. Free teachers were giving attention to duty. 18. Therefore, we shall overcome evil men in our country. 19. If you (sg.) overcome (lit., will overcome) your anger, you will overcome yourself. 20. Because of our courage many men are free. 21. Free fatherland, we always used to love you and we always shall love (you). 22. You (pl.) will not preserve wisdom by means of money. 23. Does your (sg.) soul possess enough wisdom?

KEY FOR CHAPTER 6

1. See Ch. 6, p. 38, s.v. "Complementary Infinitive."
2. (1) we; (2) they; (3) you (sg.); (4) he, she, it; (5) I; (6) I; (7) you (pl.).
3. See p. 38.
4. (1) he, she, it was; (2) he, etc., was able; (3) he will be; (4) he will be able; (5) we are; (6) we are able; (7) we were able; (8) we shall be able; (9) I was able; (10) I was; (11) I shall be; (12) I shall be able; (13) they will be; (14) they will be able; (15) they were able; (16) to be; (17) to be able.
5. (1) sumus; (2) erāmus; (3) erimus; (4) poterimus; (5) potest; (6) poterit; (7) poterat; (8) posse; (9) poterant; (10) possunt; (11) poterunt; (12) sunt; (13) esse; (14) poteram.

6. Your (pl.) country was free.   7. I was able to be a tyrant.   8. Your friend will be a tyrant.   9. Where (there) is a tyrant, there men cannot be free.   10. He could not remain in our country yesterday.   11. Tyrants will always have many faults.   12. We were not able to overcome the tyrants.   13. We ought to overcome our tyrant. 14. The tyrant was able to overcome (the) good men; but he will not be able to remain there.   15. You (pl.) will be able to see the dangers of a tyrant.   16. We cannot tolerate the faults of tyrants.   17. You (sg.) were not tolerating (did not tolerate) the treachery of the tyrant.   18. The peace in your (pl.) country cannot be perpetual.   19. You (sg.) ought to warn free men about tyrants.   20. Your (pl.) teacher always used to like (liked) fine books.   21. Good and true books were able to save the country.   22. You (pl.) will be able to save your country with good books. 23. Tyrants will not be able to overcome the wisdom of good books.   24. Bad men cannot tolerate good books.

KEY FOR CHAPTER 7

1. No.
2. Yes: nom. and acc. pl.
3. (1) nom. and acc. pl. of masc. and fem.; (2) nom. and acc. pl. neut.; (3) acc. sg. masc. and fem.
4. (1) dat. and abl. pl.; (2) dat. sg.; (3) abl. sg.; (4) acc. sg. masc. and fem.; (5) gen. pl.; (6) gen. sg.; (7) nom. and acc. pl. masc. and fem.
5. (1) magnum tempus; (2) magna virtūs; (3) magnus labor; (4) magna cīvitās; (5) magnus mōs; (6) magna pāx; (7) magnus rēx; (8) magnum corpus; (9) magna vēritās; (10) magnus amor.
6. (1) by/with much labor; (2) to/for much labor; (3) of much labor; (4) many labors (nom.); (5) of perpetual peace; (6) by/with perpetual peace; (7) to/for perpetual peace; (8) of small states; (9) a small state (acc.); (10) small states (acc.); (11) small states (nom.); (12) by a small state; (13) bad times (nom. or acc. pl.); (14) bad time (nom. or acc. sg.); (15) to/for a bad time; (16) of bad times; (17) of a bad time; (18) to/for your habit; (19) by your habit; (20) of your habit; (21) your character (nom.); (22) your character (acc.); (23) of your character.
7. (1) magnae virtūtī; (2) magna virtūs; (3) magnās virtūtēs; (4) magnārum virtūtum; (5) magnā virtūte; (6) tempus nostrum; (7) tempora nostra; (8) tempora nostra; (9) temporibus nostrīs; (10) temporī nostrō; (11) temporis nostrī; (12) temporum nostrōrum; (13) amōrem meum; (14) amōrēs meōs; (15) amōrī meō; (16) amōre meō; (17) amōris meī; (18) amōrum meōrum.

8. My time for leisure is small.   9. Your (sg.) courage is great.   10. Money is nothing without good character.   11. The virtues of many human beings are great. 12. The character of a good man will be good.   13. They will give a letter to the man.   14. We were able to see many men in the great state.   15. We used to see (saw, were seeing) a great love of money in many men.   16. Few men give attention to excellence.   17. Our state will give peace to many men.   18. Peace cannot be perpetual.   19. Without good peace the states of our times will not be strong. 20. Times are bad after many wars.   21. In many states and lands peace could not be strong.   22. Without great labor the man will have nothing.   23. The beautiful

maiden loves friends of good character.   24. Men of great courage were daring to overcome tyrants.   25. Love of country was strong in our state.

KEY FOR CHAPTER 8

1. (1) Future. (2) See Ch. 8. Perhaps a better device is found in the fact that our word "future" ends in **-e**: futur/e. The **-a-** in **dūcam** is the only exception among six forms.

2. (1) Present. (2) See Ch. 8.

3. (1) 1st pers. pl. pres.; (2) 2nd sg. fut.; (3) 3d pl. pres.; (4) 3d sg. fut.; (5) 2nd pl. pres.; (6) 1st pl. fut.; (7) 1st sg. pres.; (8) 3d pl. fut.; (9) 3d sg. pres.; (10) 2nd pl. fut.; (11) 2nd sg. pres.; (12) 1st sg. fut.; (13) 3d pl. impf.

4. (1) imper. sg.; (2) pres. inf.; (3) imper. pl.

5. (1) they were sending; (2) he is sending; (3) they are sending; (4) I shall send; (5) send (sg.); (6) we are sending; (7) you (pl.) were sending; (8) you (sg.) are sending; (9) send (pl.); (10) you (pl.) send; (11) he will send; (12) we shall send; (13) he does; (14) they will do; (15) they are doing; (16) you (pl.) will do; (17) we were doing; (18) I shall do; (19) we shall do; (20) you (sg.) are doing; (21) you (pl.) are doing; (22) he will write; (23) they are writing; (24) I shall write; (25) I was writing; (26) you (pl.) are writing; (27) we shall write; (28) he is writing; (29) you (sg.) are writing; (30) they will write; (31) write!

6. (1) pōnēbant; (2) pōnēmus; (3) pōne; (4) pōnit; (5) pōnent; (6) pōnam; (7) pōnēbās; (8) pōnētis; (9) pōnite; (10) pōnimus; (11) pōnitis; (12) pōnet.

7. What are they doing? What will you (pl.) do?   8. They were leading the man to me.   9. Lead (sg.) the man to me, and I shall thank the man.   10. While the tyrant leads the troops, we can do nothing.   11. He is writing a letter to the maiden. 12. You (sg.) were writing a great book.   13. You (sg.) will write good books. 14. We shall write books about peace.   15. Do you (pl.) have an abundance of good books?   16. The teacher teaches many boys.   17. The boys do not thank the teacher.   18. Few men were thanking our state.   19. The tyrant will lead great forces out of our state.   20. A great abundance of money does not lead men to wisdom.   21. Will good books lead many men to reason?   22. Do we often lead men to reason?   23. Reason can lead men to a good life.   24. Are you (pl.) leading a good life?   25. Always thank (pl.) a good friend.

KEY FOR CHAPTER 9

1. See p. 55.

2. (1) to/for that (m., f., n.); those (nom. m.)
   (2) that (nom. f.); those (nom./acc. n.)
   (3) of that (m., f., n.)
   (4) that (nom. m.)
   (5) by that (f.)
   (6) that (nom./acc. n.)
   (7) of those (m., n.)
   (8) those (nom. f.)
   (9) those (acc. m.)
   (10) to/for by/w./fr. those (m., f., n.)
   (11) by that (m., n.)
   (12) of those (f.)
   (13) by this (m., n.)
   (14) this (nom./acc. n.)
   (15) this (nom. f.); these (nom./acc. n.)
   (16) these (nom. f.)
   (17) by this (f.)

(18) this (acc. f.)
(19) of this (m., f., n.)
(20) this (acc. m.)
(21) these (acc. m.)
(22) to this (m., f., n.)
(23) of these (m., n.)
(24) these (acc. f.)
(25) to/for these; by these (m., f., n.)
(26) of one (m., f., n.)
(27) to/for one (m., f., n.)
(28) by one (f.)

(29) to/for the whole (m., f., n.);
    whole (nom. pl. m.)
(30) of the whole (m., f., n.)
(31) the whole (nom. f.);
    whole (nom./acc. pl. n.)
(32) the whole (acc. m.; nom./acc. n.)
(33) of no (sg. m., f., n.)
(34) to/for no (sg. m., f., n.); no (nom.
    pl. m.)
(35) no (nom. sg. f.; nom./acc. pl. n.)
(36) no (acc. pl. m.)

3. See text and examples on p. 56.

4. (1) haec puella
(2) hae puellae
(3) haec tempora
(4) huic temporī
(5) huic puerō
(6) huius temporis
(7) illīus temporis
(8) hōc librō
(9) illō librō
(10) illa puella
(11) illa tempora

(12) illa tempora
(13) illud tempus
(14) huic cīvitātī sōlī
(15) huius cīvitātis sōlīus
(16) illī puerō sōlī
(17) illī puellae sōlī
(18) illīus puellae sōlīus
(19) tyrannōrum sōlōrum
(20) tōtam cīvitātem
(21) tōtīus patriae
(22) tōtī patriae

(23) nūllīus ratiōnis
(24) nūllam ratiōnem
(25) nūllae puellae
(26) nūllī librō
(27) nūllōs librōs
(28) ūnī cīvitātī
(29) ūnī puellae
(30) ūnīus temporis
(31) ūnīus bellī
(32) alterī librō
(33) aliō librō

5. These men will lead (lead, were leading) the whole state.   6. That man will see (sees, was seeing/saw) these things in that land.   7. In that book he will write (I shall write, I was writing) those things about this man.   8. One man is leading (will lead) those forces into this land.   9. The teacher gives these things to the other boy. 10. We are writing (shall write) this book about another war.   11. The whole country thanks (will thank, was thanking) this man alone.   12. They are now giving their entire attention to that plan.   13. This man's friend will save this state by that plan. 14. The other friend will lead (his) entire life in another land.   15. This man alone was able to warn me about the faults of this tyrant.   16. You (pl.) had no forces in the other land.   17. Those men alone see no dangers in this plan.   18. You (sg.) dare to praise not only the character but also the treachery of that man.   19. In fact, on account of the treachery of one man this state was not strong.

KEY FOR CHAPTER 10

1. (1) 3d; (2) 2nd; (3) 4th; (4) 1st.

2. (1) 3d pl. pres.; (2) 2nd sg. fut.; (3) 2nd sg. pres.; (4) 1st pl. impf.; (5) 1st pl. pres.; (6) imper. sg.; (7) 2nd pl. fut.; (8) imper. pl.; (9) 2nd pl. pres.; (10) 1st sg. pres.; (11) 3d sg. pres.; (12) imper. sg. (13) 2nd sg. impf. Note: nos. 3, 5, 6, 8, 9 are 4th only; 12 is 3d only. The chief difference is the -ī- of the 4th and the -i- of the 3d. See p. 64.

3. (1) pres. inf.; (2) imper. sg.; (3) short stem vowels in 2nd sg. and 1st and 2nd pl. of pres. ind. and in the imper. pl.

4. (1) he will come
   (2) he is coming
   (3) they are coming
   (4) they will come
   (5) you (sg.) hear
   (6) you (pl.) will hear
   (7) you (pl.) hear
   (8) come (pl.)
   (9) you (sg.) will come
   (10) come (sg.)

   (11) to come
   (12) he makes/does
   (13) he will make/do
   (14) we shall make
   (15) we are making
   (16) they make
   (17) you (sg.) make
   (18) I shall make
   (19) you (sg.) will make
   (20) to make

5. (1) sentiam
   (2) sentiēmus
   (3) sentit
   (4) sentītis
   (5) sentient

   (6) sentiunt
   (7) sentīre
   (8) sentī
   (9) sentiet
   (10) sentīmus

   (11) iacit
   (12) iaciet
   (13) iaciam
   (14) iacimus
   (15) iace

   (16) iacitis
   (17) iaciēmus
   (18) iacite
   (19) iacere
   (20) iacis

6. We were fleeing from this land.   7. Flee (sg.) with your daughter.   8. They will flee into that place.   9. Time flees; the hours flee; old age is coming.   10. Come (pl.) with your friends.   11. They were coming into your country.   12. O great man, come into our state.   13. You (sg.) will find your daughter in that state.   14. They can find little money in the streets.   15. The tyrant is finding a way into this state. 16. You (pl.) will capture those men there with (their) friends.   17. We are coming to you with great forces.   18. Will he find much fame and glory there?   19. That man was always making war.   20. Those men (of yours *or* such men) will not make peace.   21. Many men do those things but do not do these things.   22. We are doing and will do our duty.   23. I shall make a great supply of books.   24. The boys were living with that good man.   25. In the books of ancient men you (pl.) will find much philosophy and wisdom.

KEY FOR CHAPTER 11

1. (1) **is, ea, id** and **eī, eae, ea**; (2) **ego** and **nōs**; (3) **tū** and **vōs**.
2. (1) to/for you (pl.); by/w./fr. you; (2) to/for us; by/w./fr. us; (3) we (nom.); us (acc.); (4) you (nom. pl.); you (acc. pl.); (5) of you (sg.); (6) of me; (7) to/for me; (8) to/for you (sg.); (9) you (acc. sg.); by/w./fr. you; (10) me (acc.); by/w./fr. me.
3. (1) them (masc.); (2) them (fem.); (3) their (masc., neut.); (4) their (fem.); (5) his, her, its; (6) by/w./fr. her; (7) she (nom.); they (nom. and acc. pl. neut.); (8) by/w./fr. him, it; (9) to/for him, her, it; they (masc. nom.); (10) to/for them (masc., fem., neut.); by/w./fr. them; (11) they (nom. fem.); (12) it (nom. or acc. sg.). N.B. in the sg. any one of the three Latin genders of **is, ea, id** may be translated by *it* when the antecedent of the pronoun is a word which in English is neuter. For instance, suppose that in a preceding sentence the word **pāx** appears. Then we read: **Sine eā nūlla cīvitās valet.** The Latin feminine **eā** becomes English *it* because in English *peace* is regarded as neuter.
4. (1) eius
   (2) eius
   (3) eōrum

   (4) eārum
   (5) eās
   (6) eōs

   (7) ea
   (8) eius
   (9) eī

   (10) eī
   (11) eā
   (12) eō

(13) vōbīs	(17) eae	(21) tū	(25) nōbīs
(14) tibi	(18) eī	(22) vōs	(26) ego
(15) eī	(19) id	(23) nōs	(27) mihi
(16) ea	(20) vōs	(24) nōs	

5. These men will give it to you (sg.). 6. *I* was giving it to you (pl.). 7. *You* (pl.) will give this gift to them. 8. I shall give the same thing to him (her, it). 9. *We* shall give them (= those things) to him (her). 10. That man will give it to me. 11. We shall give you (pl.) his books. 12. You (sg.) will give us their (masc.) books. 13. We shall give their money to you (sg.). 14. They will give his (her) money to me. 15. We shall send these/those books to her. 16. I shall send his (her) book to you (sg.). 17. That man, however, was sending their money to us. 18. We are sending them (fem.) with her. 19. I am sending him with them. 20. We shall send them with his (her) friends. 21. *You* (sg.) will send me with their friend. 22. They were sending you (pl.) with me to his friend. 23. He is sending us with you (sg.) into their land. 24. They will send them (fem.) with us to their friends. 25. I shall send him with you (pl.) to their friends. 26. They will send you (sg.) with him to me.

KEY FOR CHAPTER 12

1. (1) pres. act. ind.; (2) pres. act. inf.; (3) perf. act. ind.; (4) perf. pass. partic.
2. (1) **mittō,** pres. act. ind., *I send*
   (2) **mittere,** pres. act. inf., *to send*
   (3) **mīsī,** perf. act. ind., *I sent*
   (4) **missum,** perf. pass. partic., *having been sent, sent*
3. The perfect is like a "snapshot" of a past, completed action; the imperfect looks at continuing or progressive past action, like a video.
4.
(1) mittō	(6) agō	(11) remaneō	(16) dīcō
(2) laudō	(7) sum	(12) scrībō	(17) sum
(3) vincō	(8) dō	(13) sum	(18) vīvō
(4) dīcō	(9) sum	(14) faciō	(19) faciō
(5) faciō	(10) agō	(15) fugiō	(20) videō

5. (1) you (pl. perf.) . . . ; (2) he (perf.) . . . ; (3) they (perf.) . . . ; (4) you (sg. perf.) . . . ; (5) we (perf.) . . . ; (6) he had . . . ; (7) we shall have . . . ; (8) we had . . . ; (9) you (sg.) had . . . ; (10) they will have . . . ; (11) they had . . . ; (12) he will have . . . ; (13) you (pl.) had. . . .

6.
(1) they saw, were seeing	(12) he will conquer
(2) they had seen	(13) he conquered
(3) you (sg.) saw	(14) we conquered
(4) he did	(15) we conquer
(5) he was doing	(16) you (sg.) gave
(6) we had done	(17) you (pl.) had given
(7) we did	(18) we gave
(8) we shall do	(19) he flees
(9) they did	(20) he fled
(10) you (sg.) lived	(21) they flee
(11) they lived	(22) they fled

(23) he saved	(30) he came
(24) they saved	(31) he comes
(25) you (pl.) saved	(32) you (pl.) were coming
(26) he had saved	(33) you (pl.) came
(27) he will have saved	(34) they came
(28) we remained	(35) they come
(29) we had remained	(36) they had come

7. Those men had fled (will flee; are fleeing; were fleeing; fled). 8. These men remained (remain; will remain; were remaining; had remained). 9. The king had conquered (is conquering; conquered; will conquer) Asia. 10. The kings conquered (will conquer; are conquering; had conquered) Asia. 11. Kings possessed (possess; will possess; had possessed) Asia. 12. Caesar had come (came; is coming; will come) into the same land. 13. Caesar said (says; had said; will say) the same things. 14. *You* (pl.) gave (will give; were giving; had given) us peace. 15. *You* (sg.) sent (will send; are sending; had sent) a letter to her. 16. We saw (see; had seen) them in the same street. 17. He had lived (lived; will live) a long time. 18. You (sg.) had done (will do; did; are doing) it well. 19. I saved (shall save; was saving; had saved) their (his) state. 20. They found (had found; will find) him in the same place. 21. God had given (gave; gives; will give) liberty to men. 22. They thanked (will thank; were thanking; had thanked; thank) me. 23. *You* (pl.) were (were; are; will be; had been) free men.

KEY FOR CHAPTER 13

1. See p. 82, s.v. "Reflexive Pronouns."
2. See p. 82, s.v. "Declension of Reflexive Pronouns."
3. In pronouns of the first and the second persons.
4. (1) to/for myself.
   (2) yourself (sg. acc.); by/w./fr. yourself.
   (3) to/for ourselves; by/w./fr. ourselves.
   (4) to/for himself (herself, itself); to/for themselves.
   (5) yourselves (acc.).
   (6) himself (acc.); by/w./fr. himself; themselves (acc.); by/w./fr. themselves.
   (7) to/for yourselves; by/w./fr. yourselves.
5. Since **suus, -a, -um** is an adjective, it must agree in number with the noun which it modifies. Since **suus** is a reflexive, it means *his own* or *their own* according to whether the subject of the verb is singular or plural. See, for example, sentences 15 and 20 below.
6. **Eōrum** and **eius** are fixed genitives of possession; and therefore, they do not, like **suus,** agree with the nouns on which they depend. See, for example, sentences 16–19 below.
7. See p. 85, s.v. "The Intensive Pronoun." **Sē,** being reflexive, is used in the predicate and refers to the subject. **Ipse** can be used to emphasize a noun or pronoun in any part of a sentence. See, for example, sentences 27, 28, and 31 below.

8. Caesar saved them. 9. Caesar was saving him (= another person). 10. Caesar saved himself. 11. The Romans saved themselves. 12. The Romans saved them (=

others). 13. The Romans saved him. 14. Caesar saved his own friend. 15. Caesar saved his own friends. 16. Caesar saved his (= another's) friend. 17. Caesar saved his (= another's) friends. 18. Caesar saved their friend. 19. Caesar saved their friends. 20. The Romans saved their (own) friend. 21. The Romans saved their (own) friends. 22. The Romans saved their (= others') friend. 23. The Romans saved their (= others') friends. 24. The Romans saved his friend. 25. The Romans saved his friends. 26. Caesar himself saved him. 27. Caesar himself saved himself. 28. They saved Caesar himself. 29. They were saving the friend of Caesar himself. 30. They saved the friend of the Romans themselves. 31. The friend of Caesar himself saved himself. 32. The friends of Caesar himself saved themselves. 33. The friend of Caesar himself saved him. 34. Caesar's friends themselves saved him. 35. They did not save us. 36. We saved ourselves. 37. We saved the Romans themselves. 38. The Romans themselves did not save you. 39. *You* (sg.) saved yourself. 40. *You* (sg.) saved the Romans themselves. 41. He was giving nothing to me. 42. I gave nothing to myself. 43. He gave nothing to himself. 44. They gave nothing to themselves. 45. They gave nothing to them (= others). 46. They gave nothing to him. 47. I conquered myself. 48. They conquered me. 49. They conquered their (= others') anger. 50. They conquered their own anger. 51. He conquered his own anger. 52. He conquered his own sons. 53. They conquered their own sons.

KEY FOR CHAPTER 14

1. In the gen. pl.
2. **-ī** in abl. sg.; **-ia** in nom. and acc. pl.
3.
(1) by/w./fr. art	(17) of the kings
(2) of the arts	(18) to/for the king
(3) arts (nom. or acc.)	(19) names (nom. or acc.)
(4) to/for the sea; by/w./fr. the sea	(20) animals (nom. or acc.)
(5) to/for the seas; by/w./fr. the seas	(21) to/for an animal; by/w./fr. an animal
(6) the sea (nom. or acc.)	(22) of an animal
(7) the seas (nom. or acc.)	(23) of animals
(8) bodies (nom. or acc.)	(24) of strength
(9) of bodies	(25) men (acc.)
(10) of a part	(26) of the man; men (nom.)
(11) to/for parts; by/w./fr. parts	(27) strength (nom. or acc. pl.)
(12) of parts	(28) to/for men; by/w./fr. men
(13) by/w./fr./the city	(29) force (nom.); of force
(14) to/for the city	(30) force (acc.)
(15) of cities	(31) to/for strength; by/w./fr. strength
(16) cities (nom. or acc.)	(32) to/for force; by/w./fr. force

4. (2); (4) as abl.; (7); (12); (15); (20); (21) as abl; (23); (24); (30); (32) as abl.
5.
(1) vī magnā	(6) cīve bonō	(11) vim magnam
(2) virum magnum	(7) cīvibus multīs	(12) virōrum multōrum
(3) vīrium magnārum	(8) maria multa	(13) vīribus magnīs
(4) vī magnae	(9) marī magnō	(14) vīrēs magnās
(5) cīvium multōrum	(10) mare magnum	

6. (1) accompaniment; (2) means; (3) manner; (4) means

7. (1) they ran (currō); (2) we were running (currō); (3) you (sg.) ran (currō); (4) we had dragged (trahō); (5) he will drag (trahō); (6) they are dragging (trahō); (7) he was managing (gerō); (8) he manages (gerō); (9) they manage (gerō); (10) we shall manage (gerō); (11) they hold (teneō); (12) they will hold (teneō); (13) they held (teneō); (14) we held (teneō).

8. He waged many wars with the Romans.   9. They were managing the state with great wisdom.   10. He himself held the state by the power of troops.   11. Those animals dragged many men into the sea.   12. You (sg.) said this with great skill. 13. We ran with care (carefully) across the city.   14. He was coming to us with a large part of the citizens.   15. He will conquer the rights of the citizens by force. 16. You (pl.) dragged him to death across his land.   17. We shall join ourselves with the citizens of many cities.   18. He wrote this letter to the king himself with courage (courageously).   19. The violence of those seas was great.   20. I have seen the art of the Greeks with my own eyes.   21. We have drawn many beautiful thoughts from the ancients.

22. 8, accompaniment; 9, manner; 10, means; 12, manner; 13, manner; 14, accompaniment; 15, means; 17, accompaniment; 18, manner; 20, means.

KEY FOR CHAPTER 15

1. See p. 97.
2. See p. 97–98.
3. See p. 98.
4. (1) dat./abl. pl. m. and n.; (2) indecl. adj. agreeing with noun in any case; (3) nom./acc. pl. n.; (4) nom. pl. m. and n., acc. pl. n.; (5) any form in pl.; (6) nom./acc. pl. n.; (7) any form in pl.; (8) dat./abl. pl. f.; (9) any form in pl.; (10) gen. pl. any gender; (11) any form in pl.; (12) any form in pl.
5. The word which indicates the whole number or amount out of which a part is taken is normally put in the genitive case. See p. 99 s.v. "Genitive of the Whole."
6. **Ex** or **dē** + abl.
7. (1) one citizen
   (2) ten citizens
   (3) part of the citizens
   (4) three citizens
   (5) 3 of the 6 citizens
   (6) 5 of the citizens
   (7) 5 citizens
   (8) 100 citizens
   (9) 100 of the citizens
   (10) 1000 citizens
   (11) 3000 citizens
   (12) what (is) new?
   (13) much praise
   (14) enough money
   (15) no water

8. Time when, at which, within which.
9. (1) He used to come (was coming, kept coming) with his friends. Ablative of accompaniment.
   (2) He will come in one hour. Abl. of time within which.
   (3) He came at the same time. Abl. of time when.
   (4) He wrote the book in a few hours. Time within which.
   (5) At that time he wrote a book. Time when.
   (6) He was writing the book with care. Manner.

10. At that time alone he feared those three dangers; but he always used to fear (was afraid of) death.   11. Those two kings used to throw money among the thousands of citizens.   12. That one tyrant (of yours) always used to praise himself.   13. The citizens of those five cities kept expecting liberty.   14. They saved the city in two hours by their own wisdom.   15. I used to come into the city with three of my friends.   16. You (pl.) used to wage great wars with courage (= courageously).   17. Therefore a hundred Romans conquered a thousand Greeks.   18. Fathers often used to fear their own sons—and now they have much (of) fear.   19. Did you (sg.) see our two fathers at that time?   20. Where did you (pl.) find enough freedom?   21. They came in three hours, and he kept saying the same thing to us.   22. I understood little of the argument.   23. We have changed no part of our lives.   24. Our state used to preserve the liberty and rights of the citizens.   25. The Romans used to praise the customs of ancient times.   26. The two fathers sent four of their sons.   27. The ten men had enough wisdom and much virtue.   28. What's new, my friend?

KEY FOR CHAPTER 16

1. Abl. sg. masc. and fem.: **fortī** as compared with **cīve.**
2. (1) The adjective of 2 endings.
   (2) Nom. sg. masc. and fem.: fortis, fortis; ācer, ācris; potēns, potēns.
3. **-ī,** abl. sg. of all genders; **-ium,** gen. pl. of all genders; **-ia,** nom. and acc. neut. pl.; but see p. 105 n. 2.
4. **-ī;** but see p. 105 n. 2.
5. Yes.
6. (1) to/for a sweet girl
   (2) by/w./fr. a sweet girl
   (3) by/w./fr. a sweet mother
   (4) to/for a sweet mother
   (5) to/for a happy mother
   (6) by/w./fr. a happy mother
   (7) all wars, nom. or acc. pl.
   (8) all names, nom. or acc. pl.
   (9) all seas, nom. or acc. pl.
   (10) by/w./fr. every part
   (11) of all parts
   (12) of all kings
   (13) of all wars
   (14) by/w./fr. a happy man
   (15) to/for a happy man
   (16) to/for or by/w./fr. every sea
   (17) to/for every good art
   (18) by/w./fr. every good art
   (19) of every good art
   (20) to/for, by/w./fr. swift force

7. A long life is often difficult.   8. A difficult life can be happy.   9. How brief was his sweet life!   10. The memory of a sweet period of life helps thousands of men.   11. You (sg.) wrote a short book in a hundred hours.   12. In every sea we kept finding these two powerful animals.   13. In every land you (pl.) will see many thousands of brave men.   14. Swift rumor ran through every land.   15. That short war was difficult.   16. We overcame all dangers in six hours.   17. The powerful tyrant will conquer their country with swift violence.   18. In a short time he will change all the rights of the citizens.   19. They did not understand the difficult art of sweet liberty, for they had little wisdom.   20. Men fear difficult duties in all lands.

KEY FOR CHAPTER 17

1. See Ch. 17, p. 110–11, s.v. "Usage and Agreement."
2. (1) Its use in its own clause. (2) The antecedent.

3. In gender and number.

4. (1) who. (2) which. (3) who, which.

5.   (1) to/for whom or which, masc. sg.

    (2) whom or which, masc. pl.

    (3) who/which, nom. sg. fem.
      who/which, nom. pl. fem.
      which, nom. or acc. pl. neut.

    (4) of whom/which, whose, sg.

    (5) to/for or by/w./fr. whom/which, pl.

    (6) which, nom. or acc. neut. sg.

    (7) by/w./fr. whom/which, fem. sg.

    (8) who/which, masc. sg. and pl.

    (9) whom/which, masc. sg.

  (10) whom/which, fem. pl.

  (11) of whom/which, whose, masc. pl.

  (12) whom/which, fem. sg.

6. They praised the citizen whom you (pl.) had sent.   7. They praised the ten citizens whom you (pl.) had sent.   8. They praised the citizen who had saved the country.   9. They praised the hundred citizens who had saved the country.   10. They praised the citizen whose son had saved the country.   11. They praised the citizens whose seven sons had saved the country.   12. They praised the citizen to whom they had entrusted the country.   13. They praised many of the citizens to whom they had entrusted the country.   14. They praised the citizen with whom they had come.   15. They praised the citizens with whom they had come.   16. He came with the citizen to whom he had entrusted his own life.   17. Tyrants destroy the rights of the citizens whom they capture.   18. The tyrant destroyed the city from which thousands of citizens had fled.   19. The tyrant destroyed the city into which those nine citizens had fled.   20. The tyrant destroyed the cities from which the citizens had fled.   21. The tyrant destroyed the cities into which the citizens had fled.   22. He overcame the danger which we feared.   23. He overcame the dangers which we feared.   24. He gave books to the girls whom he was praising.   25. The man whose daughter you (sg.) love kept coming into the city.   26. He entrusted his own life to the man whose daughter you (sg.) love.   27. He used to help the mother, who had much courage.   28. The king used to give money to the mothers who had many sons.

KEY FOR CHAPTER 18

1. See p. 118 s.v. "The Passive Voice."

2. See p. 118 s.v. "Ablative of Personal Agent." Note that "agent" is a person; "means" is something other than a person.

3. (1) The letter **r.**
    (2) No.

4. (1) we; (2) he; (3) I; (4) they; (5) you (sg.); (6) you (pl.).

5. (1) **-bā-**, imperf.; **-bi-** (**-bō-**, **-be-**, **-bu-**), fut.
    (2) Yes, with the minor exception of **-be-** in the 2nd pers. sg.

6. (1) we shall be . . . ; (2) you (pl.) were being . . . ; (3) he was being . . . ; (4) you

(sg.) will be . . . ; (5) they will be . . . ; (6) we were being . . . ; (7) he will be . . . ; (8) you (sg.) were being . . . ; (9) you (pl.) will be . . . ; (10) they were being. . . .

7. They terrify me; I am terrified by them; I am terrified by their violence.   8. The tyrant was destroying this city. 9. This city was being destroyed by the tyrant; it will be destroyed by a plot.   10. He used to be aroused (moved) by his friends; he used to be aroused by their plans.   11. We are not being destroyed by the strength of men, but we can be destroyed by a plot.   12. You (pl.) will be destroyed not by war but by love of leisure and by the plans of evil men.   13. You yourself (sg.) are not being changed, but your name is being changed.   14. Thousands of men are possessed by the love of money.   15. Others used to be held by tyrants.   16. A few will be possessed by love of truth and friendship.   17. The boy will be saved by his friends.   18. Books of this sort used to be given to the boys by the teacher.   19. Liberty will be given to the people by the third king in a short time.   20. Our country can even now be saved by brave citizens.   21. We ought to be warned by the fortune of other men (others).   22. We are terrified by the plans of that tyrant who lives across the sea; but we love liberty, and we shall wage war with great courage.   23. We shall be helped by powerful friends.   24. We praise all our men, who are moved by courage and truth, not by love of themselves.

KEY FOR CHAPTER 19

1. (1) The perfect passive participle plus the present of **sum.**
   (2) The perfect passive participle plus the imperfect of **sum.**
2. (1) **Vir missus est** = *a man was (has been) sent;* **vir mittitur** = *a man is (is being) sent.*
   (2) **Vir missus erat** = *a man had been sent;* **vir mittēbātur** = *a man was being (used to be) sent.*
3. An interrogative pronoun introduces a question.
4. **quis** (nom. sg. m. and f.); **quid** (nom. and acc. sg. n.).
5. See p. 124.
6. (1) he is (is being) moved   (9) we were held
   (2) he was (has been) moved   (10) we had been held
   (3) it had been moved   (11) we were being held
   (4) he was being moved   (12) he had been changed
   (5) they had been destroyed   (13) he was (has been) changed
   (6) they were being destroyed   (14) he is (is being) changed
   (7) they were destroyed   (15) he was being changed
   (8) we are held

7. (1) whose (sg.)?   (6) to whom (sg.)?
   (2) whom (sg.)?   (7) whom (fem. pl.)?
   (3) who (pl.)?   (8) who (sg.)?
   (4) what (nom. and acc. sg.)?   (9) who (fem. pl.)?;
   (5) whose (pl.)?   what (neut. nom. and acc. pl.)?

8. By whom was the book prepared (had been prepared; was being prepared)?
9. The teacher by whom the book was prepared is overcome with work.   10. To

whom was the book given (was being given, had been given)? 11. What boy was saved? 12. I myself saw the boy who was saved. 13. Whose (sg.) two sons were saved? 14. I never saw the old man whose sons were saved. 15. Who (sg.) was sent? 16. Peace and liberty were praised by the citizen who had been sent. 17. Who (pl.) were sent? 18. Friendship was praised by the ten citizens who had been sent. 19. Whom (pl.) did you (sg.) see in the city? 20. Where are the three new friends whom you (sg.) saw in the city? 21. What things were found by you (sg.) there? 22. Where are the three bodies which were found there by you (sg.)? 23. By whom was this (thing) said? 24. To whom was this said? 25. The eight wretched men to whom these things were said fled from the city. 26. Whose sons were praised by him? 27. The fathers whose sons were praised will thank him. 28. What terrifies you? 29. What danger terrifies you? 30. But the danger which terrifies you has been conquered by brave citizens.

KEY FOR CHAPTER 20

1. (1) object, acc. sg.; (2) of, pl.; (3) by/w./fr., sg.; (4) subject, sg.; (5) of (sg.); subject or object (pl.); (6) to/for, sg.

2. (1) to/for a hand (band)   (8) of fruit; fruits (subj./obj.)
   (2) a hand (subj.)   (9) of fruits
   (3) of hands   (10) by/w./fr. fruit
   (4) by/w./fr. a hand   (11) of the senate
   (5) of a hand; hands (subj./obj.)   (12) to/for the senate
   (6) to/for or by/w./fr. fruits   (13) the senate (subj.)
   (7) fruit (obj.)   (14) by/w./fr. the senate

3. (1) Masculine; (2) **manus.**

4. (1) The ablative of place from which = motion apart; the ablative of separation = distance apart.
   (2) The ablative of separation.
   (3) The ablative of place from which.

5. Place from which regularly has a preposition (**ab, dē, ex**); for separation, see p. 130.

6. Who came to us at that time? 7. An old man of great fame fled from his country to our senate. 8. What new was said by him? 9. This (thing) was said by that man: "We lack liberty." 10. Free us from slavery and heavy fear. 11. Our forces waged long war against the tyrant's fierce bands. 12. Those fierce bands which the tyrant sent against us from that land were conquered by us. 13. After this (*lit.* these things) the citizens who feared the tyrant were led from their own country into our state. 14. We freed them from the crimes of that tyrant. 15. Now they lack (are free from) every fear (anxiety). 16. Their sons eagerly (with zeal) read good books in our schools. 17. And so they have written a thousand verses with their own hands. 18. These one hundred verses give great thanks to us. 19. In these verses the senate and the Roman people are praised. 20. For those unfortunate men now have the fruits of peace and much liberty without fear. 21. Since we have helped others, even we ourselves have great enjoyment. 22. Good men will never lack an

abundance of these fruits.   23. In our age many human beings pass their life in fear and slavery.   24. We ought to free those unfortunate men from fear.   25. For who can be happy if other human beings lack the enjoyments of peace and liberty?

26. (6) time when; (7) place from which; (8) agent; (9) agent; (10) separation; (12) agent; (13) place from which; (14) separation; (15) separation; (16) manner; (17) means; (22) separation; (23) time when; (24) separation.

KEY FOR CHAPTER 21

1. See p. 116–17.
2. Check with paradigms on p. 135–36 and repeat them until you can say them without hesitation.
3. In the passive infinitive the final **-e** of the active infinitive has been changed to **-ī**: (1) **sentīrī**, *to be felt;* (2) **movērī**, *to be moved;* (3) **servārī**, *to be saved;* (4) **scīrī**, *to be known;* (5) **tenērī**, *to be held.*
4. The whole active ending **-ere** is changed to **-ī**: (1) **mittī**, *to be sent;* (2) **iacī**, *to be thrown;* (3) **tangī**, *to be touched;* **trahī**, *to be drawn.*
5.   (1) I shall be sent
    (2) you (sg.) are sent
    (3) you (sg.) will be sent
    (4) to be sent
    (5) they are sent
    (6) I am sent
    (7) he is seized
    (8) he will be seized
    (9) to be seized
    (10) we are seized
    (11) they will be seized
    (12) they are seized
    (13) you (sg.) are seized
    (14) you (sg.) will be seized
    (15) they are touched
    (16) they will be touched
    (17) to be touched
    (18) you (sg.) are touched
    (19) you (pl.) will be touched
    (20) you (sg.) will be known
    (21) you (sg.) are known
    (22) he will be known
    (23) he is known
    (24) to be known

6. Who is being sent (will be sent, used to be sent, was sent)?   7. By whom will this letter be sent (was sent, is sent)?   8. By whose hand was that letter written (will be written)?   9. What was said (was being said, will be said, is said)?   10. "Who (sg.) will be seized?" "You (sg.) will be seized."   11. "Who (pl.) will be seized?" "You (pl.) will be seized."   12. For a long time you (sg./pl.) will be neglected (were neglected). 13. After many hours we were freed (shall be freed).   14. For the sake of the state they ordered him to be seized.   15. For the sake of liberty our state ought to be managed by the other man.   16. His soul could not be touched by money.   17. In every soul the love of country used to be felt (will be felt, is felt, was felt).   18. We are joined (used to be joined, will be joined) to (*lit.,* with) other citizens by love of country.   19. Friendship is not always understood, but it is felt.   20. Wisdom and truth will not be found (are not found, were not found) in those two men.   21. Wisdom is not obtained (will not be obtained, was not obtained) by even a great deal of (= much) money.   22. Truth often is not known (will not be known, was not known), because the study of it is difficult.   23. Not without great labor will truth be found (was found, can be found).   24. Others are drawn by eagerness for (*lit.,* of) money and fame; we ought to be drawn by love of truth and wisdom.

KEY FOR CHAPTER 22

1. ē.

2. **-em, -ē; -ēs, -ēbus, -ēs, -ēbus** (also **-eī,** dat., and **-ērum,** gen.)

3. (1) Feminine. (2) **Diēs.**

4. (1) of hope; to/for hope
   (2) of hopes
   (3) hope (acc.)
   (4) to/for or by/w./fr. hopes
   (5) hope (nom.); hopes (nom., acc.)
   (6) by/w./fr. faith
   (7) faith (acc.)
   (8) of or to/for faith
   (9) of days
   (10) day (nom.); days (nom., acc.)
   (11) to/for or by/w./fr. days
   (12) thing (acc.)
   (13) of things
   (14) by/w./fr. a thing
   (15) to/for or by/w./fr. things
   (16) of or to/for a thing
   (17) of fires
   (18) fire (acc.)
   (19) to/for or by/w./fr. fires
   (20) fires (nom., acc.)

5. (1) place where; he remained in the city.
   (2) time within which; he will come in one hour.
   (3) time when; he came at that time.
   (4) accompaniment; he came with them.
   (5) place from which; he came from the city.
   (6) separation; they lack fire.
   (7) means; that was done by fire.
   (8) agent; it was done by them.
   (9) manner; it was done faithfully (with faith).

6. (1) **ab** + abl.
   (2) **cum** + abl.
   (3) abl. alone after verbs of freeing, lacking, and depriving; with other verbs **ab, dē, ex** is often used.
   (4) **in** + abl.
   (5) abl. alone
   (6) **cum** + abl.; **cum** may be omitted when the noun is modified by an adj.
   (7) **ab, dē, ex** + abl.
   (8) abl. alone.

7. At that time he faithfully preserved the liberty of those ten citizens. 8. He managed the state with great care (= very carefully). 9. The state was managed by him with great care. 10. Many good things were seen in the middle of the city. 11. On that day they prepared many things hopefully. 12. We snatched the fire from the hands of the boy. 13. In five days Cicero will rescue the republic from danger. 14. You (sg.) freed the two republics from fear. 15. The earth nourishes human beings with good fruits. 16. He nourished their uncertain hopes by his own courage. 17. In this age our hopes are being destroyed by these three tyrants. 18. Seven of our friends came from that state with great fear. 19. The whole clan came into the territory of this state with a large band of friends in one day. 20. Not all free men dare to join themselves with this republic. 21. If those men lack faith, there is no hope of friendship and peace. 22. Good faith and the love of this republic can save us. 23. You (sg.) have given (your) whole life to this state.

24. (7) time when; manner; (8) manner; (9) manner; (10) place where; (11) time when; manner; (13) time within which; separation; (14) separation; (15) means; (16) means; (17) time when; agent; (18) place from which; manner; (19) accompaniment; time within which; (21) separation.

KEY FOR CHAPTER 23

1. (1) perf. pass. = having been . . . or Eng. perf. partic.
    (2) pres. act. = -ing
    (3) fut. act. = about to . . .
    (4) pres. act. = -ing
    (5) fut. act. = about to . . .
    (6) fut. pass. = (about) to be . . .
    (7) perf. pass. = having been . . .
    (8) pres. act. = -ing.
    (9) perf. pass. = having been (e.g., nom. pl.)
    (10) perf. pass. = having been (dat. or abl. pl.)

2. (1) about to be   (13) (about) to be done
    (2) about to press   (14) seizing
    (3) pressing   (15) about to seize
    (4) (having been) pressed   (16) (having been) desired
    (5) (about) to be pressed   (17) desiring
    (6) turning   (18) (about) to be given
    (7) (having been) turned   (19) (having been) given
    (8) about to turn   (20) about to give
    (9) (having been) said   (21) giving
    (10) saying   (22) (having been) moved
    (11) about to say   (23) moving
    (12) (having been) done   (24) about to move

3. (1) vīsus   (6) scrīptus   (11) victūrus   (15) tractus
    (2) vidēns   (7) mittēns   (12) vincēns   (16) trahēns
    (3) vīsūrus   (8) missus   (13) iūnctūrus   (17) iactūrus
    (4) scrībendus   (9) missūrus   (14) iungēns   (18) iactus
    (5) scrīptūrus   (10) victus

4. When captured (*lit.,* having been captured) he said nothing.   5. Freed from slavery he will lead a pleasant life.   6. He thanked those giving the gifts.   7. I do not like someone seeking gifts.   8. To a man desiring much money he used to give only a few gifts.   9. I sent my son to your school to be taught.   10. That man, when about to conquer another people, kept wishing to destroy (their) teachers and books.   11. Terrified by this plot we shall live a wretched life.   12. Long oppressed, they began to turn themselves against the oppressing tyrant.   13. Those four unfortunate men, when seen by the tyrant, ran across the border.   14. The orator, because he feared the tyrant, always used to say pleasing things.   15. We fear someone fearing us. (= who fears us).   16. These men, if they conquer, will take away all the rights of the conquered citizens.   17. That wretched man on the point of fleeing kept seek-

ing the advice of his three friends.   18. The old man, warned by two of his friends, fled to us.   19. Having himself been helped by the second old man, he kept giving many things to those lacking money.   20. Who, when freed from these dangers, will not thank the gods?   21. Joined with you (pl.), we shall save the republic.   22. To those having faith nothing is uncertain.

KEY FOR CHAPTER 24

1. (1) A noun (pronoun) + participle in abl.
   (2) No. (See p. 155.)
2. (1) See p. 155.
   (2) As a rule commas separate an abl. abs. from the rest of the sentence. This makes it appear somewhat apart from the rest of the sentence.
3. No. Since this "absolute" construction is not too commonly favored in English, the literal translation if regularly adhered to would make rather clumsy English.
4. When, since, after, although, if. (See p. 156.)
5. (1) Incorrect because the noun (**urbe**) of the abl. abs. is used (through its pronoun **eam**) as the object.
   (2) Incorrect because **captus** means *having been* captured, not *having* captured.
   (3) Correct because **urbem captam** (*the captured city*) stands as the natural object of **dēlēvit.**
   (4) Correct because **urbe captā** is a normal abl. abs., the noun of which is not used elsewhere as subject or object.
6. (1) Obligation or necessity.
   (2) It is really a predicate adjective; and so it naturally agrees with the subject of **sum.**
   (3) **Dēbeō** + inf., though **dēbeō** more often expresses the idea of moral obligation.
7. (1) **Mihi** is dat. of agent.
   (2) **Ā mē**; abl. of agent.

8. If (since, etc.) these two men hold the power, the republic will be strong.   9. When (since, etc.) this rumor had been reported, the leader left the city without delay. 10. When every desire for (*lit.,* of) money and glory had been banished from his soul, that leader conquered himself.   11. Every desire for evil things ought to be conquered by us (= we ought to conquer . . .) if we wish to lead a good life.   12. If (since, etc.) the citizens love (their) country, we can have great hopes.   13. All citizens kept fearing that tyrant (of yours), who had to be banished.   14. When the tyrant had been overcome, the citizens regained their liberty and rights.   15. But after a tyrant has been expelled, another tyrant often gets the power.   16. Who in taking the power desires to help the state alone, not himself?   17. When many peoples had been conquered, you (sg.) desired to possess the whole world.   18. Slavery of every sort must be checked throughout the whole world.   19. If our republic is strong, nothing is to be feared by you (sg.).   20. Our country ought to be helped by each one who likes our mode of life.   21. All rights, therefore, ought to be preserved by the citizens with great care.   22. When duties have been deserted by the citizens, the state will be in great danger.   23. When these important things had

been said, the orator was praised by us.   24. Truth and virtue ought always to be sought by all men.   25. When (since) truth and virtue had been sought, the republic was saved.

26. A. (8) virīs tenentibus; (9) fāmā narrātā; (10) cupiditāte expulsā; (12) cīvibus amantibus; (14) tyrannō superātō; (15) tyrannō expulsō; (17) gentibus victīs; (22) officiīs relictīs; (23) rēbus dictīs; (25) vēritāte . . . quaesītīs.
B. (11) vincenda est; (13) expellendus erat; (18) opprimenda est; (19) timendum est; (20) adiuvanda est; (21) cōnservanda sunt; (24) quaerendae sunt.
C. (11) nōbīs; (19) tibi; (20) cuique; (21) cīvibus; (24) virīs.
D. (22) ā cīvibus; (23) ā nōbīs.

KEY FOR CHAPTER 25

1. See p. 117, 136, 162.
2. Future active infinitive.
3. Perfect passive infinitive.
4. They agree with the subject of the infinitive. See p. 163, n. 4.
5. Since it is the ending of the perfect active infinitive, **-isse** in effect means "to have. . . ."

6.   (1) to have moved
(2) to have been moved
(3) to be about to move
(4) to be moved
(5) to be said
(6) to be known
(7) to be saved
(8) to be seized
(9) to be sent
(10) to have believed
(11) to have destroyed
(12) to have drawn
(13) to have touched
(14) to have loved
(15) to have conquered

(16) to have lived
(17) to have been drawn
(18) to have been seen
(19) to have been seized
(20) to have been sent
(21) to have been sought
(22) to have been expelled
(23) to have been left
(24) to have been given
(25) to be about to give
(26) to be about to turn
(27) to be about to press
(28) to be about to seize
(29) to be about to order
(30) to be about to touch

7. See p. 164.
8.   (2) nūntiō, I announce
(4) intellegō, I understand
(7) videō, I see
(8) nesciō, I do not know
(10) crēdō, I believe
(13) audiō, I hear

(14) sentiō, I feel, think
(16) scrībō, I write
(19) ostendō, I show
(20) spērō, I hope
(22) putō, I think
(24) negō, I say that . . . not, deny

9. Saying, knowing, thinking, perceiving. See p. 167.
10. The infinitive with subject accusative; not a "that" clause.
11. The accusative.
12. No.
13. (1) The perfect infinitive = time *before* that of the main verb.

(2) The future infinitive = time *after* that of the main verb.

(3) The present infinitive = the *same time* as that of the main verb. See p. 165.

14. I know that you did (will do, are doing) this (thing).   15. I knew that you had done (would do, were doing) this.   16. We believed that they would come (had come, were coming).   17. We believe that they will come (came, are coming).   18. Tomorrow he will hear (A) that they are coming (i.e., tomorrow); (B) that they came (e.g., yesterday) *or* that they have come; (C) that they will come (e.g., in a few days).   19. Today he hears (A) that they are coming (today); (B) that they came (yesterday); (C) that they will come (soon).   20. Yesterday he heard (A) that they were coming (yesterday); (B) that they had come (e.g., the day before yesterday); (C) that they would come (in a few days).   21. They hope that you (pl.) will see him.   22. I know that this was done by you.   23. I did not know that those things had been done by him.   24. They said that the city was not being captured by the enemy (had not been captured).   25. You (pl.) know that those men are (will be, were/have been) always faithful.   26. You (pl.) knew that those men were (would be, had been) always faithful.   27. They kept thinking that the tyrant ought to be driven out by them (by themselves).   28. We believe that peace ought to be sought by all leaders.   29. He says that peace is being sought (was sought) by the ten leaders.   30. He said that the two leaders would seek (were seeking, had sought) peace.   31. The enemy hope that they will conquer all states.   32. I well know that I do not know many things, for no one can know all things.

33. **Scīre** (sentence 32) is a complementary infinitive depending on **potest.**

34.

Word	*Form*	*Reason*
(14) tē	acc.	subj. of inf. (fēcisse)
(14) fēcisse	perf. act. inf.	indir. statement
(16) eōs	acc.	subj. of inf. (ventūrōs esse)
(17) ventūrōs esse	fut. act. inf.	indir. state
(21) eum	acc.	obj. of inf. (vīsūrōs esse)
(22) hoc	acc.	subj. of inf. (factum esse)
(23) eō	abl.	agent
(24) hostibus	abl.	agent
(25) fidēlēs	acc.	pred. adj. agreeing with illōs
(27) sibi	dat.	agent w. pass. periphrastic
(28) pācem	acc.	subj. of inf. (quaerendam esse)
(28) ducibus	dat.	agent w. pass. periphr.
(29) ducibus	abl.	agent
(30) pācem	acc.	obj. of inf. (quaesitūrōs esse)
(31) rēs pūblicās	acc.	obj. of inf.

KEY FOR CHAPTER 26

1. (1) Latin **-ior** corresponds to English *-er.*

    (2) They have a slight similarity in sound and they both have a final **-r** as a sign of the comparative.

2. (1) Latin **-issimus** corresponds to English *-est.*

    (2) The **s**'s which they have in common suggest **s** as a sign of the superlative.

3. (1) They are added to the *base* of the adjective. (See p. 171–72.)

   (2) turpior, turpissimus; vēlōcior, vēlōcissimus; prūdentior, prūdentissimus

4. (1) **Acerbior** = harsher, rather harsh, too harsh.

   (2) **Acerbissimus** = harshest, very harsh.

5. (1) **Quam** with the comparative = *than* (this man was harsher than that one).

   (2) **Quam** with the superlative = *as . . . as possible, -st possible* (this man was as harsh as possible, the harshest possible).

6. There is no fixed case after **quam,** which is an adverb or conjunction of comparison. The second word of a comparison, which comes after **quam,** is put in the same case as that of the first of the two words compared. (See p. 173.)

7. (1) Most have **i**-stems.

   (2) Comparatives have consonant stems. (Note, incidentally, that *comparative* and *consonant* both begin with the same sound.)

8. They announced that the bravest possible leader had come.   9. After a very clear light had been seen by the four men, the bravest troops were sent against the enemy. 10. When that very base man had been banished, the senate gave gifts to the more faithful citizens.   11. The more fortunate citizens used to do these pleasant things on behalf of the more unfortunate citizens.   12. This author is more famous than that one.   13. Certain men said that this author was more famous than that one.   14. Read the books of wiser authors if you wish to lead the wisest (a very wise) life.   15. The six authors whose books I have read are too (rather) harsh.   16. After certain very wise books had been read, we avoided those baser faults.   17. This man, who has overcome his base faults, is braver than the very brave leader. 18. Who is the happiest man? He who leads the wisest life is happier than the most powerful tyrant.   19. The cure of your vices seems rather (too) difficult.   20. That leader thought that his country was dearer to him than life.   21. A band of the most faithful young men possible ought to be sought by the senate.

KEY FOR CHAPTER 27

1. (1) and (2)—see p. 179 item II.

2. (1) and (2)—see p. 179 item I.

3.

Positive	Comparative	Superlative
parvus	minus (minor, minus)	minimum (minimus)
malus	pejorative (peior)	pessimist (pessimus)
bonus	ameliorate (melior)	optimist (optimus)
(prō)	prior (prior)	prime (prīmus)
magnus	major (maior)	maximum (maximus)
superus	superior (superior)	supreme (suprēmus)
multus	plus (plūs)	summit (summus)

4. (1) a smaller war
    (2) the worst (very bad) war
    (3) a greater war
    (4) former wars
    (5) a very similar book
    (6) a more difficult book
    (7) the smallest boy
    (8) the better boy
    (9) a very (most) beautiful girl
    (10) a more beautiful girl
    (11) very many girls
    (12) greater faith

(13) very small faith

(14) a smaller sea

(15) in a smaller sea

(16) larger seas

(17) the best fruits

(18) worse fruit

(19) the fiercest (very fierce) men

(20) fiercer men

(21) more men

(22) most (very) difficult labor

(23) the last (supreme) labor

(24) more labor

(25) more labors

(26) the best leaders

(27) greater leaders

(28) better leaders

(29) the smallest gifts

(30) more gifts

(31) the first gifts

(32) more praise

(33) more praises

(34) the worst citizens

(35) better citizens

(36) very free citizens

5. The easiest things often are not the best. 6. The difficult things are often the greatest. 7. The better pursuits are more (rather) difficult. 8. The worst authors write very many books. 9. These books are worse than the books of better authors. 10. The smaller boy received a larger gift. 11. That very small republic had the greatest hopes. 12. More men believe that this war is worse than the first war. 13. A better leader will come with greater forces. 14. Fierce leaders often used to praise the fiercer forces of the fiercest enemy. 15. When the very evil tyrant had been banished, the citizens sought a better and a wiser leader. 16. They gave the better leader greater power and more money. 17. Citizens of the smaller cities are not better than those of the largest cities. 18. We are not better than very many men of former ages. 19. Our ancestors used to call Apollo the god of the sun.

KEY FOR CHAPTER 28

1. Something other than a fact; e.g., the command and purpose clauses learned in this chapter. See p. 186.

2. See p. 186.

3. (1) **ē**; (2) **ā** (except that in the 3rd and 4th conjugations the forms **dūcam** and **audiam** are identical in the future indicative and the present subjunctive).

4. Command, called "jussive."

5. Purpose.

6. Jussive.

7. No. (See p. 189.)

8. (1) he will send

(2) subj., 3rd sg.

(3) he is sending

(4) subj., 3rd sg.

(5) he gives

(6) subj., 3rd pl.

(7) they believe

(8) they will believe

(9) they move

(10) subj., 3rd pl.

(11) we shall be heard

(12) subj., 1st pl. pass.

(13) we are heard

(14) subj., 2nd sg.

(15) you (sg.) are seizing

(16) you (sg.) will seize

(17) they are known

(18) they will be known

(19) subj., 3rd pl. pass.

(20) you (pl.) are freed

(21) subj., 2d. pl. pass.

(22) you (pl.) will be freed

(23) they are destroyed

(24) subj., 3rd pl. pass.

(25) you (sg.) will be conquered

(26) you (sg.) are conquered

(27) subj., 2nd sg.

(28) we say

(29) we shall say

(30) subj., 1st pl.

9. Let that leader come. We are awaiting him. 10. Let the base citizens depart from (our) republic so that we may live in peace. 11. If those two men desire friends, let them do real kindnesses. 12. He shows kindnesses to others in order to be loved (so that he may be loved). 13. I say these happy words to you so that you may not depart. 14. Let us do these very difficult things for the sake of our country. 15. Give more money to those unfortunate people so that they may not lack arms against the enemy. 16. He thinks that they will do it to avoid my anger. 17. Let us prepare arms so that our liberty may not be taken away. 18. Will our freedom be rescued from danger by arms alone? 19. Let philosophers not write too difficult books. 20. For (= the truth is) we shall not receive enough wisdom from too difficult books. 21. Let him do better and greater things so that he may not lead a most wretched life. 22. Tell these things to that very famous author so that they may be written in his book. 23. Let us always seek the truth, without which the greatest souls cannot be happy.

24.	*Word*	*Form*	*Reason*
(9)	veniat	pres. subj.	command (jussive)
(10)	discēdant	pres. subj.	command
	vīvāmus	pres. subj.	purpose
(11)	faciant	pres. subj.	command
(12)	praestat	pres. ind.	statement of fact
	amētur	pres. subj.	purpose
(13)	discēdātis	pres. subj.	purpose
(14)	faciāmus	pres. subj.	command
(15)	date	imper.	command in 2nd per.
	armīs	abl.	separation
	careant	pres. subj.	purpose
(16)	eōs	acc.	subj. of inf.
	factūrōs esse	fut. act. inf.	indirect statement
	vītent	pres. subj.	purpose
(17)	parēmus	pres. subj.	command
	tollātur	pres. subj.	purpose
(18)	armīs	abl.	means
	ēripiētur	fut. ind.	fact
(19)	scrībant	pres. subj.	command
(20)	accipiēmus	fut. ind.	fact
(21)	faciat	pres. subj.	command
	agat	pres. subj.	purpose
(22)	nārrā	imper.	command in 2nd per.
	scrībantur	pres. subj.	purpose
(23)	quaerāmus	pres. subj.	command

KEY FOR CHAPTER 29

1. Present active infinitive + personal endings. See p. 194.
2. Yes.
3.   (1) impf. subj., 3 sg.   (16) pres. subj., 3 sg.
      (2) impf. subj., 3 pl.   (17) impf. subj., 3 pl.
      (3) impf. subj., 1 pl.   (18) they will depart
      (4) impf. subj., 1 sg.   (19) pres. subj., 3 pl.
      (5) impf. subj., 2 sg.   (20) pres. subj., 1 pl.
      (6) pres. subj., 3 sg.   (21) pres. subj., 1 pl.
      (7) impf. subj., 2 pl.   (22) impf. subj., 3 pl.
      (8) pres. subj., 3 sg.   (23) pres. subj., 2 sg.
      (9) you (sg.) will find   (24) you will receive
    (10) pres. subj., 2 sg.   (25) impf. subj., 2 sg.
    (11) pres. subj., 3 sg.   (26) you (pl.) will be banished
    (12) he will say   (27) impf. subj., 2 pl.
    (13) he says   (28) pres. subj., 2 pl.
    (14) pres. subj., 3 pl.   (29) impf. subj., 3 pl.
    (15) impf. subj., 3 sg.   (30) they are moved

4. **Ut** or **ut nōn** + subjunctive.
5. See p. 196.
6. See p. 196.

7. They read the best books with such great care that they learned much wisdom. 8. We used to read good books with care so that we might learn wisdom. 9. The best books ought to be read by students in order that they may learn the truth and good character. 10. Let the wisest authors write more books so that they may be able to help all peoples. 11. The souls of very many men are so foolish that they do not wish to learn. 12. But many minds are so keen that they can learn well. 13. Some teachers used to teach their pupils so skillfully (with such great skill) that even the pupils themselves wanted to learn. 14. The power of that tyrant was so great that the senate could not drive him out. 15. Let all citizens dedicate (give) themselves to the country so that the enemy may not take away their liberty. 16. Caesar was such a keen leader that the enemy did not conquer the Roman soldiers. 17. Are we leading other peoples with such great wisdom and courage that liberty is being preserved? 18. You (pl.) used to do such great kindnesses that all loved you. 19. He was so harsh that no one loved him. 20. Thousands of citizens kept fleeing from that land in order not to be oppressed by the tyrant. 21. They so loved liberty that they were never conquered by the enemy.

22.

	Word	*Form*	*Reason*
(7)	discerent	impf. subj.	result
(8)	discerēmus	impf. subj.	purpose
(9)	discant	pres. subj.	purpose
(10)	scrībant	pres. subj.	command
	possint	pres. subj.	purpose
(11)	cupiant	pres. subj.	result

(12) possint	pres. subj.	result
(13) cuperent	impf. subj.	result
(14) posset	impf. subj.	result
(15) dent	pres. subj.	command
tollant	pres. subj.	purpose
(16) vincerent	impf. subj.	result
(17) cōnservētur	pres. subj.	result
(18) amārent	impf. subj.	result
(19) amāret	impf. subj.	result
(20) opprimerentur	impf. subj.	purpose
(21) vincerentur	impf. subj.	result

KEY FOR CHAPTER 30

1. It is the perfect active infinitive (**-isse**) + personal endings; e.g., **pōnere-m** and **posuisse-m**.
2. It is the perfect passive participle + **essem** (the imperfect subjunctive of **sum**); e.g., **positus eram** and **positus essem**.
3. **Positus sit** is perfect subjunctive passive.
4. The future perfect indicative.
5. (1) impf. pass., 3 sg.   (9) impf. act., 3 pl.
   (2) plupf. act., 1 sg.   (10) plupf. pass., 1 pl.
   (3) perf. pass., 3 pl.   (11) pres. act., 3 sg.
   (4) pres. pass., 1 pl.   (12) perf. pass., 2 sg.
   (5) perf. act., 3 pl.   (13) plupf. act., 2 sg.
   (6) impf. act., 1 pl.   (14) impf. pass., 3 sg.
   (7) plupf. act., 2 pl.   (15) perf. act., 1 pl.
   (8) plupf. pass., 3 sg.   (16) plupf. act., 3 pl.

6. (1) Present and future. See p. 205.
   (2) Present and perfect.
   (3) The past tenses.
   (4) Imperfect and pluperfect.

7. (1) The same time or time after (contemporaneous or subsequent). See p. 205.
   (2) The same time or time after.
   (3) Time before (prior).
   (4) Time before (prior).

8. Where is (was) the leader?   9. They ask where the leader is (was).   10. They kept asking where the leader was (had been).   11. They will ask where the leader is (was). 12. I do not know where the money was put.   13. Do you (sg.) know where the money is being put?   14. They knew where the money was being put.   15. He did not know where the money had been put.   16. We shall tell you (pl.) why the soldier did (does) this.   17. They told me why the soldier had done (was doing) this. 18. Tell me who came (is coming).   19. The orator asked why the other citizens had not learned these plans.   20. We announced to the leader that the other soldiers were fleeing (had fled) into that land.   21. We announced to the leader into what

land the other soldiers were fleeing (had fled).   22. We heard that the citizens were so faithful that they preserved the state.   23. We heard what the citizens had done to preserve the state.   24. They kept inquiring in whose state peace could be found. 25. We learned that peace had not been found in their country.   26. Those foolish men always ask what is better than power or money.   27. We certainly think that money itself is not bad; but we believe that truth and liberty and friendship are better and greater.   28. These things we desire so that we may live a finer life; for money alone and power can make men harsh, so that they are not happy.   29. Finally, let him explain all things so that you (pl.) may now understand what great crimes have been committed against the republic.

30.

Word	*Form*	*Reason*
(15) posita esset	plupf. subj.	ind. quest.
(16) fēcerit	perf. subj.	ind. quest.
(17) fēcisset	plupf. subj.	ind. quest.
(18) vēnerit	perf. subj.	ind. quest.
(20) fugere	pres. inf.	ind. state.
(21) fugerent	impf. subj.	ind. quest.
(22) esse	pres. inf.	ind. state.
cōnservārent	impf. subj.	result
(23) fēcissent	plupf. subj.	ind. quest
cōnservārent	impf. subj.	purpose
(24) posset	impf. subj.	ind. quest.
(25) inventam esse	perf. inf.	ind. state.
(26) sit	pres. subj.	ind. quest.
(27) esse	pres. inf.	ind. state.
(28) agāmus	pres. subj.	purpose
sint	pres.subj.	result
(29) expōnat	pres. subj.	jussive
comprehendātis	pres. subj.	purpose
commissa sint	pres. subj.	ind. quest.

KEY FOR CHAPTER 31

1. When (circumstantial, which is to be distinguished from **cum** temporal), since, although.
2. Although.
3. (1) The 3rd conjugation.
   (2) They lack the connecting vowel **e/i,** which is seen in the corresponding forms of **dūcō.** (See p. 212.)
4. (1) pres. subj. act., 3 sg.   (8) pres. subj. act., 3 pl.
   (2) he bears   (9) he is borne
   (3) impf. subj. act., 3 sg.   (10) bear (2 pl.)
   (4) he will bear   (11) you (pl.) bear
   (5) to bear   (12) you (sg.) will be borne
   (6) they bear   (13) you (sg.) are borne
   (7) they will bear   (14) bear (2 sg.)

(15) to be borne   (18) to be borne (gerundive)
(16) to have borne   (19) to have been borne
(17) to be about to bear   (20) plupf. subj. act., 3 sg.

5. When we had said this, those twenty men replied that they would offer a just peace.   6. Although he had gone into another country, nevertheless he found new friends.   7. Since they offer us friendship, we shall offer them aid.   8. Since the danger was great, they brought all their troops and arms together in a short time. 9. What do *you* (sg.) bring? What does he bring? Tell me why these gifts are offered. 10. When he had explained what he was seeking, you (sg.) said that such great aid could not be offered.   11. Although they had brought pleasing gifts, I was able nevertheless to recognize their treachery.   12. Since we now understand your plans, we will not endure your treachery.   13. Such great evils are not to be endured. Go (betake yourself) into exile.   14. Finally, let these hundred citizens bear aid to the republic.   15. I kept thinking that they would bring the wine in ships (*lit.,* by ships). 16. Although our soldiers had conquered the enemy, nevertheless they offered them many kindnesses.   17. When he had learned what great benefits the other three men were offering, he himself offered equal benefits.   18. We ought to offer sufficient aid to the unfortunate citizens of small nations.   19. When the consul had spoken these words, the senate replied that money had been brought together for this purpose.

20.

Word	Form	Reason
(5) dīxissēmus	plupf. subj.	cum circumstantial
oblātūrōs esse	fut. inf.	ind. state.
(6) contulisset	plupf. subj.	cum *although*
(7) offerant	pres. subj.	cum *since*
(8) esset	impf. subj.	cum *since*
(9) offerantur	pres. subj.	ind. quest.
(10) exposuisset	plupf. subj.	cum circumstantial
peteret	impf. subj.	ind. quest.
(11) tulissent	plupf. subj.	cum *although*
(12) comprehendāmus	pres. subj.	cum *since*
(13) cōnfer	imper. 2 sg.	command
(14) ferant	pres. subj.	jussive (command)
(15) nāvibus	abl. pl.	means
lātūrōs esse	fut. inf.	ind. state.
(16) vīcissent	plupf. subj.	cum *although*
(17) offerrent	impf. subj.	ind. quest.
(19) dīxisset	plupf. subj.	cum circumstantial

KEY FOR CHAPTER 32

1. (1) **-ē**; (2) **-iter** (e.g., līberē, celeriter).
2. The ending *-ly* (e.g., freely, quickly).
3. No. For example, see the list on p. 221.
4. (1) **-ius** (e.g., līberius, celerius).
   (2) It is identical with the nom. and acc. neut. sg.

(3) It is usually formed by using *more (too, rather)* with the positive degree of the adverb (e.g., more/too freely, more quickly).

5. The base is the same in both instances.

6. (1) **līberius** = more/too/rather freely.

(2) **līberrimē** = most/very freely.

7. (1) pleasantly
    (2) more/too pleasantly
    (3) most/very pleasantly
    (4) better
    (5) very faithfully
    (6) briefly
    (7) very quickly
    (8) worse
    (9) more faithfully
    (10) more easily
    (11) very little, least of all
    (12) more, rather
    (13) longer
    (14) badly
    (15) more wretchedly
    (16) less
    (17) easily
    (18) especially, most of all
    (19) very seriously
    (20) more swiftly

8. (1) **vol-**; (2) **vel-**. See p. 221.

9. It is similar to **sum.** See p. 221.

10. (1) you (sg.) will wish
     (2) pres. subj., 2 sg.
     (3) you (sg.) wish
     (4) impf. subj., 2 sg.
     (5) he prefers
     (6) pres. subj., 1 pl.
     (7) impf. subj., 1 pl.
     (8) plupf. subj., 2 sg.
     (9) I shall wish
     (10) they kept wishing
     (11) he will wish
     (12) you (pl.) wish
     (13) to have wished
     (14) they wish
     (15) we wished
     (16) to wish
     (17) he had wished
     (18) they wished
     (19) you (sg.) wished
     (20) impf. subj., 3 sg.
     (21) they do not wish
     (22) impf. subj., 3 sg.
     (23) pres. subj., 3 sg.
     (24) he will not wish

11. Certain men prefer to believe that all men are equal.   12. Certain men say that all men's minds at least are not equal.   13. These men obtained wealth very quickly; those will be poor for a very long time.   14. This man wishes to get very many honors as easily as possible.   15. Do not lose this knowledge.   16. The citizens themselves managed the state better than the leader.   17. There the land is more level and is more open.   18. Free men will not wish to keep us from knowledge; but tyrants especially so wish.   19. The tyrant used to oppress his citizens so badly that they always wished to be free.   20. He will offer very many gifts very freely so that the army may be willing to help that tyrant.   21. Since they had very little wish to offer aid, we were unwilling to show them many favors.   22. Since the enemy are coming swiftly against us, we want to call our men to arms as quickly as possible. 23. Although they truly wanted to preserve their liberty and laws, nevertheless the crimes of the tyrant had to be endured very long.   24. He prefers to do these things more wisely so that he may not lose this occasion at least. 25. Do not leave, my friend.

KEY FOR CHAPTER 33

1. (1) The present subjunctive. (2) See p. 229.
2. (1) (A) Present contrary to fact; (B) past contrary to fact.
   (2) The conditional clause. See p. 229.
3. **Nisi.**
4. The future less vivid condition.
5. See vocabulary p. 230.

6. If reason leads, you (sg.) are happy.   7. If reason leads, you will be happy.   8. If reason should lead, you would be happy.   9. If reason were leading, you would be happy.   10. If reason had led, you would have been happy.   11. If you (sg.) love money, you lack wisdom.   12. If you love money, you will lack wisdom.   13. If you should love money, you would lack wisdom.   14. If you were in love with money, you would lack wisdom.   15. If you had loved money, you would have lacked wisdom.   16. If we seek the truth, we find knowledge.   17. If we seek the truth, we shall find knowledge.   18. If we should seek the truth, we would find knowledge.   19. If we were seeking the truth, we would find knowledge.   20. If we had sought the truth, we would have found knowledge.   21. If you do not avoid anger, you will lose your two friends.   22. If you had not avoided anger, you would have lost your five friends.   23. If you should not avoid anger (if you should fail to avoid anger), you would lose many friends.   24. If you were not avoiding anger, you would be losing many friends.   25. If you do not avoid anger, you are losing many friends.   26. If you did not avoid anger, you lost many friends.   27. If anyone has a good character, we praise him.   28. If anyone had had a good character, we would have praised him.   29. If anyone should have a good character, we would praise him.   30. If anyone had a good character, we praised (used to praise) him.   31. If anyone were in possession of a good character, we would praise him.   32. If anyone has a good character, we shall praise him.   33. If those men win, we shall depart.   34. If those men should win, we would depart.   35. If those men had won, we would have departed.   36. If you had read books well, you would have written better.   37. If you read books well, you will write better.   38. If you should read books well, you would write better.

39. (6) simple present
     (7) simple fut.
     (8) fut. less vivid
     (9) pres. contr. to fact
     (10) past contr. to fact

     (21) simple fut.
     (22) past contr. to fact
     (23) fut. less vivid
     (24) pres. contr. to fact
     (25) simple present
     (26) simple past

KEY FOR CHAPTER 34

1. See p. 234.
2.

	Indicative	
Pres.	cōnāmur	loquitur
Impf.	cōnābāmur	loquēbātur
Fut.	cōnābimur	loquētur

Perf.	cōnātī sumus	locūtus est
Plupf.	cōnātī erāmus	locūtus erat
Fut. Perf.	cōnātī erimus	locūtus erit
	Subjunctive	
Pres.	cōnēmur	loquātur
Impf.	cōnārēmur	loquerētur
Perf.	cōnātī sīmus	locūtus sit
Plupf.	cōnātī essēmus	locūtus esset

3. (1) Participles

Pres.	patiēns, *suffering*
Perf.	passus, *having suffered*
Fut.	passūrus, *about to suffer*
Ger.	patiendus, *to be endured*

(2) Infinitives

Pres.	patī, *to suffer*
Perf.	passus esse, *to have suffered*
Fut.	passūrus esse, *to be about to suffer*

4. (1) illud cōnsilium; (2) illō cōnsiliō; (3) illud cōnsilium
5. Ablative (of means) with special deponent verbs. See p. 237–38.
6. Pres. partic.; fut. partic.; fut. inf.; e.g., **patiēns, passūrus, passūrus esse** in 3 above.

7. (1) cōnor
    2 sg. cōnāre, *try*
    2 pl. cōnāminī, *try*

    (2) loquor
    loquere, *speak*
    loquiminī, *speak*

8. (1) locūtus, *having said*
(2) mortuus, *having died*
(3) cōnātus, *having tried*
(4) passus, *having suffered*

(5) secūtus, *having followed*
(6) ēgresssus, *having gone out*
(7) profectus, *having set out*

9.   (1) he will use
    (2) pres. subj., 3 sg.
    (3) he uses
    (4) impf. subj., 3 sg.
    (5) having used
    (6) plupf. subj., 3 sg.
    (7) to be about to use
    (8) you (sg.) will endure
    (9) you (sg.) are enduring
    (10) endure (imper.)

    (11) to endure
    (12) they endured
    (13) to have endured
    (14) enduring
    (15) pres. subj., 3 sg.
    (16) he endures
    (17) we shall endure
    (18) pres. subj., 3 sg.
    (19) impf. subj., 3 sg.
    (20) it must be endured

10. He thinks that these evils ought to be endured. 11. We shall try to endure these evils. 12. If you do not wish to die, endure these evils. 13. Having endured the greatest evils, the poor man died. 14. The tyrant thought that those two men would endure these evils a long time. 15. When they had endured three wars, they dared to force that tyrant into exile. 16. If you follow this new leader, you will enjoy liberty and leisure. 17. When these words had been said, we dared to follow him.

18. Having spoken these words, we set out so that we might not die in that miserable place.   19. Although he thought that you had used a bad plan, nevertheless he spoke with you freely.   20. If anyone should dare to use wine of that sort, he would quickly die.   21. His son was born and died on the same day.   22. Let us use all our resources so that our country may be saved.   23. When he tried to set out into another land, he was captured by soldiers.   24. I kept thinking that he would go out of the city with his ten friends.   25. Having set out that night, Caesar came to a certain very famous island.   26. If they had used better books, they would have learned more.   27. If you wish to have many friends, do not be arrogant.

28. (12) simple pres.; (16) simple fut.; (20) fut. less vivid; (26) past contrary to fact.

29.

Word	Form	Reason
(14) passūrōs esse	fut. inf.	ind. state.
(17) verbīs	abl.	abl. abs.
(18) locūtī	nom. pl. of perf. partic.	agrees w. subject of verb
morerēmur	impf. subj.	purpose
(19) cōnsiliō	abl.	special deponents
arbitrārētur	impf. subj.	**cum** *although*
(21) diē	abl.	time when
(22) ūtāmur	pres. subj.	jussive
(25) nocte	abl.	time when
(26) librīs	abl.	spec. deponents

KEY FOR CHAPTER 35

1. See p. 246.
2. See p. 247–48.
3. (1) eum; they recognize him.
    (2) eī; they forgive him.
    (3) eī; they serve him.
    (4) eum; they save him.
    (5) eum; I prepared him.
    (6) eī; I obeyed him.
    (7) eum; they endure him.
    (8) eum; they will find him.
    (9) eī; they injure him.
    (10) eum; they help him.
    (11) eī; they please him.
    (12) eum; they throw him.
    (13) eum; they overcome him.
    (14) eī; they trust him.
    (15) eō; they lack it.
    (16) eī; they study it.
    (17) eum; they urge him.
    (18) eum; they follow him.
    (19) eī; they persuade him.
    (20) eō; they use it (him).
    (21) eum; they strike him.
    (22) eī; they spare him.
    (23) eī; they command him.
    (24) eum; they order him.

4. He saved the leader.   5. He served the leader.   6. Slaves serve other men.   7. Brave men save others.   8. That slave served my son and saved him.   9. If anyone serves himself alone, he will never save the republic.   10. If someone had undertaken this work, he would have saved a thousand men.   11. The gods will pardon me; you, O citizens, pardon the whole army.   12. If we want God to forgive us, we ought to forgive other men.   13. They do not trust me now, and they will never be willing to trust my two sons.   14. Those friends are very dear to me.   15. Since you lacked good faith, they could not trust you.   16. Let us obey this leader so that he

may spare us and save the city. 17. If Caesar does not please the citizens, they will not spare his life. 18. I am studying Latin literature, which I like (pleases me) even if I cannot persuade my friends. 19. Let us always study and obey truth and wisdom. 20. Always study the best subjects if you wish to be truly happy. 21. As we study these subjects, let us enjoy both books and life. 22. A good man wishes to harm nobody; he spares all, he helps all. 23. My rewards are very similar to yours.

24.

Word	*Form*	*Reason*
(5) ducī	dat.	special vbs.
(8) eum	acc.	obj. of **servāvit**
(9) sibi	dat.	spec. vbs.
(11) exercituī	dat.	spec. vbs.
(12) hominibus	dat.	spec. vbs.
(13) fīliīs	dat.	spec. vbs.
(14) mihi	dat.	dat. w. adjs.
(15) fidē	abl.	separation
(16) ducī	dat.	spec. vbs.
pāreāmus	pres. subj.	jussive
servet	pres. subj.	purpose
(17) cīvibus	dat.	spec. vbs.
vītae	dat.	spec. vbs.
(18) litterīs	dat.	spec. vbs.
amīcīs	dat.	spec. vbs.
(21) rēbus	dat.	spec. vbs.
librīs	abl.	spec. depon. vbs.
ūtāmur	pres. subj.	jussive
(22) omnibus	dat.	spec. vbs.
(23) tuīs	dat.	dat. w. adjs.

KEY FOR CHAPTER 36

1. Indirect command = **ut (nē)** + subjunctive. See p. 253.
2. E.g., imperō, dīcō, cūrō, moneō, hortor, persuādeō, petō, quaerō, ōrō, rogō. See p. 254.
3. (1) it will be made/done, he will become
   (2) it is made/done, he becomes
   (3) pres. subj., 3 sg.
   (4) impf. subj., 3 sg.
   (5) to be made/done, to become
   (6) they are made/done, they become
   (7) they were being made/done, they were becoming
   (8) you (sg.) will be made, become
   (9) to have been made/done, become
   (10) impf. subj., 3 pl.
   (11) we are made, become
   (12) they will be made, become
   (13) you (sg.) are made, become
   (14) impf. subj., 1 sg.
   (15) pres. subj., 3 pl.
   (16) gerundive, to be made/done
   (17) pres. subj., 1 pl.

4. He said that they were studying Latin literature. 5. He told why they were studying Latin literature. 6. He said that they should study Latin literature (he told them to study . . .). 7. We asked them why they were studying Greek philosophy. 8. Do

you ask that we learn (= ask us to learn) the nature of all things?   9. I warn you to spare these wise men.   10. He warned the soldiers not to injure those seeking peace. 11. He will command us not to trust the enemy.   12. He commanded you to obey the leader.   13. I ask you why you did this.   14. I ask you to do this.   15. I beg of you that peace be made.   16. They kept begging me not to make war.   17. I begged him not to obey the disgraceful king.   18. We beg you to become very keen pupils. 19. Do not be like that harsh tyrant.   20. Caesar took care that his power be made greatest in the state.   21. The speaker urged us to serve our free country eagerly. 22. He persuaded us that we should always use just laws.   23. We are trying to persuade the leader not to harm the arts and laws of the country.   24. A tyrant commands that money be made; and money is made. But that fool does not perceive that this money will be nothing without good faith.   25. Let us urge more students certainly to study the Latin language.

26.

	Word	*Form*	*Reason*
(4)	studēre	pres. inf.	ind. state.
(5)	studērent	impf. subj.	ind. quest.
(6)	studērent	impf. subj.	jussive noun
(7)	studērent	impf. subj.	ind. quest.
(8)	cognōscāmus	pres. subj.	jussive noun
(9)	parcās	pres. subj.	jussive noun
(10)	eīs	dat.	spec. vbs.
	pācem	acc.	obj. **petentibus**
(11)	hostibus	dat.	spec. vbs.
(13)	fēcerīs	perf. subj.	ind. quest.
(14)	faciās	pres. subj.	jussive noun
(16)	facerem	impf. subj.	jussive noun
(18)	fīātis	pres. subj.	jussive noun
(22)	lēgibus	abl.	spec. dep. vbs.
(23)	lēgibus	dat.	spec. vbs.
(24)	futūram esse	fut. inf.	ind. state.
(25)	hortēmur	pres. subj.	jussive

KEY FOR CHAPTER 37

1. (1) Present indicative and present subjunctive.
   (2) It is **ī-.**
2. Nom. sg. = **iēns;** nom. pl. = **euntēs.**
3. In writing the synopsis of a verb one should follow the sequence of tenses in the indicative and the subjunctive as given above in #2 of the Key of Chapter 34. If this is done there is no need to label the tenses.
   Eō 2nd sg.: Indicative—īs, ībās, ībis, īstī, ierās, ieris.
   Subjunctive—eās, īrēs, ierīs, īssēs.
   Eō 3d pl.: Indicative—eunt, ībant, ībunt, iērunt, ierant, ierint.
   Subjunctive—eant, īrent, ierint, īssent.
4. (1) we went   (3) impf. subj., 1 pl.
   (2) we are going   (4) we shall go

(5) plupf. subj., 1 pl.

(6) pres. subj., 1 pl.

(7) to be about to go

(8) going (acc. sg.)

(9) they went

(10) they are going

(11) pres. subj., 3 pl.

(12) they will go

(13) I went

(14) he was going

(15) they had gone

(16) perf. subj., 1 sg.

(17) impf. subj., 3 sg.

(18) to have gone

(19) going (nom./acc. pl.)

(20) I shall go

(21) he went

(22) we were going

(23) plupf. subj., 3 sg.

(24) pres. subj., 3 sg.

5. (1) **ab, dē, ex** + abl.; ab (ex) eā terrā.

(2) **in** + abl.: in eā terrā; in eā īnsulā.

(3) **in** or **ad** + acc.: in (ad) eam terram.

6. (1) Place from which = abl. without a preposition.

(2) Place where = locative without a preposition.

(3) Place to which = accusative without a preposition.

7. The locative is the case which expresses the idea of "place where" when **domus** or the name of a city is used. See p. 262.

8. (1) Time when = abl. without a prep.: eōdem diē.

(2) Time how long = acc. usually without a prep.: multōs diēs.

(3) Time within which = abl. without a prep.: ūnō diē.

9. Since an impersonal verb lacks the 1st and the 2nd persons sg. and pl., the 1st and the 3rd principal parts are given in the 3rd pers. sg. See p. 264, Vocabulary, s.v. **licet** and n. 1. **Licet tibi īre.**

10. (1) (for) one day

(2) in one day

(3) on that day

(4) from Rome

(5) at Rome

(6) to Rome

(7) in a few days

(8) on the same night

(9) (for) many days

(10) into the ship

(11) in the ship

(12) out of the ship

(13) home (= to home)

(14) at/from Athens

(15) at home

(16) to Athens

(17) from home

(18) (for) a few hours

11. In a few hours we shall go to Rome. 12. We are going to the city; they are going home. 13. As we have often admitted, you may not (are not permitted to) go from Rome to Athens (*lit.,* to go is not permitted to you). 14. Why did you leave home (go away from home) so quickly? 15. They are coming to Rome in order to go to Athens with my brother. 16. Do not go away from Rome. 17. When your brother had been killed at Rome, we kept urging you to return to Athens. 18. If he should go into the territory of the enemy at this time, he would perish in a few hours. 19. He said that he did not want to stay in that country of yours many days. 20. You said that you would return home from Athens in one hour. 21. I beg of you to return from the ship to the island in a short time. 22. In those days we were accustomed to be at Athens. 23. If they had injured his friends at Rome, he would have returned to Rome in a very short time. 24. Although my brother stayed at home, I nevertheless went away from home into new lands. 25. The Romans, if they wanted to say something bad, often used to say: "Go to the devil." 26. He is persuading them to study Latin.

27. (11) **hōrīs** = abl.: time within which; **Rōmam** = acc.: place to which; (12) **domum** = acc.: place to which; (13) **Rōmā** = abl.: place from; **Athēnās** = acc.: place to; **īre** = pres. inf.: subject of **licet;** (14) **domō** = abl.: place from; (15) **Rōmam** = acc.: place to; (18) **frātre** = abl.: abl. abs.; (18) **tempore** = abl.: time when; **eat** = pres. subj.: fut. less vivid; **hōrīs** = abl.: time within; (19) **velle** = pres. inf.: ind. state.; **diēs** = acc.: time how long; (20) **domum** = acc.: place to; **Athēnīs** = abl.: place from; **hōrā** = abl.: time within; **reditūrum esse** = fut. inf.: ind. state.; (21) **tempore** = abl. time within; **redeās** = pres. subj.: jussive noun clause; (22) **diēbus** = abl.: time when; **Athēnīs** = locative: place where; (23) **amīcīs** = dat.: spec. verbs; **Rōmae** = locative: place where; **redīsset** = plupf. subj.: past contr. to fact condit.; (24) **domī** = locative: place where; **terrās** = acc.: place to; **domō** = abl.: place from; (26) **studeant** = pres. subj.: jussive noun clause.

KEY FOR CHAPTER 38

1. A relative clause with the indicative tells a *fact* about the antecedent.
2. A relative clause with the subjunctive tells a *characteristic* of the antecedent, indicates it to be a person or thing of such a sort. See p. 269.
3. See p. 270.
4. See p. 270–71.

5. My friend who defended the consul was himself a very famous man.   6. But there was no one who would defend that base fellow.   7. What is there which men fear more than a tyrant?   8. Who is there who would hesitate between liberty and the command of a tyrant?   9. At ancient Rome there were those who loved money more than the state.   10. Let that evil man depart from his country—he who has endured the hatred of all good citizens.   11. Catiline, who had made such a great plot against the state, was driven from the city by Cicero.   12. What life can be pleasant for that leader as he goes off into exile?   13. Who is there who would be able to bear such pain?   14. If a person is not agreeable and good, he will not live a truly happy life, it seems to me.   15. They will not trust a consul who would do base deeds.   16. Do not trust a man who is harsh to his friends.   17. Cicero was a consul who would place the state before his own safety.   18. They knew why we wanted to follow such a brave consul.   19. I know nothing which could be easier for me.   20. I am seeking a leader whom all men would praise.   21. They were going to Rome to ask for freedom.   22. The Romans, who had captured ten Greek republics with their own armies, were themselves—amazing to say—taken captive by the Greek arts!   23. For the ancient men there was nothing which was better than courage and wisdom.
24. Nothing is to be feared which cannot injure the soul.

25. The **quī ... dēfendit** states a fact about the **amīcus;** it does not describe his character. The subjunctive clause in #6 tells what kind of person the imagined **nēmō** might be.
26. Syntax: (7) **metuat** = pres. subj.: characteristic; (8) **dubitet** = pres. subj.: characteristic; (9) **Rōmae** = loc.: place where; **amārent** = impf. subj.: characteristic; (10) **abeat** = pres. subj.: jussive; **passus est** = perf. indic. rel. cl. of fact; (11) **fēcerat** = plupf. ind.: rel. cl. of fact; (12) **ducī** = dat.: reference; **potest** = pres. ind.: main verb in a direct question; (13) **possit** = pres. subj.: characteristic; (14) **erit** = fut. indic.: simple fut. condit.; **mihi** = dat.: ref.; (15) **cōnsulī** = dat.: spec. vbs.;

(16) **amīcīs** = dat.: dat. w. adjs.; (17) **salūtī** = dat.: compound vb.; **antepōneret** = impf. subj.: characteristic; (18) **vellēmus** = impf. subj.: ind. quest.; (19) **mihi** = dat.: ref.; **possit** = pres. subj.: characteristic; (21) **rogātum** = acc. supine: purpose; (22) **cēperant** = plupf. ind.: rel. cl. of fact; **dictū** = abl. supine: respect; (23) **virīs** = dat.: ref.; (24) **animō** = dat.: spec. vbs.; **possit** = pres. subj.: characteristic.

KEY FOR CHAPTER 39

1. (1) See p. 276 s.v. "The Gerund."
   (2) See p. 276.
   (3) See p. 276–77.
   (4) In its four cases it is used as a noun is used. See p. 277.
   (5) The infinitive; see p. 277.
2. (1) See p. 276 s.v. "The Gerundive."
   (2) The gerund*ive* is an adject*ive.*
   (3) As an adjective it modifies a noun or pronoun and agrees with that noun or pronoun in gender, number, and case.
   (4) The gerundive (e.g., **laudandus, -a, -um**) is declined as **magnus, -a, -um** is. See p. 276.
   (5) Since the gerund has only the endings **-ī, -ō, -um, -ō,** any feminine or any plural ending on an **-nd-** base is bound to indicate a gerundive; and also, if an **-nd-** form agrees with a noun as an adjectival modifier, it must be a gerundive.
3. (1) The Latin gerund is normally translated by the English gerund in *-ing* with any attending noun constructions or adverbial modifiers.
   (2) The gerundive is to be translated by the English as if it were a gerund with an object and any adverbial modifiers. In other words, both the gerund and the gerundive are to be translated in the same way. See p. 277–78.
   (3) (A) We learn by reading with care.
       (B) We learn by reading books with care.

4. We learn by experiencing. 5. They came to learn (for learning). 6. He gave (devoted) himself to learning. 7. They came to your school to learn (for the sake of learning). 8. The boy went to the school desirous of learning (eager to learn). 9. The fear of dying kept terrifying him. 10. The hope of living after death encourages many people. 11. By thinking (= by using his head) he overcame them.

12. He devoted (gave) himself—(1) to seeking glory. (2) to waging war. (3) to making money. (4) to getting power. (5) to destroying states. (6) to following this leader. (7) to saving his country. (8) to seeking peace. (9) to attacking wrongs. (10) to writing books. (11) to reading books. (12) to learning philosophy. (13) to learning Latin literature. (14) to understanding the truth. (15) to seeking wisdom. (16) to helping human beings.
13. He came to Rome—(1) to undertake this work. (2) to see the Roman games. (3) to see the old buildings. (4) to seek peace. (5) for the sake of undertaking this work (to undertake . . .). (6) for the sake of learning philosophy (to learn . . .). (7) for the sake of reading new books (to read . . .). (8) to see the games.
14. He wrote a book—(1) about enduring pain. (2) about overcoming fear. (3) about

living a good life. (4) about managing the state. (5) about waging war. (6) about defending liberty. (7) about conquering the enemy. (8) about giving gifts.

15. We become wiser—(1) by reading Latin literature. (2) by learning philosophy. (3) by experiencing life. (4) by conquering fear. (5) by following truth.

16. We help our very selves—(1) by always reading good books. (2) by freeing unfortunate men from fear. (3) by offering aid. (4) by helping others.

17. He consumed much time—(1) in thinking (speaking, running). (2) in doing these tasks. (3) in finding the way. (4) in preparing an army. (5) in preparing supplies (troops).

18. He had time for writing this book only.

KEY FOR CHAPTER 40

1. See p. 284–85.
2. Positive fear clauses are introduced by **nē**; negative clauses by **ut.**
3. The noun must itself be modified by an adjective.

4. I greatly fear that the general may not send us enough help.   5. She was a woman of the greatest courage and loyalty and in fact very like her mother.   6. Do not fear that all the men and women of great courage will depart from Rome.   7. This is, indeed, easy to say but difficult to do!   8. They came home to please their parents. 9. You do wish to hear something good, don't you?   10. Do you wish to have much wisdom? Study Latin!   11. He ordered the three soldiers to go to Rome to seek peace.   12. You do not hesitate to say this, do you, my friend?   13. You urge me to be of great courage and to have hope of safety, but I fear that I may be too weak. 14. For my part I place wealth ahead of wisdom. For I do not think that human beings can find a happy life without a great deal of money.   15. However, very many rich men experience much fear.   16. Poor men are often happier and have less fear. 17. Money itself is not bad; but the things of the mind and the soul offer more help for living happily.   18. Nine of the leaders urged us to supply more aid.   19. When five of the guards had been killed, my father fled into that free land with two of his sons and with a large number of friends.   20. Never will he have enough leisure; yet some leisure is better than nothing.   21. In our times we all have too much of fear and too little of hope.   22. Great faith and courage must be found by all men.

Appendix

SOME ETYMOLOGICAL AIDS

TWO RULES OF PHONETIC CHANGE

"Phonetic" derives from Greek **phōnḗ,** *sound, voice, speech* (cp. phonograph, phonology, symphony, telephone). Consequently, phonetic change means a change which occurs in original speech sounds for one reason or another. Of the many instances of this in Latin, the following two rules of phonetic change are probably the most important ones for the beginner.

A. *Vowel weakening* usually occurs in the medial syllables of compounds according to the following outline.

    1. ă > ĭ before a single consonant and before **ng.**
       ă > ĕ before two consonants.

căpiō, căptum: ac-cĭpiō, ac-cĕptum
făciō, făctum: per-fĭciō, per-fĕctum
făcilis: dif-fĭcilis
cădō, căsum: oc-cĭdō, oc-cāsum (Note that long **ā** does not change.)
tăngō, tăctum: con-tĭngō, con-tăctum

2. **ĕ > ĭ** before a single consonant.
tĕneō: con-tĭneō (*but* contentum)
prĕmō: com-prĭmō (*but* compressum)

3. **ae > ī.**
quaerō, quaesītum: re-quīrō, re-quīsītum
laedō, laesum: col-līdō, col-līsum
caedō, caesum: in-cīdō, in-cīsum; oc-cīdō, oc-cīsum
aestimō: ex-īstimō

4. **au > ū.**
claudō: in-clūdō, ex-clūdō
causor: ex-cūsō

B. *Assimilation* of the final consonant of a prefix to the initial consonant of the base word commonly occurs.

ad-capiō > ac-cipiō   in-mortālis > im-mortālis
dis-facilis > dif-ficilis   in-ruō > ir-ruō

PREFIXES

Listed here are important prefixes helpful in the analysis of both Latin words and English derivatives. The Latin prefixes have passed over into English unchanged except where indicated. Incidentally, most Latin prefixes were also used by the Romans as prepositions; but the few labeled "inseparable" appear only as prefixes.

ā-, ab-, *away, from.*
ā-vocō, *call away* (avocation)
ā-vertō, *turn away* (avert)
ā-mittō, *send away, let go, lose*
ab-sum, *be away* (absent)
ab-eō, *go away*
ab-dūcō, *lead away* (abduct)

ad- (by assimilation **ac-, af-, ag-, al-, an-, ap-, ar-, as-, at-**), *to, towards, in addition.*
ad-vocō, *call to, call* (advocate)
ad-dūcō, *lead to* (adduce)
ad-mittō, *send to, admit*
ac-cēdō, *go to, approach* (accede)
ac-cipiō (ad-capiō), *get, accept*
ap-pōnō, *put to* (apposition)
as-sentiō, *feel towards, agree to, assent*

ante-, *before.*
ante-pōnō, *put before, prefer*
ante-cēdō, *go before, precede, excel* (antecedent)

circum-, *around.*

> **circum-dūcō,** *lead around*
> **circum-veniō,** *come around, surround* (circumvent)
> **circum-stō,** *stand around* (circumstance)

com- (**com** = **cum;** also appears as **con-, cor-, col-, co-**), *with, together;* intensive force: *completely, very, greatly, deeply, forcibly.*

> **con-vocō,** *call together* (convoke)
> **con-dūcō,** *lead together* (conduct)
> **com-pōnō,** *put together, compose* (component)
> **com-mittō,** *send together, bring together, entrust* (commit)
> **cōn-sentiō,** *feel together, agree* (consent)
> **cō-gō** (**co-agō**), *drive together, force* (cogent)
> **com-pleō,** *fill completely, fill up* (complete)
> **cōn-servō,** *save completely, preserve* (conserve)
> **con-cēdō,** *go completely, go away, yield, grant* (concede)
> **con-tendō,** *stretch greatly, strive, hurry* (contend)
> **col-laudō,** *praise greatly* or *highly*
> **cor-rōborō,** *strengthen greatly* (corroborate)

contrā-, *against, opposite.* (Not common as a prefix in Latin but fairly common in English, especially in the form *counter-.*)

> **contrā-dīcō,** *speak against* or *opposite, oppose, rely* (contradict)
> **contrā-veniō** (late Latin), *come against, oppose* (contravene)

dē-, *down, away, aside, out, off;* intensive force: *utterly, completely.*

> **dē-dūcō,** *lead down* or *away, drawn down* (deduce, deduct)
> **dē-pōnō,** *put aside, lay aside, entrust* (deponent, deposit)
> **dē-mittō,** *send down, throw down, let fall* (demit)
> **dē-veniō,** *come from, arrive at, reach*
> **dē-vocō,** *call away* or *off*
> **dē-cēdō,** *go away* (decease)
> **dē-mēns,** *out of one's mind, demented*
> **dē-certō,** *fight it out, fight to the finish*

dis- (**dif-, dī-;** inseparable), *apart, away, not.*

> **dis-pōnō,** *put apart in different places, arrange* (disposition)
> **dis-cēdō,** *go away, depart*
> **dī-mittō,** *send away in different directions, let go* (dismiss)
> **dif-ferō, dī-lātus,** *bear apart, scatter, put off, differ* (different, dilate)
> **dis-similis,** *not similar, unlike, dissimilar*
> **dif-ficilis,** *not easy, difficult*

ē-, ex- (**ef-**), *from out, forth;* intensive force: *exceedingly, up.*

> **ē-dūcō,** *lead out* (educe)
> **ex-cēdō,** *go out, from, away; go beyond* (exceed)
> **ē-mittō,** *send out, forth* (emit)
> **ē-vocō,** *call out, forth* (evoke)
> **ex-pōnō,** *put out, set forth, explain* (exponent, exposition)
> **ē-veniō,** *come out, forth; turn out, happen* (event)

ef-ficiō, (ex-faciō), *produce, accomplish, perform* (efficient, effect)

ex-pleō, *fill up, complete*

ex-asperō, *roughen exceedingly, irritate* (exasperate)

in- (im-, il-, ir-; sometimes *en-* or *em-* in Eng.), *in, into, on, upon, against.* (Also see in- below.)

    in-vocō, *call in, call upon* (invoke)

    in-dūcō, *lead in* or *into, introduce, impel* (induce)

    im-mittō, *send into, send against, let loose against*

    im-pōnō, *put in, lay upon* (impose)

    in-veniō, *come upon, find* (invent)

    in-clūdō, *shut in, shut* (include, enclose)

    in-vādō, *go into, move against* (invade)

    ir-ruō, *rush into* or *upon*

    il-līdō (in-laedō), *strike* or *dash against*

    in-genium (in + gen-, from gignō, *beget, give birth to*), *inborn nature, natural capacity, talent, character* (engine, ingenious)

in- (im-, il-, ir-; inseparable prefix; cognate with Eng. *un-*), *not, un-.*

    in-certus, *not certain, uncertain*

    in-iūstus, *not just, unjust* (*cp.* injustice)

    īn-fīnītus, *not limited, unlimited* (infinite)

    īn-firmus, *not firm, weak* (infirm)

    im-mortālis, *not mortal, deathless* (immortal)

    il-litterātus, *unlearned, ignorant* (illiterate)

    ir-revocābilis, *not-call-back-able, unalterable* (irrevocable)

inter-, *between, among.*

    inter-veniō, *come between; interrupt* (intervene)

    inter-cēdō, *go between* (intercede)

    inter-mittō, *place between, leave off* (intermittent)

    inter-pōnō, *put between, bring forward* (interpose)

    inter-rēgnum, *period between two reigns* (interregnum)

intrō-, *within, in.* (Also used as adv.)

    intrō-dūcō, *lead in* (introduce)

    intrō-mittō, *send in*

    intrō-spiciō, *look within* (introspect)

ob- (oc-, of-, op-), *towards, to, opposite, against, over.*

    ob-dūcō, *lead toward* or *against*

    ob-veniō, *come opposite, meet*

    oc-currō, *run to meet, meet* (occur)

    of-ferō, *bear towards, furnish* (offer)

    op-pōnō, *put opposite, set against, oppose* (opposition)

per- (pel-), *through;* intensive force: *thoroughly, very, completely.*

    per-dūcō, *lead through* or *along*

    per-veniō, *come through to, arrive at, reach*

    per-ferō, *carry through, bear thoroughly, endure*

    per-mittō, *let go through, entrust, allow* (permit)

per-ficiō (-faciō), *do thoroughly, accomplish, finish* (perfect)
per-facilis, *very easy*
per-paucus, *very small*
pel-lūcidus, *shining through, transparent*

post-, *after.*

post-pōnō, *put after, esteem less, disregard* (postpone)
post-ferō, *put after, esteem less, disregard* (postpone)
post-scrībō, *write after, add* (postscript)

prae-, *before, in front, forth;* intensive force: *very.* (In Eng. also spelled *pre-*.)

prae-moneō, *warn before, forewarn* (premonition)
prae-cēdō, *go before, excel* (precede)
prae-pōnō, *put before, place in command of, prefer* (preposition)
prae-mittō, *send before* or *forth, set before* (premise)
prae-scrībō, *write before, order* (prescribe, prescription)
prae-ferō, *bear before, set before, prefer*
prae-clārus, *very noble, very famous, excellent*

prō-, *before, in front, forth, out, away, instead of, for.* (Sometimes *pur-* in Eng.)

prō-vocō, *call forth* or *out, challenge, excite* (provoke)
prō-videō, *see ahead, foresee, care for* (provide, provision, purvey)
prō-dūcō, *lead before* or *out, bring forth, prolong* (produce)
prō-cēdō, *go forward, advance* (proceed)
prō-pōnō, *put in front, set forth, declare* (proponent, purpose)
prō-mittō, *send forth, assure* (promise)
prō-cōnsul, *one who served in place of a consul* (proconsul)

re- (red-; inseparable), *back again.*

re-vocō, *call back, recall* (revoke)
re-dūcō, *lead back* (reduce)
re-cēdō, *go back, retire* (recede)
re-pōnō, *put back, replace, restore* (repository)
re-mittō, *send back, give up* (remit)
red-dō, *give back, restore, return*
red-eō, *go back, return*

sē- (inseparable), *apart, aside, without.*

sē-dūcō, *lead aside, separate* (seduce)
sē-cēdō, *go apart, withdraw, retire* (secede)
sē-pōnō, *put aside, select*
sē-moveō, *move aside, separate*
sē-cūrus, *without care, untroubled, serene* (secure)

sub- (suc-, suf-, sug-, sup-, sur-, sus-), *under, up (from beneath); rather, somewhat, a little, secretly.*

sub-dūcō, *draw from under, withdraw secretly*
suc-cēdō, *go under, go up, approach, prosper* (succeed)
sup-pōnō, *put under, substitute* (supposition, supposititious)
sub-veniō, *come under, help* (subvene, subvention)
sus-tineō (-teneō), *hold up, support, endure* (sustain)

super- (also *sur-* in Eng.), *over, above.*

> **super-pōnō,** *place over* or *upon, set over* (superposition)
>
> **super-sedeō,** *sit above* or *upon, be superior to, be above, refrain from, desist* (supersede)
>
> **super-sum,** *be over and above, be left, survive*
>
> **superō,** *be above, surpass, conquer* (insuperable)
>
> **superbus,** *above others, haughty, proud* (superb)
>
> **super-vīvō,** *survive*
>
> **super-ficiēs,** *surface*

trāns- (trā-), *across, over.*

> **trāns-mittō,** *send across, cross over* (transmit)
>
> **trā-dūcō,** *lead across* (traduce)
>
> **trāns-eō,** *go across* (transition)
>
> **trā-dō,** *give over, surrender, hand down* (tradition)

SUFFIXES

Of the very numerous Latin suffixes only a few of the more important ones are listed here with their English equivalents.

1. Suffix denoting the *agent,* the *doer,* the *one who* (**-tor** or **-sor,** m.; **-trīx,** f.).

-tor *or* **-sor** (cp. *Eng.* -er)

> **victor (vincō, victum,** *conquer*), *conqueror, victor*
>
> **scrīptor (scrībō, scrīptum,** *write*), *writer*
>
> **lēctor, lēctrīx (legō, lēctum,** *read*), *reader*
>
> **ōrātor (ōrō, ōrātum,** [*speak*], *plead*), *speaker, orator*
>
> **repertor, repertrīx (reperiō, repertum,** *discover*), *discoverer*
>
> **auctor (augeō, auctum,** *increase*), *increaser, author*
>
> **līberātor (līberō, līberātum,** *free*), *liberator*
>
> **tōnsor (tondeō, tōnsum,** *shave, clip*), *barber*
>
> **amātor (amō, amātum,** *love*), *lover*

These nouns have the same base as that of the perfect participle.

2. Suffixes denoting *action* or *result of action* (**-or, -ium, -tiō**).

-or (Eng. *-or*)

> **amor (amō,** *love*), *love, amour*
>
> **timor (timeō,** *fear*), *fear*
>
> **dolor (doleō,** *suffer pain*), *pain, suffering, grief*
>
> **error (errō,** *go astray, err*), *error*
>
> **terror (terreō,** *frighten, terrify*), *fright, terror*

-ium (Eng. *-y; -ce* when **-ium** is preceded by **c** or **t**)

> **studium (studeō,** *be eager*), *eagerness, study*
>
> **colloquium (colloquor,** *talk with*), *talk, conference, colloquy*
>
> **imperium (imperō,** *command*), *command, power*
>
> **odium (ōdī,** *hate*), *hate*
>
> **aedificium (aedificō,** *build*) *building, edifice*
>
> **silentium (silēns, silentis,** *silent*), *silence*

-tiō, -tiōnis, *or* **-siō, -siōnis** (Eng. *-tion* or *-sion*)

    admonitiō (admoneō, admonitum, *admonish*) *admonition*

    ratiō (reor, ratum, *reckon, think*), *reckoning, plan, reason* (*ration*)

    ōrātiō (ōrō, ōrātum, [*speak*], *plead*), *oration*

    nātiō (nāscor, nātum, *be born*), *birth, nation*

    occāsiō (occidō, occāsum, *fall down*) *a befalling, occasion, opportunity*

3. Suffixes denoting *quality, state,* or *condition* (**-ia, -tia, -tās, -tūdō**).

-ia (Eng. *-y*)

    miseria (miser, *miserable*), *misery*

    īnsānia (īnsānus, *insane*), *insanity*

    victōria (victor, *victor*), *victory*

    invidia (invidus, *envious*), *envy*

    iniūria (iniūrus, *wrong, unjust*), *injustice, injury*

-tia (Eng. *-ce*)

    amīcitia (amīcus, *friendly*), *friendship*

    sapientia (sapiēns, *wise*), *wisdom, sapience*

    scientia (sciēns, *knowing*), *knowledge, science*

    iūstitia (iūstus, *just*), *justice*

    dīligentia (dīligēns, *diligent*), *diligence*

-tās, -tātis (Eng. *-ty*)

    lībertās (liber, *free*), *freedom, liberty*

    vēritās (vērus, *true*), *truth, verity*

    paupertās (pauper, *poor*), *poverty*

    cupiditās (cupidus, *desirous, greedy*), *greed, cupidity*

    gravitās (gravis, *heavy, grave*), *weight, seriousness, gravity*

    celeritās (celer, *swift*), *swiftness, celerity*

-tūdō, -tūdinis (Eng. *-tude*)

    multitūdō (multus, *much, many*), *multitude*

    magnitūdō (magnus, *large, great*), *magnitude*

    pulchritūdō (pulcher, *beautiful*), *beauty, pulchritude*

    sōlitūdō (sōlus, *alone*), *solitude*

    sollicitūdō (sollicitus, *agitated, solicitous*), *solicitude*

4. Adjectival suffix meaning *full of* (**-ōsus**).

-ōsus, -ōsa, -ōsum (Eng. *-ous* or *-ose*)

    studiōsus (studium, *zeal*), *full of zeal, eager* (*studious*)

    imperiōsus (imperium, *command*), *full of command, imperious*

    perīculōsus (perīculum, *danger*), *full of danger, dangerous*

    vitiōsus (vitium, *fault, vice*), *faulty, vicious*

    verbōsus (verbum, *word*), *wordy, verbose*

5. Adjectival suffix meaning *able to be, worthy to be;* sometimes *able to* (**-bilis**).

-bilis, -bile (Eng. *-able, -ible, -ble*)

    laudābilis (laudō, *praise*), *worthy to be praised, laudable*

    amābilis (amō, *love*), *worthy to be loved, lovable, amiable*

      incrēdibilis (**crēdō,** *believe*), *not worthy to be believed, incredible*
      mōbilis (**moveō,** *move*), *able to be moved, movable, mobile*
      inexpugnābilis (**expugnō,** *conquer*), *unconquerable*
      stabilis (**stō,** *stand*), *able to stand, stable*

6. Adjectival suffixes denoting *pertaining to* (**-ālis** or **-āris, -ānus, -icus**).

-ālis, -āle, *or* **-āris, -āre** (Eng. *-al* or *-ar*)

      mortālis (**mors,** *death*), *pertaining to death, mortal*
      vītālis (**vīta,** *life*), *pertaining to life, vital*
      fātālis (**fātum,** *fate*), *fatal*
      populāris (**populus,** *people*), *popular*
      vulgāris (**vulgus,** *the common people*), *common, vulgar*

-ānus, -āna, -ānum (Eng. *-an* or *-ane*)

      Rōmānus (**Rōma,** *Rome*), *pertaining to Rome, Roman*
      hūmānus (**homō,** *man*), *pertaining to man, human, humane*
      urbānus (**urbs,** *city*), *urban, urbane*
      mundānus (**mundus,** *world*), *worldly, mundane*

-icus, -ica, -icum (Eng. *-ic*)

      domesticus (**domus,** *house*), *pertaining to the house, domestic*
      pūblicus (**populus,** *people*), *pertaining to the people, public*
      rūsticus (**rūs,** *country*), *rustic*
      cīvicus (**cīvis,** *citizen*), *civic*
      classicus (**classis,** *class*), *pertaining to the classes, of the highest class; classic*

SUPPLEMENTARY SYNTAX

The following constructions are listed for the benefit of students who plan to continue their study of Latin beyond the introductory year. A number of these constructions have already been encountered here and there in the 40 formal chapters of this book. However, although often these can be easily translated without benefit of syntactical labels, it seems wise to catalog them here along with the more difficult items.

GENITIVE OF MATERIAL

The genitive may indicate the material of which a thing is made.

      pōculum **aurī,** *a goblet of gold*
      Numerus **hostium** crēscit, *the number of the enemy is increasing.*
      Mōns **aquae** secūtus est et tempestās trēs nāvēs cīnxit aggere **harēnae,** *a mountain of water followed and the storm surrounded three ships with a mound of sand.*

OBJECTIVE GENITIVE

The objective genitive depends on a noun of verbal meaning and is used as the object of the verbal idea. It is sometimes translated by *for.*

amor **laudis,** *love of praise* (= amat laudem, *he loves praise.*)
cupiditās **pecūniae,** *greed for money* (= cupit pecūniam, *he longs for money.*)
metus **mortis,** *fear of death* (= metuit mortem, *he fears death.*)
spēs **salūtis,** *hope for safety* (= spērat salūtem, *he hopes for safety.*)
Fēmina erat dux **factī,** *a woman was the leader of the enterprise* (= dūxit factum.)
laudātor **temporis** āctī, *a praiser of the past* (= laudat tempus āctum.)

DATIVE OF PURPOSE

The dative may express the purpose for which a person or thing serves. A dative of reference (Ch. 38) often appears in conjunction with the dative of purpose, and this combination is called the "double dative" construction.

Petītiō mea **tibi** (dat. of ref.) summae **cūrae** (dat. of purp.) est, *my candidacy is (for) the greatest concern to you.*
Ea rēs **mihi** (ref.) summae **voluptātī** (purp.) erat, *that matter was for the greatest pleasure to me = gave me the greatest pleasure.*
Illī **nōbīs** (ref.) **auxiliō** (purp.) vēnērunt, *they came as an aid to us.*
Hōs librōs **dōnō** (purp.) mīsit, *he sent these books as a gift.*
Hoc mē iuvat et **mihi** (ref.) **mellī** (purp.) est, *this gratifies me and is (as) honey to me.*
Optant locum **tēctō** (purp.), *they desire a place for a roof (building).*

DATIVE OF POSSESSION

The dative can be used with **sum** to express the idea of possession.

Liber est **mihi,** *a book is to me = I have a book.*
   (Contrast: liber est **meus,** *the book is mine.*)
Illī maior turba clientium est, *that man has a greater throng of retainers.*
Sunt **tibi** animus et mōrēs, *you have a soul and character.*
Haec **eīs** semper erunt, *they will always have these things.*
Prūdentia est illī **puellae,** *that girl has prudence.*
Ō virgō, nōn **tibi** est vultus mortālis, *O maiden, you do not have the face of a mortal.*
Sī umquam **mihi** fīlius erit . . . , *if I ever have a son. . . .*

ABLATIVE OF SPECIFICATION

The ablative may be used to tell in what specific respect a verb or an adjective holds true.

Hī omnēs **linguā, īnstitūtīs, lēgibus** inter sē differunt, *these all differ from one another in language, customs, and laws.*
Illī **virtūte** omnibus (dat.) praestābant, *those men used to excel all in courage.*
Id genus erat intractābile **bellō,** *that race was unmanageable in war.*
Quis est praestantior aut **nōbilitāte** aut **probitāte** aut **studiō** optimārum artium? *Who is more outstanding in nobility or integrity or the pursuit of the finest arts?*
Ager bene cultus est ūber **ūsū** et ōrnātus **speciē,** *a field well cultivated is rich in usefulness and beautiful in appearance.*

Asia omnibus terrīs (dat.) antecellit **ūbertāte** agrōrum et **varietāte** frūctuum et **multitūdine** eārum quae exportantur, *Asia excels all lands in richness of fields and variety of fruits and large number of those things which are exported.*

ABLATIVE OF CAUSE

The ablative can be used to indicate a cause or reason.

Miser **timōre** dēlīrat, *the wretched man is insane with fear.*
Corpora eōrum **metū** dēbilia sunt, *their bodies are weak from fear.*
Aper **dentibus** timētur, *the boar is feared because of his teeth.*
Nihil arduum mortālibus est; caelum ipsum **stultitiā** petimus, *nothing is (too) arduous for mortals; we seek the sky itself in our folly.*
Odiō tyrannī in exsilium fūgit, *because of his hatred of the tyrant he fled into exile.*
Bonī **amōre** virtūtis peccāre ōdērunt, *good men because of their love of virtue hate to sin.*

ABLATIVE OF DEGREE OF DIFFERENCE

With comparatives and adverbs suggesting comparison the ablative can be used to indicate the degree of difference in the comparison.

Tantō melius, *the better by so much = so much the better.*
Senex nōn facit ea quae iuvenis, at **multō** maiōra et meliōra facit, *an old man does not do the things which a young man does, but he does much greater and better things (greater by much).*
Multō ācrius iam vigilābō, *I shall now watch much more keenly.*
Rōmam **paucīs** post **diēbus** vēnistī, *you came to Rome a few days afterwards (afterwards by a few days).*
Aberat ab eā urbe **tribus mīlibus** passuum, *he was three miles from that city (was away by three miles).*
Bonae Athēnae **paulō** plūs artis adiēcērunt, *good Athens added a little more skill (more by a little).*

SUBORDINATE CLAUSES IN INDIRECT DISCOURSE

In indirect discourse, subordinate clauses regularly have verbs in the subjunctive mood, even though they had the indicative in the direct form.

Lēgit librōs quōs mīserās, *he read the books which you had sent.*
Dīxit sē lēgisse librōs quōs **mīsissēs,** *he said that he had read the books which you had sent.*

Eī malī quī in urbe manent īnfīrmī erunt sine duce, *those evil men who remain in the city will be weak without their leader.*
Putō eōs malōs quī in urbe **maneant** īnfīrmōs futūrōs esse sine duce, *I think that those evil men who remain in the city will be weak without their leader.*

Sī id crēdet, errābit. *If he believes this, he will be wrong.*
Dīcō sī id **crēdat** eum errātūrum esse. *I say that if he believes this he will be wrong.*

OBJECTIVE INFINITIVE

The complementary infinitive has no subject accusative (see Ch. 6). However, when an infinitive with subject accusative is used as the object of a verb, it is called an objective infinitive.

Volunt venīre, *they wish to come.* (compl. inf.)

Iussit eōs venīre, *he ordered them to come.* (obj. inf.)

Nōn possum loquī, *I cannot speak.* (compl. inf.)

Nōn patitur mē loquī, *he does not permit me to speak.* (obj. inf.)

Nōn audet īre, *he does not dare to go.* (compl. inf.)

Coēgērunt eum īre, *they forced him to go.* (obj. inf.)

SUMMARY OF FORMS

NOUNS—DECLENSIONS

First	Second				Third	
porta, -ae	amīcus, -ī	puer, -ī	ager, -grī	dōnum, -ī	rēx, rēgis	corpus, -oris
f., *gate*	m., *friend*	m., *boy*	m., *field*	n., *gift*	m., *king*	n., *body*
Sg.						
N. port-a	amīc-us[1]	puer	ager	dōn-um	rēx	corpus
G. port-ae	amīc-ī	puer-ī	agr-ī	dōn-ī	rēg-is	corpor-is
D. port-ae	amīc-ō	puer-ō	agr-ō	dōn-ō	rēg-ī	corpor-ī
A. port-am	amīc-um	puer-um	agr-um	dōn-um	rēg-em	corpus
Ab. port-ā	amīc-ō	puer-ō	agr-ō	dōn-ō	rēg-e	corpor-e
Pl.						
N. port-ae	amīc-ī	puer-ī	agr-ī	dōn-a	rēg-ēs	corpor-a
G. port-ārum	amīc-ōrum	puer-ōrum	agr-ōrum	dōn-ōrum	rēg-um	corpor-um
D. port-īs	amīc-īs	puer-īs	agr-īs	dōn-īs	rēg-ibus	corpor-ibus
A. port-ās	amīc-ōs	puer-ōs	agr-ōs	dōn-a	rēg-ēs	corpor-a
Ab. port-īs	amīc-īs	puer-īs	agr-īs	dōn-īs	rēg-ibus	corpor-ibus

Third (I-Stems)			Fourth		Fifth
cīvis, -is	urbs, -is	mare, -is	frūctus, -ūs	cornū,-ūs	diēs, -ēī
m., *citizen*	f., *city*	n., *sea*	m., *fruit*	n., *horn*	m., *day*
Sg.					
N. cīv-is	urb-s	mar-e	frūct-us	corn-ū	di-ēs
G. cīv-is	urb-is	mar-is	frūct-ūs	corn-ūs	di-ēī
D. cīv-ī	urb-ī	mar-ī	frūct-uī	corn-ū	di-ēī
A. cīv-em	urb-em	mar-e	frūct-um	corn-ū	di-em
Ab. cīv-e	urb-e	mar-ī	frūct-ū	corn-ū	di-ē
Pl.					
N. cīv-ēs	urb-ēs	mar-ia	frūct-ūs	corn-ua	di-ēs
G. cīv-ium	urb-ium	mar-ium	frūct-uum	corn-uum	di-ērum
D. cīv-ibus	urb-ibus	mar-ibus	frūct-ibus	corn-ibus	di-ēbus
A. cīv-ēs	urb-ēs	mar-ia	frūct-ūs	corn-ua	di-ēs
Ab. cīv-ibus	urb-ibus	mar-ibus	frūct-ibus	corn-ibus	di-ēbus

Vīs is irregular: Sg., N., vīs, G. (vīs), D. (vī), A. vim. Ab. vī; Pl., N. vīrēs, G. vīrium, D. vīribus, A. vīrēs, Ab. vīribus.

[1] The vocative singular of nouns like **amīcus** and of masculine adjectives like **magnus** ends in **-e**. The vocative singular of **fīlius** and of names in **-ius** ends in a single **-ī** (**fīlī, Vergilī**); the vocative singular of the masculine adjective **meus** is **mī**; the vocative singular of masculine adjectives in **-ius** ends in **-ie** (**ēgregius; ēgregie**). Otherwise, the vocative has the same form as the nominative in all declensions.

ADJECTIVES—DECLENSIONS

First and Second Declensions

	Adjs. in -us, -a, -um			Adjs. in -er, -era, -erum; -er, -ra, -rum		
M.	**F.**	**N.**		**M.**	**F.**	**N.**
	Singular				**Singular²**	
N. magnus	magna	magnum		līber	lībera	līberum
G. magnī	magnae	magnī		līberī	līberae	līberī
D. magnō	magnae	magnō		līberō	līberae	līberō
A. magnum	magnam	magnum		līberum	līberam	līberum
Ab. magnō	magnā	magnō		līberō	līberā	līberō
	Plural				**Singular²**	
N. magnī	magnae	magna		pulcher	pulchra	pulchrum
G. magnōrum	magnārum	magnōrum		pulchrī	pulchrae	pulchrī
D. magnīs	magnīs	magnīs		pulchrō	pulchrae	pulchrō
A. magnōs	magnās	magna		pulchrum	pulchram	pulchrum
Ab. magnīs	magnīs	magnīs		pulchrō	pulchrā	pulchrō

Third Declension

Two endings fortis, forte *brave*		**Three endings** ācer, ācris, ācre *keen, severe*		**One Ending** potēns³ *powerful*		**Comparatives⁵** fortior, fortius *braver*	
M. & F.	**N.**	**M. & F.**	**N.**	**M. & F.**	**N.**	**M. & F.**	**N.**
Sg.							
N. fortis	forte	ācer ācris	ācre	potēns	potēns	fortior	fortius
G. fortis		ācris		potentis		fortiōris	
D. fortī		ācrī		potentī		fortiōrī	
A. fortem	forte	ācrem	ācre	potentem	potēns	fortiōrem	fortius
Ab. fortī		ācrī		potentī		fortiōre	
Pl.							
N. fortēs	fortia	ācrēs	ācria	potentēs	potentia	fortiōrēs	fortiōra
G. fortium		ācrium		potentium		fortiōrum	
D. fortibus		ācribus		potentibus		fortiōribus	
A. fortēs⁴	fortia	ācres⁴	ācria	potentēs⁴	potentia	fortiōrēs	fortiōra
Ab. fortibus		ācribus		potentibus		fortiōribus	

² The plural follows the pattern of the singular except that it has the plural endings.

³ Present participles follow the declension of **potēns** except that they have **-e** in the ablative singular when used as genuine participles.

⁴ For **-īs** (acc. pl.) see Ch. 16.

⁵ For irregular **plūs** see Ch. 27.

PRONOUNS

Demonstrative

hic, *this*   ille, *that*

	M.	F.	N.	M.	F.	N.
Sg.						
N.	hic	haec	hoc	ille	illa	illud
G.	huius	huius	huius	illīus	illīus	illīus
D.	huic	huic	huic	illī	illī	illī
A.	hunc	hanc	hoc	illum	illam	illud
Ab.	hōc	hāc	hōc	illō	illā	illō
Pl.						
N.	hī	hae	haec	illī	illae	illa
G.	hōrum	hārum	hōrum	illōrum	illārum	illōrum
D.	hīs	hīs	hīs	illīs	illīs	illīs
A.	hōs	hās	haec	illōs	illās	illa
Ab.	hīs	hīs	hīs	illīs	illīs	illīs

Relative   **Interrogative**[6]   **Intensive**
quī, *who, which*   quis, *who?*   ipse, *himself,* etc.

	M.	F.	N.	M. & F.	N.	M.	F.	N.
Sg.								
N.	quī	quae	quod	quis	quid	ipse	ipsa	ipsum
G.	cuius	cuius	cuius	cuius	cuius	ipsīus	ipsīus	ipsīus
D.	cui	cui	cui	cui	cui	ipsī	ipsī	ipsī
A.	quem	quam	quod	quem	quid	ipsum	ipsam	ipsum
Ab.	quō	quā	quō	quō	quō	ipsō	ipsā	ipsō
Pl.								
N.	quī	quae	quae	(Plural is same		ipsī	ipsae	ipsa
G.	quōrum	quārum	quōrum	as that of		ipsōrum	ipsārum	ipsōrum
D.	quibus	quibus	quibus	relative.)		ipsīs	ipsīs	ipsīs
A.	quōs	quās	quae			ipsōs	ipsās	ipsa
Ab.	quibus	quibus	quibus			ipsīs	ipsīs	ipsīs

[6] The interrogative adjective **quī? quae? quod?** meaning *what? which? what kind of?* has the same declension as that of the relative pronoun.

PRONOUNS
Demonstrative

is, *this, that, he, she, it*			idem, *the same*		
M.	**F.**	**N.**	**M.**	**F.**	**N.**

Sg.

N. is	ea	id	īdem	eadem	idem
G. eius	eius	eius	eiusdem	eiusdem	eiusdem
D. eī	eī	eī	eīdem	eīdem	eīdem
A. eum	eam	id	eundem	eandem	idem
Ab. eō	eā	eō	eōdem	eādem	eōdem

Pl.

N. eī, iī	eae	ea	eīdem, īdem	eaedem	eadem
G. eōrum	eārum	eōrum	eōrundem	eārundem	eōrundem
D. eīs, iīs	eīs, iīs	eīs, iīs	eīsdem[7]	eīsdem	eīsdem
A. eōs	eās	ea	eōsdem	eāsdem	eadem
Ab. eīs	eīs	eīs	eīsdem	eīsdem	eīsdem

Irregular Adjectives[8]			Personal[9]		Reflexive[9]
sōlus, *alone, only*					suī, *himself,*
M.	**F.**	**N.**	ego, *I*	tū, *you*	*herself, itself*

Sg.

N. sōlus	sōla	sōlum	ego	tū	———
G. sōlīus	sōlīus	sōlīus	meī	tuī	suī[10]
D. sōlī	sōlī	sōlī	mihi	tibi	sibi
A. sōlum	sōlam	sōlum	mē	tē	sē[11]
Ab. sōlō	sōlā	sōlō	mē	tē	sē[11]

Pl.

N. sōlī	sōlae	sōla	nōs	vōs	———
G. sōlōrum	sōlārum	sōlōrum	nostrum / nostrī	vestrum / vestrī	suī
D. sōlīs	sōlīs	sōlīs	nōbīs	vōbīs	sibi
A. sōlōs	sōlās	sōla	nōs	vōs	sē[11]
Ab. sōlīs	sōlīs	sōlīs	nōbīs	vōbīs	sē[11]

[7] Also **īsdem.**

[8] Similarly **ūnus, tōtus, ūllus, nūllus, alius, alter, uter, neuter** (see Ch. 9).

[9] All forms of the pronouns of the first and second persons except the nom. sg. and the nom. pl. may also be used as reflexive pronouns.

[10] These forms are reflexive only. The nonreflexive forms of the third person are supplied by **is, ea, id** (see Chs. 11, 13).

[11] The form **sēsē** is also frequently found.

COMPARISON OF ADJECTIVES

Positive	Comparative	Superlative
Regular		
longus, -a, -um (*long*)	longior, -ius	longissimus, -a, -um
fortis, -e (*brave*)	fortior, -ius	fortissimus, -a, -um
fēlīx, *gen.* fēlīcis, (*happy*)	fēlīcior, -ius	fēlīcissimus, -a, -um
sapiēns, *gen.* sapientis (*wise*)	sapientior, -ius	sapientissimus, -a, -um
facilis, -e (*easy*)	facilior, -ius	facillimus, -a, -um
līber, -era, -erum (*free*)	līberior, -ius	līberrimus, -a, -um
pulcher, -chra, -chrum (*beautiful*)	pulchrior, -ius	pulcherrimus, -a, -um
ācer, ācris, ācre (*keen*)	ācrior, -ius	ācerrimus, -a, -um
Irregular		
bonus, -a, -um (*good*)	melior, -ius	optimus, -a, -um
magnus, -a, -um (*large*)	maior, -ius	maximus, -a, -um
malus, -a, -um (*bad*)	peior, -ius	pessimus, -a, -um
multus, -a, -um (*much*)	—, plūs	plūrimus, -a, -um
parvus, -a, -um (*small*)	minor, minus	minimus, -a, -um
(prae, prō)	prior, -ius (*former*)	prīmus, -a, -um
superus, -a, -um (*that above*)	superior, -ius	summus (suprēmus), -a, -um

COMPARISON OF ADVERBS

Positive	Comparative	Superlative
Regular		
longē (*far*)	longius	longissimē
fortiter (*bravely*)	fortius	fortissimē
fēlīciter (*happily*)	fēlīcius	fēlīcissimē
sapienter (*wisely*)	sapientius	sapientissimē
facile (*easily*)	facilius	facillimē
līberē (*freely*)	līberius	līberrimē
pulchrē (*beautifully*)	pulchrius	pulcherrimē
ācriter (*keenly*)	ācrius	ācerrimē
Irregular		
bene (*well*)	melius	optimē
magnopere (*greatly*)	magis	maximē
male (*badly*)	peius	pessimē
multum (*much*)	plūs	plūrimum
parum (*little*)	minus	minimē
(prae, prō)	prius (*before*)	prīmum; prīmō
diū (*a long time*)	diūtius	diūtissimē

NUMERALS

Cardinals	Ordinals	Roman Numerals
1. ūnus, -a, -um	prīmus, -a, -um	I
2. duo, duae, duo	secundus, alter	II
3. trēs, tria	tertius	III
4. quattuor	quārtus	IIII; IV
5. quīnque	quīntus	V
6. sex	sextus	VI
7. septem	septimus	VII
8. octō	octāvus	VIII
9. novem	nōnus	VIIII; IX
10. decem	decimus	X
11. ūndecim	ūndecimus	XI
12. duodecim	duodecimus	XII
13. tredecim	tertius decimus	XIII
14. quattuordecim	quārtus decimus	XIIII; XIV
15. quīndecim	quīntus decimus	XV
16. sēdecim	sextus decimus	XVI
17. septendecim	septimus decimus	XVII
18. duodēvīgintī	duodēvīcēsimus	XVIII
19. ūndēvīgintī	ūndēvīcēsimus	XVIIII; XIX
20. vīgintī	vīcēsimus	XX
21. vīgintī ūnus, ūnus et vīgintī	vīcēsimus prīmus	XXI
30. trīgintā	trīcēsimus	XXX
40. quadrāgintā	quadrāgēsimus	XXXX, XL
50. quīnquāgintā	quīnquāgēsimus	L
60. sexāgintā	sexāgēsimus	LX
70. septuāgintā	septuāgēsimus	LXX
80. octōgintā	octōgēsimus	LXXX
90. nōnāgintā	nōnāgēsimus	LXXXX; XC
100. centum	centēsimus	C
101. centum ūnus	centēsimus prīmus	CI
200. ducentī, -ae, -a	duocentēsimus	CC
300. trecentī	trecentēsimus	CCC
400. quadringentī	quadringentēsimus	CCCC
500. quīngentī	quīngentēsimus	D
600. sescentī	sescentēsimus	DC
700. septingentī	septingentēsimus	DCC
800. octingentī	octingentēsimus	DCCC
900. nōngentī	nōngentēsimus	DCCCC
1000. mīlle	mīllēsimus	M
2000. duo mīlia	bis mīllēsimus	MM

Declension of Numerals

For the declension of **ūnus** see Ch. 9 or **sōlus** above.

For **duo, trēs,** and **mīlle** see Ch. 15.

The forms from **trecentī** through **nōngentī** are declined in the plural like **ducentī, -ae, -a.**

The ordinals are declined like **prīmus, -a, -um.**

The other forms are indeclinable.

CONJUGATIONS 1–4

Principal Parts

1*st:* laudō	laudāre	laudāvī	laudātum
2*nd:* moneō	monēre	monuī	monitum
3*rd:* agō	agere	ēgī	āctum
4*th:* audiō	audīre	audīvī	audītum
3*rd* (**-iō**): capiō	capere	cēpī	captum

Indicative Active

Present

laudō	moneō	agō	audiō	capiō
laudās	monēs	agis	audīs	capis
laudat	monet	agit	audit	capit
laudāmus	monēmus	agimus	audīmus	capimus
laudātis	monētis	agitis	audītis	capitis
laudant	monent	agunt	audiunt	capiunt

Imperfect

laudābam	monēbam	agēbam	audiēbam	capiēbam
laudābās	monēbās	agēbās	audiēbās	capiēbās
laudābat	monēbat	agēbat	audiēbat	capiēbat
laudābāmus	monēbāmus	agēbāmus	audiēbāmus	capiēbāmus
laudābātis	monēbātis	agēbātis	audiēbātis	capiēbātis
laudābant	monēbant	agēbant	audiēbant	capiēbant

Future

laudābō	monēbō	agam	audiam	capiam
laudābis	monēbis	agēs	audiēs	capiēs
laudābit	monēbit	aget	audiet	capiet
laudābimus	monēbimus	agēmus	audiēmus	capiēmus
laudābitis	monēbitis	agētis	audiētis	capiētis
laudābunt	monēbunt	agent	audient	capient

Perfect

laudāvī	monuī	ēgī	audīvī	cēpī
laudāvistī	monuistī	ēgistī	audīvistī	cēpistī
laudāvit	monuit	ēgit	audīvit	cēpit
laudāvimus	monuimus	ēgimus	audīvimus	cēpimus
laudāvistis	monuistis	ēgistis	audīvistis	cēpistis
laudāvērunt	monuērunt	ēgērunt	audīvērunt	cēpērunt

Pluperfect

laudāveram	monueram	ēgeram	audīveram	cēperam
laudāverās	monuerās	ēgerās	audīverās	cēperās
laudāverat	monuerat	ēgerat	audīverat	cēperat
laudāverāmus	monuerāmus	ēgerāmus	audīverāmus	cēperāmus
laudāverātis	monuerātis	ēgerātis	audīverātis	cēperātis
laudāverant	monuerant	ēgerant	audīverant	cēperant

Future Perfect

laudāverō	monuerō	ēgerō	audīverō	cēperō
laudāveris	monueris	ēgeris	audīveris	cēperis
laudāverit	monuerit	ēgerit	audīverit	cēperit
laudāverimus	monuerimus	ēgerimus	audīverimus	cēperimus
laudāveritis	monueritis	ēgeritis	audīveritis	cēperitis
laudāverint	monuerint	ēgerint	audīverint	cēperint

Subjunctive Active

Present

laudem	moneam	agam	audiam	capiam
laudēs	moneās	agās	audiās	capiās
laudet	moneat	agat	audiat	capiat
laudēmus	moneāmus	agāmus	audiāmus	capiāmus
laudētis	moneātis	agātis	audiātis	capiātis
laudent	moneant	agant	audiant	capiant

Imperfect

laudārem	monērem	agerem	audīrem	caperem
laudārēs	monērēs	agerēs	audīrēs	caperēs
laudāret	monēret	ageret	audīret	caperet
laudārēmus	monērēmus	agerēmus	audīrēmus	caperēmus
laudārētis	monērētis	agerētis	audīrētis	caperētis
laudārent	monērent	agerent	audīrent	caperent

Perfect

laudāverim	monuerim	ēgerim	audīverim	cēperim
laudāverīs	monuerīs	ēgerīs	audīverīs	cēperīs
laudāverit	monuerit	ēgerit	audīverit	cēperit
laudāverīmus	monuerīmus	ēgerīmus	audīverīmus	cēperīmus
laudāverītis	monuerītis	ēgerītis	audīverītis	cēperītis
laudāverint	monuerint	ēgerint	audīverint	cēperint

Pluperfect

laudāvissem	monuissem	ēgissem	audīvissem	cēpissem
laudāvissēs	monuissēs	ēgissēs	audīvissēs	cēpissēs
laudāvisset	monuisset	ēgisset	audīvisset	cēpisset
laudāvissēmus	monuissēmus	ēgissēmus	audīvissēmus	cēpissēmus
laudāvissētis	monuissētis	ēgissētis	audīvissētis	cēpissētis
laudāvissent	monuissent	ēgissent	audīvissent	cēpissent

Present Imperative Active

laudā	monē	age	audī	cape
laudāte	monēte	agite	audīte	capite

Indicative Passive

Present

laudor	moneor	agor	audior	capior
laudāris(-re)	monēris(-re)	ageris(-re)	audīris(-re)	caperis(-re)
laudātur	monētur	agitur	audītur	capitur
laudāmur	monēmur	agimur	audīmur	capimur
laudāminī	monēminī	agiminī	audīminī	capiminī
laudantur	monentur	aguntur	audiuntur	capiuntur

Imperfect

laudābar	monēbar	agēbar	audiēbar	capiēbar
laudābāris(-re)	monēbāris(-re)	agēbāris(-re)	audiēbāris(-re)	capiēbāris(-re)
laudābātur	monēbātur	agēbātur	audiēbātur	capiēbātur
laudābāmur	monēbāmur	agēbāmur	audiēbāmur	capiēbāmur
laudābāminī	monēbāminī	agēbāminī	audiēbāminī	capiēbāminī
laudābantur	monēbantur	agēbantur	audiēbantur	capiēbantur

Future

laudābor	monēbor	agar	audiar	capiar
laudāberis(-re)	monēberis(-re)	agēris(-re)	audiēris(-re)	capiēris(-re)
laudābitur	monēbitur	agētur	audiētur	capiētur
laudābimur	monēbimur	agēmur	audiēmur	capiēmur
laudābiminī	monēbiminī	agēminī	audiēminī	capiēminī
laudābuntur	monēbuntur	agentur	audientur	capientur

Perfect

laudātus[12] sum	monitus sum	āctus sum	audītus sum	captus sum
laudātus es	monitus es	āctus es	audītus es	captus es
laudātus est	monitus est	āctus est	audītus est	captus est
laudātī sumus	monitī sumus	āctī sumus	audītī sumus	captī sumus
laudātī estis	monitī estis	āctī estis	audītī estis	captī estis
laudātī sunt	monitī sunt	āctī sunt	audītī sunt	captī sunt

Pluperfect

laudātus eram	monitus eram	āctus eram	audītus eram	captus eram
laudātus erās	monitus erās	āctus erās	audītus erās	captus erās
laudātus erat	monitus erat	āctus erat	audītus erat	captus erat
laudātī erāmus	monitī erāmus	āctī erāmus	audītī erāmus	captī erāmus
laudātī erātis	monitī erātis	āctī erātis	audītī erātis	captī erātis
laudātī erant	monitī erant	āctī erant	audītī erant	captī erant

Future Perfect

laudātus erō	monitus erō	āctus erō	audītus erō	captus erō
laudātus eris	monitus eris	āctus eris	audītus eris	captus eris
laudātus erit	monitus erit	āctus erit	audītus erit	captus erit
laudātī erimus	monitī erimus	āctī erimus	audītī erimus	captī erimus
laudātī eritis	monitī eritis	āctī eritis	audītī eritis	captī eritis
laudātī erunt	monitī erunt	āctī erunt	audītī erunt	captī erunt

Subjunctive Passive

Present

lauder	monear	agar	audiar	capiar
laudēris(-re)	moneāris(-re)	agāris(-re)	audiāris(-re)	capiāris(-re)
laudētur	moneātur	agātur	audiātur	capiātur
laudēmur	moneāmur	agāmur	audiāmur	capiāmur
laudēminī	moneāminī	agāminī	audiāminī	capiāminī
laudentur	moneantur	agantur	audiantur	capiantur

Imperfect

laudārer	monērer	agerer	audīrer	caperer
laudārēris(-re)	monērēris(-re)	agerēris(-re)	audīrēris(-re)	caperēris(-re)
laudārētur	monērētur	agerētur	audīrētur	caperētur
laudārēmur	monērēmur	agerēmur	audīrēmur	caperēmur
laudārēminī	monērēminī	agerēminī	audīrēminī	caperēminī
laudārentur	monērentur	agerentur	audīrentur	caperentur

[12] The participles **laudātus (-a, -um)**, **monitus (-a, -um)**, etc., are used as predicate adjectives, and so their endings vary to agree with the subject.

Perfect

laudātus sim	monitus sim	āctus sim	audītus sim	captus sim
laudātus sīs	monitus sīs	āctus sīs	audītus sīs	captus sīs
laudātus sit	monitus sit	āctus sit	audītus sit	captus sit
laudātī sīmus	monitī sīmus	āctī sīmus	audītī sīmus	captī sīmus
laudātī sītis	monitī sītis	āctī sītis	audītī sītis	captī sītis
laudātī sint	monitī sint	āctī sint	audītī sint	captī sint

Pluperfect

laudātus essem	monitus essem	āctus essem	audītus essem	captus essem
laudātus essēs	monitus essēs	āctus essēs	audītus essēs	captus essēs
laudātus esset	monitus esset	āctus esset	audītus esset	captus esset
laudātī essēmus	monitī essēmus	āctī essēmus	audītī essēmus	captī essēmus
laudātī essētis	monitī essētis	āctī essētis	audītī essētis	captī essētis
laudātī essent	monitī essent	āctī essent	audītī essent	captī essent

Present Imperative Passive

In classical Latin, passive form imperatives are found chiefly in deponent verbs (for forms, see Ch. 34).

Participles

Active

Pres.	laudāns	monēns	agēns	audiēns	capiēns
Fut.	laudātūrus	monitūrus	āctūrus	audītūrus	captūrus

Passive

Perf.	laudātus	monitus	āctus	audītus	captus
Fut.	laudandus	monendus	agendus	audiendus	capiendus

Infinitives

Active

Pres.	laudāre	monēre	agere	audīre	capere
Perf.	laudāvisse	monuisse	ēgisse	audīvisse	cēpisse
Fut.	laudātūrus esse	monitūrus esse	āctūrus esse	audītūrus esse	captūrus esse

Passive

Pres.	laudārī	monērī	agī	audīrī	capī
Perf.	laudātus esse	monitus esse	āctus esse	audītus esse	captus esse
Fut.	laudātum īrī	monitum īrī	āctum īrī	audītum īrī	captum īrī

DEPONENT VERBS

Principal Parts

1st Conj.:	hortor	hortārī	hortātus sum (*urge*)
2nd Conj.:	fateor	fatērī	fassus sum (*confess*)
3rd Conj.:	sequor	sequī	secūtus sum (*follow*)
4th Conj.:	mōlior	mōlīrī	mōlītus sum (*work at*)
3rd (-iō):	patior	patī	passus sum (*suffer*)

Indicative

Present

hortor	fateor	sequor	mōlior	patior
hortāris(-re)	fatēris(-re)	sequeris(-re)	mōlīris(-re)	pateris(-re)
hortātur	fatētur	sequitur	mōlītur	patitur
hortāmur	fatēmur	sequimur	mōlīmur	patimur
hortāminī	fatēminī	sequiminī	mōlīminī	patiminī
hortantur	fatentur	sequuntur	mōliuntur	patiuntur

Imperfect

hortābar	fatēbar	sequēbar	mōliēbar	patiēbar
hortābāris(-re)	fatēbāris(-re)	sequēbāris(-re)	mōliēbāris(-re)	patiēbāris(-re)
hortābātur	fatēbātur	sequēbātur	mōliēbātur	patiēbātur
hortābāmur	fatēbāmur	sequēbāmur	mōliēbāmur	patiēbāmur
hortābāminī	fatēbāminī	sequēbāminī	mōliēbāminī	patiēbāminī
hortābantur	fatēbantur	sequēbantur	mōliēbantur	patiēbantur

Future

hortābor	fatēbor	sequar	mōliar	patiar
hortāberis(-re)	fatēberis(-re)	sequēris(-re)	mōliēris(-re)	patiēris(-re)
hortābitur	fatēbitur	sequētur	mōliētur	patiētur
hortābimur	fatēbimur	sequēmur	mōliēmur	patiēmur
hortābiminī	fatēbiminī	sequēminī	mōliēminī	patiēminī
hortābuntur	fatēbuntur	sequentur	mōlientur	patientur

Perfect

hortātus sum	fassus sum	secūtus sum	mōlītus sum	passus sum
hortātus es	fassus es	secūtus es	mōlītus es	passus es
hortātus est	fassus est	secūtus est	mōlītus est	passus est
hortātī sumus	fassī sumus	secūtī sumus	mōlītī sumus	passī sumus
hortātī estis	fassī estis	secūtī estis	mōlītī estis	passī estis
hortātī sunt	fassī sunt	secūtī sunt	mōlītī sunt	passī sunt

Pluperfect

hortātus eram	fassus eram	secūtus eram	mōlītus eram	passus eram
hortātus erās	fassus erās	secūtus erās	mōlītus erās	passus erās
hortātus erat	fassus erat	secūtus erat	mōlītus erat	passus erat
hortātī erāmus	fassī erāmus	secūtī erāmus	mōlītī erāmus	passī erāmus
hortātī erātis	fassī erātis	secūtī erātis	mōlītī erātis	passī erātis
hortātī erant	fassī erant	secūtī erant	mōlītī erant	passī erant

Future Perfect

hortātus erō	fassus erō	secūtus erō	mōlītus erō	passus erō
hortātus eris	fassus eris	secūtus eris	mōlītus eris	passus eris
hortātus erit	fassus erit	secūtus erit	mōlītus erit	passus erit
hortātī erimus	fassī erimus	secūtī erimus	mōlītī erimus	passī erimus
hortātī eritis	fassī eritis	secūtī eritis	mōlītī eritis	passī eritis
hortātī erunt	fassī erunt	secūtī erunt	mōlītī erunt	passī erunt

Subjunctive

Present

horter	fatear	sequar	mōliar	patiar
hortēris(-re)	fateāris(-re)	sequāris(-re)	mōliāris(-re)	patiāris(-re)
hortētur	fateātur	sequātur	mōliātur	patiātur
hortēmur	fateāmur	sequāmur	mōliāmur	patiāmur
hortēminī	fateāminī	sequāminī	mōliāminī	patiāminī
hortentur	fateantur	sequantur	mōliantur	patiantur

Imperfect

hortārer	fatērer	sequerer	mōlīrer	paterer
hortārēris(-re)	fatērēris(-re)	sequerēris(-re)	mōlīrēris(-re)	paterēris(-re)
hortārētur	fatērētur	sequerētur	mōlīrētur	paterētur
hortārēmur	fatērēmur	sequerēmur	mōlīrēmur	paterēmur
hortārēminī	fatērēminī	sequerēminī	mōlīrēminī	paterēminī
hortārentur	fatērentur	sequerentur	mōlīrentur	paterentur

Perfect

hortātus sim	fassus sim	secūtus sim	mōlītus sim	passus sim
hortātus sīs	fassus sīs	secūtus sīs	mōlītus sīs	passus sīs
hortātus sit	fassus sit	secūtus sit	mōlītus sit	passus sit
hortātī sīmus	fassī sīmus	secūtī sīmus	mōlītī sīmus	passī sīmus
hortātī sītis	fassī sītis	secūtī sītis	mōlītī sītis	passī sītis
hortātī sint	fassī sint	secūtī sint	mōlītī sint	passī sint

Pluperfect

hortātus essem	fassus essem	secūtus essem	mōlītus essem	passus essem
hortātus essēs	fassus essēs	secūtus essēs	mōlītus essēs	passus essēs
hortātus esset	fassus esset	secūtus esset	mōlītus esset	passus esset
hortātī essēmus	fassī essēmus	secūtī essēmus	mōlītī essēmus	passī essēmus
hortātī essētis	fassī essētis	secūtī essētis	mōlītī essētis	passī essētis
hortātī essent	fassī essent	secūtī essent	mōlītī essent	passī essent

Present Imperative

hortāre	fatēre	sequere	mōlīre	patere
hortāminī	fatēminī	sequiminī	mōlīminī	patiminī

Participles

Pres.	hortāns	fatēns	sequēns	mōliēns	patiēns
Perf.	hortātus	fassus	secūtus	mōlītus	passus
Fut.	hortātūrus	fassūrus	secūtūrus	mōlītūrus	passūrus
Ger.	hortandus	fatendus	sequendus	mōliendus	patiendus

Infinitives

Pres.	hortārī	fatērī	sequī	mōlīrī	patī
Perf.	hortātus esse	fassus esse	secūtus esse	mōlītus esse	passus esse
Fut.	hortātūrus esse	fassūrus esse	secūtūrus esse	mōlītūrus esse	passūrus esse

IRREGULAR VERBS

Principal Parts

sum	esse	fuī	futūrum	(*be*)
possum	posse	potuī		(*be able, can*)
volō	velle	voluī		(*wish, be willing*)
nōlō	nōlle	nōluī		(*not to wish, be unwilling*)
mālō	mālle	māluī		(*prefer*)
eō	īre	iī	itum	(*go*)

Indicative[13]

Present

sum	possum	volō	nōlō	mālō	eō
es	potes	vīs	nōn vīs	māvīs	īs
est	potest	vult	nōn vult	māvult	it
sumus	possumus	volumus	nōlumus	mālumus	īmus
estis	potestis	vultis	nōn vultis	māvultis	ītis
sunt	possunt	volunt	nōlunt	mālunt	eunt

Imperfect

eram	poteram	volēbam	nōlēbam	mālēbam	ībam
erās	poterās	volēbās	nōlēbās	mālēbās	ībās
erat	poterat	volēbat	nōlēbat	mālēbat	ībat
erāmus	poterāmus	volēbāmus	nōlēbāmus	mālēbāmus	ībāmus
erātis	poterātis	volēbātis	nōlēbātis	mālēbātis	ībātis
erant	poterant	volēbant	nōlēbant	mālēbant	ībant

Future

erō	poterō	volam	nōlam	mālam	ībō
eris	poteris	volēs	nōlēs	mālēs	ībis
erit	poterit	volet	nōlet	mālet	ībit
erimus	poterimus	volēmus	nōlēmus	mālēmus	ībimus
eritis	poteritis	volētis	nōlētis	mālētis	ībitis
erunt	poterunt	volent	nōlent	mālent	ībunt

Perfect

fuī	potuī	voluī	nōluī	māluī	iī
fuistī	potuistī	voluistī	nōluistī	māluistī	īstī
fuit	potuit	voluit	nōluit	māluit	iit
fuimus	potuimus	voluimus	nōluimus	māluimus	iimus
fuistis	potuistis	voluistis	nōluistis	māluistis	īstis
fuērunt	potuērunt	voluērunt	nōluērunt	māluērunt	iērunt

Pluperfect

fueram	potueram	volueram	nōlueram	mālueram	ieram
fuerās	potuerās	voluerās	nōluerās	māluerās	ierās
etc.	etc.	etc.	etc.	etc.	etc.

Future Perfect

fuerō	potuerō	voluerō	nōluerō	māluerō	ierō
fueris	potueris	volueris	nōlueris	mālueris	ieris
etc.	etc.	etc.	etc.	etc.	etc.

Subjunctive

Present

sim	possim	velim	nōlim	mālim	eam
sīs	possīs	velīs	nōlīs	mālīs	eās
sit	possit	velit	nōlit	mālit	eat
sīmus	possīmus	velīmus	nōlīmus	mālīmus	eāmus
sītis	possītis	velītis	nōlītis	mālītis	eātis
sint	possint	velint	nōlint	mālint	eant

[13] Note that the verbs in this list have no passive voice (except for the idiomatic impersonal passive of **eō,** which is not used in this book).

Imperfect

essem	possem	vellem	nōllem	māllem	īrem
essēs	possēs	vellēs	nōllēs	māllēs	īrēs
esset	posset	vellet	nōllet	māllet	īret
essēmus	possēmus	vellēmus	nōllēmus	māllēmus	īrēmus
essētis	possētis	vellētis	nōllētis	māllētis	īrētis
essent	possent	vellent	nōllent	māllent	īrent

Perfect

fuerim	potuerim	voluerim	nōluerim	māluerim	ierim
fuerīs	potuerīs	voluerīs	nōluerīs	māluerīs	ierīs
fuerit	potuerit	voluerit	nōluerit	māluerit	ierit
fuerīmus	potuerīmus	voluerīmus	nōluerīmus	māluerīmus	ierīmus
fuerītis	potuerītis	voluerītis	nōluerītis	māluerītis	ierītis
fuerint	potuerint	voluerint	nōluerint	māluerint	ierint

Pluperfect

fuissem	potuissem	voluissem	nōluissem	māluissem	īssem
fuissēs	potuissēs	voluissēs	nōluissēs	māluissēs	īssēs
fuisset	potuisset	voluisset	nōluisset	māluisset	īsset
fuissēmus	potuissēmus	voluissēmus	nōluissēmus	māluissēmus	īssēmus
fuissētis	potuissētis	voluissētis	nōluissētis	māluissētis	īssētis
fuissent	potuissent	voluissent	nōluissent	māluissent	īssent

Present Imperative

es	———	———	nōlī	———	ī
este	———	———	nōlīte	———	īte

Participles

Pres.	———	potēns	volēns	nōlēns	———	iēns (*gen.* euntis)
Perf.	———	———	———	———	———	itum
Fut.	futūrus	———	———	———	———	itūrus
Ger.	———	———	———	———	———	eundus

Infinitives

Pr.	esse	posse	velle	nōlle	mālle	īre
Pf.	fuisse	potuisse	voluisse	nōluisse	māluisse	īsse
Fu.	futūrus esse	———	———	———	———	itūrus esse
	or fore					

IRREGULAR: ferō, ferre, tulī, lātum, *to bear, carry*

Indicative

Present Act.	Pass.	Imperfect Act.	Pass.	Future Act.	Pass.
ferō	feror	ferēbam	ferēbar	feram	ferar
fers	ferris(-re)	ferēbās	ferēbāris(-re)	ferēs	ferēris(-re)
fert	fertur	ferēbat	ferēbātur	feret	ferētur
ferimus	ferimur	ferēbāmus	ferēbāmur	ferēmus	ferēmur
fertis	feriminī	ferēbātis	ferēbāminī	ferētis	ferēminī
ferunt	feruntur	ferēbant	ferēbantur	ferent	ferentur

Perfect		Pluperfect		Future Perfect	
Act.	Pass.	Act.	Pass.	Act.	Pass.
tulī	lātus sum	tuleram	lātus eram	tulerō	lātus erō
tulistī	lātus es	tulerās	lātus erās	tuleris	lātus eris
tulit	lātus est	tulerat	lātus erat	tulerit	lātus erit
etc.	etc.	etc.	etc.	etc.	etc.

Subjunctive

Present		Imperfect		Perfect	
Act.	Pass.	Act.	Pass.	Act.	Pass.
feram	ferar	ferrem	ferrer	tulerim	lātus sim
ferās	ferāris(-re)	ferrēs	ferrēris(-re)	tulerīs	lātus sīs
ferat	ferātur	ferret	ferrētur	tulerit	lātus sit
ferāmus	ferāmur	ferrēmus	ferrēmur	etc.	etc.
ferātis	ferāminī	ferrētis	ferrēminī		
ferant	ferantur	ferrent	ferrentur		

Pluperfect

tulissem	lātus essem
tulissēs	lātus essēs
tulisset	lātus esset
etc.	etc.

Pres. Imper.		Participles		Infinitives	
Act.	Pass.	Act.	Pass.	Act.	Pass.
fer	———	*Pres.* ferēns	———	ferre	ferrī
ferte	———	*Perf.* ———	lātus	tulisse	lātus esse
		Fut. lātūrus	ferendus	lātūrus esse	lātum īrī

IRREGULAR: fīō, fierī, factus sum, to happen, become; be made, be done

Indicative

Pres.	Impf.	Fut.	Perf.	Pluperf.	Fut. Perf.
fīō	fīēbam	fīam	factus sum	factus eram	factus erō
fīs	fīēbās	fīēs	factus es	factus erās	factus eris
fit	fīēbat	fīet	factus est	factus erat	factus erit
fīmus	fīēbāmus	fīēmus	factī sumus	factī erāmus	factī erimus
fītis	fīēbātis	fīētis	factī estis	factī erātis	factī eritis
fīunt	fīēbant	fīent	factī sunt	factī erant	factī erunt

Subjunctive

Pres.	Impf.	Perf.	Pluperf.
fīam	fierem	factus sim	factus essem
fīās	fierēs	factus sīs	factus essēs
fīat	fieret	factus sit	factus esset
fīāmus	fierēmus	factī sīmus	factī essēmus
fīātis	fierētis	factī sītis	factī essētis
fīant	fierent	factī sint	factī essent

Part.	Inf.
Pres. ———	fierī
Perf. factus	factus esse
Fut. faciendus	factum īrī

Imperative: fī, fīte

English-Latin Vocabulary

An Arabic (1) in parentheses after a verb shows that this is a regular verb of the first conjugation with a sequence of principal parts ending in **-āre, -āvī, -ātum.** For prefixes and suffixes see the lists in the Appendix. For more complete definitions of the Latin words, see the Latin-English Vocabulary.

A

abandon, relinquō, -ere, -liquī, -lictum
able (be), possum, posse, potuī
about (concerning), dē + *abl.*
absolute ruler, tyrannus, -ī, *m.*
abundance, cōpia, -ae, *f.*
accomplish, faciō, -ere, fēcī, factum; **be accomplished,** fīō, fierī, factus sum
across, trāns + *acc.*
advice, cōnsilium, -iī, *n.*
advise, moneō, -ēre, -uī, -itum
affect, adficiō, -ere, -fēcī, -fectum
afraid (be), metuō, -ere, -uī
after, post + *acc.*
afterwards, posteā
after all, postrēmum
again, iterum
against, contrā + *acc.*
age, aetās, -tātis, *f.*
alas, heu, vae
all, omnis, -e
alone, sōlus, -a, -um

also, quoque
although, cum + *subj.*
always, semper
among, inter + *acc.*
ancestors, maiōrēs, maiōrum, *m. pl.*
ancient, antīquus, -a, -um
and, et, -que, ac, atque
anger, īra, -ae, *f.*
angry, īrātus, -a, -um
animal, animal, -mālis, *n.*
announce, nūntiō (1)
another, alius, -a, -ud
answer, respondeō, -ēre, -spondī, -spōnsum
any, ūllus, -a, -um
any (anyone, anything, *after* sī, nisi, nē, num), quis, quid
argument, argūmentum, -ī, *n.*
army, exercitus, -ūs, *m.*
arms, arma, -ōrum, *n. pl.*
arrest, comprehendō, -ere, -ī, -hēnsum
arrogant, superbus, -a, -um
art, ars, artis, *f.*

as, ut + *indic.*
as . . . as possible, quam + *superlative*
Asia, Asia, -ae, *f.*
ask, rogō (1)
assure (I assure you, you may be assured), *use personal pron. in dat. case* (*dat. of reference, e.g.,* tibi)
at (= *time*), *abl. of time;* (= *place*), *loc. of names of cities*
Athens, Athēnae, -ārum, *f. pl.*
attack, oppugnō (1)
author, auctor, -tōris, *m.*
avert, āvertō, -ere, -ī, -versum
away from, ab + *abl.*

B

bad, malus, -a, -um
band, manus, -ūs, *f.*
banish, expellō, -ere, -pulī, -pulsum
base, turpis, -e
be, sum, esse, fuī, futūrum
beard, barba, -ae, *f.*
beautiful, pulcher, -chra, -chrum; bellus, -a, -um
beauty, fōrma, -ae, *f.*
because, quod
become, fīō, fierī, factus sum
before, ante + *acc.*
beg, ōrō (1)
began, coepī, coepisse, coeptum (*pres. system supplied by* incipiō)
begin, incipiō, -ere, -cēpī, -ceptum (*see* **began** *above*)
believe, crēdō, -ere, -didī, -ditum
benefit, beneficium, -iī, *n.*
best, optimus, -a, -um
better, melior, -ius
blind, caecus, -a, -um
body, corpus, -poris, *n.*
(be) born, nāscor, -ī, nātus sum
book, liber, -brī, *m.*
both . . . and, et . . . et
boy, puer, puerī, *m.*
brave, fortis, -e
brief, brevis, -e.
bright, clārus, -a, -um
bring, ferō, ferre, tulī, lātum
bring (back), referō, -ferre, -ttulī, -lātum
brother, frāter, -tris, *m.*
bull, bōs, bovis, *m./f.*

but, sed, at
by (= *agent*), ā *or* ab + *abl.;* (= *means*), *simple abl.*

C

Caesar, Caesar, -saris, *m.*
call, vocō (1); appellō (1)
can, possum, posse, potuī
capture, capiō, -ere, cēpī, captum
care, cūra, -ae, *f.*
certain (definite, sure), certus, -a, -um; (*indef.*) quīdam, quaedam, quiddam (*pron.*) *or* quoddam (*adj.*)
certainly, certē
change, mūtō (1)
character, mōrēs, mōrum, *m. pl.*
cheer, recreō (1)
Cicero, Cicerō, -rōnis, *m.*
citizen, cīvis, -is, *m./f.*
citizenship, cīvitās, -tātis, *f.*
city, urbs, urbis, *f.*
come, veniō, -īre, vēnī, ventum
come back, reveniō, -īre, -vēnī, -ventum
comfort, sōlācium, -iī, *n.*
command (*noun*), imperium, -iī, *n.;* (*vb.*), imperō (1)
common, commūnis, -e
commonwealth, rēs pūblica, reī pūblicae, *f.*
compare, comparō (1)
complain, queror, -ī, questus sum
concerning, dē + *abl.*
confess, fateor, -ērī, fassus sum
conquer, superō (1); vincō, -ere, vīcī, victum
conspirators, coniūrātī, -ōrum, *m. pl.*
constellation, sīdus, -deris, *n.*
consul, cōnsul, -sulis, *m.*
country, patria, -ae, *f.;* terra, -ae, *f.*
courage, virtūs, -tūtis, *f.*
create, creō (1)
custom, mōs, mōris, *m.*
crime, scelus, -leris, *n.*

D

danger, perīculum, -ī, *n.*
dare, audeō, -ēre, ausus sum
daughter, fīlia, -ae, *f.* (*dat. and abl. pl.* fīliābus)
day, diēs, -ēī, *m.*
dear, cārus, -a, -um

death, mors, mortis, *f.*
dedicate, dēdicō (1)
deed, factum, -ī, *n.*
defend, dēfendō, -ere, -ī, -fēnsum
delay, mora, -ae, *f.*
delight, dēlectō (1)
deny, negō (1)
depart, discēdō, -ere, -cessī, -cessum; abeō, -īre, -iī, -itum
deprived of (be), careō, -ēre, -uī, -itūrum
descendant, nepōs, -pōtis, *m.*
desire (*vb.*), cupiō, -ere, -īvī, -ītum; dēsīderō (1); (*noun*), voluptās, -tātis, *f.*
despise, contemnō, -ere, -tempsī, -temptum
destroy, dēleō, -ēre, -ēvī, -ētum
destruction, exitium, -ī, *n.*
die, morior, -ī, mortuus sum
difficult, difficilis, -e
dignity, dignitās, -tātis, *f.*
dine, cēnō (1)
dinner, cēna, -ae, *f.*
discover, reperiō, -īre, -pperī, -pertum
disgraceful, turpis, -e
dissimilar, dissimilis, -e
do, faciō, -ere, fēcī, factum; **be done,** fīō, fierī, factus sum
doctor, medica, -ae, *f.;* medicus, -ī, *m.*
drag, trahō, -ere, trāxī, tractum
dread (*vb.*), metuō, -ere, -uī; (*noun*), metus, -ūs, *m.*
drive out, expellō, -ere, -pulī, -pulsum

E

eagerness, studium, -iī, *n.*
ear, auris, -is, *f.*
easy, facilis, -e
eight, octō
either, uter, utra, utrum
either . . . or, aut . . . aut
eleven, ūndecim
emperor, imperātor, -tōris, *m.*
end, fīnis, -is, *m.*
endure, ferō, ferre, tulī, lātum; patior, -ī, passus sum
enemy, hostis, -is, *m.* (*usually pl.*)
enjoy, ūtor, -ī, ūsus sum + *abl.*
enjoyment, frūctus, -ūs, *m.*
enough, satis
entire, tōtus, -a, -um

entrust, committō, -ere, -mīsī, -missum
envy, (be) envious, invideō, -ēre, -vīdī, -vīsum + *dat.*
err, errō (1)
esteem, dīligō, -ere, -lēxī, -lēctum
even, etiam; **not even,** nē . . . quidem
ever, umquam
every(one), omnis, -e
evil (*adj.*), malus, -a, -um; (*noun*), malum, -ī, *n.*
exhibit, ostendō, -ere, -ī, -tentum
expect, exspectō (1)
expel, expellō, -ere, -pulī, -pulsum
eye, oculus, -ī, *m.*

F

face, vultus, -ūs, *m.*
faith, fidēs, -eī, *f.*
faithful, fidēlis, -e
fall, cadō, -ere, cecidī, casūrum
false, falsus, -a, -um
fame, fāma, -ae, *f.*
family, familia, -ae, *f.*
farmer, agricola, -ae, *m.*
father, pater, -tris, *m.*
fault, culpa, -ae, *f.;* vitium, -iī, *n.*
fear (*vb.*), timeō, -ēre, -uī; (*noun*), metus, -ūs, *m.;* timor, -mōris, *m.*
feel, sentiō, -īre, sēnsī, sēnsum
feeling, sēnsus, -ūs, *m.*
ferocious, ferōx, *gen.* ferōcis
few, paucī, -ae, -a (*pl.*)
fidelity, fidēs, -eī, *f.*
fierce, ācer, ācris, ācre; ferōx, *gen.* ferōcis
fifth, quīntus, -a, -um
finally, dēnique
find, inveniō, -īre, -vēnī, -ventum
first (*adj.*), prīmus, -a, -um; (*adv.*) prīmum, prīmō
five, quīnque
flee, fugiō, -ere, fūgī, fugitūrum
follow, sequor, -ī, secūtus sum
foolish, stultus, -a, -um
for (*conj.*), nam, enim; (= **since, because**), quod, quoniam; (*prep.*), prō + *abl.; often simply the dat. case.*
force, vīs, vīs, *f.*
forces (troops), cōpiae, -ārum, *f. pl.*
forgive, ignōscō, -ere, -nōvī, -nōtum + *dat.*
former, prior, prius
fortunate, fortūnātus, -a, -um

fortune, fortūna, -ae, *f.*
forum, forum -ī, *n.*
four, quattuor
free (*vb.*), līberō (1); (*adj.*), līber, -era, -erum
freedom, lībertās, -tātis, *f.*
freely, līberē
friend, amīca, -ae, *f.;* amīcus, -ī, *m.*
friendly, amīcus, -a, -um
friendship, amīcitia, -ae, *f.*
frighten, terreō, -ēre, -uī, -itum
from (away), ab; **(out)** ex; **(down)** dē: *all + abl.*
fruit, frūctus, -ūs, *m.*
full, plēnus, -a, -um

G

game, lūdus, -ī, *m.*
gate, porta, -ae, *f.*
general, dux, ducis, *m.;* imperātor, -tōris, *m.*
gift, dōnum, -ī, *n.*
girl, puella, -ae, *f.*
give, dō, dare, dedī, datum
(be) glad, gaudeō, -ēre, gāvīsus sum
glory, glōria, -ae, *f.*
go, eō, īre, iī, itum
go astray, errō (1)
go away, abeō, -īre, -iī, -itum
god, deus, -ī, *m.* (*voc. sg.* deus, *nom. pl.* deī *or* dī, *dat. and abl. pl.* dīs)
goddess, dea, -ae, *f.* (*dat. and abl. pl.* deābus)
good, bonus, -a, -um
gratitude, grātia, -ae, *f.*
great, magnus, -a, -um
greedy, avārus, -a, -um
Greek, Graecus, -a, -um; **a Greek,** Graecus, -ī, *m.*
grieve, doleō, -ēre, -uī, -itūrum
ground, humus, -ī, *f.;* terra, -ae, *f.*
guard, custōdia, -ae, *f.*

H

hand, manus, -ūs, *f.*
happy, beātus, -a, -um; fēlīx, *gen.* fēlīcis
harm, noceō, -ēre, -uī, -itum + *dat.*
harsh, dūrus, -a, -um; acerbus, -a, -um
have, habeō, -ēre, -uī, -itum
he, is; *often indicated only by the personal ending of vb.*
head, caput, -pitis, *n.*

healthy, sānus, -a, -um
hear, audiō, -īre, -īvī, -ītum
heart (in one's), *use personal pron. in dat. case* (*dat. of reference, e.g.,* mihi, tibi)
heavy, gravis, -e
help (*vb.*), adiuvō, -āre, -iūvī, -iūtum; (*noun*), auxilium, -iī, *n.*
her (*possessive*) eius (*not reflexive*); suus, -a, -um (*reflexive*)
herself, suī (*reflexive*); ipsa (*intensive*)
hesitate, dubitō (1)
high, altus, -a, -um
higher, altior, -ius; superior, -ius
himself, suī (*reflexive*); ipse (*intensive*)
his, eius (*not reflexive*); suus, -a, -um (*reflexive*)
hold, teneō, -ēre, -uī, tentum
home, domus, -ūs, *f.;* **at home,** domī; **(to) home,** domum; **from home,** domō
honor, honor, -nōris, *m.*
hope (*noun*), spēs, -eī, *f.;* (*vb.*), spērō (1)
horn, cornū, -ūs, *n.*
horse, equus, -ī, *m.*
hour, hōra, -ae, *f.*
house, casa, -ae, *f.*
however, autem (*postpositive*)
how great, quantus, -a, -um
how many, quot
human, hūmānus, -a, -um
human being, homō, -minis, *m.*
humane, hūmānus, -a, -um
humble, humilis, -e
hundred, centum
hurt, noceō, -ēre, -uī, -itum + *dat.*

I

I, ego, meī; *often expressed simply by the personal ending of vb.*
if, sī; **if . . . not,** nisi
ill, malum, -ī, *n.*
illustrious, clārus, -a, -um
immortal, immortālis, -e
in, in + *abl.*
infancy, īnfantia, -ae, *f.*
injustice, iniūria, -ae, *f.*
into, in + *acc.*
invite, invītō (1)
iron, ferrum, -ī, *n.*
it, is, ea, id; *often indicated only by personal ending of vb.*

Italy, Italia, -ae, *f.*
itself, suī (*reflexive*); ipsum (*intensive*)

J

join, iungō, -ere, iūnxī, iūnctum
judge, iūdex, -dicis, *m.*
judgment, iūdicium, -iī, *n.*
just, iūstus, -a, -um

K

keen, ācer, ācris, ācre
keenly, ācriter
kindness, beneficium, -iī, *n.*
king, rēx, rēgis, *m.*
kiss, bāsium, -iī, *n.*
knee, genū, -ūs, *n.*
know, sciō, -īre, -īvī, -ītum; **not know,** nesciō, -īre,
    -īvī, -ītum
knowledge, scientia, -ae, *f.*

L

labor, labor, -bōris, *m.*
lack, careō, -ēre, -uī, -itūrum + *abl.*
land, patria, -ae, *f.*; terra, -ae, *f.*
language, lingua, -ae, *f.*
large, magnus, -a, -um
Latin, Latīnus, -a, -um
law, lēx, lēgis, *f.*
lead, dūcō, -ere, dūxī, ductum
leader, dux, ducis, *m.*
learn (*in the academic sense*), discō, -ere, didicī;
    (*get information*), cognōscō, -ere, -nōvī, -nitum
leave, abeō, -īre, -iī, -itum
left, sinister, -tra, -trum
leisure, ōtium, -iī, *n.*
let (someone do something), *express this with*
    jussive subj.
letter (epistle), litterae, -ārum, *f. pl.*
liberty, lībertās, -tātis, *f.*
life, vīta, -ae, *f.*
light, lūx, lūcis, *f.*
listen (to), audiō, -īre, -īvī, -ītum
literature, litterae, -ārum, *f. pl.*
little, parvus, -a, -um; **little book,** libellus, -ī, *m.*
live, vīvō, -ere, vīxī, vīctum; **live one's life,** vītam
    agō, -ere, ēgī, āctum
long (for a long time), diū

lose, āmittō, -ere, -mīsī, -missum
love (*vb.*), amō (1); (*noun*), amor, amōris, *m.*
loyal, fidēlis, -e
luck, fortūna, -ae, *f.*

M

make, faciō, -ere, fēcī, factum
man, vir, virī, *m.*; homō, -minis, *m.*;
    often expressed by masc. of an adj.
many, multī, -ae, -a
master, magister, -trī, *m.*; dominus, -ī, *m.*
may (*indicating permission to do something*), licet
    + *dat.* + *inf.*
me. *See* **I.**
memory, memoria, -ae, *f.*
mercy, clēmentia, -ae, *f.*
method, modus, -ī, *m.*
middle, medius, -a, -um
mind, mēns, mentis, *f.*
mix, misceō, -ēre, -uī, mixtum
mob, vulgus, -ī, *n. (sometimes m.)*
modest, pudīcus, -a, -um
money, pecūnia, -ae, *f.*
monument, monumentum, -ī, *n.*
more, plūs, plūris; *comp. of adj. or adv.*
most, plūrimus, -a, -um; *superl. of adj. or adv.*
mother, māter, -tris, *f.*
mountain, mōns, montis, *m.*
move, moveō, -ēre, mōvī, mōtum
much, multus, -a, -um
murder, necō (1)
must, dēbeō, -ēre, -uī, -itum; *or, for passive, use*
    passive periphrastic
my, meus, -a, -um (*m. voc. sg.* mī)
myself (*reflexive*), meī, mihi, *etc.*;
    (*intensive*) ipse, ipsa

N

name, nōmen, -minis, *n.*
narrate, narrō (1)
nation, gēns, gentis, *f.*
nature, nātūra, -ae, *f.*
neglect, neglegō, -ere, -glēxī, -glēctum
neighbor, vīcīna, -ae, *f.*; vīcīnus, -ī, *m.*
neither . . . nor, neque . . . neque
never, numquam
nevertheless, tamen
new, novus, -a, -um

night, nox, noctis, *f.*

nine, novem

no, nūllus, -a, -um

nobody, no one, nēmō, *m./f.; for decl. see Lat.-Eng. Vocab.*

not, nōn; nē *with jussive, jussive noun, and purp-clauses;* ut *with fear clauses*

nothing, nihil *(indecl.), n.*

now, nunc

number, numerus, -ī, *m.*

O

obey, pāreō, -ēre, -uī + *dat.*

offer, offerō, -ferre, obtulī, oblātum

office, officium, -iī, *n.*

often, saepe

old, antīquus, -a, -um; senex, senis

old man, senex, senis, *m.*

on (= *place*), in + *abl.*; (= *time*), *simple abl.*

on account of, propter + *acc.*

once, semel

one, ūnus, -a, -um

only (*adv.*), tantum; (*adj.*), sōlus, -a, -um

opinion, sententia, -ae, *f.;* (**in one's**) **opinion,** *use personal pron. in dat. case (dat. of reference, e.g.,* mihi, tibi)

opportunity, occāsiō, -ōnis, *f.*

or, aut

oration, ōrātiō, -ōnis, *f.*

orator, ōrātor, -tōris, *m.*

order, iubeō, -ēre, iussī, iussum; imperō (1) + *dat.*

(**in**) **order to,** ut (+ *subj.*); **in order not to,** nē (+ *subj.*)

other, another, alius, alia, aliud;

 the other (of two), alter, -era, -erum;

 (**all**) **the other,** cēterī, -ae, -a

ought, dēbeō, -ēre, -uī, -itum; *or, for passive, use passive periphrastic*

our, noster, -tra, -trum

out of, ex + *abl.*

overcome, superō (1)

overpower, opprimō, -ere, -pressī, -pressum

own, his own, suus, -a, -um; **my own,** meus, -a, -um

P

pain, dolor, -lōris, *m.*

part, pars, partis, *f.*

passage, locus, -ī, *m.*

passion, cupiditās, -tātis, *f.*

patience, patientia, -ae, *f.*

pay. *See* **penalty.**

peace, pāx, pācis, *f.*

penalty, poena, -ae, *f.;* **pay the penalty,** poenās dare

people, populus, -ī, *m.*

perceive, sentiō, -īre, sēnsī, sēnsum

perhaps, fortasse

period (of time), aetās, -tātis, *f.*

perish, pereō, -īre, -iī, -itum

permit, patior, -ī, passus sum;

 it is permitted, licet, licēre, licuit (*impers.*)

perpetual, perpetuus, -a, -um

persuade, persuādeō, -ēre, -suāsī, -suāsum + *dat.*

philosopher, sapiēns, -entis, *m.;* philosopha, -ae, *f.;* philosophus, -ī, *m.*

philosophy, philosophia, -ae, *f.*

place, locus, -ī, *m.; pl.,* loca, -ōrum, *n.*

plan, cōnsilium, -iī, *n.*

pleasant, iūcundus, -a, -um

please, placeō, -ēre, -uī, -itum + *dat.; with a request,* amābō tē

pleasure, voluptās, -tātis, *f.*

plebeians, plēbs, plēbis, *f.*

plot, īnsidiae, -ārum, *f. pl.*

poem, carmen, -minis, *n.*

poet, poēta, -ae, *m.*

(**as . . . as**) **possible** (*or* **greatest possible, brightest possible,** *etc.*), quam + *superl. of adj. or adv.*

power (command), imperium, -iī, *n.*

powerful, potēns, *gen.* potentis

praise (*vb.*), laudō (1); (*noun*), laus, laudis, *f.*

prefer, mālō, mālle, māluī

prepare, parō (1)

preserve, cōnservō (1)

press, premō, -ere, pressī, pressum

pretty, bellus, -a, -um; pulcher, -chra, -chrum

priest, sacerdōs, -dōtis, *m.*

prohibit, prohibeō, -ēre, -uī, -itum

promise, prōmittō, -ere, -mīsī, -missum

provided that, dummodo + *subj.*

pupil, discipula, -ae, *f.;* discipulus, -ī, *m.*

pursuit, studium, -iī, *n.*

put, pōnō, -ere, posuī, positum

Q

queen, rēgīna, -ae, *f.*

quick, celer, -eris, -ere

quickly, celeriter, cito

R

raise, tollō, -ere, sustulī, sublātum
rather: *express this with comp. degree of adj. or adv.*
read, legō, -ere, lēgī, lēctum
real, vērus, -a, -um
reason, ratiō, -ōnis, *f.*
receive, accipiō, -ere, -cēpī, -ceptum
recite, recitō (1)
recognize, recognōscō, -ere, -nōvī, -nitum
refuse, recūsō (1)
regain, recipiō, -ere, -cēpī, -ceptum
region, loca, -ōrum, *n.*
remain, remaneō, -ēre, -mānsī, -mānsum
report, nūntiō (1)
republic, rēs pūblica, reī pūblicae, *f.*
reputation, fāma, -ae, *f.*
rescue, ēripiō, -ere, -uī, -reptum
rest, the rest, cēterī, -ae, -a
restrain, teneō, -ēre, -uī, -tentum
return (go back), redeō, -īre, -iī, -itum
return (in return for), prō + *abl.*
riches, dīvitiae, -ārum, *f. pl.*
right (*noun*), iūs, iūris, *n.*; (*adj.*), dexter, -tra, -trum
road, via, -ae, *f.*
Roman, Rōmānus, -a, -um
Rome, Rōma, -ae, *f.*
rose, rosa, -ae, *f.*
rule (*noun*), regnum, -ī, *n.*; (*vb.*), regō, -ere, rēxī, rēctum
rumor, rūmor, -mōris, *m.*
run, currō, -ere, cucurrī, cursum

S

sad, tristis, -e
safe, salvus, -a, -um
safety, salūs, -lūtis, *f.*
sailor, nauta, -ae, *m.*
sake (for the sake of), *gen.* + causā
salt, sāl, salis, *m.*
same, īdem, eadem, idem
satisfy, satiō (1)
save, servō (1); cōnservō (1)
say, dīcō, -ere, dīxī, dictum
school, lūdus, -ī, *m.*
sea, mare, -is, *n.*
second, secundus, -a, -um; alter, -era, -erum
see, videō, -ēre, vīdī, vīsum

seek, petō, -ere, -īvī, -ītum; quaerō, -ere, -sīvī, -sītum
seem, videor, -ērī, vīsus sum
seize, rapiō, -ere, -uī, raptum
senate, senātus, -ūs, *m.*
send, mittō, -ere, mīsī, missum
serious, gravis, -e
serve, serviō, -īre, -īvī, -ītum + *dat.*
service, officium, -iī, *n.*
seven, septem
she, ea; *often indicated only by the personal ending of vb.*
ship, nāvis, -is, *f.*
short, brevis, -e
show, ostendō, -ere, -ī, -tentum
shun, vītō (1); fugiō, -ere, fūgī, fugitūrum
sign, signum, -ī, *n.*
similar, similis, -e
since, quoniam + *indic.;* cum + *subj.;* abl. abs.
sister, soror, -rōris, *f.*
six, sex
skill, ars, artis, *f.*
slave, servus, -ī, *m.;* **slavegirl,** serva, -ae, *f.*
slavery, servitūs, -tūtis, *f.*
sleep (*vb.*), dormiō, -īre, -īvī, -itum; (*noun*), somnus, -ī, *m.*
slender, gracilis, -e
small, parvus, -a, -um
so, ita, sīc (*usually with vbs.*), tam (*usually with adjs. and advs.*); **so great,** tantus, -a, -um
soldier, mīles, -litis, *m.*
some, a certain one (*indef.*), quīdam, quaedam, quiddam; (*more emphatic pron.*), aliquis, aliquid
some . . . others, aliī . . . aliī
son, fīlius, -iī, *m.*
soon, mox
sort, genus, -neris, *n.*
soul, animus, -ī, *m.*
sound, sānus, -a, -um; salvus, -a, -um
spare, parcō, -ere, pepercī, parsūrum + *dat.*
speak, dīcō, -ere, dīxī, dictum; loquor, -ī, locūtus sum
spirit, spīritus, -ūs, *m.*
stand, stō, stāre, stetī, statum
start, proficīscor, -ī, -fectus sum
state, cīvitās, -tātis, *f.;* rēs pūblica, reī pūblicae, *f.*
story, fābula, -ae, *f.*
street, via, -ae, *f.*
strength, vīrēs, -ium, *f. pl.*
strong, fortis, -e; **be strong,** valeō, -ēre, -uī, -itūrum
student, discipula, -ae, *f.;* discipulus, -ī, *m.*

study (*noun*), studium, -iī, *n.*; (*vb.*), studeō, -ēre, -uī
  + *dat.*
suddenly, subitō
summer, aestās, -tātis, *f.*
sun, sōl, sōlis, *m.*
support, alō, -ere, -uī, altum
suppose, opīnor, -ārī, -ātus sum; putō (1)
suppress, opprimō, -primere, -pressī, -pressum
supreme power, imperium, -iī, *n.*
sure, certus, -a, -um
surrender, trādō, -ere, -didī, -ditum
sweet, dulcis, -e
swift, celer, -eris, -ere
sword, ferrum, -ī, *n.*; gladius, -iī, *m.*
Syracuse, Syrācūsae, -ārum, *f. pl.*

T

talk, loquor, -ī, -cūtus sum
teach, doceō, -ēre, -uī, doctum
teacher, magister, -trī, *m.; magistra, -ae, f.*
tear, lacrima, -ae, *f.*
tell, dīcō, -ere, dīxī, dictum
ten, decem
terrify, terreō, -ēre, -uī, -itum
territory, fīnēs, -ium, *m. pl.*
than, quam; *or simple abl.*
thank, grātiās agō, -ere, ēgī, āctum + *dat.*
that (*demonstrative*), ille, illa, illud; is, ea, id;
  that (of yours), iste, ista, istud
that (*subord. conj.*), *not expressed in ind. state.;* ut
  (*purp. and result*); nē (*fear*)
  that . . . not, nē (*purp.*); ut . . . nōn (*result*); ut
  (*fear*)
that (*rel. pron.*), quī, quae, quod
their, suus, -a, -um (*reflexive*); eōrum, eārum (*not
  reflexive*)
them. *See* **he, she, it.**
then, tum, deinde
there, ibi
therefore, igitur (*postpositive*)
these. *See* **this,** *demonstrative.*
they. *See* **he, she, it;** *often expressed simply by the
  personal ending of vb.*
thing, rēs, reī, *f.; often merely the neut. of an adj.*
think, putō (1); arbitror, -ārī, -ātus sum
third, tertius, -a, -um
this, hic, haec, hoc; is, ea, id
those. *See* **that,** *demonstrative.*
thousand, mīlle (*indecl. adj. sg.*), mīlia, -ium, *n.*
  (*noun in pl.*)

three, trēs, tria
through, per + *acc.*
throughout, per + *acc.*
throw, iaciō, -ere, iēcī, iactum
thus, sīc
time, tempus, -poris, *n.;* **(period of) time,** aetās,
  -tātis, *f.*
to (*place to which*), ad + *acc.;* (*ind. obj.*), *dat.;*
  (*purp.*), ut + *subj.,* ad + *gerund or gerundive*
today, hodiē
tolerate, tolerō (1)
tomorrow, crās
too, nimis, nimium; *or use comp. degree of adj. or
  adv.*
touch, tangō, -ere, tetigī, tāctum
travel (abroad), peregrīnor, -ārī, -ātus sum
trivial, levis, -e
troops, cōpiae, -ārum, *f. pl.*
Troy, Trōia, -ae, *f.*
true, vērus, -a, -um
truly, vērē
trust, crēdō, -ere, -didī, -ditum + *dat.*
truth, vēritās, -tātis, *f.*
try, experior, -īrī, expertus sum
turn, vertō, -ere, -ī, versum
twenty, vīgintī
two, duo, duae, duo
type, genus, -neris, *n.*
tyrant, tyrannus, -ī, *m.*

U

unable (be) nōn possum
uncertain, incertus, -a, -um
under, sub + *abl.* (= *place where*),
  + *acc.* (= *place to which*)
understand, intellegō, -ere, -lēxī, -lēctum;
  comprehendō, -ere, -ī, -hēnsum
unfortunate, miser, -era, -erum
unless, nisi
unwilling (be), nōlō, nōlle, nōluī
urban, urbāne, urbānus, -a, -um
urge, hortor, -ārī, -ātus sum
use, ūtor, -ī, ūsus sum + *abl.*

V

verse, versus, -ūs, *m.*
very, *express this by the superl. degree of adj. or
  adv.*
vice, vitium, -iī, *n.*

Virgil, Vergilius, -iī, *m.*
virtue, virtūs, -tūtis, *f.*

W

wage, gerō, -ere, gessī, gestum
walls, moenia, -ium, *n. pl.*
want, volō, velle, voluī
war, bellum, -ī, *n.*
warn, moneō, -ēre, -uī, -itum
water, aqua, -ae, *f.*
we. *See* **I;** *often expressed simply by the personal ending of vb.*
wealth, dīvitiae, -ārum, *f. pl.*
weapons, arma, -ōrum, *n. pl.*
well, bene
what (*pron.*), quid; (*adj.*), quī, quae, quod
whatever, quisquis, quidquid
when, *participial phrase; abl. abs.;* cum + *subj.;* (*interrogative*), quandō; (*rel.*), ubi
whence, unde, *adv.*
where, ubi
wherefore, quārē
which (*rel. pron. and interrogative adj.*), quī, quae, quod
while, dum
who (*rel.*), quī, quae, quod; (*interrogative*), quis, quid
whole, tōtus, -a, -um
why, cūr
wicked, malus, -a, -um
wife, uxor, uxōris, *f.*

willing (be), volō, velle, voluī
window, fenestra, -ae, *f.*
wine, vīnum, -ī, *n.*
wisdom, sapientia, -ae, *f.*
wise, sapiēns, *gen.* sapientis
wisely, sapienter
wish, cupiō, -ere, -īvī, -ītum; volō, velle, voluī
with, cum + *abl.; abl. of means* (*no prep.*)
without, sine + *abl.*
woman, fēmina, -ae, *f.; often expressed by fem. of an adj.*
word, verbum, -ī, *n.*
work, labor, -bōris, *m.;* opus, operis, *n.*
world, mundus, -ī, *m.*
worse, peior, -ius
worst, pessimus, -a, -um
write, scrībō, -ere, scrīpsī, scrīptum
writer, scrīptor, -tōris, *m.*

Y

year, annus, -ī, *m.*
yesterday, herī
yield, cēdō, -ere, cessī, cessum
you, tū, tuī; *often expressed simply by the personal ending of vb.*
young man, adulēscēns, -centis, *m.*
your (*sg.*), tuus, -a, -um; (*pl.*), vester, -tra, -trum
yourself (*reflexive*), tuī, tibi, *etc.;* (*intensive*), ipse, ipsa
youth, iuvenis, -is, *m.*

Latin-English Vocabulary

An Arabic numeral after a vocabulary entry indicates the chapter in which the word is first introduced as an item of required vocabulary. Arabic (1) in parentheses after a verb shows that this is a regular verb of the first conjugation with a sequence of principal parts ending in **-āre, -āvī, -ātum.** For prefixes and suffixes see the lists in the Appendix.

A

ā *or* **ab,** *prep. + abl.,* from, away from; by (*agent*). 14

abeō, -īre, -iī, -itum, go away, depart, leave. 37

absconditus, -a, -um, hidden, secret

absēns, *gen.* **-sentis,** *adj.,* absent, away. 37

absum, -esse, āfuī, āfutūrum, be away, be absent

abundantia, -ae, *f.,* abundance

ac. *See* **atque.**

accēdō, -ere, -cessī, -cessum, come near, approach. 36

accipiō, -ere, -cēpī, -ceptum, take, receive, accept. 24

accommodō (1), adjust, adapt

accūsātor, -tōris, *m.,* accuser

accūsō (1), accuse

ācer, ācris, ācre, sharp, keen, eager, severe, fierce. 16

acerbitās, -tātis, *f.,* harshness

acerbus, -a, -um, harsh, bitter, grievous. 12

Achillēs, -is, *m.,* Achilles, Greek hero, chief character in the *Iliad*

aciēs, -ēī, *f.,* sharp edge, keenness, line of battle

acquīrō, -ere, -quīsīvī, -quīsītum, acquire, gain

ācriter, *adv.,* keenly, fiercely. 32

ad, *prep. + acc.,* to, up to, near to. 8

addiscō, -ere, -didicī, learn in addition

addūcō, -ere, -dūxī, -ductum, lead to, induce

adeō, -īre, -iī, -itum, go to, approach. 37

adferō, -ferre, attulī, allātum, bring to. 31

adficiō, -ere, -fēcī, -fectum, affect, afflict, weaken

adiciō, -ere, -iēcī, -iectum, add

adiuvō, -āre, -iūvī, -iūtum, help, aid, assist; please. 4

admīror, -ārī, -ātus sum, wonder at, admire

admittō, -ere, -mīsī, -missum, admit, receive, let in. 17

admoneō = moneō

adnuō, -ere, -nuī, nod assent

adoptō (1), wish for oneself, select, adopt

adsum, -esse, -fuī, -futūrum, be near, be present, assist

adūlātiō, -ōnis, *f.,* fawning, flattery

adulēscēns, -centis, *m. and f.,* young man or woman. 12

adulēscentia, -ae, *f.,* youth, young manhood; youthfulness. 5

adultus, -a, -um, grown up, mature, adult

adūrō, -ere, -ussī, -ustum, set fire to, burn, singe

adveniō, -īre, -vēnī, -ventum, come (to), arrive

adversus, -a, -um, facing, opposite, adverse. 34

adversus, *prep.* + *acc.*, toward, facing; against

advesperāscit, advesperāscere, advesperāvit, *impers.*, evening is coming on, it is growing dark

aedificium, -iī, *n.,* building, structure. 39

aegrē, *adv.,* with difficulty, hardly, scarcely

aequitās, -tātis, *f.,* justice, fairness, equity

aequus, -a, -um, level, even, calm, equal, just, favorable. 22

aes, aeris, *n.,* bronze. 40

aestās, -tātis, *f.,* summer. 35

aestus, -ūs, *m.,* heat, tide

aetās, -tātis, *f.,* period of life, life, age, an age, time. 16

aeternus, -a, -um, eternal

Agamemnon, -nonis, *m.,* Agamemnon, commander-in-chief of the Greek forces at Troy

ager, agrī, *m.,* field, farm. 3

agō, -ere, ēgī, āctum, drive, lead, do, act; *of time or life,* pass, spend; **grātiās agere** + *dat.,* thank. 8

agricola, -ae, *m.,* farmer. 3

agrīcultūra, -ae, *f.,* agriculture

āit, āiunt, he says, they say, assert. 25

Alexander, -drī, *m.,* Alexander the Great, renowned Macedonian general and king, 4th cen., B.C.

aliēnus, -a, -um, belonging to another (*cp.* **alius**), foreign, strange, alien

aliōquī, *adv.,* otherwise

aliquī, aliqua, aliquod, *indef. pronominal adj.,* some

aliquis, aliquid (*gen.* **alicuius;** *dat.* **alicui**), *indef. pron.,* someone, somebody, something. 23

aliter, *adv.,* otherwise

alius, alia, aliud, other, another; **aliī . . . aliī,** some . . . others. 9

alō, -ere, aluī, altum, nourish, support, sustain, increase; cherish. 13

alter, -era, -erum, the other (of two), second. 9

altus, -a, -um, high, deep

ambitiō, -ōnis, *f.,* a canvassing for votes; ambition; flattery

ambulō (1), walk. 39

āmēn, *adv. from Hebrew,* truly, verily, so be it

amīca, -ae, *f.,* (female) friend. 3

amīcitia, -ae, *f.,* friendship. 10

amiculum, -ī, *n.,* cloak

amīcus, -a, -um, friendly. 11

amīcus, -ī, *m.,* (male) friend. 3

āmittō, -ere, -mīsī, -missum, lose, let go. 12

amō (1), love, like; **amābō tē,** please. 1

amor, amōris, *m.,* love. 7

āmoveō, -ēre, -mōvī, -mōtum, move away, remove

an, *adv. and conj. introducing the second part of a double question* (*see* **utrum**), or; *used alone,* or, can it be that

ancilla, -ae, *f.,* maidservant

angelus, -ī, *m.,* angel

angulus, -ī, *m.,* corner

angustus, -a, -um, narrow, limited

anima, -ae, *f.,* soul, spirit. 34

animal, -mālis, *n.,* a living creature, animal. 14

animus, -ī, *m.,* soul, spirit, mind; **animī, -ōrum,** high spirits, pride, courage. 5

annus, -ī, *m.,* year. 12

ante, *prep.* + *acc.,* before (*in place or time*), in front of; *adv.,* before, previously. 13

anteā, *adv.,* before, formerly

antepōnō, -ere, -posuī, -positum, put before, prefer + *dat.* 35

antīquus, -a, -um, ancient, old-time. 2

Apollō, -linis, *m.,* Phoebus Apollo, god of sun, prophecy, poetry, etc.

apparātus, -ūs, *m.,* equipment, splendor

appellō (1), speak to, address (as), call, name. 14

approbō (1), approve

appropinquō (1) + *dat.,* approach, draw near to

aptus, -a, -um, fit, suitable

apud, *prep.* + *acc.,* among, in the presence of, at the house of. 31

aqua, -ae, *f.,* water. 14

āra, -ae, *f.,* altar

arānea, -ae, *f.,* spider's web

arbitror, -ārī, -ātus sum, judge, think. 34

arbor, -boris, *f.,* tree. 38

arcus, -ūs, *m.,* bow

argentum, -ī, *n.,* silver, money

argūmentum, -ī, *n.,* proof, evidence, argument. 19

arma, -ōrum, *n.,* arms, weapons. 28

arō (1), plow

ars, artis, *f.,* art, skill. 14

arx, arcis, *f.,* citadel, stronghold. 23

as, assis, *m.,* an as (a small copper coin roughly equivalent to a cent). 31

Asia, -ae, *f.,* Asia, commonly the Roman province in Asia Minor. 12

asper, -era, -erum, rough, harsh. 21

aspiciō, -ere, -spexī, -spectum, look at, behold

assentātor, -tōris, *m.,* yes-man, flatterer

astrum, -ī, *n.,* star, constellation

at, *conj.,* but; but, mind you; but, you say; *a more emotional adversative than* **sed.** 19

āter, ātra, ātrum, dark, gloomy

Athēnae, -ārum, *f. pl.,* Athens. 37

Athēniēnsis, -e, Athenian; **Athēniēnsēs, -ium,** the Athenians

atque *or* **ac,** *conj.,* and, and also, and even. 21

atquī, *conj.,* and yet, still

auctor, -tōris, *m.,* increaser; author, originator. 19

auctōritās, -tātis, *f.,* authority

audācia, -ae, *f.,* daring, boldness, audacity

audāx, *gen.* **audācis,** daring, bold

audeō, -ēre, ausus sum, dare. 7

audiō, -īre, -īvī, -ītum, hear, listen to. 10

audītor, -tōris, *m.,* hearer, listener, member of an audience. 16

auferō, -ferre, abstulī, ablātum, bear away, carry off

Augustus, -ī, *m.,* Augustus, the first Roman emperor

aureus, -a, -um, golden

auris, -is, *f.,* ear. 14

aurum, -ī, *n.,* gold

aut, *conj.,* or; **aut . . . aut,** either . . . or. 17

autem, *postpositive conj.,* however; moreover. 11

auxilium, -iī, *n.,* aid, help. 31

avāritia, -ae, *f.,* greed, avarice

avārus, -a, -um, greedy, avaricious. 3

āvehō, -ere, -vexī, -vectum, carry away

āvertō, -ere, -vertī, -versum, turn away, avert. 23

āvocō (1), call away, divert

B

balbus, -a, -um, stammering, stuttering

barba, -ae, *f.,* beard

bāsium, -iī, *n.,* kiss. 4

beātus, -a, -um, happy, fortunate, blessed. 10

bellicus, -a, -um, relating to war, military

bellum, -ī, *n.,* war. 4

bellus, -a, -um, pretty, handsome, charming. 4

bene, *adv. of* **bonus,** well, satisfactorily, quite. 11 (*comp.* **melius;** *superl.* **optimē.** 32)

beneficium, -iī, *n.,* benefit, kindness, favor. 19

benevolentia, -ae, *f.,* good will, kindness

bēstia, -ae, *f.,* animal, beast

bibō, -ere, bibī, drink. 30

bis, *adv.,* twice

bonus, -a, -um, good, kind. 4 (*comp.* **melior;** *superl.* **optimus.** 27)

bōs, bovis, *m./f.,* bull, ox, cow

brevis, -e, short, small, brief. 16

brevitās, -tātis, *f.,* shortness, brevity

breviter, *adv.,* briefly

Britannia, -ae, *f.,* Britain

Brundisium, -iī, *n.,* important seaport in S. Italy

Brūtus, -ī, *m.,* famous Roman name: L. Junius Brutus, who helped establish the Roman republic; M. Junius Brutus, one of the conspirators against Julius Caesar

C

C., abbreviation for the common name **Gāius**

cadō, -ere, cecidī, cāsūrum, fall. 12

caecus, -a, -um, blind. 17

caelestis, -e, heavenly, celestial

caelum, -ī, *n.,* sky, heaven. 5

Caesar, -saris, *m.,* Caesar, especially Gaius Julius Caesar. 12

calamitās, -tātis, *f.,* misfortune, disaster

calculus, -ī, *m.,* pebble

campana, -ae, *f.,* bell (*late Lat.*)

candidus, -a, -um, shining, bright, white; beautiful. 33

canis, -is (*gen. pl.* **canum**), *m./f.,* dog

canō, -ere, cecinī, cantum, to sing about

cantō (1), sing

capillus, -ī, *m.,* hair (*of head or beard*)

capiō, -ere, cēpī, captum, take, capture, seize, get. 10

captō (1), grab, seek to get, hunt for (legacies, etc.)

caput, -pitis, *n.,* head; leader; beginning; life; heading, chapter. 11

carbō, -bōnis, *m.,* coal, charcoal

careō, -ēre, -uī, -itūrum + *abl. of separation,* be without, be deprived of, want, lack, be free from. 20

cāritās, -tātis, *f.,* dearness, affection

carmen, -minis, *n.,* song, poem. 7

carpō, -ere, carpsī, carptum, harvest, pluck; seize. 36

Carthāgō, -ginis, *f.,* Carthage (city in N. Africa). 24

cārus, -a, -um, dear. 11

casa, -ae, *f.,* house, cottage, hut. 21

cāsus, -ūs, *m.,* accident, chance

catēna, -ae, *f.,* chain
Catilīna, -ae, *m.,* L. Sergius Catiline, leader of the conspiracy against the Roman state in 63 B.C.
Catullus, -ī, *m.,* Gaius Valerius Catullus, 1st cen. B.C. lyric poet
cattus, -ī, *m.,* cat (*late word for classical* **fēlēs, -is**)
causa, -ae, *f.,* cause, reason; case, situation; **causā** *with a preceding gen.,* for the sake of, on account of. 21
caveō, -ēre, cāvī, cautum, beware, avoid
cavus, -ī, *m.,* hole
cēdō, -ere, cessī, cessum, go, withdraw; yield to, submit, grant. 28
celer, -eris, -ere, swift, quick, rapid. 16
celeritās, -tātis, *f.,* speed, swiftness
celeriter, swiftly, quickly
cēna, -ae, *f.,* dinner. 26
cēnō (1), dine. 5
centum, *indecl. adj.,* a hundred. 15
cernō, -ere, crēvī, crētum, distinguish, discern, perceive. 22
certē, *adv.,* certainly
certus, -a, -um, definite, sure, certain, reliable. 19
cervus, -ī, *m.,* stag, deer
cēterī, -ae, -a, the remaining, the rest, the other. 30
Cicerō, -rōnis, *m.,* Marcus Tullius Cicero. 8
cicūta, -ae, *f.,* hemlock (*poison*)
cinis, -neris, *m.,* ashes
circēnsēs, -ium, *m. pl.* (*sc.* **lūdī**), games in the Circus
cito, *adv.,* quickly. 17
cīvīlis, -e, civil, civic
cīvis, -is, *m./f.,* citizen. 14
cīvitās, -tātis, *f.,* state, citizenship. 7
clārus, -a, -um, clear, bright; renowned, famous, illustrious. 18
claudō, -ere, clausī, clausum, shut, close
clēmentia, -ae, *f.,* mildness, gentleness, mercy. 16
coepī, coepisse, coeptum (*defective vb.; pres. system supplied by* **incipiō**), began. 17
coërceō, -ēre, -uī, -itum, curb, check, repress
cōgitō (1), think, ponder, consider, plan. 1
cognōscō, -ere, -nōvī, -nitum, become acquainted with, learn, recognize; *in perf. tenses,* know. 30
cōgō, -ere, coēgī, coāctum, drive *or* bring together, force, compel. 36
colligō, -ere, -lēgī, -lēctum, gather together, collect
collocō (1), place, put, arrange

collum, -ī, *n.,* neck
colō, -ere, coluī, cultum, cultivate; cherish
color, -ōris, *m.,* color
commemorō (1), remind, relate, mention
commisceō, -ēre, -uī, -mixtum, intermingle, join
committō, -ere, -mīsī, -missum, entrust, commit. 15
commūnis, -e, common, general, of/for the community. 20
comparō (1), compare
compōnō, -ere, -posuī, -positum, put together, compose
comprehendō, -ere, -hendī, -hēnsum, grasp, seize, arrest; comprehend, understand. 30
concēdō, -ere, -cessī, -cessum, yield, grant, concede
concilium, -iī, *n.,* council
condō, -ere, -didī, -ditum, put together or into, store; build, found, establish. 29
cōnferō, -ferre, contulī, collātum, bring together, compare; **sē cōnferre,** betake oneself, go. 31
cōnfīdō, -ere, -fīsus sum, have confidence in, believe confidently, be confident
cōnfiteor, -ērī, -fessus sum, confess
congregō (1), gather together, assemble
coniciō, -ere, -iēcī, -iectum, throw, hurl, put with force; put together, conjecture
coniūrātiō, -ōnis, *f.,* conspiracy
coniūrātī, -ōrum, *m. pl.,* conspirators. 20
cōnor, -ārī, -ātus sum, try, attempt. 34
cōnscientia, -ae, *f.,* consciousness, knowledge; conscience
cōnscius, -a, -um, conscious, aware of
cōnservō (1), preserve, conserve, maintain. 1
cōnsilium, -iī, *n.,* counsel, advice, plan, purpose; judgment, wisdom. 4
cōnsistō, -ere, -stitī + in, depend on
cōnstō, -āre, -stitī, -stātūrum + ex, consist of
cōnsuēscō, -ere, -suēvī, -suētum, become accustomed
cōnsul, -sulis, *m.,* consul. 11
cōnsulō, -ere, -suluī, -sultum, look out for, have regard for
cōnsultum, -ī, *n.,* decree
cōnsūmō, -ere, -sūmpsī, -sūmptum, use up, consume. 30
contemnō, -ere, -tempsī, -temptum, despise, scorn. 36
contendō, -ere, -tendī, -tentum, strive, struggle, contend, hasten. 29
contineō, -ēre, -tinuī, -tentum, hold together, keep, enclose, restrain, contain. 21

contingō, -ere, -tigī, -tāctum, touch closely, befall, fall to one's lot

contrā, *prep.* + *acc.,* against. 19

contundō, -tundere, -tudī, -tūsum, beat, crush, bruise, destroy. 36

conturbō (1), throw into confusion

convertō, -ere, -vertī, -versum, turn around, cause to turn

convocō (1), call together, convene

cōpia, -ae, *f.,* abundance, supply; **cōpiae, -ārum,** supplies, troops, forces. 8

cōpiōsē, *adv.,* fully, at length, copiously

Corinthus, -ī, *f.,* Corinth

cornū, -ūs, *n.,* horn. 20

corōna, -ae, *f.,* crown

corpus, -poris, *n.,* body. 7

corrigō, -ere, -rēxī, -rēctum, make right, correct

corrōborō (1), strengthen

corrumpō, -ere, -rūpī, -ruptum, ruin, corrupt

cōtīdiē, *adv.,* daily, every day. 36

crās, *adv.,* tomorrow. 5

creātor, -tōris, *m.,* creator

creātūra, -ae, *f.,* creature (*late Lat.*)

crēber, -bra, -brum, thick, frequent, numerous

crēdō, -ere, crēdidī, crēditum, believe, trust. 25; + *dat.* 35

creō (1), create. 12

crēscō, -ere, crēvī, crētum, increase. 34

crūdēlis, -e, cruel

crūstulum, -ī, *n.,* pastry, cookie

cubiculum, -ī, *n.,* bedroom, room

culpa, -ae, *f.,* fault, blame. 5

culpō (1), blame, censure. 5

cultūra, -ae, *f.,* cultivation

cum, *conj., with subj.,* when, since, although; *with ind.,* when. 31

cum, *prep.* + *abl.,* with. 10

cūnctātiō, -ōnis, *f.,* delay

cūnctātor, -tōris, *m.,* delayer

cūnctor (1), delay

cupiditās, -tātis, *f.,* desire, longing, passion; cupidity, avarice. 10

cupīdō, -dinis, *f.,* desire, passion. 36

cupidus, -a, -um, desirous, eager, fond; + *gen.,* desirous of, eager for. 39

cupiō, -ere, cupīvī, cupītum, desire, wish, long for. 17

cūr, *adv.,* why. 18

cūra, -ae, *f.,* care, attention, caution, anxiety. 4

cūrō (1), care for, attend to; heal, cure; take care. 36

currō, -ere, cucurrī, cursum, run, rush, move quickly. 14

cursus, -ūs, *m.,* running, race; course. 28

curvus, -a, -um, curved, crooked, wrong

custōdia, -ae, *f.,* protection, custody; *pl.,* guards. 32

custōs, -tōdis, *m.,* guardian, guard

D

damnō (1), condemn

Dāmoclēs, -is, *m.,* Damocles, an attendant of Dionysius

dē, *prep.* + *abl.,* down from, from; concerning, about. 3

dea, -ae, *f.* (*dat. and abl. pl.* **deābus**), goddess. 6

dēbeō, -ēre, -uī, -itum, owe, ought, must. 1

dēbilitō (1), weaken

dēcernō, -ere, -crēvī, -crētum, decide, settle, decree. 36

dēcertō (1), fight it out, fight to the finish, contend

decimus, -a, -um, tenth. 15

dēcipiō, -ere, -cēpi, -ceptum, deceive

decor, -cōris, *m.,* beauty, grace

dēcrētum, -ī, *n.,* decree

dēfendō, -ere, -fendī, -fēnsum, ward off, defend, protect. 20

dēficiō, -ere, -fēcī, -fectum, fail

dēgustō (1), taste

dehinc, *adv.,* then, next. 25

deinde, *adv.,* thereupon, next, then. 18

dēlectātiō, -ōnis, *f.,* delight, pleasure, enjoyment. 27

dēlectō (1), delight, charm, please. 19

dēleō, -ēre, dēlēvī, dēlētum, destroy, wipe out, erase. 17

dēlīberō (1), consider, deliberate

dēmēns, *gen.* **-mentis,** *adj.,* out of one's mind, insane, foolish

dēmittō, -ere, -mīsī, -missum, let down, lower

dēmōnstrō (1), point out, show, demonstrate. 8

Dēmosthenēs, -is, *m.,* Demosthenes, the most famous Greek orator, 4th cen. B.C.

dēnique, *adv.,* at last, finally. 29

dēns, dentis, *m.,* tooth

dēpōnō, -ere, -posuī, -positum, put down, lay aside

dēportō (1), carry off

dēsīderō (1), desire, long for, miss. 17

dēsidiōsus, -a, -um, lazy

dēsinō, -ere, -sīvī, -situm, cease, leave off. 34

dēsipiō, -ere, act foolishly

dēstinātus, -a, -um, resolved, resolute, firm

dētrīmentum, -ī, *n.,* loss, detriment

deus, -ī, *m. (voc. sg.* deus, *nom. pl.* deī *or* dī, *dat. and abl. pl.* dīs), god. 6

dēvocō (1), call down *or* away

dexter, -tra, -trum, right, right-hand. 20

diabolus, -ī, *m.,* devil

dīcō, -ere, dīxī, dictum, say, tell, speak; call, name. 10

dictāta, -ōrum, *n. pl.,* things dictated, lessons, precepts

dictātor, -tōris, *m.,* dictator

dictō (1), say repeatedly, dictate

diēs, -ēī, *m.,* day. 22

difficilis, -e, hard, difficult, troublesome. 16

digitus, -ī, *m.,* finger, toe. 31

dignitās, -tātis, *f.,* merit, prestige, dignity. 38

dignus, -a, -um + *abl.,* worthy, worthy of. 29

dīligēns, *gen.* -gentis, *adj.,* diligent, careful. 27

dīligenter, *adv.,* diligently

dīligentia, -ae, *f.,* diligence

dīligō, -ere, dīlēxī, dīlēctum, esteem, love. 13

dīmidium, -iī, *n.,* half

dīmittō, -ere, -mīsī, -missum, send away, dismiss

Dionȳsius, -iī, *m.,* Dionysius, tyrant of Syracuse

discēdō, -ere, -cessī, -cessum, go away, depart. 20

discipula, -ae, *f.,* and discipulus, -ī, *m.,* learner, pupil, disciple. 6

discō, -ere, didicī, learn. 8

disputātiō, -ōnis, *f.,* discussion

disputō (1), discuss

dissimilis, -e, unlike, different. 27

dissimulō (1), conceal

distinguō, -ere, -stīnxī, -stīnctum, distinguish

diū, *adv.,* long, for a long time. 12

dīves, *gen.* dīvitis *or* dītis, *adj.,* rich. 32

dīvīnus, -a, -um, divine, sacred

dīvitiae, -ārum, *f. pl.,* riches, wealth. 13

dō, dare, dedī, datum, give, offer. 1

doceō, -ēre, -uī, doctum, teach. 8

doctrīna, -ae, *f.,* teaching, instruction, learning

doctus, -a, -um, taught, learned, skilled. 13

doleō, -ēre, -uī, -itūrum, grieve, suffer; hurt, give pain. 31

dolor, -lōris, *m.,* pain, grief. 38

domesticus, -a, -um, domestic; civil

domina, -ae, *f.,* mistress, lady. 40

dominātus, -ūs, *m.,* rule, mastery, tyranny

dominicus, -a, -um, belonging to a master; the Lord's

dominus, -ī, *m.,* master, lord. 40

domus, -ūs (-ī), *f.,* house, home; domī, at home; domum, (to) home; domō, from home. 37

dōnum, -ī, *n.,* gift, present. 4

dormiō, -īre, -īvī, -ītum, sleep. 31

dubitō (1), doubt, hesitate. 30

dubium, -iī, *n.,* doubt

dūcō, -ere, dūxī, ductum, lead; consider, regard; prolong. 8

dulcis, -e, sweet, pleasant, agreeable. 16

dum, *conj.,* while, as long as; at the same time that; until. 8

dummodo, *conj., with subj.,* provided that, so long as. 32

duo, duae, duo, two. 15

dūrō (1), harden, last, endure

dūrus, -a, -um, hard, harsh, rough, stern, unfeeling, hardy, tough, difficult. 29

dux, ducis, *m.,* leader, guide, commander, general. 23

E

ē. *See* ex.

ecclēsia, -ae, *f.,* church (*ecclesiastical Lat.*)

ēducō (1), bring up, educate. 23

ēdūcō, -ere, -dūxī, -ductum, lead out

efferō, -ferre, extulī, ēlātum, carry out; bury; lift up, exalt

efficiō, -ere, -fēcī, -fectum, accomplish, perform, bring about, cause

effugiō, -ere, -fūgī, -fugitūrum, flee from, flee away, escape

egeō, -ēre, eguī + *abl. or gen.,* need, lack, want. 28

ego, meī, I. 11

ēgredior, -ī, -gressus sum, go out, depart. 34

ēiciō, -ere, -iēcī, -iectum, throw out, drive out. 15

elementum, -ī, *n.,* element, first principle

elephantus, -ī, *m.,* elephant. 31

ēloquēns, *gen.* -quentis, *adj.,* eloquent

ēloquentia, -ae, *f.,* eloquence

ēmendō (1), correct, emend

emō, -ere, ēmī, ēmptum, buy

ēmoveō, -ēre, -mōvī, -mōtum, move away, remove

enim, *postpositive conj.,* for, in fact, truly. 9

Ennius, -iī, *m.,* Quintus Ennius, early Roman writer

ēnumerō (1), count up, enumerate

eō, īre, iī (*or* īvī), itum, go. 37

epigramma, -matis, *n.,* inscription, epigram

epistula, -ae, *f.,* letter, epistle

eques, equitis, *m.,* horseman

equidem, *adv. especially common with 1st pers.,* indeed, truly, for my part

equitātus, -ūs, *m.,* cavalry

equus, -ī, *m.,* horse. 23

ergā, *prep. + acc.,* toward. 38

ergō, *adv.,* therefore

ēripiō, -ere, -ripuī, -reptum, snatch away, take away, rescue. 22

errō (1), wander; err, go astray, make a mistake, be mistaken. 1

error, -rōris, *m.,* a going astray, error, mistake

et, *conj.,* and; even (= **etiam**); **et . . . et,** both . . . and. 2

etiam, *adv.,* even, also. 11

etsī, *conj.,* even if (**et-sī**), although. 38

ēveniō, -īre, -vēnī, -ventum, come out, turn out, happen

ēventus, -ūs, *m.,* outcome, result

ex or **ē,** *prep + abl.,* out of, from within, from; by reason of, on account of; *following cardinal numerals,* of. **Ex** *can be used before consonants or vowels;* **ē,** *before consonants only.* 8

excellentia, -ae, *f.,* excellence, merit

excipiō, -ere, -cēpī, -ceptum, take out, except; take, receive, capture. 24

exclāmō (1), cry out, call out

exclūdō, -ere, -clūsī, -clūsum, shut out, exclude

excruciō (1), torture, torment

excūsātiō, -ōnis, *f.,* excuse

exemplar, -plāris, *n.,* model, pattern, original. 14

exemplum, -ī, *n.,* example, model

exeō, -īre, -iī, -itum, go out, exit. 37

exercitus, -ūs, *m.,* army. 32

exigō, -igere, -ēgī, -āctum (*ex + agō*), drive out, force out, extract, drive through, complete, perfect. 36

eximius, -a, -um, extraordinary, excellent

exitium, -iī, *n.,* destruction, ruin. 4

expellō, -ere, -pulī, -pulsum, drive out, expel, banish. 24

experior, -īrī, -pertus sum, try, test; experience. 39

expleō, -ēre, -plēvī, -plētum, fill, fill up, complete. 28

explicō (1), unfold; explain; spread out, deploy. 40

expōnō, -ere, -posuī, -positum, set forth, explain, expose. 30

exquīsītus, -a, -um, sought-out, exquisite, excellent

exsilium, -iī, *n.,* exile, banishment. 31

exspectō (1), look for, expect, await. 15

exstinguō, -ere, -stīnxī, -stīnctum, extinguish

externus, -a, -um, foreign

extorqueō, -ēre, -torsī, -tortum, twist away, extort

extrā, *prep. + acc.,* beyond, outside

extrēmus, -a, -um, outermost, last, extreme

F

Fabius, -iī, *m.,* Roman name; especially Quintus Fabius Maximus Cunctator (the Delayer), celebrated for his delaying tactics (Fabian tactics) against Hannibal

fābula, -ae, *f.,* story, tale; play. 24

facile, *adv.,* easily. 32

facilis, -e, easy; agreeable, affable. 16

faciō, -ere, fēcī, factum, make, do, accomplish, 10; *passive:* **fīō, fierī, factus sum.** 36

factum, -ī, *n.,* deed, act, achievement. 13

facultās, -tātis, *f.,* ability, skill, opportunity, means

falsus, -a, -um, false, deceptive

fāma, -ae, *f.,* rumor, report; fame, reputation. 2

familia, -ae, *f.,* household, family. 19

fās (*indecl.*), *n.,* right, sacred duty; **fās est,** it is right, fitting, lawful

fateor, -ērī, fassus sum, confess, admit. 34

fatīgō (1), weary, tire out. 40

fātum, -ī, *n.,* fate; death; *often pl.,* the Fates. 29

faucēs, -ium, *f. pl.,* jaws; narrow passage.

fēlīciter, *adv.,* happily. 32

fēlīx, *gen.* **-līcis,** *adj.,* lucky, fortunate, happy. 22

fēmina, -ae, *f.,* woman. 3

fenestra, -ae, *f.,* window. 21

ferē, *adv.,* almost, nearly, generally

ferō, ferre, tulī, lātum, bear, carry, bring; suffer, endure, tolerate; say, report. 31

ferōx, *gen.* **-rōcis,** fierce, savage. 25

ferrum, -ī, *n.,* iron, sword. 22

ferus, -a, -um, wild, uncivilized, fierce

festīnātiō, -ōnis, *f.,* haste

festīnō (1), hasten, hurry

fīcus, -ī *and* **-ūs,** *f.,* fig tree

fidēlis, -e, faithful, loyal. 25

fidēs, -eī, *f.,* faith, trust, trustworthiness, fidelity; promise, guarantee, protection. 22

fīlia, -ae, *f.* (*dat. and abl. pl.* **fīliābus**), daughter. 3

fīlius, -iī, *m.,* son. 3

fīnis, -is, *m.,* end, limit, boundary; purpose; **fīnēs, -ium** (boundaries) territory. 21

fīō, fierī, factus sum, occur, happen; become, be made, be done. 36

fīrmus, -a, -um, firm, strong; reliable. 38

flamma, -ae, *f.,* flame, fire

fleō, -ēre, flēvī, flētum, weep

flūctus, -ūs, *m.,* billow, wave

flūmen, -minis, *n.,* river. 18

fluō, -ere, flūxī, flūxum, flow. 18

for, fārī, fātus sum, speak (prophetically), talk, foretell. 40

forīs, *adv.,* out of doors, outside. 37

fōrma, -ae, *f.,* form, shape, beauty. 2

formīca, -ae, *f.,* ant

fōrmō (1), form, shape, fashion

fors, fortis, *f.,* chance, fortune

forsan, *adv.,* perhaps

fortasse, *adv.,* perhaps. 36

fortis, -e, strong, brave. 16

fortiter, *adv.,* bravely. 32

fortūna, -ae, *f.,* fortune, luck. 2

fortūnātē, *adv.,* fortunately

fortūnātus, -a, -um, lucky, fortunate, happy. 13

forum, -ī, *n.,* market place, forum. 26

foveō, -ēre, fōvī, fōtum, comfort, nurture, support. 35

frāter, -tris, *m.,* brother. 8

frōns, frontis, *f.,* forehead, brow, front

frūctus, -ūs, *m.,* fruit; profit, benefit, enjoyment. 20

frūgālitās, -tātis, *f.,* frugality

frūstrā, *adv.,* in vain

fuga, -ae, *f.,* flight

fugiō, -ere, fūgī, fugitūrum, flee, hurry away; escape; go into exile; avoid, shun. 10

fugitīvus, -ī, *m.,* fugitive, deserter, runaway slave

fugō (1), put to flight, rout

fulgeō, -ēre, fulsī, flash, shine

furor, -rōris, *m.,* rage, frenzy, madness

fūrtificus, -a, -um, thievish

fūrtim, *adv.,* stealthily, secretly. 30

G

Gāius, -iī, *m.,* Gaius, a common praenomen (first name); usually abbreviated to **C.** in writing

Gallus, -ī, *m.,* a Gaul. The Gauls were a Celtic people who inhabited the district which we know as France.

gaudeō, gaudēre, gāvīsus sum, be glad, rejoice. 23

gaudium, -iī, *n.,* joy, delight

geminus, -a, -um, twin. 25

gēns, gentis, *f.,* clan, race, nation, people. 21

genū, genūs, *n.,* knee. 20

genus, generis, *n.,* origin; kind, type, sort, class. 18

gerō, -ere, gessī, gestum, carry; carry on, manage, conduct, wage, accomplish, perform. 8

gladius, -iī, *m.,* sword

glōria, -ae, *f.,* glory, fame. 5

gracilis, -e, slender, thin. 27

Graecia, -ae, *f.,* Greece. 19

Graecus, -a, -um, Greek; **Graecus, -ī,** *m.,* a Greek. 6

grātia, -ae, *f.,* gratitude, favor; **grātiās agere** + *dat.,* to thank. 8

grātus, -a, -um, pleasing, agreeable; grateful. 37

gravis, -e, heavy, weighty; serious, important; severe, grievous. 19

gravitās, -tātis, *f.,* weight, seriousness, importance, dignity

graviter, *adv.,* heavily, seriously

gustō (1), taste

H

habeō, -ēre, -uī, -itum, have, hold, possess; consider, regard. 3

hāmus, -ī, *m.,* hook

Hannibal, -balis, *m.,* Hannibal, celebrated Carthaginian general in the 2nd Punic War, 218–201 B.C.

hasta, -ae, *f.,* spear. 23

haud, *adv.,* not, not at all (*strong negative*)

herī, *adv.,* yesterday. 5

heu, *interjection,* ah!, alas! (*a sound of grief or pain*). 33

hic, haec, hoc, *demonstrative adj. and pron.,* this, the latter; *at times weakened to* he, she, it, they. 9

hīc, *adv.,* here. 25

hinc, *adv.,* from this place, hence

hodiē, *adv.,* today. 3

Homērus, -ī, *m.,* Homer, the Greek epic poet

homō, hominis, *m.,* human being, man. 7

honor, -nōris, *m.,* honor, esteem; public office. 30

hōra, -ae, *f.,* hour, time. 10

horrendus, -a, -um, horrible, dreadful

hortor, -ārī, -ātus sum, urge, encourage. 34

hortus, -ī, *m.,* garden

hospes, -pitis, *m.,* stranger, guest; host

hostis, -is, *m.,* an enemy (of the state); **hostēs, -ium,** the enemy. 18

hui, *interj., sound of surprise or approbation not unlike our* "whee"

hūmānitās, -tātis, *f.,* kindness, refinement

hūmānus, -a, -um, pertaining to man, human; humane, kind; refined, cultivated. 4

humilis, -e, lowly, humble. 27

humus, -ī, *f.,* ground, earth; soil. 37

hypocrita, -ae, *m.,* hypocrite (*ecclesiastical Lat.*)

I

iaceō, -ēre, -uī, lie; lie prostrate; lie dead. 25
iaciō, -ere, iēcī, iactum, throw, hurl. 15
iaculum, -ī, *n.,* dart, javelin
iam, *adv.,* now, already, soon. 19
iānua, -ae, *f.,* door. 35
ibi, *adv.,* there. 6
īdem, eadem, idem, the same. 11
identidem, *adv.,* repeatedly, again and again
idōneus, -a, -um, suitable, fit, appropriate. 37
igitur, *postpositive conj.,* therefore, consequently. 5
ignārus, -a, -um, not knowing, ignorant
ignis, -is, *m.,* fire. 22
ignōscō, -ere, -nōvī, -nōtum + *dat.,* grant pardon
 to, forgive, overlook. 35
illacrimō (1) + *dat.,* weep over
ille, illa, illud, *demonstrative adj. and pron.,* that,
 the former; the famous; *at times weakened to*
 he, she, it, they. 9
illūdō, -ere, -lūsī, -lūsum, mock, ridicule
imāgō, -ginis, *m.,* image, likeness
imitor, -ārī, -ātus sum, imitate
immineō, -ēre, overhang, threaten
immodicus, -a, -um, beyond measure, moderate,
 excessive
immortālis, -e, not subject to death, immortal. 19
immōtus, -a, -um, unmoved; unchanged;
 unrelenting. 37
impedīmentum, -ī, *n.,* hindrance, impediment
impediō, -īre, -īvī, -ītum, impede, hinder,
 prevent. 38
impellō, -ere, -pulī, -pulsum, urge on, impel
impendeō, -ēre, hang over, threaten, be imminent
imperātor, -tōris, *m.,* general, commander-in-chief,
 emperor. 24
imperiōsus, -a, -um, powerful, domineering,
 imperious
imperium, -ī, *n.,* power to command, supreme
 power, authority, command, control. 24
imperō (1), give orders to, command + *dat.* + **ut.**
 35
impleō, -ēre, implēvī, implētum, fill up, complete
imprīmīs, *adv.,* especially, particularly
imprōvidus, -a, -um, improvident
impudēns, *gen.* **-dentis,** *adj.,* shameless, impudent
impudenter, *adv.,* shamelessly, impudently
impūnītus, -a, -um, unpunished, unrestrained,
 safe
in, *prep.* + *abl.,* in, on, 3; + *acc.,* into, toward,
 against. 9

inānis, -e, empty, vain
incertus, -a, -um, uncertain, unsure, doubtful
incipiō, -ere, -cēpī, -ceptum, begin, commence. 17
inclūdō, -ere, -clūsī, -clūsum, shut in, inclose
incorruptus, -a, -um, uncorrupted, genuine, pure
incrēdibilis, -e, incredible
indicō (1), indicate, expose, accuse
indignus, -a, -um, unworthy
indūcō, -ere, -dūxī, -ductum, lead in, introduce,
 induce
industria, -ae, *f.,* industry, diligence
industrius, -a, -um, industrious, diligent
ineō, -īre, -iī, -itum, go in, enter. 37
ineptiō, -īre, play the fool, trifle
inexpugnābilis, -e, impregnable, unconquerable
īnfantia, -ae, *f.,* infancy
īnferī, -ōrum, *m. pl.,* those below, the dead
īnferō, -ferre, intulī, illātum, bring in, bring upon,
 inflict
īnfīnītus, -a, -um, unlimited, infinite
īnfīrmus, -a, -um, not strong, weak, feeble. 38
īnflammō (1), set on fire, inflame
īnfōrmis, -e, formless, deformed, hideous
īnfortūnātus, -a, -um, unfortunate
ingenium, -iī, *n.,* nature, innate talent. 29
ingēns, *gen.* **-gentis,** *adj.,* huge. 16
ingrātus, -a, -um, unpleasant, ungrateful
iniciō, -ere, -iēcī, -iectum, throw on *or* into, put
 on; inspire
inimīcus, -ī, *m.,* (personal) enemy
inīquus, -a, -um, unequal, unfair, unjust
initium, -iī, *n.,* beginning, commencement. 33
iniūria, -ae, *f.,* injustice, injury, wrong. 39
iniūstus, -a, -um, unjust. 10
inops, *gen.* **-opis,** *adj.,* poor, needy
inquam. See inquit.
inquit, *defective verb,* he says, *placed after one or
 more words of a direct quotation; other forms:*
 inquam, I say, **inquis,** you say. 22
īnsānia, -ae, *f.,* insanity, folly
īnsciēns, *gen.* **-entis,** unknowing, unaware
īnscrībō, -ere, -scrīpsī, -scrīptum, inscribe, entitle
īnsidiae, -ārum, *f. pl.,* ambush, plot, treachery. 6
īnsōns, *gen.* **-sontis,** guiltless, innocent
īnstituō, -ere, -stituī, -stitūtum, establish, institute
īnsula, -ae, *f.,* island. 23
īnsurgō, -ere, -surrēxī, -surrēctum, rise up
integer, -gra, -grum, untouched, whole, unhurt
intellegō, -ere, -lēxī, -lēctum, understand. 11
intempestīvus, -a, -um, untimely
inter, *prep.* + *acc.,* between, among. 15

intercipiō, -ere, -cēpī, -ceptum, intercept
interdum, *adv.,* at times, sometimes
intereā, *adv.,* meanwhile
interficiō, -ere, -fēcī, -fectum, kill, murder. 37
interrogātiō, -ōnis, *f.,* interrogation, inquiry
intrō (1), walk into, enter
intrōdūcō, -ere, -dūxī, -ductum, lead in, introduce
intus, *adv.,* within
invādō, -ere, -vāsī, -vāsum, enter on, move against, assail
inveniō, -īre, -vēnī, -ventum, come upon, find. 10
inventor, -tōris, *m.,* inventor
invēstīgō (1), track out, investigate
invictus, -a, -um, unconquered; unconquerable
invideō, -ēre, -vīdī, -vīsum, be envious; + *dat.,* look at with envy, envy, be jealous of. 31
invidia, -ae, *f.,* envy, jealousy, hatred. 31
invīsus, -a, -um, hated; hateful
invītō (1), entertain; invite, summon. 26
invītus, -a, -um, unwilling, against one's will
iocus, -ī, *m.,* joke, jest
ipse, ipsa, ipsum, *intensive pron.,* myself, yourself, himself, herself, itself, *etc.;* the very, the actual. 13
īra, -ae, *f.,* ire, anger. 2
īrāscor, -ī, īrātus sum, be angry
īrātus, -a, -um, angered, angry. 35
irrītō (1), excite, exasperate, irritate
is, ea, id, *demonstrative pron. and adj.,* this, that; *personal pron.,* he, she, it. 11
iste, ista, istud, *demonstrative pron. and adj.,* that of yours, that; such; *sometimes with contemptuous force.* 9
ita, *adv. used with adjs., vbs., and advs.,* so, thus. 29
Italia, -ae, *f.,* Italy. 15
itaque, *adv.,* and so, therefore. 15
iter, itineris, *n.,* journey; route, road. 37
iterō (1), repeat
iterum, *adv.,* again, a second time. 21
iubeō, -ēre, iussī, iussum, bid, order, command. 21
iūcunditās, -tātis, *f.,* pleasure, charm
iūcundus, -a, -um, agreeable, pleasant, gratifying. 16
iūdex, -dicis, *m.,* judge, juror. 19
iūdicium, -iī, *n.,* judgment, decision, opinion; trial. 19
iūdicō (1), judge, consider
iungō, -ere, iūnxī, iūnctum, join. 13
Iuppiter, Iovis, *m.,* Jupiter, Jove
iūrō (1), swear

iūs, iūris, *n.,* right, justice, law. 14; **iūs iūrandum, iūris iūrandī,** *n.,* oath
iussū, *defective noun, abl. sg. only, m.,* at the command of
iūstus, -a, -um, just, right. 40
iuvenis, -is (*gen. pl.* **iuvenum**), *m./f.,* a youth, young person
iuvō, -āre, iūvī, iūtum, help, aid, assist; please. 4

L

lābor, -ī, lāpsus sum, slip, glide
labor, -bōris, *m.,* labor, work, toil. 7
labōrō (1), labor; be in distress. 21
labrum, -ī, *n.,* lip
lacessō, -ere, -īvī, -ītum, harass, attack
lacrima, -ae, *f.,* tear. 40
lacūnar, -nāris, *n.,* paneled ceiling
laetāns, *gen.* **-tantis,** *adj.,* rejoicing
laetus, -a, -um, happy, joyful
Latīnus, -a, -um, Latin. 22
laudātor, -tōris, *m.,* praiser
laudō (1), praise. 1
laus, laudis, *f.,* praise, glory, fame. 8
lēctor, -tōris, *m.,* **lēctrīx, -trīcis,** *f.,* reader. 36
lectus, -ī, *m.,* bed
lēgātus, -ī, *m.,* ambassador, deputy
legiō, -ōnis, *f.,* legion
legō, -ere, lēgī, lēctum, pick out, choose; read. 18
lēnis, -e, smooth, gentle, kind
lentē, *adv.,* slowly
Lentulus, -ī, *m.,* P. Cornelius Lentulus Sura, chief conspirator under Catiline, left in charge of the conspiracy when Catiline was forced to flee from Rome
Lesbia, -ae, *f.,* Lesbia, the name which Catullus gave to his sweetheart
levis, -e, light; easy, slight, trivial. 17
lēx, lēgis, *f.,* law, statute. 26
libellus, -ī, *m.,* little book. 17
libenter, *adv.,* with pleasure, gladly. 38
līber, -era, -erum, free. 5
liber, -brī, *m.,* book. 6
līberālis, -e, of, relating to a free person; worthy of a free man, decent, liberal, generous. 39
līberālitās, -tātis, *f.,* generosity, liberality
līberātor, -tōris, *m.,* liberator
līberē, *adv.,* freely. 32
līberī, -ōrum, *m. pl.,* (one's) children
līberō (1), free, liberate. 19
lībertās, -tātis, *f.,* liberty, freedom. 8

libō (1), pour a libation of, on; pour ritually; sip; touch gently. 39

licet, licēre, licuit, *impers.* + *dat. and inf.,* it is permitted, one may. 37

ligō (1), bind, tie

līmen, -minis, *n.,* threshold. 26

lingua, -ae, *f.,* tongue; language. 25

linteum, -ī, *n.,* linen, napkin

littera, -ae, *f.,* a letter of the alphabet; **litterae, -ārum,** a letter (epistle); literature. 7

lītus, -toris, *n.,* shore, coast. 23

locō (1), place, put

locuplētō (1), enrich

locus, -ī, *m.,* place; passage in literature; *pl.,* **loca, -ōrum,** *n.,* places, region; **locī, -ōrum,** *m.,* passages in literature. 9

longē, *adv.,* far. 32

longinquitās, -tātis, *f.,* distance, remoteness

longus, -a, -um, long. 16

loquāx, *gen.* **-quācis,** *adj.,* talkative, loquacious

loquor, -ī, locūtus sum, say, speak, tell, talk. 34

lucrum, -ī, *n.,* gain, profit

lūdō, -ere, lūsī, lūsum, play

lūdus, -ī, *m.,* game, sport; school. 18

lūna, -ae, *f.,* moon. 28

lupus, -ī, *m.,* wolf

lūx, lūcis, *f.,* light. 26

luxuria, -ae, *f.,* luxury, extravagance

M

Maecēnās, -ātis, *m.,* Maecenas, unofficial "prime minister" of Augustus, and patron and friend of Horace

magis, *adv.,* more, rather

magister, -trī, *m.,* master, schoolmaster, teacher. 4

magistra, -ae, *f.,* mistress, schoolmistress. 4

magnanimus, -a, -um, great-hearted, brave, magnanimous. 23

magnopere, *adv.,* greatly, exceedingly (*comp.* **magis;** *superl.* **maximē**). 32

magnus, -a, -um, large, great; important. 2 (*comp.* **maior;** *superl.* **maximus.** 27); **maiōrēs, -um,** *m. pl.,* ancestors. 27

maiestās, -tātis, *f.,* greatness, dignity, majesty

maior. *See* **magnus.**

maiōrēs, -um, *m. pl.,* ancestors. 27

male, *adv.,* badly, ill, wrongly (*comp.* **peius;** *superl.* **pessimē**). 32

mālō, mālle, māluī, to want (something) more, instead; prefer. 32

malum, -ī, *n.,* evil, misfortune, hurt, injury. 30

malus, -a, -um, bad, wicked, evil. 4 (*comp.* **peior;** *superl.* **pessimus.** 27)

mandātum, -ī, *n.,* order, command, instruction

maneō, -ēre, mānsī, mānsum, remain, stay, abide, continue. 5

manus, -ūs, *f.,* hand; handwriting; band. 20

Mārcellus, -ī, *m.,* Marcellus, Roman general who captured Syracuse in 212 B.C.

Mārcus, -ī, *m.,* Marcus, a common Roman first name, usually abbreviated to **M.** in writing

mare, -is, *n.,* sea. 14

marītus, -ī, *m.,* husband

māter, -tris, *f.,* mother. 12

māteria, -ae, *f.,* material, matter

mātrimōnium, -iī, *n.,* marriage

maximus. *See* **magnus.**

medicus, -ī, *m.,* **medica, -ae,** *f.,* doctor, physician. 12

mediocris, -e, ordinary, moderate, mediocre. 31

meditor, -ārī, -ātus sum, reflect upon, practice

medius, -a, -um, middle; *used partitively,* the middle of. 22

mel, mellis, *n.,* honey

melior. *See* **bonus.**

meminī, meminisse, *defective,* remember

memor, *gen.* **-moris,** *adj.,* mindful

memoria, -ae, *f.,* memory, recollection. 15

mendōsus, -a, -um, full of faults, faulty

mēns, mentis, *f.,* mind, thought, intention. 16

mēnsa, -ae, *f.,* table; dining; dish, course; **mēnsa secunda,** dessert. 26

mēnsis, -is, *m.,* month

merces, -cēdis, *f.,* pay, reward, recompense

merīdiānus, -a, -um, of midday, noon; southern

merus, -a, -um, pure, undiluted. 33

mēta, -ae, *f.,* turning point, goal, limit, boundary. 40

metuō, -ere, metuī, fear, dread; be afraid for + *dat.* 38

metus, -ūs, *m.,* fear, dread, anxiety. 20

meus, -a, -um (*m. voc.* **mī**), my. 2

mīles, mīlitis, *m.,* soldier. 23

mīlitāris, -e, military

mīlle, *indecl. adj. in sg.,* thousand; **mīlia, -ium,** *n., pl. noun,* thousands. 15

minimus. *See* **parvus.**

minor. *See* **parvus.**

minuō, -ere, minuī, minūtum, lessen, diminish. 30

mīrābilis, -e, amazing, wondrous, remarkable. 38

mīror, -ārī, -ātus sum, marvel at, admire, wonder. 35

mīrus, -a, -um, wonderful, surprising, extraordinary

misceō, -ēre, miscuī, mixtum, mix, stir up, disturb. 18

miser, -era, -erum, wretched, miserable, unfortunate. 15

miserē, *adv.,* wretchedly

misericordia, -ae, *f.,* pity, mercy

mītēscō, -ere, become *or* grow mild

mītis, -e, mild, gentle; ripe

mittō, -ere, mīsī, missum, send, let go. 11

modo, *adv.,* now, just now, only; **modo . . . modo,** at one time . . . at another

modus, -ī, *m.,* measure, bound, limit; manner, method, mode, way. 22

moenia, -ium, *n. pl.,* walls of a city. 29

molestus, -a, -um, troublesome, disagreeable, annoying

mōlior, -īrī, mōlītus sum, work at, build, undertake, plan. 34

molliō, -īre, -īvī, -ītum, soften; make calm *or* less hostile. 29

mollis, -e, soft, mild, weak

moneō, -ēre, -uī, -itum, remind, warn, advise, 1; **moneō eum ut** + *subj.* 36

monitiō, -ōnis, *f.,* admonition, warning

mōns, montis, *m.,* mountain. 20

mōnstrum, -ī, *n.,* portent; monster

monumentum, -ī, *n.,* monument. 40

mora, -ae, *f.,* delay. 4

morbus, -ī, *m.,* disease, sickness. 9

morior, -ī, mortuus sum, die. 34

mors, mortis, *f.,* death. 14

mortālis, -e, mortal. 18

mortuus, -a, -um, dead. 28

mōs, mōris, *m.,* habit, custom, manner; **mōrēs, mōrum,** habits, morals, character. 7

moveō, -ēre, mōvī, mōtum, move; arouse, affect. 18

mox, *adv.,* soon. 30

mulier, -eris, *f.,* woman. 39

multō (1), punish, fine

multum, *adv.,* much (*comp.* **plūs;** *superl.* **plūrimum**). 32

multus, -a, -um, much, many, 2 (*comp.* **plūs;** *superl.* **plūrimus.** 27)

mundus, -ī, *m.,* world, universe. 21

mūnīmentum, -ī, *n.,* fortification, protection

mūniō, -īre, -īvī, -ītum, fortify, defend; build (a road)

mūnus, -neris, *n.,* service, office, function, duty; gift

mūs, mūris, *m./f.,* mouse

Mūsa, -ae, *f.,* a Muse (one of the goddesses of poetry, music, etc.)

mūtātiō, -ōnis, *f.,* change

mūtō (1), change, alter; exchange. 14

N

nam, *conj.,* for. 13

nārrō (1), tell, narrate, report. 24

nāscor, -ī, nātus sum, be born, spring forth, arise. 34

nāsus, -ī, *m.,* nose. 40

nāta, -ae, *f.,* daughter. 29

nātālis, -is (*sc.* **diēs**), *m.,* birthday

nātiō, -ōnis, *f.,* nation, people

nātūra, -ae, *f.,* nature. 10

nauta, -ae, *m.,* sailor. 2

nāvigātiō, -ōnis, *f.,* voyage, navigation

nāvigō (1), sail, navigate. 17

nāvis, -is, *f.,* ship. 21

nē, *conj. with subj.,* that . . . not, in order that . . . not, in order not to, 28, 36; that, 40; *adv. in* **nē . . . quidem,** not . . . even. 29

-ne, *enclitic added to the emphatic word at the beginning of a question the answer to which may be either "yes" or "no." It can be used in both direct and indirect questions.* 5

nec. *See* **neque.**

necessārius, -a, -um, necessary

necesse, *indecl. adj.,* necessary, inevitable. 39

necō (1), murder, kill. 7

nefās (*indecl.*), *n.,* wrong, sin

neglegō, -ere, -lēxī, -lēctum, neglect, disregard. 17

negō (1), deny, say that . . . not. 25

nēmō, (nūllīus), nēminī, nēminem, (nūllō, -ā), *m./f.,* no one, nobody. 11

nepōs, -pōtis, *m.,* grandson, descendant. 27

neque *or* **nec,** *conj.,* and not, nor; **neque . . . neque,** neither . . . nor. 11

nesciō, -īre, -īvī, -ītum, not to know, be ignorant. 25

neuter, -tra, -trum, not either, neither. 9

nēve, and not, nor (*used to continue* **ut** *or* **nē** + *subj.*)

niger, -gra, -grum, black

nihil (*indecl.*), *n.,* nothing. 1, 4

nihilum, -ī, *n.,* nothing

nimis *or* **nimium,** *adv.,* too, too much, excessively. 9

nisi, if . . . not, unless, except. 19

niveus, -a, -um, snowy, white

noceō, -ēre, nocuī, nocitum + *dat.,* do harm to, harm, injure. 35

nōlō, nōlle, nōluī, not . . . wish, be unwilling. 32

nōmen, nōminis, *n.,* name. 7

nōn, *adv.,* not. 1

nōndum, *adv.,* not yet

nōnne, *interrog. adv. which introduces questions expecting the answer "yes."* 40

nōnnūllus, -a, -um, some, several

nōnnumquam, sometimes

nōnus, -a, -um, ninth

nōs. *See* **ego.**

nōscō. *See* **cognōscō.**

noster, -tra, -trum, our, ours. 5

notārius, -iī, *m.,* writer of shorthand, stenographer

novem, *indecl. adj.,* nine. 15

novus, -a, -um, new, strange. 7

nox, noctis, *f.,* night. 26

nūbēs, -is, *f.,* cloud. 14

nūbō, -ere, nūpsī, nūptum, cover, veil; + dat. (*of a bride*) be married to, marry. 35

nūllus, -a, -um, not any, no, none. 9

num, *interrogative adv.:* (1) *introduces direct questions which expect the answer "no"*; (2) *introduces indirect questions and means* whether. 40

numerus, -ī, *m.,* number. 3

numquam, *adv.,* never. 8

nunc, *adv.,* now, at present. 6

nūntiō (1), announce, report, relate. 25

nūntius, -iī, *m.,* messenger, message

nūper, *adv.,* recently. 12

nūtriō, -īre, -īvī, -ītum, nourish, rear

O

Ō, *interjection,* O!, oh! 2

obdūrō (1), be hard, persist, endure

obeō, -īre, -iī, -itum, go up against, meet; die. 37

obiciō, -ere, -iēcī, -iectum, offer; cite (*as grounds for condemnation*)

oblectō (1), please, amuse, delight; pass time pleasantly. 36

obruō, -ere, -ruī, -rutum, overwhelm, destroy

obsequium, -iī, *n.,* compliance

obstinātus, -a, -um, firm, resolved

occāsiō, -ōnis, *f.,* occasion, opportunity. 28

occidō, -ere, -cidī, -cāsum (cadō, fall), fall down; die; set (*of the sun*). 31

occīdō, -ere, -cīdī, -cīsum (caedō, cut), cut down; kill, slay

occultē, *adv.,* secretly

occupō (1), seize

oculus, -ī, *m.,* eye. 4

ōdī, ōdisse, ōsūrum (*defective vb.*), hate. 20

odium, -iī, *n.,* hatred. 38

Oedipūs, -podis, *m.,* Oedipus, Greek mythical figure said to have murdered his father and married his mother

offerō, -ferre, obtulī, oblātum, offer. 31

officium, -iī, *n.,* duty, service. 4

ōlim, *adv.,* at that time, once, formerly; in the future. 13

omittō, -ere, -mīsī, -missum, let go, omit

omnīnō, *adv.,* wholly, entirely, altogether. 40

omnipotēns, *gen.* **-tentis,** *adj.,* all-powerful, omnipotent

omnis, -e, every, all. 16

onerō (1), burden, load

onus, oneris, *n.,* burden, load

opera, -ae, *f.,* work, pains, help

opīnor, -ārī, -ātus sum, suppose. 40

oportet, -ēre, oportuit (*impers.*), it is necessary, proper, right. 39

oppōnō, -ere, -posuī, -positum, set against, oppose

opportūnē, *adv.,* opportunely

opportūnus, -a, -um, fit, suitable, advantageous, opportune

opprimō, -ere, -pressī, -pressum, suppress, overwhelm, overpower, check. 23

opprobrium, -iī, *n.,* reproach, taunt, disgrace

oppugnō (1), fight against, attack, assault, assail. 39

ops, opis, *f.,* help, aid; **opēs, opum,** power, resources, wealth. 33

optimus. *See* **bonus.**

optō (1), wish for, desire

opus, operis, *n.,* a work, task; deed, accomplishment. 38

ōrātiō, -ōnis, *f.,* speech. 38

ōrātor, -tōris, *m.,* orator, speaker. 23

orbis, -is, *m.,* circle, orb; **orbis terrārum,** the world, the earth

ōrdō, ōrdinis, *m.,* rank, class, order

orior, -īrī, ortus sum, arise, begin, proceed, originate

ōrnō (1), equip, furnish, adorn. 39

ōrō (1), speak, plead; beg, beseech, entreat, pray. 36

ōs, ōris, *n.,* mouth, face. 14

ōsculum, -ī, *n.,* kiss. 29

ostendō, -ere, -tendī, -tentum, exhibit, show, display. 23

ōstium, -iī, *n.,* entrance, door

ōtium, -iī, *n.,* leisure, peace. 4
ovis, -is, *f.,* sheep

P

paedagōgus, -ī, *m.,* slave who attended children
(*particularly at school*)
pāgānus, -ī, *m.,* a countryman, peasant; pagan
palam, *adv.,* openly, plainly
palma, -ae, *f.,* palm
pānis, -is, *m.,* bread
pār, *gen.* **paris,** *adj.,* equal, like. 32
parcō, -ere, pepercī, parsūrum + *dat.,* be lenient
to, spare. 35
parēns, -rentis, *m./f.,* parent. 28
pāreō, -ēre, -uī + *dat.,* be obedient to, obey. 35
pariēs, -ietis, *m.,* wall
pariō, -ere, peperī, partum, beget, produce
parmula, -ae, *f.,* little shield
parō (1), prepare, provide; get, obtain. 19
pars, partis, *f.,* part, share; direction. 14
parum, *adv.,* little, too little, not very (much)
(*comp.* **minus;** *superl.* **minimē**). 32
parvus, -a, -um, small, little, 4 (*comp.* **minor;** *superl.*
minimus. 27)
passer, -seris, *m.,* sparrow
patefaciō, -ere, -fēcī, -factum, make open, open;
disclose, expose. 25
pateō, -ēre, -uī, be open, lie open; be accessible; be
evident. 32
pater, -tris, *m.,* father. 12
patiēns, *gen.* **-entis,** *adj.,* patient; + *gen.,* capable
of enduring
patientia, -ae, *f.,* suffering; patience, endurance. 12
patior, -ī, passus sum, suffer, endure; permit.
34
patria, -ae, *f.,* fatherland, native land, (one's)
country. 2
patrōnus, -ī, *m.,* patron, protector
paucī, -ae, -a, *usually pl.,* few, a few. 3
pauper, *gen.* **-peris,** *adj.,* of small means, poor. 32
paupertās, -tātis, *f.,* poverty, humble
circumstances. 32
pāx, pācis, *f.,* peace. 7
peccō (1), sin, do wrong
pectus, -toris, *n.,* breast, heart. 35
pecūnia, -ae, *f.,* money. 2
peior. *See* **malus.**
pellō, -ere, pepulī, pulsum, strike, push; drive out,
banish. 24

per, *prep.* + *acc.,* through; *with reflex. pron.,* by. 13
percipiō, -ere, -cēpī, -ceptum, gain, learn, perceive
perdō, -ere, perdidī, perditum, destroy, ruin, lose
pereō, -īre, -iī, -itum, pass away, be destroyed,
perish. 37
peregrīnor, peregrīnārī, peregrīnātus sum, travel
abroad, wander. 37
perfectus, -a, -um, complete, perfect
perferō, -ferre, -tulī, -lātum, bear, endure, suffer
perficiō, -ere, -fēcī, -fectum, do thoroughly,
accomplish, bring about
perfugium, -iī, *n.,* refuge, shelter. 24
perīculōsus, -a, -um, dangerous
perīculum, -ī, *n.,* danger, risk. 4
perimō, -ere, -ēmī, -ēmptum, destroy
perītus, -a, -um, skilled, expert
permittō, -ere, -mīsī, -missum, permit, allow
perniciōsus, -a, -um, destructive, pernicious
pernoctō (1), spend *or* occupy the night. 39
perpetuus, -a, -um, perpetual, lasting,
uninterrupted, continuous. 6
perscrībō, -ere, -scrīpsī, -scrīptum, write out, place
on record
persequor, -ī, -secūtus sum, follow up, pursue, take
vengeance on
Persicus, -a, -um, Persian
persuādeō, -ēre, -suāsī, -suāsum, succeed in
urging, persuade, convince
perterreō, -ēre, -uī, -itum, frighten thoroughly,
terrify
pertineō, -ēre, -uī, -tentum, pertain to, relate to,
concern
perturbō (1), throw into confusion, trouble,
disturb, perturb
perveniō, -īre, -vēnī, -ventum + **ad,** come through
to, arrive at, reach
pēs, pedis, *m.,* lower leg, foot. 38
pessimus. *See* **malus.**
pestis, -is, *f.,* plague, pestilence, curse, destruction
petō, -ere, petīvī, petītum, seek, aim at, beg,
beseech, 23; **petō ab eō ut** + *subj.* 36
philosophia, -ae, *f.,* philosophy, love of wisdom. 2
philosophus, -ī, *m.,* **philosopha, -ae,** *f.,* philosopher.
33
piger, -gra, -grum, lazy, slow, dull
pīpiō (1), chirp, pipe
piscātor, -tōris, *m.,* fisherman
piscis, -is, *m.,* fish
placeō, -ēre, -uī, -itum + *dat.,* be pleasing to,
please. 35
plācō (1), placate, appease

plānē, *adv.,* plainly, clearly
platea, -ae, *f.,* broad way, street
Platō, -tōnis, *m.,* Plato, the renowned Greek
philosopher
plēbs, plēbis, *f.,* the common people, populace,
plebeians. 33
plēnus, -a, -um, full, abundant, generous. 6
plūrimus. *See* **multus.**
plūs. *See* **multus.**
poēma, -matis, *n.,* poem
poena, -ae, *f.,* penalty, punishment; **poenās dare,**
pay the penalty. 2
poēta, -ae, *m.,* poet. 2
pōmum, -ī, *n.,* fruit, apple
pōnō, -ere, posuī, positum, put, place, set. 27
pōns, pontis, *m.,* bridge
populus, -ī, *m.,* the people, a people, nation. 3
porta, -ae, *f.,* gate, entrance. 2
possessiō, -ōnis, *f.,* possession, property
possum, posse, potuī, be able, can, have power. 6
post, *prep.* + *acc.,* after, behind. 7
posteā, *adv.,* afterwards. 24
postpōnō, -ere, -posuī, -positum, put after, consider
secondary
postquam, *conj.,* after
postrēmum, *adv.,* after all, finally; for the last
time. 40
potēns, *gen.* **-tentis,** *pres. part. of* **possum** *as adj.,*
able, powerful, mighty, strong. 16
potestās, -tātis, *f.,* power, ability, opportunity
potior, -īrī, potītus sum + *gen.* or *abl.,* get
possession of, possess, hold
potius, *adv.,* rather, preferably
prae, *prep.* + *abl.,* in front of, before. 26
praebeō, -ēre, -uī, -itum, offer, provide. 32
praeceptum, -ī, *n.,* precept
praeclārus, -a, -um, noble, distinguished, famous,
remarkable
praeferō, -ferre, -tulī, -lātum, bear before, display;
place before, prefer
praeficiō, -ere, -fēcī, -fectum, put in charge of
praemittō, -ere, -mīsī, -missum, send ahead *or*
forward
praemium, -iī, *n.,* reward, prize. 35
praesidium, -iī, *n.,* guard, detachment, protection
praestō, -āre, -stitī, -stitum, excel (+ *dat.*); exhibit,
show, offer, supply. 28
praesum, -esse, -fuī, be at the head of, be in
charge of
praeter, *prep.* + *acc.,* besides, except; beyond,
past. 40

praetereō, -īre, -iī, -itum, go by, pass, omit
praeteritus, -a, -um, *perf. part. of* **praetereō** *as adj.,*
past
premō, -ere, pressī, pressum, press; press hard,
pursue. 23
pretium, -iī, *n.,* price, value, reward
prex, precis, *f.,* prayer
prīmō, *adv.,* at first, first, at the beginning. 30
prīmum, *adv.,* first, in the first place; **quam
prīmum,** as soon as possible
prīmus. *See* **prior.** 27
prīnceps, *gen.* **-cipis,** chief; *m./f. noun,* leader,
prince, emperor. 28
prīncipium, -iī, *n.,* beginning. 12
prior, prius, *comp. adj.,* former, prior; **prīmus, -a,
-um,** first, foremost, chief, principal. 27
prīstinus, -a, -um, ancient, former, previous. 38
prius, *adv.,* before, previously
prīvātus, -ī, *m.,* private citizen
prīvō (1), deprive
prō, *prep.* + *abl.,* in front of, before, on behalf of,
in return for, instead of, for, as. 12
probitās, -tātis, *f.,* uprightness, honesty, probity. 18
probō (1), approve; recommend; test. 27
prōcōnsul, -sulis, *m.,* proconsul, governor of a
province
prōditor, -tōris, *m.,* betrayer, traitor
proelium, -iī, *n.,* battle
prōferō, -ferre, -tulī, -lātum, bring forward,
produce, make known, extend
proficīscor, -ī, -fectus sum, set out, start. 34
profor, -ārī, -ātus sum, speak out
prōfundō, -ere, -fūdī, -fūsum, pour forth
prohibeō, -ēre, -uī, -itum, prevent, hinder, restrain,
prohibit. 20
prōiciō, -ere, -iēcī, -iectum, throw forward *or* out
prōmittō, -mittere, -mīsī, -missum, send forth,
promise. 32
prōnūntiō (1), proclaim, announce; declaim;
pronounce. 20
prōpōnō, -ere, -posuī, -positum, put forward,
propose
proprius, -a, -um, one's own, peculiar, proper,
personal, characteristic
propter, *prep.* + *acc.,* on account of, because of. 5
prōtinus, *adv.,* immediately. 22
prōvideō, -ēre, -vīdī, -vīsum, foresee, provide, make
provision
proximus, -a, -um (*superl. of* **propior**), nearest, next
prūdēns, *gen.* **-dentis,** *adj.,* wise, prudent
prūdenter, *adv.,* wisely, discreetly

prūdentia, -ae, *f.,* foresight, wisdom, discretion
pūblicus, -a, -um, of the people, public;
  rēs pūblica, reī pūblicae, *f.,* the state
pudīcus, -a, -um, modest, chaste. 26
pudor, -dōris, *m.,* modesty, bashfulness
puella, -ae, *f.,* girl. 2
puer, puerī, *m.,* boy; *pl.* boys, children. 3
puerīliter, *adv.,* childishly, foolishly
pugna, -ae, *f.,* fight, battle
pugnō (1), fight. 29
pulcher, -chra, -chrum, beautiful, handsome;
  fine. 5
pulchrē, *adv.,* beautifully, finely. 32
pulchritūdō, -dinis, *f.,* beauty
pūniō, -īre, -īvī, -ītum, punish
pūrgō (1), cleanse
pūrus, -a, -um, pure, free from
putō (1), reckon, suppose, judge, think,
  imagine. 25
Pȳthagorās, -ae, *m.,* Pythagoras, Greek
  philosopher and mathematician of 6th cen. B.C.

Q

quā, *adv.,* by which route, where
quadrāgintā, *indecl. adj.,* forty
quaerō, -ere, quaesīvī, quaesītum, seek, look for,
  strive for; ask, inquire, inquire into. 24
quam, *adv.,* how, 16; *conj.,* than, 26; as . . . as
  possible (*with superl.*), 26
quamvīs, *adv. and conj.,* however much, however;
  although
quandō, *interrogative and rel. adv. and conj.,* when;
  sī quandō, if ever. 5
quantus, -a, -um, how large, how great, how
  much. 30
quārē, *adv.,* because of which thing, therefore,
  wherefore, why. 6
quārtus, -a, -um, fourth. 15
quasi, *adv. or conj.,* as if, as it were. 39
quattuor, *indecl. adj.,* four. 15
-que, *enclitic conj.,* and. *It is appended to the
  second of two words to be joined.* 6
quemadmodum, *adv.,* in what manner, how
queror, -ī, questus sum, complain, lament. 38
quī, quae, quod, *rel. pron.,* who, which, what,
  that. 17
quī? quae? quod?, *interrog. adj.,* what? which? what
  kind of? 19
quia, *conj.,* since, because
quid, what, why. *See* **quis.**

quīdam, quaedam, quiddam (*pron.*) *or* **quoddam**
  (*adj.*), *indef. pron. and adj.:* as *pron.,* a certain
  one *or* thing, someone, something; as *adj.,* a
  certain. 26
quidem, *postpositive adv.,* indeed, certainly, at
  least, even; **nē . . . quidem,** not even. 29
quiēs, -ētis, *f.,* quiet, rest, peace
quīn, *adv.,* indeed, in fact. 40
quīn etiam, *adv.,* why even, in fact, moreover
Quīntus, -ī, *m.,* Quintus, a Roman praenomen,
  abbreviated to **Q.** in writing
quis? quid?, *interrogative pron.,* who? what? which?
  19
quis, quid, *indef. pron.,* after **sī, nisi, nē,** *and* **num,**
  anyone, anything, someone, something. 33
quisquam, quidquam (*or* **quicquam**), *indef. pron.
  and adj.,* anyone, anything
quisque, quidque, *indef. pron.,* each one, each
  person, each thing. 13
quisquis, quidquid, *indef. pron.,* whoever,
  whatever. 23
quō, *adv.,* to which *or* what place, whither, where
quod, *conj.,* because. 11
quōmodo, *adv.,* in what way, how
quondam, *adv.,* formerly, once. 22
quoniam, *conj.,* since, inasmuch as. 10
quoque, *adv.,* also, too. 17
quot, *indecl. adj.,* how many, as many. 27
quotiēnscumque, *adv.,* however often, whenever

R

rapiō, -ere, rapuī, raptum, seize, snatch, carry
  away. 21
rārus, -a, -um, rare
ratiō, -ōnis, *f.,* reckoning, account; reason,
  judgment, consideration; system, manner,
  method. 8
recēdō, -ere, -cessī, -cessum, go back, retire, recede
recipiō, -ere, -cēpī, -ceptum, take back, regain;
  admit, receive. 24
recitō (1), read aloud, recite. 17
recognōscō, -ere, -nōvī, -nitum, recognize,
  recollect. 38
recordātiō, -ōnis, *f.,* recollection
recreō (1), restore, revive; refresh, cheer. 36
rēctus, -a, -um, straight, right; **rēctum, -ī,** *n.,* the
  right, virtue
recuperātiō, -ōnis, *f.,* recovery
recuperō (1), regain
recūsō (1), refuse. 33

reddō, -ere, -didī, -ditum, give back, return
redeō, -īre, -iī, -itum, go back, return. 37
redūcō, -ere, -dūxī, -ductum, lead back, bring back
referō, -ferre, -ttulī, -lātum, carry back, bring back; repeat, answer, report. 31
rēgīna, -ae, *f.,* queen. 7
rēgius, -a, -um, royal
rēgnum, -ī, *n.,* rule, authority, kingdom
regō, -ere, rēxī, rēctum, rule, guide, direct. 16
relegō, -ere, -lēgī, -lēctum, read again, reread
relevō (1), relieve, alleviate, diminish
relinquō, -ere, -līquī, -lictum, leave behind, leave, abandon. 21
remaneō, -ēre, -mānsī, -mānsum, remain, stay behind, abide, continue. 5
remedium, -iī, *n.,* cure, remedy. 4
remissiō, -ōnis, *f.,* letting go, release; relaxation. 34
removeō, -ēre, -mōvī, -mōtum, remove
repente, *adv.,* suddenly. 30
reperiō, -īre, -pperī, -pertum, find, discover, learn; get. 40
repetītiō, -ōnis, *f.,* repetition
repetō, -ere, -īvī, -ītum, seek again, repeat
rēpō, -ere, rēpsī, rēptum, creep, crawl
repugnō (1) + *dat.,* fight against, be incompatible with
requiēscō, -ere, -quiēvī, -quiētum, rest. 37
requīrō, -ere, -quīsīvī, -sītum, seek, ask for; miss, need, require. 36
rēs, reī, *f.,* thing, matter, business, affair; **rēs pūblica, reī pūblicae,** state, commonwealth. 22
resistō, -ere, -stitī, make a stand, resist, oppose
respondeō, -ēre, -spondī, -spōnsum, answer. 29
restituō, -ere, -stituī, -stitūtum, restore
retrahō, -ere, -trāxī, -tractum, drag *or* draw back
reveniō, -īre, -vēnī, -ventum, come back, return
revertor, -ī, -vertī (*perf.* is *act.*), **-versum,** return
revocō (1), call back, recall
rēx, rēgis, *m.,* king. 7
rhētoricus, -a, -um, of rhetoric, rhetorical
rīdeō, -ēre, rīsī, rīsum, laugh, laugh at. 24
rīdiculus, -a, -um, laughable, ridiculous. 30
rogō (1), ask, ask for. 30; **rogō eum ut** + *subj.,* 36
Rōma, -ae, *f.,* Rome. 14
Rōmānus, -a, -um, Roman. 3
rosa, -ae, *f.,* rose. 2
rōstrum, -ī, *n.,* beak of a ship; **Rōstra, -ōrum,** the Rostra, speaker's platform
rota, -ae, *f.,* wheel
rotundus, -a, -um, wheel-shaped, round

rūmor, -mōris, *m.,* rumor, gossip. 31
ruō, -ere, ruī, rutum, rush, fall, be ruined
rūs, rūris, *n.,* the country, countryside. 37
rūsticor, -ārī, -ātus sum, live in the country. 34
rūsticus, -a, -um, rustic, rural

S

sabbatum, -ī, *n.,* the Sabbath
sacculus, -ī, *n.,* little bag, purse
sacrificium, -iī, *n.,* sacrifice
sacerdōs, sacerdōtis, *m.,* priest. 23
sacrilegus, -a, -um, sacrilegious, impious
saepe, *adv.,* often. 1
saeta equīna, -ae -ae, *f.,* horse-hair
sagitta, -ae, *f.,* arrow
sāl, salis, *m.,* salt; wit. 33
salsus, -a, -um, salty, witty
salūbris, -e, healthy, salubrious
salūs, salūtis, *f.,* health, safety; greeting. 21
salūtō (1), greet
salveō, -ēre, be well, be in good health. 1
salvus, -a, -um, safe, sound. 6
sānctificō (1), sanctify, treat as holy
sānctus, -a, -um, sacred, holy
sānitās, -tātis, *f.,* health, soundness of mind, sanity
sānō (1), heal
sānus, -a, -um, sound, healthy, sane. 5
sapiēns, *gen.* **-entis,** *adj.,* wise, judicious; *as a noun, m.,* a wise man, philosopher. 25
sapienter, *adv.,* wisely, sensibly. 32
sapientia, -ae, *f.,* wisdom. 3
sapiō, -ere, sapīvī, have good taste; have good sense, be wise. 35
satiō (1), satisfy, sate. 3
satis, *indecl. noun, adj., and adv.,* enough, sufficient(ly). 5
sator, -tōris, *m.,* sower, planter; begetter, father. 38
satura, -ae, *f.,* satire. 16
saxum, -ī, *n.,* rock, stone. 40
scabiēs, -ēī, *f.,* the itch, mange
scelerātus, -a, -um, criminal, wicked, accursed
scelestus, -a, -um, wicked, accursed, infamous
scelus, -leris, *n.,* evil deed, crime, sin, wickedness. 19
schola, -ae, *f.,* school
scientia, -ae, *f.,* knowledge, science, skill. 18
sciō, -īre, -īvī, -ītum, know. 21
scrībō, -ere, scrīpsī, scrīptum, write, compose. 8
scrīptor, -tōris, *m.,* writer, author. 8
sēcernō, -ere, -crēvī, -crētum, separate

secundus, -a, -um, second; favorable. 6
sēcūrus, -a, -um, free from care, untroubled, safe
sed, *conj.,* but. 2
sedeō, -ēre, sēdī, sessum, sit. 34
sēductor, -tōris, *m.* (*ecclesiastical Lat.*), seducer
semel, *adv.,* a single time, once, once and for all, simultaneously. 31
semper, *adv.,* always. 3
senātor, -tōris, *m.,* senator
senātus, -ūs, *m.,* senate. 20
senectūs, -tūtis, *f.,* old age. 10
senex, senis, *adj. and n.,* old, aged; old man. 16
sēnsus, -ūs, *m.,* feeling, sense. 20
sententia, -ae, *f.,* feeling, thought, opinion, vote; sentence. 2
sentiō, -īre, sēnsī, sēnsum, feel, perceive, think, experience. 11
septem, *indecl. adj.,* seven. 15
sepulchrum, -ī, *n.,* grave, tomb
sequor, -ī, secūtus sum, follow. 34
serēnō (1), make clear, brighten; cheer up, soothe. 36
sēriō, *adv.,* seriously
sērius, -a, -um, serious, grave
sermō, -mōnis, *m.,* conversation, talk
serō, -ere, sēvī, satum, sow
serviō, -īre, -īvī, -ītum + *dat.,* be a slave to, serve. 35
servitūs, -tūtis, *f.,* servitude, slavery. 20
servō (1), preserve, keep, save, guard. 1
servus, -ī, *m.,* and **serva, -ae,** *f.,* slave. 24
sevēritās, -tātis, *f.,* severity, sternness, strictness
sī, *conj.,* if. 1
sīc, *adv.* (*most commonly with verbs*), so, thus. 29
sīcut, *adv. and conj.,* as, just as, as it were
sīdus, -deris, *n.,* constellation, star. 29
signum, -ī, *n.,* sign, signal, indication; seal. 13
silentium, -iī, *n.,* silence
silva, -ae, *f.,* forest, wood
similis, -e, similar to, like, resembling. 27
simplex, *gen.* **-plicis,** *adj.,* simple, unaffected
simulātiō, -ōnis, *f.,* pretense
sine, *prep.* + *abl.,* without. 2
singulī, -ae, -a, *pl.,* one each, single, separate
singultim, *adv.,* stammeringly
sinister, -tra, -trum, left, left-hand; harmful, ill-omened. 20
sitiō, -īre, -īvī, be thirsty
socius, -iī, *m.,* companion, ally
Sōcratēs, -is, *m.,* Socrates

sōl, sōlis, *m.,* sun. 27
sōlācium, -iī, *n.,* comfort, relief. 24
soleō, -ēre, solitus sum, be accustomed. 37
sōlitūdō, -dinis, *f.,* solitude, loneliness
sollicitō (1), stir up, arouse, incite
sollicitūdō, -dinis, *f.,* anxiety, concern, solicitude
sollicitus, -a, -um, troubled, anxious, disturbed
Solōn, -lōnis, *m.,* Solon, Athenian sage and statesman of the 7th-6th cen. B.C.
sōlum, *adv.,* only, merely; **nōn sōlum . . . sed etiam,** not only . . . but also. 9
sōlus, -a, -um, alone, only, the only. 9
somnus, -ī, *m.,* sleep. 26
Sophoclēs, -is, *m.,* Sophocles, one of the three greatest writers of Greek tragedy
sopor, -pōris, *m.,* deep sleep
sordēs, -dium, *f. pl.,* filth; meanness, stinginess
soror, -rōris, *f.,* sister. 8
spargō, -ere, sparsī, sparsum, scatter, spread, strew
spectāculum, -ī, *n.,* spectacle, show
spectō (1), look at, see. 34
speculum, -ī, *n.,* mirror. 33
spernō, -ere, sprēvī, sprētum, scorn, despise, spurn
spērō (1), hope for, hope. 25
spēs, -eī, *f.,* hope. 22
spīritus, -ūs, *m.,* breath, breathing; spirit, soul. 20
stabilis, -e, stable, steadfast
stadium, -iī, *n.,* stadium
statim, *adv.,* immediately, at once
statua, -ae, *f.,* statue
stēlla, -ae, *f.,* star, planet. 28
stilus, -ī, *m.,* stilus (*for writing*)
stō, stāre, stetī, statum, stand, stand still *or* firm. 13
studeō, -ēre, -uī + *dat.,* direct one's zeal to, be eager for, study. 35
studiōsus, -a, -um, full of zeal, eager, fond of
studium, -iī, *n.,* eagerness, zeal, pursuit, study. 9
stultus, -a, -um, foolish; **stultus, -ī,** *m.,* a fool. 4
suāvis, -e, sweet. 33
sub, *prep.* + *abl. with verbs of rest,* + *acc. with verbs of motion,* under, up under, close to. 7
subitō, *adv.,* suddenly. 33
subitus, -a, -um, sudden
subiungō, -ere, -iūnxī, -iūnctum, subject, subdue
sublīmis, sublīme, elevated, lofty; heroic, noble. 38
subrīdeō, -rīdēre, -rīsī, -rīsum, smile (down) upon. 35
succurrō, -ere, -currī, -cursum, run up under, help
sufficiō, -ere, -fēcī, -fectum, be sufficient, suffice

suī (sibi, sē, sē), *reflex. pron. of 3rd pers.,* himself, herself, itself, themselves. 13

sum, esse, fuī, futūrum, be, exist. 4; **est, sunt** *may mean* there is, there are. 1

summa, -ae, *f.,* highest part, sum, whole

summus, -a, -um. *See* **superus.**

sūmō, -ere, sūmpsī, sūmptum, take, take up, assume

sūmptus, -ūs, *m.,* expense, cost

supellex, -lectilis, *f.,* furniture, apparatus

superbus, -a, -um, arrogant, overbearing, haughty, proud. 26

superior. *See* **superus.**

superō (1), be above, have the upper hand, surpass, overcome, conquer. 5

superus, -a, -um, above, upper; **superī, -ōrum,** *m.,* the gods (*comp.* **superior, -ius,** higher; *superl.* **suprēmus, -a, -um,** last, *or* **summus, -a, -um,** highest). 27

supplicium, -iī, *n.,* punishment

suprā, *adv. and prep.* + *acc.,* above

suprēmus. *See* **superus.**

surculus, -ī, *m.,* shoot, sprout

surgō, -ere, surrēxī, surrēctum, get up, arise. 29

suscipiō, -ere, -cēpī, -ceptum, undertake. 25

suspendō, -ere, -pendī, -pēnsum, hang up, suspend; interrupt. 38

sustineō, -ēre, -uī, -tentum, hold up, sustain, endure

suus, -a, -um, *reflexive possessive adj. of 3rd pers.,* his own, her own, its own, their own. 13

synagōga, -ae, *f.,* synagogue

Syrācūsae, -ārum, *f. pl.,* Syracuse. 37

T

tabella, -ae, *f.,* writing tablet; **tabellae, -ārum,** letter, document

taceō, -ēre, -uī, -itum, be silent, leave unmentioned. 28

tālis, -e, such, of such a sort. 34

tam, *adv. used with adjs. and advs.,* so, to such a degree; **tam . . . quam,** so . . . as. 29

tamen, *adv.,* nevertheless, still. 8

tamquam, *adv.,* as it were, as if, so to speak. 29

tandem, *adv.,* at last, finally

tangō, -ere, tetigī, tāctum, touch. 21

tantum, *adv.,* only. 26

tantus, -a, -um, so large, so great, of such size. 29

tardus, -a, -um, slow, tardy

tēctum, -ī, *n.,* roof, house

tegō, -ere, tēxī, tēctum, cover, hide, protect

temeritās, -tātis, *f.,* rashness, temerity

temperantia, -ae, *f.,* moderation, temperance, self-control

tempestās, -tātis, *f.,* period of time, season; weather, storm. 15

templum, -ī, *n.,* sacred area, temple

temptātiō, -ōnis, *f.,* trial, temptation

tempus, -poris, *n.,* time; occasion, opportunity. 7

tendō, -ere, tetendī, tentum *or* **tēnsum,** stretch, extend; go

teneō, -ēre, -uī, tentum, hold, keep, possess, restrain. 14

terō, -ere, trīvī, trītum, rub, wear out

terra, -ae, *f.,* earth, ground, land, country. 7

terreō, -ēre, -uī, -itum, frighten, terrify. 1

tertius, -a, -um, third. 15

thema, -matis, *n.,* theme

Themistoclēs, -is, *m.,* Themistocles, celebrated Athenian statesman and military leader who advocated a powerful navy at the time of the Persian Wars

timeō, -ēre, -uī, fear, be afraid of, be afraid. 15

timor, -mōris, *m.,* fear. 10

titulus, -ī, *m.,* label, title; placard

toga, -ae, *f.,* toga, the garb of peace

tolerō (1), bear, endure, tolerate. 6

tollō, -ere, sustulī, sublātum, raise, lift up; take away, remove, destroy. 22

tondeō, -ēre, totondī, tōnsum, shear, clip

tōnsor, -sōris, *m.,* barber

tōnsōrius, -a, -um, of *or* pertaining to a barber, barber's

tot, *indecl. adj.,* that number of, so many. 40

tōtus, -a, -um, whole, entire. 9

tractō (1), drag about; handle, treat, discuss

trādō, -ere, -didī, -ditum, give over, surrender, hand down, transmit, teach. 33

tragoedia, -ae, *f.,* tragedy

trahō, -ere, trāxī, tractum, draw, drag; derive, acquire. 8

trāns, *prep.* + *acc.,* across. 14

trānseō, -īre, -iī, -itum, go across, cross; pass over, ignore. 39

trānsferō, -ferre, -tulī, -lātum, bear across, transfer, convey

trānsitus, -ūs, *m.,* passing over, transit; transition. 39

trēdecim, *indecl. adj.,* thirteen. 15

tremō, -ere, tremuī, tremble

trepidē, *adv.,* with trepidation, in confusion

trēs, tria, three. 15

trīgintā, *indecl. adj.,* thirty

trīstis, -e, sad, sorrowful; joyless, grim, severe. 26

triumphus, -ī, *m.,* triumphal procession, triumph

Trōia, -ae, *f.,* Troy. 23

Trōiānus, -a, -um, Trojan

tū, tuī, you. 11

Tullius, -iī, *m.,* Cicero's family name

tum, *adv.,* then, at that time; thereupon, in the next place. 5

tumultus, -ūs, *m.,* uprising, disturbance

tumulus, -ī, *m.,* mound, tomb

tunc, *adv.,* then, at that time

turba, -ae, *f.,* uproar, disturbance; mob, crowd, multitude. 14

turpis, -e, ugly; shameful, base, disgraceful. 26

tūtus, -a, -um, protected, safe, secure

tuus, -a, -um, your, yours (*sg.*). 2

tyrannus, -ī, *m.,* absolute ruler, tyrant. 6

U

ubi, *rel. adv. and conj.,* where; when; *interrogative,* where? 6

ulcīscor, -ī, ultus sum, avenge, punish for wrong done

ūllus, -a, -um, any. 9

ultimus, -a, -um, farthest, extreme; last, final. 25

ultrā, *adv. and prep.* + *acc.,* on the other side of, beyond. 22

umbra, -ae, *f.,* shade; ghost

umerus, -ī, *m.,* shoulder, upper arm

umquam, *adv.,* ever, at any time. 23

unde, *adv.,* whence, from what *or* which place; from which, from whom. 30

ūnus, -a, -um, one, single, alone. 9

urbānus, -a, -um, of the city, urban, urbane, elegant. 26

urbs, urbis, *f.,* city. 14

ūsque, *adv.,* all the way, up (to), even (to), continuously, always. 31

ūsus, -ūs, *m.,* use, experience, skill, advantage

ut, *conj.;* A. *with subj., introducing* (1) *purpose,* in order that, that, to (28); (2) *result,* so that, that (29); (3) *jussive noun clauses,* to, that (36); (4) *fear clauses,* that . . . not (40); B. *with indic.,* just as, as, when. 24

uter, utra, utrum, either, which (of two). 9

ūtilis, -e, useful, advantageous. 27

ūtilitās, -tātis, *f.,* usefulness, advantage

ūtor, -ī, ūsus sum + *abl.,* use; enjoy, experience. 34

utrum . . . an, *conj.,* whether . . . or. 30

uxor, -ōris, *f.,* wife. 7

V

vacō (1), be free from, be unoccupied

vacuus, -a, -um, empty, devoid (of), free (from)

vae, *interjection,* alas, woe to. 34

valeō, -ēre, -uī, -itūrum, be strong, have power; be well, fare well; **valē (valēte),** good-bye. 1

valētūdō, -dinis, *f.,* health, good health, bad health

varius, -a, -um, various, varied, different

-ve, *conj.,* or 33

vehemēns, *gen.* **-mentis,** *adj.,* violent, vehement, emphatic, vigorous

vehō, -ere, vexī, vectum, carry, convey

vel, *conj.,* or (*an optional alternative*)

vēlōx, *gen.* **-lōcis,** *adj.,* swift

vēndō, -ere, vēndidī, vēnditum, sell. 38

venia, -ae, *f.,* kindness, favor, pardon

veniō, -īre, vēnī, ventum, come. 10

ventitō (1), come often

ventus, -ī, *m.,* wind. 39

Venus, -neris, *f.,* Venus, goddess of grace, charm, and love

verbera, -rum, *n. pl.,* blows, a beating

verbum, -ī, *n.,* word. 5

vērē, *adv.,* truly, really, actually, rightly

vereor, -ērī, veritus sum, show reverence for, respect; be afraid of, fear. 40

Vergilius, -iī, *m.,* Virgil, the Roman epic poet

vēritās, -tātis, *f.,* truth. 10

vērō, *adv.,* in truth, indeed, to be sure, however. 29

versus, -ūs, *m.,* line, verse. 20

vertō, -ere, vertī, versum, turn, change. 23

vērus, -a, -um, true, real, proper. 4

vesper, -peris *or* **-perī,** *m.,* evening; evening star. 28

vespillō, -lōnis, *m.,* undertaker

vester, -tra, -trum, your, yours (*pl.*). 6

vestiō, -īre, -īvī, -ītum, clothe

vetus, *gen.* **-teris,** *adj.,* old. 34

via, -ae, *f.,* road, street, way. 10

vīcīnus, -ī, *m.,* **vīcīna, -ae,** *f.,* neighbor. 21

vicissitūdō, -dinis, *f.,* change, vicissitude

victor, -tōris, *m.,* victor

victōria, -ae, *f.,* victory. 8

vīctus, -ūs, *m.,* living, mode of life

videō, -ēre, vīdī, vīsum, see, observe; understand, 1; **videor, -ērī, vīsus sum,** be seen, seem, appear. 18

vigilō (1), be awake, watch, be vigilant

vigor, -gōris, *m.,* vigor, liveliness

vīlla, -ae, *f.,* villa, country house

vincō, -ere, vīcī, victum, conquer, overcome. 8

vinculum, -ī, *n.,* bond, chain. 36

vīnum, -ī, *n.,* wine. 31

vir, virī, *m.,* man, hero. 3

virgō, -ginis, *f.,* maiden, virgin. 7

virtūs, -tūtis, *f.,* manliness, courage; excellence, virtue, character, worth. 7

vīs, vīs, *f.,* force, power, violence; **vīrēs, vīrium,** strength. 14

vīta, -ae, *f.,* life, mode of life. 2

vitiōsus, -a, -um, full of vice, vicious. 34

vitium, -iī, *n.,* fault, vice, crime. 6

vītō (1), avoid, shun. 14

vīvō, -ere, vīxī, vīctum, live. 10

vīvus, -a, -um, alive, living. 30

vix, *adv.,* hardly, scarcely, with difficulty

vocō (1), call, summon. 1

volō, velle, voluī, wish, want, be willing, will. 32

volō (1), fly

voluntārius, -a, -um, voluntary

voluntās, -tātis, *f.,* will, wish

voluptās, -tātis, *f.,* pleasure. 10

vōs. *See* **tū.**

vōx, vōcis, *f.,* voice, word. 34

vulgus, -ī, *n.* (*sometimes m.*), the common people, mob, rabble. 21

vulnus, -neris, *n.,* wound. 24

vultus, -ūs, *m.,* countenance, face, 40.

X

Xenophōn, -phontis, *m.,* Xenophon, Greek general and author

Abbreviations

AUTHORS AND WORKS CITED

Aug., St. Augustine (Confessions)
Caes., Caesar
    B.C., Bellum Civile
    B.G., Bellum Gallicum
Catull., Catullus (Poems)
Cic., Cicero
    Am., De Amicitia
    Arch., Oratio pro Archia
    Att., Epistulae ad Atticum
    Cat., Orationes in Catilinam
    De Or., De Oratore
    Div., De Divinatione
    Fam., Epistulae ad Familiares
    Fin., De Finibus
    Inv., De Inventione Rhetorica
    Leg., De Legibus
    Marcell, Oratio pro Marcello
    Off., De Officiis
    Or., Orator
    Phil., Orationes Philippicae in M. Antonium
    Pis., Oratio in Pisonem
    Planc., Oratio pro Plancio
    Q. Fr., Epistulae ad Q. Fratrem

    Rep., De Re Publica
    Sen., De Senectute
    Sex. Rosc., Oratio pro Sex. Roscio
    Sull., Oratio pro Sulla
    Tusc., Tusculanae Disputationes
    Verr., Actio in Verrem
Enn., Ennius (Poems)
Hor., Horace
    A.P., Ars Poetica (Ep. 2.3)
    Ep., Epistulae
    Epod., Epodes
    Od., Odes (Carmina)
    Sat., Satires (Sermones)
Juv., Juvenal (Satires)
Liv., Livy (Ab Urbe Condita)
Lucr., Lucretius (De Natura Rerum)
Mart., Martial (Epigrams)
Macr., Macrobius (Saturnalia)
Nep., Nepos
    Att., Atticus
    Cim., Cimon
    Milt., Miltiades
Ov., Ovid

A.A., Ars Amatoria
Am., Amores
Her., Heroides
Met., Metamorphoses
Pers., Persius (Satires)
Petron., Petronius (Satyricon)
Phaedr., Phaedrus (Fables)
Plaut., Plautus
  Aul., Aulularia
  Mil., Miles Gloriosus
  Most., Mostellaria
  Stich., Stichus
Plin., Pliny the Elder
  H.N., Historia Naturalis
Plin., Pliny the Younger
  Ep., Epistulae
Prop., Propertius (Elegies)
Publil. Syr., Publilius Syrus (Sententiae)
Quint., Quintilian
  Inst., Institutiones Oratoriae
Sall., Sallust
  Cat., Catilina
Sen., Seneca the Elder
  Contr., Controversiae
Sen., Seneca the Younger
  Brev. Vit., De Brevitate Vitae
  Clem., De Clementia

Cons. Polyb., Ad Polybium de
  Consolatione
Ep., Epistulae
Suet., Suetonius
  Aug., Augustus Caesar
  Caes., Julius Caesar
Tac., Tacitus
  Ann., Annales
  Dial., Dialogus de Oratoribus
Ter., Terence
  Ad., Adelphi
  And., Andria
  Heaut., Heauton Timoroumenos
  Hec., Hecyra
  Phorm., Phormio
Veg., Vegetius Renatus
  Mil., De Re Militari
Vell., Velleius Paterculus (Histories)
Virg., Virgil
  Aen., Aeneid
  Ecl., Eclogues
  Geor., Georgics
Vulg., Vulgate
  Eccles., Ecclesiastes
  Exod., Exodus
  Gen., Genesis

OTHER ABBREVIATIONS

abl.	ablative case
abs.	absolute
acc.	accusative case
act.	active voice
A.D.	after Christ (Lat. *annō dominī*, lit., *in the year of the Lord*)
adj.	adjective
adv.	adverb
App.	Appendix
B.C.	before Christ
ca.	about (Lat. *circā*)
cen(s).	century(ies)
Ch(s).	Chapter(s)
cl(s).	clause(s)
comp.	comparative (degree)
compl.	complementary

conj.	conjunction
contr. to fact	contrary to fact
cp.	compare (Lat. *comparā*)
dat.	dative case
decl.	declension
dep.	deponent
e.g.	for example (Lat. *exemplī grātiā*)
Eng.	English
etc.	and others (Lat. *et cētera*)
f./F./fem.	feminine gender
ff.	and the following (lines, pages)
Fr.	French
fr.	from
fut.	future tense
fut. perf.	future perfect tense
gen.	genitive case

Ger.	German	pass.	passive voice
Gk.	Greek	perf.	perfect (present perfect) tense
ibid.	in the same place (Lat. *ibidem*)	pers.	person
id.	the same (Lat. *idem*)	pl.	plural
i.e.	that is (Lat. *id est*)	plupf.	pluperfect (past perfect) tense
imper.	imperative mood	P.R.	Practice and Review (sentences)
impers.	impersonal	prep.	preposition
impf.	imperfect tense	pres.	present tense
ind. quest.	indirect question	pron.	pronoun
ind. state.	indirect statement	purp.	purpose
indecl.	indeclinable	ref.	reference
indef.	indefinite	rel.	relative
indic.	indicative mood	Russ.	Russian
inf.	infinitive	sc.	supply, namely (Lat. *scīlicet*)
interj.	interjection	sent.	sentence
Introd.	Introduction	sg.	singular
irreg.	irregular	Sp.	Spanish
It.	Italian	spec.	special
L.A.	*Locī Antīquī*	S.A.	*Sententiae Antīquae*
Lat.	Latin	S.S.	Supplementary Syntax
L.I.	*Locī Immūtātī*		(p. 442–45)
lit.	literally	subj.	subjunctive mood
loc.	locative case	superl.	superlative
m./M./masc.	masculine gender	s.v.	under the word (Lat. *sub verbō*)
mid.	middle	vb(s).	verb(s)
n./N./neut.	note *or* neuter gender	voc.	vocative case
no(s).	number(s)	Vocab.	Vocabulary
nom.	nominative case	vs.	as opposed to, in comparison with
obj.	object *or* objective		(Lat. *versus*)
p.	page(s)	w.	with
part.	participle		

Index

Page references to illustrations are italicized.

Location of the
Sentēntiae Antīquae

1. (1) Pers., Sat. 6.27.   (2) Plaut., Most. 1.3.30.
(3) Suet., Aug. 25 (4) Hor., Sat. 1.2.11.
(5) Sen., Clem. 1.2.2.   (6) Cic., Sest. 67.141.
(7) Cic., Cat. 4.3.   (8) Virg., Aen. 3.121 and
4.173 and 184.   (9) Ter., Heaut. 190 et passim.   (10) Cic., Fam. 2.16.4.   (11) Hor., Sat.
1.9.78.   (12) Hor., Sat. 1.10.81–83.
(13) Cic., Cat. 1.12.30.   (14) Cic., Inv. 1.1.1.
(15) Publil. Syr. 321.

2. (1) Plaut., Stich. 5.2.2.   (2) Virg., Aen. 3.121.
(3) Ter., Ad. 5.8.937.   (4) Cic., Marcell. 4.12.
(5) Cic., Verr. 2.4.54.   (6) Hor., Sat. 2.7.22–
24.   (7) Sen., Ep. 8.1.   (8) Sen., Ep. 17.5.
(9) Cic., Fin. 3.1.2.   (10) Sen., Ep. 8.5.
(11) Sen., Ep. 18.14, De Ira 1.1.2; cp. Ch. 16
S.A.8.   (12). Sen., Ep. 18.15.   (13) Sen., Ep.
115.16.   (14) Hor., Od. 3.11.45.   (15) Cic.,
Pis. 10.22.

3. (1) Cic., Cat. 4.1.   (2) Hor., Sat. 2.6.41.
(3) Phaedr., Fab. I. Prologus 4.   (4) Cic.,
Tusc. 5.3.9.   (5) Hor., Sat. 2.7.84 and 88.
(6) Nep., Cim. 4.   (7) Hor., Ep. 1.2.56.
(8) Sen., Ep. 94.43.   (9) Publil. Syr., 56.
(10) Publil. Syr. 697.   (11) Sen., Clem. 1.2.2.

4. (1) Cic., Am. 15.54.   (2) Ter., Heaut. 2.3.295–
296.   (3) Ter., Ad. 5.9.961.   (4) Hor., Sat.
1.4.114.   (5) Proverbial; cp. Cic., Phil. 12.2.5.
(6) Hor., Od. 2.16.27–28.   (7) Sen., De Ira II
18ff. and III init.; cp. Ter., Phor. 1.4.185.
(8) Virg., Ecl. 5.61.   (9) Hor., Sat. 1.1.25.
(10) Ter., Ad. 4.5.701–702.   (11) Catull. 5.7.
(12) Vulg., Eccles. 1.15.   (13) Cic., Am.
21.79.   (14) Pers., Sat. 6.27.   (15) Cic., Cat.
1.4.9.

5. (1) Cic., Cat. 1.9.23.   (2) Cic., Cat. 1.13.31.
(3) Cic., Off. 1.20.68.   (4) Ov., Her. 3.85.
(5) Cic., Fam. 14.3.1   (6) Ter., Ad. 5.8.937.
(7) Ter., Ad. 5.9.992–993.   (8) Cic., Att. 2.2.
(9) Sen., Cons. Polyb. 9.6.   (10) Ter., Ad.
5.8.937.   (11) Sen., Ep. 17.5.   (12) Virg., Ecl.
5.78.   (13) Hor., Ep. 2.3.445–446 (Ars Poetica).

6. (1) Cic., Tusc. 5.20.57.   (2) Cic., Tusc. 5.21.61.
(3) Cic., Cat. 3.1.3.   (4) Cic., Cat. 3.12.29.
(5) Cic., Cat. 1.6.13.   (6) Liv. 21.1.2.
(7) Cic., Arch. 3.5.   (8) Sen., Ep. 73.16.
(9) Publil. Syr. 302.   (10) Publil. Syr. 282.

7. (1) Ter., Heaut. 1.1.77.   (2) Vulg., Eccles. 1.10.
(3) Hor., Od. 3.1.2–4.   (4) Hor., Sat. 2.7.22–
23.   (5) Hor., Ep. 1.16.52.   (6) Mart.
12.6.11–12.   (7) Hor., Sat. 1.6.15–16.
(8) Cic.; cp. graffiti.   (9) Sen., Ep. 82.2.
(10) Cic., Phil. 10.10.20.   (11) Hor., Sat.
1.9.59–60.   (12) Cic., Cat. 3.12.29.
(13) Vulg., Luke 2.14.

8. (1) Ter., Ad. 5.4.863.   (2) Ter., Heaut. 3.1.432.
(3) Laberius; see Macr. 2.7.   (4) Cic., Cat.
3.1.3.   (5) Publil. Syr. 507; also Macr. 2.7.
(6) Sen., Ep. 8.3.   (7) Catull. 49.   (8) Liv.
26.50.1.   (9) Cic., Tusc. 1.42.98.   (10) Cic.,
Arch. 11.26.   (11) Cic., Marcell. 5.15.
(12) Hor., Ep. 2.2.65–66.   (13) Hor., Ep.
1.2.1–2.   (14) Sen., Ep. 106.12.   (15) Sen.,
Ep. 7.8.   (16) Liv. 22.39.21.

9. (1) Ter., Phor. 4.5.727.   (2) Ter., Phor. 4.3.670.
(3) Ter., Heaut. 4.3.709.   (4) Cic., Am.
27.102.   (5) Ter., Phor. 3.3.539.   (6) Cic.,
Cat. 1.13.31.   (7) Cic., Cat. 1.4.9.   (8) Mart.
10.72.4.   (9) Liv. 22.39.10.

10. (1) Cic., Off. 1.20.68.   (2) Ter., Ad. 4.3.593.
(3) Ter., Ad. 3.2.340.   (4) Mart. 6.70.15.
(5) Cic., Clu. 18.51.   (6) Lucr. 6.93–95.
(7) Pers. 5.153.   (8) Hor., Epod. 13.3–4.
(9) Cic., Sen. 19.67.   (10) Virg., Georg. 3.284.
(11) Virg., Aen. 3.395.   (12) Publil. Syr. 764.
(13) Cic., Am. 24.89.

11. (1) Hor., Sat. 2.5.33.   (2) Ter., Ad. 1.1.49.
(3) Plin., Ep. 1.11.1.   (4) Plin., Ep. 5.18.1.
(5) Ter., Hec. 1.2.197.   (6) Cic., Cat. 1.8.20.
(7) Cic., Marcell. 11.33.   (8) Cic., Fam.
1.5.b.2.   (9) Liv. 120.   (10) Hor., Ep. 2.2.58.
(11) Mart. 12.47.   (12) Cic., Am. 21.80.

12. (1) Vulg., Gen. 1.1 and 27.   (2) Suet., Caes. 37.
(3) Ter., Hec. 3.5.461.   (4) Cic., Sen. 19.68.
(5) Sen., Brev. Vit.; see Duff, Silver Age p.
216.   (6) Ter., Phor. 2.1.302.   (7) Cic., Sen.
7.22.   (8) Cic., Off. 1.24.84.   (9) Tac., Ann.
1.1.1.   (10) Laber. in Macr. 2.7.

13. (1) Caes., B.G. 1.21.   (2) Cic., Sull. 24.67.
(3) Cic. Cat. 3.10.   (4) Cic., Am. 21.80.
(5) Publil. Syr. 206.   (6) Sen., Ep. 7.8.
(7) Sen., Ep. 80.3.   (8) Phaedr. 4.21.1.

14. (1) Vulg., Gen. 1.10.   (2) Lucr. 5.822–823.
(3) Virg., Ecl. 2.33.   (4) Hor., Sat. 1.1.33–

34. (5) Ter., Phor. 3.2.506. (6) Hor., Od.
3.1.13. (7) Enn. in Cic., Rep. 3.3.6.
(8) Sall., Cat. 3.4. (9) Hor., Od. 3.30.6–7.
(10) Hor., Ep. 2.3.268–269. (11) Cic., Sen.
6.17. (12) Hor., Ep. 1.11.27.

15. (1) Ter., Hec. 3.4.421–422. (2) Cic., Fam. 16.9.2.
(3) Cic., Arch. 3.5. (4) Tac., Ann. 12.32.
(5) Cic., Cat. 3.2.3. (6) Cic., Verr. 2.5.62.
(7) Catull. 3.5 and 10. (8) Ter., Ad. 5.4 passim. (9) Cic., Tusc. 5.20.58.

16. (1) Phaedr., 3.7.1. (2) Virg., Geor. 1.145.
(3) Ter., Phor. 1.4.203. (4) Cic., Or. 59.200.
(5) Virg., Aen. 3.657–658. (6) Virg., Aen.
4.569–570. (7) Mart. 7.85.3–4. (8) Hor.,
Ep. 1.2.62; cp. Ch. 2 S.A. 11. (9) Servius on
Aen. 1.683. (10) Hor., Od. 2.16.27–28.
(11) Phaedr., Fab. 1. Prologus 3–4. (12) Cic.,
Leg. 1.22.58. (13) Sen., Clem. 1.19.6.
(14) Sen. Brev. Vit. (15) Cic., Sen. 19.70.
(16) Vell. 2.66.3 (cp. Duff., Silver Age p. 91).

17. (1) Ter., Phor. 2.1.287–288. (2) Cic., N.D.
3.34.83. (3) Cic., Cat. 1.12.30. (4) Publil.
Syr. 321. (5) Hor., Ep. 1.2.40–41.
(6) Publil. Syr. 353. (7) Publil. Syr. 232.
(8) Cic., Am. 15.54. (9) Publil. Syr. 86.
(10) Cic., Am. 25.92. (11) Cic., Am. 27.102.
(12) Sen., Ep. 7.1 and 8.

18. (1) Virg., Aen. 5.231. (2) Tac., Ann. 15.59.
(3) Cic., Cat. 1.3.6. (4) Publil. Syr. 393.
(5) Ov., Met. 4.428. (6) Plin., Ep. 9.6.1.
(7) Cic., Fam. 9.20.3. (8) Lucr. 3.830–831.
(9) Publil. Syr. 37. (10) Cic., Marcell. 2.7.
(11) Enn. (See Duff, Golden Age p. 148.)
(12) Hor., Sat. 1.2.11. (13) Juv. 1.74.

19. (1) Lucr. 1.112. (2) Cic., Cat. 3.5.13. (3) Cic.,
Sest. 67.141. (4) Ter., Hec. 1.2.132.
(5) Cic., Cat. 1.4.9. (6) Cic., Planc. 33.80.
(7) Cic., Am. 15.55.

20. (1) Mart. 13.94.1. (2) Cic., Fin. 5.29.87.
(3) Cic., Am. 12.42. (4) Cic., De Or.
1.61.261. (5) Hor., Od. 1.38.1. (6) Hor.,
Sat. 1.3.66. (7) Cic., Sen. 5.15. (8) Sen.,
Clem. 1.6.2–3. (9) Cic., Off. 1.2.4.
(10) Quint., Inst. 8.3.41. (11) Hor., Od.
1.22.1–2. (12) Cic., Fam. 16.9.3. (13) Cic.,
Cat. 3.5.10.

21. (1) Publil. Syr. 507. (2) Mart. 1.86.1–2.
(3) Cic., Cat. 1.11.27. (4) Hor., Epod.
16.1–2. (5) Cic., Am. 6.22. (6) Cic., Sen.
19.69. (7) Cic., N.D. 2.62.154. (8) Cic.,
Sen. 17.59. (9) Phaedr., App. 27.
(10) Vulg., Job 28.12. (11) Liv., 22.39.19.

22. (1) Cic., Att. 9.10.3. (2) Hor., Od. 2.3.1–2.
(3) Cic., Rep. 3.31. (4) Cic., Cat. 1.1.3.
(5) Cic., Marcell. 10.32. (6) Cic., Cat.

1.12.30. (7) Cic., Cat. 3.1.1. (8) Liv.
32.33.10. (9) Plaut., Aul. 4.10.772.
(10) Cic., Am. 17.64. (11) Hor., Ep. 2.3.148–
149. (12) Virg., Georg. 2.490 and 493.
(13) Sen., Ep. 17.12. (14) Hor., Ep. 1.1.19.
(15) Hor., Sat. 1.1.106–107. (16) Mart.
10.76.1

23. (1) Cic., Cat. 1.2.6. (2) Liv. 44.42.4. (3) Hor.,
Sat. 1.1.68–69. (4) Cic., N.D. 2.4.12.
(5) Hor., Ep. 2.1.156. (6) Nep., Att. 4.
(7) Quint., Inst. Praef. 5. (8) Hor., Sat.
1.10.72. (9) Quint., Inst. 11.3.157.
(10) Cic., N.D. 3.33.82. (11) Cic., Sen. 3.9.
(12) Hor., Ep. 1.16.66. (13) Sen., Ep. 61.3.
(14) Hor., Ep. 1.18.71.

24. (1) Cp. Plutarch, Cato ad fin. (2) Plin., H.N.
33.148. (3) Caes., B.C. 2.43. (4) Cic., Sex.
Rosc. 1.3. (5) Cic., Marcell. 8.24. (6) Hor.,
Od. 3.14.14–16. (7) Cic., Rep. 2.30.
(8) Tac., Dial. 5.

25. (1) Ter., Heaut. Prolog. 18. (2) Cic., 1.11.27.
(3) Cic., Cat. 1.11.27. (4) Cic., Cat. 3.2.4.
(5) Cic., Cat. 4.10.22. (6) Cic., Off. 1.1.1.
(7) Ter., Phor. 4.1.581–582. (8) Cic., Sen.
16.56. (9) Enn. in Cic., Div. 2.56.116.
(10) Cic., Tusc. 1.42.101. (11) Cic., Tusc.
5.37.108. (12) Cic., quoted in Dumesnil's
Lat. Synonyms s.v. abnuere. (13) Cic., Tusc.,
5.40.118. (14) Cic., Sen. 21.77. (15) Cic.,
Sen. 19.68. (16) Plin., Ep. 7.9.15.

26. (1) Cic., Sen. 16.55. (2) Cic., Cat. 1.3.6.
(3) Sen., Contr. 6.7.2; Publil. Syr. 253.
(4) Cic., Cat. 3.1.5. (5) Sen., Ep. 61.3.
(6) Ov., Her. 17.71–72. (7) Hor., Epod.
2.1,7,8. (8) Cic., Am. 26.99. (9) Cic.,
Sen. 19.68. (10) Mart. 1.107.1–2.
(11) Mart. 14.208. (12) Cic., Off. 1.22.74.
(13) Catull. 12.

27. (1) Ov., Met. 7.21–22. (2) Mart. 1.16.1.
(3) Ter., Ad. 5.5.884, 5.7.922. (4) Plin., Ep.
10.88. (5) Cic., Sen. 6.19. (6) Cic., Off.
1.22.78. (7) Cic., Off. 1.22.77. (8) Cic., Sen.
2.5. (9) Sen., Ep. 17.9. (10) See Ch. 4
S.A.7. (11) Cic., Marcell. 3.8. (12) Cic.,
Tusc. 5.20.57–5.21.62. (13) Virg., Aen. 7.312.

28. (1) Liv. 22.39.21. (2) Cic., Off. 1.22.77.
(3) Cic., Cat. 1.7.18. (4) Ter., Phor. 5.5.831.
(5) Hor., Epod. 13.3–4. (6) Sen., Ep. 80.3.
(7) Sen. (8) Diog. Laert.: a Latin translation
from his Greek. (9) Quint., Inst. 2.2.5.
(10) Cic., Am. 24.89. (11) Ov., A.A. 1.97.
(12) Virg., Aen. 1.1–2.

29. (1) Virg., Ecl. 10.69. (2) Virg., Aen. 4.653, 655
(3) Ter., Phor. 3.2.497–498. (4) Hor., Ep.
1.1.40. (5) Juv. 1.30. (6) Cic., Cat. 1.1.3.

(7) Cic., Phil. 10.10.20.   (8) Cic., Phil. 4.5.9.
(9) Nep., Milt. 5.   (10) Cic., De Or. 1.61.260.
(11) Hor., A.P. (Ep. 2.3) 335–336.   (12) Ter.,
Heaut. 4.2.675.   (13) Cic., Off. 1.23.80.
(14) Cic., Am. 9.29.

30. (1) Cic., Cat. 4.3.6.   (2) Phaedr. 3.7.1.   (3) Hor.,
Sat. 1.5.67–68.   (4) Virg., Ecl. 8.43.
(5) Hor., Sat. 1.4.16.   (6) Cic., Marcell.
10.30.   (7) Lucr. 1.55–56.   (8) Lucr. 2.4.
(9) Hor., Ep. 1.2.1–4.   (10) Hor., Ep. 1.18.96–
97, 100–101.   (11) Sen., Ep. 115.14.
(12) Prop. 2.15.29–30.   (13) Cic., Tusc.
1.41.99.

31. (1) Cic., Cat. 1.6.15.   (2) Cic., Am. 12.42.
(3) Cic., Cat. 1.5.10 and 1.9.23.   (4) Hor.,
Od. 1.14.1–2.   (5) Cic., Marcell. 7.22.
(6) Cic., Q. Fr. 1.2.4.14.   (7) Cic., Cat. 3.5.12.
(8) Cic., Sen. 10.33.   (9) Liv. 45.8.   (10) Ter.,
Ad. 2.1.155.   (11) Ter., Phor. 1.2.137–138.
12. Cic., Cluent. 53.146.

32. (1) Publil. Syr. 512.   (2) Cic., Cat. 1.5.10.
(3) Hor., Ep. 1.6.29.   (4) Ter., Ad. 5.9.996.
(5) Ter., Heaut. 4.1.622.   (6) Cic., Sen. 3.7.
(7) Ter., Ad. 4.5.701.   (8) Caes., B.G. 3.18.
(9) Plaut., Trin. 2.2.361.   (10) Publil. Syr.
129.   (11) Sall., Cat. 8.   (12) Cic., Fin.
3.7.26.   (13) See Ch. 18 S.A. 11.   (14) Sen.,
Ep. 80.6.   (15) Hor., Sat. 1.1.25–26.
16. Hor., Ep. 2.3.102–103 (Ars Poetica).

33. (1) Veg., Mil. Prolog. 3.   (2) Cic., Off. 1.22.76.
(3) Cic., Sull. 31.87.   (4) Cic., Q. Fr. 1.3.5.
(5) Phaedr. App. 18.   (6) Hor., Sat. 2.7.22–
24.   (7) Publil. Syr. 412.   (8) Hor., Od.
4.10.6.   (9) Juv. 3.152–153.

34. (1) Virg., Aen. 3.188.   (2) Hor., Sat. 1.3.68–69.
(3) Cic., N.D. 2.62.154.   (4) Cp. Sen., De Ira
2.9.1 and Cic., Tusc. 3.9.19.   (5) Cic., Cat.
1.5.10.   (6) Hor., Od. 3.16.7.   (7) Cic., Fam.
7.10.1.   (8) Publil. Syr. 350.   (9) Mart. Bk. I
Praef. 1–2.   (10) Cic., Sen. 19.69.   (11) Ter.,
Heaut. 1.2.239–240.   (12) Cic., Am. 6.22.
(13) Cic., De Or. 2.67.274.   (14) Virg., Aen.
1.199.

35. (1) Sen., cp. Ep. 8.7; and Hor., Sat. 2.7.83 ff. and
Ep. 1.16.66.   (2) Publil. Syr. 290.   (3) Publil.
Syr. 99.   (4) Hor., Sat. 1.1.86–87.   (5) Cic.,
Fin. 1.18.60, 4.24.65; De Or. 1.3.10 et pas-
sim.   (6) Publil. Syr. 767 and 493.   (7) Vulg.,
Gen. 1.26.   (8) Cic., Rep. 2.24.59.   (9) Caes.,
B.G. 4.23 and 5.45.   (10) Quint., Inst.

10.1.112.   (11) Hor., Ep. 2.2.41–42.
(12) Publil. Syr. 687.   (13) Hor., Sat. 2.2.135–
136.   (14) Virg., Aen. 1.630.   (15) Publil.
Syr. 288.

36. (1) Vulg., Gen. 1.3.   (2) Lucr. 1.205.   (3) Ter.,
Heaut. 2.3.314.   (4) Caes., B.C. 2.43.
(5) Ter., Ad. 3.4.505.   (6) Ter., Heaut.
5.5.1049 and 1067.   (7) Hor., Od. 1.11.7–8.
(8) Pers. 5.151–152.   (9) Sen., Ep. 61.2.
(10) Cic., Sen. 8.26.   (11) Hor., Ep. 2.2.206–
211.   (12) Hor., Od. 1.24.19–20.   (13) Ov.,
Am. 1.2.10.   (14) Cic., Am. 5.7.   (15) Cic.,
Arch. 2.3.

37. (1) Hor., Ep. 2.3.68.   (2) Virg., Aen. 6.127.
(3) Ov., A.A. 3.62–65.   (4) Ter., Hec. 1.2.132;
Ad. 1.1.26.   (5) Ter., Ad. 5.5.882.   (6) Ter.,
Ad. 4.1.517, 4.2.556.   (7) Hor., Sat. 1.9.1.
(8) Cic., Tusc. 5.21.62.   (9) Cic., Verr.
2.4.54.120.   (10) Ter., Hec. 3.4.421 and 423.
(11) Cic., Cat. 1.9.23.   (12) Nep., Att. 8; Cic.,
Phil. 2.12.28, Tusc. 5.37.109 (names
changed).   (13) Cic., Att. 12.50.   (14) Cic.,
Sen. 7.24.   (15) Prop., 2.15.23–24.

38. (1) Caes., B.G. 1.31.   (2) Cic., Cat. 1.4.9.
(3) Cat., 4.7.16.   (4) Cic., Am. 7.23.
(5) Cic., Cat. 1.6.13.   (6) Cic., Am. 15.53.
(7) Cic., Cat. 1.7.18.   (8) Cic., Cat. 4.11.24.
(9) Virg., Ecl. 1.7.   (10) Cic., Fam. 4.5.6.
(11) Sen., Ep. 17.11.   (12) Cic., Marcell. 4.11.
(13) Plin., Ep. 5.16.4–5.   (14) Hor., Od.
1.37.1–2.

39. (1) Cic., Cat. 1.12.30.   (2) Cic., Cat. 1.13.32.
(3) Cic., Off. 1.22.74.   (4) Publil. Syr. 762.
(5) Cic., Off. 1.25.89.   (6) Cic., Verr. 2.4.54.
(7) Cic., Off. 3.32.113.   (8) Cic., Sest. 2.5
(9) Cic., Sen. 5.15.   (10) Cic., Att. 2.23.1.
(11) Publil. Syr. 704.   (12) Cic., Leg. 1.23.60.
(13) Virg., Aen. 4.175.   (14) Cic., Fam.
5.12.4.

40. (1) Cic., Cat. 4.7.14.   (2) Hor., Od. 3.30.6–7.
(3) Cic., Tusc. 1.41.97.   (4) Ter., Ad. 5.4.856.
(5) Sen., Ep. 7.7.   (6) Plin., Ep. 9.6.2.
(7) Lucr. 4.1286–87.   (8) Cic., Fam. 14.12.
(9) Liv.: see Loci Immutati #17.   (10) Cic.,
Marcell. 10.32.   (11) Catull. 43.1–3.
(12) Ter., Heaut. 1.1.77.   (13) Cic., Am.
21.81.   (14) Vulg., Exod. 20.11.   (15) Caes.,
B.G. 1.47.   (16) Cic., Cat. 1.4.8.   (17) Cic.,
Planc. 42.101.

ABOUT THE AUTHORS

Frederic M. Wheelock (1902–1987) received the A.B., A.M., and Ph.D. degrees from Harvard University. His long and distinguished teaching career included appointments at Haverford College, Harvard University, the College of the City of New York, Brooklyn College, Cazenovia Junior College (where he served as Dean), the Darrow School for Boys (New Lebanon, NY), the University of Toledo (from which he retired as full Professor in 1968), and a visiting professorship at Florida Presbyterian (now Eckerd) College. He published a number of articles and reviews in the fields of textual criticism, palaeography, and the study of Latin; in addition to *Wheelock's Latin* (previously titled *Latin: An Introductory Course Based on Ancient Authors*), his books include *Wheelock's Latin Reader* (previously titled *Latin Literature: A Book of Readings*) and *Quintilian as Educator* (trans. H. E. Butler; introd. and notes by Prof. Wheelock). Professor Wheelock was a member of the American Classical League, the American Philological Association, and the Classical Association of the Atlantic States. Biographies of Professor Wheelock authored by Professor Ward Briggs appear in his book, *A Biographical Dictionary of American Classicists* (Westport, CT: Greenwood Press, 1994), as well as in the Winter, 2003, issue of the *Classical Outlook*.

Richard A. LaFleur received the B.A. and M.A. in Latin from the University of Virginia and the Ph.D. in Classical Studies from Duke. He has taught since 1972 at the University of Georgia, where he served for 21 years as head of one of the largest Classics programs in North America and has held since 1998 the chair of Franklin Professor of Classics. He has numerous publications in Latin language, literature, and pedagogy, including the books *The Teaching of Latin in American Schools: A Profession in Crisis, Latin Poetry for the Beginning Student, Love and Transformation: An Ovid Reader, Latin for the 21st Century: From Concept to Classroom, A Song of War: Readings from Vergil's Aeneid* (with Alexander G. McKay), *Wheelock's Latin* (revised 5th and 6th eds.), *Wheelock's Latin Reader* (revised 2nd ed.), and (with Paul Comeau) *Workbook for Wheelock's Latin* (revised 3rd ed.). Professor LaFleur also served as editor of *The Classical Outlook* (1979–2003) and is past President of the American Classical League (1984–1986). He has been recipient of over one million dollars in grants from the National Endowment for the Humanities and other agencies, and of state, regional, and national awards for teaching and professional service, including, in 1984, the American Philological Association's award for Excellence in the Teaching of Classics.

Wheelock's Latin is better than ever!

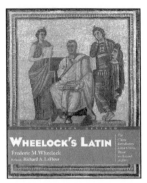

560 pages; illustrated
$21.95 paperback (0-06-078371-0)
$29.95 hardcover (0-06-078423-7)

Wheelock's Latin, Sixth Edition, Revised
Frederic M. Wheelock • Revised by Richard A. LaFleur

The new, revised sixth edition of *Wheelock's Latin* has all the features that have made it the best-selling single-volume beginning Latin textbook: forty chapters with grammatical explanations and readings based on ancient Roman authors • self-tutorial exercises with an answer key for independent study • extensive English-Latin/Latin-English vocabularies • supplementary original Latin readings—unlike other textbooks which contain primarily made-up sentences and passages • etymological aids • maps of the Mediterranean, Italy, and the Aegean area • numerous photographs illustrating aspects of classical culture, mythology, and historical and literary figures presented in the chapter readings.

Also new to the sixth edition, revised, are: further expansion of the English-Latin vocabulary • audio for the chapter vocabularies and other pronunciation aids, online at www.WheelocksLatin.com • an online teacher's guide and answer key, available to instructors only and password/gatekeeper-protected at www.HarperAcademic.com.

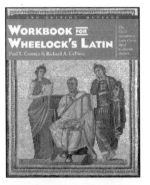

352 pages
$17.95 paperback (0-06-095642-9)
An answer key is available gratis for teachers at:
www.HarperAcademic.com

Workbook for Wheelock's Latin, Third Edition, Revised
Paul T. Comeau • Revised by Richard A. LaFleur

From two of the country's leading Latinists comes this updated edition of the *Workbook for Wheelock's Latin*. Each of the forty lessons presented in this newly revised edition begins with a detailed set of objectives and continues with a series of questions designed to focus directly on the newly introduced grammar, a variety of transformation drills, word and phrase translations, and other exercises designed to test and sharpen the student's skills. A section on word power focuses on vocabulary and derivatives, and the final section includes reading comprehension questions and sentences for translation practice. Lessons are presented in an easy to read, clear layout, with perforated pages for hand-in homework assignments and space for the student's name and date.

Wheelock's Latin Reader, Second Edition
Frederic M. Wheelock • Revised by Richard A. LaFleur

This second edition marks the first time this classic book has ever been significantly revised. Featuring expanded notes, and all new photos and maps, *Wheelock's Latin Reader* is the ideal intermediate Latin reader to follow the best-selling *Wheelock's Latin* and other introductory texts. It includes extensive selections from writers such as Cicero, Livy, Ovid, Pliny, the Vulgate, Bede, and others, along with useful introductions, translation notes, and a full Latin-English vocabulary.

"[*Wheelock's Latin Reader*] is a solid companion to [*Wheelock's Latin*] and deserves wide circulation as a practical introduction to the humanism of Ancient Rome."
— *The Classical Bulletin*

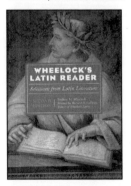

448 pages; illustrated
$19.00 paperback (0-06-093506-5)

www.WheelocksLatin.com